THE IDEALISTIC ARGUMENT

IN

RECENT BRITISH AND AMERICAN
PHILOSOPHY

The Century Philosophy Series
STERLING P. LAMPRECHT, Editor

THE IDEALISTIC ARGUMENT IN RECENT BRITISH AND AMERICAN PHILOSOPHY

BY

G. WATTS CUNNINGHAM

SAGE SCHOOL OF PHILOSOPHY, CORNELL UNIVERSITY

GREENWOOD PRESS, PUBLISHERS
WESTPORT, CONNECTICUT

Originally published in 1933
by the Century Co.

First Greenwood Reprinting 1969

SBN 8371-2833-1

To the memory

of

JAMES EDWIN CREIGHTON

UNDER WHOSE TUTELAGE I FIRST BECAME ACQUAINTED WITH
IDEALISTIC PHILOSOPHY
AND WHO I LIKE TO THINK
WOULD NOT BE WHOLLY OUT OF SYMPATHY WITH THE SPIRIT OF
THIS TREATMENT OF IT

PREFACE

This study is not, and does not pretend to be, a general history of British and American idealism. Many aspects of that complex movement are left wholly on one side; the historical circumstances of the movement's inauguration in Great Britain, of its transplantation to America, and of its nurture and growth in both countries are only incidentally considered; and some names prominent on the roster of representatives of the movement are only casually mentioned, while others are omitted. The sole aim of the study is to give a somewhat detailed account, both expository and critical, of the chief arguments in support of an idealistic metaphysics expressed by British and American philosophers since the middle of the last century.

This limitation in the scope of the study was deliberately accepted as the alternative to a general survey of the movement as a whole—an alternative which, if undertaken by the writer at any rate, would in all probability have resulted in nothing more significant than a relatively barren catalogue of names and doctrines more or less loosely put together. It is recognized that the limitation *ab initio* excludes from consideration many tendencies and tenets which are both interesting and important aspects of the theory under survey. But it is hoped that compensation for this lies in the opportunity offered to direct the reader's undivided attention to the foundations which any serious account of the movement must touch in the end and which, despite the controversies that have for so long turned about the idealistic tradition, have not yet perhaps received adequate analytical treatment.

The authors chosen for detailed consideration are those who presumably would not themselves object (at least in principle) to being classed as idealists and who have either given independent formulations of the argument or have aided significantly in its clarification. But no living author has been included. Whether the choice is wholly fortunate may, of course, be questioned; and there are obvious omissions. But the line had to be drawn somewhere. Presumably, no omission has led to the neglect of essential principles.

The first part of the volume is made up entirely of summaries, to a degree historically oriented, of what have been judged to be the main formulations. As far as possible, these summaries have been framed in the terminologies of the several authors—the aim was exclusively so to frame them—to the end of keeping at a minimum the writer's own interpretation of what they intended to say. Critical remarks made by the authors about each other have occasionally been introduced into the summaries, and, so far, the story is a self-critical one; but no effort has been made to gather these comments exhaustively or to stress the ones inserted. The effort has been, rather, to present succinctly and accurately each author's independent statement, with particular attention to his own special contribution to the historical development. Ideally at least, the effort seems called for. In most of the formulations, condensation obviously makes for clarity; and even in such a closely reasoned statement as that of McTaggart—which an expositor bent on summary can approach only with trepidation—selection and coördination of emphases in respect of the main drift of the complicated argument is perhaps not without its advantages. The extent to which this part of the study is successful the instructed reader must judge; but there can be no doubt that the task is important and that, if it is in any degree successfully accomplished here, the present study cannot be wholly worthless.

The second part is exclusively critical, and it assumes throughout that the reader is familiar with the content of the first part. In it liberties have frankly been taken with the historical material. This material has here been forced into classification convenient for the critical discussion, statements which appeared to be identical in principle have been merged, and emphases which seemed to be of secondary significance or merely repetitious have been largely neglected. In all of this, naturally, issues have been weighed and in some measure prejudged. But at no point, it is believed, has the arrangement of the material involved misinterpretation of doctrines or the neglect of difficulties in order to facilitate the criticisms. Whether this faith is mistaken the reader, once more, must decide; and, if at any point he is suspicious, he will presumably find the corrective in the first part of the book. The summaries there given were designed to guard the writer against hasty interpretation set in the midst of criticism and, on the other side, to indicate references which lead directly to the relevant source-material.

The primary aim of the critical comments is to fix, as precisely as possible, sundry difficulties that appear to be involved in the several historical formulations summarized in the first part of the study and to make explicit the underlying assumptions. What in the end seems to remain, despite the criticisms, has here and there been indicated; and it is hoped that the reader will not overlook these more positive statements. Of special importance is the theory of knowledge expressed in the assumptions underlying the argument *a contingentia mundi*. There are, indeed, in the basal concepts of this theory as stated, certain troublesome ambiguities—such, for example, as the 'ultimate' and 'immediate' or 'proximate' subjects in judgment both of which are to be 'real,' the concept of the 'given' with which we start, 'internal' and 'external' meanings, and the 'whole' whose 'spirit' is the guiding principle throughout. And these ambiguities are on occasion intimately linked with important steps in the argument, which seems to break down once the ambiguities are cleared up. But such ambiguities are not integral to the theory, the main tenets of which stand out more clearly when the ambiguities are removed.

These tenets are chiefly two—namely, that the cognitive situation is essentially self-transcendent and that 'reality' is the context within which such transcendence finds its logical ground —and they appear to be quite important. At least they mark the parting of the ways for epistemological theories, and much depends on their acceptance or rejection. It is the writer's conviction that the present study gives some reasons for their acceptance in principle.

Within these tenets and what they entail is to be found perhaps the major contribution which the British and American
idealistic tradition has to make to a fruitful consideration of
the issues that have merged out of the revolts against it. These
revolts have, in intent, been consciously directed against the
idealistic theory of knowledge; but in the main they seem to
have failed to distinguish between the theories underlying the
different types of idealistic argument and to have assumed that
there is only one—namely, the one which denies in principle
the logical possibility of transcending the subject-object relationship. The theory here in question, however, still remains, and
to neglect it is an oversight which is without historical warrant.
It is true, as is argued in some detail below, that this theory
cannot support the weight of the ontology historically laid upon
it by those idealists who set it in the forefront of their argument; and, so far indeed, the idealistic tradition must apparently be set aside. But the theory apparently stands essentially untouched by the attacks of the revolutionists, and is
perhaps even surreptitiously appropriated by some of them; and
it stands as the foundation for a constructive handling of the
problems raised by them—and justly raised within the compass
of the premises adopted.

The present study does not, of course, undertake to justify
in detail this contention—a task requiring another volume. But,
in the writer's mind at least, the study does something towards
clearing the ground for such an undertaking and to that extent
may be said to be a prolegomenon to it.

It has not seemed necessary to burden this volume with a
bibliography, since all the major works of the authors discussed
are indicated in the footnotes appended to the summaries of
the first part. If the summaries send the uninitiated reader to
these works with fairly accurate views as to what essentially
is to be found there, the chief purpose of this part of the study
will have been accomplished. And, if he does not find there basal
doctrines which are wholly neglected in the critical remarks
of the second part, that part too may, so far at least, be regarded
as successful.

CONTENTS

PART II

CRITICAL

THE IDEALISTIC ARGUMENT
IN
RECENT BRITISH AND AMERICAN
PHILOSOPHY

INTRODUCTION

The historical period with which this book is primarily concerned begins about the middle of the nineteenth century with the writings of J. F. Ferrier. At the background of Ferrier's thought, however, lies the story of Locke's "way of ideas" and the development it received at the hands of Berkeley and Hume and, later, of Reid and Hamilton. This story is, therefore, relevant to the present undertaking and, despite the fact it has often been told, it must here be told once again. Fortunately, the merest outline is all that is called for in the present context, since only the crucial points are here significant. These introductory remarks, then, will concern themselves only with a very brief sketch of the main results of this development. And we begin with the "way of ideas" itself.

Locke's definition of an 'idea,' it will be recalled, is (i) "Whatever is the object of the understanding when a man thinks." By *thinking* Locke means perceiving, remembering, imagining, conceiving, in short, the sundry cognitive operations of the mind: and, on this side of its nature, mind is 'understanding.' By being an "object of the understanding" Locke means being presented to, or apprehended by, the understanding. As "an object of the understanding," then, an idea is 'in' mind; it is, as Locke tells us elsewhere, an "immediate" object of the understanding. But (ii) ideas may be divided, Locke teaches, into two basal groups, namely, those of "sensation" and those of "reflexion." By the former is meant the set of ideas which come to us through the senses of seeing, hearing, tasting, smelling, and the like; by the latter is meant the set of ideas derived by the mind through observation of its own operations, such as willing, feeling, and thinking.

Ideas of the first group are most relevant for our present purpose, and it is very important to notice that (iii) they are not in mind without cause. What is their cause? To this question

3

Locke's answer is simple: These ideas are not created by the mind itself, but are derived from things outside of mind and in commerce with the body. The causes of ideas of sense, then, are things existing in the world and independent of mind. Thus it happens that (iv) each idea of sense, like a color or an odor, is in the mind in a representative capacity; it is present there as a sort of ambassador from the external object to which it refers, from which it is derived, and which it represents in the mind. Its ambassadorial function (its 'objective reference') is guaranteed largely by its causal connection with the object, though Locke does at times seem to suggest that the idea's reference to the external object is *logically* necessary, since apart from such a reference, the distinction between real (true) and unreal (false or illusory) ideas would be meaningless. (This, however, is not consistent with his major assumptions about the sharp separation between the 'idea' in the mind and the 'object' outside of the mind.)

If we may summarize for the sake of clarity, the net result of Locke's analysis of our knowledge of the external world is this: There is always a mind which knows, an outside and independent object which is known, and an idea 'in' mind through which, as a medium, the knowing of the external object takes place. This is the theory of knowledge which Ferrier later called "the theory of representative perception."

The first step, logically as well as historically, in the development of this theory was taken by Bishop Berkeley. He found himself unable to accept the distinction Locke makes between the idea 'in' mind and the object external to and independent of mind. Consequently he was driven to his famous doctrine "to be is to be perceived" (*esse est percipi*), the cardinal doctrine of the earliest form of British idealism.

The reasoning which brought Berkeley to this doctrine is essentially as follows: (i) Since by hypothesis (assuming Locke's theory of representative perception as the starting point) ideas alone are present 'in' mind in the act of knowing, it follows at once that there is no knowable object different from ideas. All we can mean by an 'object,' therefore, in so far as the object is known or knowable, is merely an idea or a "collection of ideas."

(ii) But ideas have existence only in so far as they are present to a mind, since it is nonsense to speak of an idea unrelated to mind; the existence of ideas consists in their being perceived. Consequently, seeing that when we speak of *objects* all we mean or can mean by the term is ideas, when we speak of the *existence* of objects all we mean or can mean is that they are perceived. (iii) To suppose that there is matter outside of the mind, existing independently, is to make an assumption which, when rendered explicit, shows itself either to be meaningless or to involve a contradiction. If such an independently existing matter is identified with sensible objects, then it involves a contradiction, since *sensible objects* manifestly are ideas, and ideas exist only in relation to mind. If the independent matter is supposed to be some material 'substance' underlying the sensible qualities of objects, then it is nothing more than a meaningless abstraction without assignable content.

The thesis that the existence of things consists in their being perceived, Berkeley thinks, states nothing really novel. It is only a precise and explicit formulation of what is generally accepted by common sense and philosophy alike. "I do not pretend to be a setter-up of new notions," he tells us in the conclusion of the third of the *Three Dialogues between Hylas and Philonous.* "My endeavours tend only to unite and place in a clearer light that truth which was before shared between the vulgar and the philosophers—the former being of the opinion, that *those things they imediately perceive are the real things;* and the latter, that *those things immediately perceived are ideas which exist only in the mind.* Which two notions put together, do, in effect, constitute the substance of what I advance."

The upshot of Berkeley's argument, thus, is to modify Locke's analysis of the cognitive situation by eliminating from it *objects* as distinct from, and represented by, *ideas in the mind.* And he deems this modification logically necessary because objects, in this sense, are by hypothesis unknown and unknowable; they do not in any manner function in the knowing experience. For him, then, the only real existents are minds and their ideas; objects exist only in the sense in which objects are ideas, that is, are related to mind. He denies outright "the independent existence of unthinking things."

Under the analysis of Hume, as is well known, Locke's "way of ideas" yields much more skeptical conclusions. Hume holds in effect that if you accept Locke's view of representative perception as your point of departure, you will find yourself logically driven to the conclusion, not only that there is no reason for supposing the existence of an independent object, as Berkeley had insisted, but also that the existence of an independent 'mind' is equally, and on essentially similar grounds, open to the same skepticism. For the mind, too, is not an idea and therefore cannot be "the object of the understanding when a man thinks." Consequently, it is either unknowable or it is known in some way other than the "way of ideas." But there is no other way of knowing, and mind as distinct from ideas is therefore a meaningless word. The mind is only a "heap or collection of different perceptions," that is, in Locke's terminology, a collection of 'ideas.' It is "a kind of theater, where several perceptions successively make their appearance; pass, re-pass, glide away, and mingle in an infinite variety of postures and situations. . . . The comparison of the theater must not mislead us. They are the successive perceptions only that constitute the mind; nor have we the most distant notion of the place where these scenes are represented, or of the materials of which it is composed."[1] Thus 'minds' like 'objects,' dissolve into 'ideas' or 'perceptions.' As there is no reason for holding that there are objects beyond the ideas which are supposed to represent them, so there is no reason for holding that there is a mind in which ideas reside. On the contrary, the very reasoning which leads to the former conclusion leads with equal cogency to the latter—a consequence which Berkeley had failed to see only because he was not willing to follow to the end the road along which he started.[2]

With Hume, then, the "way of ideas" leads into an abyss of skepticism. Objects dissolve into 'perceptions' (ideas) on the one

[1] Hume, *A Treatise of Human Nature*, Book I, Part IV, section vi.
[2] As a matter of fact, Berkeley did have some hesitancy on the point. Note his denial that we can have an 'idea' of the 'mind,' and his use of the vague term *notion* to justify his acceptance of mind's existence (*Principles of Human Knowledge*, addition to section 27 in the second edition).

side, and a similar fate befalls mind on the other. Under Hume's rigorous analysis, the ideas, which according to Locke are 'in' mind as representatives of an independent world of objects, stand exposed as self-appointed ambassadors to no court. Such a skeptical conclusion, however, seems a scandal to philosophy, and some of Hume's contemporaries (though not as many as he had hoped) were scandalized by it.

The successors of Hume in British philosophy were generally concerned to find a way of escape from his skepticism. Among them was a group of thinkers, known as the Scottish School, who advocated what they called the philosophy of common sense, by which they sought at once to undermine the foundations of their fellow-Scotsman's negations and to avoid the 'idealism' of Berkeley. Of this group the most important for the present survey are the founder of the school, Thomas Reid, and his editor and critic, Sir William Hamilton.

In his *Inquiry into the Human Mind on the Principles of Common Sense* (1764), Reid undertakes to show that the idealism of Berkeley and the skepticism of Hume are alike based upon false premises. In order to accomplish this, however, he thinks it is necessary first to call in question the principles of Locke's theory of knowledge—a theory, Reid insists, which Locke took over from Descartes and developed into the "way of ideas." This view of knowledge, Reid is convinced, necessarily involves the conclusions of both Berkeley and Hume; if these conclusions are to be escaped, therefore, the "way of ideas" must be abandoned.

"I acknowledge," he says in the dedicatory letter prefixed to the *Inquiry*, "that I never thought of calling in question the principles commonly received with regard to the human understanding, until the *Treatise of Human Nature* was published, in the year 1739. The ingenious author of that treatise, upon the principles of Locke, who was no skeptic, hath built a system of skepticism, which leaves no ground to believe any one thing rather than its contrary. His reasoning appeared to me to be just; there was therefore a necessity to call in question the principles upon which it is founded, or to admit the conclusion."

That these principles necessarily lead to skepticism through idealism, Reid thinks is shown in their historical development from Descartes to Hume. "Des Cartes no sooner began to dig in this mine, than skepticism was ready to break in upon him. He did what he could to shut it out. Malebranche and Locke, who dug deeper, found the difficulty in keeping out this enemy still to increase; but they laboured honestly in the design. Then Berkeley, who carried on the work, despairing of securing all, bethought himself of an expedient: by giving up the material world, which he thought might be spared without loss, and even with advantage, he hoped by an impregnable partition, to secure the world of spirits. But, alas! the *Treatise of Human Nature* wantonly sapped the foundation of this partition, and drowned all in one universal deluge." [3] In order to escape such a catastrophe, Reid turns back to an inquiry into the principles which had thus, historically and logically, led to it. He critically examines the "way of ideas" (or, as he prefers to call it, "the ideal system") and undertakes to disclose its "original defect."

This original defect he discovers in the foundational hypothesis "that nothing is perceived but what is in the mind which perceives it: that we do not really perceive things that are external, but only certain images and pictures of them imprinted upon the mind, which are called *impressions* and *ideas*." [4] This hypothesis, Reid contends, is directly at variance with common sense, and this, in his opinion, is ample reason for discarding it. In justice to Reid, however, it should be noted that he does not here refer to uncritical common sense; he is not quite willing to submit the issue to a popular referendum. What he has in mind is, rather, what he calls the "principles" of common sense. These he conceives as follows: "If there are certain principles, as I think there are, which the constitution of our nature leads us to believe, and which we are under a necessity to take for granted in the common concerns of life, without being able to give a reason for them; these are what we call the principles of common sense; and what is manifestly contrary to them, is what we call absurd." [5] And it is to such principles that Reid appeals

[3] *Inquiry*, Chapter I, section vii.
[4] *Ibid.*, Dedication.
[5] *Ibid.*, Chapter II, section vi.

in his argument against the validity of the hypothesis here in question.

This hypothesis, Reid maintains, is manifestly contrary to the principles of common sense as above defined. It is contrary to such principles to hold that in perception what are perceived are merely images and pictures in the mind, for the "constitution of our nature" forces us to believe that what is perceived is the independently existing external object, and not any mere image of it. The hypothesis must therefore be given up, and since it is the basal tenet of the "ideal system," that system stands refuted.

Positively, what we are forced by the constitution of our nature to believe about perception is, in the first instance, that in the act of perceiving there is a direct and irrefragable experience of an external object beyond the intervening image or idea. In the smell of a rose, for example, "by the original constitution of our nature, we are both led to believe that there is a permanent cause of the sensation, and prompted to seek after it; and experience determines us to place it in the rose." [6] Why we should thus believe we cannot explain, nor can we prove that the belief is true; all we can say is that the belief is a "principle of common sense." But this is sufficient and Berkeley is thereby refuted.

By the same necessity, in the second place, we are compelled to accept the existence of 'mind' or self. That mind or self exists cannot be demonstrated, since the very attempt to prove it presupposes it; we are infallibly certain of its existence. "It is certain, no man can conceive or believe smelling to exist of itself, without a mind, or something that has the power of smelling, of which it is called a sensation, an operation, or feeling. Yet if any man should demand a proof, that sensation cannot be without a mind or sentient being, I confess that I can give none; and that to pretend to prove it, seems to me almost as absurd as to deny it." [7] Once again, then, belief in the existence of mind is a "principle of common sense." There is consequently nothing more to be said, and with this Hume is refuted.

[6] *Ibid.*, Chapter II, section ix.
[7] *Ibid*, section vi.

Reid's reply to both Berkeley and Hume thus resolves itself into a denial, based on the principles of common sense which themselves are ultimate, of the premises upon which he thinks their conclusions finally rest. Starting with the "ideal system" and following its logic, he says in effect, one cannot in the end escape these conclusions. But why start with that system? To do so is to go contrary to the "original constitution of our nature" and to mistake an absurdity for certainty. Applying the principles of common sense to the case, we may see clearly that the "ideal system" is in error, and that the conclusions following from it lack compulsion.

In his critical comments on the theory of Locke, Reid advances a theory of knowledge on his own account, which is succinctly stated in the following passage: "How or when I got such first principles, upon which I build all my reasoning, I know not; for I had them before I can remember: but I am sure they are parts of my constitution, and that I cannot throw them off. That our thoughts and sensations must have a subject, which we call *ourself*, is not therefore an opinion got by reasoning but a natural principle. That our sensations of touch indicate something external, extended, figured, hard or soft, is not a deduction of reason, but a natural principle. The belief of it, and the very conception of it, are equally parts of our constitution. If we are deceived in it, we are deceived by him that made us, and there is no remedy." Such is the theory of perception which Reid accepts in opposition to the "ideal system," and which he thinks is itself grounded in certainty.[8] But little inspection of it is required to disclose the fact that some rather disturbing questions arise out of it.

In the first place, Reid's theory places him in the position of one who maintains that mere belief is prior to knowledge and furnishes reason with its basal principles. Whether such a position is tenable or not, it certainly does raise some very important questions for a theory of knowledge. In any event, one who maintains it can hardly be said certainly to have accomplished what Reid claims he has accomplished—the task, namely, of bridging

[8] *Inquiry*, Chapter II, *passim*.

the "abyss of skepticism" in which he seems to think Hume delights to wander.

The second, and for our present survey the more important, question arising out of Reid's theory concerns the quite ambiguous status in which he leaves that peculiar aspect of the perceptual situation which he calls *sensation*. Nowhere does he formulate a precise definition of it, but he lists the several senses (smelling, seeing, hearing, and so forth) as instances. What he *prima facie* means by it is perhaps clear enough. When one smells a rose, for example, Reid intends to say that there are the mind which smells, the rose which is smelt, and the smelling of the rose; and that within the complex experience the smelling is the 'sensation.' It is to be noted, however, that, on the one side, there is a difference between the act of smelling and the mind which smells and, on the other side, between the act of smelling (the sensation) and that which is smelt (something in the rose as an external object). And distressing difficulties arise on both sides. How is the 'sensation' of smelling related to the mind which 'has' the sensation? How is the sensation in the mind related to the something in the rose—the act of smelling to the smelt?

Though Reid seems to be more or less vaguely aware of these difficulties,[9] he does not meet either of them satisfactorily. He asserts that the object produces on mind an effect which we call the sensation in the mind and which "suggests" or "signifies" the object as its "concomitant." And with this quite general answer he leaves the matter. He does indeed call attention to the fact that the sensation seems more closely related to mind than to the object, although we are compelled to think of it as primarily in the object. But this is intolerably obscure, and he fails to give any sort of analysis of the quite fundamental point at issue. He is content to remain in the dubious conviction that "the smell of the rose signifies two things. *First*, A sensation, which can have no existence but when it is perceived, and can only be in a sentient being or mind. *Secondly*, it signifies some power, quality or virtue, in the rose, or in effluvia proceeding from it, which hath a permanent existence, independent of the mind, and which

[9] Cf. *Ibid.*, Chapter II, section ix, and Chapter VI, section iii.

by the constitution of nature, produces the sensation in us." [10]
In other words, a sensation is something in the mind which
exists only as it is present there, and it is also something in the
object which has an existence wholly independent of any relation to mind.

It would thus appear that the only change which Reid makes
in the "ideal system" he sets out to criticize is a purely terminological one. For him, as for Locke, there are three elements
in the perceptual experience: mind, sensation (Locke's idea),
and object. And the question is inevitable whether, with this
result on his hands, the "original defect" of the "ideal system"
which he was so concerned to avoid is not still present to plague
him. He seems to have succeeded only in introducing a quite
minor change in Locke's terminology, and in adding to the perceptual situation a criterion of doubtful significance. In the place
of Locke's 'idea' he has substituted a 'sensation,' and he has
introduced as logically basal to the certainty of perception a
peculiar belief whose sole guarantee is the deep-seated conviction
on the part of common sense that it must be accepted. With
these modifications, however, he has hardly accomplished what
he set out to do; he has not overcome the difficulties which he
quite clearly sees in Locke's theory, and presumably neither
Berkeley nor Hume would agree that he has successfully undermined the conclusions which they drew from that theory.

Largely because of the ambiguities in it, Reid's theory of
perception speedily gave rise to lively debates among his successors in the Scottish School. Some of them, like Thomas
Brown, subjected the theory to quite vigorous criticism and
insisted upon modifying it in more or less important respects,
while others were staunch defenders of it in principle, though
not wholly satisfied with the formulation which Reid himself
had given. Among the latter group the most prominent figure is
that of Sir William Hamilton, whose painstaking devotion to the
arduous task of editing Reid's writings seemed, to at least one
of his contemporaries, a fruitless loyalty to an unworthy cause.[11]

[10] *Inquiry*, Chapter II, section ix.
[11] "For thirty years past," writes J. F. Ferrier of Hamilton in the appendix to his *Institutes of Metaphysics*, "I have been of opinion that the
dedication of his powers to the service of Dr. Reid was a perversion of

But the fortunes of Reid's epistemological theory at the hands of his successors in the School are of no direct concern to us here. An independent doctrine advanced by Hamilton, however, is of importance for our later survey, and to a brief statement of one aspect of that doctrine we must now turn.

The doctrine in question is what Hamilton calls the "philosophy of the conditioned." As actually developed by him, this is a doctrine of many meanings. But the aspect of the doctrine here relevant is expressed in the following passage: "Our whole knowledge of mind and of matter is relative,—conditioned,—relatively conditioned. Of things absolutely or in themselves, be they external, be they internal, we know nothing, or know them only as incognizable; and we become aware of their incomprehensible existence, only as this is indirectly and accidentally revealed to us, through certain qualities related to our faculties of knowledge, and which qualities, again, we cannot think as unconditioned, irrelative, existent in and of themselves. All that we know is therefore phenomenal,—phenomenal of the unknown. The philosopher speculating the worlds of matter and mind, is thus, in a certain sort, only an ignorant admirer. . . . With the exception, in fact, of a few late Absolutist theorizers in Germany, this is, perhaps, the truth of all others most harmoniously re-echoed by every philosopher of every school. . . ." [12] And hereupon follows documented evidence of the last statement in the form of a list of seventeen quotations beginning with Protagoras's dictum, "Man is the measure of all things," and ending with the statement of Kant in the Preface to the *Kritik der reinen Vernunft*: "In perception everything is known in conformity to the constitution of our faculty."

His doctrine of the conditioned, Hamilton informs us, aims to express precisely the converse of the philosophy of the Absolute—and here he has explicitly in mind the post-Kantian philosophy in Germany. "For this asserts to man a knowledge of the Unconditioned,—of the Absolute and Infinite; while that

his genius, that this was the one mistake in his career, and that he would have done far better if he had built entirely on his own foundation."

[12] *Philosophy of the Conditioned*, Chapter II, section II, subdivision ii. For the ambiguities in Hamilton's general theory, the reader should consult A. K. Rogers, *English and American Philosophy Since 1800*, pp. 17 ff.

denies to him a knowledge of either, and maintains, all which we immediately know, or can know, to be only the Conditioned, the Relative, the Phenomenal, the Finite." The one asserts philosophic omniscience; the other asserts philosophic nescience. "In other words: the doctrine of the Unconditioned is a philosophy confessing relative ignorance, but professing absolute knowledge; while the doctrine of the Conditioned is a philosophy professing relative knowledge, but confessing absolute ignorance." [13] And in Hamilton's view the former is wholly unjustified, while the latter alone is tenable.

Reid's theory of perception, on the one side, and Hamilton's philosophy of the conditioned, on the other, constitute two very important elements in the historical background of the idealistic argument of another Scotsman, J. F. Ferrier, who is the earliest British philosopher to give a systematic formulation of so-called 'absolute' idealism. To a statement of this argument we turn in Chapter I.

[13] Hamilton, *op. cit.*, Chapter II, section I.

PART I

EXPOSITORY

JAMES FREDERICK FERRIER (1808-1864)

DESPITE the fact that Sir William Hamilton, especially in his later years, judged the philosophy of his younger contemporary, James Frederick Ferrier, to be of slight significance, Ferrier himself held to the end the highest appreciation of Hamilton both as a man and as a philosopher. In the Appendix to the *Institutes of Metaphysics* (1854), Ferrier expressed his appreciation as follows: "I have learnt more from him than from all other philosophers put together; more, both as regards what I assented to and what I dissented from. His contributions to philosophy have been great; but the man himself was greater far. I have studied both. I approve of much in the one; in the other I approve of all. He was a giant in every field of intellectual action. I trust that I have profited by whatever is valuable in the letter of his system: at any rate, I venture to hope that, from my acquaintance, both with himself and his writings, I have imbibed some small portion of his philosophic spirit; and that spirit, when left freely to itself, was as gentle as the calm, and yet also as intrepid as the storm."

This high regard for the elder philosopher on Ferrier's part grew out of an unusually intimate association during many years when "scarcely a day passed in which I was not in his company for many hours." Ferrier's estimate is therefore colored by a deep and loyal friendship, and should be evaluated in the light of that fact. However, in spite of his friendly loyalty to the man, Ferrier was not by any means blind to the shortcomings of Hamilton's philosophy, as is intimated in the quotation above. Particularly was he displeased with the Hamiltonian doctrine of the 'conditioned,' which seemed to him to rest upon an inadequate analysis of the nature of knowledge. Ferrier's own 'agnoiology,' or theory of ignorance, was developed in explicit opposition to this doctrine. His reasons for the rejection

17

of the doctrine and his own counter-theory will appear as we follow his formulation of his general theory.

Ferrier's estimate of Reid is on quite a different plane. Of the man himself he thinks well enough, and he is, in general, sympathetic to what Reid was trying to do. But of the philosophic acumen which Reid brought to bear upon his task Ferrier holds a very qualified opinion. Such an opinion he thinks is amply warranted by a consideration of the outcome of Reid's attempt to deal critically with the issue before him. He was sound, Ferrier agrees, in his conviction that the only way of escape from the idealism of Berkeley and the skepticism of Hume lies through a denial of the premise from which the argument starts, namely, Locke's theory of perception. But the bare denial of a given point of view is in itself of no special philosophical significance; the basis of the denial, and the construction built upon it, is the important matter philosophically considered.

It is Ferrier's conviction that Reid not only failed to get beyond a mere denial so far as his critical efforts are concerned, but that in his constructive efforts he fell back into the very position which his denial and subsequent construction were supposed to eliminate. "He [Reid] was among the first to *say* and to *write* that the representative theory of perception [namely, Locke's 'ideal system'] was false and erroneous, and was the fountainhead of scepticism and idealism. But this admission of his merits must be accompanied by the qualification that he adopted, as the basis of his philosophy, a principle which rendered nugatory all his protestations. It is of no use to disclaim a conclusion if we accept the premises which inevitably lead to it. Dr. Reid disclaimed the representative theory, but he embraced its premises, and thus he virtually ratified the conclusions of the very system which he clamorously denounced." [1] And most of Ferrier's further consideration of Reid's argument is in support of this general accusation.

That Reid remained to the end caught in the clutches of

---

[1] J. F. Ferrier, *Philosophical Works*, Vol. III, p. 418; author's italics. I quote from the edition of 1883 by Sir Alexander Grant and E. L. Lushington.

Locke's representative theory of perception is to Ferrier quite obvious. For Reid's analysis of perceptual knowledge leaves him in the position of accepting the object of knowledge as essentially dual in nature; and any theory of perception which accepts this, Ferrier contends, is to be denominated a representative theory.[2] "His analysis gave him more than he bargained for. He wished to obtain only one, that is, only a proximate object in perception; but his analysis necessarily gave him two: it gave him a remote as well as a proximate object. The mental mode or operation which he calls the perception of matter, and which he distinguishes from matter itself, this, in his philosophy, is the proximate object of consciousness, and is precisely equivalent to the species, phantasms, and representations of the older psychology; the real existence, matter itself, which he distinguishes from the perception of it, this is the remote object of mind, and is precisely equivalent to the mediate or represented object of the older psychology."[3] And so Reid remains essentially at one with the theory of Locke, despite his 'clamorous' denunciation of that theory.

Logically, therefore, Reid on his own showing should have been an idealist like Berkeley, or a skeptic like Hume, and for precisely the same reasons. He thinks he escapes both idealism and skepticism by an appeal to "our instinctive and irresistible belief" in the independent existence of matter. But such a belief is non-existent, because it is logically impossible; and it is logically impossible, because it involves a flat contradiction. In the case of a man's perception of a tree, for example, "unless he believes in the existence of the tree disengaged from its perception, he does not believe in the independent existence of the tree, in the existence of the tree *per se*. Now, can the mind by any effort effect this disengagement? The thing is an absolute impossibility. The condition on which the belief hinges cannot be purified, and consequently the belief itself cannot be enter-

---

[2] "It is the very essence and definition of the representative theory to recognize, in perception, a remote as well as a proximate object of the mind. Every system which does this is necessarily a representative system." (*Ibid.*, p. 415.)

[3] *Ibid.*, p. 417.

tained." [4] This belief, then, cannot offer a logical way of escape from the idealism or skepticism implicit in the representative theory of perception; at best, it is but a comforting illusion.

In Ferrier's opinion, there is one, and only one, way of escape from Hume's skeptical conclusions; and that way lies through an adequate analysis of the nature of perceptual experience. This lesson, at least, he thinks, is taught by Reid's futile attempt at escape; and it is the lesson that is basal to any sound philosophy. The nature of perceptual experience, adequately apprehended, and its implications for philosophical theory Ferrier undertakes to set forth in the positive formulation of his own argument given below.

From the beginning, however, he would have it understood that the escape from Hume does not involve a return to Berkeley. Though convinced that Berkeley was "a speculator in the truest sense of the word," since he was highly endowed with "the power of seeing true facts and of *unseeing* false ones," Ferrier holds that the idealism of the bishop is no more ultimately satisfactory than is the skepticism of Hume or the common sense philosophy of Reid and his group. He is indeed willing to admit that, on its negative side, Berkeley's idealism expresses an important truth; any sane philosophy, he thinks, must deny what Berkeley was primarily concerned to deny, namely, "an occult something which, in itself, is *not* touched, *not* seen, *not* heard, *not* smelled, and *not* tasted; a phantom-world lying behind the visible and tangible universe, and which . . . is never itself brought within the sphere or apprehension of the senses." [5]

The affirmative implication of this, namely, that matter depends on mind for its existence, is in Ferrier's opinion a tenet which is fundamental within any philosophy that really knows what it is about. But the argument which Berkeley advances in support of the tenet he regards as wholly unsatisfactory. *Esse est percipi* is tantamount to the assertion that there are trees, houses, and the like, solely *because* they are perceived or thought

---

[4] Ferrier, *op. cit.*, p. 423.
[5] *Ibid.*, p. 296. The italics are in the original text.

of as perceived; and this seems to imply that they would not be *unless* they were perceived. But precisely in this implication is found the major weakness of the Berkeleyan position. "The realist may laugh it to scorn by saying, 'Then, I suppose, there are no trees and no houses when there is no man's mind either seeing or thinking of them!' " [6] The realist here tacitly assumes a distinction between the object and our perception of the object, and that distinction is of course precisely the point at issue. But Berkeley's argument as it stands is not sufficient to meet the realist's objection; it must be enlarged, if the baselessness of the realist's assumption is to be adequately exposed. And this enlargement must include the affirmation that "in the case of *every* phenomenon, that is, even in the case of the *phenomenon of the absence of all phenomena,* a subject-mind must be thought of as incarnated with the phenomenon."

When Berkeley's argument is thus expanded, "it is then proof against all cavils and objections whatever. It is perfectly true that the existence of matter depends entirely on the presence, that is, either the real or the ideal presence, of a conscious mind. But it does not follow from this that there would be *no-matter* if no such conscious mind were present or thought of as present, because *no-matter* depends just as much upon the real or ideal presence of a conscious mind. Thus are spiked all the cannon of false realism; thus all her trenches are obliterated, all her supplies cut off, and all her resources rendered unserviceable. Thus, too, we may add, is the flank of false idealism turned, and her forces driven from their ground, while absolute real idealism, or the complete conciliation of common sense and philosophy, remains in triumphant possession of the field." [7] How Ferrier thinks this campaign should be conducted so as to insure the consummate victory of "absolute real idealism" will appear in detail below.

Ferrier is particularly enthusiastic about his theory of ignorance (developed in the Part of the *Institutes of Metaphysics* entitled "Agnoiology"), which he thinks is "an entire novelty in philosophy" and which, as we shall see, plays a very important

---

[6] Ferrier, *op. cit.,* p. 314.
[7] *Ibid.,* pp. 314, 315-316. The italics are in the text.

part in the campaign leading to the victory forecast above. Its major thesis and its place in the argument as a whole will be considered in the proper context. Here it is sufficient to note that the theory was projected with special reference to the doctrine of nescience advocated by Hamilton and, as he supposed, accepted in principle by most of the major philosophers from Protagoras to Kant. It is true that Ferrier does not specifically mention Hamilton in this connection, but he clearly has in mind the doctrine of which Hamilton was the most eminent contemporary exponent.

The doctrine of nescience Ferrier deems wholly without significance, because its proponents have never seriously inquired precisely what it is they are talking about when they speak of ignorance. And they have failed to raise this question concerning the nature of ignorance largely because they have been too much occupied with contemplating its immensity and bewailing its existence. "Its quantity has distracted their attention from its quality. *'Heu, quantum est quod nescimus!'* exclaim they pathetically. 'What an immensity of ignorance is ours!' True; but these whinings will never teach us what ignorance is, what its law is, and what its object is: and this alone is what we, as searchers after truth, are interested in finding out." [8] And unless we do find out, Ferrier maintains, the whole ontological problem becomes intrinsically insoluble, for, then, reality continuously falls away into the misty vastness of nescience undefined and, so, forever eludes our grasp. "Any reasoned ontological conclusion establishing what alone absolutely exists, is obviously impossible in a system which admits our ignorance without entering into any critical inquiry as to its nature; while, on the other hand, the ontology of a system which denies our ignorance, or passes it over *sub silentio*, must either rest upon a false ground, or upon no ground at all,—on a false ground if our ignorance is denied—on no ground at all if it is not taken into account. . . . A reasoned and systematic ontology has remained until this day a desideratum in speculative science, because a reasoned and systematic agnoiology has never yet

---

[8] Ferrier, *Institutes of Metaphysics,* p. 437. I quote from the third edition, published in 1875.

been projected." [9] Hence both Ferrier's estimate of the importance of his own agnoiology and the fondness with which he was inclined to regard it.

It is now time to turn from these preliminary and more or less negative remarks to Ferrier's systematic formulation of his own position. Henceforward, he will be permitted, so far as possible, to speak directly and in his own terminology. The argument as here summarized is taken in the main from the *Institutes of Metaphysics*, which, of course, is the author's major work.[10] For the headings under which the summary is given, I am responsible; but the order of the argument, as well as the terminology, is my author's.

1. NATURE AND METHOD OF PHILOSOPHY

Philosophy is bound by two main requisitions: It ought to be true, and it ought to be reasoned. It is more important that philosophy be reasoned than that it be true. For, if it be not reasoned, even though it be true, it will have no scientific value and will also lack value as a mental discipline. Furthermore, it will be true provided it is adequately reasoned.

What, then, are we to understand by an adequately reasoned philosophy? Such a philosophy is a system of propositions arranged in accordance with the "right use" of reason. And reason is used rightly when it concerns itself only with necessary truths, that is, with truths or propositions the opposites of which are inconceivable because contradictory. The law of contradiction, then, is the criterion of the right use of reason. When reason proceeds according to this law it is *right reason,* and the system of propositions thus established will be a rightly reasoned system of true propositions—will, in short, be philosophy. The basal canon of all philosophy, therefore, is this: *"Affirm* nothing except what is enforced by reason as a necessary truth—that is, as a truth the reversal of which would involve a contradiction;

---

[9] *Ibid.,* pp. 407-408.

[10] Other discussions, important for Ferrier's argument, were published under "Philosophical Remains" in Vol. III of his *Works.* Among these should be mentioned particularly the lengthy "Introduction to the Philosophy of Consciousness" (1838-1839) and "The Crisis of Modern Speculation" (1841).

and *deny* nothing, unless its affirmation involves a contradiction —that is, contradicts some necessary truth or law of reason." Whoever follows this canon rigorously in his deliberations will inevitably emerge with a rightly reasoned and therefore true philosophy.

2. THE PROBLEM AND STARTING POINT OF PHILOSOPHY

When one sets about the application of the method above described, it at once becomes evident that there is a difficulty involved in determining precisely what truths are necessary truths, and which among such truths are important for philosophy. Not all conclusions accepted as truths are necessary truths; on the contrary, it is often difficult to distinguish necessary truths from generally accepted erroneous beliefs. The only way of surmounting this difficulty is to penetrate to a necessary truth as a point of departure for reason, and from that to proceed to other necessary truths through the application of the law or principle of contradiction. This necessary point of departure, for philosophy, is to be obtained by an analysis of the problem of philosophy. The starting point of philosophical reasoning must be a proposition the necessity of which is fixed in its relevancy to the general problem of which philosophy is seeking the solution, and relevancy can be apprehended only when the problem to be solved is clearly defined. Consequently, we must first inquire what the problem of philosophy is, and then proceed to ask what necessary truth discloses itself as a point of departure for one seeking to attain a reasoned solution of that problem.

(a) *The Problem of Philosophy*. As has been generally admitted throughout the ages of speculation, the problem of philosophy turns upon the connection between the mind of man and the order of things. But the problem has been variously formulated because of the ambiguities of the terms *mind* and *things*. Our first task, then, is to remove these ambiguities.

In the tradition it has been commonly assumed that mind and things are sharply sundered entities, each definable in its own right without reference to the other. On this assumption, the problem of philosophy has been identified with the following question: How is mind *per se* related to the thing *per se?* The attempt to solve the problem thus formulated led to the representative theory of preception—the theory, namely, that outward objects cause within mind perceptions which somehow represent or stand for the objects. The *prima facie* implication of this theory is that there can be no direct knowledge of objects *per se*, since what is immediately known is not the object but its representative in the mind. From this it is not a long step to the question as to whether there can be any inferential knowledge of objects *per se*. So the problem of the relation between mind and things, as thus understood, sooner or later transforms itself logically, as it did historically, into the question as to whether there is logical ground for belief in an external world at all.

In answer to this question, three historical systems have been formulated: (i) Hypothetical Realism, according to which there must be assumed to be, though there cannot be proved to be, a real external order as the source of our perceptions; (ii) Idealism, which flatly identifies things with perceptions, and holds that a belief in an external order of things is an illogical encumbrance; and (iii) Skepticism, which, while not denying the possibility of an external order of things, urges that, if there be such an order, it must be something very different from what appears to us in perception and must therefore remain for us an object of ignorance. Each of these theories has something to say for itself, but no one of them is in the end entirely satisfactory. Once mind and things are sharply sundered, there is no logical way to bring them together. Speculation is thereby brought into inextricable perplexities.

The source of these perplexities is, of course, the assumption that leads to them. But this assumption is false, arising as it does from a mistaken view of the nature of actual perception. According to this view the difference between what are called things and our perceptions of them is an absolute difference The true view is that the difference is only a relative difference —describable in terms of shifting points of view with reference to one and the same factual situation. The total fact is the perceptual-situation. Of this situation, there is an objective side and a subjective side, but they are merely two aspects of the same total situation. Furthermore, they are strictly logical correlatives; the objective aspect cannot even be thought except in reference to the subjective, and the thought of the subjective just as inevitably involves reference to the objective.

One thinks of light, for example, by and through the thought of seeing, and one can think of it in no other manner. Conversely, seeing is thought through the thought of light, and it can be thought in no other way. When we think the object, then, we are compelled "by an invincible law of our nature" to think the subject along with it; and when we think the subject, on the other side, we are by the same necessity compelled to think the object also. Subject and object, mind and thing, are not existentially two; they are aspects of that which exists as one. Subject-object in inseparable union is the basal knowledge-fact, as disclosed by observation and substantiated by speculative analysis. And the failure to see this is the fatal oversight which gives rise to the representative theory of knowledge and its philosophical offspring.

From the preceding considerations it follows that knowledge is not in mind, if by *mind* is intended something which exists in isolation from things; nor are things external to, and independent of, mind. Human knowledge, at any rate, is subject in inseparable union with object, object in inseparable union with subject. To attempt to go beyond this relation is to try to achieve that which is logically impossible; to confuse the relation leads to inescapable perplexities, as is evidenced by the older theories; to hold the relation clear is the beginning of wisdom in philosophy.

The problem of philosophy is now seen in an entirely new light. It can no longer be identified with the question: What is the connection between the mind of man *and* the external world? For these are now seen to be, not two things, but one thing. The question is, therefore, identical with asking about the nature of the connection between one thing—a question which "no one but an Irishman would think of asking, or expecting an answer to." This formulation of the problem is simply an irrational absurdity; the question posed cannot be answered, not because it is unanswerable, but because it is un-askable. The real problem, on the other hand, is quite different from this: it concerns the implications of the subject-object situation. There is, and can be, no question as to how knowledge is made. The only possible question is: What is the nature of knowledge? And this is the genuine problem of philosophy.

(b) *The Starting Point of Philosophy*. Having arrived at the formulation of the philosophical problem, we are in posi-tion to advance towards the statement of the necessary truth on which our system of philosophy may safely be founded. But we cannot go directly to an apprehension of this necessary truth. A further step in analysis of the problem is requisite before we can clearly discern the starting point of our reasoned solution.

The question: What is the nature of knowledge? is in its turn vague,* since it is open to more than one interpretation; and its meaning must be fixed before we can proceed. "Now, when well considered, it will be found that the question, What is knowledge? must mean one of two things. It must mean either, *first*, What is knowledge in so far as its kinds differ? In plainer words—What different kinds of knowledge are there? Or it must mean, *secondly*, What is knowledge in so far as its various kinds agree? In plainer words—What is the one invari-able feature, quality, or constituent, common to all our cogni-tions, however diverse and multifarious these, in other respects, may be?" The question: What is knowledge? is not susceptible of being analyzed into any other meanings than these two.[11]

Our next step, then, is to inquire which of these two possible forms of the question is logically fundamental. This inquiry may be very brief, since little reflection is needed to see that the question concerning the different kinds of knowledge is itself not fundamental. It is, therefore, of no interest to philos-ophy, which is not required to teach us that the different kinds of knowledge are the mathematical, historical, and the like. The

[11] The meaning of the question in the sense in which it might be equivalent to: What is the genesis of the knowledge situation? is, in Ferrier's opinion, ruled out by the analysis which we have summarily traced above under section (a). The reader may find Ferrier's detailed statement of that analysis in the essay, "The Crisis of Modern Specula-tion," *Works*, Vol. III.

alternative question alone is left, and it must give us the basal
problem of philosophy. The complete answer to it must, therefore,
constitute philosophy, and within it must be found the necessary
truth which is to serve as the foundation of the system.

What is this necessary truth? Let us see. The common point,
quality, or feature in all our knowledge is necessarily that element which is essential to every datum of cognition, and without which cognition would be impossible. "In other words, it must
be such an element that, if taken away, the whole datum is,
of necessity, extinguished, and its restoration rendered absolutely impossible until the missing element is restored." What,
now, is this element? That which must be known along with
whatever else is known and which alone is common to all knowledge is the self, or ego, or subject which knows. That is the
common center in which all our cognitions meet, and apart from
which no cognition is possible. Giving explicit recognition to
this basal fact in the form of a general proposition, then, we
derive this fundamental law: "Along with whatever any intelligence knows, it must, as the ground or condition of its knowledge, have some cognisance of itself." And this is the first
necessary truth of our reasoned solution of the problem of knowledge.[12]

Since this proposition is the foundation of the whole system
and every proposition which follows hinges on its stability, we
may pause to consider for a moment its necessity. (i) The
first point to be noted is that experience does not disprove the
proposition but, on the contrary, supports it. It is a fact of
experience, to be sure, that, when we are engaged in the active
pursuits of life or absorbed in contemplation, we are not conscious of ourselves. But this fact is not in opposition to our
proposition; it is only an illustration of a general law, the law
of familiarity, which is expressed in the adage: "Familiarity
breeds neglect." We are so familiar with ourselves that we tend
to neglect ourselves in the datum of cognition. It must be care-

---

[12] John Grote, a younger contemporary of Ferrier, has some critical comments to make on this first proposition of Ferrier's system and on the
method (called by Grote the "Euclidic method") which he follows in his
argument. The comments will be found in the *Exploratio Philosophica*,
Part I, 54 ff. See below, Chapter III, pp. 67-70.

fully noted, however, that our proposition affirms only that the self or subject is always in some sense present in cognition as that to which perceptions and thought are (it may be, only latently) referred. And experience supports this: let a man search his cognitive experience as diligently as he may, he will invariably find that his cognizance of any content is a cognizance of it as *his*. (ii) More important, however, is the consideration that reason shows our proposition to be axiomatic. "If it were possible for an intelligence to receive knowledge at *any one* time without knowing that it was *his* knowledge, it would be possible for him to do this at *all* times. So that an intelligent being might be endowed with knowledge without once, during the whole term of his existence, knowing that he possessed it." But this is absurd, since it involves a contradiction. A man who is not aware that his perceptions and thoughts are his cannot be aware of them at all. Hence a man who knows anything must always know that he knows it, must, in other words, be self-conscious. Consequently our first proposition is a necessary truth of reason, the denial of which involves a contradiction.

3. FURTHER INFERENCES

From this basal proposition it follows directly that the object of all knowledge is not an object in the usual meaning of the term, but object-*plus*-subject—thing *mecum*. As our preceding analysis has already disclosed, this is really only another form of our original proposition; but it is not a useless repetition, since it has the advantage of explicitly guarding us against the fatal error (above referred to) of supposing that object is independent of subject. This new formulation also emphasizes another fundamental truth, namely, that the objective part of the object of knowledge and the subjective part of the object of knowledge, though clearly distinguishable, are in fact inseparable and together constitute the unit of knowledge. And from this it immediately follows that matter *per se*, together with its qualities whether 'primary' or secondary,' is absolutely unknowable—cannot be an object of knowledge. Therefore the epistemological foundation of the older Realism is swept away.

Again, every object of cognition must contain an element that is common to all and an element that is peculiar to itself. In other words knowledge is a synthesis of that which is unchangeable, necessary, and universal on the one side, and that which is changeable, contingent, and particular on the other. This is proved by the dual fact that all cognitions may be classed together *as cognition*, and yet they are all quite distinct from one another. There are, thus, two parts—that which is the same in all and that which is different in each—involved in the constitution of every cognition.[13] And all knowledge is necessarily a synthesis of both factors.[14]

The element common to all cognitions is the ego or mind, while matter is the element peculiar to particular cognitions. The first clause of this statement is simply a repetition of our original proposition: The ego is of necessity known along with whatever is known. The second clause is established by the consideration (a) that cognitions in which no material element is apprehended are conceivable, and, therefore, matter is not an element common to all cognitions; but (b) that matter is an element in some cognitions and, when it is so, is known as the differential part of them. We may, therefore, say that the ego is immaterial, if by immateriality be meant universality in cognition. Since the ego is the universal element in cognition and cannot be known as particular, it, therefore, cannot be known as material. Furthermore, the ego *per se* is unknowable, since the ego is the common element of all cognitions, and every cognition must contain a differential part; or, otherwise expressed, the ego is known only along with some determinate modification; but always, be it

---

[13] The word *cognition* here signifies the known, the *cognitum*, the object of knowledge, not the act of knowing.

[14] This truth, Ferrier maintains, renders nugatory the traditional interpretation of Plato's theory, which identifies it with the doctrine that there is an inferior kind of knowledge occupied with particulars, and a superior kind of knowledge occupied with universals—an interpretation which, in point of historical fact, he thinks, is contrary to the main drift of Plato's thought. And the truth also undermines the controversy among the realists, conceptualists, and nominalists of the Middle Ages about universals—a controversy which ultimately rested upon nothing more significant than this misinterpretation of Plato's doctrine of Ideas.

remembered, as the universal which remains unchanged and permanent in the midst of changing particulars.[15]

Since the ego must form a part of every cognition and since the ego cannot be known as material (that is, cannot be apprehended by the senses), it follows that *mere* objects of sense can never be objects of cognition. Mere objects of sense are inherently contradictory, since whatever is known must be known along with that which itself cannot possibly be a mere object of sense. With this conclusion we have destroyed the foundation upon which rests the doctrine of "sensualism" in all its forms—the doctrine, namely, that all knowledge is referable to, and originally derived from, the senses. Of course, there is involved here no denial of the thesis that all knowledge comes from experience. Knowledge is itself experience, and to say that knowledge comes from experience is simply to say that knowledge is knowledge, a tautological truism. What is denied, however, is the view that "*nihil est in intellectu quod non prius fuit in sensu*"—in other words, the view that all knowledge comes from sensible experience. Sense experience is not itself a cognition, it is only an element of cognition. Sense and intellect "constitute one capacity of cognition, and can bring knowledge to mind only when in joint operation."

It is possible to draw a distinction between (a) knowledge or knowing and (b) thought or thinking, using the first to express our original cognitive experiences—the perceptions, for example, which we have of things when they are actually before us—and the second to express our cognition of that previous knowledge. On the basis of this distinction it might be supposed that it is possible for us to think what it is impossible for us to know. Such a supposition, however, would be mistaken. It is impossible

[15] For the sake of clarity, it must be borne in mind that the discussion here concerns the ego and matter only in so far as they function in the cognitive situation. The point made is: not that the self or ego cannot *be* material, but that it cannot *be known* to be such; not that it cannot *exist per se* (that is, in an indeterminate state), but that it cannot *be known per se*.

Problems of ontology or of existence are not as yet raised in the argument; they enter only after the nature of ignorance is considered, since it is Ferrier's conviction that the agnoiology logically precedes any consideration of ontological issues.

for us to think what it is impossible for us to know, since thinking is nothing but a representation of what was formerly presented in knowing. Of course, thought can alter the arrangement of the data of knowledge and mold them into new combinations, as when one thinks of a centaur; and this power of thought is not intended here to be denied. The important point is that thought cannot transcend knowledge on the one side, nor on the other subtract from it any essential element. The unit or minimum of thought is commensurate, in its essential constituents, with the unit or minimum of cognition. Whatever is basically unknowable, therefore, is basically unthinkable, and whatever is foundational in knowledge is likewise foundational in thought. Hence matter *per se* and its qualities, as well as the ego *per se*, having been shown to be unknowable, are of necessity absolutely unthinkable also.

Further, since the only universe that can be known is objects in relation to subject, it follows that only such a universe is thinkable. The only sense in which any mind can think of an *independent* universe is the sense in which it can think of objects in synthesis with some *other* mind. If it be objected that this assumes a logical impossibility (namely, that another self is knowable by a mind), the answer is that what is assumed is clearly logical, since in the apprehension by a given mind of itself in synthesis with objects, it has a pattern or instance according to which it can cogitate another mind in the same state. Finally, object in synthesis with subject is the only knowable, and therefore, the only thinkable, substance or absolute; for subject-object alone is that which can be known or thought without anything else, of necessity, being known or thought along with it.

All that has hitherto been said holds true, not only of human knowing and thinking, but of all knowing and thinking whatsoever. We have been dealing, not with contingent aspects of knowing and thinking, but with the universal and unchangeable laws of thought and knowledge—the conditions apart from which all cognition and all intelligence are simply impossible. In this connection it is important to observe that our senses are not laws of cognition which are universally binding; on the contrary, they are contingent conditions of knowledge. It is conceivable that intelligences other than human should apprehend objects in ways other than those of hearing, seeing, touching, tasting, and smelling; for it is conceivable that our senses might be entirely changed and knowledge still be possible—knowledge of quite a different content, of course, from that which we now possess. The senses, therefore, are not indispensable conditions of knowledge and thought; they are contingent only.[16] What is indispensable is that apart from which knowing and thinking are alike inconceivable, namely, subject and object in inseparable union.

Hereupon we may explicitly state the final answer to the question with which we began: What is knowledge? The answer is: The apprehension of the self along with all that one apprehends—this, and this alone, is knowledge. To the question: What is known? the answer is: The synthesis of subject and object is the minimum, the unit, of any possible knowledge; these two factors are required to constitute any cognition. And to the question: What is absolutely unknowable? the answer is: Any object without a subject, or any subject without an object, is absolutely unknowable. Finally, to the question: What is thinkable or unthinkable? the answer must be: Anything that is knowable is thinkable, and anything that is unknowable is unthinkable. These are the major results of the science of epistemology.

4. NATURE OF EXISTENCE

It is a mistake to suppose that we can pass directly from the conclusion of our epistemological inquiry to the task of determining the nature of that which exists. Such procedure would leave a fatal gap in the logic of our argument. For if, in answer to

---

[16] Ferrier thinks that it is in forgetfulness of precisely this point that the theory of representative perception and the theory of Berkeley alike go astray. The advocates of representationism waver between the alternatives of elevating the senses to the same footing of necessity with the ego on the one hand, and of reducing the ego to the same footing of contingency with the senses on the other; while Berkeley accepts unequivocally the first alternative. But both are in error, and in the same error; for both alike fail to see that the ego is the necessary condition of all knowledge and thought, whether human or not, while the senses are merely contingent and of significance only with reference to human knowing and thinking.

the question: What truly and absolutely is? we should fall back on our epistemology and reply that it is what is absolutely knowable and thinkable, namely, objects *plus* a subject, it would still be open to the skeptic to assert that such a reply does not necessarily follow, even granting our epistemological conclusions, since that which exists may be that of which we are profoundly ignorant. And to such a skeptical objection, we have not yet developed principles for an adequate rejoinder.

Such principles can be set forth only in an agnoiology, or theory of ignorance. It remains to be shown that the object of ignorance is necessarily identical with the object of knowledge. But this can readily be shown.

Ignorance is nothing more than an intellectual defect, since it is merely a deprivation of something which is consistent with the nature of intelligence, that is, knowledge. Ignorance is also *logically* remediable; if it were not so, the knowledge by which the ignorance in question might be remedied would be inconsistent with the nature of all intelligence, and this is an absurdity. Hence there can be ignorance only of that which can possibly be known, since any ignorance of that which cannot possibly be known would not be logically remediable. Therefore the object of all ignorance is identical with the object of all knowledge.[17]

With this conclusion established, we are in position to proceed without fear of the skeptic to a definition of the nature of absolute being or existence. That which truly and absolutely exists is either that which we know, or that which we are ignorant of, or that which we neither know nor are ignorant of; and no other alternative is possible. But that which we neither know nor are ignorant of must be the contradictory; for if it were not the contradictory it would be knowable, and therefore either an object of knowledge or an object of ignorance.[18] That

---

[17] For a criticism of this theory of ignorance, the reader is referred to Grote's comments in his *Exploratio Philosophica,* Part I, 56, 74-75. See below, Chapter III.

[18] The contradictory "is either of the factors of cognition taken by itself, or apart from its co-factor." In other words, it is either the object *per se* or the subject *per se.* (*Institutes of Metaphysics,* Section III, Proposition I, Observation 10.)

which truly and absolutely exists is not the contradictory, however, since there is no contradiction involved in the proposition that something (whatever it may be) truly and absolutely exists. Consequently, that which exists must be either an object of knowledge or an object of ignorance—that is, it can be neither matter *per se* nor mind or ego *per se*, but only some-object-plus-some-subject. Any absolute existent, then, is necessarily mind-together-with-that-which-it-apprehends.

In answer to the question: How many absolute existents are there? one need be neither hesitant nor vague. It is abstractly possible that there are many absolute existents, but only one is logically necessary. We can therefore say that there is only one absolutely necessary existent—the abstractly possible ones are contingent, not necessary. The one necessary absolute existent is an Absolute Mind in synthesis with all things, and it is necessary because it must be postulated to save the world from presenting reason with a contradiction. Other existents (finite-minds-together-with-things), however, do not require to be postulated to save the world from contradiction, and they are therefore contingent. "The universe is rescued from contradiction as effectually by the supposition of one intelligence in connection with it, as by the supposition of ten million, and reason never postulates more than is necessary. Therefore all absolute existences are contingent except one. In other words, there is One, but only One, Absolute Existence which is strictly necessary; and that existence is a supreme, and infinite, and eternal Mind in synthesis with all things." [19]

5. Summary of Argument

The argument advanced by Ferrier may conveniently be reduced to the following theses, which summarily state the major points:

[19] *Institutes of Metaphysics,* Section III, Proposition XI. Compare: "There was a time when the world was without man. . . . This is intelligible to reason. But in the judgment of reason there never can have been a time when the universe was without God. *That* is unintelligible to reason; because time is not time, but is nonsense, without a mind; space is not space, but is nonsense, without a mind; all objects are not objects, but are nonsense, without a mind; in short, the whole universe is neither anything nor nothing, but is the sheer contradictory, without a mind."

(a) Reality is either (i) that which we know, or (ii) that of which we are ignorant, or (iii) that of which we neither have knowledge nor are ignorant; and there is no other alternative.

(b) If reality is (iii), it must be the contradictory; but this is impossible, since there is no contradiction involved in the proposition that something is real.

(c) If reality is (ii), it must also be (i); for the object of ignorance is necessarily identical in its basal characteristics with the object of knowledge.

(d) But if reality is (i), then it must unequivocally be equated with some object *plus* some subject; for subject-object is the atomic fact of the cognitive situation.

(e) Only one subject is necessary to define reality and redeem the world from contradiction, and this subject must have for its object all that in any sense can be said to exist. Absolute Reality, therefore, is one subject which has as object all there is; there are indeed other subjects, but these are contingent and not logically necessary.

These theses, Ferrier maintains, are reasoned and true—reasoned, because they necessarily follow from an initial proposition; true, because this initial proposition is a necessary proposition. Hence "absolute real idealism" is the only philosophy, and it is certain.[20]

[20] The statement of Ferrier's idealism given in this chapter leaves out of account much of the richness and suggestiveness of his thought as contained in the numerous "Observations" which supplement the formal proofs of the "Propositions" in the *Institutes of Metaphysics*. But, in his own view it would appear, Ferrier's chief contribution to philosophical speculation lies in his rigorous deduction of the idealistic view; and the logic of that deduction is fairly presented, both in form and content, in the preceding statement.

Chapter II

THOMAS HILL GREEN (1836-1882)

Some of Ferrier's contemporaries asserted that his philosophy was borrowed largely from Continental thinkers—its method from Spinoza and its content from Hegel, whose system was then coming into prominence in British circles. Such an accusation Ferrier resented with some heat. "My philosophy," he writes in the Appendix to the *Institutes*, "is Scottish to the very core; I disclaim for it the paternity of Germany or Holland: I assert that in every fibre it is of home growth and national texture." And there seems little reason to doubt that his assertion is in principle correct, despite the fact that his thought, in both method and result, differs rather radically from the Scottish main tradition.

Of course, there is a general similarity in method between the *Institutes of Metaphysics* and Spinoza's famous work. But, after all, the similarity is not sufficiently striking to warrant any inference that Ferrier was consciously following Spinoza. They have nothing in common except that each, in his own way, attempts to construct his philosophy in the form of a series of propositions rigorously deduced from a point of departure held to be necessary. This much, Ferrier maintains, must be common to all philosophers who seriously try to follow the method of reason itself and are not content simply to indulge in idle flights of fancy. The parallelism in method between the two thinkers may readily be explained by the fact that each was undertaking to develop a reasoned philosophy and both were agreed concerning the demands which such a philosophy makes.

As to the accusation that Ferrier parades the content of Hegel's philosophy in a new dress, one must say simply that there is not the slightest evidence in support of it. He claims that he did not understand the Hegelian system, despite the fact that he had read Hegel's writings many times and even

37

wrote an article about him for publication in the *Imperial Dictionary of Universal Biography*.[1] Whether this protestation of ignorance of Hegel's meaning is to be taken seriously may be questioned, though I think there is evidence that in the main it is justified. And, in any event, there is no evidence of Hegelian influence traceable in the argument as formulated in the *Institutes* and summarized in the preceding chapter. That argument is linked primarily—though, indeed, negatively—with the British tradition culminating in Reid and Hamilton, as Ferrier understood that tradition. The argument shows no trace of the principles developed in post-Kantian German idealism.[2]

The year after Ferrier's death there was published a book which is generally said to mark a new attitude, and even a new era, in British philosophy. That book is James Hutchison Stirling's *The Secret of Hegel, being the Hegelian-System in Origin, Principle, Form, and Matter*.[3] As its title suggests, the primary purpose of this book is to disclose the historical background and the basal meaning of Hegel's system of philosophy. The assumption underlying the author's exposition is that, once understood, the secret of Hegel will prove to be the *open sesame* for all troublesome philosophical perplexities, the thread of Ariadne

---

[1] Ferrier's full statement of his relation to Hegel is, "The exact truth of the matter is this: I have read most of Hegel's works again and again, but I cannot say that I am acquainted with his philosophy. I am able to understand only a few short passages here and there in his writings; and these I greatly admire for the depth of their insight, the breadth of their wisdom, and the loftiness of their tone. More than this I cannot say. If others understand him better and to a larger extent, they have the advantage of me, and I confess I envy them the privilege. But, for myself, I must declare that I have not found one word or one thought in Hegel which was available for my system, even if I had been disposed to use it. If Hegel follows (as I do) the demonstrative method, I own I cannot see it, and would feel much obliged to any one who would point this out and make it clear." (Appendix to the *Institutes*.) And he confesses elsewhere that he finds Hegel to be "impenetrable almost throughout as a mountain of adamant."

[2] In the articles on Schelling and Hegel, published in the *Imperial Dictionary of Universal Biography*, there is perhaps some evidence that Ferrier did in the end grasp more of the basal principles of German idealism, and especially of so-called Hegelianism, than he was willing to admit in the *Institutes*. But, even so, what is said above in the text about his own formulation of the idealistic argument still holds true.

[3] First published in 1865; new edition in 1898.

that guides one safely through the hitherto untraversable labyrinth of metaphysical speculation.

In itself, the book is quite remarkable. It consists of translation, commentary, and discussion; it lacks clarity and order; and its terminological difficulties are frequently as great as those of its original—so great, in fact, that some unkind critics have suggested that it was apparently designed to keep, rather than disclose, the great secret. Despite its deficiencies, the book is not without merit; it is at least forceful and imaginative, and at times it throws into clear light the deeper drifts of the Hegelian dialectic. Historically, it is perhaps the first important fruitage of a movement which for some years had been under way in Britain—the movement, namely, to go beyond the insularity of the main tradition in British philosophy and to seek for new outlets in Continental thought, and particularly in German idealism.[4] And there is no doubt that Stirling's work exerted great influence on the British thought of the day, particularly in the direction of emphasizing the significance of the Hegelian philosophy as a solution for the problems raised by the traditional British empiricism.

Stirling's volume was speedily followed by a long list of other works devoted to essentially the same task, though independently of him. In this list a prominent place must be assigned to the writings of Edward Caird, especially to his comprehensive two-volume work entitled *The Critical Philosophy of Immanuel Kant* (1889), which undertakes to interpret and evaluate the Kantian philosophy in the light of Hegelian principles. Attention must be paid also to Caird's extraordinarily lucid account of the Hegelian system in the little volume on *Hegel* previously published (1883) in the Blackwood's Philosophical Classics series. His brother, John Caird, was also influential in applying

---

[4] For a statement of some of the more important details of this movement, the reader should consult the article by J. H. Muirhead on "How Hegel Came to England," *Mind*, N. S. XXXVI, 423 ff. See also the same author's books, *Coleridge as Philosopher* (1930) and *The Platonic Tradition in Anglo-Saxon Philosophy* (1931). The latter defends the thesis that the movement here under survey owed its inception, not only to the influx of German thought, but also to the revival of an idealistic tradition indigenous to British thought since John Scotus Erigena.

Hegelian principles to the problems of the philosophy of religion in *An Introduction to the Philosophy of Religion* (1880).

William Wallace, who succeeded Thomas Hill Green in the chair of moral philosophy at Oxford, published translations of two of Hegel's works: *The Logic of Hegel* (translated in 1874 from Hegel's *Encyklopaedie*), and the *Philosophy of Mind* (1894). These translations introduced the text of two of Hegel's most important works to those who found it difficult, if not impossible, to follow the author's crabbed German; and the translator's "Prolegomena" accompanying the translation of the *Logic* were of service in calling attention to important applications of the principles of the system.

To this list numerous other titles and authors might be added, but the name which stands out most prominently in the development here under consideration, and which is by far the most important for the purpose of the present survey, is that of Green, the man Wallace succeeded at Oxford. By common consent of his associates in the movement, Green is the leader; and his argument in support of an idealistic philosophy is unquestionably the outstanding constructive expression of the period. We shall therefore turn to a detailed study of his formulation of the idealistic argument.[5]

Like Ferrier, Green is definitely of the conviction that the English speculation of the preceding century had reached an impasse and that the only hope for further progress lay in a thorough revision of the premises which had, logically enough, brought it to such a predicament. But, unlike Ferrier, he avowedly looked toward German philosophy for a way of escape. At the end of the second of the two very detailed *Introductions to Hume's Treatise of Human Nature*, Green tells us that his

[5] The most important writings of Green published during his life are the two lengthy *Introductions to Hume's Treatise of Human Nature* (1874), and his detailed analyses of the views of Herbert Spencer and George Henry Lewes (published as articles in the *Contemporary Review* for December, 1877, March, 1878, July, 1878, and January, 1881). These, together with some unpublished material in the form of lectures, were collected and published (1885, 1886) by R. L. Nettleship in two volumes as the *Works of Thomas Hill Green. The Prolegomena to Ethics*, which contains the fundamentals of Green's idealistic argument, was left unfinished at the author's death and was published the following year (1883) under the editorship of A. C. Bradley.

elaborate and critical analysis ("an irksome labour") of the British tradition was designed "to show that the philosophy based on the abstraction of feeling, in regard to morals no less than to nature, was with Hume played out, and that the next step forward in speculation could only be an effort to rethink the process of nature and human action from its beginning in thought."[6] He also there states his further conviction (painstakingly defended in the course of his survey) that this step forward would necessarily lead around the "anachronistic systems hitherto prevalent" in England, and through the systems of Kant and Hegel. He sought to give this conviction deeper grounding by a detailed critical study of current British theories of knowledge as expressed particularly in the writings of Herbert Spencer and George Henry Lewes.[7]

It is commonly asserted that Green is essentially a disciple of Hegel, but this is true only with quite important reservations. The basal principles of his idealistic argument derive from Kant rather than from Hegel, though he was not satisfied with Kant's final conclusions and felt that Hegel had, in principle, though somewhat hesitantly and vaguely, pointed the way beyond. Green did not doubt that something like Hegel's idealism is the inevitable outcome of the logical development of Kant's fundamental doctrines, but he was equally convinced that the substructure upon which Hegel built his system is of very doubtful stability.

In his important review (1880) of John Caird's *An Introduction to the Philosophy of Religion*—which, he holds, "represents a thorough assimilation" of Hegel's philosophy of religion— Green expresses his attitude towards Hegel's doctrine as follows: "When we think out the problem left by previous inquirers, we find ourselves led to it [that is, to Hegel's doctrine] by an intellectual necessity; but on reflection we become aware that we are Hegelian, so to speak, with only a fraction of our thoughts—on the Sundays of 'speculation,' not on the weekdays of 'ordinary thought.' . . ." And the main weakness he finds in Hegel's doctrine lies in its failure to supply "the need

[6] *Works*, Vol. I, 371.
[7] Cf. *Ibid.*, Vol. I, 373-520.

of some such mediation between speculative truth and our judgments concerning matters of fact as will help philosophy to come to an understanding with science." So he concludes that Hegel's doctrine, though essentially sound in its final tenets, "must all be done over again." In some important sense, he is convinced, we must go back to Kant for the foundational principles. Consequently, in his own attempt to face the philosophical problem we find him orienting his argument primarily with reference to the *Kritik der reinen Vernunft* as the main point of departure.

The problem bequeathed to philosophy by Hume, but largely ignored in its crucial features by his English followers, Green holds to be precisely the problem which Kant explicitly raised: How is knowledge possible? Kant's solution of the problem is, he thinks, not satisfactory, but at least it has the merit of directing attention to fundamentals; and this is the reason why he insists, first, upon a return to Kant and, then, upon going beyond him towards the results obtained by Hegel.

The upshot of British empiricism in its development from Locke to Hume, Green maintains, was the elimination of 'mind' from knowledge and the reduction of knowledge to mere passive sensations—as becomes clearly evident in Hume's analysis. It is for this reason, he thinks, that the traditional British philosophy "was with Hume played out." It is for this reason also that he feels impelled to raise once again the question concerning the nature of knowledge. "We have to return once more," he tells us in the Introduction to the *Prolegomena to Ethics*, "to that analysis of the conditions of knowledge, which forms the basis of all Critical Philosophy whether called by the name of Kant or no, and to ask whether the experience of connected matters of fact, which in its methodical expression we call science, does not presuppose a principle which is not itself any one or number of such matters of fact, or their result."

Green is convinced that such a principle is presupposed, and upon this conviction he builds his argument for an idealistic *Weltanschauung*. The argument is somewhat involved and repetitious, but four theses stand out fairly clearly as constituting its major parts. They are: (a) the principle of consciousness or understanding is foundational within knowledge as its principle of objectivity; (b) this principle is itself natural and 'eternal'; (c) nature implies an analogous spiritual principle, because (i) nature *for us* means an "unalterable order of relations" which (ii) presupposes a principle of relations analogous to that in us called consciousness or understanding and (iii) nature *in itself* must be as it is *for us;* (d) the spiritual principle (consciousness or understanding) in human beings is a "limited mode" of the analogous principle in nature, and herein lies the basis of man's true freedom both practical and theoretical. In summarizing the argument, we shall draw out these four points.[8]

1. The Object in Knowledge

Among the objects of our knowledge we constantly distinguish some which, as we say, are 'real' and 'objective' as contrasted with others which are 'unreal' and 'illusory.' For one interested in the critical analysis of knowledge, the first important question concerns precisely this distinction. When we ask whether any particular mental state is, or represents, anything which is 'real' and 'objective,' what exactly does the question mean and how do we set about answering it?

It is to be observed, in the first place, that this question is not equivalent to asking whether a given feeling is felt. Some feeling must be felt as a ground of the possibility of the question's being raised at all. Assuming that a feeling is felt, the question is whether it "is what it is taken to be; or, in other words, whether it is related as it seems to be related." The question whether a particular feeling is real as felt, then, is always translatable into the form: "Is a feeling, which is undoubtedly felt, really related as some one thinking about it takes it to be?" And this is its precise meaning.

How do we set about answering the question in any given case? Simply by observing whether the object which is taken for 'real' involves a permanent and unalterable order of re-

---

[8] This summary is based on the first Book of the *Prolegomena to Ethics,* from which all the quotations are drawn. The point of view here developed is, of course, implicit in the author's two *Introductions to Hume's Treatise of Human Nature* and his critical articles in the *Contemporary Review* dealing with the theories of Spencer and Lewes.

lations, or an order of relations which is impermanent and contingent. If the former, the object is 'real' and 'objective'; if the latter, it is 'unreal' and 'illusory.' The distinction between 'real' and 'unreal' objects, therefore, in the end reduces to the distinction between an order of relations which is permanent and an order of relations which is contingent upon circumstances. It is specially to be noted that the so-called 'unreal' or 'illusory' object is itself a set of relations. As distinguished from the object which is 'real' or 'objective,' it is simply a peculiar sort of relationship—one, to repeat, which is not unalterable, but is contingent upon circumstances.

"If an engine-driver, under certain conditions, permanent with him or temporary, 'sees a signal wrong,' as we say, his disordered vision has its own reality just as much as if he saw right. There are relations between combinations of moving particles on the one side and his visual organs on the other, between the present state of the latter and certain determining conditions, between the immediate sensible effect and the secondary impressions which it in turn excites, as full and definite— with sufficient enquiry and opportunity, as ascertainable—as in any case of normal vision. There is as much reality in the one case as in the other, but it is not the same reality: *i.e.*, it does not consist in the same relations. The engine-driver mistakes the effect of one set of relations for that of another, one reality for another, and hence his error in action." Every object, thus, stands in relations, and it is real as related; if it is contrasted with another object which is more 'real,' this means, and can mean, only that the other object stands in relations which are more permanent.

The upshot of our inquiry into the distinction between real and unreal objects is: (a) anything which is experienced as standing in certain relations is called real as thus experienced; and (b) the 'real' as contrasted with the 'unreal,' 'matter of fact' as opposed to 'illusion,' means one experienced set of relations standing in contrast with another experienced set of relations, the former of which is unalterable and the latter contingent.

From this emerges a consideration of fundamental importance.

The terms *real* and *objective* have no meaning except for a consciousness or understanding "which presents its experiences to itself as determined by relations, and at the same time conceives a single and unalterable order of relations determining them, with which its temporary presentation, as each experience occurs, of the relations determining it may be contrasted." The understanding or consciousness, therefore, is the principle of objectivity. Through it, and through it alone, there is for us an objective world or an order of nature, with which we must reconcile our interpretations of phenomena if they are to be other than 'subjective' illusions. In this sense, at least, we must agree with Kant's dictum that "the understanding makes nature."

2. CONSCIOUSNESS NOT 'NATURAL'

Consciousness or understanding itself is not, and cannot be, a natural event or an effect of natural events. If it were so, it would have to be conceived in one of the following three ways: (a) as identical with one of the events in the series of which it is the consciousness; (b) as the sum of all the events of the series; or (c) as the after-product of such a series, upon which it supervenes as an effect. But it cannot intelligibly be conceived in either of these ways. It cannot be identical with any one event in the series, because it belongs to the series as a whole; it cannot be identified with the sum of the events in the series taken seriatim, because it is characteristic of each and every event as constituting, when taken together, a series of related events which in some sense is one; nor, finally, can it be conceived an as after-effect of the series, because then there would be no consciousness of the series while in progress, and a series of which there is no consciousness is not a set of conditions into which consciousness can be analyzed.

"A consciousness of events as a related series—experience in the most elementary form in which it can be the beginning of knowledge—has not any element of identity with, and therefore cannot properly be said to be developed out of, a mere series of related events, of successive modifications of body or soul. . . . No one and no number of a series of related events can be the conseiousness of the series as related. Nor can any product of the series be so either. Even if this product could be anything else than a further event, it could at any rate only be something that supervenes at a certain stage upon such of the events as have so far elapsed. But a consciousness of certain events cannot be anything that thus succeeds them. It must be equally present to all the events of which it is the consciousness. For this reason an intelligent experience, or experience as the source of knowledge, can neither be constituted by events of which it is the experience, nor be a product of them." Thus, consciousness of events as a related series cannot be explained by any natural history; properly speaking, it has no genesis.[9] One might indeed fairly characterize consciousness as being non-temporal or eternal. This should not be understood to mean, however, that the consciousness of this or that man does not change; it means only that within consciousness itself there is "no relation of before and after, of here and there, between its constituent members—between the presentation, for instance, of point A and that of point B in the process which forms the object of consciousness."[10]

[9] Compare Ferrier's position on the point: "The question is, What are the conceivable causes in existence which generate knowledge? And the answer is, That no existence at all can be conceived by any intelligence anterior to, and aloof from, knowledge. Knowledge of existence—the apprehension of oneself and other things—is alone true existence. This is itself the First, the Bottom, the Origin—and this is what all intelligence is prevented by the laws of all reason from ever getting beyond or below. To inquire what this proceeds from, is as inept as to ask what is the Beginning. All the explanations which can be proposed can find their data only by presupposing the very knowledge whose genesis they are professing to explain." (Ferrier, *Institutes of Metaphysics*, Section III, Proposition IX, Observation 35.)

[10] To this notion of timeless consciousness F. H. Bradley objects. He is willing to admit that "without an identity, to which all its members are related, a series is not one, and is therefore not a series"; and the "person who denies this unity is able to do so merely because he covertly supplies it from his own unreflecting mind." But to suppose that the unity of the series is itself timeless or has no duration is to misinterpret an interesting and important fact so as to convert it into "a monster." Of course, "there is a permanent in the perception of change, which goes right through the succession and holds it together." But the permanent is only "a piece of duration, not experienced *as* successive." Viewed in this aspect, it may be said to include succession and itself not to lapse; nevertheless, this absence of lapse is only relative, and to take it for absolute is to mistake it. It has an assignable place in a history; it is an event with a before and after in time. How then, and in what sense can it be said to be 'timeless'?

3. SPIRITUAL PRINCIPLE IN NATURE

Thus far in our analysis we have been concerned with objects of knowledge; and we have seen that the spiritual principle of consciousness or understanding is deeply involved in knowledge as the basis of objectivity. The question now arises whether we must hold that such a principle is involved in nature as well. And we shall see that there is reason for answering this question in the affirmative.

(a) As we have already noted, there are two meanings of the *real*. In the first meaning, the *real* is identical with a contingent and more or less arbitrary set of relations; it is relative to an individual, and to the individual as existing under peculiar circumstances—as in the example given above, the 'wrong' signal is also 'real,' but only as a set of relations that are dependent upon the disordered vision of the engine-driver and the circumstances under which the vision takes place. In the second meaning of the term, however, the *real* is an unalterable order of relations which is independent of the accidental circumstances of perceptual experience on the part of the individual—as the 'right' signal seen by an engine-driver with normal vision which, unlike the 'wrong' signal, is not relative to peculiar circumstances, but is permanent and unalterable. In this meaning, "whatever anything is really it is unalterably." We must now inquire further into the significance of this dual meaning.

In the first place, it is to be observed that the term *real* has no meaning except the two already indicated. Some have indeed supposed that there is a sense in which the real stands opposed to unreal as something sharply distinguished and characterized by contradictory attributes. Such a supposition, however, is false. As opposed to the unreal in this sense, the real is whatever exists—the unreal being simply the non-existent. The only significant question concerning the real as contrasted with the unreal, then, is the one with which we have dealt above. The genuine contrast is that between an existent set of relations which is 'really' as it seems to be and a set of relations which is 'really' not as it seems to be.

The criterion by which we distinguish between such sets of relations is unalterableness. This is "the test by which we ascertain whether what we have believed to be the nature of any event is really so or not." It may indeed be difficult to apply this test in special cases, and it may well be that in the end it is impossible for us to arrive at the complete determination of the real nature of any event. "But that there *is* an unalterable order of relations, if we could only find it out, is the presupposition of all our inquiry into the real nature of appearances. . . ." And this unalterable order of relations constitutes the really real nature of the appearance in question.

The clause omitted from the immediately preceding quotation is this: "and such unalterableness implies their inclusion in one system which leaves nothing outside itself." I place this clause in a separate paragraph, because of its basal import for the argument as a whole. The monistic position which it asserts is, of course, of the most fundamental significance for Green's idealism. Here would be the appropriate paragraph for the proof of such a position. But the only proof which the author presents is in the assertion itself, which apparently is supposed to be self-evident—an unalterable order of relations is *ipso facto* an all-inclusive order of relations. The best the expositor can do, therefore, is to set the assertion apart by itself as its importance demands, to direct attention to its inadequacy, and to turn to the next step in the argument.

(b) The question next arises: What is the condition of the possibility of such an all-inclusive system of unalterable relations? That there is such a system is implied in the distinction we necessarily make between 'real' objects and 'apparent' objects. Can such a system stand alone, or does it logically require something else to render it intelligible? To see the answer to this question we must first observe what frequently is overlooked, namely, that a relation involves all the mystery of the existence of many in one. A thing is nothing when abstracted from its relations, for without relations it could not exist at all. It is therefore impossible that the thing "first exists in its unity, and then is brought into various relations." Likewise, from the other side, a relation is precisely a unity of many things which in their manifold being constitute the relation. Hence, since the relation is the several things in their common nature, the relation is not produced by the combination of disparate things. Thus it turns out that a system of relations is equivalent to a multiplicity of things which, in order to support the relations, must retain their several natures and yet, as related, are possessed of a common nature. How is such a system intelligible? Not when taken as a mere set of terms in relation. "There must be something other than the manifold things themselves, which combines them without effacing their severalty." What, then, is this "something"?

We have already seen, following Kant, that we have in our experience such a combining principle in the form of what in ourselves we call *consciousness* or *understanding*. No one can deny that in experience there is a principle of unity which makes knowledge possible. And this principle cannot be identified either with matter or with particular feelings or with mental states— not with matter, because it "so organises experience that the relations expressed by our definitions of matter and motion arise therein" and "it cannot itself be determined by those relations"; and not with particular mental states, because the unity of experience is not immediately given in an impression but, on the contrary, is presupposed in such an immediate state. There is, therefore, in knowledge, a spiritual principle which is connected to relations as faculty to function; and this we call *understanding* or *consciousness*.

We are therefore justified in saying that such a spiritual principle is involved in that "unalterable order of relations" which, we have seen, is presupposed in the distinction between reality and appearances. The principle in us is the source of relations, and it is the only empirical source of relations; it must, therefore, be held to be foundational to that unalterable order of relations with which, from the standpoint of experience, we are compelled to identify objects as they really are. The condition of the possibility of our "inquiry into the real nature of appearances" is "the action of some unifying principle analogous to that of our understanding." Hence, the "unalterable order of relations" involves a spiritual principle analogous to that of our understanding or consciousness.[11]

(c) May we now proceed at once to the conclusion that a similar spiritual principle is involved in nature itself? We may, indeed, proceed ultimately to such a conclusion; but not directly, since such procedure would assume that our conception of an unalterable order of relations and nature itself are identical, and this remains to be considered. Our immediate task, therefore, is to see why the two must, in the end, fall together.

Kant, as is well known, drew a sharp distinction between the two. The work of the understanding he limited to phenomena (things as they appear in our experience); and he denied that the 'nature' thus constituted implies any conclusions with reference to noumena (things as they are in themselves), since such a 'nature' is merely a unity in the relations of phenomena. Nevertheless, he does admit that noumena after a fashion are connected with phenomena. He insists upon a further distinction within the 'nature' constituted by our intelligence—the distinction, namely, between the form and the matter of 'nature' itself. By *form* he means the relations by which phenomena are connected in the one world of experience; and by *matter* he means the mere phenomena or sensations undetermined by those relations. Form he regards as the work of understanding, while he holds matter to be the work of unknown things-in-themselves, acting upon us in unknown ways. Thus are things-in-themselves

---

[11] Strictly interpreted, the conclusion here established amounts to this: The principle of the understanding is logically foundational to our *conception* of an all-inclusive and unalterable order of relations. And the argument is by analogy: As the unifying principle of consciousness is basal within our experience of 'objects,' we must for the same reasons hold it to be basal within our experience of 'really real objects'—objects, that is, which are constituted by unalterable relations.

At this point, however, the author confuses the argument—and his reader—by injecting the statement: "The same or an analogous action is necessary to account for any relation whatever—for a relation between material atoms as much as any other." For this assertion no proof is here offered. It assumes that, since consciousness is the source of relations within empirical objects, it, or an analogous principle, must be the source of relations among things themselves. But this assumption clearly begs the question which yet remains to be considered, namely, whether our conception of the "unalterable order of relations" is to be identified with the ultimate nature of things themselves—with nature *per se*.

connected with experience; they are the alien source whence come the sensations which are constituted 'nature' by the forms of understanding.

Hereupon, however, we are met by a formidable logical difficulty. We have on our hands two natures—one the nature of phenomena as related to each other in the universe of our experience, and the other the nature of phenomena as effects of things-in-themselves. And these two natures are logically disparate; the nature which belongs to phenomena in experience springs from their relations which the action of the principle of understanding brings about, while the nature which belongs to them as effects of things-in-themselves springs from a source to which no experience or interrogation of experience brings us any nearer. The one belongs to a world of which a unifying self-consciousness is the organizing principle; the other belongs to another world which is assumed to have some principle of unity of its own, but of which, because it is a world of things-in-themselves, the principle must be taken to be the pure negation of that which determines the world of experience. If this be so, what logically follows? Simply that "the conception of a universe is a delusive one. Man weaves a web of his own and calls it a universe; but if the principle of this universe is neither one with, nor dependent on, that of things-in-themselves, there is in truth no universe at all, nor does there seem to be any reason why there should not be any number of such independent creations. We have asserted the unity of the world of our experience only to transfer that world to a larger chaos." [12]

[12] In connection with the argument of this paragraph, it is important for the reader to bear in mind the author's conviction that the nature of phenomena as springing from things-in-themselves cannot, on Kant's principles, be identified with their nature "as conditioned by a particular mode of matter and motion—the nature which the man of science investigates. . . . The nature of a sensation, as dependent upon any motion or configuration of molecules, is still a nature determined by its relation to other data of experience—a relation which (like every other relation within, or capable of coming within, experience) the single self-distinguishing principle, which Kant calls understanding, is needed to constitute." Not nature in this sense is to be attributed to phenomena as 'appearances.' It is rather a nature "to which no experience or interrogation of experience brings us any nearer, that we must suppose to belong to the phenomenon as an appearance of a thing-in-itself, if Kant's antithesis is to be maintained."

If we try to escape this difficulty by reducing the world of experience to dependence on that of things-in-themselves (through the device of taking the intellectual principle of the world of experience itself as the product of things-in-themselves), we succeed only in committing ourselves either to a meaningless assertion or to a denial of the independence of things-in-themselves. If the intellectual principle is to be dependent on things-in-themselves, these 'things' must be understood to mean something other than any objects we know or can know, since the action of the principle is already implied in the existence of such objects.[13] There is, therefore, no meaning to be attached to the assertion that the principle of unity in experience is dependent on things-in-themselves.

If, on the other side, any significant assertion of the dependence is possible and something can be understood by the relation asserted, then the independence of things-in-themselves is definitely compromised; for such a relation, like all relations, cannot exist except through the unifying action of spirit, and the things-in-themselves are thus determined by a spiritual action of exactly that kind which is alleged to depend on them. There is in this direction, therefore, no way of escape. If the two worlds are to be kept wholly separated, then the organizing subject of the world of experience cannot be dependent on that of things-in-themselves as in any sense its product.

Essentially the same inconsistency is involved in Kant's own view of the relation between things-in-themselves and the 'matter' of experience. For it is impossible to hold, as Kant does, that phenomena in respect of their 'matter' are effects of things-in-themselves without making the latter a member of the causal relation—a relation which, Kant himself is ready to remind us, we have no warrant for extending beyond the world of experience. If all that can be said about things-in-themselves is that they belong to a world other than the world of our experience, then to say that sensations, or the matter of experience, are

---

[13] A psycho-genetic account of consciousness, for example, which undertakes to trace it from simpler beginnings in protoplasm is an account which must be written in terms that represent, not independent agents, but "substantial relations between phenomena."

connected as effects with things-in-themselves is self-contradictory or unmeaning.

It would appear, then, that we cannot take the matter of
experience to be the effect of things-in-themselves, since these
things, if they are to be things-in-themselves, cannot exist in
a relation which only holds for the world of experience. Nevertheless, it seems equally impossible that the matter of experience
should be taken as a product of the intelligent subject. Granting
to that subject every function that can be claimed for it in the
way of uniting in a related system the material of sensation,
we must still deny it the function of generating that material.
Thus we are apparently left, after all our protests against dualism, with an unaccountable residuum in experience itself—an
element which is essential to the world of experience, but which
cannot be traced to what we regard as the organizing principle
of that world. Is not this irreducible element a thing-in-itself,
alien and opposite to anything that we can explain as the construction of the unifying principle of the understanding? We
must next seek an answer to this question, and with the answer
we shall be in position to reach a conclusion with reference to
the general question with which we began—the question,
namely, whether we must hold that there is in nature a spiritual
principle analogous to that which in ourselves we call *consciousness*.

Reflecting on the process by which we have come to know
anything, we find that any stage in the process consists in the
further qualification of given material by the consideration
of that material under relations before unconsidered. As contrasted with its further qualification, the given material may be
regarded as unformed matter; but, on the other hand, when we
investigate it more closely we find that it is already formed
by the previous synthesis of less determinate data. There is a
point in this retrospective analysis of the knowing process, however, at which one must stop. Beyond that point, it is natural
to assume, there is something with which the process begins and
which itself is not involved in previous formative intellectual
processes. This something is then taken to be the irreducible
residuum of experience alien to the organizing principle—the

absolute matter of experience, matter excluding all form. Thus it is that the notion of the mere matter of experience as opposed to the formative influence of intelligence is derived.

Whether this account holds true in fact even of the mental history of the individual may legitimately be doubted. But the question before us is not whether any such thing as mere sensation, a matter wholly unformed by intelligence, exists as a stage in the process by which the individual becomes acquainted with the world. The main question is, rather, whether there is any such element in the world of knowable facts; and this is the question with which we shall deal. It may be put in either of two forms: (i) Among the facts that form the objects of possible experience, are there sensations which do not depend on thought for being what they are? (ii) Is sensation, as unqualified by thought, an element in the consciousness which is necessary to there being such a thing as a world of phenomena? The answer to one of these questions is in principle the answer to the other, but they may be separated for clarity of discussion.

(i) If it is admitted that we know of no other medium but a thinking or self-distinguishing consciousness in and through which that unification of the manifold can take place as it must to constitute relation, then it is clear that the first question must be answered in the negative. For it follows at once from this admission that sensation would *eo ipso* be unrelated, and an unrelated sensation cannot amount to a fact. It could neither occur in this or that order of succession nor with this or that degree of intensity, and these relations constitute the minimum determination of a sensible fact. And the admission underlying this conclusion must in principle be accepted; relations spring from a source which in us is consciousness or understanding and which elsewhere is, in principle, identical with it. On this there can be no difference of opinion; differences turn, in the end, upon the secondary question concerning the fitness of the term to be applied to the agency.[14] The first form of our question must

[14] "If by thought is necessarily understood a faculty which is born and dies with each man; which is exhausted by labour and refreshed by repose; which is exhibited in the constructions of chains of reasoning, but not in the common ideas which make mankind and its experience one; on which the 'great thinker' may plume himself as the athlete on the strength

therefore be answered negatively: Sensations which do not depend on thought for being what they are are not found among the facts that form the objects of possible experience.

(ii) The answer to the second form of the question, Can sensation exist as an independent element in a consciousness to which facts can appear? is virtually contained in the answer to the first. To that thinking subject, whose action is the universal bond of relation that renders facts what they are, their existence and their appearance must be one and the same; their appearance is their existence. Hence, sensation can no more be an independent element in that subject, as the subject to which they appear, than it can be an independent element in it as the subject through whose action they exist. And with this conclusion, our second question is answered negatively: Mere sensation, as matter unformed by thought, has no place in the world of facts, in the cosmos of possible experience.

Mere sensation, then, is only an abstraction and offers no difficulty to a monistic view of the world of experience. Nor does it need to be accounted for as a product of things-in-themselves, as if it were an opposite to thought and its work. "Feeling and thought are inseparable and mutually dependent in the consciousness for which the world of experience exists, inseparable and mutually dependent in the constitution of the facts which form the object of that consciousness. Each in its full reality includes the other." And the two thus taken together in insepa-

---

of his muscles; then to say that the agency which makes sensible facts what they are can only be that of a thinking subject, is an absurd impropriety. But if it appears that a function in the way of self-consciousness is implied in the existence of relations, and therefore of determinate facts —a function identical in principle with that which enables the individual to look before and after, and which renders his experience a connected system—then it is more reasonable to modify some of our habitual notions of thought as exercised by ourselves than, on the strength of these notions, to refuse to recognise an essential identity between the subject which forms the unifying principle of the experienced world, and that which, as in us, qualifies us for an experience of it. It becomes time to consider whether the characteristics of thought, even as exercised by us, are not rather to be sought in the unity of its object as presented to all men, and in the continuity of all experience in regard to that object, than in the incidents of an individual life which is but for a day, or in abilities of which any man can boast that he has more than his neighbour." (*Prolegomena to Ethics,* Book I, Chapter I, section 47.)

rable union constitute the activity of consciousness—"one and the same living world of experience which, considered as the manifold object presented by a self-distinguishing subject to itself, may be called feeling, and, considered as the subject presenting such an object to itself, may be called thought." Taken separately, each becomes a mere abstraction to which no reality corresponds, either in the facts of the world or in the consciousness to which those facts are relative.

There is, therefore, no meaning in the question concerning the origin of either thought or feeling, in the sense in which it is intended to trace them to some more ultimate source—such as a world of things-in-themselves. The explanatory connection between a phenomenon and its conditions is one that obtains only in and for consciousness; no such connection can obtain between consciousness and anything else, since the consciousness itself, whether considered as feeling or as thought, is that by reference to which everything is accounted for and does not in its turn admit of being accounted for, in the sense that any 'whence' or 'why' can be assigned for it. All of our explanatory principles fall within the world of possible experience and spring from the spiritual principle of unity which is basal within that world; neither that world nor its organizing principle can be explained in the ordinary sense of the word. In short, the world of possible experience is the only intelligible world.

We are now at length in position to see the necessity of the conclusion that there is a spiritual principle in nature. The obstacle that stood in the way of our reaching this conclusion in the first place was due to the distinction (insisted upon especially by Kant) between two natures—the nature of phenomena and the nature of things-in-themselves—and our consequent doubt as to whether what is characteristic of the one may legitimately be said to be characteristic of the other, since they were supposed to be quite opposite. We have meanwhile seen, however, that there is no ground for the distinction; we have seen that the nature of things-in-themselves is a meaningless abstraction, and that the only intelligible nature is that of phenomena —existence under definite and unalterable relations. We may therefore set aside our doubt, and say finally that nature, in the only sense in which it can for us have any meaning, namely, as a knowable order of connected facts, implies something other than itself as the condition of its being what it is.

"Of that something else we are entitled to say, positively, that it is a self-distinguishing consciousness; because the function which it must fulfil in order to render the relations of phenomena, and with them nature, possible, is one which, on however limited a scale, we ourselves exercise in the acquisition of experience, and exercise only by means of such a consciousness. We are further entitled to say of it, negatively, that the relations by which, through its action, phenomena are determined are not relations *of* it—not relations by which it is itself determined. They arise out of its presence to phenomena, or the presence of phenomena to it, but the very condition of their thus arising is that the unifying consciousness which constitutes them should not itself be one of the objects related." In short, the spiritual principle in nature is a self-distinguishing self-consciousness, which is the ground of all relations whatsoever among phenomena and does not itself stand in any relations to something outside and beyond; it is an eternal and all-inclusive self-consciousness.

4. HUMAN CONSCIOUSNESS AND THE SPIRITUAL PRINCIPLE IN NATURE

The final point for consideration concerns the relation which obtains between the spiritual principle in nature and our own consciousness. And, first, we must be clear as to the point at issue.

The spiritual principle in nature is, as we have just seen, an eternal self-consciousness. It is a self-consciousness, because of the function it fulfils in rendering nature possible; it is eternal, because it is the source of all relations and time involves relations. But human consciousness is *prima facie* through-and-through temporal; it seems to be an order of events which is adequately pictured by the figure of the stream, and so we speak of the 'stream of consciousness' as if consciousness were only a bare succession of states. Thus arises the question: How is the purely temporal human conciousness related to the eternal consciousness implied in nature? And at first glance there seems to be no intelligible answer to the question.

But the difficulty is more apparent than real, based as it is on the false assumption that the *prima facie* view of finite consciousness is the final view. That such an assumption is false we have, indeed, already seen. It may once again be exposed by the following considerations.

There is an important difference between an act of thought and an object of thought. The act of thought is a particular state of perceiving, conceiving, and the like; an object of thought is that of which in those particular states we are conscious. Now consciousness may be, and frequently is, identified with an act of thought; and when this identification is made it naturally follows that consciousness is merely temporal, since acts of thought are only successive apprehensive attitudes and as such are temporal events. It follows also, if the identification is made, that the object of thought stands over against consciousness as something alien to it. But the identification of consciousness with an act of thought is based on a confusion, and at best expresses but half of the truth. The full truth is that consciousness is exhibited in the structure of the object as well as in separate acts of thought. This is a general truth, but we may turn to the case of perception for its illustration. There is general agreement that no perception is possible apart from what Locke called "actual present sensation." But the actual present sensation is never quite the object perceived, otherwise the object would be exactly the same for all perceivers and this is notoriously not the case. The object perceived is, rather, a synthesis of sensations—a synthesis which "implies the action of a subject which thinks of its feelings, which distinguishes them from itself and can thus present them to itself as facts." The object perceived, therefore, is not alien to nor independent of consciousness, but is a construction of it; consciousness enters into the very texture of the object. "It is relations of which the percipient consciousness is the sustainer, which exist only through its action, that make the object, as in each case the percipient perceives it, what it is to him."

And this is true of all objects, whether of the act of perceiving or of any other act of thought.

Now, as thus basal within the constitution of objects of thought, consciousness cannot be merely one event among other events in a mental history, or "any sort of succession of phenomena." On the contrary, it is strictly out of time. The sensation which forms the nucleus of the perception is indeed an event in time, and its presentation to consciousness is also an event in time; but "the content of the presentation, the perception of this or that object, depends on the presence of that which in occurrence is past, as a fact united in one consciousness with the fact of the sensation now occurring." And that consciousness itself cannot be subject to the conditions of time; it must be non-temporal.[15]

Thus it would appear that the difficulty before us is, in principle, overcome. When we speak of 'our' consciousness, we may mean either of two things. We may mean (a) a process of time, a stream of states, contingent and intermittent; or we may mean (b) a non-temporal synthesis which is foundational within the temporal process as the 'sustainer' of its content and order. Of course, this does not mean that in man there is a double consciousness; it means only that "the one indivisible reality of our consciousness cannot be comprehended in a single conception." The consciousness of man is at once temporal and non-temporal —as consisting of states or 'acts' it is temporal; as constituting relations among states (objects) it is non-temporal.

There is a sense, to be sure, in which the non-temporal aspect of human consciousness seems to change; the very consciousness which holds together successive events as equally present apparently has itself a history in time and comes to be what it has not been. But this must not blind us to the other side of the matter: such consciousness, in coming to be what it has not been, is still coming to be itself. "Every step forward in real intelligence, whether in the way of addition to what we call the stock of human knowledge, or of an appropriation by

[15] Compare Bradley's views on the 'timeless' self referred to in the footnote on p. 46 above. Bradley's criticism should be read in connection with the point which Green here makes.

the individual of some part of that stock, is only explicable on supposition that successive reports of the senses, successive efforts of attention, successive processes of observation and experiment, are determined by the consciousness that all things form a related whole—a consciousness which is operative throughout their succession and which at the same time realises itself through them." So we seem free to maintain that on this side of human consciousness is found the link that logically binds it to the eternal consciousness in nature. For on this side, consciousness has no history; into it time does not enter; only the reproduction or expression of it is subject to time. It is, therefore, in principle identical with the eternal consciousness, which gathers all things into "the timeless unity of knowledge." And this is our answer to the question before us: The finite consciousness in its non-temporal aspect is an imperfect reproduction of the eternal consciousness in nature; and through its various states, its history in time, it gradually becomes the vehicle of this eternally complete consciousness.

Herein, it should be noted, lies the true freedom of man, both as intelligence and as will. And in conclusion we may comment briefly on each of these points.

As has just been shown in the preceding analysis of the characteristics of man's knowledge, it is evident that "his consciousness would not be what it is, *as knowing*, or as a subject of intelligent experience, but for the self-realization or reproduction in it . . . of an eternal consciousness, not existing in time but the condition of there being an order in time, not an object of experience but the condition of there being an intelligent experience." And on the basis of this fact we may say that man is a "free cause" as an intelligent being. The spiritual principle implied in nature is such a cause, since nature has no character which is not given it by the action of this principle. This principle, in turn, cannot be an 'effect' of natural events, and is not determined as an ordinary event is determined, since its character is given by its own action and self-determination. Now the action of man's 'mind' in knowledge is a reproduction of that principle in nature, and is essentially at one with it; therefore, man as intelligence is a "free cause" in the same sense.

Of course, it must not be denied that human consciousness, on one side, is empirically determined; and there is here no intention to deny this. What is affirmed is merely a reiteration of what has been already shown at length and what is clearly the fact, namely, that the successive phenomena of our mental history, together with the mechanical and biological processes presupposed in them, do not make up the complete account of *consciousness as knowing*, but imply a non-temporal principle which underlies and makes possible that history itself. And herein lies the freedom of man as intelligence.

Essentially the same is true of man as will. The problem of the freedom of will resolves itself, on analysis, into the problem of the strongest motive, since in any given case the will is precisely the strongest motive—"such a motive is the will in act." Now a motive is "an idea of an end, which a self-conscious subject presents to itself, and which it strives and tends to realise." Thus, for example, when Esau sells his birthright for a mess of pottage, his real motive is not his hunger, but his conception of himself as finding for the time his greatest good in the satisfaction of his hunger. Consequently, that which is basal in the motivation of human conduct is the self or the man. When we ask what is to be understood by this 'self' or 'man,' we find that we are dealing with precisely the same principle as that implied in knowledge. "We mean by it a certain reproduction of itself on the part of the eternal self-conscious subject of the world—a reproduction of itself to which it makes the processes of animal life organic, and which is qualified and limited by the nature of those processes, but which is so far essentially a reproduction of the one supreme subject, implied in the existence of the world, that the product carries with it under all its limitations and qualifications the characteristic of being an object to itself. It is the particular human self or person, we hold, thus constituted, that in every moral action, virtuous or vicious, presents to itself some possible state or achievement of its own as for the time its greatest good, and acts for the sake of that good." And this is what we mean by the 'free will.' The freedom of the will, thus, is identical in principle with the freedom of intelligence; in both instances freedom is grounded in the same

eternal consciousness which is implied in the constitution of
nature and which reproduces itself in the special succession of
phenomena we call a finite 'mind,' whether as knowing or as
acting.

Chapter III

JOHN GROTE (1813-1866)

In the preceding chapter the statement was made that the argument of Green shows little of the influence of Hegel, but is oriented in the direction of the Critical Philosophy. A detailed justification of this statement is not possible here and would be out of keeping with the main purpose of the present survey. However, a few observations in support of it will help to carry us forward in our historical task.

Green himself avows that he is following Kant quite closely in the earlier stages of his argument, and he is at pains to indicate the points of essential agreement between him and his guide. "So far," he says in the thirty-eighth section of the *Prolegomena to Ethics,* "we have been following the lead of Kant in enquiring what is necessary to constitute, what is implied in there being, a world of experience—an objective world, if by that is meant a world of ascertainable laws, as distinguished from a world of unknowable 'things-in-themselves.' We have followed him also, as we believe every one must who has once faced the question, in maintaining that a single active self-conscious principle, by whatever name it be called, is necessary to constitute such a world, as the condition under which alone phenomena, *i.e.* appearances to consciousness, can be related to each other in a single universe. This is the irrefragable truth involved in the proposition that 'the understanding makes nature.' "

In this frank statement of his indebtedness to Kant, Green is without doubt correct. For up to the point at which this statement is inserted, his argument is little more than the reassertion of the principles advocated in the earlier portions of the *Kritik der reinen Vernunft,* with special emphasis upon the principles involved in the deduction of the categories. In his insistence that consciousness or understanding is foundational in the experience

63

of nature and that, consequently, consciousness or understanding is implied in nature as an object of knowledge and is itself non-empirical—in all of this Green clearly follows the lead of Kant with no deviation in principle.

He departs from Kant's principles in his contention that, in the last analysis, there is no justification for distinguishing between nature as an object of knowledge and nature as a system of things-in-themselves; but that, on the contrary, the two must be identified. From this identification follow all the major consequences of Green's argument which are at variance with the principles of the Critical Philosophy. Even here, however, it is Green's opinion that his argument varies only from the letter, and not from the spirit of Kant's analysis. For he holds that whatever plausibility such a distinction as that drawn by Kant between phenomena and noumena may have, arises either from an identification of things-in-themselves with the material conditions of sensations or from the assumption that sensations are effects of things-in-themselves. And either position, Green urges, is untenable and contravenes the spirit of the Kantian principles. (1) To identify things-in-themselves with the ascertainable material conditions of sensations is virtually to identify things-in-themselves with phenomena, for "the nature of a sensation, as dependent upon any motion or configuration of molecules, is still a nature determined by its relation to other data of experience—a relation which (like every other relation within, or capable of coming within, experience) the single self-distinguishing principle, which Kant calls understanding, is needed to constitute." And (2) the assumption that sensations are effects of things-in-themselves, as differentiated from the ascertainable material conditions of those sensations, obviously cannot stand in the face of Kant's doctrine of causation, for "we cannot assert such a relation of cause and effect between the things and sensation without making the former a member of a relation which, as Kant himself on occasion would be ready to remind us, we have no warrant for extending beyond the world of experience. . . . Causation has no meaning except as an unalterable connexion between changes in the world of our experience—an unalterableness of which the basis is the relation of that world throughout, with all its changes, to a single subject." [1] Therefore, the denial of the distinction between nature *per se* and nature as an object of knowledge is more in harmony with Kant's principles than is the assertion of the distinction. Thus, even in his major departure from the Critical Philosophy, Green is, in his own view, still a loyal Kantian at heart.

In all of this there is no evidence of Hegelian influence. There is, of course, agreement with Hegel (as, in fact, with most of Kant's immediate successors in Germany) that Kant had failed to live up to the logic of his doctrine and had unwittingly fallen into the inconsistency of making an abysmal separation between appearance and reality. There is also an essential similarity between the conclusions reached by the two thinkers. The "eternal consciousness" at which Green finally arrives through his analysis of the implications of the knowledge of nature has much in common with the "Weltgeist" of Hegel. But in the argument by which Green attains that result there is little reminiscent of the Heglian dialectical method. In fact, Green is averse to that method and speaks rather slightingly of it. He thinks that whoever would convincingly present the basal truth for which Hegel contends, "though he cannot drink too deep of Hegel, should rather sit loose to the dialectical method." Thus, so far as Green's idealistic argument is concerned at any rate, it is inaccurate to speak of him as an Hegelian; the truth is that, from this angle, he is not Hegelian at all.

But John Grote, who was one of Green's contemporaries and who held the chair of moral philosophy at Cambridge from 1855 to his death in 1866, outlines an idealistic argument which, though apparently independently conceived, is quite in the spirit of the Hegelian dialectical method. In fact in some of its details it is strikingly reminiscent of the earlier stages of consciousness as set forth in Hegel's remarkable "voyage of discovery," the *Phœnomenologie des Geistes*. So far as I am aware, Grote's is the earliest formulation of this type of argument to be found in British philosophy; and, since it has generally been over-

[1] Green, *Prolegomena to Ethics*, sections 39, 41.

looked by the historians, it needs to be presented here at some length.[2]

The *Exploratio Philosophica* is, as the author himself describes it, "rough notes." There is nothing systematic about it. The argument as developed is quite sketchy, and it is expounded by the aid of running critical comments on sundry aspects of the views of Ferrier, Hamilton, Mill, Whewell, and Spencer. Despite its unsystematic and incomplete nature, however, the *Exploratio* contains a fairly definite body of doctrines, worked out with a logic which is intrinsically important in the movement of British idealism and which deserves more consideration than it has received at the hands of the historians of that movement. That logic I wish here briefly to sketch.

In stating his own views on "the highest matters of philosophy" Grote quotes with entire approval the following assertions of doctrine from the later pages of Ferrier's *Institutes of Metaphysics*. "Neither the existence nor the non-existence of things is conceivable out of relation to our intelligence, and therefore the highest and most binding law of all reason is, that under no circumstances can a supreme mind be conceived as abstracted from the universe. . . . To save the universe from presenting a contradiction to all reason, intelligence must be postulated along with it. . . . In the judgment of reason there never can have been a time when the universe was without God. . . . Every mind thinks, and *must* think of God (however little it may be conscious of the operation which it is performing), whenever it thinks of anything as lying beyond all human

---

[2] During his lifetime Grote issued only one volume on philosophy. This was Part I of the *Exploratio Philosophica,* and was published in 1865. His intention, expressed in the Preface to this volume, was to follow it with a second volume which was to constitute Part II of the work; but this intention was frustrated by his death in 1866. He left to his literary executor, Joseph B. Mayor, a mass of manuscripts with the instruction that they be published in whole or in part or not at all, as the executor might think fit. From these manuscripts the executor selected and published, besides several incidental papers on various subjects, three substantial volumes as follows: *Examination of the Utilitarian Philosophy* (1870); *Moral Ideals* (1876); and *Exploratio Philosophica,* Part II (1900).

The argument summarized in the text is drawn primarily from the *Exploratio Philosophica.*

observation, or as subsisting in the absence or annihilation of all finite intelligences." [3]

1. CRITICISMS OF FERRIER

Though Grote finds himself in the end thus in whole-hearted agreement with Ferrier's idealistic and theistic conclusion, he is by no means committed to the argument by which that conclusion is established. On the contrary, he is convinced that Ferrier's argument is in some quite important respects faulty in its logic and, therefore, unconvincing.

For one thing, Grote does not attach any great importance to Ferrier's "Euclidic method" and the "show of demonstration" which it rather ostentatiously exhibits. Indeed, he feels very strongly that such a method is quite impossible in philosophy. The basal defect which he finds in Ferrier's own development of it is the omission of "that most important preliminary, the definitions and axioms." These, Grote urges, are logically fundamental within the "Euclidic method" and until they are supplied the method is entirely inconsequential. "Till axioms are agreed upon, representing a ground common to various thinkers on the subject, the most perfect consecution in the demonstration is not important." [4] Such axioms and definitions, upon which agreement is possible, Grote holds to be entirely lacking in Ferrier's formulation. Furthermore, he is quite doubtful as to whether it is possible to find such a point of departure for serious philosophical discussion, primarily for the reason that the method itself permits only bare and fruitless repetition, not significant explanation and elaboration, of the propositions that are set down at the beginning as axiomatic. This, he thinks, is illustrated in Ferrier's saying "so repeatedly and so barely" that his first proposition is a necessary truth of reason.

In the second place, Grote is not very greatly impressed by Ferrier's fervent and persistent claims to originality in his theory of ignorance. He is, indeed, willing to admit that the point stressed in the agnoiology is of considerable logical significance; but he is not at all convinced that Ferrier was, as he claims to

---

[3] These passages are quoted in *Exploratia Philosophica*, Part I, 79.
[4] *Ibid.*, p. 54.

have been, the first philosopher to see it. The passage in which Grote states his view of the matter deserves to be set down in full: "Mr. Ferrier claims for himself much merit for his 'agnoiology,' or theory of ignorance, of that kind which Sir William Hamilton is very fond of claiming, namely, that he is here original, and the first to break new ground. This merit does not seem to me so great in philosophy as in some other branches of thought or literature, for the reason that the problems of philosophy are all so intertwined together, that from the first, in the touching of any of them, they have all been more or less touched, and to distinguish between what is really new, and what is only the same thing in other words, is difficult. But the calling attention to the difference between ignorance (so to call it) of the knowable and that mere nescience (so to call it) which must be the state of mind in regard of that which is not matter of knowledge, is an observation of much importance. If borne in mind, it would prevent much foolish talk in depreciation of human intelligence." [5]

The preceding general comments indicate clearly enough that the form of Ferrier's argument and even one of the parts of it which Ferrier himself regarded as quite foundational leave Grote somewhat cold, despite his general agreement with the conclusion which the argument is designed to establish. The real significance of the *Institutes* he seeks, rather, "in the incidental remarks, and the *whole* manner of thought which they exhibit." As thus appraised, the argument strongly appeals to him; in principle it seems to him to stand. He finds, however, that Ferrier's phraseology is ambiguous on two matters of fundamental importance, and he comments critically on these at some length. A short summary of these comments will conveniently serve as a transition to the consideration of Grote's own constructive formulation, as well as direct the reader's attention to what undoubtedly are basal difficulties in Ferrier's argument.

The first point is the distinction drawn by Ferrier between contingency and necessity—a distinction which plays an important rôle in his argument. As Ferrier defines it, the distinction is that between what can be conceived otherwise than as it

[5] *Exploratio Philosophica*, Pt. I, p. 56. See also pp. 74-75.

is and what cannot be so conceived; the former is contingent, and the latter is necessary. For example, it is conceivable that the sun should turn round the earth, but it is not conceivable that two straight lines should enclose a space. The proposition that the earth rotates about the sun is therefore contingent, while the proposition that two straight lines cannot enclose a space is necessary. Such is Ferrier's view. Now, while Grote agrees that the distinction is not without meaning, he is by no means willing to admit that it is so sharp and clear-cut as Ferrier would have it. "The difference between the necessary and contingent," seems to him, rather, "only a difference of our manner of arriving at knowledge; that knowledge which we arrive at chiefly by the way of thought and reason has to us more of the character which we call necessity: that which is more of experience, acquaintance, testimony, is contingential: but we cannot draw a line: we cannot say, one portion of knowledge is and must be known to us in the one way, another part in the other: so far as the contingential is true *knowledge*, is *certain*, not approximate only or hypothetical, it might have been arrived at by the road of thought, and then it would have been to be called necessary: and, on the other hand, there is no thought which is not experience: . . . we *find out* everything: *after* that which we start with, our own existence." [6] The difference between Ferrier and his critic here concerns a basal epistemological issue, and it marks a significant attitude on the part of Grote with reference to the nature of knowledge—an attitude which, as we shall see below, underlies much of his metaphysical doctrine.

The other point of difference between the two is related to a matter closely connected with the foregoing, and is involved in the first proposition with which Ferrier's argument begins. Here, despite the fact that Ferrier holds the proposition to be axiomatic and necessary, Grote discovers an ambiguity in the very meaning of the proposition—an ambiguity which, he thinks, vitiates Ferrier's argument, and which when cleared away discloses its correct emphasis. "When Mr. Ferrier says that we think the subject with the object, I rather question the term

[6] *Ibid.*, p. 75. Italics are in the text. Cf. also pp. 80-82.

'object' in this application: if, till the subject is added to it, there is no knowledge, it is not as yet, or itself, the *object*. And Mr. Ferrier hardly sufficiently explains whether he means to pass from the notion of ourselves as knowing, or from knowledge being 'knowledge that we know,' which of itself, I think, is not very important, to the notion of ourselves, or part of ourselves, known in the object, which *is* the important one. It is *this* which really leads on, in the chain of thought, to the notion of knowledge being the meeting, through the intervention of phenomenal matter and the conversion of it into intellectual objects, with the thoughts, proceeding in the opposite direction, of mind or a mind like our own, however, wider and vaster." [7]

2. The Constructive Argument: Philosophy and Phenomenalism

The view adumbrated in the last sentence of the preceding quotation is the view which, though here attributed with doubtful accuracy to Ferrier, is avowedly accepted by Grote himself. His main quarrel over the point is that the ambiguity involved in Ferrier's original proposition darkens the entire argument. What formulation Grote himself prefers we shall henceforth try to let him state in his own manner.

(a) In the first place, we are called upon to note a distinction of importance—that, namely, between the view of phenomenalism and the view of philosophy. "The point of difference is that in the former we look upon what we find out by physical research as ultimate fact, so far as we are concerned, and upon conformity with it as the test of truth: so that nothing is admitted as true except so far as it follows by some process of inference from this. In opposition to this, the contrasted view is to the effect, that for philosophy, for our *entire* judgment about things, we must go beyond this, or rather go further back than it, the ultimate fact *really* (however for the purposes of physical science we may assume the former) for us—the basis upon which all rests—being not that things exist, but that we know them, *i.e.*, think of them as existing: the order of things in this view is not, existence first, and then knowledge with

[7] *Exploratio Philosophica*, pp. 67-68. Author's italics.

regard to this or to parts of it arising in whatever manner; but knowledge first, involving or implying the existence of what is known, but logically at least, prior to it, and conceivably more extensive than it, and not all meeting with application. In the former view, knowledge about things is looked upon as a possibly supervening accident to them or of them: in the latter view, their knowableness is a part, and the most important part, of their reality or essential being. In the former view, mind is supposed to follow, desultorily and accidentally, after matter of fact: in the latter view mind or consciousness begins with recognising itself as a part of an entire supposed matter of fact or universe, and next as correspondent, in its subjective character, to the whole of this besides as object, while the understanding of this latter as *known*, germinates into the notion of the recognition of other mind or reason in it." [8]

The distinction between the two views Grote expresses more technically, and perhaps more precisely, in the following passage: "The phenomenal verb is 'is' in the sense of 'exist,' with immediate application of it to certain objects of our thought: the thought itself, the nature of the existence, the grounds of our supposition of it, not entering into consideration. The verb of philosophy, or when our point of departure is consciousness or our own personality, is one which has scarcely existence in popular language: we might consider it to be 'feel' used neutrally, or 'feel ourselves' (the Greek ἔχω) with an adverb. In this consciousness, in the philosopher's view, is the root of all certainty or knowledge." [9] By phenomenalism, then, is meant that view which sharply abstracts the objects of knowledge from the fact of knowledge, and undertakes to deal with those 'objects' [10]

---

[8] *Ibid.*, p. 59.

[9] *Ibid.*, p. 4. "The problem of philosophy," Grote adds to the above quotation, "is the finding the relation between existence and this." It is important for an understanding of Grote's general argument to note that he is not willing to admit that the 'object' can be wholly neglected in the view of philosophy; on the contrary, it is quite important. The faculties of knowledge which "might know anything" indifferently are the "counterpart abstraction to phenomenalism" and are not worth discussing. In this abstraction, he thinks, lies the basal mistake of Kant's analysis. (Cf. also *op. cit.*, pp. 17-18.)

[10] Grote is particularly insistent upon clarity in the use of this term. "If we wish to try the clearness of a philosopher's thought, it seems to me that

taken in this abstraction. By the view of philosophy (sometimes called by Grote the view of the "higher logic"—not, however, with "reference to any comparative superiority"), on the other hand, is meant the view which emphasizes the fact of knowledge or consciousness as fundamental, rather than the 'objects' taken in abstraction from the fact of knowledge.

(b) Within its own province, and in its own way, phenomenalism is true enough; and if any alien elements are introduced into it, false science results. Nevertheless, it is an abstract view and is therefore not entirely satisfactory; one must go beyond it to the philosophical view. That such is the case may be made evident by a consideration and analysis of the view itself.

Viewed phenomenally, the universe is the universe as conceived by physical science. And what sort of a universe is this? Space and time are realities in virtue of their relation (which Grote conceives as that of being 'filled') to matter and movement. What they are filled with is not 'things,' but matter (which is a changing notion) and what we may loosely term "natural agents" or forces in matter. Through the action of these upon our own bodies matter comes to have what, in reference to ourselves, may be called sensible qualities (taste, pressure, weight, and the like). From the phenomenal point of view, *things* remain puzzles; for each involves unity, and unity from the standpoint of phenomenalism is a mystery. Nor is there anything to be gained here by appealing to 'law'; for on the phenomenal level law is itself a puzzle.

The root difficulty in phenomenalism, however, if phenomenalism be taken as final, lies in the very knowledge of which phenomenalism itself is supposed to be an expression. In the first place, there is for phenomenalism no 'mind' in the philosophical sense of the term. 'We' can here mean only our animated bodies. Consequently 'knowing,' in so far as it has any meaning at all on this level, is merely physical contact between the space-time order of events and our bodies—a contact, the circuit of which in the animated body, the physiologist may or may not be able to complete. In other words, knowledge here can mean only the

the crucial test is his use of the term 'object' in application to knowledge."
(*Exploratio Philosophica*, Part I, 61.)

complicated and mutual action of the various "natural agents" between the bodily frame of each of us and the rest of the material universe. And it is not easy to see how such knowledge could give us the sort of world which in fact we do know, and which even phenomenalism supposes that we know. Furthermore, the only test of truth which is open to phenomenalism is that of "harmonizing all our sensitive powers and all the different experience of different men"—unless one wishes to add the test of utility, which in the end reduces to the other.

This criterion does apply in distinguishing illusions. What is not true for all our sensitive powers, so far as they can be brought into comparison, is not phenomenally true at all. But where only one sensitive power is involved there is no test whether there is illusion or not, and it is difficult to stretch the test to apply to all cases where the question of truth is involved. Finally, knowledge for phenomenalism is an inessential accident; existence is the basal fact, while knowledge is a mere possibility which may on occasion supervene.

Thus, in "the simply phenomenalist spirit" there is something "inexpressibly depressing and desolate." Knowledge here is largely meaningless, and the object of knowledge is vague and inchoate. "The progress of knowledge, so far as we can be true to this manner of thought, is the passing on unmeaningly, we might say the falling helplessly, from one view to a fresh one in a course which is not advance towards an end but the getting further and further into a hopeless infinity." [11] We are compelled, then, to pass on from the phenomenalist view to the philosophical.

(c) The philosophical view, as we have already seen, starts from consciousness. We find here a certainty which is beyond cavil, and which is much more intimate than any phenomenal certainty can possibly be. "Whether anything beyond ourselves exist or not, we are at least certain that we feel, *i.e.*, that feeling, pleasure and pain, are realities, and individual to what, in virtue of this feeling or consciousness, we call *ourselves:* and that so far as consciousness is a proof or a fit suggestive of existence, '*cogito*' of '*sum*,' *we* ourselves exist." [12] And it is to be

11 *Ibid.*, Pt. I, p. 15.
12 *Ibid.*, pp. 18-19.

particularly noted that the 'we' of consciousness is quite different from the 'we' of phenomenalism; the former is feeling, while the latter is simply our bodies.

The certainty of consciousness, with which we thus begin, is also certainly double. We no sooner feel ourselves to exist than we feel something besides ourselves to exist also. The two feelings are the same fact looked at from different points of view, not two distinct facts. The feeling of existence is inherently dual and on analysis resolves itself into 'being' and 'feeling,' the difference between the two being that the first is sharablé between ourselves and something else while the second is not thus sharable. Thus the distinction between the notion of individuality and that of being is coeval with consciousness; consciousness involves both. "The matter may be best understood thus: if we, any of us, were the solitary existence, the simple monad, of the universe, though the notion of feeling or individuality would exist in us, I do not think that of existence would—we *feel* for ourselves, but we *are* not for and by ourselves, we *are* something; that is, in other words, in the notion *be* there is something quasi-generic, and it implies already a state of things, an universe." [13]

We may therefore say that intellectually we are born into a universe. "It is not really correct to say, as an ultimate fact which cannot and need not be accounted for, that we refer our first feelings of pleasure and pain (or some of them) to a cause independent of us, for the distinction begins earlier than this, and as early as we have the consciousness which answers to the language 'our feelings' we have the idea of an universe, large or small, of which *we* are a part." All of our later knowledge is contained 'seminally' in this first experience; our so-called progress in knowledge consists simply "in the gradual making acquaintance with that which is thus revealed to us." Knowledge, therefore, is a process which consists largely in self-correction. "It proceeds as it were by hitches, and every step in it together with truth contains error, which the next or an after step corrects." It is through such a process "that the dim universe which is the ground or counter-notion of primitive con-

[13] *Exploratio Philosophica*, Pt. I, pp. 22-23. Author's italics.

sciousness, the reality or state of things in which, so soon as
we understand anything, we understand ourselves as existing,
takes form and fullness and particularity." [14] This gradual making acquaintance with that which is thus revealed to us and
giving it content and form, fullness and particularity, is the
process of philosophical speculation.

(d) Hereupon Grote enters upon an account of some of the
details of this growing universe. Space, time, matter, and things,
as they present themselves from this point of view, are dealt
with at some length, as are also the notions of causality and
unity. A 'scale' of consciousness is roughly suggested, in which
consciousness, as progressively sensation, will, and intelligence,
is rather vaguely differentiated. And in parts of the second
volume of the *Exploratio,* especially in Book II, the question
of immediate knowledge is taken up and the distinction between
"knowledge of acquaintance" and "knowledge of judgment" is
drawn and more or less fully discussed. But all of this survey
is sketchy, and some portions of it are now quite outgrown;
nor does it readily lend itself to systematic summary. There
are involved in it, however, some principles which are important
for Grote's general argument; and these may here be set down
in conclusion of our expository statement.

The first and most basal of these is the thesis that consciousness or feeling develops in conjunction with phenomenal fact,
from which, as has been noted above, he holds, it can be separated only by abstraction. The historical development of
knowledge "is the continued exercise of the mind in judgment
in conjunction with the continued communication, by the senses,
with phenomenal fact." Knowledge is not simply a matter of
successive experiences on the one side, nor is it the vague and
loose exercise of judgment on the other; it is rather the two in
conjunction. "In judgment, for *it* to be knowledge, there must
be something to judge or be judged; in experience, for *it* to be
knowledge, there must be *notice* or exercise of the will." [15] And

[14] *Ibid.,* pp. 23, 24.
[15] *Ibid.,* p. 30. The point here is emphasized by Grote in numerous places
and various contexts. Compare, for example, the following: "We are every
moment, by means of the sensitive and motive nerves of our body, hitting,
knocking ourselves against, one thing after another in nature: but all this

this dual nature of knowledge is for Grote's argument of quite
foundational significance.

In it lies the basis for his denial of such a sharp distinction
between necessary and contingent truth as is drawn by Ferrier.
For Grote, as we have already noted, the difference between
the two is only a difference in our manner of arriving at truth—
not a difference in the nature of the truth arrived at. And we
can now see why he holds this view. The fragmentary and contingent nature of the sort of knowledge called experimental is
not to be attributed to our faculties of knowledge at all, but
to "our sensive powers and our corporeal frame"; its inco-
herence and unsatisfactoriness arise "because our powers of
sensitive communication do not constitute a consistent and universal *physiometer* so to call it." If they were such, then experi-
ential knowledge would be necessary knowledge; for, then, it
would adequately meet the demands of intelligence.

Again, the universe of 'things' is based on, and arises in,
consciousness alone. Such a universe is not possible for phenomenalism, since no principle of unity is, at this level, available. At this level, all we can possibly have is invariable connection (causation) between different portions of matter, or
that which fills space. It is by no means clear, however, how
the phenomenalist is really to know either things or causal connections, in the only sense in which knowledge is strictly possible
for him at his level. For a 'thing' is only a given portion of
matter, and a 'cause' is only an invariable antecedent; but fact
is continuous, and in phenomenalism there is no ground for dis-
criminating between one thing and another or for saying that
one thing is antecedent to another. 'Things' are, as it were,
carved out of the continuous and undiscriminated phenomenal
whole by consciousness itself; consciousness is the principle of
individuation. There are, to be sure, certain lines or nuances
in the phenomenal continuum which consciousness follows in
this operation. We distinguish one thing from another in space,
for instance, partly at least because it is of such a size and

(and this is all that our *experience* of itself is) would be fruitless, unless
we were *thinking* all the while." (*Exploratio*, II, 305. The italics here, as in
the quotation given in the text, are all in the original.)

shape. But in the notion of 'thingness' there is always involved
more than this phenomenal discreteness. A reference of the portion of matter called a 'thing' to our consciousness is required,
since our notice of things is from the first *interested*. "A 'thing'
is what we may use or make, or if not we, what others may
use or have made. Our notice of things is in this way from the
first . . . *interested:* what makes them individualities or things
to us is originally a supposed relation to ourselves." [16] A world
of 'things' and relations among things, thus, involves a necessary
reference to consciousness.

The major problem at issue in the preceding discussion of
the 'thing' is, of course, the problem of unity. And the principle
defended in that discussion, Grote thinks, holds universally.
Therefore, in thinking the universe as systematic we 'humanize'
it, since system is of mind alone. Progress in knowledge does
not consist in merely following fact; it consists rather in
"actively speculating, imagining, anticipating, meeting the fragmentariness of experience by belief in the reason of things and
in the connectedness of all." [17] Thus it is that mind gradually
discovers itself in experience, and so comes at last to find itself
'at home' there.

The instructed reader will, of course, observe much in the
argument of Grote which is quite in the spirit of the Hegelian
tradition, but there is no apparent evidence that Hegel actually
exerted any very great influence on him. The argument, however, is inadequately formulated; there are many gaps in it
and underlying assumptions are not developed. Nevertheless
Grote deserves credit for being the first among British idealists
to emphasize, however inadequately, the importance of an argument which in principle was foundational in the work of some
of his successors in the movement, such as Bradley, Bosanquet,
and Royce.

[16] *Ibid.*, p. 51. Compare Hegel's discussion of the 'This' in the first part
of the *Phaenomenologie des Geistes.*
[17] *Exploratio Philosophica*, Part II, 312. I may venture to translate the
meaning of Grote here to be that progress in knowledge consists in transforming 'contingent' into 'necessary' truth, or, perhaps better, in appre-
hending 'contingent' truth as 'necessary.'

CHAPTER IV

FRANCIS HERBERT BRADLEY (1846-1924)

"FRANCIS HERBERT BRADLEY is the most important English representative of the tendency which may be described as the *New Idealism.*" This is the opinion of Harald Höffding as expressed in his *Brief History of Modern Thought.* In his lectures on *Modern Philosophers* the same critic refers to Bradley as "England's most renowned thinker of recent times." Professor J. H. Muirhead, in his Preface to the first volume of *Contemporary British Philosophy,* asserts: "Mr. F. H. Bradley has been by general acknowledgment the foremost figure in British philosophy (perhaps in the philosophy of our time in any country) for the last generation." By common consent of the contributors to the second volume of this work, it was dedicated to Bradley as one "to whom British philosophy owed the impulse that gave it new life in our time."

All of these estimates of Bradley's importance in the history of British philosophy are, without doubt, justified. No British philosopher of Bradley's generation deserves to be placed above him, and there are few to compare with him in scope of vision or in vigor and incisiveness of analytical ability. No one has exerted a greater influence on his contemporaries, in England or outside. Certainly in the history of British idealism his position is an outstanding one.

Like Green, Bradley is an unsparing critic of the traditional British philosophy. Its atomistic view of experience seemed to him, as it had seemed to Green, a hopelessly blind alley in epistemology and ethics; and in both his *Ethical Studies* and his *Principles of Logic* he subjected it to a merciless criticism which, in some of its aspects at least, may well be taken as final. The principles underlying this criticism are essentially the same as those at the basis of Green's elaborate *Introductions* to his edition of the works of Hume, but Bradley's formulation of these principles is his own, and in many respects. it marks a decided advance beyond Green.

In his statement of the idealistic argument, Bradley's departure from Green is quite marked. His emphasis is rather in the spirit of John Grote. Of course, Bradley is more or less consciously under the influence of Hegel, to whom he occasionally acknowledges his indebtedness. But whether he should be called an Hegelian and in what sense, is a question which is of no concern to us here and the discussion of it would be largely idle.[1] He is no mere borrower of other men's ideas, and, though there can be no doubt of the influence of German thinkers, particularly Hegel, Bradley's construction is always his own. In that construction his peculiar genius appears in its fullest incisiveness and gives us perhaps the first statement of the case of British idealism, wholly freed from theological bias and imbued with a healthy skepticism—a statement which had to be reckoned with by all later thinkers, idealist and non-idealist alike. It is that statement with which we are concerned in this chapter.

Replying directly to certain criticisms of his most important metaphysical treatise, *Appearance and Reality*, Bradley writes in the Appendix to the second edition of that work: "The actual starting-point and basis of this work is an assumption about truth and reality. I have assumed that the object of metaphysics is to find a general view which will satisfy the intellect, and I have assumed that whatever succeeds in doing this is real and true, and that whatever fails is neither. This is a doctrine which, so far as I see, can neither be proved nor questioned. The proof or the question, it seems to me, must imply the truth of the doctrine, and, if that is not assumed, both vanish." In 1911 he described his general position as follows: "Reality for me . . . is one individual Experience. It is a higher unity above our immediate experience, and above all ideality and relations. It is above thought and will and aesthetic perception. But, though transcending these modes of experience, it includes them all fully. Such a whole is Reality, and, as against this whole, truth

---

[1] In any event, it seems to me wrong to say of Bradley, as Höffding does, that "he must be called far more a Kantian than a Hegelian." (*Modern Philosophers,* p. 66.) This is true of Green no doubt, but hardly of Bradley.

is merely ideal. It is indeed never a mere idea, for certainly there are no mere ideas. It is Reality appearing and expressing itself in that one-sided way which we call ideal. Hence truth is identical with Reality in the sense that, in order to perfect itself, it would have to become Reality. On the other side truth, while it is truth, differs from Reality, and, if it ceases to be different, would cease to be true. But how in detail all this is possible, cannot be understood." [2]

These two quotations together state in summary fashion Bradley's view of the assumption with which he begins, the general conclusion of his philosophy, and the direction of the argument by which the conclusion it reached. The aim of the following exposition is to draw out the points here involved, and particularly to elaborate the argument indicated. The argument falls conveniently under several heads, which may be set down as an aid in the exposition—(1) The Given: Immediate Experience; (2) The Relational Level: Its Genesis; (3) Terms and Relations: Appearance; (4) Reality: the Absolute; (5) Reality and Appearance: Degrees of Reality. [3]

1. THE GIVEN: IMMEDIATE EXPERIENCE

What is directly given in experience must constitute the point of departure for philosophical speculation. On this proposition

[2] From an article in *Mind*, July, 1911, reprinted in *Essays on Truth and Reality*, pp. 343-344. The position here suggested with reference to 'mere ideas' is different from that advocated earlier in *Principles of Logic* (1883); and the difference is important. The position here, that there are no 'mere' ideas but all ideas qualify reality, is the one which Bradley in the end holds to be true. (Cf. *Essays on Truth and Reality*, Chapter III, especially the foot-note p. 29.)

[3] Bradley's chief works are: *Ethical Studies* (1876); second edition, with additional notes by the author (1927); *Principles of Logic* (1883); *Appearance and Reality* (1893); second edition, with an Appendix (1897); *Essays on Truth and Reality* (1914). The last volume is composed of articles previously published in the journals, mostly in *Mind*.

The argument presented in this chapter is taken primarily from *Appearance and Reality* and the *Essays on Truth and Reality*, since these are the volumes in which the author's principles are set forth in their latest form. The *Ethical Studies* is drawn upon for the treatment of the ethical and religious consciousness, however, while the general principles of the *Logic*, of course, underlie the whole. From the earlier to the later of Bradley's writings there is no important change of principle in his philosophy.

there is general agreement, but widely divergent views are held concerning the nature of immediate experience. So our first step must be to inquire into the form of experience which is immediate and given.

It is sometimes supposed that immediate experience is a manifold of different objects, and that the business of philosophy is to bring this manifold into a unity and to explain how this is both possible and necessary. At other times, however, it is maintained that immediate experience is an unanalyzable correlation of subject and object, knower and known, and that the problem of philosophy is simply to read off the implications of this correlation for a theory of the world.[4] Neither of these views can in the end be justified. Both are vitiated by a common false assumption, namely, that the immediate type of experience is to be found at the relational level. As relational, experience is already an ideal construction and yields to analysis; it is therefore not immediate experience. Such experience is to be sought, and found, only below the relational level; and this fact we now proceed to establish.

If, looking for immediate experience and following the genetic method, you push your analysis back to the simplest form of experience, what you seem always to find is a type of experience which can be described only as a simply felt manifold in which there are no distinctions among qualities. In it "there is nothing beyond what is presented, what is and is felt, or is rather felt simply. There is no memory or imagination or hope or fear or thought or will, and no perception of difference or likeness. There are in short no relations and no feelings, only feeling. It is all one blur with differences that work and that are felt, but not discriminated." [5] Considered genetically, then, immediate experience is a simply felt whole in which differences are functionally present but not distinguished.

Again, if you turn your attention to the level of experience

[4] Compare the views of Ferrier, Green, and Grote on the point.

[5] "Association and Thought," *Mind,* Vol. XII, 363. Compare the view of "pure experience" as held by William James and stated by him, for instance, in his *Essays in Radical Empiricism,* Chapters II and III. Note Bradley's criticism of this view and the distinction he draws between it and his notion of "immediate experience" in Appendix III to Chapter V of his *Essays on Truth and Reality.*

where terms and relations are explicitly distinguished and search there for the immediate, what you find is the same undifferentiated whole of feeling. You find a deep-lying felt totality which is non-relational in nature, and on which the relational features characteristic of this higher level are seen to depend. Of course, at this higher level you do have subject and object together with all the distinctions which these involve. But subject and object and their relation to each other are themselves not given as defying analysis. On the contrary, subject and object are derived aspects of the undifferentiated whole of feeling which lies there as their indispensable background. It is this undifferentiated whole which alone may be taken as immediate experience; subject and object and all distinctions and differences experienced as such arise out of it through ideal construction, as we shall see in some detail below. At the relational level, therefore, immediate experience is, as at the pre-relational level, a felt unity of a manifold which comprises within itself an indefinite amount of difference, but without felt distinctions; it is a many simply felt as one.

For our later argument, it is quite important to note that immediate experience is present within the relational level as foundational. It functions as the background or nucleus in which terms and relations germinate, so to say, and from which they grow; it is the felt unity which is the immediate center of all mediated experience. It "is not a stage, which may or may not at some time have been there and has now ceased to exist. It is not in any case removed by the presence of a not-self and of a relational consciousness. All that is thus removed is at most, we may say, the *mereness* of immediacy. Every distinction and relation still rests on an immediate background of which we are aware, and every distinction and relation (so far as experienced) is also felt, and felt in a sense to belong to an immediate totality. Thus in all experience we still have feeling which is not an object, and at all our moments the entirety of what comes to us, however much distinguished and relational, is felt as comprised within a unity which itself is not relational." [6]

[6] *Essays on Truth and Reality,* Chapter VI, p. 178; cf. *Appearance and Reality,* second edition, p. 459.

2. THE RELATIONAL LEVEL: ITS GENESIS

Viewed from within, immediate experience is unstable because it carries within itself the impulse towards its own transcendence. We must now undertake to see in some detail how this is so and where, following this impulse, we are finally led. In this section we are to notice how the sort of immediate experience which characterizes the primitive consciousness is broken, by its inherent flux, into explicit relations of subject and object. Here we shall be dealing with the genesis (whether historical or merely theoretical makes no difference in principle) of the relational consciousness.

As we have noted in the preceding section, immediate experience is not a bare and atomic simple; it is rather a manifold in unity, simply felt as a whole and without explicit differentiations. As such a manifold, it involves, at the least, sensations and the feelings of pleasure and pain. Now it happens that there are certain regularities in the flow of sensations due to the order of the environment, and these regularities are emphasized in experience by the pleasure and pain which attach to them. Thus the sensations are gradually conjoined and fashioned into groups, and here we have the beginnings of the formation of objects and of the basal distinction between subject and objects. Some of the groups of sensations are relatively stable, while others are shifting and loose; the relatively stable ones are 'objective' in a sense in which the relatively shifting ones are not.

Among the stable groups there is one which has a unique status: it is always present in experience, while others are intermittent; and it is more intimately connected with the feelings of pleasure and pain than is any other group. It thus becomes 'permanent' and 'essential' as against any other group, which in comparison is variable and 'accidental.' The core of this privileged group of sensations is a bundle of feelings directly linked with pleasure and pain. This relatively permanent feeling-mass is gradually dissociated from all other groups, because (a) these other groups are linked with pleasure and pain only under occasional conditions, while the feeling-mass is persistently qualified by pleasure and pain and (b) the instability and variations of these other groups gradually loosen them from contact with this feeling-mass. The content of this feeling-mass, however, is, in its turn, not definitely and unalterably fixed; and, as we shall see later, this shifting of its limits is of importance in connection with the right understanding of the meaning of the 'subject' into which this feeling-mass finally develops.

At first, this feeling-mass seems to be identical with the body-group of sensations. Even at the higher level, where the full-fledged relational consciousness with the distinction of subject and object is clearly present—so far as it is possible, after contrast has done its work, we experience this feeling-mass most of all in organic sensation. But the feeling-mass is not confined exclusively to the body-group of sensations, for this group may be differentiated from it in varying degrees of sharpness. The truth of the matter is that "it will contain more or less of *whatever in the environment has not been dissociated from itself.*" [7]

When the dissociation of this central group from all the other groups, more loosely linked with pleasure and pain, has been carried far enough to give rise to the perception of a relation (for instance, the relation of difference) between them—a result obtained, we must suppose, only through a long and devious course of evolutionary conflict among cohesions and discrepancies—we have consciousness with its subject-object relation. This development, it would appear, is the outcome of a practical collision between the feeling-group and other groups dissociated from it, when the latter fail to give the satisfaction which the former is led to expect as the dissociated groups are approached. If persistent, this antagonism results in a rupture within the total whole of feeling, and the feeling-group is more or less permanently set over against the discrepant and disappointing 'outer' group, which is then distinguished as its 'other.' The feeling-group itself becomes the 'subject' to which this other is an 'object.' However, there is never a final and sharp cleavage between the two. Elements of the one may on occasion pass over into the other without any assignable limit, but each remains in some sense an element in a common, felt whole. The

[7] *Mind,* Vol. XII, 370. Italics are in the original text.

distinction, however, is fairly definite in any case, and the 'object' felt as distinct recurs often and is mainly the same. Hence the 'object' gradually acquires relative permanence on its own account and an apparent independence of the 'subject.' When it attains this status it is ready to function as a *theoretical* object, controlling thought and desire and playing its rôle in the search for truth as well as in the moral and aesthetic relations of life.[8]

Precisely how the 'perception' of the relation of subject to object arises within the genesis of experience we are wholly unable to explain, except to point out one very significant condition of it. That condition lies in the felt unity which functions throughout and makes the collisions whence the distinction emerges a significant conflict within a single whole, rather than a mere antagonism between discrete entities or separate wholes. If the collisions were of the latter sort, nothing could result from them; only because they occur among elements of a whole do they result in the distinction indicated by the subject-object relation. Immediate experience, then, is logically, as well as psychologically and historically, foundational to the relational consciousness.

The preceding account of the genesis of relational experience puts us in position to answer the question as to why, starting with immediate experience, we cannot stay there. We have seen that the felt unity with which we begin necessarily develops into the relational level of consciousness through its own inner diremption, and that the unity, far from being destroyed in the process, functions throughout and is even basal. The felt whole gradually differentiates itself into groups related in various ways, and the process of differentiation is one in which the unity tends to complete its inner drive through what, in the later stages, we know as ideation. Out of the conflicts within the felt unity, therefore, terms and relations are born, and the unity itself persists beneath them. Thus, beginning with immediate experience we cannot stay there, because such experience is by

[8] The details of Bradley's analysis here are very interesting and touch on many basal psychological questions. They may be found in his articles on "Thought and Will" published in *Mind* during the year 1887, and the years 1902-1904.

its very nature precarious and unstable and must seek itself beyond itself. There is within it a tendency towards its own transcendence, following which thought is forced to seek its satisfaction elsewhere than in immediate experience itself.[9]

3. TERMS AND RELATIONS: APPEARANCE

We are seeking for that which will satisfy the intellect. Immediate experience will not do so, since it dissolves on analysis. We turn now to inquire whether such satisfaction can be found at the level into which immediate experience develops—the level of terms and relations.

First, let us be clear as to what is to be understood by thought's satisfaction. That which satisfies thought must be of such a nature as to meet thought's peculiar need. Now the need of thought is twofold: on the one side, it seeks the self-consistent and the harmonious; on the other side, it seeks the self-complete and the all-inclusive. Whatever involves any inconsistency jars with the demands of thought, and until the inconsistency is removed thought cannot rest. Nor can that which is incomplete satisfy, for the limited involves an environment beyond into which thought is necessarily pushed on its quest for satisfaction. In last analysis, both of these demands of thought are one and the same; incompleteness is disclosed by some sort of inconsistency, and inconsistency betokens some sort of incompleteness. So we may summarily say that thought seeks consistency, and that which would satisfy it is a harmonious whole —a consistent, and therefore all-inclusive, system.

Such a system thought is able to find nowhere at the level of the relational consciousness, for here it is everywhere confronted by the inherent contradiction involved in the distinction between terms and relations. What, then, is this contradiction?

It is apparent that terms are inseparable from relations and are meaningless apart from them. Terms are never found without relations, since one term is always together with one other

---

[9] "We start . . . from the immediate union of one and many, of sameness and difference, which we have given to us in feeling and in the inherence of qualities in a sensuous whole. This immediate union is of necessity dissolved in our judgement, and it never in any judgement is completely made good." (*Essays on Truth and Reality*, p. 256.)

term at least. Again, though we may possibly conceive terms as distinct from relations and suppose that the relations have existence only for us, while the terms exist independently, this proves, not that terms and relations are really separate, but only that by a process of abstraction we can imagine them separately. Finally, terms are intrinsically related, since they must in any case be distinct; distinctness implies difference and, so, a relation. Terms, we may therefore conclude, are inseparable from relations.

On the other hand, terms cannot be identified with relations, since the term necessarily is, and remains, itself. It is, therefore, something different from its relations. But with this conclusion we are caught in a contradiction, for each term is now seen to have a double character which remains unintelligible. The term is at once both itself as term and itself as related, and there is no intelligible way in which this variety within its nature can be combined. It is one and also dual, and this duality is such as to dissipate its unity. To preserve its unity there is need within it of a relation between itself as term and itself as related, and such a relation cannot be found in the nature of the term. Its unity does not include within it a relation which combines the term's duality, but must seek always beyond for a new relation between the proposed combining relation and the duality to be combined. Thus the combining relation, introduced into the term to unify it, succeeds only in generating a greater complexity within its nature without removing the contradiction it was invoked to explain. The combining relation, in' its turn, demands new combining relations for more complicated terms which presuppose further relations without limit. Thus we are involved in an infinite regress, following which we are only carried farther and farther from our goal. Within the term there is a diremption which is incurable; the term must be, yet cannot intelligibly be, related.

The same dilemma is disclosed from the side of relations. A bare relation without terms is meaningless, but how the relation can stand to the terms is unintelligible. If the relation is nothing to the terms, then the terms are not related and so are not terms. If, on the other hand, the relation is to hold between the terms, then the relation must be related to the terms, and this demands a new relation *ad infinitum*. Thus we find ourselves in the infinite regress once more, and our problem, far from being solved, only grows in complexity. "The links are united by a link, and this bond of union is a link which also has two ends; and these require each a fresh link to connect them with the old. The problem is to find how the relation can stand to its qualities; and this problem is insoluble." [10]

Thus it turns out that at the relational level of experience thought can never find the satisfaction it seeks. Terms and relations alike demand a unity which they cannot achieve, and so they are irremediably self-contradictory. Our general conclusion, then, must be "that a relational way of thought—any one that moves by the machinery of terms and relations—must give appearance, and not truth." And this conclusion leads at once to the further conclusion that the whole spatial and temporal world must be set down as appearance, for in this world we are confronted throughout by terms and relations.

To enter upon some of the details here, let us take space and time themselves. Analysis discloses that each is riddled with inconsistencies and cannot, therefore, be called real or true. Space, for instance, is, and yet is not, nothing but a relation. It is at once infinitely divisible and infinitely extensible, and in either direction analysis resolves it into bare relations. Consider its divisibility: Here the parts of space cannot be solid, since they are extended and consequently consist of parts which, in turn, are extended indefinitely Thus, the infinitesimal parts of space are only relations for which terms are ever lacking. Or, on the other side, consider its extensibility: In this direction it vanishes into an illusory whole beyond, and is therefore a bare relation to a non-existent other. Nevertheless, space is a whole made up of parts and must in some sense be itself a term made

[10] *Appearance and Reality*, second edition, p. 33. The word Bradley actually uses throughout the discussion here summarized is 'qualities,' rather than 'terms.' This usage is perhaps better fitted to point precisely the difficulty he is developing—"the old puzzle," namely, "as to the connection of diversity and unity." In my summary I have changed the terminology in order to generalize the thesis. This generalization Bradley himself in the end insists upon; and he must insist upon it, of course, if the thesis is to bear the weight of the conclusion which he grounds in it.

up of terms; for as a whole it is more than merely relation, and as consisting of parts it is more than a bare infinite regress of relations. Thus space is inherently contradictory.

The same holds in principle of time. "If you take time as a relation between units without duration, then the whole time has no duration, and it is not time at all. But, if you give duration to the whole time, then at once the units themselves are found to possess it; and they thus cease to be units. Time in fact is 'before' and 'after' in one; and without this diversity it is not time. But these differences cannot be asserted of the unity; and, on the other hand and failing that, time is helplessly dissolved. Hence they are asserted under a relation. 'Before in relation to after' is the character of time; and here the old difficulties about relation and quality recommence." Time, thus, like space, involves contradiction. In both, terms are ever vanishing into relations, and relations are ever seeking for terms which evade them. Both must therefore be set down as appearance only.

Essentially the same must be said of motion and change, causation, activity, and things—all are vitiated by the difficulty with reference to terms and relations, and if taken as real are self-contradictory. An analysis of them, however, would add nothing to the principles already advanced, and consequently it may be omitted from this summary statement.[11]

There is, however, one type of unity at the relational level which has commonly been supposed to be a type of unity in which thought can rest, namely, the self. It seems obvious at once that such a supposition must be false, since the self does not transcend the relational type of experience. But further inquiry into the supposition will carry us into important matters, and we begin with the self taken in isolation.

In the first place, it must be noted that, while we are all sure that we in some sense exist as individuals, we are by no means certain of the answer to the very pertinent question: In what sense and with what character? Indeed, there are widely

[11] Bradley examines these types of experience at some length. His analysis will be found in Chapters V-VIII of *Appearance and Reality,* and should be read; it contains helpful elaboration of the principles above outlined.

divergent views as to the nature of the self, and all of them on rigorous analysis disclose more or less serious deficiencies. We may mean by the self (a) a cross-section of experience at any given moment; but this quite obviously does not satisfy, since even in its least significant aspects the self must be something beyond the present moment. Or (b) we may identify the self, not with the mass of a given moment, but with the constant average mass. "Take a section completely through the man, and expose his total psychical contents; only now take this section at different times, and remove what seems exceptional. The residue will be the normal and ordinary matter, which fills his experience; and this is the self of the individual." [12] But such a view is quite as unsatisfactory as the other one, because of the fluctuations of the 'average' and because of the accidental circumstances that enter into its determination. On this view, either we take the man's history as his self, and then it is hardly one; or we identify his self with separate periods of that history, and then the single self entirely disappears.

Can we, then, discover (c) an 'essential' self? Where shall we seek for it, and how shall we describe it? Change is so radical a feature of experience that there seems to be nothing therein untouched by it; or, if there be, it is so poor and barren that it cannot meaningfully be identified with the self. If we seek for the self (d) in some single being or 'monad' which exists as a unit and in some sphere presumably free from change, our search is vain. We soon discover that this view is hopelessly wrecked on the difficulty of reconciling the simplicity and unity of the monad with the diversity of experience. If the unity is not sundered from the diversity, it loses its privileged status; if it is so sundered, it is certainly not the self whatever else it may be. Nor do we fare any better, but rather worse, if the self be equated with (e) personal interest, for in this sense the self is extremely variable and even self-contradictory. "If the self means merely what interests us personally, then at any one time it is likely to be too wide, and perhaps also to be too narrow; and at different times it seems quite at variance with itself." [13]

[12] *Appearance and Reality*, second edition, p. 78.
[13] *Ibid.*, p. 88.

Finally, despairing of these views, one may fall back on the traditional view which (f) identifies the self with an ego, or subject, standing over against an object of which it is aware as its content and from which it is sharply distinguished. This view has often been held, but whatever may be its attractions, there are at least three basal difficulties in it. In the first place, as we have already seen, the relation of subject and object is a relatively late development. It is not found everywhere in experience, for "every soul either exists or has existed at a stage where there was no self and no not-self, neither Ego nor object in any sense whatever." Again, subject as well as object is a concrete psychical existent, and the supposition that the subject is something apart from and beyond its psychical filling is not based upon, and cannot be supported by, observation. Finally, the contents of subject and object, so far as observation carries us, are constantly shifting from one to the other side in both the theoretical and the practical relations of life; and this takes place to such an extent that "the main bulk of the elements on each side is interchangeable."

Thus, we are apparently unable to find a meaning of the self which will justify us in saying that the self is real, for whatever meaning we hit upon we are unable to maintain it. But may not our difficulties be due to our abstract procedure? We have taken the self in its individual reference, and have tried to fix its meaning in isolation. The question arises whether this is justifiable and whether, viewing the self more concretely in its social setting, a meaning of it may be found in which thought may finally rest. To a consideration of this question we now turn.

That the self cannot justifiably be taken in abstraction from its social context may be safely affirmed, for whatever the individual may be, he is at any rate essentially social, and the self that is his is inextricably mingled in the communal life. He finds his life in "the life of the whole, he lives that in himself, 'he is a pulse-beat of the whole system, and himself the whole system.' " [14] The institutional life which encompasses him enters

---

[14] *Ethical Studies,* second edition, p. 172. The full discussion of the point here should be noted; it is foundational to Bradley's ethics. The last part of the quotation given above is taken from Hegel.

into his very being. Let us then broaden our view of the self so as to include this social reference, and inquire whether, taken in this reference, there is a meaning of the self wherein may be found the satisfaction of thought for which we have sought elsewhere in vain. Clearly, we are now undertaking to deal with moral experience, and we must first ask what morality essentially is.

In morality something is to be done; a good is to be realized; an end is to be attained. And that end, in a word, is self-realization, for morality implies, not only that something is to be done, but also that it is to be done by me as my act. "The act for me means my act, and there is no end beyond the act. This we see in the belief that failure may be equivalent morally to success—in the saying, that there is nothing good except a good will. In short, for morality the end implies the act, and the act implies self-realisation." [15] Such seems to be the fundamental characteristic of moral consciousness as involving an end to be attained. And the same is evident when, leaving on one side what we think we ought to do, we inquire into what it is we actually do, for all motivating objects have been associated with our satisfaction, or, more correctly, have been felt in and as ourselves. The only reason why they move us now is because, when they are presented to our minds as motives, we feel ourselves asserted or affirmed in them. The essence of desire is the feeling of the affirmation of our self in the idea of something not our self, without which the self is felt as void and negated. Thus from the standpoint of motivation, as from that of obligation, self-realization is the end.[16]

---

[15] *Ethical Studies,* pp. 65-66.

[16] Compare the view advocated by Green in *Prolegomena to Ethics,* Book II, Chapter I, section 96. "When Esau sells his birthright for a mess of pottage, his motive, we might be apt hastily to say, is an animal want. On reflection . . . we shall find that it is not so. The motive lies in the presentation of an idea of himself as enjoying the pleasure of eating the pottage. . . . If the action were determined directly by the hunger, it would have no moral character, any more than have actions done in sleep, or strictly under compulsion, or from accident, or (so far as we know) the actions of animals. Since, however, it is not the hunger as a natural force, but his own conception of himself, as finding for the time his greatest good in the satisfaction of hunger, that determines the act, Esau recognises himself as the author of the act."

But it is all-important to comprehend the full import of this. The self to be realized is not the self as this or that particular feeling, or as a mere collection of states. In actual life "no man has disconnected particular ends; he looks beyond the moment, beyond this or that circumstance or position; his ends are subordinated to wider ends; each situation is seen (consciously or unconsciously) as part of a broader situation, and in this or that act he is aiming at and realizing some larger whole, which is not real in any particular act as such, and yet is realized in the body of acts which carry it out . . . and so far we may say that the self we realize is identified with wholes. . . ."[17] And, further, we must see that these wholes are ultimately included in one whole. This is not true, of course, in the sense that every individual consciously aims at such a whole, since much more reflection is required for this than is present in every life and in every act. Again, not every man's actions are consistent in detail, and in some cases there is hardly enough consistency to be called a system or whole at all. But, in the large, human life does exemplify in its activity that which at least roughly may be called systematic; the individual's life is a whole.

On reflection, this is fairly evident in both theoretical and practical activity. In each, the self as a whole is that at which (at least, ideally) we aim. What we want in theory is primarily to understand the object, to get at the truth of it; but this end is not attained till the whole mind of the thinker finds itself at home in the object. "So long as our theory strikes on the mind as strange and alien, so long do we say we have not found truth; we feel the impulse to go beyond and beyond, we alter and alter our views, till we see them as a consistent whole. There we rest, because then we have found the nature of our own mind and the truth of facts in one." And the same, in principle, holds in practice. Here there is the same demand for system, in which alone the will may ultimately rest. "Here our aim is not, leaving the given as it is, to find the truth of it; but here we want to force the sensuous fact to correspond to the truth of ourselves. We say, 'My sensuous existence is thus, but I truly am not thus; I am different.' On the one hand, as a matter of

[17] *Ethical Studies,* second edition, p. 69.

fact, I and my existing world are discrepant; on the other hand, the instinct of my nature tells me that the world is mine. On that impulse I act, I alter and alter the sensuous facts, till I find in them nothing but myself carried out. Then I possess my world, and I do not possess it until I find my will in it; and I do not find that, until what I have is a harmony or a whole in system." [18] As in the case of thought, then, so in that of will, the end is the whole; and for both thought and will the whole is the self.

It is of crucial importance for our further progress in analysis to make explicit what is here implied—namely, that the self which is willed in morality is always beyond. It is not the self here and now, at this time and under these particular circumstances, which is the end; it is rather the self as it may be, in its farther deepening and expansion. "It is no human ideal to lead 'the life of an oyster.' We have no right first to find out just what we happen to be and to have, and then to contract our wants to that limit. We cannot do it if we would, and morality calls to us that, if we try to do it, we are false to ourselves. Against the sensuous facts around us and within us, we must forever attempt to widen our empire. . . ." [19] The moral end, thus, "is the realisation of ourselves as the will which is above ourselves."

With this we are brought face to face with a contradiction which lies deep within moral experience. This experience commands me to realize myself; and yet the self which is the end is always other than the actual self and can never be attained *in propria persona*. "I *am* finite; I am both infinite *and* finite, and that is why my moral life is a perpetual progress. I must progress, because I have another which is to be, and yet never quite is, myself; and so, as I am, am in a state of contradiction."

In the history of ethical theory various ways out of this contradiction have been proposed, but without success. On the one side is the way of all hedonisms, which undertake to construct

[18] *Ethical Studies,* second edition, pp. 73-74.
[19] *Ibid.,* p. 74. The full discussion of the point is quite enlightening with reference to Bradley's general position, and it touches fundamental issues in a very helpful manner.

the universal of morality by the simple expedient of adding together (with variations in details, of course) the pleasurable feelings of this or that moment, or the pleasurable states of momentary selves. But instead of a true universal this gives us "a futile and bastard product, which carries its self-destruction within it, in the continual assertion of its own universality, together with its unceasing actual particularity and finitude." On the other side there are the sundry attempts to find the moral ultimate in a supposed pure will, independent of particular states. But this also involves contradiction, since such a will could never be an end without losing its 'purity'; or, stated otherwise, the will which this view says is to be realized in conduct is, by its nature, such that it cannot be realized, since to realize it would be to particularize it. Furthermore, such a will is meaningless even psychologically. Will apart from desire, will which wills nothing in particular, is a pure fiction. By neither of these ways, therefore, may we escape from the contradiction which moral experience involves. Neither "pleasure for pleasure's sake" nor "duty for duty's sake" can stand; the self to be realized in morality is neither "the feeling of self-realizedness" nor the sort of self which is the flat negation of the actual.[20]

Another attempt to remove the contradiction, though more nearly successful, is not in the end any more satisfactory. As we have already seen, the self is essentially social and is not an isolated point or atom. May it not then be true that the will above ourselves, which we are to realize in the process of realizing ourselves, is to be found in the community? Do we not, in performing the duties attached to our station in the social whole, realize our own true being? Here, it would seem, we have found a will above us which is yet within us, and which through self-expression we may attain. And such, in a measure at least, is doubtless the case. For here "is a universal which can confront our wandering desires with a fixed and stern imperative, but which yet is no unreal form of the mind, but a living soul that penetrates and stands fast in the detail of actual existence. It

[20] For the author's extended criticism of these ethical theories the reader should refer to Essays III and IV in the *Ethical Studies;* also to Chapter XXV of *Appearance and Reality.*

is real, and real for me. It is in its affirmation that I affirm myself, for I am but as 'a heart-beat in its system.' And I am real in it; for, when I give myself to it, it gives me the fruition of my own personal activity, the accomplished ideal of my life which is happiness. In the realized idea which, superior to me, and yet here and now in and by me, affirms itself in a continuous process, we have found the end, we have found self-realization, duty, and happiness in one—yes, we have found ourselves, when we have found our station and its duties, our function as an organ in a social organism." [21] This view is much more nearly satisfactory than is either of the other two considered above. "It satisfies us, because in it our wills attain their realization; the content of the will is a whole, is systematic; and it is the same whole on both sides. On the outside and inside alike we have the same universal will in union with the particular personality; and in the identity of inside and outside in one single process we have reached the point where the 'is to be,' with all its contradictions, disappears, or remains but as a moment in a higher 'is.' " [22]

Hereupon it might be assumed that we have at last reached our final goal, but such an assumption would be an error, for the community as the whole-which is an end does not satisfy; its "higher 'is' " is not ultimate yet. That the conception of "my station and its duties" expresses a basal insight into the demands of morality, that the self which is to be realized in the moral life finds here the concrete content of its imperative and higher will—all of this may readily be granted. "The basis and foundation of the ideal self is the self which is true to my station and its duties." But the ideal self reaches still beyond this 'visible' community; and, even within the circle of my station and its duties, the opposition between the ideal self and the actual self is not completely resolved.

Taking the latter point first, we observe that within this

[21] *Ethical Studies*, p. 163. Following the author's footnote in the second edition, I have inserted 'a' in place of 'the' as the third word from the end of this quotation. The author's detailed statement in Essay V of the view of "my station and its duties" is a justly famous passage of recent philosophical literature.

[22] *Ibid.*, p. 202.

sphere the actual self is not identified with the ideal self in such a manner that the bad self entirely disappears. There is always a discrepancy between the two, and each is in some genuine sense my real self. "I feel at times identified with the good, as though all my self were in it; there are certain good habits and pursuits and companies which are natural to me, and in which I feel at home. And then again there are certain bad habits and pursuits and companies in which perhaps I feel no less at home, in which also I feel myself to be myself. . . ." But when one tries to fix the content of the bad self, one is at a loss to do so except by opposing it to the good. And yet, on the other side, the content of the good self cannot be definitely fixed. It cannot always be identified with the social, the bad self standing over against it as the selfish; for it sometimes happens that the duties of the good self apparently lie on the 'selfish' side, since even altruism may be carried too far. Within the sphere of my station and its duties, therefore, the opposition between the world beyond and the 'ought' in me is not overcome.[23]

Furthermore, the ideal self tends to fall beyond the sphere of my station and its duties, in two directions. On the one hand, the 'ought,' in general, cannot be limited to any actual social order; for any actual social order is in development and always points to a better. The imperative of morality transcends particular times and countries; it is featured by non-temporal and cosmopolitan attributes. On the other hand, the imperative does not appear always to involve relations to others. The search for beauty and truth, for example, may be recognized as a duty; and yet it is not easy to discover the compulsion within the social order. "To say, without society science and art could not have arisen, is true. To say, apart from society the life of an artist or man of science cannot be carried on, is also true; but neither truth goes to show that society is the ultimate end, unless by an argument which takes the basis of a result as its final cause, and which would prove the physical and physiological conditions of society to be the end for which it existed. Man is not man at all unless social, but man is not

[23] *Ibid.*, pp. 276 ff.

much above the beasts unless more than social." [24] Thus the moral 'ought' leads beyond any actual social order, and there are claims that cannot be included within the duties of my station.

The view of my station and its duties, therefore, fails to resolve the contradiction within morality. All along we have seen that the self which morality bids us realize falls outside of our actual self, and we here see it going beyond the bounds of any describable community. It thus remains merely ideal and, contrasted with it, the actual self remains imperfect and incomplete. We must now note further that the contradiction is ineradicable, because morality is inherently self-contradictory. It tells you to realize yourself, and then shows you that your self cannot be realized; it insists upon your doing that which you can never do, and the doing of which (were it possible) would destroy morality itself. "No one ever was or could be perfectly moral; and, if he were, he would be moral no longer. Where there is no imperfection there is no ought, where there is no ought there is no morality, where there is no self-contradiction there is no ought. The ought is a self-contradiction. . . . Morality aims at the cessation of that which makes it possible; it is the effort after non-morality, and it presses forward beyond itself to a super-moral sphere where it ceases as such to exist." [25] This super-moral sphere to which morality itself thus brings us is, of course, the sphere of the religious consciousness. And we must now inquire whether thought can find its satisfaction in this type of experience.[26]

There is an inseparable connection between morality and religion. Religion includes morality within itself, and one who is on the whole immoral could not be called religious in any defensible meaning of the term. "Religion is essentially a doing,

[24] *Ethical Studies*, p. 223.

[25] *Ibid.*, pp. 234-235; compare *Appearance and Reality*, pp. 401-436. Apropos of the notion of "endless moral progress," Bradley adds this note to the above quotation: "Progress to an end which is completeness and the end of progress and morality, is one thing. Endless progress is progress without an end, is endless incompleteness, endless immorality, and is quite another thing."

[26] For the author's detailed consideration of this question see *Ethical Studies*, Concluding Remarks; *Appearance and Reality*, p. 436 ff.; and *Essays on Truth and Reality*, Chapter XV, with Supplementary Notes.

and a doing which is moral. It implies a realizing, and a realizing of the good self." But, though inseparably joined, religion and morality are by no means identical. As in the moral consciousness, so in the religious, there are two poles—namely, the actual self and the ideal self. In the moral consciousness, however, the ideal self remains to the end a mere 'ought to be' which 'is' not and which stands to the actual self as always beyond; while in the religious consciousness the ideal self becomes real (as God) and within it the actual self (as finite) is supposed in some sense to fall. Thus religion supplements morality in two ways: in religion (a) the 'ought' in general, or as ideal, becomes 'is'; and (b) the 'ought' in the finite individual is raised to some sort of identity with the universal.[27]

The relation here between the individual and the universal, between man and God, however, remains unstable; and because of its instability, religion proves to be unsatisfactory and in the end breaks under analysis. Religion is essentially practical, yet it assumes the perfection and completeness of its object; and these two sides of it, though essential to its nature, stand in irreconcilable conflict with each other. There is, on the one side, the 'ought' in me, and, on the other, the 'ought' (God's will) as an ideal which is realized; and there is neither an identity between the two nor any way in which they can intelligibly be brought together if religion is to stand. "We have a perfect real will, and we have my will, and the practical relation of these wills is what we mean by religion. And yet, if perfection is actually realized, what becomes of my will which is over against the complete Good Will? While, on the other hand, if there is no such Will, what becomes of God?" [28] Apart from a practical relation between man and God, such that the two are separate, there is no religion; but so long as this separation continues the religious consciousness is, like the moral, inherently self-contradictory. Thus the religious consciousness offers thought no satisfactory resting place; its goal is not here.

[27] "Our wills are ours to make them thine." Compare Hegel's analysis of what he calls the "unhappy consciousness" (das unglückliche Bewusstsein) in the Phänomonologie des Geistes, section B.

[28] Essays on Truth and Reality, p. 429. Cf. Ethical Studies, second edition, p. 314 ff.; and Appearance and Reality, second edition, p. 442 ff.

We have now sought throughout the ranges of the self for a meaning of it which would meet the demands of thought, and we have sought in vain. All of the meanings have proved inadequate; the self cannot be a punctual center or particularized individual, and equally it cannot be a socialized center. Taken as either it involves contradictions. This result, however, might have been foreseen from the beginning, since the nature of the self, however taken, is inherently relational and is consequently burdened with the inconsistency attaching to the machinery of terms and relations. It always implies a unity which it nowhere includes, and a diversity in which it cannot abide; the distinction between its two aspects always remains, and it remains as a relation for which there are no precise and intelligible terms. We should, then, without more ado, accept what inevitably must follow: The self cannot be taken as real. "The self is no doubt the highest form of experience which we have, but, for all that, is not a true form. It does not give us the facts as they are in reality; and, as it gives them, they are appearance, appearance and error." [29]

Our general conclusion thus far, then, is that so long as thought remains at the relational level of experience it finds itself everywhere brought to a stand by contradictions and, so, unable to attain its satisfaction. Nowhere at this level does it reach reality; everywhere it meets only appearance. Are we, then, forced to hold that appearance only is the proper object of thought, while reality falls wholly beyond and is to us unknowable?

To rest in such a position is clearly impossible—unless, indeed, we are resolved to put up with mere confusion. Appearances exist, and they are either related to reality or they are not. If they are, then reality can no longer be said to be something by itself and beyond; it is then qualified by appearances, but on the basis of what principle we do not know. If appearances are not reality, then reality lacks qualities utterly and becomes a mere abstraction which may indifferently be called 'being' or 'nothing.' Furthermore, a logical dichotomy between appearances and reality is theoretically useless and practically even danger-

[29] *Appearance and Reality*, p. 119.

ous. So sundered, reality is unknowable and, therefore, cannot help us to understand appearances. If we try to take appearances in connection with such reality, they are not thereby rendered one whit less confused. On the contrary, their confusion and inconsistencies are left standing untouched. And viewed practically, the dichotomy is dangerous; reality may then all too easily serve "only as a poor and irrelevant excuse for neglecting our own concerns." The separation must therefore be denied in the interest of both sanity and integrity. Reality (whatever else it may be) must at least include appearances; they exist, and so must belong to reality. Reality is for us nothing at all, or it appears; it cannot, therefore, be less than appearance. And this thesis we must hold fast in the sequel.

One other conclusion of positive import follows from the preceding considerations, and that conclusion should here be made explicit as an aid to further progress. Through the survey we have been following, we have gained some detailed insight into the nature of the goal, the whole, which, if attained, would satisfy the demands of thought. We have seen that thought is persistently balked at the relational level, because here terms and relations are everywhere present and standing opposed to each other in irreconcilable conflict. Relations seek for terms which elude them, and terms demand relations which are not available. It follows directly from this that a manifold unity from which relational inconsistencies are removed—a whole which has nothing outside of itself in the form of an 'elsewhere' or a 'not-yet' or an 'ought' and which within itself is unity in multiplicity—would meet the demands of thought. This is a positive conclusion, and so much is gain. It now remains to inquire whether from this result we may go forward. Is such a whole attainable by thought, and what, in more detail, may be said concerning its nature?

4. REALITY: THE ABSOLUTE

In the first place, let it be repeated that such a whole would be what we must mean by reality. That which ultimately satisfies thought, we have agreed, is reality and not appearance. This is an assumption; but it is a necessary assumption, and the denial of it is self-refuting. But can thought attain this, its final satisfaction?

At first glance, it would appear that the answer to this question must be negative. The goal which thought seeks is, as we have just seen, a non-relational whole; but thought itself is essentially relational, moving as it does only by the machinery of terms and relations. From these two propositions the conclusion seems to be inevitable: Thought is by its very nature incompetent to attain that which would satisfy it. In a sense this conclusion is inescapable; we shall in the end be forced to abide by it, but not in the sense in which it is understood to imply that the goal is wholly unintelligible. Some preliminary observations on the nature of judgment may enable us to understand the precise sense in which the conclusion must be accepted.

Every judgment is of a twofold nature. On one side, there is a something, a 'that,' about which the judgment is made; on the other side, there is a something, a 'what,' attached by the judgment to the 'that' as a qualification of it. In other words, there are in every judgment a subject and a predicate; the judgment is precisely the attribution of a predicate (a 'what') to the subject (a 'that'). Further, the two are inseparably joined. "If we try to get the 'that' by itself, we do not get it, for either we have it qualified, or else we fail utterly. If we try to get the 'what' by itself, we find at once that it is not all. It points to something beyond, and cannot exist by itself and as a bare adjective." [30] But, though the 'that' and the 'what' are inseparable, they are never in judgment identical and their distinction is essential. The 'what' is always alienated from its 'that' in the sense that it works beyond it, and this transcendence of the 'what' is essential to judgment; the two are always held asunder, and the judgment expresses their relation. Thus judgment is basically relational.

And with this we are confronted by the impasse noted above. The non-relational whole which would satisfy thought is such

[30] *Appearance and Reality*, pp. 162-163. Cf. *Esays on Truth and Reality*, Chapter III, and various passages on 'floating' ideas. Cf. also *Principles of Logic*, Book I.

that within it the 'what' and the 'that' would seem to collapse into a blank identity. It is a whole, then, which apparently cannot possibly be an object of judgment; and, if thought is to lead us to it, it must do so through its own suicide. But there is another aspect of judgment, equally essential, which we have so far failed to notice and a consideration of which may serve to render this difficulty less obdurate.

Not only is judgment dual in nature, as above described; it also involves a synthesis of its dual aspects. The 'that' and the 'what' in judgment do not stand over against each other as merely alien and estranged; on the contrary, the 'what' is always *of* the 'that' and the 'that' involves the 'what.' Turning our attention to this side of the matter, two important considerations are forced upon us. First, the subject of judgment is not an 'idea'; it is always an existent, a factual situation, which can be said to be ideal only in so far as its predicate (the 'what,' which is always an ideal content) is contained in it. And, second, the nisus of thought is to heal the breach between the two, by bringing the predicate or ideal content more and more into unity with the subject or factual situation. If thought were successful in this, "it would have a predicate consistent in itself and agreeing entirely with the subject." Since these two considerations are foundational within our further argument, it will be well to dwell for a moment upon them; and we take them in order.

In the judgment the predicate is involved in the subject. Though the two are distinct, and must remain distinct if the judgment is to exist, they are distinct only as aspects of a whole. In 'This horse is a mammal,' for example, the character of 'mammality' is involved in 'this horse,' and could not (at least meaningfully) be predicated of it unless it were so involved. This fact must be held fast as we proceed. Now the subject of judgment is, we have said, an existent, not a mere ideal construction. There is a sense, to be sure, in which one might say that the subject of judgment is an ideal content; but this is true only when the grammatical subject is meant. The grammatical subject, however, is not the real subject of the judgment; there is always something given in immediate presentation to which the grammatical subject together with its predicate refers, and this is the real subject. "Let us fancy ourselves in total darkness hung over a stream and looking down on it. The stream has no banks, and its current is covered and filled continuously with floating things. Right under our faces is a bright illuminated spot on the water, which ceaselessly widens and narrows its area, and shows us what passes away on the current. And this spot that is light is our now, our present." [31] This spot represents the real subject of the perceptual judgment that refers to it; it is the 'that' judged about. This holds in principle of every judgment; there is always a real subject, different from and basal to the grammatical subject, and this real subject is presented in immediate experience. The subject of every judgment, we may say then, is an aspect of reality; when we judge 'S is P' what we mean, if we understand ourselves, is 'reality is such that S is P.' [32]

But the reality which is directly the subject of judgment is that which appears in the immediacy of feeling and which is consequently arbitrarily narrowed. This is the basis of explanation of the second point, namely, the nisus of thought to unify subject and predicate. The subject, we can now see, is an element within, an aspect of, a more comprehensive whole; and it is this whole which acts as the drive within the judgment towards its own completion. To return to the figure of the stream, the brightly illuminated spot has transparent edges through which the contents of the center are more or less vaguely seen to come from elsewhere and to pass on. "We have not only an illuminated place, and the rest of the stream in total darkness. There is a paler light which, both up and down the stream, is shed on what comes before and after our now. And this paler light is the off-spring of the present." Thus there is within the immediately presented datum, the direct real subject of the judgment, a call, so to say, to its own transcendence; and there is also an inescapable tendency on the part of thought to obey this call. So

---

[31] *Principles of Logic*, second edition, Vol. I, 54.

[32] What has been said above about the relation between reality and appearances should be borne in mind in connection with the point here.

it turns out that thought can be adequately described only as a process which progressively idealizes reality.

Pausing for a moment to gather the lesson disclosed by this analysis, we must emphasize the fact that thought is a progressive qualification of reality. It is a qualification of *reality*, because the subject of judgment is always reality as apprehended through the immediacy of feeling; the 'that' is basically a real existent which judgment strives to qualify by the 'what' or ideal content. It is a *progressive* qualification of reality, because the reality given in the immediacy of feeling is never complete, but is inherently incomplete, and thought is therefore driven to seek its qualification through indefinite expansion.[33]

With this we are brought to the conclusion that thought is ever descriptive of reality and yet is by its nature ever barred from a complete description. It is always a qualification of the real, but through the medium of an ideal content which perforce remains in some degree abstract. The important point for the present purpose, however, is that thought is always in touch with reality and is therefore competent to reveal, at least in broad outline, something of its ultimate nature. Thus it happens that thought, while it can never bring itself to final rest in the sense that it seizes reality in its fullness, nevertheless is able to disclose what in broad outline the real must be; and in this vision it sees the necessity of its own transcendence. "Thought desires for its content the character which makes reality. These features, if realized, would destroy mere thought; and hence they are an Other beyond thought. But thought, nevertheless, can desire them, because its content has been already in an incomplete form. And in the desire for the completion of what one has there is no contradiction. . . . Thought can form the idea of an apprehension, something like feeling in directness, which contains all the character sought by its relational efforts. Thought can understand that, to reach its goal, it must get beyond relations. Yet in its nature it can find no other working means of progress. Hence it perceives that somehow this relational side of its

---

[33] See the author's discussion of the ideal nature and essential incompleteness of truth in *Essays on Truth and Reality*, p. 114 ff., and throughout.

nature must be merged and must include somehow the other side. Such a fusion would compel thought to lose and to transcend its proper self. And the nature of this fusion thought can apprehend in vague generality, but not in detail; and it can see the reason why a detailed apprehension is impossible. Such anticipated self-transcendence *is* an Other; but to assert that Other is *not* a self-contradiction." [34] Thus thought can bring us to the verge of the promised land, to a general vision of the whole in which it would find its own complete satisfaction, but it itself is not permitted to enter and possess it; and there is no contradiction involved in these two statements.

If at this juncture an unfriendly critic should raise the objection that the position here attained is not different from the doctrine that reality is unknowable, since it leaves reality unintelligible, an adequate reply may be found in the answer to the question: What is to be understood by the term 'unintelligible'? Until this question is definitely raised, the objection is utterly vague and without significance. When the question is raised and fairly faced, the objection will then be seen to be of no serious moment.

If by the unintelligible we are to understand that which is inexplicable in detail, it must be frankly admitted, and even urged, that reality is in this sense unintelligible to us. But it is no business of philosophy to explain everything; if so, then obviously philosophy is a hopeless and even an absurd enterprise. Some aspects of the world must, on any finite view, be left unexplained. The real question is whether what is thus left is unintelligible in the further sense that, falling outside our explanatory system, it stands over against it as a negative instance. It is only in this meaning that unintelligibility has any sinister implication. But reality, for us, is not unintelligible in this sense. For, as we have seen, it is involved in every judgment and in the finite center which is the very core of our being. It is not something beyond thought and lying against it in flat contradiction, but is rather a Beyond with which thought is always in touch and by which it is controlled. Therefore, while

[34] *Appearance and Reality*, pp. 180-182. Cf. *Essays on Truth and Reality*, Chapter VI, and elsewhere.

thought cannot explain reality in detail, it can apprehend it; it can descry its general features, and these, so far, are certain. We turn, then, to inquire what these are, assured meanwhile that the skeptical objection to our procedure is based upon nothing more significant than an ambiguity.[35]

In the first place, we can readily see that reality must at least be sentient experience. It is this, or for us it is nothing; for we can in no sense envisage the real except as an element within experience. Outside of experience it is an empty word. "Find any piece of existence, take up anything that any one could possibly call a fact, or could in any sense assert to have being, and then judge if it does not consist in sentient experience. Try to discover any sense in which you can still continue to speak of it, when all perception and feeling have been removed; or point out any fragment of its matter, any aspect of its being, which is not derived from and is not still relative to this source. When the experiment is made strictly, I can myself conceive of nothing else than the experienced. Anything, in no sense felt or perceived, becomes to me quite unmeaning. And as I cannot try to think of it without realizing either that I am not thinking at all, or that I am thinking of it against my will as being experienced, I am driven to the conclusion that for me experience is the same as reality. The fact that falls elsewhere seems, in my mind, to be a mere word and a failure, or else an attempt at self-contradiction. It is a vicious abstraction whose existence is meaningless nonsense, and is therefore not possible." Thus "to be real is to be indissolubly one thing with sentience. It is to be something which comes as a feature and aspect within one whole of feeling, something which, except as an integral element of such sentience, has no meaning at all."[36]

This sentience with which reality is to be identified must be an immediate experience. Within it the inconsistencies attaching to terms and relations must be removed; otherwise it could not

[35] Cf. *Appearance and Reality,* pp. 159-161 for a summary statement of the author's position; also *Essays on Truth and Reality,* Chapter XI.

[36] *Appearance and Reality,* pp. 145 and 146. I have quoted this particular argument at length because of its importance for Bradley's idealistic conclusion. Its validity will be questioned below when we come (in Part II) to inquire critically into the argument as a whole.

meet the demands of thought, which, as we have seen, can find no satisfaction at the level of relational consciousness. But it must differ from immediate experience as known to us. Our immediate experience is fragmentary and incomplete, and therefore leads to its own transcendence; but the immediate experience which is to be real must be complete and self-contained. It must, therefore, include our immediate experience and its idealization by thought; in it the inconsistencies of our entire relational experience must be done away. So we may say that reality is an immediate experience, which is like our prerelational immediate experience in that it is a unity in multiplicity, but unlike it in that it is a post-relational immediacy and inclusive of the idealization of experience through the medium of terms and relations. The sentient experience which is real is a harmonious unity in which the inconsistencies of relational consciousness are removed.

Again, we can see that reality must be one in another sense. There is only one reality. A plurality of independent reals is self-contradictory. For such reals would at least have to be coexistent; but coexistence is a way of togetherness, and the question at once arises whether this togetherness can be understood in a manner which avoids the destruction of the independence of the reals. On inquiry we find that such is impossible. Where can one find the unity implied in such togetherness? If we seek for it in a form of feeling below the relational level, what we find is only an undivided whole of which the diversity is an integral character and apart from which it is meaningless. The mode of togetherness which we can verify in our own immediate feeling, thus, renders logically impossible anything like independent reals. If we try to conceive this togetherness in some other fashion (as, for instance, a mere collection or aggregation), we are at once balked by the consideration that the reals, thus conceived, necessarily stand in relations, and relations are at once necessarily fatal to the self-sufficiency of each; for relations are unmeaning and even self-contradictory except on the basis of some unity, and among independent reals a basis of unity is wholly lacking. Since these alternatives exhaust the logical possibilities, we are driven to the conclusion that independent reals are unintelligible and reality must be one only. "We cannot maintain a plurality save as dependent on the relations in which it stands. Or if desiring to avoid relations we fall back on the diversity given in feeling, the result is the same. The plurality then sinks to become merely an integral aspect in a single substantial unity, and the reals have vanished." [37] Reality, then, must be the Absolute—an all-inclusive and non-relational sentient whole of experience.

Another characteristic of this whole stands out fairly clearly, but it needs to be emphasized. It must satisfy desire and will, as well as intellect. In fact, if it satisfies the intellect it *ipso facto* satisfies both desire and will. For if reality is to be harmonious intellectually, none of its elements must collide; but either unsatisfied desire or unfulfilled will would introduce a note of discord arising from an ideal element not at one with present feeling. Therefore, if the Absolute is to satisfy the demands of thought—and this is our basal assumption throughout—desires must within it be cancelled and will must be set at rest. "We must believe that reality satisfies our whole being. Our main wants—for truth and life, for beauty and goodness—must all find satisfaction. . . . Every element of the universe, sensation, feeling, thought and will, must be included within one comprehensive sentience." [38]

It would be a serious error, however, to draw from this the conclusion that the Absolute is personal, at least in the ordinary meaning of the term. As commonly understood, a person is a finite self amongst and over against other finite selves and moved by feelings towards them. Obviously, the Absolute cannot be personal in this sense. There is indeed another meaning of the term personal in which it might be attributed even to the Absolute; but in that case a warning should be raised. "If by calling it personal you mean only that it is nothing but experience, that it contains all the highest that we possibly can know and feel, and is a unity in which the details are utterly

---

[37] *Appearance and Reality*, p. 143.
[38] *Ibid.*, pp. 158-159. Cf. *Essays on Truth and Reality*, p. 243.

pervaded and embraced," there is perhaps no serious objection
to your doing so. But the question is important whether such
usage does not rob the term of its ordinary meaning and leave
us caught in a dangerous ambiguity. For with this usage it is
an easy, one might indeed say an inescapable, step to identify
the Absolute with the God of those religions that insist upon
a personal deity. And with this identification we are at once
threatened with ruin. We have then fallen back into the view of
personality which defines it in terms of relations, and have assumed that this view holds of the Absolute; but therewith we
have attributed to reality characteristics which, when understood,
land us in inescapable inconsistencies and a hopeless skepticism.
It is, therefore, the counsel of wisdom not to speak of the Absolute as personal. But the alternative, it should be carefully
noted, is not to conceive it as impersonal; this would be even
farther from the truth. Certainly the Absolute stands above, not
below, its own distinctions; and since persons are among its
appearances and do in fact exist within it, it can hardly be
supposed to be less than personal. The truth is, the Absolute is
neither personal nor impersonal; it is supra-personal—a sentient
unity which includes persons within its diversity, but which
itself stands in no relations ('personal' or other) to anything
other than itself.

When it is said that the Absolute 'includes' persons within
its diversity, however, this must not be understood to mean
that the Absolute 'consists' of persons or finite centers of experience. "Such a phrase implies a mode of union which we
cannot regard as ultimate. It suggests that in the Absolute finite
centers are maintained and respected, and that we may consider
them, as such, to persist and to be merely ordered and arranged.
But not like this . . . is the final destiny and the last truth of
things." [39] This last truth is, rather, that finite centers or persons
are so included in the Absolute that they "are there transmuted
and have lost their individual natures." And for this reason
we must hold that "Humanity, or an organism, kingdom, or
society of selves, is not an ultimate idea." It holds of persons
as appearances; it does not hold of them as being included in

[39] *Appearance and Reality,* p. 529.

the Absolute. In this inclusion we have a rearrangement of their internal elements.

Finally, the Absolute cannot change and there is no sense in which it itself can be said to be featured either by progress or by retrogression. To predicate change of the Absolute is to deny its all-inclusiveness and to introduce into its harmony the fateful discord of terms and relations. To *change* means to become that which not yet is, but for the Absolute there is no 'not yet'; to *change* means to pass into an other, but for the Absolute there is no 'other.' Of course, there is change among appearances, and there is no occasion to deny that change exists. But change is not real. As temporal and changing, appearances are abstractions and as such are transmuted in the Absolute. "The Absolute has no history of its own, though it contains histories without number. These, with their tale of progress or decline, are constructions starting from and based on some one given piece of finitude. They are but partial aspects in the region of temporal appearance. Their truth and reality may vary much in extent and in importance, but in the end it can never be more than relative . . . nothing perfect, nothing genuinely real, can move. The Absolute has no seasons, but all at once bears its leaves, fruit, and blossoms." [40]

5. Reality and Appearances: Degrees of Reality

We have seen that the whole world of relations is contradictory and, as such, must be denominated unreal and mere appearance. On the other hand, we have also seen that the Absolute is involved in appearances and that, viewed from this side, every appearance must be said to be real. We come now, in conclusion, to inquire concerning the relation between the Absolute and its appearances.

No appearance, nor any combination of appearances, is the Absolute; yet every appearance is in the Absolute and the Absolute is in each and all of its appearances. But the Absolute is not equally present in every appearance; appearances do not lie side by side, as it were, in the Absolute. On the contrary, there are degrees of reality attaching to appearances. The Ab-

[40] *Ibid.,* pp. 499-500.

solute is not identical with appearances taken singly or with all taken together as an aggregate, nor is it in all equally. It is, as we have already seen, a systematic whole which includes all appearances. We are now to note that it is a whole, such that appearances are included within it at different levels and with varying degrees of completeness. This follows from the systematic nature of the Absolute. Any given appearance is incomplete and implicates other aspects of the relational level; thus no appearance can in itself be called real. But it can be said to be more or less real, its degree of reality depending on the extent to which it expresses the nature of the Absolute.

The criterion by which degrees of reality are distinguished is the criterion which we have been following throughout, namely, the criterion of coherence. More or less real means participation in the Absolute to a greater or less extent, and this is measured by means of the ideal of inclusiveness and self-consistency. "The truth and the fact, which, to be converted into the Absolute, would require less rearrangement and addition, is more real and truer. And this is what we mean by degrees of reality and truth." [41]

For the sake of clarity, it is necessary to recall that the criterion which we are here applying is of a twofold nature. It is the ideal of inclusiveness on the one side, and of harmony or consistency on the other. In last analysis these are, of course, inseparable. The more inclusive an appearance may be the more harmonious it is, and *vice versa*. The Absolute is the perfection of both at once. As entirely harmonious and self-consistent it is also necessarily all-inclusive, and as all-inclusive it is also necessarily harmonious. But in attempting to apply the criterion in the determination of degrees of reality of appearances these two aspects of it should be kept distinct. In seeking to define the degree of reality of a given event, for example, we proceed more prosperously by inquiring in turn what is its extent in space or time or both and how far it is internally systematic and coherent. What needs less rearrangement to make it consistent, or, again, what spreads more widely in space or lasts longer in time, is more real.

[41] *Appearance and Reality*, pp. 364-365.

This criterion is universally applicable to appearances, though the details of its application are often confused and at times even beyond our powers. In many cases we do apply it with fair success. In any event, it is the only means whereby we can concretely distinguish between the more and the less real and significant. It is our criterion of beauty and ugliness, of good and evil, of truth and error. It is the criterion which distinguishes and gives meaning to the 'higher' and 'lower' in all their forms. Looking back over the course we have followed in this survey, we can see that the various stages in our journey exemplify its application at least in a general way. From immediate experience, through the relational level in all its sundry ramifications from lower to higher, from nature to the self, we have, broadly speaking, ascending degrees of truth and reality. The criterion by which these degrees are distinguished is the criterion of coherence—the criterion of inclusiveness and consistency. And the denial of reality to any of these stages taken in its isolation is based on the same criterion. No stage, thus taken, is completely inclusive and consistent, but only partially so. To the extent that it is so, any given appearance is real; its degree of truth and reality is its degree of coherence, of systematic stability.

CHAPTER V

BERNARD BOSANQUET (1848-1923)

IN his personal statement contributed to the First Series of *Contemporary British Philosophy*, Bosanquet speaks of the publication of Bradley's *Ethical Studies* as "an epoch-making event, not merely as restating and concluding the discussion of Hedonism, but because of a philosophical significance which far transcended that particular subject-matter." In his opinion, this book "is to most books on philosophy like Dickens or Meredith to most novels; a page of it would dilute into a hundred of any other." And throughout his writings Bosanquet refers to other works of Bradley with the same enthusiasm and always with an acknowledgment of his indebtedness to them. But the indebtedness is not entirely one-sided. Bradley, on his part, at times confesses obligations to his colleague, particularly in the realm of logical theory. Especially did he thank Bosanquet for holding steadfastly to the "true doctrine" of ideas, as against some of his own earlier statements in which he approached the view (later explicitly repudiated) that there are at least some ideas which do not directly qualify reality but merely "float." [1] And the "true doctrine" of ideas—namely, that all ideas are "adjectives of the real" and that "except in a relative sense, there are no ideas which float or are suspended"—is of foundational importance to the idealistic argument which Bradley and Bosanquet alike advocate.

Bradley's formulation of this argument we have summarized in the preceding chapter, and we now turn to Bosanquet's way of stating it. There is in this nothing new in principle beyond

[1] Cf. Bradley, *Essays on Truth and Reality*, Chapter III. The earlier statements referred to are in the *Principles of Logic*, p. 4 and elsewhere. In a foot-note on page 29 of the *Essays*, Bradley adds this: "I should have added that, from the first and throughout, Professor Bosanquet has consistently advocated the true doctrine. The debt which philosophy owes to him here has not been adequately recognized."

Bradley; but there is a new emphasis which, in at least some respects, adds to Bradley's formulation and perhaps in the end escapes some of the difficulties attaching to it.

"The positive and constructive principle of non-contradiction —in other words, the spirit of the whole—is," Bosanquet agrees in principle with Bradley, "the operative principle of life as of metaphysical thought. We might call it the argument *a contingentia mundi*, or inference from the imperfection of data and premisses." And he adds: "It is this, essentially, and over-looking differences of degree, in virtue of which alone we can at all have progressive and continuous experience, whether as inference, or as significant feeling, or as expansion through action. It is this through which my perception of the earth's surface makes one system with my conception of the Antipodes, or the emotion attending the parental instinct passes into the wise tenderness of the civilised parent, and the instinct itself, as we are told,[2] develops into the whole structure of social beneficence. And it is this, only further pursued, that forces us to the conception of the Absolute. I am aware of no point at which an arrest in the process can be justified."[3]

It is the aim of philosophy, as Bosanquet views it, to enter into this "spirit of the whole" and to follow its development through the sundry types of experience (individual and social) on to the Absolute, where alone it finds its completest realization and fulfilment. In other and more technical phraseology, the aim of philosophy is to follow "the passage from the contradictory and unstable in all experience alike to the stable and satisfactory." Such is the Pilgrim's Progress of philosophy as Bosanquet conceives it. Our exposition of his argument, then, must undertake to set forth the main stages in this Pilgrim's Progress, and we begin with the point of departure.[4]

[2] The reference here is to McDougall, *Social Psychology*, p. 79.
[3] Bernard Bosanquet, *The Principle of Individuality and Value*, pp. 267-268.
[4] The argument here summarized is taken primarily from Bosanquet's *Logic, or the Morphology of Knowledge* (1888); second edition (1911); and his Gifford Lectures, *The Principle of Individuality and Value* (1912); and *The Value and Destiny of the Individual* (1913).

1. The Given: Central Experiences

Of course, it is in some sense inevitable that any one who starts to reflect must begin with experience; and it is also obvious that experience is in some important sense given. To say this, however, is to say very little that is of significance; the statement is too general to have any precise meaning. The important question is: With what sort of experience are we to begin, and what is the criterion of our choice?

Only a minimum of observation is required to disclose the fact that *experience* is only a general name for many different sorts of things—that *experience* really means 'experienc*es*,' and that experiences appear to be of an indefinite variety. The admonition to base reflection on experience, then, is in itself largely empty and is not a sufficient guide. Thus admonished we are still poorly instructed, and the framework of our theory will vary according as we hit upon this or that type of experience as specially significant. "It is obvious that if we take our idea of the individual from what he is at the minimum of his conscious being, say in the state of fear or ineffective desire, we shall get a wholly different reading of his nature from that which will suggest itself if we take into account the social, aesthetic, or religious consciousness and their characteristic or their highest development." [5] Thus it turns out that one's initial attitude towards experience, rather than the mere facts of experience, is the important matter for philosophical inquiry. Behind and foundational to the framework of a theory there is always something more than the bare observation of experiences taken at random and accepted at face value. "And this something is our attitude to experience; or more strictly, the mode of experience in which each of us more especially sees and feels his continuity with reality." [6]

Now it is of the greatest importance in philosophical speculation that the philosopher's attitude to experience be correct. This is the ground of sane inference, and apart from it thought is without chart and compass. But what is the correct attitude

[5] *The Principle of Individuality and Value,* pp. **269-270.**
[6] *Ibid.,* p. 2.

to experience, and how is it to be determined? This, of course, is the crucial question. The complete answer to it lies in the entire view which is summarized below. In this preliminary statement only a general answer can be suggested.

It is to be noted, in the first place, that not all experiences are equally significant. Some are more 'central' than others. It is these central experiences which should control in the speculative enterprise, and the correct attitude to experience lies in submission to them. The determination of what experiences are central is one of the most delicate, and in some ways one of the most difficult, tasks confronting the philosopher. In the end, to be sure, central experiences are much more certain than are those so-called unmediated immediates, such as 'facts' or 'life' or 'self,' which are often called obvious and taken for absolute and reliable data. But despite their certainty central experiences are not obvious and, indeed, are generally overlooked. More often than not, we are neither sufficiently simple nor sufficiently profound to seize them. On the one side our lack of sensitiveness stands in our way; on the other our sophistication.

How, then, are central experiences to be found? The full answer to this question lies in the analysis of the nature of thought to be given below, since it is only through thought that *centrality* may be defined. The important point to be emphasized in this preliminary statement is that thought which is foundational to centrality is inclusive of will and significant feeling as well as of cognition. Hence *centrality* is not merely *relevancy* in the commonly accepted meaning of the term; it involves evaluation as well. The determination of centrality, therefore, demands a special attitude of mind which, in Ruskin's phrase, we might call "penetrative imagination—what Wordsworth was unmatched in." This "penetrative imagination," however, is not non-intellectual; on the contrary, it is precisely intelligence, taken in its true connotation as the life of a critical mind. It is an error, therefore, to suppose that centrality may be determined by some 'mystical' (in the sense of non-intellectual) sort of insight. But it is equally erroneous, and much more common, to suppose that it is determinable by pure cognition.

Only "a serious lack of sympathetic insight prevents us

from understanding that to be right in one's bird's-eye view of centrality and the scheme of values, demands a higher intellectual character and even a more toilsome intellectual achievement than to formulate whole volumes of ingenious ratiocination. . . . Bad taste is bad logic, and bad logic is bad taste. Simply to be right, as the greatest men are right, means to have traversed hundreds and thousands of ingenuities, to have rejected them as inadequate, and come back to the centre enriched by their negative results." [7] There is, then, no simple formula for the determination of central experiences. Thought alone discloses them, and thought, when fully taken, is no mere deduction from postulated principles, but is penetrative insight into both relevancy and value.

Our point of departure in the Pilgrim's Progress of philosophy, therefore, lies in central experiences—centrality being determined by thought in its fullest meaning as penetrative or interpretative and evaluative. These central experiences are the "informing spirit" of sane philosophical speculation, in respect of both its beginning and its procedure. "We begin then with the principle—the truism if you like—that in our attitude to experience, or through experience to our world, we are to put central things in the centre, to respect the claims of the obvious which is neglected—to take for our standard what man recognizes as value when his life is fullest and his soul at its highest stretch." [8]

2. The Guide: Coherence

There is no immediate experience in the sense of a primary and absolute datum on which, if we chose, we could remain standing. For every experience that is, or can be, immediately given is linked with a larger context. "You cannot anywhere, whether in life or in logic, find rest and salvation by withdrawing from the intercourse and implications of life; no more in the world of individual property and self-maintenance than in the world of international politics and economics; no more in

---

[7] *The Principle of Individuality and Value*, pp. 6-7.

[8] *Ibid.*, p. 3. The contrast between Bosanquet's position here and that of Ferrier, or even that of Green, is quite marked. Compare with the view of Fichte as expressed in his famous statement that the sort of philosophy one has depends on the sort of man one is.

the world of logical apprehension than in that of moral service and religious devotion." [9] In the abstract immediate there is no abiding place for life or logic; willy-nilly, one is driven beyond. Thus our Pilgrim's Progress is inevitable, in life generally as in technical philosophy. In each alike, "to cling to our initial standing ground—or to strive or pretend to do so, for it is not really possible—is without any question to abide in the City of Destruction." But whither shall we flee, and what shall lead us on?

So far at least as philosophy is concerned, thought alone is the guide; whither thought will lead will appear in the sequel. Meanwhile it is to be observed that *thought* is a very vague term, and we must be careful to note its true nature; otherwise we may be led astray, all the while under the mistaken impression that it is thought which leads us. What then are we to understand by *thought?*

Thought is simply the spirit of totality within experience. As we have already seen, there is no immediate experience in which we may remain standing; for every supposed immediate experience is linked with a context and harbors within itself the impulse to its own transcendence. This impulse is away from fragmentariness and towards totality—towards the system within which the immediate experience falls. This is the impulse of thought, which is precisely the "spirit of the whole."

The same point may be expressed by saying that thought is the universalizing function within or among experiences. And there is much to be gained by expressing the matter so, provided —but only provided—we are clear as to the nature of this function. What, we must ask, is the universal of thought?

In the first place, we must sharply distinguish between the true universal of thought and the universal which is generated by the principle of abstraction. The latter type of universal is the result of the sort of generalization which seeks identity apart from differences. It "is framed by attending to the common qualities of a number of individuals, and disregarding their differences." It therefore turns out to a bare generality which at best is of indefinite meaning—as, for example, man, animal,

[9] *Ibid.,* p. 7.

organism, body, as mere abstract notions. And if the process of generalization is carried to its logical goal, the resulting universal tends to vanish into complete emptiness—as, for instance, the notion of being in general, or mere being. The true universal of thought, however, is quite other than this sort of blank abstraction. It is the totality or system wherein contradictions are removed. It is attained, not through the omission of differences, but through the explication and eduction of the unity or identity involved in them.

Stated more technically, genuine thought is at once analytic and synthetic in that it expresses both identity and difference. The analytic aspect is inseparably linked with the synthetic, the synthetic is inseparably linked with the analytic—in short, analysis and synthesis are only two aspects of one and the same process of thinking. "To see the escapement wheel lying inside the watch does *not* 'give' me this wheel as a part of a mechanical arrangement; to know it as a part of *such* a whole I must understand it; and in understanding it, i.e. in my analysis, perform the synthesis of the watch as a definite mechanical contrivance." [10] The true universal of thought, thus, is an identity within or among differences—a universal arrived at through the interpretation of differences within a system. As such it is quite distinct from the universal of mere generalization mentioned above; the latter is an abstract, while the former is a concrete, universal.

There is another sense in which the true universal of thought is concrete, though in last analysis this meaning reduces in principle to the other. This is the sense in which the universal of thought includes within itself sensible, and emotive, and conative, as well as purely discursive or cognitive, experiences. That the universal of thought is concrete in this sense is evident from the consideration that thought is the impulse towards completeness within experience and experience is basically the same in all of its forms. Sensation, for instance, receives or, rather, manifests new meaning when it is thought, since new characters

[10] *Logic*, Vol. I, p. 95. The italics are in the original. The reference is to the second edition.

appear in it when it becomes an element in a more comprehensive whole.

This is especially evident in the realm of beauty; here sensations have a logic and necessity of their own, and when they are thought they fall within a system. "The universal—the straining towards the whole—is in them as in all experience; and it is idle to deny their constructive and creative nisus the name of thinking, because it does not operate through what we call *par excellence* logical language and conceptions attached to words. The rhythm that completes a rhythm, the sound that with other sounds satisfies the educated ear, the colour that is demanded by a colour-scheme, are I take it as necessary and as rational as the conclusion of a syllogism." [11]

The same in principle holds of feeling, which becomes richer in significance and, therefore, a deeper feeling, as it enters into a thought-whole. "As with sensation, so with emotion or pleasure-pain, it is the concrete universal that draws them out of their blankness and exhibits them as aspects of the difference made to a living world by contents in which it is affirmed or negated; and thus makes explicit the 'more' and 'greater' of which they are capable." [12]

Nor is the case any different with voluntary experiences, as has been emphasized by all of the great idealists since the Greeks. "Will and activity mean the operation of the nature of thought through the expansion of ideas into fact." [13] Thus in all forms of experience the nisus of the logical universal is manifest. "If we view experience *bona fide,* and follow where its connections lead us, noting the relation of incompleteness to completeness in all the responses of mind, it does not matter from what point we start. It is like going up a hill; you only need to keep

[11] *Principle of Individuality and Value,* p. 62. In this connection Bosanquet refers to Nettleship, *Remains,* I, 178, and adds the following remark about Whistler (cf. Whistler's *Life,* I, 185): "A visitor to Whistler's studio remarked that the upright line in the panelling of the wall was wrong . . . adding, 'of course, it's a matter of taste.' To which Whistler replied . . . 'remember, so that you may not make the mistake again, it's not a matter of taste at all, it's a matter of knowledge.' I do not say he was precisely right but he was right as implying a necessity of the type of rational necessity."

[12] *The Principle of Individuality and Value,* p. 64.

[13] *Ibid.,* p. 67.

ascending, and you must reach the top. You cannot study thought and not be led to will and feeling, nor will or feeling and not be led back to thought." [14]

Thus the universal of thought is concrete, both because it is the result of the systematization of particulars and not of the negation of them and because it is inclusive of all forms of experience. In last analysis, both of these reduce to the thesis that thought is simply the nisus of experience towards completeness. We may therefore say that the universal of thought is system, provided we mean thereby "a system of members, such that every member, being *ex hypothesi* distinct, nevertheless contributes to the unity of the whole in virtue of the peculiarities which constitute its distinctness." [15] The universal of thought is indifferently a concrete universal, a system, a world, or the individual. And this nature of the universal must be borne in mind throughout.

From the above considerations it follows that coherence is the criterion of truth. To doubt intelligently is to assert a ground for doubting, and the aim of thought (ideally at least, however inadequately realized in practice) is to leave no ground for doubting. This, we may now see, is accomplished through the systematization of experience by thought, in such a way that whatever may be urged against the resulting system is already anticipated by, and implied in, the system itself. Furthermore, every doubt raised against such a system, if the doubter makes a positive assertion, is simply a demand that the system be so modified as to include within itself the basis of the doubt supposedly standing against it.

For instance, if, doubting the revelations of modern astronomy, "you say the sun is a lantern, lit up every morning and put out at night, or the stars are holes in a sort of dish cover, through which the light beyond shines through [*sic*], then, I presume, the competent astronomer has you in his power. . . .

[14] *The Principle of Individuality and Value*, p. 39.
[15] *Ibid.*, p. 37. Compare *Social and International Ideals*, pp. 162-163. The same point is frequently emphasized by Bosanquet elsewhere in *The Principle of Individuality and Value* and in the *Logic*; in the latter, see especially Vol. II, Chapters VIII, IX, X. Compare his *Science and Philosophy*, Chapter II.

You have picked up a fragment of experience which you are attempting to push against the system of sciences, a something which you treat as outside it and as thus destroying its universality. In doing so, however, you acknowledge universality as the test. . . . But, so far as it is the whole, the system can reply: 'We know all that already; we already possess your interpretation, but in a shape which effects the object implied in every interpretation of appearances, which, in the shape you gave it, it failed to do. You wanted, of course, to connect your vision of the starry heavens with other experiences and ideas so as to express what it was for you in the completest way. But we possess the experiences which you need for that purpose, together with an enormous mass of others. And we can show you that by using them as you did it is impossible to attain the complete expression you desired, because in that way they cannot be united with the full appearances in question, or with the mass of other experience. On the other hand, we can show you a set of connections which will at all events draw out the nature of your experience very much more completely and in a far greater union with the rest of experience. We can show you that you were only attempting imperfectly and in confusion what is here, at least comparatively, perfect and complete.' " [16] This instance is typical, and the thesis is plain: Truth is the whole, because the whole alone can maintain itself against all doubt—a thesis which is familiar in philosophy from Plato downwards.

If one desires further confirmation of the point, however, one may readily find it in a consideration of the nature of so-called 'fact.' It is commonly supposed that a fact is immediately given, and in a sense the supposition is true. But it is equally true, and very important to note, that what is thus immediately given is never quite the full fact. For what is immediately given always comes in a context, and itself is never quite simple and ultimate. To get at the fact in its fullness one must penetrate this context and, so, go beyond that which *prima facie* is presented. The full fact is the fact as true; and the fact as true is

[16] *Ibid.*, pp. 42-43. Cf. *Logic*, Vol. II, Chapter IX.

the immediate datum plus the implications which lie in the surrounding context of which the datum is a fragment. In short, the fact as true is the entire system. To seek facts is to seek concrete universals.

The appeal to the concrete universal as the criterion is thus seen to be essentially an appeal to the principle of coherence and non-contradiction. Truth is that which does not contradict itself, but is self-consistent and impervious to doubt; and that which thus stands is a self-sustaining system—a system which is internally coherent. But it must not be forgotten what sort of system and what sort of consistency are here in question: the system is organized experience, and the consistency is "the consistency, so far as attainable, of the whole body of experience with itself." To take thought as our guide in the philosophical enterprise, then, means to seek for the completest organization of the whole body of experience; coherence is our criterion, and we must look for truth only in the direction it indicates.

A further point to be noted in this connection is that the criterion of truth is the criterion of all value. And this point is of sufficient significance for the argument to justify brief expansion.

We value that which gives us satisfaction, and the judgment of value is, therefore, in a sense relative to feeling. But, as we have already urged, feeling cannot be ultimately sundered from thought, since it is a special sort of reason; and satisfaction is a matter of degrees, definable only in terms of experience as a whole. Thus the criterion of value is the criterion of thought, namely, positive non-contradiction developed through comprehensiveness and consistency.

This position is exemplified in the fields of art and morals. The work of art is indeed the expression of a spiritual mood of the artist, and in the strictest sense it excludes construction by explicit or abstract ratiocination. The artistic mood is not to be identified with cognitive reflection, nor can it be reproduced in the observer by any mere discursive analysis. Nevertheless, the work of art is a systematic whole, charged with intelligence and exemplifying the sort of rational coherence in which all knowledge consists. Though springing primarily from feeling and embodying feeling, it is still the product of thought; it is "thoroughly penetrated with reason in the form of feeling." From another angle, the same point is illustrated in moral judgments. Here that which gives positive pleasure and ultimate satisfaction "depends on the character of logical stability of the whole inherent in the objects of desire." The logically stable whole is the standard by which the good, as the beautiful, must be determined. "And by this standard any judgment as to ultimate end or value can be criticised or estimated."

Standing in opposition to the view here advanced, of course, are other theories of value; but a thorough analysis of them reduces each in principle to the position which they in common oppose. If you hold that value is relative to feeling, your position is in a sense sound; but only in the sense in which feeling is taken as a form of thought, and not as sharply separate from it. If there were no feeling there could be no value—this is true enough. But it is equally true that if there were no values there could be no value-feelings—feelings, that is, which are permeated by reason. Feelings of value are relative to that which reaches beyond them, namely, the totality of experience in which lies their ultimate satisfaction.

Again, to seek value in the conscious states of conscious beings is to seek it where it can not possibly be found, if such states are taken in abstraction from the world; for when so taken they are not only valueless but also meaningless. But if they are taken as they should be taken, namely, as continuous with objects, then their value lies in the whole beyond them: ". . . you cannot value the fragment without appreciation of the whole." And, finally, to conceive all values as relative to 'persons' is not to escape the criterion which lies ahead; for 'persons' are essentially linked to 'persons' indefinitely, and ultimately with the universe, where lies their complete individuality and where alone is to be found the ultimate standard of all their values.[17]

[17] For the author's discussion of the problem of value see *Principle of Individuality and Value*, Lecture VIII; *Value and Destiny of the Individual*, Lectures V-VII; and *Three Lectures on Aesthetic* (1915). A lengthy discussion linked with historical systems may be found in Bosan-

The criterion of the beautiful and the good, then, is identical with that of the true. "Positive non-contradiction, developed through comprehensiveness and consistency"—this is the one standard of thought in all of its forms.

As we proceed in the application of this criterion in our Pilgrim's Progress, we must not forget that the search for truth and value is also and *ipso facto* a search for reality. The nisus of thought is towards reality, not away from it; the concrete universal is the real, because it is the true, fact. "The ultimate tendency of thought, we have seen, is not to generalise, but to constitute a world. It is true that it presses beyond the given, following the 'what' beyond the limits of the 'that.' But it is also true that in following the 'what' it tends always to return to a fuller 'that.' If its impulse is away from the given it is towards the whole—the world. And as constituting a world it tends to return to the full depth and roundness of experience from which its first step was to depart. In a 'world,' a 'concrete universal,' we do not lose directness and significance as we depart from primary experience; on the contrary, every detail has gained incalculably in vividness and in meaning, by reason of the intricate interpretation and interconnection, through which thought has developed its possibilities of 'being.' The watchword of concrete thinking is 'Philosophiren ist dephlegmatisiren, vivificiren.' " [18] The main results of this process we shall see more fully below. Meanwhile it must be remembered that thought progresses towards the real always and that, following its guidance, we are penetrating into reality itself. For the criterion adopted is adopted not "by arbitrary preference for use in logical discussion, but as a simple and necessary corollary from our conception of experience and of the universe when seriously taken." [19]

The recognition of the true logical universal, thus, is "the key to all sound philosophy." Whither, when persistently and consistently followed through, does this recognition carry us?

quet's *History of Aesthetic* (1892). For his ethical approach *Some Suggestions in Ethics* (1918) should be consulted.

[18] *The Principle of Individuality and Value*, pp. 55-56. Cf. *Logic*, Vol. II, pp. 174 ff. (2nd ed.).

[19] Bosanquet, *The Meeting of Extremes in Contemporary Philosophy*, pp. 188-189.

3. The Pilgrim's Progress

The main stages in our journey lie through (a) nature, (b) life, (c) mind, and (d) the Absolute. And we must inquire into some of the details resulting from the application of our criterion in each of these four fields.

(a) To begin with nature, we must in the first place once for all take our stand against any sort of 'idealism' that would reduce nature to states of consciousness or mind. So far from being mere idea, nature exists in its own right independent of any finite mind; in fact, as we shall see later, it provides the very foundation of finite mind. "It is not created by the self taken apart from the detail of the environment; for so taken the self would be nothing. The self may indeed be said to make its own environment. But this is only by selection; it depends on the given; and even within the given it cannot be arbitrary. . . . The self, which makes the environment, is itself all soaked in environment." [20] There is then no question of reducing nature to states of any self.

Nor can nature any more successfully be equated with psychical centers, as is attempted by Pan-psychism. Such an attempt ends at last in destroying the very contrast between nature and mind, "the complementary functions of subjective mind on the one hand and externality on the other," upon which the essential nature of mind itself seems to depend. "There cannot be spirit, it would seem, constituted by nothing but pure spiritual centres. Spirit is a light, a focus, a significance, which can be only by contact with a 'nature,' an external world." [21]

Nature, then, must be taken to have existence in its own right, and not as "a masked and enfeebled section of the subject-world." As the indispensable environment of the self, it "can hardly be reckoned as less than the whole detail of thing and fact which enters into the world of the self."

But it is of the greatest importance to note that nature, so taken, expresses everywhere within itself the nisus towards totality. For everywhere within it there is system and intelligibility, and intelligibility precisely in and through system. This

[20] *The Principle of Individuality and Value,* p. 360.
[21] *Ibid.,* p. 240; compare pp. 363, 366, 369.

is exemplified in every formulation of what is commonly called scientific laws. The theory of gravitation, for example, is the expression of a system. "The point which constitutes the theory is the conception of the systematic relation between the distance and the attraction, and the contribution which this conception makes to the further determination of the nature of the physical world." And the same principle holds true of every law in whatever field; law is essentially the expression of a 'world.' "Every nexus, so far as a universal law, is a necessary determination within and hypothetical upon an Individual whole—whether a world-whole or a member of it, a macrocosm or microcosm, makes no difference of principle." [22] Nature is everywhere enlivened by "the spirit of the whole."

From this it follows that there is no essential antagonism between law and individuality, despite the widespread idea that such is the case. [23] The idea that there is an antagonism between them, that law or the principle of uniformity is incompatible with the principle of individuality, in the end is based upon a "confusion between the abstract and the concrete universal; between the recurrence of similars and the identity of a differentiated system." Once this confusion is cleared away, it is readily seen that there is no incompatibility between the two principles; on the contrary, it becomes clear that the two principles are really one—that the principle of uniformity is precisely system or "the coherence of differences in a whole," and that this is also the principle of individuality. [24] This, of course, is no reason why one should seek for, or expect to find, mentality in nature, which would be a serious blunder; but it is a reason for holding that there is no break in principle between nature and mind, and this is important.

(b) In the course of time and according to some nexus un-

[22] *The Principle of Individuality and Value*, p. 117. The immediately preceding quotation is from pp. 100-101.

[23] In this connection Bosanquet cites Ward, *Naturalism and Agnosticism*, Vol. I, 108, and Vol. II, 241 and 280; Taylor, *Elements of Metaphysics*, p. 221 ff.; and Royce, *The World and the Individual*, Second Series, pp. 191, 195.

[24] Compare Hegel's discussion of the relation between law, the infinite, and self-consciousness in the *Phänomenologie des Geistes*, section A, sub-section III.

known to us in detail, external nature becomes the vehicle of finite centers. These, in turn, assume the active form of totality which we call life, while the centers themselves we call living things or organisms. They appear in the process of nature, we must suppose, as the result of natural causes and are maintained by natural selection. But whatever may have been their ultimate origin, or whatever may be the factors involved in their maintenance, we know that they are centers of activity reacting to a surrounding world from which they draw their content. They are shaped by the environment, not as alien entities bent to the harsh demands of extraneous laws, but as new forms of the nisus towards totality inherent in inorganic nature herself. "Natural selection means the operation of a realm of externality in modelling its responsive centre, and thereby coming alive itself in a partial individuality which represents it. . . . In all life we find . . . a certain relative individuality—that is to say, a self-maintaining system, consistent and coherent in the main when taken together with the environment to which it is adapted, and which, taking present and past as a single system, has dictated its form. The creation of such a system is due to the operation of the positive principle of non-contradiction in a definite embodiment and environment. . . . Non-contradiction, as we saw, is the principle of individuality; and here we observe it at work in the initial formation of the finite centre of experience." [25] Thus life is in principle continuous with nature.

(c) Organic forms are the foundation on which those other finite centers, called minds, rest. At precisely what stage in the evolution of these forms mind first makes its appearance it is as yet impossible for us to determine with any assurance. But we know that mind appears relatively late in the series, and we know further that it is built up through the processes of life and as a continuation of the same development of systems in active commerce with the environment. When we reach the level of mind in the evolutionary order we are on surer ground and can describe with more precision the main features of the nisus towards totality.

The chief peculiarity of mind is that it is a more or less

[25] *The Value and Destiny of the Individual*, pp. 75-76.

explicit world of experience working itself out to harmony and completeness through linkage with its environment. We can clearly see that mind is not a self-encased punctual center, shut up, so to say, in its own shell and standing over against a merely external environment as if it were "some angel or genius, or some spark of intelligence coming from out-of-doors." On the contrary, we can see that mind is a center of activity thoroughly soaked in an environment whence it springs, which it progressively (in part at least) creates, and which enters into its very texture. Thus mind is at once original and conditioned by its environment, and we shall be helped forward in our inquiry if we pause to note some of the details of this, its dual nature.

It is clear that finite mind is oriented in two directions. (i) On one side it is linked with a long evolutionary process lying back of, and resulting in, a complex and highly organized body to which it is somehow attached. (ii) On the other side mind is bound by the course of institutional history, the structure of which is founded on creative individual minds in active inter-communication. "Everywhere finite consciousness makes its appearance, so far as this is obvious and unmistakable, at a relatively high level, focusing and revealing the significance of a huge complication of mute history and circumstance behind it and surrounding it." [26] What, we now ask, is the import of this for theory?

(i) The linkage of finite mind with a complex set of conditions which are below it and on which it stands is now obvious and must be admitted by all open-minded theories concerning mind. Conscious mind is a late comer in evolution, but the fact that it is intimately connected with a physical body, which in some very important manner conditions it, is in this day and age taken for granted. It is also commonly accepted knowledge that this physical body reaches back indefinitely into the stages of the evolutionary process which has produced it and that it is in some sense served by the mind. The important question is: What does all this mean for a theory of mind?

Our answer to this question is already prepared by the pre-

---

[26] *The Principle of Individuality and Value*, p. 154. Compare *The Value and Destiny of the Individual*, pp. 9 ff.

ceding considerations. In the first place, we are committed to the position that mind is not brought into nature from out-of-doors, but through the body on which it rests. It is continuous with an evolutionary series which reaches far into the past, in which it temporarily emerges, and through which it receives the mechanisms for its peculiar activity. "After all, we must not shut our eyes to the fact that, though we cannot see life coming out of inorganic matter, we can, every day and everywhere, see souls, with full human capacities, apparently being brought into existence by the fulfilment of certain very elementary conditions of cell-conjugation and division; and we see that soul is emphatically . . . a thing or power or quality (whatever we like to call it), of which there can be more and less in every conceivable degree, and the more and less vary with the complication of the material system in connection with which it is observed." [27]

Hereupon it might be supposed that we are committed further to a mechanistic view of mind. But this would be a serious error, arising from inadequate observation of the facts in the case. For, in the second place, it must be noted that, while mind is continuous with nature and life and is not brought in from the outside as an alien entity, it is not merely a more complicated form or system of material elements. It is rather a fuller expression of the nisus towards totality which is inherent in nature from the beginning and which emerges in living forms or, more adequately, in souls or spirits. It is not something added to nature, nor is it nature as merely material; it is, rather, nature featured by the peculiar quality of consciousness. "Mind is not so much a something, a unit, exercising guidance upon matter, as the fact of self-guidance of that world which appears as matter, when that reaches a certain level of organisation." [28]

The main point here may be drawn out more clearly perhaps by a brief survey of the vexed question of the mind-body relationship. No one doubts that the relation between mind and body

[27] *The Principle of Individuality and Value,* p. 189.
[28] *Ibid.,* pp. 193-194. Compare the view of "emergent evolution" as expressed, for instance, by Lloyd Morgan in his Gifford Lectures, *Emergent Evolution,* and *Life, Mind and Spirit.* See, for a somewhat different emphasis, S. Alexander's, *Space, Time and Deity.*

is an intimate one; the real question at issue concerns the nature of that relation. In the light of the preceding considerations, it would appear to be erroneous to conceive that relation in terms of causation. To suppose that mind is causally connected with body is to destroy the continuity between them by setting them over against each other as more or less independent entities. Nor is the parallelistic view of the relation any better; it assumes virtually the same abstract separation.

The only satisfactory conception of the relation is that mind is the 'inner' or 'meaning' side of bodily processes; mind is not itself an event, but is the appreciation or interpretation of what is taking place. "Take as an example the incoming sensation—the feeling of the prick of a pin. Is this feeling, a sensation with a painful tone, an effect of the physical prick or not? I should reply, 'No; not an effect but an interpretation.' An effect is a continuation of a process into a further stage. The pin-prick sets up neural change, and ultimately some degree of motor stimulus. That is an effect. An interpretation is a going into, an appreciating, the nature of a process as it happens. It is an interpretation when we hear certain shocks as music, instead of regarding them, on physical evidence, as transmitted vibrations . . . an interpretation is not an effect; it is not a new happening; it is an appreciation of what is happening." Nor is this view a matter of mere words; it is precisely the view involved in the line of thought thus far advanced. The environment, we have urged, is a continuum in which the nisus towards totality or system is evident. Organic forms are stages in which the nisus comes alive, and consciousness or mind is only a further manifestation of the same spirit of the whole. However, it is one in which new qualities appear and which may therefore be said to be a new type of whole. Here we are only attempting to describe more closely what those new qualities are—namely, a wider apprehensiveness and responsiveness than are to be found at the lower levels. The universal implicit in the lower, at this level becomes more explicit and emerges into new significance.

Mind, then, we are driven to hold, is the meaning side of bodily processes. "All that happens, on our view, is that when you come to matter which has been granted life or consciousness, its capacities of apprehension and response open up a new significance and become the focus of a new kind of whole. Sensation and pain, it is submitted, are what the prick is when the apprehension of it is deepened; they are no additional reaction, but the reaction as apprehended by a certain kind of system. They are what the effect on the sentient organism is like when you come to realise it." And in principle the same holds of other phases of mental activity, such as volition and speculative thought.[29]

Does the view of mind here defended destroy the significance of ideals by cutting the foundation from freedom and initiative? The supposition that it does so is based upon a total misapprehension of the nature of freedom, or upon a failure to grasp the full significance of the view in question. To see how this is so one must observe the second aspect of the nature of mind, namely its linkage with its social context.

(ii) Mind is a center of activity arising out of conditions which antedate it and on which it rests. Thus viewed, mind may be said to be dependent upon the external and mechanical order of nature, since it is "erected on a foundation of habit and determinate reaction, to which no injustice could be done by connecting it with a physical counterpart, and equating it with a sum of mechanical energy." [30] This we have already seen. But, we are now to note, mind is much more than this. It is also a nisus towards totality and harmony, of a sort which gives rise to genuine freedom and initiative.

In its earlier stages, mind is largely limited by its own bodily mechanisms. "It takes over its household furniture, or at any rate enough to keep house with, from Life; and is itself at first merely a better order and a clearer purpose in making use of the same, or of that portion of it which specially demands order and purpose." [31] And so we may say that mind is in a sense full before it exists; certainly it does not first exist, and then have to be filled from experience. But it is not thus completely full;

---

[29] *The Principle of Individuality and Value*, pp. 196 ff.
[30] *Ibid.*, p. 178.
[31] *The Value and Destiny of the Individual*, pp. 82-83.

the exigencies of its domestic economy, to continue the metaphor, soon compel it to supplement the furniture which it receives from Life. Being a system of content come alive and conscious of itself, it is by this very nature dissatisfied with its bequeathed possessions and is forced to acquire others. It is speedily driven beyond the sort of activity that is possible to the mere bodily mechanisms with which it is connected. It has to seek its heritage elsewhere—namely, in a new world of "universal consciousness or social Mind." For it "is essentially reciprocal . . . and lives in the medium of recognition; and therefore, when a certain *de facto* continuity of centres, each with itself and with others, is attained in the correlation of organisms, the recognition of the continuity is generated *pari passu* in a plurality of centres." [32]

Thus a new environment is added to mind; the environment as external nature and organic forms is now supplemented by the social, and to the set of conditions 'below' mind is added a set of conditions 'above' mind. With this, a new level of mind, a new type of individuality, is attained—the type of individuality, namely, which is manifested in the forms of the scientific, moral, artistic, and religious consciousness. "Not only are particular centres of experience moulded by natural selection into a deeper harmony with their surroundings, but in so far as the surroundings form a mental or spiritual system—a social mind—the particular centres begin to be adapted as members of an individuality transcending their own." [33] This larger individuality is what we mean broadly by culture and civilization.

Now the freedom of the finite center of experience lies precisely in its penetration into, and its appropriate adaptation of itself towards, the environment both above and below it. For this is the response of the mind to its content through which it progressively realizes its own nature, creates itself—is free. The principle of individuality which first comes alive in conscious-

[32] *The Value and Destiny of the Individual,* p. 85. Bosanquet here is reproducing in principle Hegel's discussion of the same point, to which he refers. Cf. Hegel's analysis of the "master" and "servant" forms of consciousness in the *Phänomenologie des Geistes,* section B, sub-section IV.

[33] *Ibid.,* p. 90. Cf. *The Principle of Individuality and Value,* pp. 153-155, 179.

ness, or the finite center, is also the principle which is basal within the environment; in immersing itself in its environment, therefore, mind is only attaining contact with its own nature writ on a larger scale. Seeking through the environment, it finds itself.

An example taken from the field of art may clarify the issue. The creative activity of the artist at its best is no mere flight of fancy freed from the drag of relevant facts; it is, rather, precisely the vivid revelation of the subtleties of the content which is before the artist's mind. "Not the invention of novelty, but the logic which lays bare the heart and structure of things, and in doing so purifies and intensifies the feeling which current appearances are too confused and contradictory to evoke, is the true secret of art." Of course, the imagination of the true artist is creative; but it is creative "because profound penetration reveals positive treasures beyond the scope of the average mind; not because it deviates into paths of arbitrary phantasy." Creative imagination is penetrative imagination, and it is created in precisely the degree it is penetrative. The principle holds true of all the activities of mind, as might readily be disclosed by a survey of moral and cognitive insight. So we may conclude generally that "all logical activity is a world of content reshaping itself by its own spirit and laws in presence of new suggestions; a syllogism is in principle nothing less, and a Parthenon or 'Paradise Lost' is in principle nothing more." [34]

Penetration into its environment, then, is the basal characteristic of mind in all of its activities. And this constitutes its freedom—the only type of freedom which our argument will vindicate, but also the only type of freedom which can be attributed to a mind that is anything at all. For, after all, freedom is not synonymous with license to pursue a lawless course. Our thought is most free when it is most definitely under control of relevant facts, for only under such control is it brought to the realization of its own deeper demands. Likewise, our will is free when it is corrected and amended through criticism in the light of factual situations, for only so does it attain its own basal ends. Freedom, "as the condition of our being ourselves,

[34] *Ibid.*, pp. 332, 333.

cannot simply be something which we have, still less something which we have always had—a *status quo* to be maintained. It must be a condition relevant to our continued struggle to assert the control of something in us, which we recognise as imperative upon us or as our real self, but which we only obey in a very imperfect degree. Thus it is that we can speak, without a contradiction, of being forced to be free." [35]

Our view of mind, in sum, amounts to this. Mind is a finite center of activity within which the "spirit of the whole" progressively and in varying degrees of clarity manifests itself. On one side it is linked with nature below it through the mechanisms of the body; on the other side, it is attached to that "higher individuality" or social mind which is above and beyond it. Viewed from either side, however, it is a nisus towards the whole of which it is an incomplete expression. Through penetration into this whole it enriches itself and realizes more and more its own nature. Nor is there anything mysterious about this; it is in fact obvious, if we would but observe without prejudice. "So far from its being a strange or unwarranted assumption that the experience of conscious units is transformed, reinforced, and rearranged, by entrance into a fuller and more extended experience, the thing is plainly fact, which, if we were not blinded by traditional superstition, we should recognise in our daily lives as a matter of course. We, our subject selves, are in truth much more to be compared to a rising and falling tide, which is continually covering wider areas as it deepens, and dropping back to narrower and shallower ones as it ebbs, than to the isolated pillars with their fixed circumferences, as which we have been taught to think of ourselves." When once we have freed ourselves from the superstition of regarding ourselves as "substances, crystal nuclei, fallen or celestial angels, or both at once," the view here advanced will seem plain enough. Our experience everywhere supports it and forces it upon us. [36]

There is a point implied in the preceding analysis which now

[35] Bosanquet, *The Philosophical Theory of the State,* third edition, pp. 117-118. Compare Hegel's analysis of "the unhappy consciousness," *Phänomenologie des Geistes,* section B, sub-section IV.

[36] Cf. *The Principle of Individuality and Value,* p. 372; and the fragment *Three Chapters on the Nature of Mind.*

must be made explicit. Mind, we have said, is a finite center which in principle is continuous with the environment above and below it. In seeking itself, then, mind must penetrate into this environment; here alone can it find its own completion and fulfilment. Thus the philosopher—who is simply one set upon attaining mind's satisfaction—must undertake to disclose the nature of the environment in which mind is engulfed. And here-upon he is face to face with the Absolute, which is merely this environment adequately understood.[37]

(d) In passing to a consideration of the Absolute, we are not entering upon a wholly new stage in our Pilgrim's Progress; we are only taking a fuller survey of what has been with us from the beginning. The "spirit of the whole" is, in fact, the spirit of the Absolute. We have seen it manifesting itself in nature, life and mind; but only incompletely and in varying degrees. Now, we are to behold it in its full significance and adequate embodiment. The exposition upon which we are entering, while rehearsing many of the principles with which we are already familiar, will present them in a new and richer context; for we are now concerned with reality and not, as above, with appearances.

The argument leading to the Absolute is involved in what has already been advanced, and all that is needed here is to disclose it. To this end the argument must be more concisely stated, and we begin with a purely logical consideration.

In the perceptive judgment, for example, we find that the subject is never a mere idea. "If I say, pointing to a particular house, 'That is my home,' it is clear that in this act of judgment

---

[37] That the Absolute is no far-off entity set on a hill, but is precisely the all-encompassing environment of finite minds, is a thesis which is quite important for an understanding of Bosanquet's idealism or, as he prefers to call his view, "speculative philosophy." And one who fails to get the point misses much of what he wishes to say. "We all of us experience the Absolute," he insists, "because the Absolute is in everything. And as it is in everything we do or suffer, we may even say that we experience it more fully than we experience anything else, especially as one profound charac-teristic runs through the whole. And that is, that the world does not let us alone; it drives us from pillar to post, and the very chapter of accidents, as we call it, confronts us with an extraordinary mixture of opportunity and suffering, which is itself opportunity." (*Principle of Individuality and Value*, p. 27; cf. p. 378 ff.). Compare the metaphor of the tide, noted above.

the reference conveyed by the demonstrative is indispensable. The significant idea, 'my home,' is affirmed, not of any other general significant idea in my mind, but of something which is rendered unique by being present to me in perception. In making the judgment, 'That is my home,' I extend the present sense-perception of a house in a certain landscape by attaching to it the ideal content or meaning of 'home'; and moreover, in doing this, I pronounce the ideal content to be, so to speak, of one and the same tissue with what I have before me in my actual perception. That is to say, I affirm the meaning of the idea, or the idea considered as a meaning, to be a real quality of that which I perceive in my perception." And this holds true of every perceptive judgment. In every case, "there is a presence of a something in contact with our sensitive self, which, as being so in contact, has the character of reality; and there is the qualification of this reality by the reference to it of some meaning *such as can be* symbolised by a name." But "as all reality is continuous," the subject of the judgment "is not *merely* this given spot or point. It is impossible to confine the real world within this or that presentation. Every definition or qualification of a point in present perception is affirmed of the real world which is continuous with present perception. The ultimate subject of the perceptive judgment is the real world as a whole, and it is of this that, in judging, we affirm the qualities or characteristics."[38]

The same is true in principle of all sorts of judgments. In universal judgments, to be sure, the element of present sense-perception is displaced by descriptive ideas; and so also in hypothetical or conditional judgments. But in no judgment is the reference to reality ever lost, however much it may be disguised, for in every judgment the subject, whatever it may be, "is not *merely* in my mind; not relative purely to me as a conscious organism; not a psychical fact in my individual history. Every judgment, perceptive or universal, might without altering its meaning be introduced by some such phrase as 'Realty is such that——,' 'The real world is characterised by——.' "

---

[38] *Logic*, Vol. I, 71-74. Italics are in the text. Compare with Bradley's account of the 'that' and the 'what' in judgment, and his figure of the illuminated spot on the stream (pp. 102-105 above).

Speaking quite generally, then, we may say that judgment is "the intellectual function which defines reality by significant ideas, and in so doing affirms the reality of those ideas." Judgment "always refers to a Reality which goes beyond and is independent of the act itself." [39]

The reality to which every cognitive judgment thus necessarily refers always runs on ahead, and it is through penetration into this reality that judgment seeks its final completion and stability—its truth. But no final stability, no ultimate truth, can be attained until a self-contained and all-inclusive system is reached, since anything less would involve a nisus to its own transcendence and completion and so could not be an ultimate subject. Such a self-contained and all-inclusive system is precisely what we mean by the Absolute; the Absolute, therefore, is the genuine subject of every congitive judgment. Our principle of coherence and non-contradiction expressing itself in cognitive judgments, thus, implicates the Absolute; the true is the whole, and the whole is the Absolute—the system of all that is.

But the criterion of non-contradiction holds equally true of the other types of experience, and is not confined exclusively to the cognitive. "It holds good . . . of significant sensation as in beauty, and of feeling in the sense of emotion, or of pleasure and pain, no less than of strictly logical structures, such as science and philosophy, or of the ideas which operate in morality, in social behavior, or in religion." It holds good, in short, of life itself. Everywhere the "spirit of the whole" is the controlling principle; personality in the end is nothing else.

And here, from this angle, the same logic is operative and drives us to the Absolute. Taking the individual as including the moral, aesthetic, and religious consciousness and forms of experience, it is clear that there are degrees of individuality and that individuality grows in significance as a foreign environment

[39] *Logic*, Vol. I, p. 97. For Bosanquet's meaning of 'independence' here, the reader should refer to the *Logic*, Vol. II, pp. 264 ff. "When I speak of this Reality as independent of our act of judgment, as it is in an enormous proportion, I do not mean to exclude the truth that our judgment, in an infinitesimal degree, contributes to sustain it, and forms an element in its life. In this limited sense the two forms of Reality are interdependent. But their interdependence is not correspondence, and their independence is not that of original and copy."

falls away. No finite individual is self-contained or self-depend-
ent, and all finite individuals differ in their degree of approximation to these characteristics. The important point, however,
is that selfhood is attained, is deepened and broadened and
enriched, through the transcendence of isolation. Every self has
its deeper significance beyond its mere uniqueness, its *prima
facie* preferences and interests. Nor is there anything mysterious
in this. It follows from the fact that "the finite self is plainly a
partial world, yet possesses within it the principle of infinity,
taken in the sense of the nisus towards absolute unity and self-
completion." [40] "What we call 'the individual' is not a fixed
essence, but a living world of content, representing a certain
range of externality, which in it strives after unity and true
individuality or completeness because it has in it the active spirit
of non-contradiction, the form of the whole." [41] And this "true
individuality or completeness" towards which the finite individual is driven by its very nature is the Absolute. The Absolute,
thus, is directly involved in finite individuality; it "is simply
the high-water mark of fluctuations in experience, of which, in
general, we are daily and normally aware." [42]

The foundation of the inference to the Absolute, then, everywhere lies close to hand—in morality and social behavior generally, in religion, as well as in the more formal logical structures. It is "the passage from the contradictory and unstable
in all experience alike to the stable and satisfactory." But what,
in more detail, are we to understand by the Absolute and what
is its relation to finite individuals? The answer to this question
will bring us to the end of our pilgrimage

From what has preceded, it is clear that the Absolute must
be the ultimate self-contained and all-inclusive system. It is
clear also that the Absolute must be said to be spiritual; it is
precisely the 'whole' which comes alive in finite conscious centers
and is there imperfectly realized. But the Absolute cannot be
a self or person; it is not characterized by will, and is not to
be identified with the God of religion. On the contrary, it tran-

[40] *The Value and Destiny of the Individual*, p. 4.

[41] *The Principle of Individuality and Value*, p. 289.

[42] A convenient summary of the main points is given by Bosanquet himself in the second edition of the *Logic*, Vol. II, Chapter VIII.

scends all such characterizations, since it can have no 'other.'
It is all that is, and cannot, therefore, be described in terms
appropriate to its appearances. What can positively be said
about it is that it is the all-comprehensive and self-harmonious
system, which includes all appearances though in a manner
which transmutes them. The nature of the relation between the
Absolute and its appearances may be made clearer by the following considerations.

A basal characteristic of the Absolute is 'negativity.' But
negativity must be distinguished from contradiction. Contradiction, to be sure, falls within system and is meaningless apart
from it; there is no contradiction among predicates taken at
random, but only among predicates ascribed to one term. Beautiful and ugly (not-beautiful), for example, are not *per se*
contradictory; they become contradictory only when they are
predicated of the same conditions. "It is a formal contradiction
if you say, 'This colour is both beautiful and ugly, i.e. not
beautiful.' It ceases to be a contradiction if you say, 'This colour
by daylight is beautiful and by candle-light is ugly.' " Contradiction, thus, "is not a dead fact about certain predicates; it is
an imperfection in the organisation of systems." From this it
follows that contradiction cannot characterize the Absolute, for
in the Absolute there is no imperfection of organization. In what
sense, then, does negativity belong to the Absolute?

If we inquire what ordinarily survives when a contradiction
is resolved, we find, not a bare denial of opposition, but rather
a successful emendation of it. In the example given above, for
instance, the removal of the contradiction between beauty and
its opposite is not equivalent to the removal of the opposition
between them; it lies, rather, in the inclusion of the opposites
within a more comprehensive system wherein the opposed predicates, though still opposed, are reconciled. When a contradiction
is resolved "nothing is changed, except what was attempted has
been achieved. The contents are diverse, as they were . . . the
change is merely that now they and their world have been read-
justed, and can carry out their union." In other words, contradiction has now become negativity; the bare opposition has been
transformed into a systematic and harmonious arrangement of

'differents.' We may, therefore, say that contradiction and negation are logically the same principle viewed, on the one side, as
incomplete and, on the other, as complete. "Contradiction . . .
is an unsuccessful or obstructed Negativity; Negativity is a
successful or frictionless contradiction." From this we can see
that negativity plays its rôle in all experience. "It is the same
characteristic which has been described as the fact that experience is always beyond itself—the character, indeed, which we
have described from the beginning as that of the universal, or,
in other words, the tendency of every datum to transcend itself
as a fragment and complete itself as a whole." [43] It is a point
full of significance, however, that negativity plays a larger, not
a smaller, rôle as contradiction diminishes; negativity is really
affirmation—affirmation of differences, with contradiction removed—and the affirmative side must not be lost sight of. When
we say, then, that negativity is a characteristic of the Absolute,
what is to be understood is that, in the Absolute, contradiction
has entirely disappeared, while the spirit of difference survives
in its highest form. The Absolute negates conflict and confusion,
it affirms system and significant oppositions; and, to put the
matter paradoxically, its negation and its affirmation are one
and the same.

Taking this paradox seriously and applying it to the reality
of appearances, we can explain the troublesome problem of
evil and finiteness generally. These, to be sure, are no illusions;
on the contrary, they are actual features of reality, and indeed
essential to it. But they are real only when, and as, taken for
what they are—namely, aspects of finite systems with a limited
range of externality, aspects demanding their own expansion
and completion. Ultimately they are negated in the Absolute,
but only in the sense that this complete system carries within
itself the principle through which their antagonisms and contradictions are finally set at rest. The perfection of the Absolute,
however, must not be conceived as excluding the process through
which these finite systems are completed. For its own self-com-
pletion the Absolute presupposes the temporal order, the hazards

[43] *The Principle of Individuality and Value*, pp. 228, 231. Cf. *Science
and Philosophy*, Chapter V.

and hardships of finite selfhood; apart from this order and the content it furnishes the Absolute would be nothing at all. Its very perfection is dependent upon the temporal instruments through which that perfection is achieved; its negativity belongs as much to them as to itself. But this is not to be understood to imply that the Absolute is in time, or that it is characterized by purpose or will. What appears to finite minds as the temporal order or as purpose and will are, of course, included in the Absolute and so are real; but as included in the Absolute they are negated—they are subsumed within that totality of system which itself is non-temporal, non-purposive, non-volitional, and as thus subsumed they are transmuted. Time and its children are all within the Absolute, but they are there as aspects of a harmonious whole in which all oppositions and contradictions are finally resolved.

There is, indeed, a sense in which teleology may be predicated of the Absolute, and it is important to determine in precisely what sense this is permissible. To this end it is necessary to note that the term 'teleology' has two meanings which are quite distinct and which must be kept separate in any intelligent discussion of the problem. In its *prima facie* meaning teleology is not a metaphysical, but only a psychological, idea and cannot without contradiction be applied to the totality of things. In its profounder meaning it is essentially a non-temporal category and when applied to the universe, as it must be, it not only does not imply that the Absolute is in time, but it implies precisely the reverse.

The two meanings of 'teleology' stand out fairly clearly. On the one hand, and most obviously, it refers to a purposive order involving items related to each other as 'end' and 'means.' Taken in this sense it is applicable only to a series in which conscious purposes are fulfilled and is essentially identical with accomplishment, perfectibility. But there is a deeper interpretation in which the term qualifies a nexus of relations within a perfect whole; here it means completion, perfection. The distinction can be made clearer, perhaps, by reference to the dual meaning of *end* from which the double meaning of teleology arises. *End* means both conclusion and completeness. In the first meaning, a teleological situation is constituted by a series of events in which certain ones are set off as 'end' and more or less sharply sundered from others taken as 'means.' Here *purpose* in the sense of want or incompleteness is prominent; a finite individual life exemplifies it. In the second meaning of the term, *end*, however, the teleological situation is not at all a series of events loosely joined and separable as 'end' and 'means,' but rather a nexus of relations so delicately conjoined that the distinction between 'end' and 'means' loses, or threatens to lose, all significance. Here "purpose *qua* purpose is negligible. . . . It is the nexus of relations held together by the distinctly apprehended whole which determines the implications of one in another and *vice versa*. And in such a nexus, in proportion to the completeness of its interconnection, no part can be idle; and if it presents on one side the aspect of a purpose—say, like the total embodied will of a society—it must be a purpose—it must be a purpose such that every so-called means is a modification of the end and every feature of the end imparts a character to something which might also be called a means." [44]

The transition of thought from the first to the second of these meanings of teleology is necessary. It is forced upon us as we penetrate further into the nature of reality. Starting with the sharp separation between end and means as it appears in the ordinary affairs of practical experience, we soon discover that the temporal distinctness between end and means loses its sharpness. Deeper penetration leads us to see that we can no longer think of the end as out yonder in the future, and of the means as present devices whose sole function is to lead up to it. "We soon come to recognise that what we have called an end, as if it were a goal and a stopping-place is in reality 'not a point, but a line,' or even a solid; that it expands itself, irregularly, over the whole process of our activity. When, for example, we are dealing with a total system, whether of life or of nature, how are we to discriminate between end and means?" [45] On further reflection, thus, end and means tend to blend inextrica-

---

[44] From the author's article, "The Relation of Coherence to Immediacy and Specific Purpose," *Philosophical Review* (1917), Vol. XXVI, p. 271.
[45] *The Principle of Individuality and Value*, p. 125.

bly; and we are driven from the principle of purposiveness to the principle of individuality or non-contradiction in our analysis of the concept of teleology.[46]

This inevitable blending of end and means points a moral of great importance, namely, that teleology in its *prima facie* meaning is only an 'arbitrary and eclectic' notion. As so construed, it cannot without manifest contradiction be predicated of the totality of things; as a metaphysical concept it breaks down completely. The whole cannot want anything; it has no unfulfilled desires; there are within it no non-adjustments to be adjusted, no incompletion to be removed, and hence it cannot be conceived as being a will or as involving an ought.[47] To speak of it as teleological, as using means to accomplish ends, is, consequently, unmeaning because contradictory. In this sense teleology is a temporal, psychological, and ethical concept; it has no metaphysical value, and to attempt to give it a cosmic status is merely to attempt the impossible.

In the second meaning of the term, however, it is not only permissible, it is necessary, to affirm teleology of reality. For this view of teleology substitutes for the principle of purposive-

---

[46] *Ibid.*, pp. 126-127. "In this transition, the principle of purposiveness, of a nature imperative on every element of a whole, expands into the principle of Individuality, or positive non-contradiction. In working with it, we substitute the idea of perfection or the whole—a logical or metaphysical, non-temporal, and religious idea—for that of *de facto* purpose—a psychological, temporal, and ethical idea. We deal with a substantive criterion of value applicable to every detail of a totality, and equally valid if Time is treated as an appearance."

[47] "A purpose, or a will, can never be the whole of a world. A purpose always means that, founding yourself on matter accepted as a basis, you recognise a certain alteration as essential in view of the admitted situation, for the restoration or partial restoration of harmony. *Ex nihilo nihil.* You cannot gather material for purpose out of no situation. The content you are impelled to produce must be relative to a content which you admit. The same is true of Will, and of Ought. . . . Will and Ought, in a word, are the properties of a world that mends discrepancies within itself by a process in time. There can be no will or ought except on the basis of a presupposed reality, within which non-adjustment calls for adjustment. . . . Therefore, it seems unintelligible for the Absolute or for any perfect experience to be a will or purpose. It would be a meaningless pursuit of nothing in particular." (*Principle of Individuality and Value*, Appendix I, 3, pp. 391-393.) The same argument is advanced in *Meeting of Extremes*, Chapters V, VI, and IX.

ness and incompletion the principle₁ of non-contradiction and completion—in a word, individuality; and this is precisely what reality is. To be sure, this is teleology in a very different sense from what is ordinarily understood by the term. "In extending the idea of teleology to the universe as a whole we are turning from the question whether this fact or that has the appearance of being contrived for a purpose, to the question whether the totality . . . can be apprehended or conceived as satisfactory, *i. e.*, as a supreme value." [48] But it is teleology still, or may be so called. And with this application of teleology to the world-whole time is, of course, *ipso facto*, excluded from the notion. Now we are conceiving of the whole, not as purposive and hence temporal, but as a nexus of relations which is ultimately satis-factory, non-contradictory, perfect, and which consequently is strictly non-temporal. As thus teleological the whole is in a state of perfect logical equilibrium.

The upshot of the whole matter, then, would seem to be that the question whether teleology is an ultimate category depends altogether on what is to be understood by the term. If by it is meant a purposive system such that part is set temporally over against part as end and means, the end being a goal towards which the present runs, then teleology is only a sub-form of human intelligence and cannot without contradiction be predi-cated of the whole; in this meaning it is sharply distinct from the concept of a 'world.' If, on the other hand, it is taken to mean a 'world,' a system in which the interpenetration of ele-ments is such that no one 'remains idle,' but each is touched by all and all by each, and no trace of contradiction or incom-pleteness mars the perfect harmony—then teleology is predic-able of reality, or, perhaps, more accurately, is reality; in this construction it is not meaningless to say that reality is teleo-logical. So we may without contradiction say that reality is, and is not, teleological. It is *not* teleological in the sense of a process in time going on to the realization of unrealized pur-poses, but it *is* teleological in the sense of a perfect system of absolutely harmoniously interpenetrating elements. Thus we can understand the apparently paradoxical statement: "Things

[48] *The Principle of Individuality and Value*, p. 127.

are not teleological because they are purposed, but are purposed because they are teleological." [49]

The question concerning the relation between the Absolute and those finite centers called 'selves' is answered in principle by the immediately preceding considerations, and the answer may in conclusion be here summarily set down. The finite self, though an indispensable center or focus of activity through which the Absolute expresses and maintains itself, is in the Absolute so transmuted as to be hardly identical with what we ordinarily intend by the term 'self.' The leading function of the spatio-temporal and the social order may, from one angle, be said to be that of soul-making: "souls are cast and moulded by the externality of nature, and of other finite souls." But the soul which is thus being moulded manifests an active principle which is the spirit of the whole, and what we call its being moulded is but one aspect of the self-determination by which it transforms its partial world. Thus the finite soul is torn between its existential character and its self-transcendence; it maintains its finiteness only at the expense of contradiction. But, by virtue of the spirit of the whole present within it, it "is bound in its intolerance of all contradiction to contradict its own existence. Thus the self, in the striving to complete itself, will break in pieces every partial form of its own crystallised being, will welcome the chapter of accidents, and clothe itself in conflict and adventure."

Practically, the self seeks its security in the religious consciousness, but this practical attitude is not in the end satisfactory. Only in the Absolute, "the whole considered as a perfection in which the antagonism of good and evil is unnoted" because overcome, does the finite self attain its genuine stability and security "by which alone the vice of finiteness can be

---

[49] *Ibid.*, p. 137. The view of teleology here defended by Bosanquet is quite different from that advocated in the first edition of the *Logic*, in which purpose is made an active principle of system. The later view summarized above is, however, the one which Bosanquet explicitly supports as against his earlier view. See his reply (*Philosophical Review*, Vol. XXVI, 271) to Sabine's statement of the apparent inconsistency (same journal, Vol. XXI, 562-564).

cured." [50] And when it has thus attained, it is changed; its opposition to externality, which is so essential to its finite nature, is removed and it is one with the whole.

This may, indeed, be called a sort of mysticism. But it is a higher mysticism for which finite experience is not "an accidental disturbance of the Quiet, nor a regrettable deviation from the Perfect." It is rather an imperfect approximation of a consummation which, when attained, must result in something more positive for the finite self than bare extinction. For the finite self at its best tends more and more to unite itself with the not-self or other. Thus it gives definite indication of the positive result of its own transcendence, though in achieving the complete reconciliation it must surrender its claims to a substantival nature, and become an element in, or aspect of, the Absolute. So we may say, without contradiction, that the finite self finds itself in the Absolute; but in finding itself it must also lose itself—in expressing fully the "spirit of the whole" within it, it must lose its opposition to an alien environment. The Absolute absorbs into its being all that the finite self exists to achieve, but in its finiteness can never achieve—self-maintenance in self-transcendence.

[50] *The Value and Destiny of the Individual,* pp. 16, 17, and Lecture VIII.

CHAPTER VI

ANDREW SETH PRINGLE-PATTISON (1856-1931)

IN his *Gifford Lectures,* delivered at the University of Aberdeen in the years 1912 and 1913 under the title, *The Idea of God in the Light of Recent Philosophy,* Pringle-Pattison describes the type of idealism, for which in these lectures he is arguing, as follows: "It is sufficient for the purposes of Idealism that nature as a whole should be recognised as complementary to mind, and possessing therefore no absolute existence of its own apart from its spiritual completion; just as mind in turn would be intellectually and ethically void without a world to furnish it with the materials of knowledge and of duty. Both are necessary elements of a single system."

In the same lectures he states his conception of method thus: "The logical principle of non-contradiction, or, to express it more largely, the principle of intellectual coherence, we must and do accept as absolute. We accept it as a necessity of reason involved in the possibility of knowing anything—involved therefore in all practical living as well as in the immovable belief in law and order which inspires all scientific investigation. And, needless to say, life and science alike vindicate the principle; all experience may be looked upon as its progressive verification. But if we ask what is the nature of our certainty that existence, the world of facts, is ultimately and throughout intellectually coherent—that we have to do, in short, not with a chaos but with a cosmos, a world whose laws may be infinitely complex and difficult to unravel, but which will never put us to permanent intellectual confusion—we are bound to reply that in a sense it is an unproved belief. It is unproved in the sense that we have not explored the whole of existence, and in the nature of the case can never hope to include all the facts within the net of reason. And hence it may perhaps be called a postulate of reason, a supreme hypothesis." But it is the inescapable presupposition of all thinking, as of all acting; and, "although a little philosophy may lead us for a time into the wilderness of scepticism and relativism, depth in philosophy brings us back with fuller insight to the sanity of our original position."[1]

These quotations set before us our author's conception of the idealistic thesis and of the general method by which he thinks it can in the end be justified. That his view of method and result is much in the spirit of Bradley and Bosanquet is evident even from this summary statement; the similarity will become clearer as we proceed into the details of his argument. But he differs from his colleagues on important matters, particularly in his conception of the Absolute and of the ultimate significance of the finite individual. Indeed, his differences here are sufficiently marked to place him as the first and most important representative of the transition in the development of British philosophy from the type of idealism commonly called *absolute idealism* to that known as *personalism*. One is tempted to classify him as a personalistic absolutist. But these matters may best be left for further consideration after the statement of his own idealistic argument, to which we now turn.

1. THE EPISTEMOLOGICAL ARGUMENT

The attempt to prove the idealistic thesis by purely epistemological considerations Pringle-Pattison holds to be fruitless, as exemplified in the procedure of Berkeley, Ferrier and Green.

The argument advanced by Berkeley is quite obviously circular. It undertakes to establish the thesis that material things cannot exist independently of mind on the premise—which, indeed, must be granted—that we cannot without contradiction conceive of the existence of things apart from, and independent of, a mind which so conceives them. Clearly, this argument moves in a vicious circle. The assumption on which it patently rests is that things as they exist must be things as they are known, and this assumption is precisely what is supposed to be proved by the argument. So the Berkeleian argument for idealism is entirely inadequate. It may indeed be said to prove, if proof is needed, that things "cannot exist *in the knowledge rela-*

[1] *The Idea of God,* pp. 189, 239, 240.

tion without implying a mind or ego, and also that we cannot say anything about them except as known, so that out of that relation they are to us, in a Kantian phrase, as good as nothing at all. But this method of approach cannot possibly prove that they do not exist out of that relation; it cannot prove Berkeley's thesis that being-in-that-relation constitutes their existence. On the contrary, we should all say, *prima facie*, that being known makes no difference to the existence of anything real." [2] Hence the argument of Berkeley for idealism must be set aside as logically incompetent.

And Ferrier's argument is in no better case. It is in fact little more than "Berkeleianism universalised and applied on the cosmic scale," and is of the same circular character. For Ferrier simply appeals to a cosmic mind to save the world from contradiction, and nothing is gained in principle by appealing to an Absolute mind instead of a finite one. *"If knowledge has the same meaning in the two cases,* the existence of a thing can no more depend on God's knowing it than on my knowing it," for it is a basal principle "that in every case knowledge presupposes a reality, which it knows but does not make." Furthermore, the result of Ferrier's argument, even if taken as proved, gives us nothing of philosophical significance. For the mind in synthesis with all things, which the argument purports to establish, is a mind standing over against its content in a purely external relationship analogous to that between the eye and its objects in the field of vision. It is therefore not a principle of explanation, but only an abstract point of reference—a mere spectator of the world. It is philosophically useless. So we are driven to hold, in the first place, that Ferrier's argument does not prove his thesis; and, in the second place, that even if it did the thesis is fruitless for philosophical interpretation.

Essentially the same criticism holds of Green's argument. The argument rests on the assumption of atomistic and unrelated sensations as its point of departure, and apart from this assumption it has no significance whatever. But the assumption

---

[2] *Ibid.*, p. 192. The criticism here is in avowed agreement with that of the realists. Cf. R. B. Perry, *Present Philosophical Tendencies,* Chapter VI, especially p. 126 ff.

is false—as false as is the defunct psychology (that of **Locke and Hume**) on which it rests. What is, in fact, given to us in sensation is not a mere multiplicity of unrelated elements, but a unified whole. "The unity of experience, so far as it *is* unified and connected, is just as real and primitive a fact as its variety." This fact William James in his character as 'radical empiricist' has unanswerably shown, and it may be taken as generally admitted in recent discussion. We do not therefore require the apparatus of 'consciousness' or 'understanding,' as a "combining agency," to sustain relations; the supposed factual basis of this conception is lacking. Whether there are other grounds for admitting the conception is, of course, another question; the point here is that the ground laid by the argument of Green cannot stand. And, furthermore, even granting that the argument does establish the conception of an "all-uniting consciousness" through whose agency alone relations exist, the conception itself is entirely empty. Such a consciousness is, as it was in the case of Ferrier, a mere abstract point of reference which cannot function as a principle of philosophical explanation—it is the eye that sees, but does not support or maintain.

This abstract result, however, is the inevitable outcome of any argument based on purely epistemological considerations, and is not merely derived from the special formulations which such an argument receives at the hands of Berkeley, Ferrier, and Green. At the very most, the epistemological argument yields only a formal ego or mind—finite or infinite; there is no difference in principle—which in Balfour's expressive figure is little more than "the bare geometrical point through which must pass the threads which make up the web of nature." And such a point is, for philosophical speculation, of no genuine account. Certainly, it is not capable of supporting an idealistic metaphysics. There is little difference between conceiving nature as being present to, or registered in, a mind and conceiving it as existing *per se*.

But the epistemological argument is not the only argument for idealism; if it were, the case of the idealist would be hopeless. The argument for idealism springs, rather, from the necessity under which reason labors of conceiving the world as a *res com-*

pleta and the impossibility of thus conceiving it apart from value. Not the speculative impossibility of a world unperceived or unthought of, but the moral impossibility of a world devoid of value is the driving power of the argument for an idealistic philosophy. We are now to see, in some detail, how this is so.[3]

2. THE HIGHER NATURALISM

"If, as men of science tell us, scientific explanation is in the end description, the same is ultimately true of philosophy itself. Philosophy, or perhaps I should qualify the statement and say, sane philosophy, is not really the quest of some transcendent reason why the nature of things is as it is; it does not attempt, in Lotze's phrase, to tell us 'how being is made.' 'All that can be asked of philosophy,' I ventured to say in my first volume, published more than thirty years ago, 'is, by the help of the most complete analysis, to present a reasonable synthesis of the world as we find it. The difference between a true and a false philosophy is that a false philosophy fixes its eye on a part only of the material submitted to it, and would explain the whole, therefore, by a principle which is adequate merely to one of its parts or stages; a true philosophy, on the other hand, is one which "sees life steadily and sees it whole"—whose principle, therefore, embraces in its evolution every phase of the actual.' " [4]

All explanation, then, is merely a matter of applying to that which is to be explained those categories that are appropriate to its nature. Adequate explanation involves, further, the determination of the relative significance attaching to the several categories used in describing different aspects of the real. What categories are appropriate to a given set of data is a problem which falls within the scope of some special science. The deter-

---

[3] The details of the argument here given are taken primarily from Pringle-Pattison's Gifford Lectures, *The Idea of God in the Light of Recent Philosophy* (1917).

Pringle-Pattison's other important works are: *The Development from Kant to Hegel* (1882); *Hegelianism and Personality* (1887), in which the author's emphasis on the significance of finite personality is pronounced; *Man's Place in the Cosmos* (1897); *The Philosophical Radicals* (1907); and *The Idea of Immortality* (1922), a second series of Gifford Lectures and a development of some of the theses of the first.

[4] *The Idea of God*, pp. 108-109. The first volume referred to in the quotation is the author's *The Development from Kant to Hegel*, p. 66.

mination of the relative significance of the various categories thus discovered with particular reference to their proper application is the main task of philosophy. "Correct explanation depends in any department on the employment of appropriate categories, and philosophy consists in an insight into the relation of the categories in question and the realm of facts which they describe, to other categories and other realms or aspects of reality. We must have some notion of their significance in an account of the nature of the universe as a whole. The function of philosophy is, in this connexion, comparable to that of a 'Warden of the Marches' between the various sciences, resisting the pretensions of any particular science to be the exclusive exponent of reality and assigning to each its hierarchical rank in a complete scheme of knowledge." [5]

Applying the principles above emphasized, we note in the first place that what is commonly called naturalism must be a false philosophy. Of course, in so far as naturalism may be understood to mean merely a negation of super-naturalism, an insistence that all events and existences must be explained by what are called natural as contrasted with super-natural causes or conditions, there is nothing to be said against it. On the contrary, in this sense it must not only be accepted but insisted upon by all since it represents an awakened intelligence which desires to be honest and to assent only to what can be proved. But, as a philosophy, naturalism has come to mean something very different from this straightforward emphasis. It has come to mean "the type of theory which so emphasizes the continuity between man and the non-human nature from which he springs as to minimize, if not entirely to deny, any difference between them." [6] And in this meaning naturalism is fundamentally false.

It is quite important to understand, however, precisely where the basal error of the naturalistic philosophy lies. No legitimate objection to naturalism can be raised because of its emphasis on continuity within nature. In this emphasis it is simply directing attention to one aspect, and a very important aspect, of the

[5] *Idea of God*, p. 108. Cf. the author's essay on "Philosophy as a Criticism of Categories," in the coöperative volume, *Essays in Philosophical Criticism* (1883), edited by A. Seth and R. B. Haldane.

[6] *Ibid.*, pp. 88-89.

world as we find it. No one who is not blind to the facts can fail to see that there is continuity throughout the various stages and transformations of the natural order, including man and his works. *Non fit saltus in natura;* so far as this thesis is concerned naturalism is impregnable, and in that fact lies the secret of its vitality as a philosophical doctrine.

Naturalism falls into error when it so interprets the principle of continuity as to exclude another equally obvious and equally important aspect of the order of nature, namely, the emergence of significant differences among the stages or levels in that order. That there are such differences seems to be beyond legitimate question. Between the inorganic and the organic, for instance, or between mere animal and human life, there are differences so radical as to mark different orders of fact. The categories which adequately describe inorganic events are wholly inadequate for the description of organic events, and the psychology of human beings demands categories which are not applicable to earthworms or bees or even the higher sub-human vertebrates. But naturalism denies all these differences by reading the principle of continuity as necessitating "the reduction of all nature's facts to the dead level of a single type"—ultimately, the type of the inorganic and merely physical. In so doing, however, it is guilty of a serious misapplication of categories and, consequently, gives a false description. It aims at simplification which in itself is a worthy goal of intellectual analysis, but the simplification it achieves is attained by a process of leveling down without regard to the claims of significant differences— "a process of abstraction which leaves out the characteristic features of the concrete facts supposed to be explained." The result is not an explanation of the facts; it is simply a falsification of them.

If we eliminate from naturalism its basal error, while holding to the truth involved in its emphasis on the principle of continuity, we obtain a view which is much more in harmony with the facts of the natural order. This view we might call the higher naturalism, as distinguished from the lower naturalism just criticized. The higher naturalism whole-heartedly accepts the principle of continuity, and is entirely averse to the introduction of a *deus ex machina* at any point in the order of nature.[7] But it is also averse to the abstract process of leveling down, which is the chief characteristic and the basal error of the lower naturalism. "It does not hesitate to recognize differences where it sees them, without feeling that it is thereby creating an absolute chasm between one stage of nature's processes and another—a chasm which can only be cleared by supernatural assistance expressly invoked." For in such recognition of differences it holds that it is but faithfully following the method of any sane philosophy—the method, namely, of applying categories in a critical manner. "When the dog develops a system of astronomy or the cow pauses on the hill-top to admire the view," the higher naturalism will "gladly welcome them to the logician's company of 'rational animals.'" Till then, however, it "will be content to recognize a difference which is real"; and it will follow this principle in all cases where there are real differences, from star-dust to symphony. *"Continuity of process and the emergence of real differences*—these are, in short, the twin aspects of the cosmic history, and it is essential to clear thinking that the one be not allowed to obscure the other."[8] It is equally essential to clear thinking that the intimate connection between the two be borne in mind, and that continuity among the emergents be specifically recognized. Both emphases are essential to the higher naturalism.

Herewith we have reached a conclusion which for philosophy is foundational. The force of this whole conclusion can only be expressed in two propositions: Man is organic to nature, and Nature is organic to man. These, of course, are correlative propositions, but both are necessary to bring into the open the full implication of the higher naturalism. The emphasis of the first serves to distinguish the higher from the lower naturalism, since by its light the assumption of the lower naturalism that nature is complete in itself—a system finished without man —is clearly seen to be a vicious abstraction. The emphasis of the second proposition, or the other side, differentiates the

---

[7] Cf. Bosanquet's insistence on the naturalness of finite mind in his chapter on "The Bodily Basis of Mind," *Principle of Individuality and Value,* and summarized above, pp. 129-137.

[8] *The Idea of God,* pp. 91, 103. The italics are Pringle-Pattison's.

higher naturalism from all forms of panpsychism, which would resolve the natural order without remainder into an assemblage of subjective centers of experience, thus abolishing altogether the conception of nature in the ordinary sense of the word. This emphasis notes the fact that the system of nature, as an independent order, furnishes both the conditions of individuation and the means of communication among individuals. Both propositions taken together furnish the bed-rock upon which alone a true philosophy may be founded.

This philosophy, which hitherto we have called the higher naturalism, may equally well be called idealism. For it nature is complementary to mind, and mind is complementary to nature; neither by itself is a *res completa*. The attempt to conceive either alone as the real involves the conversion of abstractions into realities by forcibly separating facts which are given together and cannot even be conceived apart. For this philosophy, both man and nature are necessary elements within a single system, and the system alone is the real. "The doctrine of the self-conscious life as organic to the world or of the world as finding completion and expression in that life, so that the universe, as a complete or self-existent fact, is statable only in terms of mind"—this is the doctrine to which we are brought by the argument. And this is the doctrine historically known as idealism, or, as it is sometimes called in distinction from the Berkeleian view, *objective* or *absolute idealism*.

The fuller significance of this general conclusion may be more clearly grasped by noting some of the detailed implications of the argument by which it has been reached.

(a) In the first place, the so-called epistemological problem is set aside as essentially meaningless; it is of as little significance as is the assumption from which it arises. "The so-called epistemological problem which obsesses modern philosophy, from Descartes and Locke to Kant and Spencer and the most recent magazine discussions—this problem, with all the varieties of subjective idealism, agnosticism, phenomenalism, and sceptical relativism to which it gives rise, depends upon the presupposition of a finished world, as an independently existing fact, and an equally independent knower, equipped, from heaven knows where, with a peculiar apparatus of faculties." When the theorist has thus extruded man from the world which he seeks to know and treats him "as if he were, so to say, a stranger visitant, contemplating *ab extra* an independent universe," the epistemological problem is inevitable—and insoluble. Once this abstract separation of man from his world is denied, as it must be by any sane philosophy, the epistemological problem falls of its own weight. "If we keep steadily in view the fact that man is from beginning to end, even *qua* knower, a member and, as it were, an organ of the universe, knowledge will appear to us in a more natural light, and we shall not be tempted to open this miraculous chasm between the knower and the realities which he knows." Rather, with the pragmatists we shall hold that things are what they are experienced as, with the neo-realists, that knowledge is a direct relation between the knower and the reality known.[9]

(b) But we must not forget upon what grounds this position rests, nor be half-hearted in our acceptance of the principle involved. If we are to be consistent, we must frankly follow the principle the whole way. The principle is that man *qua* knower and experiencer is within, and a part of, the system which he knows and experiences. And if we are to take this principle seriously, we are by it committed to the conclusion that what man apprehends of his environment is, so far and in its own way, a true account of that environment. The old distinction between 'primary' and 'secondary' qualities which regards the former as 'real' and the latter as 'imaginary' must, consequently, be surrendered. It is based upon a bifurcation of mind and nature, which by our principle is denied. The so-called 'secondary' qualities, we must hold, are in their own manner as objective and 'real' as are spatial and temporal qualities. Essentially the same must be said of the aesthetic qualities—those aspects of beauty and sublimity which we recognize in nature, as well as the results of the poetic imagination. "These things also are not subjective imaginings; they give us a deeper truth than ordinary vision, just as the more developed eye or ear

[9] Cf. *The Idea of God*, pp. 111-112, and entire Lecture VI.

carries us farther into nature's refinements and beauties." [10] To suppose that they are mere "subjective imaginings," dependent for their existence merely upon our psychological states, is to deny essentially that man is organic to nature.

More important for the idealistic argument, however, is the further consideration that human values, especially moral ones, are trustworthy indices to the nature of reality. This, of course, has often been denied; in fact, it is precisely at this point that the sharp dualism between man and nature has historically been most pronounced. The positivism of Comte is a noteworthy example of it. "Nature and man are not part of one scheme of things; nature is just, as it were, a brute fact with which man finds himself confronted. Hence man appears in the universe like a moral Melchizedek without ancestry, owing everything to himself, his own Providence, bringing into the universe for the first time the qualities which merit the attribute divine. And accordingly, the deification of man is equivalent to the dethronement of God. As Comte puts it in a notable, if somewhat blustering paradox, the heavens declare the glory, not of God, but of Kepler and Newton." [11] And many others, differing widely from Comte in their religious views, have accepted the initial dualism between man and nature upon which Comte's religion of Humanity is built.

This dualism, however, is wholly without warrant. Man is rooted in nature, as we have already urged, and this holds of him as a moral and religious, as well as an intelligent being. Therefore, we must hold that the significance of the world is disclosed by man's moral insight as truly as it is by his cognitive insight. Indeed, more so, for morality belongs to the higher ranges of human experience, and must consequently be accepted as revelatory of the nature of the world in a deeper sense. "Man is the child of nature, and it is on the basis of natural impulses and in commerce with the system of external things, that his ethical being is built up. The characteristics of the ethical life must be taken, therefore, as contributing to determine the nature of the system in which we live. Nay, according to the interpreta-

[10] *Ibid.*, p. 127.
[11] *Ibid.*, p. 153.

tion we have put upon the principle of value and upon the evolutionary distinction between lower and higher ranges of experience, the ethical predicates must carry us nearer to a true definition of the ultimate Life in which we live than the categories which suffice to describe, for example, the environmental conditions of our existence." [12] In the "essential greatness of man and the infinite nature of the values revealed in his life," then, we find, and by our principle of continuity and the emergence of real differences, must find the most significant index to the real nature of the world.

If we are pressed for an answer to the question why this higher significance is attached to values, especially moral values, in the interpretation of reality, we are forced to admit that, in last analysis, it is an assumption that cannot be justified in set terms. It is a profound conviction, however, from which we cannot escape. Granted the thesis that man and nature are organic to each other and that there is a distinction between lower and higher ranges of experience, the conclusion necessarily follows. But if one presses the question why such a thesis must be granted, it must be admitted that there is an assumption woven into the very texture of this philosophical theory without which, perhaps, the theory would never have been arrived at—the conviction, namely "of the essential greatness of man and the infinite nature of the values revealed in his life." It is not clear, however, that we can escape this assumption. "Without this absolute judgment of value, how could we argue, how could we *convince ourselves* that, in our estimates, it is not we who judge as finite particulars, but Reality affirming, through us, its inmost nature? It is not on the mere fact of consciousness or self-consciousness that we take our stand, but on the nature of the content experienced, the inexhaustible wonder and greatness of the worlds which it opens up to us. Every form of philosophical idealism appears to involve this

---

[12] *The Idea of God,* p. 156. The author is in essential agreement with Bradley and Bosanquet on the question of the criterion of value. With them he accepts the principle "that the nature of reality can only mean the systematic structure discernible in its appearances, and that this must furnish us with our ultimate criterion of value." (*Ibid.,* p. 225; cf. the entire Lecture XII.)

conviction of the profound significance of human life, as capable
of appropriating and realizing these values. And without such
a conviction, argument about God or the universe would seem
to be a mere waste of time; for the man to whom his own life
is a triviality is not likely to find a meaning in anything
else." [13] Nor must it be forgotten that this conviction is logically
on a par with another conviction, which underlies all of our
science—the conviction, namely, that the world of fact is ultimately and throughout intellectually coherent. This, too, is an
unproved assumption; and it is unprovable, since no finite mind
can possibly compass the entire world of fact. But we accept it,
and build our science upon it, nevertheless. And we do so
because we cannot avoid the assumption that "the best we think,
or can think, must *be*." Likewise, in the case of values, we
assume that the best we can achieve, or envisage as worthy of
achievement, must *be*. Both assumptions rest on the same
ground; nature, existence, is the matrix within which our ideas
and values bud and grow to fruition.

(c) The preceding considerations lead us to the conclusion
that the universe is a spiritual system. The All of existence
cannot be other than the temporal process taken as a whole.
"But the whole process wears the appearance of a progressive
revelation, not of a sheer addition to the life of the universe. It
is impossible to get away from the conception of a *natura
rerum*, whether we call it Nature, the Absolute, or God." If
it be called "Nature," however, the term cannot be taken in
any other meaning than that attributed to it by the higher
naturalism. By the principle of continuity Nature includes within herself man and his values, and must be interpreted as including them. The more appropriate term to apply to the whole
process, therefore, is the Absolute or God—the Whole in which
human values are conserved as eternal qualities. We cannot
escape the conception of the Whole, for we must look to the end
as well as to the process of its becoming, if we would envisage
the whole truth; and the Whole must be spiritual, since spirit is
the highest aspect of it known to us. As philosophers, therefore,
we cannot "rest in any principle of explanation short of that

[13] *Ibid.*, p. 236.

which we name the Absolute or God. All experience might not
unfitly be described, from the human side, as the quest of God—
the progressive attempt, through living and knowing, to reach a
true conception of the Power whose nature is revealed in all
that is." [14] That such a conception must be identified with the
Absolute, a spiritual Whole, is made necessary by the principle of
continuity; such a conception alone does justice to the fullest
implications of the thesis that man and nature are organic to
each other.

3. Finite Individuals, God, and the Absolute

From the preceding discussion the following principles and
conclusions emerge: The nature of reality must be sought
through a systematic interpretation of appearances; by such
a systematic interpretation is meant applying appropriate categories to appearances and noting the proper interrelation of
these categories; the principle of continuity among appearances
must not, therefore, be interpreted as necessitating the leveling
down of all appearances to one type of category, as is done
by the lower naturalism, but, on the contrary, real differences
in the order of nature must be frankly recognized and explicitly
admitted; the principle of continuity, however, must not be
forgotten and the different levels of the order must be held to
be organic to each other; the later stages of the process are
higher, more complex, and more significant, than the earlier
and consequently the intellectual and moral life of human
beings must be reckoned among the highest; human values must
be foundational in our explanation of the universe, since they are
the highest manifestations of it with which we are acquainted;
hence the world as a complete fact is statable only in terms of
conscious values, intellectual and moral, and the least inadequate name we can apply to it is that of the Absolute or God.

[14] *The Idea of God,* pp. 154-155, 156. "Man weighs in a balance the earth
on which he moves, an insignificant speck; he calculates the distance, the
mass, and the movements of the farthest stars; he dissolves the solid
framework of material things into a whirl of invisible elements and forces;
he traces the history of his own and of other worlds 'in the dark backward
and abysm of time'; he foresees his own death and the death of his race.
He asks the meaning of it all, and he names the name of God" (p. 237).

The upshot of our discussion, thus, is objective or absolute idealism.

Thus named, the view would appear to be identical with that advocated by Bradley and Bosanquet. And the argument by which it is justified is in principle the argument upon which they chiefly depend—the argument *a contingentia mundi*, as Bosanquet calls it. There are, however, differences of importance between Pringle-Pattison and his idealistic colleagues. They concern the nature of the Absolute and the status of the finite individual, and must in conclusion be made explicit. We begin with the nature of the finite individual, as being logically fundamental in the discussion.

(a) At the outset, it is well to be clear as to the points on which there is agreement here. And these are mainly two. The first is that no finite individual exists "strong in solid singleness," lik a Lucretian atom. On the contrary, it is agreed that in every self there is a universal aspect and that this is essential to its nature. "A self," Pringle-Pattison holds with Bosanquet, "can exist only in vital relation to an objective system of reason and an objective world of ethical observance from which it receives its content, and of which it is, as it were, the focus and depositary. Apart from these it would be a bare point of mere existence. Historically the individual is organic to society . . . it is only by a convenient (though often misleading) abstraction that we can discuss the nature and conduct of the individual apart from the social whole in which he is, as it were, embedded, and of which he appears to be the product. And as the individual is organic to society, so in a still larger philosophical reference the individual is organic to a universal life or world, of which he is similarly a focus, an organ or expression. And he cannot possibly be regarded as self-contained in relation to that life, for such self-containedness would mean sheer emptiness." [15] All of this is common ground between Pringle-Pattison and Bradley and Bosanquet. And on another point, intimately linked with this, there is also agreement—the conviction, namely, "that in the making of souls we have the typical business, or, as one might put it, the central interest

[15] *Ibid.*, pp. 258, 259.

of the universe." [16] This also is common ground. The two points of agreement, then, are: the intrinsically universal nature of the finite individual; and the view of the universe as, in Keat's phrase borrowed by Bosanquet, "a place of soul-making."

But Bradley and Bosanquet, the former perhaps more than the latter, tend to hold that finite selfhood is a vanishing distinction which disappears in the Absolute. Otherwise expressed, they maintain that finite centers of experience possess only adjectival, not a substantival, mode of being. With such a position Pringle-Pattison does not agree, and for the following considerations.

From the point of view of finite individuals themselves, it seems clear that selfhood means uniqueness and that apart from uniqueness selfhood vanishes utterly. It is "a little world of content which . . . constitutes an expression or focalization of the universe which is nowhere exactly repeated." And unless it is at least this, it is nothing at all. Nor does the admittedly universal aspect of individuality in the smallest degree 'impair' its formal distinctness. "The fabric of two minds may, as Professor Bosanquet has suggested, be so nearly identical that the one seems to reduplicate the other rather than to supplement it, and yet they remain two minds to the end of the chapter. Finite centers may 'overlap' indefinitely in content, but, *ex vi termini,* they cannot overlap at all in existence; their very *raison d'être* is to be distinct and, in that sense, separate and exclusive focalizations of a common universe." We must not forget that, after all, it is *we* who act and think; that in all questions of moral causation the person is necessarily a *terminus ad quem* or a *terminus a quo;* that, in short, the existence of the self for the self is an experienced certainty in all fields of experience. If we are to take seriously the principle which has guided us throughout, namely, the principle of the reality of appearances, this fact must be given its due weight in the final

---

[16] *The Idea of God,* p. 260. For Bosanquet this idea is quite central: "The universe is not a place of pleasure, nor even a place compounded of probation and justice; it is, from the highest point of view concerned with finite beings, a place of soul-making. Our best experience carries us without hesitation thus far. . . . It is the moulding and the greatness of souls that we really care for." (*Principle of Individuality and Value,* p. 26.)

reckoning. Nor, on the other hand, when we contemplate the universal aspect of the self, must we overlook the fact that the social whole, which is the sustaining life of its individual members, melts into insignificance if treated as an entity apart from them; taken by itself, 'society' is nothing more than an abstraction hypostatized.[17] The uniqueness of the finite individual, then, cannot be denied or explained away; it is an experienced certainty and is foundational to all thinking and acting, as to the social structure itself.

From this it would appear to follow that the Absolute cannot be so conceived as to negate finite selfhood. From the side of the Absolute itself, the existence of unique finite centers is a fact which is as true and as important as it is from the side of these finite centers. With the denial of the reality of such finite centers the whole superstructure of our experience is robbed of its foundation, and falls utterly; and with it falls the conception of the Absolute, which then becomes a meaningless word. "God becomes an abstraction if separated from the universe of his manifestation, just as the finite subjects have no independent subsistence outside of the universal Life which mediates itself to them in a world of objects. We may conceive God as an experience in which the universe is felt and apprehended as an ultimately harmonious whole; and we must, of course, distinguish between such an infinite experience and the experiences of ourselves and other finite persons. But we have no right to treat either out of relation to the other. We have no right to suppose the possibility of such an infinite experience as a solitary monad—an absolute . . . self-sufficient and entirely independent of the finite intelligences to whom, in the actual world which we know, it freely communicates itself. . . . The infinite in and through the finite, the finite in and through the infinite —this mutual implication is the ultimate fact of the universe as we know it."[18] Nor must the mutuality of the implication be neglected: The infinite is as dependent on the ultimacy of

[17] *The Idea of God*, pp. 264, 265, 266, 288, 291, 292, 193, 296. Cf. the author's contribution to the symposium on the question, "Do finite Individuals possess a Substantival or an Adjectival Mode of Being?" *Proceedings of the Aristotelian Society*, July, 1918.

[18] *The Idea of God*, pp. 314, 315.

the finite as the finite is dependent upon the ultimacy of the infinite.

Herewith we are brought to a view of the nature of the Absolute and its relation to the order of the world different from that upon which absolutists of the type of Bradley and Bosanquet insist.

In the first place, it is clear that the Absolute cannot be a mere timeless system of abstract truth. It is on the basis of our own experiences, and especially our experiences of value, that we make the inference to the Absolute; and these experiences would lose their ultimate significance unless there is in the Absolute something which represents and preserves the facts which in ourselves we call conation and fruition. The Absolute must therefore be conceived as essentially of a teleological nature—and teleological in the sense in which "the ideas of activity and purpose are indispensable" to that nature. Otherwise, there is in it nothing to represent the facts of conation and fruition; it becomes logically indistinguishable from Spinoza's Substance, from a timeless system of abstract truth as at times it appears to be in the thought of Hegel, or even from the purely mechanical ideal of the lower naturalism. And, on the other side, the basal characteristics of our deepest experience are denied reality by such a conception; unless the universe is, in last analysis, an Experience and not merely a system of timeless truth, the verities of our own spiritual life wither away into subjective prejudices which have not the slightest guaranty of permanence or of cosmic significance.

We must hold, then, that the Absolute is a personal experience in the sense, at least, that within that experience the facts of process and ultimate achievement through effort are included as fundamental. In short, we must hold that the Absolute is identical with God as foundational within the deeper drifts of the religious consciousness. "No God, or Absolute, existing in solitary bliss and perfection, but a God who lives in the perpetual giving of himself, who shares the life of his finite creatures, bearing in and with them the whole burden of their finitude, their sinful wanderings and sorrows, and the suffering without which they cannot be made perfect"—such is the God of religion, and such is the Absolute to which we are brought by our argument.[19]

Activity and purpose, however, seem to imply time apart from which they are without precise meaning. And in so far as this is true, time must be retained in any conception we can form of God or the Absolute. Strictly speaking, therefore, we cannot say that the Absolute is timeless. The world of abstract truth, as logic conceives it, is timeless; the time-process is irrelevant to it. But the Absolute is not identical with this; as we have seen, it must be an experience in which our values are conserved and guaranteed. And as such it cannot be timeless; into that experience the time-process must somehow enter.

But this must not be understood to mean that the Absolute or God is in time, that progress is predicable of the Absolute. "From an ultimate metaphysical point of view . . . our conclusion must be that progress is predicable only of the part which can interact with other parts, and, in such interaction, has the nature of the whole to draw upon. It is unintelligible as applied to the whole, and the temporal view of things cannot therefore be ultimate." [20] In God, then, time must be somehow transcended, even though in a sense it remains. How in detail this is possible we cannot, of course, clearly apprehend, and the relation bebetween finite centers and the infinite Person is to us incomprehensible. The infinite experience includes within itself the time-process and finite individuals within that process in a manner which falls beyond our human perspective. The analogy of the work of art may aid us. Here the end is inseparable from the process of its accomplishment, and yet the end is not the final stage which succeeds and supplants its predecessors, but is, rather, the meaning and spirit of the whole.[21] We may say that the Absolute or God is, in a somewhat analogous manner,

[19] Contrast the views of Bradley and Bosanquet on the inherent contradiction involved in religious experience and the necessity of transcending it (*supra*, pp. 98, 109, 140). Cf. Bradley, *Ethical Studies, Concluding Remarks; Appearance and Reality*, pp. 436-464; and *Essays on Truth and Reality*, Chapter XV; Bosanquet, *The Value and Destiny of the Individual*, Lecture VIII.

[20] *The Idea of God*, p. 383; cf. the whole of Lecture XIX.

[21] Cf. *Ibid.*, pp. 361 ff.

inseparable from the time-process and yet falls beyond it as the meaning or spirit of it—is present in it only as its sustaining and inclusive principle. In other words, we may say that God or the Absolute though not timeless is nevertheless eternal —the everlasting which perdures through time.[22] But in this emphasis upon the eternity of God, important as it is for metaphysics, the still more important point must not be forgotten—namely, that in the experience of the Absolute the time-process must in some significant fashion be retained "if our life experience is not to be deprived of all meaning and value. The temporal process is not simply non-existent from the Absolute point of view; it is not a mere illusion, any more than the existence of the finite world, of which, indeed, it is the characteristic form and expression . . . the existence of that world must represent a necessity of the divine nature and must possess a value for the divine experience. Hence the time-process must enter somehow into that experience." [23] But precisely how this is to be remains for us incomprehensible in detail.

[22] Compare Green's view of "eternal" consciousness (*supra*, pp. 45-46), and Bradley's criticism of it there cited.

[23] *The Idea of God*, p. 363.

CHAPTER VII

JAMES WARD (1843-1925)

As we have seen in the preceding chapter, there are two closely related, though clearly distinguishable, emphases in the argument of Pringle-Pattison—emphases which in his own opinion mark the major differences between his type of idealism and that of his more absolutistic colleagues. These emphases are: the ultimate significance of human values, especially moral values, for an interpretation of reality; and the substantival nature of the finite individual. The first emphasis is found in Bradley and Bosanquet, who are by no means content to rest the argument for idealism on purely epistemological considerations but are quite critical of abstract 'intellectualism.' In the argument of Pringle-Pattison, however, this emphasis is more insistently dwelt upon, and its importance for an idealistic view of the world is more pointedly set forth. In his second emphasis Pringle-Pattison departs more or less radically from the absolutists and directs attention to a thesis which they in principle tend to deny. Here, as he himself observes, one comes upon the parting of the ways between his own view of reality and theirs. For them, finite individuality as such is appearance and error and is transmuted in the Absolute; for him, finite individuality must be said to have reality in its own right—a right so fundamental and tenacious that the conception of the Absolute must be modified to accommodate it.

The first of these two emphases has received even more detailed exposition at the hands of W. R. Sorley (b. 1855), Knightbridge Professor of Moral Philosophy in Cambridge University. As the title of his Gifford Lectures indicates,[1] they are concerned exclusively with the question as to whether the facts of morality and the principles of ethics have any bearing—and if

---

[1] *Moral Values and the Idea of God* (1919). The lectures were delivered at the University of Aberdeen in 1914 and 1915.

so what bearing—on our conception of ultimate reality. And his answer to that question is that values are fundamental to our conception of reality and in the end force us to accept an idealistic, even a theistic, view of the world.

The tenor of Sorley's argument is summarily stated in a passage which he quotes, for that purpose, from Rashdall: "An absolute Moral Law or moral ideal cannot exist *in* material things. And it does not exist in the mind of this or that individual. Only if we believe in the existence of a Mind for which the true moral ideal is already in some sense real, a Mind which is the source of whatever is true in our own moral judgments, can we rationally think of the moral ideal as no less real than the world itself. Only so can we believe in an absolute standard of right and wrong, which is as independent of this or that man's actual ideas and actual desires as the facts of material nature. The belief in God, though not (like the belief in a real and an active self) a postulate of there being any such thing as Morality at all, is the logical presupposition of an 'objective' or absolute Morality. A moral ideal can exist nowhere and 'nohow but in a mind; an absolute moral ideal can exist only in a Mind from which all reality is derived. Our moral ideal can only claim objective validity in so far as it can rationally be regarded as the revelation of a moral ideal eternally existing in the mind of God." [2]

Developing his argument in support of this general position, Sorley emphasizes and defends the following theses: that moral values attach only to persons; that moral values constitute a system and, so, a moral order; that this moral order is 'objective,' that is, not relative to finite persons; that finite persons belong to a causal order by virtue of their bodily existence; that the moral order and the causal order (the order of nature) are ultimately aspects of one and the same order, which is the world-order; that values are thus inherent in the world-order as constituent elements; and that, consequently, this world-order can be conceived only as a Mind in which values find their source and conservation. In the development of these

[2] *Moral Values and the Idea of God*, p. 351. The passage is quoted from H. Rashdall, *The Theory of Good and Evil* (1907), Vol. II, p. 212.

theses, however, Sorley adds nothing in principle to the "higher naturalism" of Pringle-Pattison. A detailed statement of Sorley's formulation may therefore be omitted here. This omission is all the more permissible, since Sorley himself has given two quite adequate summaries in readily accessible texts.[3]

In his insistence upon a supreme Mind or God as the ground of reality, however, Sorley does not wish to deny freedom and initiative to finite individuals. On the contrary, he urges that only on the basis of the postulate of freedom is it possible to explain how it is that finite persons, in whom alone moral values are progressively realized, do as a matter of historical fact realize them so imperfectly and make such slow and halting progress in their efforts to realize them. Freedom of the finite individual, thus, is for Sorley a basal tenet and he would so define the conception of God as to make room for it. In this, again, he is in essential agreement with Pringle-Pattison. Reality cannot be identified with the Absolute as conceived by Bradley and Bosanquet; it is, rather, a system characterized by purpose, but a purpose which is gradually reproduced through the activity of free human selves, who are substantival in nature—who are, that is, free agents within the system and not to be dissolved or merged into mere adjectival aspects of it.

This emphasis upon the substantival nature of the finite individual is carried much farther in the systems of James Ward and J. E. McTaggart. The remaining part of the present chapter will be devoted to a statement of Ward's formulation, and the chapter following to that of McTaggart.

Ward's argument falls into two main parts. The first undertakes to establish the general idealistic, or, as he prefers to call it, the spiritualistic, view of the world. The second seeks to ascertain what we can know, or reasonably believe, concerning the constitution of the world interpreted throughout and strictly in terms of mind. Our summary statement of the argument will therefore follow this division.[4]

[3] These may be found in *Moral Values and the Idea of God*, Lecture XX; and *Contemporary British Philosophy* (ed. by J. H. Muirhead), Second Series, pp. 247 ff.

[4] The first part of the argument is presented in the first series of Ward's Gifford Lectures, *Naturalism and Agnosticism* (1899); fourth edition

1. NATURALISM, DUALISM, AND SPIRITUALISM

The basal postulates in the argument in support of the priority of spirit are three. (a) Naturalism is a wholly inadequate, because abstract view of the world. (b) A dualistic view of reality as composed of two distinct types of being, namely, mind and matter, is in the end untenable. (c) Only a monistic view of reality is permissible, and a monism interpreted in terms of mind; Nature, therefore, is Spirit. The reasons for these three postulates constitute the main body of the argument for the spiritualistic view of the world.

(a) In any intelligent discussion of the claims of naturalism, clearness as to what naturalism is, is, of course, indispensable. Naturalism is not science; it is, rather, a philosophy professedly built on science. It is a general view of the world supposedly based on the results of the natural sciences, and especially the science of physics. Founding itself on these results, naturalism undertakes to subordinate spirit to matter and to make ultimate principles of the laws of matter and motion. On careful analysis, naturalism turns out to be a complex theory made up of three subordinate theories: (i) that nature is a single vast mechanism; (ii) that evolution is simply the process through which this mechanism works itself out in detail; and (iii) that mental phenomena may on occasion accompany, but may never determine, the movements and interactions of different parts of the machine.

A critical examination of naturalism, then, resolves itself into an evaluation of the claims of these three theories. Detailed scrutiny discloses that none of the three is tenable, and we must therefore conclude that naturalism cannot stand. The major considerations in support of this conclusion are the following.

(i) The fundamental, and fatal, objection to the mechanical

(1915). These lectures were delivered at the University of Aberdeen during the years 1896-1898. The second part of the argument is given in the second series, *The Realm of Ends or Pluralism and Theism* (1911); third edition (1920), delivered at the University of St. Andrews during the years 1907-1910. The following statement of the argument is based upon these two works.

Ward's other writings include: *Psychological Principles* (1918); second edition (1920); *A Study of Kant* (1922); and the very important article, "Psychology," in the *Encyclopaedia Britannica* (eleventh edition, Vol. XXII).

theory of nature is that it is based upon the false assumption that the concepts of the natural sciences set before us what verily is and happens. It is supposed that the laws of matter and motion, the mechanical formulae of abstract dynamics, or molar and molecular mechanics, when once carefully defined, disclose the complete nature of existing things. These laws are assumed to be universal, to hold of all events in the universe, and to express the ultimate nature of all events. But this assumption is entirely erroneous. The conceptions of the natural sciences are not adequate descriptions of events. On the contrary, they are abstractions from events—generalizations, that is, which are arrived at through the process of omitting from consideration many of the concrete and factual aspects of events. Of course, these conceptions have scientific value, and as used by the scientist they are in no way open to criticism. They may be allowed to stand so long as they are taken for what they are, namely, convenient devices whereby the human mind can deal with certain aspects of its environment. But naturalism takes them for much more than this. It takes them to be adequate, and hence ultimate, accounts of what exists, including organisms and the mind of man. And precisely in this assumption lies its fatal weakness. In the end this assumption is nothing more significant than an expression of the tendency of the human mind to give objective significance to its own abstractions—a tendency which is none the less unjustifiable because it is quite common. This tendency alone is at the bottom of the mechanical theory of nature and gives it support. That theory, therefore, is without secure foundation and must be abandoned.[5]

(ii) In so far as the postulate that cosmic evolution can be deduced from mechanical principles is simply an application of the mechanical theory to the details of the cosmic process the objections against the mechanical theory hold of it directly. It, then, is nothing more significant than are the hypostatized

[5] The points here summarily and dogmatically set down are developed by Ward at length and with a wealth of illustrative detail in the first six lectures, Part I, of *Naturalism and Agnosticism*. But these details cannot here be reproduced, and must be sought there. Though doing poor justice to Ward's complete account, the above summary has at least the advantage of focusing attention on the crucial issue in the discussion. Compare the view of William James on what he calls "vicious intellectualism."

abstractions on which it is based. Thus conceived, evolution would indeed give us change, "but only change of motion, change of grouping of unchangeable elements, unchangeable because utterly devoid of qualitative diversity or internal character. Progress, development, history, meaning—of these there would be nothing. It is obviously impossible to get such conceptions out of space, time, and mass, as quantities; or out of any relations between them, for these in turn are only quantities. We have only the night—to appropriate a *mot* of Hegel's—when all cows are black." [6] To get meaning into the evolutionary process, a teleological factor must be introduced; and this factor is entirely inconsistent with the mechanical theory. If evolution is to mean more than merely a series of quantitative changes without qualitative differences, it is not deducible from bare mechanical principles; unless it means more than this it has no application to the world of concrete fact.

For the world of concrete fact is obviously a world of different levels, and throughout it there are teleological factors which defy the leveling-down process involved in the mechanical view of evolution. This world of concrete fact "is only intelligible to us so far as we can regard it as a world of individuals, a world full of purpose and of adaptations, a world to which such notions as worth, progress, and perfection are applicable." But the mechanical view of evolution, strictly interpreted and rigorously applied, would eliminate from the world all of these conceptions. Furthermore, the concrete world of fact presents "an ascending order of complexity and value—physical, biological, psychological, social" and the like. And "as we make this ascent we have at every advance to take up new conceptions: the facts of biology cannot be expressed in purely physical terms; psychology will not resolve into biology nor sociology into psychology." [7] But the mechanical view of evolution would, if followed to its logical conclusion, reduce all of these to the dead level of purely quantitative concepts—matter and motion, mass and energy. One who is not willing to do injustice to the most obvious facts

[6] *Naturalism and Agnosticism*, p. 240. All references are to the fourth edition of this work.

[7] *Ibid.*, pp. 240 and 241. Compare Pringle-Pattison's discussion of the 'lower' and 'higher' naturalism in *The Idea of God*, Lecture V.

of experience, then, cannot accept the view which interprets cosmic evolution in terms exclusively of mechanical principles.

When evolution is taken in the narrower and more definite sense of biological evolution, the impossibility of its being reduced to mechanical principles becomes quite apparent. The teleological factor in this sort of evolution is obvious, since apart from it the notions of the 'good' or 'welfare' of the organism and the 'struggle' for existence—notions which are fundamental in the formulation of the larger conception—utterly lack intelligibility. Nor can these notions be translated into mere mechanical concepts; they are empty words unless linked with mind. "Correlated with mind these characteristics are intelligible; but to interpret them literally in terms of physical interaction, and apart from mind, is surely impossible. However we resolve the problem as to the connexion of mind and matter, it is then, we may conclude, unquestionably a simplification to infer that wherever a material system is organised for self-maintenance, growth and reproduction, as an individual in touch with an environment, that system has a psychical as well as a material aspect." [8]

This advocacy of the view that mind is coextensive with life must not, however, be misinterpreted. It is not intended to assert that a clear prevision of ends is assumed to be characteristic of all living forms. It asserts only that, since in organic evolution there are always involved the principles of self-conservation and of subjective or hedonic selection and since these principles imply the existence of mind in some sense, wherever there is life there must be mind.[9] Only where there is an impulse towards self-maintenance and betterment, towards the satisfaction of needs, appetites, or desires, is there any meaning in the notion of a struggle to survive. This impulse presupposes conscious, or at

[8] *Naturalism and Agnosticism,* p. 279.

[9] The principle of self-conservation is the principle of "the conservation of the self by the self," which "presupposes the will to live and the pain of dying." (Cf. *Naturalism and Agnosticism,* p. 285, and the Index.)

The principle of hedonic selection is the fact "that, out of all the manifold changes of sensory presentation which a given individual experiences, only a few are the occasion of such decided feeling as to become objects of possible appetite or aversion." (Cf. *Encyclopaedia Britannica,* eleventh edition, article entitled "Psychology.")

least sentient, activity—psychical activity, in a word, as distinct from physical passivity and inertness. And this is what is intended by the assertion, as well as the ground for the assertion, that mind is concomitant with life.

Biological evolution, thus, is no merely mechanical process. It involves teleological factors, and these imply "not a nondescript force called vital, but a psychical something endowed with feeling and will." [10] We may also conclude that cosmic evolution, in so far as such evolution may be said to have any meaning at all, must likewise involve an indwelling Life and Mind. For, as we have already noted, if evolution is to mean anything more than purely quantitative changes without qualitative differences, it must involve a teleological factor; and we now see that teleology, where we unmistakably have it, is inseparably linked with life and mind. Thus, when confronted by ascertainable fact, the mechanical view of evolution breaks down; theoretically, it is a vacuous concept.

(iii) The third postulate of naturalism, namely epiphenomenalism, is likewise untenable; and on this side naturalism again fails. We are now to see how this is so.

In the first place, it should be clearly noted that epiphenomenalism is the only theory of the relation between mind and body which is open to the naturalist—unless, that is, he is willing to commit himself to the absurdities of materialism.[11] He cannot maintain a parallelism between the two, and at the same time hold on to an absolute separation of them. The view that they are fundamentally disparate renders impossible any intelligible explanation of their parallelism. What is left to him, therefore, is the doctrine of epiphenomenalism—the doctrine, namely, that the psychical series is a 'collateral product' of the physical series, but not causally connected with it. For naturalism holds to the mechanical view of nature, which postulates a complete and rigorous concatenation of all physical changes in one vast undeviating process; it cannot therefore admit any causal inter-

[10] *Naturalism and Agnosticism,* p. 296.

[11] In his discussion Ward does not consider in detail the claims of materialism. He dismisses it as a theory of mind which is absurd on its face, and which scientists themselves have given up. Mind, he thinks, can never be identified with matter.

action between the physical and psychical (non-physical). So naturalism must hold, and if consistent does hold, that the physical series is a closed causal order and that the mental series accompanies it (where it does) as a succession of shadows.

This view is untenable, however, for the following reasons. In the first place, it is strictly self-contradictory; it at once affirms and denies a causal relation between the physical and the mental series. Constant coexistence and correspondence imply a causal connection of some description, but a causal connection is wholly out of keeping with the naturalistic assumption. If a causal relation is denied, then parallelism between the two series fails; if a causal relation is affirmed, then the mechanical principle is abandoned. Nor can one escape the dilemma through the application of the adjective 'epiphenomenal' to the mental series. "To say that consciousness is an *aura* or epiphenomenon of the organism, which itself is but a mechanical automaton, is to shirk the difficulty, not to face it. If mental states are not simply products of material conditions, then matter must interact with something else to produce them. The clock will not sound in a vacuum nor cast shadows in the dark." [12]

In the second place, this view if accepted renders mind useless in the evolutionary process, since by hypothesis the psychical series is absolutely excluded from efficient participation in the physical series. And here, once more, naturalism is at variance with itself. For throughout its exposition of biological evolution it assumes, and must assume, that mind *is* an efficient factor in the struggle for existence. It is everywhere taken for granted that instincts, habits, and inclinations are factors equally as potent as anatomical structure or physiological processes. It is assumed, not only that there is a constant concomitance between the physical and the psychical series, but also that the concomitance is teleological. But such an assumption must be false if the epiphenomenalistic view of mind is to be retained. For on this view we must say, if we are consistent, that "the physical world is a complete whole in itself, and goes along together by itself"; that "the very same laws fundamentally, that determine the varying motions of the solar system, bring together from the

[12] *Naturalism and Agnosticism*, pp. 331-332.

four corners of the earth the molecules that from time to time join in the dance we know as the brain of a Dante creating immortal verse, or as the brain of a Borgia teeming with unheard of crimes"; and that "the presence of mental epiphenomena is as irrelevant and immaterial to the one result as is their absence to the other."

The apparent participation of mind in the course of the physical series as a determining factor is, thus, an illusion. And here, once more and finally, naturalism is at variance with itself. Even on the basis of its principles the appearance of this illusion is inexplicable. For illusory experience obviously implies a counterpart experience by which its illusory character is made manifest; but the epiphenomenalistic assumption excludes precisely the sort of experience—namely, participation by mind in the physical series—on the basis of which its claim to participation in that series is shown to be illusory. If the epiphenomenalistic view of mind is true, then the fact that it is known to be true is an inexplicable mystery; knowledge that it is true is inconsistent with its being true.[13]

Thus on detailed examination, the three postulates which together make up the complex theory of naturalism turn out to be incoherent and untenable. Naturalism must consequently be surrendered. It defies again and again the basic canon of thought "that to understand the world as a whole we must take it as a whole." On this rock it is in the end hopelessly wrecked. It resolves qualities into quantities and discards all relations except the mathematical; these it makes logically fundamental. That it is a fascinating ideal there is, of course, no question; it seems to afford us the unity and permanence of being without mystery, and so to give us certainty freed from doubt. "But, alas, for the vanity of human dreams! though everything that is has quantity, has spatial and temporal relations, there is nothing that entirely consists of these." Everywhere in the concrete world in which we live and struggle we find variety and diversity; nowhere do we find anything which suggests its ultimate resolution into homogeneous mass-points mechanically interconnected. And it is for this reason we must hold the naturalistic philosophy to be the

[13] Cf. *Naturalism and Agnosticism*, pp. 335 ff.

merest abstraction and its claims to be illusory. Within the
scheme of things which it offers us there is, to be sure, exactness
and precision; but there is in it no true unity and no meaning,
for these things are dependent on spirit, and spirit is utterly
banished.

(b) From the disastrous consequences of naturalism a way of
escape must be found—unless, that is, we are willing to abide in
mere confusion and a view of things that gives the lie to our
direct experience. Dualism has at times been proposed as a way
out, and we are now to inquire whether it is available.

As every one knows, the metaphysics of Descartes is founded
on a sharp dualism between things mental and things material,
res cogitantes and *res extensae;* and this dualism has been a
prolific source of problems for philosophers since. The breach
between the two substances, emphasized by Descartes, was
speedily widened by the development of the sciences—the natural
sciences on the one side and psychology on the other. For the
natural scientist, the problem was to get from matter to mind;
and the solution attempted by naturalism through the hypothesis
of psycho-physical parallelism was, as we have just seen, highly
defective and unsatisfactory. For the psychologist, the problem
was to get from mind to matter, the problem of external perception.

In British thought from Locke to Reid the problem remained
unresolved: Locke slyly remarked that it seemed "not to want
difficulty"; Hume boldly declared it to be insoluble, and fell
into skepticism; Berkeley thought to resolve it by denying Descartes's outer circle of things, and escaped solipsism only through
an inconsistency; Reid took refuge in outer things, but avoided
the Cartesian inner circle of ideas only by shutting his eyes to it.
Meanwhile, the rationalistic thinkers of the Continent looked to
"clear and distinct conceptions" for a solution of the difficulty;
but this procedure presently proved futile, and its futility became
even evident when Wolff finally made the abstract law of contradiction the touchstone of philosophy. With Kant, however,
the problem assumed a new status, and he first set philosophical
speculation on the road to its solution.

In his three *Critiques*, Kant turns the problem of external perception into the wider one of the nature of experience. And his major contribution to the solution of the problem thus modified lies in his insistence on the essential duality in unity of subject and object. In the details of Kant's analysis we are not here interested; our only concern is with his insistence on this basal feature of experience and the significance of it for the solution of the problem before us.

First, we must note that his emphasis is sound in principle. The proof of his thesis which Kant himself offers may in some of its details be legitimately called in question; but in the main it stands against criticism. Kant's analysis aside, however, one may readily show that, when concretely considered, experience is a duality in unity and cannot be dismembered into two independent halves. Three characteristics of experience prove this: (i) range in time, (ii) familiarity or expertness, and (iii) intellective synthesis.

(i) That experience possesses a range in time is clear enough—memory is precisely that, and memory is a basal fact. Without it, experience simply would not be experience as we know it. But memory is both subjective and objective at once. What we remember is our own past experience, and we can remember nothing else; on the other side, what we remember is the concrete 'filling' or content of experience. Memory or range of experience in time, therefore, exemplifies the essential duality of experience. But the duality implies the unity and is meaningless apart from it; time as lived belongs neither to the subject apart from object, nor to object apart from subject, but to both at once and in their interdependence.

(ii) Again, experience is a developing familiarity with the nature of objects and expertness in dealing with them. And here, once more, we note the interplay of subject and object in inseparable union and yet in irresolvable duality, for objects are relative to subject, and apart from subject they have no meaning. They cannot be explained in terms of any such abstraction as the *uniformity of nature* which means, and can mean, only the uniformity of experience. Objects are selected by the subject, and the selection is basal within them. But objects are not made by the subject; they are appropriated by it, so to say, through the very process by which it grows to definiteness and uniqueness. "This increasing definiteness reveals no trace of unrelated and unrelatable elements that can only be conceived apart, but shows rather a duality in unity which we may fitly describe as an organic whole." [14]

(iii) Finally, there is another type of duality in experience disclosed in the contrast between individual and collective (or universal) experience, which results from the fact of intersubjective intercourse among individuals. This duality involves unity, however, and is impossible apart from it, since there must be an intellective synthesis which first makes intersubjective intercourse possible at all. Taking experience as individual on the one side and universal on the other, we have four terms to deal with. We have "the subject and object of individual or perceptual experience, and the subject and object of universal or conceptual experience; and we have to ascertain the relation of the second pair to the first."

So far as the objects are concerned, it is clear that there is no discontinuity between them and that the object of universal or conceptual experience is an extension of the object of individual or perceptual experience. Without the content which immediate experience contributes, the universal forms are wholly empty. "It would seem, then, that as regards objects there is no discontinuity between universal and individual experience, since the intellectual form which characterises the one consists exclusively in establishing relations within the concrete real that constitutes the other. Relations necessarily presuppose *fundamenta;* and though we cannot advance to universal experience without relations, there is nothing but these *fundamenta* of individual experience to advance from."

But what of the relation between the subject of individual experience and the subject of universal experience? Here, once again, the answer is not far to seek. "The subject of universal experience is not numerically distinct from the subject of individual experience; but is this same subject advanced to the level of self-consciousness, and so participating in all that is com-

[14] *Naturalism and Agnosticism,* p. 456. Compare Bradley's account of the genesis of the relational consciousness.

municable, that is, in all that is intelligible, in the experience of other self-conscious subjects. Universal experience is not distinct from all subjects, but common to all intelligents, peculiar to none." [15]

Thus throughout all experience there is unity in duality, duality in unity. The subject and object of universal experience are continuous with the subject and object of individual experience; and within individual experience, subject and object are indissolubly joined but never blankly identical. Experience, in short, is one and dual. "What a subject without objects, or what objects without a subject, would be, is indeed, as we are often told, unknowable; for in truth the knowledge of either apart is a contradiction." [16] So much seems clear.

From this it follows that analysis cannot possibly penetrate beyond this characteristic of experience; indeed, it underlies all of our analyses and interpretations. It is ultimate, and for it there can be no explanation. Furthermore, the demand for its explanation may be taken as sufficient evidence that the facts have been misconceived. Any theory, therefore, which calls for an explanation of this aspect of experience may justly be held suspect; such a theory is clearly guilty of doing violence to the dual unity of experience, by abstracting the aspects and treating them as separate wholes.

All forms of dualism involve precisely this abstraction, and it is for this reason that in the end they must all be set aside. They seek to analyze the subject-object relationship, forgetting that this relationship is unique and not reducible. They fall into the absurdity of seeking for a connection between correlatives, as if the correlatives were absolute terms. Ferrier has put the point as concisely as any one: "Our intercourse with the external universe was the given whole with which we had to deal. The older philosophers divided this given whole into the external universe on the one hand, and our perception of it on the other; but they

[15] *Naturalism and Agnosticism,* pp. 471, 476-477, 489. The point in the last quotation is illustrated by the author (pp. 480-487) by an analysis of the category of causation, which, he maintains, we owe "to the interaction of active subjects with their environment, and to their intercourse with each other."

[16] *Ibid.,* p. 404. Compare Ferrier's view that subject-object is the primary fact of cognition.

were unable to show how these two, the objective and the subjective, could again be understood to coalesce. Like magicians with but half the powers of sorcery, they had spoken the dissolving spell which severed man's mind from the universe; but they were unable to articulate the binding word which again might bring them into union. It was reserved for the speculation of a later day to utter this word. And this it did by admitting *in limine* the distinction; but, at the same time, by showing that *each* of the divided members again resolves itself into *both* the factors, into which the original whole was separated; and that in this way the distinction undoes itself. . . . [But] unless we are able to think two things *as two* and separated from each other, it is vain and unreasonable to ask how they become one. . . . In the same way, with respect to the question in hand. There is not a subjective *and* objective before us, but there is what we find to be an indivisible subjective-objective, when we commence by regarding what we imagined to be the pure subjective, and there is what we find to be an indivisible subjective-objective also, when we commence by regarding what we imagined to be the pure objective. So that the question respecting the nature of the connexion between the subjective and the objective comes to be either this, What is the nature of the connexion between two subjective-objectives (but this is not the question to which an answer was wished), or else this, What is the nature of the connexion *between one* thing, one thing which no effort of thought can construe as really two?" [17]

Starting from dualism, then, we can never arrive at experience. The unity which is basal within experience and apart from which experience simply does not exist is by dualism denied, and it cannot by dualism be restored. But we can see how dualism naturally arises through a process of illegitimate abstraction within experience. The steps in this process may be briefly noted in conclusion of the refutation of the claims of dualism.

These steps are chiefly three: the notion of the trans-subjective; the hypothesis of introjection; and the reification of abstractions.

---

[17] *Ibid.*, pp. 491-492; the italics are as given. The passage is quoted from Ferrier, *Works,* Vol. III, pp. 278-284. Cf. above, pp. 24 ff.

(i) The notion of the trans-subjective, developing as the consequence of intersubjective intercourse, is the conception of an object which is taken as independent of any and all observers. The sun as trans-subjective object, for example, is not the sun of any given observer, my sun or yours, but the sun supposedly out of relation to all observers; it is *the* sun, as distinguished from the several impressions of several observers. The reasoning by which the conception of such an object is arrived at is essentially as follows: Since the sun (or any object) is independent of all observers taken severally, it is and remains an object independent of them taken collectively. This is the first step towards dualism.

(ii) The second step is introjection. The essence of introjection consists, first, in assuming that the experiences of others are distinct from mine; and, second, in assuming that their experiences are in them in the form of sensations, perceptions, and other 'internal states'—of the sun in my environment, for example—I say there is a perception in them. And since these assumptions are by others applied to me, I naturally apply them to myself and say that the sun and my perception of the sun are quite distinct. Thus is the distinction between 'internal states' and 'external objects' emphasized, and with it dualism is essentially complete.

(iii) The full-blown theory emerges when these distinctions are converted into separate entities. Then the abstractions are reified; two quite distinct worlds are set over against each other, namely, the internal or subjective and the external or objective, and each is regarded as independent of the other. Hereupon we are committed to an out-and-out dualism, and to the insoluble problems it brings.

It should be easy to see, however, that this whole process is throughout erroneous. In the first place, there is no warrant for concluding that because an object is independent of any and every *particular* subject it is therefore independent of any subject. "Such reasoning is about on a par with maintaining that the British House of Commons is an estate of the realm independent of each individual member and that therefore it might be addressed from the throne, for instance, though there were no members." [18] The process of interjection is also fallacious. It first applies to the experience of my fellows' conceptions which have no counterpart in my own, and then it reflects back into my own experience the abstraction thus derived. "Thus it comes about that instead of construing others' experience exactly and precisely on the lines of our own,—as a duality of subject and object,—we are induced to misconstrue our own experience on the lines of a false but highly plausible assumption as to others' experience, which actually contradicts our own." [19] And the reification of abstractions is merely the final and inevitable step in this erroneous procedure. It is but the implications of the whole process of abstraction made fully explicit, and of course it falls with the substructure on which it solely rests.

The conclusion of the whole matter, then, is that dualism is not available as the way out of the difficulties raised by naturalism. It springs from an abstract handling of experience; sunders its essential unity into two disparate parts, and then treats them as wholly separate and distinct entities. Furthermore, in its every step it runs counter to the very experience with which it would deal. It is at once abstract and futile—futile because abstract. Monism therefore alone remains, and we are now to inquire what sort of monism is in the end acceptable.

(c) The essential characteristic of experience we have found to be duality in unity, and this can neither be denied nor explained; it is for us ultimate. Dualism fails because it is incompatible with the unity; naturalistic monism or materialism fails because it is incompatible with the duality. Some thinkers have supposed that they might take refuge in an agnostic or neutral monism, which maintains that reality in the end is unknown and unknowable, and that it is neutral as regards matter and mind— that it is not more matter than mind, not more subject than object. Such a neutral monism, however, is quite unstable and gives no final resting place for theory. The Unknown, even though written with an initial capital, is too hazy a notion to furnish ground for a stable system; it is not, and cannot be, a principle of explanation. Furthermore, strict neutrality as regards

[18] *Naturalism and Agnosticism,* p. 463.
[19] *Ibid.,* p. 464; cf. p. 608.

the significance of mind and matter cannot be maintained in its name; for the question: Which of the two is better known? will not down. However we settle it the result is bound to affect our theory. In point of fact the advocates of this view, preferring calculability to intelligibility, simplification to meaning, have leaned to the materialistic side. With the varying pressure of social issues, they have oscillated between an unmediated dualism and a pronounced materialism, the obscurity of the conception of the unknowable only serving to cover their vacillations. But the basal inconsistency in the view is no less fatal because overlooked by the advocates of the view.

If dualism is unsound, as we have reason to hold it is, there seems to be no agnostic resting place between materialism and spiritualism. And it is an interesting historical fact that at least some of the advocates of agnostic monism have shown signs of moving in the direction of spiritualism.[20] This drift is significant as well as interesting. It indicates that an honest and intelligent attempt to face the facts necessarily leads one away from a materialistic, and towards a spiritualistic, view of nature. How this is so we must next inquire.

Nature, as science conceives it, may be described as a system involving invariable conformity to law. Knowledge of nature is an indispensable means to its control, and upon that control human welfare and progress in large measure depend. Such knowledge is, therefore, teleological, as truly as are other practical pursuits and achievements of human activity. But what of the conception of nature? It is not in any sense an axiom, which it would be absurd to deny; it is neither self-evident nor a deduction from anything that is self-evident. Nor, again, is it given to us as a brute fact. Experience of a sort would be possible without it; purely formal knowledge, such as that of logic or mathematics, is independent of it. The conception is entirely hypothetical, admitting of question and awaiting verification. Yet it seems to be an indispensable hypothesis; without it scientific experience, at any rate, is impossible. Why must we assume it, and whence is it derived? The answer to this question is in the

[20] See the author's account of Huxley's drift in this direction, *Naturalism and Agnosticism,* p. 500 ff.

end grounded on what we ourselves are—self-conscious, self-determining individuals. And this must be shown at some length.

There are three basal characteristics or elements involved in the conception of nature, namely unity, causality, and regularity. These are inherent in the structure of nature, conceived as a systematic unity subject to invariable law. We are now to see that each of these is intimately bound up with the self-activity of subjects.

Before passing to these considerations, however, two points in connection with the self-activity of the subject should be emphasized. The first is that such self-activity is a basal fact of experience; it is of the essence of the subject-object relation. One may indeed find difficulty in giving accurate statement of the conditions of the fact; but the fact itself cannot be denied, and this for our present purpose is sufficient. The second point to be noted is that this activity is not merely intellective or perceptive; it is also, and perhaps primarily, a practical or conative activity. However much for purposes of exposition we may abstract intellection from volition, we cannot keep them separate; they are indissolubly linked in fact, and this must be borne in mind through the following discussion. With these two characteristics of the self-activity of subjects premised,[21] we may pass on to the main considerations before us.

(i) The unity of nature, as we have already seen in principle, is the ideal counterpart of the actual unity of each individual experience—an ideal towards which we first advance when inter-subjective intercourse and reasoning begin, and which becomes clearer and more distinct as mythological explanation gives way to scientific. We have also seen, in our discussion of the claims of dualism, that experience is fundamentally monistic. The point now to be stressed is that this monism must be interpreted ideal-istically, since all that is formative in experience is primarily due to the activity of the subject. However advanced or however elementary the experience may be, "The one activity complexly

[21] For the author's detailed justification of the points here stated the reader should turn to the Index of *Naturalism and Agnosticism* and the passages there noted, especially p. 422 ff. and 532 ff.

expressed as 'I think, I feel, I do' is implied throughout, connecting all that is presented or presentable with the one subjective centre." And from this it follows directly that the system of nature must be interpreted idealistically. For "In so far as Nature and *possible* experience are one and the same, what holds of possible experience will hold of Nature, because it holds of experience." But unless nature is identified with experience, actual or possible, then it is for us meaningless. The immanence of experience is thus absolute; it is on this ground, and on this ground alone, that we say all phenomena exist in one nature and in complete community in one continuous space and one continuous time. The unity of nature, therefore, is grounded in the activity of subject.[22]

(ii) The causal relation, likewise, is based on the same foundation. We do not find causality in the relation between one objective situation and another, between sunshine and the melting snow, for instance, or between sunshine and the hardening clay. In such relations there is no experience of cause and effect but only, as Hume urged, spatial and temporal proximity. To transform spatial and temporal proximity into the notion of causality, we must import into them the notions of activity and passivity; and this we do only by analogical reasoning on the basis of our experience. The experience of intersubjective intercourse yields a complete knowledge of causal efficiency. "I know that my fellowman is determined or influenced by my action, as I, in turn, am determined or influenced by his. Society, civilisation, and science itself are the result of such interaction."[23] But so far as the bare events of the physical environment are concerned, there is no evidence of *inter*-action, and the application of the notion of causality is dubious; if it is applied, the physical environment is in principle conceived "as primitive man does when he personifies sun and moon, winds and stream, fire and pestilence." And in the universal experience of science, where objective changes are regarded solely in relation to each other,

[22] Cf. *Naturalism and Agnosticism*, pp. 525-526. The author refers here to Kant's *Prolegomena*, section 36. Compare the argument of Green (*supra*, pp. 47 ff).

[23] *Naturalism and Agnosticism*, p. 529.

there is no evidence of action at all; indeed, ideally there can be no action here. "The whole is one thing and the procession of its changes one continuous event." In the scientific scheme, therefore, there is no causation strictly so-called; there are here no efficient causes. There may indeed be causal uniformity, ordered sequences of events; but this is quite a different conception. Efficient causation is absent. This does not mean, however, that efficient causes are denied by science; it means only that the scientific scheme of the world is so abstract that efficient causes are *ab initio* excluded from it. And here we have further evidence of the inadequacy of naturalism as a philosophy, which forgets the abstract nature of scientific concepts and supposes that science extirpates the notion of efficient causation root and branch.

(iii) Finally, the regularity of nature is postulated by mind and is meaningless apart from it. The laws of nature are at times interpreted as if they were self-existent entities "binding nature fast in fate." This interpretation, however, overlooks the very pertinent fact that law is of an essentially teleological character —and is but another example of the short-sightedness of the naturalistic view of the world. If we do not find efficient causes among our data, neither do we find laws among them. Genetically, the conception of law is of course the outcome of social coöperation, of intersubjective intercourse; and this holds true of the conception, whether as civil or as scientific law.

Society as a lawful order is possible only where there is a common understanding and a common purpose; nature as a lawful order is possible only where there is an accord between thinking and being. In each case the laws are postulates, and in each case the conditions are imposed by mind. If there is to be accord between thinking and being—to turn our attention at once to the point of basal interest in the present context—then being must be an object of possible experience; and the conditions of possible experience are in us who know, not in' the things known or to be known. Thus the scientific ideal of orderly and systematic knowledge, in which every item has its place by virtue of universal and necessary laws, is conditioned by subject. The whole notion of universal and necessary laws of nature is a postulate; it is postulated by the regularity of mind, which is its *a priori* basis.[24]

The preceding discussion has shown that the material and the mechanical are not ultimate, but that the teleological and the spiritual are presupposed by them. The unity and regularity of nature are grounded in intelligence, and efficient causality is the unassailable possession of mind alone. Adding to this the consideration that we have already transcended the dualistic separation between matter and mind and are logically bound by the duality in unity of concrete experience, we have this as a final formulation of our position: "It being in general granted that our conception of the unity and regularity of Nature is entitled to the name of knowledge—being ever confirmed, never falsified, by experience—we are now equally entitled to say that this unity and regularity of Nature proves that *Nature itself* is teleological, and *that* in two respects: (i) it is conformable to human intelligence and (ii), in consequence, it is amenable to human ends." [25] Thus the very necessity, which constitutes the boast of science as well as the ground of its utility and the criterion of its perfection, constitutes also the ground of spiritualistic philosophy. For all necessary truths "are, as Leibniz rightly called them, truths of *reason*. They originate in the subject of experience, not in the object; but if the objects conform to them, then all experience is rational; our reason is confronted and determined by universal reason. Such is the world of spiritualistic monism. . . . The Realm of Nature turns out to be a Realm of Ends." [26]

[24] In this connection the author takes occasion to warn us against the fallacy involved in the assumption of naturalism that there is a necessary conflict between natural law and individual spontaneity. "How absurd it would be to argue," he urges, "that in constituting a commonwealth in order to obtain greater freedom and security, men thereby become slaves, because as citizens they can no longer each one do whatever is right in his own eyes. Equally absurd is it to argue that, in postulating regularity in nature as the one ground of rational experience, we are deprived of all power and initiative, because in a system of universal and necessary law nothing can be arbitrary and there can be no gaps. . . . The very fact that it [mechanism] is our conception, that we devised it and use it, see its imperfections and amend them, shews that we are outside it and above it: its *a priori* condition and not its helpless consequence." (*Naturalism and Agnosticism*, p. 541.) Compare Bosanquet's view on the same point (*supra*, p. 128).

[25] *Naturalism and Agnosticism*, p. 544. Ward's italics.

[26] *Ibid.*, p. 573.

2. THE REALM OF ENDS

"Having satisfied ourselves, then, that mechanism is not the secret of the universe; that, if it is to have any meaning, it must subserve some end; and finding generally that increased knowledge of Nature's laws means increased control of Nature's processes, we accept the facts of experience in which subject and object interact, rather than the conclusions of dualism that mind and matter are for us two alien worlds and all knowledge of Nature an inexplicable mystery—we accept the spiritualistic standpoint and its Realm of Ends as the more fundamental." [27] And we are now to inquire concerning the characteristics of this spiritualistic standpoint.

Since we have already shown that spirit is foundational, our further task may be simply stated. It is "to ascertain what we can know, or reasonably believe, concerning the constitution of the world, *interpreted throughout and strictly in terms of Mind.*" And our starting point is also clear. We must begin with mind as we know it in self-consciousness, both in ourselves and in others. We must start from what we ourselves are, namely cognitive and conative subjects; and from where we are—so to say, *in mediis rebus,* in a world consisting to an indefinite extent of other like subjects. We start here because we can start nowhere else. "If the speculative enterprises of the past can be any guide for the future, they show that we have no choice but to begin where we are, and that we only deceive ourselves when we try to start by transcending experience. Accepting this teaching of history then, we began our inquiry about the universe as a realm of ends from the pluralistic standpoint." [28]

Our general assumption, then, is that "the whole world is made up of individuals, each distinguished by its characteristic behaviour." These individuals are to be interpreted on the analogy of the self of which we are conscious, since the conscious self "furnishes us with our first paradigm of what we are to under-

---

[27] *The Realm of Ends or Pluralism and Theism,* p. 13. The larger part of this quotation is taken by Ward from his *Philosophical Orientation and Scientific Standpoints* (Berkeley, California, 1904).

[28] Ward's summary statement at the end of his argument, *The Realm of Ends,* p. 432.

stand by the individuals of our plurality." Thus we are to work backwards from the facts of human personality and social intercourse. Our method of thought, therefore, is anthropomorphic; on the basis of the analogy of ourselves we are to build our interpretation of the universe. But, though frankly anthropomorphic, our method is not crudely so; we do not regard a mountain or a river as a person. Rather, we assume "that there exists an indefinite variety of selves, some indefinitely higher, some indefinitely lower than ourselves"; and we make use of this variety among selves in our explanation of the world. But we do maintain that the individuals or selves which make up the world, though not all properly to be called conscious persons or minds, must be understood as essentially like unto ourselves—the highest, if there be a highest, being only *primus inter pares;* and the lowest possessing whatever may be the irreducible minimum essential to being in any sense a self at all. And we are not following this method arbitrarily; on the contrary, we are forced to it by the argument thus far. For that argument has shown us that spirit is logically foundational in philosophical explanation; and in trying to give content to this general thesis by further elaboration of it we must proceed outwards from our own self-conscious experience, since in that experience we have direct acquaintance with the nature of spirit.

The principle on the basis of which we may logically pass from ourselves to higher or lower selves in the world order is the principle of continuity. This is the principle emphasized by Leibniz and formulated by him in the concise statement: "Nature makes no leaps." It is the principle which must be accepted by every thoroughgoing system of spiritualistic pluralism, and it receives progressive verification with our advancing knowledge of the world. Thus our assumption that there are higher and lower selves is not a mere assumption; it rests on our thesis that spirit is basal in the world-order and that the principle of continuity holds within that order.

One further preliminary observation is necessary. The irreducible minimum essential to being in any sense a subject or self at all "implies behaviour directed towards self-conservation or self-realisation." Only that which has an impulse towards, or an interest in, its own conservation is a true individual. But self-conservation implies, because it demands, effort and perseverance. Thus self-conservation means growth, self-realization—"a new standard, so to say, of the self to be conserved." And throughout the process as basal runs the principle of intersubjective intercourse; in the struggle for existence self acts on self. "It is plain then that when we talk of self-conservation the main stress is not to be laid on the bare conservation of some metaphysically simple entity, such as the soul of the old rationalist psychologists. What is meant is rather the maintenance of the most advantageous position attained by the actual self in relation to the world as a whole. This implies that each one is in touch with all the rest collectively and with some more specially." [29] In other words, self-conservation means the activity of an individual in interaction with other individuals and the preservation, in some form, of the results of such activity. It means 'betterment'; "the idea of the good is the master clue." And this clue must not be lost sight of in what follows.

(a) On the basis of the assumption that the world is made up of individuals in the sense above defined and that they vary indefinitely in degree, though always retaining the essentials of a subject or self, it is possible adequately to account for all the main orders of fact, as the following considerations may serve to indicate at least in outline.

In the world which we ordinarily call 'historical'—the world, that is, of the social life of human beings—we find a multitude of beings, varying widely in tastes and endowments, progressing from apparent chaos towards an ever-expanding and ever-deepening unity of organization. At the outset each must needs fend for himself, selecting the vocation and the habitat left open to him by fortune's favor and making the most of the situation allottéd to him by chance. Gradually this is changed; custom and imitation more and more determine the behavior of the less gifted; discoveries and inventions of the more gifted improve the conditions of life for all; coöperation and division of labor supplement individual enterprise and at the same time entail a more intimate and far-reaching dependence of each on his fellows;

[29] *The Realm of Ends,* p. 53; cf. p. 433.

public and private ends tend more and more to fall together. Thus the advance from insecurity and conflict to stability and unity takes place; the incoherent aggregate develops into a social organization in which different members have their respective places and functions and the unity of this organization is progressively emphasized. All of this is perfectly intelligible on the pluralist's assumption concerning the nature of the historical world, namely, that it is composed of an indefinite number of separate selves in intersubjective intercourse and struggling towards self-conservation.

The broad analogy which fairly obviously holds between the historical and the biological worlds seems to warrant the extension of the spiritualistic pluralist's theory to the latter also. Whether we have regard to the external correlations of organisms to each other (bionomics) or to the correlations of activities within each organism (physionomics), the main result is the same. In the former case there is a close parallel with human history; ". . . we find a multitude of comparatively isolated and independent units gradually advancing, by the survival of the fittest among innumerable random variations, towards the realisation of 'a vast and complex web of life,' whose myriad fibres are all intertwined, though every one is unique." And in the latter case, "we note again the same progress from relatively independent parts, barely conjoined and hardly differentiated, to highly specialised organs intimately associated together in a single living whole." And though in both cases the *prima facie* explanation of the facts is given in purely descriptive terms, it may be questioned whether this is real explanation; it may still be reasonably held that such facts are "only to be intelligibly interpreted like the facts of economics and social interaction; as implying, that is to say, percipient and conative subjects behaving as severally or jointly intent on self-conservation and betterment. It is easy throughout to recognise more or less striking evidence of experiences discriminated, retained, and turned to account." [30]

When we come to the inanimate world, however, we find a serious difficulty in applying the thesis of the spiritualistic

[30] *The Realm of Ends,* pp. 58, 59.

pluralist. For here "we can discern, *prima facie* at all events, no
signs of active striving or selective preference or progressive
organization: we find no unique individuals, no competing purposes to be adjusted, no tentative efforts to be followed at length
by success. First and last, everywhere and always, there seems
to be only fixity and uniformity." But the difficulty is more
apparent than real; at any rate, it is not insuperable.

In the first place, one must observe that it is perfectly conceivable that a uniform order of events may be the manifestation
of the behavior of individuals severally bent on self-conservation.
In fact, we have ample evidence that such is not infrequently the
case. The progress and development of individuals or species or
societies, we certainly know, may halt at a certain point at which
habit or instinct or custom is supreme. Witness, for example,
existing forms of life, like the Nautilus, which have remained
practically unaltered almost from the beginning of the geologi-
cal record; or certain savage people who to-day are still as
backward as the primeval men of the stone age; or advanced
societies, like that of the Chinese, which have remained practically stationary for thousands of years; or the thousands of
individuals at various cultural levels who are the slaves of habit
and custom and whose chief concern is to avoid disturbance and
let well alone. It is not unreasonable to suppose—on the contrary, the principle of continuity would lead us to suppose—that
what is characteristic of the known historical and biological
world may hold true of the inanimate world also. There the
individuals may invariably act with such regularity as always
to conform to what we call the principle of the uniformity of
inanimate nature.

In the second place, this principle of uniformity may readily
be explained on the theory of spiritualism. There are numberless
instances known to us in which what is sensibly simple and
homogeneous turns out, on analysis, to be extremely complex and
heterogeneous; and there seems to be ample ground for holding
with Leibniz that "there are no two indiscernible individuals."

In last analysis, it would appear, strict homogeneity is a
feature of pure quantities only, not of qualities. Again, we know
that where large numbers of individuals are concerned their

behavior presents aggregate results which are uniform. This is unmistakably shown in statistics. Now the physicist, like the statistician, "is always dealing with aggregates, but unlike the statist he finds the constituent individuals to be beyond his ken. The statist is aware that individual variations underlie his aggregates, but they do not interest him: the physicist is ignorant of those underlying his, and assumes that they do not exist." For such an assumption, however, there is no compelling reason. On the contrary, there must be some ground for these uniformities; and the spiritual pluralist is well within his logical rights when he maintains that it is reasonable to suppose that such a ground "is analogous to that which we know to underlie the law and order of the historical world." [31]

Thus we conclude that the hypothesis that "the whole world is made up of individuals, each distinguished by its characteristic behaviour" may reasonably be said to be an intelligible interpretation of the historical, biological, and physical aspects of the world-order. In the historical realm we find contingency, but we also find uniformity; these are here correlatives, and both result from the behavior of individuals seeking self-conservation and betterment. This characteristic of the historical world the spiritualistic pluralist generalizes to the utmost. "All nature is regarded as plastic and evolving like mind; its routine and uniformity being explained on the analogy of habit and heredity in the individual, of custom and tradition in society; while its variety is attributed to spontaneity in some form." [32] Such, broadly described, is the *Weltanschauung* of spiritualistic pluralism; and such, in general outline, are the considerations which underlie its detailed justification.

(b) It is to be carefully noted, however, that the pluralism here maintained is not a bare pluralism devoid of unity. On the contrary, unity is fundamental within it. The individuals of the plurality, we have seen, are characterized by behavior directed

---

[31] *The Realm of Ends,* pp. 66, 67.

[32] *Ibid.,* p. 74. For the author's further discussion of this matter, with special reference to the problems of contingency and uniformity, the reader should consult Lectures IV-VI of *The Realm of Ends.* Lecture V is especially important because of the analysis of the notion of evolution there given.

towards self-conservation; and self-conservation means betterment. This implies that each individual is in touch with all the
rest collectively and the common good of all is the goal of
endeavor. Thus there is within the plurality a tendency "to re-
place an initial state of comparative isolation and conflict by
progressively higher forms of unity and coöperation." This is a
necessary consequence of the interaction of a plurality of individuals intent on self-conservation and self-betterment.

At the lower levels of organization we must suppose that this
tendency is a mere blind impulse; but it is more open in what
we call biological evolution, the cardinal characteristic of which
is, in Wundt's happy phrase, creative synthesis. When the level
of the historical is reached, this tendency becomes a conscious
ideal—an ideal towards unity which is there progressively embodied in both theory and practice. It is true, of course, that the
ideal is never completely expressed in the historical process, in
which there are always many lapses. But in this process the ideal
stands out quite clearly, and we can see what sort of unity the
complete realization of the ideal would secure. It would be the
unity characteristic of a plurality of independently acting individuals intent on a common objective, namely, the good of all.
Through its attainment the natures of the different individuals
are severally deepened and enriched.

This, then, in sum is the unity of the world as spiritualistic
pluralism envisages it. It is a multiplicity of interacting individuals permeated by an informing spirit immanent in the group.
This spirit, when it grows self-conscious, reveals itself as the
ideal of the good. This unity is not to be understood, however,
in the sense of unity emphasized either by the theist or by the
absolute idealist. It "is a whole of experiences, but not a whole
experience, a whole of lives but not a living whole, a whole of
beings but without a complete and perfect being." Such is the
goal of the pluralistic standpoint carried as far as its premises
will allow. But the question arises whether we can stop here and
hold this to be final.

Applying his own principle of continuity, the spiritualistic
pluralist seems compelled to go beyond this position. And he is
forced beyond in two directions. Upwards, he is driven to assume

a hierarchy of intelligences of a higher order than human, and so is led to conceive a Highest of all; this we may call the upper limit of pluralism. Downwards, the principle of continuity leads back towards origins, and posits the necessity of an ultimate ground for the pluralist's individuals; this we may call pluralism's lower limit. Both of these limits are apparently inescapable, and yet the principles of the pluralist enable him to attain neither. Pluralism strictly interpreted, therefore, needs to be transcended. And the question is: How and to what end?

There are two reasons why a merely pluralistic world cannot in the end be regarded as sufficient for philosophy.[33] The theoretical reason is that such a world is ontologically incomplete. There is in it no ultimate ground either for the existence or for the unity of the finite individuals which by hypothesis make it up. The second reason is a practical one. In such a world there is neither definiteness in character, nor guaranty of attainment, of the ideal involved in the very structure of that world. For these two reasons pluralism must be held to be an inadequate philosophy. What is demanded for its completion is that its ideal unity be also real, that in addition to the Many an existent One be posited; then, and only then, does the pluralist's world become self-contained and absolute.[34]

At this point in the construction of our *Weltanschauung* we take leave of knowledge and put our trust in faith. This should be frankly acknowledged. But what faith means should also be clearly understood, since an understanding of it will clear our procedure of the charge of being arbitrary. What, then, is to be understood by faith?

Conation is, in a very important sense, foundational to cognition. This is quite evident in experience, since experience "means becoming expert by experiment." We gain knowledge by doing, and solely by doing; this is true both psychologically and historically. And it *must* be true, if our pluralistic standpoint is

---

[33] Ward's personal statement under the heading of "A Theistic Monadism" in *Contemporary British Philosophy* (edited by J. H. Muirhead), Second Series, p. 46 ff. Compare *The Realm of Ends*, Lectures IX and X.
[34] The author thinks that the postulate of immortality, as well as that of the existence of God, is involved in this demand. For his discussion of the point see *The Realm of Ends*, Lecture XVIII.

accepted; for on its premises the main endeavor of life is self-betterment, and knowledge is attained only as far as this paramount interest prompts to new ventures. Thus we may say that conation is the fundamental fact or characteristic of experience, and is the source of knowledge; it is a sort of "primitive credulity which leads us to trust and to try before we know."

Now this "credulity" runs through an ascending series from mere instinctive belief to what we ordinarily call rational belief. When it attains this latter form we name it 'faith.' Thus faith, in principle, implicit at all levels of experience, comes to its full expression at the level of rational self-consciousness. It is "a certain trustfulness (πίστις) of a kind which is implicit throughout all life and makes knowledge itself first of all possible. It is the highest phase of that continuous striving that conation involves; the highest because it emerges as a motive only at the self-conscious or rational level of experience." [35] Faith then, we may say, is a form of reason; it is a venture of intelligence, a *systematic* venture. And herein lies its cardinal characteristic, by which it is differentiated from the "primitive credulity" of the conative attitude in its earlier stages.

But herein also is the characteristic of faith which renders it amenable to philosophical criticism. For, after all, faith is but a form of reason; it is reason taken in its practical, rather than in its theoretical function. And therefore faith is subject to rational criteria and, so, amenable to philosophical (though not, strictly speaking, to scientific) critical evaluation.[36]

Now the hypothesis of an existent One, as supplementary to the ideal unity involved in the pluralist's conception of the world, is a postulate of faith. It is, however, open to philosophical evaluation, and to this task we now turn in concluding our ex-

[35] *Contemporary British Philosophy*, Second Series, p. 53; cf. *The Realm of Ends*, p. 413 ff. Compare the view of William James in *The Will to Believe*, to which Ward in this connection makes reference.

[36] Cf. *The Realm of Ends*, pp. 417-418. On the difference between science and philosophy see pp. 245-246. Compare: "Philosophy is not directly concerned with matters-of-fact: it cannot, of course, contradict experience; but its one aim is to understand this as a whole, to find a unity and a meaning in the entire sum of things beyond the so-called system of nature as science describes it." (*Contemporary British Philosophy*, Second Series, p. 47.)

position. We have already seen reason for holding that such an One must be posited; it remains for us to inquire what can be its nature and how it is related to the Many.

In the first place, it is clear that the One cannot be the Absolute in the sense in which that conception is defined by the absolute idealists. Such an Absolute meets neither of the demands for positing an existent unity within the pluralist's world. It does not account for the existence of the finite individuals that make up that world, but logically destroys them; nor does it guarantee the actualization of the pluralistic ideal, but rather negates it. It "reduces the world to an inexplicable appearance which, somehow seeming to be there, it can only explain away." Into the Absolute the Many, which by the pluralist are taken to be real, "are absorbed and vanish." Pluralism and absolutism (singularism, Ward usually calls it) are in fact antithetical views. If the one is accepted, the other cannot stand. The pluralist, therefore, cannot identify the One of his *Weltanschauung* with the Absolute as conceived, for instance, by Bradley and Bosanquet.

The theist's conception of God, however, is acceptable to the pluralist, provided God is defined in such manner as to assure personality and initiative to finite individuals. If God is conceived as an infinite personal Spirit, possessing intelligence and will, who creates the world and through the process of creation limits himself with respect to the wills of finite persons, then we may say that God is a postulate of rational faith; for in such a conception we have, in principle—the details are, of course, beyond us—that existent Unity of the world demanded by spiritualistic pluralism but not logically attained within the limits of its premises. Such a God, it may be admitted, might in a sense be said to be a 'finite' God, but only in the sense in which the term means "a living God with a living world, not a potter God with a world of illusory clay, not an inconceivable abstraction that is only infinite and absolute, because it is beyond everything and means nothing." Such a living world is "a world of self-determining, free agents, severally intent on attaining more good or at least on retaining the good they have." And God, if he is to be admitted into this world at all, must leave these agents free and self-determining; otherwise, the living world falls and God with it.[37]

Thus in the end we are forced to interpret the principles of the pluralist's standpoint so as to accommodate them to the theistic ideal—the ideal, that is, of a Person who creates the world and limits himself in respect of his creation. This ideal we may indeed call the Absolute, provided we hold clearly to its meaning, namely a "realm of ends" in which God is supreme and yet all his subjects free to work together with him. Such an ideal cannot be theoretically proved; but it is a postulate of practical reason, rational faith, and, if accepted, it bodies forth in existence the deeper implications of the principles of spiritual pluralism.

[37] For the author's view of the place of evil in such a world see *The Realm of Ends,* Lectures XVI, XVII.

Chapter VIII

JOHN McTAGGART ELLIS McTAGGART (1866-1925)

"ONTOLOGICALLY I am an Idealist, since I believe that all that exists is spiritual. I am also, in one sense of the term, a Personal Idealist. For I believe that every part of the content of spirit falls within some self, and that no part of it falls within more than one self; and that the only substances are selves, parts of selves, and groups of selves or parts of selves." This is McTaggart's summary statement of his own position as given in the personal statement which he contributed to *Contemporary British Philosophy* in 1924. There is much in it which is obviously in the spirit of Ward, but the argument which McTaggart employs is quite different from that of Ward.

This argument falls into two main parts. In the first part, the aim is to inquire "what can be determined as to the characteristics which belong to all that exists, or, again, which belong to existence as a whole."[1] Here the method of argument is necessarily *a priori*. It cannot be the ordinary method of inductive inference for two reasons: (i) because the validity of induction is not self-evident and must be proved, and yet its proof could be had only by showing that it discloses the nature of that which exists—that is, the proof would be circular, since the method trusted for finding the goal would presuppose that the goal may by that method be found; and (ii) because the goal here sought cannot be attained by induction, however valid it may be, since induction proceeds from particular to particular within a class,[2]

---

[1] McTaggart, *The Nature of Existence*, Section 41. The summary of the argument given below is taken from this book, and all the references are to it unless otherwise indicated. With the summary here given the reader should compare McTaggart's own formulation as presented in *Contemporary British Philosophy*, First Series, pp. 249-269.

[2] Induction "starts by observing that the same characteristic is to be found in several members of the same class—for example, that this man, that man, and the other man are mortal." (Section 43.) Contrast the view of Bosanquet on the point. See especially his *Implication and Linear*

and therefore cannot reach the characteristics of "existence as a whole" which is one, and only one, thing. The method, then, must be *a priori*. And as such it will result in absolute demonstration, if successfully carried through. Here "our results will either be fallacious through some error in the argument, or they will be certain." [3] In the second part of the argument, however, no claim is made for absolute demonstration, except in certain stages of it where the solution of the problem immediately under discussion is directly deducible from the results of the first part. On the whole, the conclusions here are admitted to be only probable. In this second part the aim is to show what consequences follow when the nature of the existent, as determined *a priori* in the first part, is brought to bear on what is empirically known to us. The argument here must, therefore, rely to some extent on purely empirical observation, and the best we can hope for our conclusions is a high degree of probability; but that at least we may expect to attain, if the discussion is carefully oriented with reference to the *a priori* conclusions of the first part.

1. EXISTENCE AND SUBSTANCE

It would be entirely possible to carry forward the first part of the argument without raising the question as to whether anything exists. Ignoring this question, we might inquire what characteristics necessarily belong to whatever exists and then hold that, if anything exists, it must have these characteristics thus *a priori* determined. But this procedure would leave our argument without practical interest or importance. So we begin with the question: Does anything exist?

(a) *The Existent.* The answer to this question is necessarily

Inference and *Science and Philosophy,* Essay IV. See also his observations on the general question of the *a priori* determination of the field of philosophy in the first Essay of the latter volume.

[3] Section 54. McTaggart admits that the argument here involves two appeals to empirical considerations. The first empirical premise is "something exists," and the second is "what exists is differentiated." But this empirical element, he thinks, does not render his results less certain. The appeal in each instance is to a single perception (awareness of the existent) and, so, does not involve induction from the results of various perceptions. The question remains, however, whether in point of fact the author's argument is not based ultimately on the principles of induction. But see Section 45.

empirical, but it is nevertheless certain. And the answer must be in the affirmative. If one denies that something exists, this denial involves the existence of the doubter or, at the very least, of the doubt. And if the doubt itself be an illusion, the existence of the illusion still remains. Thus the denial that something exists is self-refuting; the denial at least exists, if only as an illusion. "And a similar argument is applicable in the case of a thinker who should simply contemplate the question whether anything does exist, without either affirming it, denying it, or doubting it." [4]

Something, then, exists. With this proposition established, empirically but certainly, we can go forward by purely *a priori* considerations to other conclusions with the assurance that they are of practical interest and, if no mistake occurs in our reasoning, absolutely certain.

(b) *Quality*. The assertion that something exists raises the further question as to what this 'something' is. If we should suppose that we may answer the question by saying simply that this something is that which exists, we should find ourselves at once caught in a contradiction. "If we stop with existence, and refuse to go any further, the existent is a perfect and absolute blank, and to say that only this exists is equivalent to saying that nothing exists." [5] Thus, starting with the premise that something exists, we arrive at the conclusion that nothing exists. But we cannot rest in this contradiction, and are forced to go further. Of that which certainly exists something besides its own existence must be true. Now that which is true of something is a quality of that something. Hence we are compelled to say of anything which exists that it must have some quality besides that of mere existence. [6]

But we can go yet further, and say that what exists must have a plurality of qualities. This conclusion is necessary. Since there are qualities which are incompatible with each other and which cannot together belong to the same thing, there must necessarily

---

[4] Section 56. Compare the *cogito ergo sum* of Descartes.

[5] Section 59. Compare McTaggart's treatment of the first Hegelian triad in his *Studies in the Hegelian Dialectic*.

[6] Strictly, quality is indefinable. Examples are: redness, sweetness, goodness, happiness. Cf. *The Nature of Existence*, Section 60.

be some qualities which any given thing cannot possess; and the non-possession of a quality is itself a quality. If a thing is round, it is not square; and this involves that it is possessed of the quality of not-squareness. This may at first seem trivial; but it illustrates an important principle, namely, that negation has its positive aspect. And it is by this principle that we may certainly know *a priori* that what exists must possess a plurality of qualities.

Qualities may be subdivided into simple, compound, and complex. A simple quality is one which does not admit of analysis, and which consequently is strictly indefinable; redness is such a quality. A compound quality is one which can be analyzed into other qualities, and the qualities into which it can be analyzed are its parts. Thus the qualities redness and sweetness, when for any reason taken together, would be a compound quality (for which we have no name) of which redness and sweetness is each a part. A complex quality differs from a compound quality in that it does not consist of an aggregate of other qualities, though it can be analyzed into other qualities or relations or both; and these are, not its parts, but its elements. Thus a negative quality (not-squareness, for instance) is complex. It may be analyzed into two qualities (the negative and the corresponding positive quality), but it is not an aggregate of these. The parts of a compound quality, like the elements of a complex quality, need not be simple qualities; they may be either compound or complex, but their analysis leads in the end to simple characteristics. Finally, and quite importantly for the later argument, all the qualities possessed by a particular thing form a compound quality which is identical with the *nature* of that thing. The nature of a triangle is the compound quality composed of all its qualities.

(c) *Substance*. A quality, we have seen, is that which is true of something; an existent quality is that which is true of something which exists. The question now arises concerning what that is of which a quality is true. In the first place, it is to be noted that to predicate a quality of itself leads to absurdity—the quality of happiness, for example, cannot itself be happy. Again, a quality is not predicable of the group of qualities of which it is one of the members. It is clear that when, for example, we say that Smith is happy we do not and cannot mean or intend to say that the qualities which together constitute Smith's nature are themselves happy, whether those qualities be taken severally or in the aggregate. In short, it is impossible to hold that nothing exists but qualities; the attempt to do so leads to the absurdity of predicating qualities of qualities without end. There must therefore be something which has qualities without being itself a quality. A similar argument holds of relation; for a relation, like a quality, cannot exist in its own right. Thus in the end we are driven to the conclusion that something must exist of which qualities and relations are predicable, and which is itself neither a quality nor a relation. This is what is meant by substance.

In connection with this conception of substance three points should be specially noted. (i) The conception is of cardinal importance for the following argument, and its definition must be clearly grasped and kept in mind throughout.[7] (ii) As here defined, a substance is any existent aggregate which has qualities or is related, but itself is neither a quality nor a relation; and the significance or triviality of the aggregate is indifferent to its being a substance—a sneeze or a party at whist or all red-haired archdeacons is a substance as genuine as is a solar system or a man. (iii) A substance is nothing apart from its qualities, as existent qualities are nothing apart from substance; substance is always in conjunction with its qualities, and existent qualities always belong to substances.

Are there many substances, or is there one substance only? More technically expressed: Are we compelled to hold that substance is differentiated? To this question the answer must be affirmative, and the basis for it is found in perception.[8] At most

[7] Note that substance is distinguished from fact. "I should define a Fact as being either the possession by anything of a quality, or the connection of anything with anything by a relation"—in this definition 'anything' is used to include both substances and characteristics, that is qualities and relations (Section 10).

[8] "Perception is the awareness of what Mr. Russell calls particulars, as distinct from the awareness of what he calls universals. In the terminology which I propose to adopt, it is the awareness of substances as distinct from the awareness of characteristics." (Section 44.) By 'characteristics' is always intended qualities and relations.

moments our field of perception is differentiated. In such moments we are directly aware of more than one perception-datum, and perception-data are substances. Therefore direct perception proves that substance is differentiated. Even the perception of a single datum proves the same point; for, besides the perception-datum, there is always the perception itself, and each perception is a substance. And this holds true, it should be noted, whether the perception be interpreted as a mental state or as a relation of which the datum is one term. In the first interpretation, the perception and the datum are obviously two substances; and in the second interpretation, there must be another substantive term—presumably, a self or mind—of the perceptual relation of which the perception-datum is the other substantive term.

Substance is, therefore, differentiated, and there is more than one substance. This is certain, even though the proof of it is empirical. For the existence of even one perception proves the proposition; and the doubt or denial that perception exists is itself an instance of perception, if the skeptic is to know that he doubts or denies.

(d) *Relations.* That there are relations there can be no possible doubt. They are necessarily involved in the conception of a plurality of substances. For different substances will be at least similar to each other, since all are substances; they will also be diverse from each other, since they are separate substances. But similarity and diversity are relations. Thus it is certain that some relations do exist.

Like qualities, relations are indefinable. When asked what is to be understood by relations we can only give examples of them, such as similarity, diversity, above, greater than, father of, and the like. But we can classify them. And it is fairly obvious that there are three classes of relations, corresponding to the three classes of qualities mentioned above. A simple relation is one which does not admit of analysis; a compound relation is analyzable into simple relations; a complex relation is not an aggregate of simple relations, but may be analyzed into other relations or qualities or both. Again, relations may be grouped into: (i) reflexive, unreflexive, or not reflexive; (ii) symmetrical, asymmetrical, or not symmetrical; (iii) transitive, intransitive, or not transitive.[9]

(e) *Characteristics.* Notwithstanding the fact that qualities and relations are alike indefinable, it is clear that neither can be reduced to the other and that both are indispensable in describing existence. It is convenient to have a term to refer to both, since it is necessary on occasion to speak of both together. The term we shall henceforth employ for this purpose is 'characteristics.' By characteristics, then, is to be understood qualities and relations.

Though a relation may be based on a quality or may determine a quality of any whole which contains all the terms of the relation, in no case can a relation be replaced by a quality or a quality by a relation. Qualities inhere in something, while relations are not in anything but hold between something and something; and the conceptions 'in' and 'between' are alike ultimate and irreducible. It is very important to note, however, that relations may generate qualities. The occurrence of any relation involves the occurrence of a special quality in each of its terms. Designating terms-in-relation as a 'relationship,' we may say generally that each relationship generates a quality in each of the terms in that relationship. To illustrate: if A admires B, or if X is equal to Y, the admiration of A for B and the equality of X to Y are relationships; in the first relationship A has the quality of 'admirer of B' while B has the quality 'object of A's admiration' and, in the second, X has the quality 'being equal to Y' while Y has the quality 'being equal to X.' Qualities thus generated by relations may be called 'relational qualities' to distinguish them from 'original qualities' which are not so generated.

Besides generated or relational qualities, there are also generated relationships. Every quality indeed generates such a relationship, since the possession of any quality by a substance generates a relationship between the substance and that quality. Furthermore, every relationship generates another; for if a sub-

[9] Not much use of these classifications of relations is made by McTaggart in his later argument, so it seems unnecessary to labor them further in this summary statement. For a more detailed explanation of them the reader should consult Section 84 of McTaggart's text.

stance stands in a relationship, it necessarily stands in relation to that relationship as well as to the term with which that relationship connects it. Thus there are derivative relations as well as relational (derivative) qualities.

Making use of our general term 'characteristics,' we may say shortly that there are two sorts of characteristics, namely original and derivative. Derivative characteristics include all generated qualities and relations; original characteristics include all qualities and relations not generated as above described.

(f) *Substance and Characteristics*. From the preceding analysis it follows at once that within any given substance there is an infinite series of characteristics. Starting with an original quality of the substance, we find that there are the derivative relationship between the substance and that quality, the relational quality of standing in that relationship, and so on without end. And starting with an original relationship, we find that there are the relational quality of standing in that relationship, the derivative relationship between the substance and that relational quality, and so on without end. Furthermore, each relationship generates a relationship which involves an infinite series of derivative characteristics.

All the qualities in these infinite series are parts of the nature of the substance which possesses them. Therefore the nature of substance may be said to be a compound quality with an infinite number of parts. But it is quite important to note that the meaning of the later members in these infinite series is determined by the meaning of the earlier members, and not *vice versa*. And from this it follows that there is no necessity of completing any given series (which would be logically impossible) in order to determine the meaning of the original characteristics that generate it. On the contrary, the meaning of the original characteristics determines the meaning of each of the members in the derivative series of characteristics. Hence the nature of substance is not rendered logically unintelligible by virtue of the fact that it involves an infinite series of derivative characteristics.[10] Such

---

[10] In this connection the author remarks: "I venture to suggest that this consideration removes the force of Mr. Bradley's argument for rejecting the validity of the conceptions of quality and relation." (Section 88, foot-

would be the case, indeed, if it were true that the characteristics of a characteristic were genuine *parts* of that characteristic; for then it would follow that the meaning of the original characteristic would be logically dependent upon the meanings of its generated characteristics *ad infinitum,* and so the series of generated characteristics would be a vicious one. But the characteristics of a characteristic are parts only of the *nature* of the original characteristic, and that nature determines the meanings of the derivative characteristics and is not determined by them.[11] There can be no difference in 'repeating' qualities which does not arise from some difference in 'primary' qualities; but knowledge of the primary qualities does not presuppose knowledge of the repeating qualities, since repeating qualities can be deduced at will by the application of the formula of generation given above.[12]

(g) *Dissimilarity and Description of Substances.* We have already seen that there must necessarily be a plurality of substances. Must we go forward from this to hold that substances are necessarily dissimilar in the sense that they are not, and cannot possibly be, exactly similar? The conclusion that such is the case is involved in the very conception of a plurality of substances, and this may be made evident by the following considerations. A substance has no individuality apart from and other than its own nature, for an explanation of what is to be understood by such a supposedly distinct aspect of substance could be stated only by asserting qualities of substance, and these qualities we have already seen to be parts of the nature of substance. The nature of a given substance, then, expresses

note.) For the argument of Bradley referred to, see *Appearance and Reality,* Chapter III; the argument is summarized above, pp. 86-88.

[11] The distinction here made use of between a characteristic *per se* and its 'nature' is of considerable importance to McTaggart's later argument; and it becomes particularly significant when it is introduced (as we shall see below in some detail it is introduced) into the consideration of the meaning of substance. For McTaggart's discussion, see Chapters X and following.

[12] By 'primary' qualities is meant those qualities which are original or which are immediately derived from original relationships. By 'repeating' qualities is meant all other derivative qualities. All qualities in the second class are generated, directly or indirectly, by those in the first class. For the definition of 'presuppose,' see below, p. 219.

completely what the substance is. And from this it immediately follows that, if there be two substances, the nature of the one cannot be exactly similar to the nature of the other; if the natures of the two substances were exactly similar, the substances would be identical. A plurality of substances, thus, involves the dissimilarity of substances.[13]

Since every substance is particular, it cannot be defined. Definition applies only to characteristics—which are universal—and only to those characteristics which are not simple. But a substance may be described,—for instance, by indicating the qualities it possesses or the relations between it and other substances. Such description, however, is imperfect unless the substance described were the only substance to which the description applies; if it were, the description would be an 'exclusive' description. By an exclusive description, then, is to be understood a description which applies to only one substance, so that the substance is absolutely identified by the description.

But an exclusive description need not be a 'complete' description. A complete description of a substance would consist of all of its qualities and so would be an exhaustive account of its nature. A complete description would, of course, be an exclusive description also, since no two substances have their natures exactly the same and a complete account of the nature of one substance could consequently never be true of the nature of any other substance. But an exclusive description need not be a complete description. "The most virtuous of all beings" could not be a complete description of any possible being, but it would be an exclusive description of any being of whom it is true since it could not possibly be true of more than one being.

An exclusive description may contain undescribed substances, or it may be stated entirely in terms of characteristics. If it is stated entirely in terms of characteristics, it is what we may call a 'sufficient' description. A sufficient description of a substance,

---

[13] Note especially the view of substance and its nature which lies at the bottom of the argument here. The argument later seems to depart from it. The general thesis here defended is, of course, in the spirit of the doctrine of Leibniz which is usually called the Identity of Indiscernibles (cf. his fourth letter to Clark, and his *Nouveaux Essais*, Book II, Chapter 27, section 3). This McTaggart admits, though he objects to the name.

then, is an exclusive description in which are to be found nothing but the characteristics of the substance described. "The most virtuous of all beings" would be an example of a sufficient description.

It is clear that every substance must have an exclusive description, because no substance can' have exactly the same nature as any other. And from this it follows that every substance must also have a sufficient description; for if a substance had no sufficient description, its exclusive description would involve a vicious infinite. This very important point may be made clear by the following considerations. A given substance, A, must be dissimilar to all other substances. "The possibility of this depends on the existence of B, and the existence of B depends on its dissimilarity to all other substances. And this depends on the existence of C, and this on its dissimilarity to all other substances, and so on. If this series is infinite, it is vicious. For, starting from the existence of A, each earlier term requires all the later terms, and therefore requires that the series should be completed, which it cannot be. If, therefore, the series is infinite, A cannot be dissimilar to all other substances—cannot, in other words, have an exclusive description—and so cannot exist. Therefore, if A does exist, the series cannot be infinite. And if the series is not infinite, A has a sufficient description. Every substance, therefore, must have a sufficient description." [14]

(h) *Extrinsic Determination and Manifestation.* The nature of a substance, we have seen, consists of all the qualities which belong to that substance. And we have also seen that the nature of a substance expresses completely what the substance is. From these two propositions it follows that an alteration in any one of the qualities of a substance would necessarily change the substance itself. If X, Y, Z be a complete list of the qualities of the substance, S, then any alteration in X, Y, or Z, either by addition

<hr/>

[14] Section 105. I have quoted this particular argument verbatim because of its foundational importance for McTaggart's later discussion. Note that the argument seems to rest on the assumption that substance, if it is to be, must be knowable; and consider McTaggart's denial that such is the case: "The necessity that a substance should have an exclusive description arises from the fact that two substances cannot be completely similar, and that a substance which is not completely similar to any other has necessarily an exclusive description." (*Ibid.*)

or subtraction or substitution, would involve a change in the nature of S, and S would then become a different substance. If Snowden is a mountain which is m feet high, then any mountain which is $m-1$ feet high is not Snowden even though all its other qualities are the same; for the nature of Snowden is, by hypothesis, to be exactly m feet in height and any change in that height changes the nature, and consequently the substance, designated by the name Snowden.

The relation among the qualities of a substance described in the preceding paragraph may be called the relation of *extrinsic determination*. The qualities of a substance are so related to each other by virtue of their relation to the substance to which they belong that, if one is changed, there is no reason to suppose that the others remain; they may indeed remain, but there is no ground for supposing that they do. By changing any quality we have modified the substance, and the other qualities were there only as parts of the nature of that substance. The same principle holds of relations also. And so we may say that extrinsic determination is valid for the characteristics (qualities and relations) of a substance.

The point above expressed may be expressed in another way, but with a difference of emphasis which is quite important. Instead of saying that the nature of substance is composed of all its characteristics in the relation of extrinsic determination, we may say that the characteristics in this relation are united in the nature of the substance. These are two expressions of the same fact, but the former emphasizes plurality while the latter emphasizes unity. A convenient term for stressing the second emphasis is *manifestation*, where manifestation means nothing more than the relation between a whole and its parts with the emphasis placed on the unity of the whole rather than on the plurality of the parts. Thus we may say that the nature of substance is manifested in the characteristics of substance; and by this is meant the emphasis that the characteristics are to be regarded as differentiations of the nature of substance.

(i) *Groups and Substances*. It is clear that, since there is a plurality of substances which stand in relations to each other, these substances may be arranged in various collections by virtue of some common quality or qualities. It is clear, further, that such collections may include other collections indefinitely. For such collections we may use the name *groups*, the constituent elements of any group being called *members* of that group. A group, then, would mean any collection of substances, or of collections of substances, or of both; and the members of the group would mean the substances or collections of substances which form the group. But it is quite important to distinguish clearly between the members of a group and the parts of a group; for all members of a group are also parts of it, but not every part of a group is also a member of it. The member-group relation and the part-group relation, though alike indefinable, are nevertheless distinguishable. The main difference is that the part-group relation is transitive, while the member-group relation is not transitive. If A is a part of B, and B is a part of C, then A is a part of C; but if L is a member of M, and is itself a group of which N is a member, then N is not a member of M though it is a part of M. Neither England nor Whitechapel, for example, is a member of the group of all the counties of Great Britain, but they are parts of the group; any particular county would be a member of the group of all counties, but a member of that county would not be a member (though it would be a part) of the group of all the counties.

Strictly speaking, it is not true that a whole consists of all its parts; it consists rather of a *set of parts*. A set of parts is any collection of parts which together make up the whole, and do not more than make it up, so that the whole would not be made up if any of those parts, or any of their parts, should be subtracted. Thus England, Scotland, and Wales are a set of parts of Great Britain; they entirely make it up, and it would not be made up if any of them, or any of their parts, were subtracted. It should also be noted that the relation between a group and its set of parts is transitive. If one collection of counties is a set of parts of England, another a set of parts of Scotland, and a third a set of parts of Wales, then the aggregate of the three sets of parts taken together is a set of parts of Great Britain. Furthermore, it should be noted that the members of a group are a set of parts of that group. England, Scotland, and Wales, which are members of Great Britain, are also a set of parts of Great Britain.

One and the same group may consist of different sets of parts and hence of different groups, but it has only one *content;* and two groups will have the same content if there is no part of one which is not also a part of the other. Thus Great Britain has different sets of parts, and each set of parts is a different group; but the content is the same for all the sets of parts, since there is not any part of one which is not also a part of the others. By content, then, is to be understood that plurality which is identical in different sets of parts of a group.

Every group has qualities and stands in relations, but is not itself either a quality or a relation. Every group is therefore a substance. And from this it immediately follows that some substances at least have substances for their parts. Such substances we may call *compound substances.* The question whether all substances are compound is a very important question, which will have to be considered at a later stage in the argument.

Though every group is a substance, not every different group is a different substance. The group of the counties of Great Britain and the group of the parishes of Great Britain, for instance, are two distinct groups; but they have the same content and are therefore the same substance. Nor is there any logical difficulty here. 'To be the group whose members are X and Y' is a quality; and 'To be the group whose members are V and W' is another quality. Now, since every substance has many qualities, there is no reason why one and the same substance should not have both these qualities, provided the content of X and Y is identical with the content of V and W.[15]

(j) *The Universe.* Any two, or more, substances will form a compound substance. There must therefore be one compound

[15] Despite McTaggart's claim, the reader should carefully consider whether the position here taken is sound. The position seems to be: There is a meaning of the term 'substance' in which one can say that two substances (groups) may have the same content and still remain two, but there is another meaning of the term in which two substances (groups) with the same content must be one substance (in what sense?). The point is of basal significance for the later argument, and the question is inevitable whether there is not a subtle change in meaning of 'substance.' See Section 128 for the full discussion.

substance which includes all substances. For any content which is not in any given substance, A, must be in some substance or substances outside of A; and by adding these to A we shall have a compound substance which contains all content and *ipso facto* all substances. This compound substance is what we call the *universe*.

It is clear that the universe must exist, since something exists. It is also clear that there cannot be more than one universe. If there were two, each would contain all existent content; the two would therefore have the same content and there cannot be more than one substance with the same content.

Any fact [16] about any substance in the universe is also a fact about the universe. If it is a fact that the substance X has the quality y, then it is a fact about the universe that it possesses the quality of having a part, X, with certain qualities among which is the quality y. We may call this quality of the universe y'.

It has already been proved that all the qualities of any substance are connected with each other by extrinsic determination so that it would be unjustifiable to assert that any of them would remain the same if any one were different from what it is. On the basis of this principle, since the universe is a substance, we may conclude that it is unjustifiable to hold either that any of the qualities of the universe would remain the same if X did not have the quality y, or that X could have quality y if any other qualities of the universe were not the same. For every fact about every other substance extrinsically determines every fact about the universe, and every fact about the universe extrinsically determines every fact about every other substance. And from this it follows that substances themselves are determined in the same way; for, as we have seen above, the individuality of a substance is inseparable from the qualities it possesses, and therefore a determination of its qualities is at once a determination of the substance. Hence the general conclusion: All that exists, both substances and characteristics

---

[16] A 'fact' is defined as the possession by anything of a quality, or the connection of anything with anything by a relation.

(qualities and relations), are bound together in one system of extrinsic determination.[17]

Just as we saw above that the nature of a substance *manifests* itself, taken as a whole, in the qualities which are its parts, so here we may observe that a compound substance, as a unity, manifests itself in the substances of which it is composed. But for clarity it is important to distinguish between the manifestation of a substance and the manifestation of the nature of a substance. The compound substance A is manifested in the several substances which are the parts of A, while the nature of A is manifested in the qualities and relations of A, which are parts of that nature (including, of course, the qualities of having as its parts B and the other substances which are its parts). For, in the sense in which we are using the word *manifestation*, nothing can be manifested except in its own parts, and it is obvious that the parts of substance are substances, while the parts of the nature of substance are characteristics. When we speak of the manifestation of a substance, therefore, we are to understand that the relation of unity holds between the substance *per se* (not its nature taken as a whole) and the substances *per se* (not their several natures) of which it is composed.[18]

[17] It must be carefully noted that *intrinsic* determination is not here asserted. Intrinsic determination is defined as follows: "The quality X will be said to determine intrinsically the quality Y whenever the proposition that something has the quality X implies the proposition that something has the quality Y." (Section 108.) The two qualities may be in the same thing, or in different things. For example, the occurrence of blueness as the quality of anything intrinsically determines the occurrence of spatiality as a quality of the same thing, but if one person has the quality of being a husband this intrinsically determines the occurrence in some other person of the quality of being a wife. The position stated in the text above, however, is not that all substances and characteristics are bound together in a system of intrinsic determination (cf. section 142). Compare the view of the absolutists.

[18] Because the point here involved is so very important for McTaggart's argument, I have quoted verbatim most of his formulation of it. For the full text the reader should consult Chapter XX of his book.

A difficulty seems to be involved here. We have frequently been told before this that the nature of substance and substance itself are inseparable, that "the nature of a substance expresses completely what the substance is." (Section 94.) And yet here we are explicitly warned that the manifestation of the one is quite different from that of the other, since the part of a substance (which is a substance) and the part of the nature

And here we are confronted by a new relation of the whole to its parts, and of the parts to one another. It has already been shown that all the substances in the universe are interdependent, and the reason given for that conclusion would equally justify us in concluding of any whole, besides the universe, that its parts are interdependent. If any part were different, the whole would no longer be the same whole; and, if it were not the same whole, we should have no reason for maintaining that any of the other parts would exist. But now we can go further, for the parts are now seen to manifest the whole taken as a unity. No one part could do this if the others did not do so. For, if any part were wanting, then the whole containing that part could not be manifested at all. Thus no part could manifest the whole if the others did not do so also. And thus the parts may be said to *coöperate* in manifesting the whole. We no longer say, negatively, that if one of the parts were different the whole would be different, and we should then have no ground for supposing that the other parts would remain. We say, rather and affirmatively, that the parts have a common function to perform, namely, the manifestation of the whole. To the idea of mutual indispensability is now added the more positive idea of mutual coöperation.[19]

To express this more positive relation of the whole to the parts and of the parts to one another, we may use the term *organic unity*. This term is not without its misleading associations, and these should be rigidly excluded from its connotation as here used.[20] But some term is needed, and this one on the whole seems to be the least objectionable. What is here meant by it is simply that the parts manifest the whole, that since the whole as unity is what it is the parts must be what they

of a substance (which is a characteristic) are radically diverse. But in the same section (144), when the author undertakes to tell us more explicitly what the difference is, he seems to say only that the substance which is manifested in such and such parts (substances) is that which has such and such characteristics. It seems fairly clear that the distinction between substance and its nature is at best an elusive distinction, and it should be watched.

[19] This paragraph is, once more, quoted practically verbatim (section 145) because of its crucial importance.

[20] For McTaggart's consideration of these misleading associations, see Sections 149-154.

are. And in this meaning of the term we may say the universe is an organic unity, and so are all substances, whether a heap of stones, the group composed of a table and a dose of medicine and the oldest rabbit in Australia, a biological form, or any social group.

(k) *Infinite Divisibility of Substance*. There can be so simple substance. This proposition cannot be proved from any other proposition; but it needs no proof, since it is self-evident. Obviously, every substance must have content, that is, must be characterized by a plurality which is identical in different sets of parts. This is equivalent to saying that no substance can be simple. Every substance, therefore, has parts. But this involves that every substance has an unending series of sets of parts, since each part in any set will be a substance which has content, and therefore parts, and the parts of the parts will always form a fresh set of parts of the original substance. Every substance, consequently, is infinitely divisible.

But here we are met by a difficulty. We have already seen that every substance has a sufficient description, and the question now raised is: How is this possible? Can substance, which is infinitely divisible, have a sufficient description? If so, on what conditions? If it has a sufficient description, that involves that there must be a sufficient description of its parts which, as we have just seen, constitute an infinite series; and the question which meets us concerns the conditions on which this is possible.

In undertaking to answer this question we must note, in the first place, that there are only two ways in which the nature of a substance may be related to the sufficient descriptions of its parts: it may presuppose them, or it may supply them. And each of these possibilities must be considered in turn.

By presupposition is meant the relation between X and either Y or Z, when X intrinsically determines [21] the alternative Y-or-Z but does not determine intrinsically either the occurrence of Y or the occurrence of Z. In such a case, X is said to presuppose either the occurrence of Y or the occurrence of Z. For

---

[21] See foot-note, p. 217 above. Intrinsic determination is the relation among qualities corresponding to the relation of implication among propositions. The notion of implication is itself indefinable.

example, the possession by any substance of the quality of
being human intrinsically determines that that substance is
male-or-female, and presupposes either that it is male or that it
is female.

Now it sometimes happens that there may be several presuppositions involved in the nature of a substance, and that there
is also presupposed among these presuppositions a relation of
intrinsic determination such that when one presupposition is
known the other presuppositions are *fixed*—that is, are known
also. For example, that a substance is triangular presupposes
(i) either that it is equilateral or that it is isosceles or that it
is scalene, and (ii) that there are certain relations in which the
magnitude of its three interior angles (which themselves are
intrinsically determined as to number) may stand to each other
—namely, as all equal or two equal or none equal. And if the
second of these presuppositions is known, the first is thereby
fixed. If the angles are all equal, the triangle is equilateral; if
two of the angles are equal, the triangle is isosceles; if no two
of the angles are equal, the triangle is scalene. On the basis of
this principle, we may distinguish between mere presupposition
and *total ultimate presupposition*. By total ultimate presupposition is meant the aggregate of all the presuppositions left over
after there have been removed those presuppositions, the fixing
of which is implied in any of those which remain. It should be
further noted that whatever has a presupposition has also, necessarily, a total ultimate presupposition, which may be either one
presupposition or several.

Turning to our present problem with these definitions in
mind, we see that substance cannot *presuppose* sufficient descriptions of any of its sets of parts without involving a contradiction in the nature of substance. And that contradiction,
stated in its simplest terms, is, that on this hypothesis, substance would have a presupposition and yet could not have a
total ultimate presupposition.

This can be shown as follows. The fact that A is a substance
implies (since no substance is simple) that it has parts within
parts to infinity, and that each of these must have a sufficient
description. If, then, A presupposes sufficient descriptions of its

sets of parts, its presuppositions are infinite, since its sets of parts are infinite. But no given presupposition in this infinite series could be a part of the total ultimate presupposition, because the sufficient descriptions of any given set of parts would be fixed only in reference to sufficient descriptions of sequent sets of parts and therefore could not fall within the total ultimate presupposition. Sufficient descriptions of the members of the set of parts, M, for instance, would be fixed with reference to sufficient descriptions of the members of the sequent set of parts, N, and these in turn with reference to sufficient descriptions of the members of the sequent set of parts, O, and so on without end. Hence neither the presuppositions of sufficient descriptions of the members of M, nor of those of N, nor of those of O, nor of those of any sequent set of parts could belong to the total ultimate presupposition of A, the substance in question. For the total ultimate presupposition cannot contain any presupposition which is fixed only in reference to some sequent presupposition. Thus we are forced to conclude that any substance which presupposes sufficient descriptions of its sets of parts cannot have a total ultimate presupposition. And this is absurd.

We are therefore driven to accept the other alternative. Since substance cannot presuppose descriptions of its sets of parts without contradiction, it must *supply* them. Now there are two, and only two, ways in which it might supply them: it might *include* them, or it might *imply* them. But it cannot include them without implying them; inclusion without implication could be nothing more than an endless series. For substance to supply sufficient descriptions of its sets of parts, then, it must imply them.[22] Thus, in order to avoid contradiction in the very nature of substance, we must find in substance itself the basis for a chain of implications running downwards from preceding to sequent sets of parts to infinity, such that sufficient descriptions of members of the precedent sets imply sufficient descriptions of members of all the sequent sets. In what way can such implications be determined?

(1) *Determining Correspondence.* There is one, and only one, relation among substances which can serve as the basis for the

[22] For the details of the argument on this point see Sections 193, 194.

chain of implications we require, and that is the relation of
determining correspondence. This relation may be defined as
follows. Any relation between a substance, C, and part of another
substance, B, is a relation of determining correspondence if a
certain sufficient description of C which includes the fact that
it is in that relation to *some* part of B (i) intrinsically determines a sufficient description of the part of B in question,
namely, the part of B which corresponds to C and indicated by
the convention B!C, and (ii) intrinsically determines sufficient
descriptions of each member of a set of parts of B!C, and of
each member of a set of parts of each of such members, and so
on to infinity.[23] The second clause of this definition could only be
true in cases in which three conditions are also true, and these
conditions must be grasped if the full meaning of the definition is
to be understood. These conditions are: (i) the sufficient description of C also includes a statement that each member of
a set of parts of C's points has some substance to which it stands
in a relation of determining correspondence, as the part of B
does to C itself; (ii) either B and C form a group, or part of a
group, in which determination is reciprocal, or else each of them
is itself determined, either directly or indirectly, by a relation
of determining correspondence to substances which are in such
a reciprocal relation to each other;[24] and (iii) when one determinant is part of another determinant, and any part determined by the first will be part of a part determined by the
other.

The principle of determining correspondence, above defined,
may be illustrated as follows. Let A have a set of parts, B and
C (the number of parts in the set may, of course, be any
number). The principle of determining correspondence will ob-

[23] The relation of determining correspondence is to be distinguished
carefully from the relation of intrinsic determination. Determining correspondence is a relation between *substances;* the relation of intrinsic determination is a relation between descriptions of substances. (The conven-
tions are as follows: B!C is to be read as 'that part of B which corresponds to C'; B!C!D is to be read as 'that part of B which corresponds
to that part of C which corresponds to D': and so on.)

[24] Determination is said to be *reciprocal* when each member of the group
of substances in this relation determines, either directly or indirectly,
parts of each of the other members, and when no part of any member is
determined by any substance outside of the group. (Section 201.)

tain if the following conditions are fulfilled: (i) each of these parts has a set of parts corresponding to each set of parts of A; (ii) the correspondence is of the same sort throughout, that is, is a one-to-one relation between the members of the sets of parts, and is such that a certain sufficient description of C, which includes the fact that it is in this relation to *some* part of B, will determine a sufficient description of the part of B in question; and (iii) the correspondence is such that, when one determinant is part of another determinant, then any part determined by the first will be part of a part determined by the second. Under these conditions we have in B the part corresponding to B (B!B), and the part corresponding to C (B!C); and in C, the part corresponding to C (C!C) and the part corresponding to B (C!B). All of these, it is to be noted, are parts of A. And each of the four will have parts in both B and C corresponding to it, as follows: in B there will be the part of B corresponding to the part of B corresponding to B (B!B!B), the part of B corresponding to the part of B corresponding to C (B!B!C), the part of B corresponding to the part of C corresponding to B (B!C!B), and the part of B corresponding to the part of C corresponding to C (B!C!C); likewise, in C, there will be C!C!C, C!C!B, C!B!C, and C!B!B. These eight parts are parts of A, and each will have parts corresponding to it in both B and C; and so on without end. And all of these parts within parts to infinity will be determined by sufficient descriptions of B and C.[25]

By this principle of determining correspondence we are enabled to escape the apparent contradiction involved in the infinite divisibility of substance. For we have thus got an infinite series of parts of parts of any substance, A, in which the sufficient descriptions of each set of parts imply, and do not presuppose, the sufficient descriptions of sequent sets of parts. And so the difficulty, above explained, with reference to the total ultimate presupposition is removed.

With this we are brought to the general conclusion that sub-

---

[25] See Section 197 ff. In the example given above, A would be a *primary whole* and B and C would be *primary parts*. For formal definitions of these see Section 202.

stance must necessarily be such that the relation of determining correspondence holds. For the relation of determining correspondence is the only relation through which a contradiction in the nature of infinitely divisible substance can be avoided, and we have already proved that substance does exist and is infinitely divisible. The theory of determining correspondence may therefore be taken as proved.

2. SUBSTANCE AS SPIRITUAL

The question now arises whether we may say more about substance than has hitherto been said, in view of the fact that the principle of determining correspondence has been shown to hold true within it. In order to answer this question we are forced to turn to empirical considerations. *Prima facie*, the universe appears to contain substances of three different kinds, namely, matter, sensa, and spirit. We must investigate the claims of each of these, and we begin with matter.

(a) *Substance as Material*. On the basis of the considerations advanced in the preceding part of the argument, it is evident that substance is infinitely divisible and that such infinite divisibility involves a contradiction unless the parts of substance are determined by determining correspondence. If matter exists as substance, then, it must have infinite parts determined by determining correspondence. Is this possible?

It is to be noted, in the first place, that the required sufficient descriptions of the primary parts cannot be expressed in non-spatial qualities.[26] Take, for instance, color. Let the primary parts be sufficiently described, one as blue, one as red, and so on. Then the part of a primary part corresponding to another primary part would have to be two colors at once; the part of a primary part which is red, if it corresponded to the blue primary part, would have to be red and also blue. But it is obvious that this is impossible; a thing cannot be blue if a part of it is red. Nor could the difficulty be obviated if we suppose that, while the primary parts are sufficiently described by one sort of non-

---

[26] By non-spatial qualities are meant those qualities which are not strictly spatial—the strictly spatial qualities being three only, namely size, shape, and position.

spatial qualities, the secondary parts [27] are described by other sorts—that, for instance, the primary parts are sufficiently described by their color and the secondary parts by their taste. For, in the first place, there is no reason to suppose that matter possesses an infinite number of sorts of qualities analogous to color, taste, and so on—one sort for each of the infinite series of grades of secondary parts—as would have to be the case if this hypothesis is to hold. And, in the second place, there would have to be a separate law of determining correspondence for each of the infinite number of grades of parts, since no one kind of determining correspondence could hold throughout. Therefore, the determining correspondence could not be of such a nature as to remove the contradiction involved in substance.

It is clear that every material substance, in addition to its non-spatial qualities, must have spatial qualities (size, shape, and position) also. And, if a contradiction in the structure of material substance is to be avoided, these spatial qualities must be determined by determining correspondence. For otherwise, even if it were possible to give sufficient descriptions of spatial parts of parts of matter to infinity by means of their non-spatial qualities, the concurrence of the spatial qualities with the non-spatial qualities would be undetermined—and of these concurrences there would be an infinite number, since the number of parts is infinite. Furthermore, since the spatial qualities of the members of a set of parts imply the spatial qualities of the whole of which they are a set of parts, while themselves are only presupposed and not implied by the whole, we should, without determining correspondence among the spatial qualities, have an infinite series of parts in which the subsequent parts imply the precedent, while the precedent only presuppose the subsequent. Such a series would involve a contradiction, since every term in it would have a presupposition and yet could not have a total ultimate presupposition.

Thus we are driven to the conclusion that the spatial qualities

[27] A *secondary part* is any member of a set of parts sequent to the primary. For example: if A is a substance whose set of parts are B and C, then B!C would be a secondary part. As has already been said above, A would be a primary whole and B or C would be a primary part. For McTaggart's discussion of the terminology see Sections 197, 202.

of matter must be determined by determining correspondence. We are now to see that this is impossible unless we can establish determining correspondence in respect of the non-spatial qualities also (which, we have seen, cannot be done). And this holds whether space be taken as relative or as absolute. If we take space to be relative, then all the spatial qualities of matter are relational qualities which arise from the relationship of one piece of matter with another; and there cannot be such relationships unless the pieces of matter are otherwise differentiated from each other. M and N cannot be differentiated from each other merely by the fact that M's relation to N is different from N's relation to M. If, on the other hand, we take space as absolute, the same conclusion is inevitable. For spatial division to infinity by spatial qualities is only possible if each part is also differentiated by non-spatial qualities, since for each spatial part there must be some quality which is shared by all the parts of that part and is not shared by anything that is in spatial contact with that part, and this quality must necessarily be non-spatial. Thus determining correspondence in respect of the spatial qualities of matter is impossible apart from determining correspondence in respect of the non-spatial qualities.[28]

Our conclusion is, then, that matter cannot be divided into parts of parts to infinity in respect of its spatial dimensions. For, if so, there would have to be determining correspondence based either on non-spatial qualities or on spatial qualities. And we have seen (i) that it could not be based on non-spatial qualities, (ii) that, if it could, it would be necessary to base it also on spatial qualities, (iii) that the possibility of basing it on spatial qualities depends on its being independently based on non-spatial qualities, which is impossible. We turn, now, to inquire whether matter can be divided into parts of parts to infinity in respect of its temporal dimensions.

On consideration it seems clear that what has been said about space is true also of time. Therefore, by arguments similar to those outlined above in the case of space, we are brought to essentially the same conclusion in regard to time: (i) that the

[28] For the details of the argument here Sections 357-360 should be consulted.

JOHN—ELLIS McTAGGART (1866-1925)

necessary determining correspondence could not be based on non-temporal qualities; (ii) that, if it could, it would be necessary to base it also on temporal qualities; and (iii) that the possibility of basing it on temporal qualities depends on its being independently based on non-temporal qualities, which is impossible.[29]

If we suppose that matter as real is not in time and therefore is not possessed by a temporal dimension,[30] then, indeed, the fact that it could not be divided into parts of parts to infinity in respect of its temporal dimension is irrelevant to the question of its existence. For, in that supposition, matter could have no temporal dimension. But it would have a dimension that appears as temporal; and the question is raised whether in its trans-temporal, or real, dimension, which appears as temporal, matter is possessed of a basis for its being divided according to the principle of determining correspondence. This, however, is clearly not possible. For such a dimension of matter could be characterized only by spatial or non-spatial qualities; and we have just shown that these qualities can give no ground for the differentiation of matter into parts of parts to infinity. Therefore there can be no differentiation of matter, in respect of its trans-temporal dimension, on the principle of determining correspondence.

Thus matter cannot be divided into parts of parts to infinity in respect either of its spatial dimension, or of that dimension which is temporal or which is trans-temporal and appears as temporal. And matter, at least as usually defined, has no other dimensions. It cannot therefore be divided into parts of parts to infinity; and therefore it cannot exist.[31]

[29] The terms temporal and non-temporal are used here in senses analogous to those in which we have used the terms spatial and non-spatial above.

[30] McTaggart thinks that we must not merely assume that matter as real is non-temporal, but that we must hold this as a positive conviction. For, he maintains, it can be shown that nothing real is in time, and that everything which is perceived as in time is misperceived. For a summary statement of his argument in support of this conviction see the Appendix to the present chapter.

[31] McTaggart recognizes other possible definitions of matter to which the arguments above stated would hardly apply except with modifications. In his opinion, however, these modifications are of no basal importance

This conclusion is at variance with what is a universal belief, namely, that matter does exist. It may therefore be worth while to inquire into the justification of that belief.

We judge matter to exist, but we do not perceive it as existing. Our belief in the existence of matter is, thus, an inference. Now the basis on which this inference rests is the existence of sensa which, *prima facie* at any rate, are perceived as existing and not merely judged to exist. Our question therefore resolves itself into the question whether the existence of sensa is a sufficient ground for the inference that matter exists.[32]

The reason in support of an affirmative answer to this question is to be found in the two following propositions: (i) sensa must have causes, and it is highly improbable that each percipient is the sole cause of the sensa he perceives; (ii) the cause of sensa must have those qualities which constitute the nature of matter, since the sensa have those qualities. There is no need to object to the first of these propositions. Only when it is taken in conjunction with the second proposition, does it tend to prove the existence of matter; taken by itself, it does not exclude such conclusions as those of Berkeley, of Leibniz, and of Hegel, all of whom assigned to the sensa of each percipient a cause outside of himself, and all of whom denied the existence of matter. But the second proposition cannot be admitted, because it rests upon a principle which must be rejected as invalid. That principle is that there is always a special resemblance between cause and effect. Sometimes, of course, there is such a special resemblance; but often there is not, and this is sufficient to destroy the principle as a basis of argument in the case before us. Even if the principle were valid, its application as a proof of the existence of matter would involve us in many inconveniences. For instance, it would prove the existence of matter in the case of sensa in dreams; it would involve the

and mark no fundamental change in the arguments; nor does he think that these other views of matter can escape the general conclusion that matter does not exist. For his discussion of these points the reader should consult Sections 429-431.

[32] Sensa are those data of perception (percepta) which appear *prima facie* to be given us by means of the sense organs of our bodies—data of sight, touch, hearing, smell, and taste, together with those given in motor and organic sensation.

denial of the distinction between primary and secondary qualities and thus lead to the conclusion that one and the same piece of matter may have, for example, many colors at once; and, even if the distinction between primary and secondary qualities were inconsistently maintained, the principle would still force us to accept the inference that one and the same piece of matter may have several shapes at once. This line of argument for the existence of matter, then, must be rejected; it is based upon a principle which is invalid and which, if valid, would involve us either in inconsistencies or in absurdities.

Another argument in support of the judgment that matter exists has been advanced by Dr. Broad.[33] Summarily stated, the argument reduces to these two propositions: (i) there is no inner contradiction in the qualities of shape and size, since sensa at least have shape and size and sensa certainly exist; and (ii) the only hypothesis, on which the variations in the shape of visual sensa as the observer changes position can be explained, is the hypothesis that something, at least analogous to shape, belongs to the permanent conditions of visual sensa. And the conclusion based on these propositions is that, if the existence of matter is not thus proved, it is at least rendered highly probable.

Two observations, however, considerably weaken the force of this argument and render it inadequate to establish a ground for the belief that matter exists. The first observation is that proposition (i) rests on a questionable assumption, namely, that erroneous perception is impossible; and, since this assumption may reasonably be called in question, even though there can be no doubt that we do perceive things as sensa having shape and size, it is still possible that there should be an inner contradiction in the qualities of shape and size. The second observation is that proposition (ii) does not seem to be correct. For it is clear that we can bring under a general law—and this is all we can mean by explaining anything—the variations referred to without attributing to their permanent conditions anything analogous to shape. The permanent conditions might be spiritual (non-material) substances misperceived as bodies in spatial and

33 In *Scientific Thought*, p. 278.

temporal relations to each other, and yet all conditions for the explanation of variations in shape as the observer changes position would be supplied. For the substances in question, since they appear as being in space, would have their appearances connected together by the laws of space as much as real substances in space would have their real natures connected by the laws of space.

Consequently our conclusion with reference to the question, how belief in the existence of matter is to be justified, is that there is no justification for it. The argument from the qualities of sensa to the qualities of their causes is unwarranted, and the facts of sense-experience can be explained on the hypothesis that there is no matter. This would, by itself, compel us to refrain from believing that matter exists but could not, of course, justify us in believing that matter does not exist. The justification for this belief rests on the argument advanced in the earlier part of this section.

(b) *Substance as Sensa.* The objects which we perceive are called percepta, and they are divided into two classes. The first is the class of those data which the percipient perceives by introspection; such data are *prima facie* spiritual and will be considered under the following heading. The second class is made up of those data which appear to be given us by means of the sense organs of our bodies and which are called sensa. It has sometimes been supposed that sensa are parts of the percipient and are therefore spiritual; but this view seems to arise from a failure to distinguish between the sensum and the perception of it, and when this distinction is clearly made there appears to be no reason to regard the sensum itself as part of the percipient, but only the perception of the sensum. There is consequently no reason to suppose that the sensum is spiritual. On the other hand, however, it is clear that there is a *prima facie* distinction between sensa and matter. For example, two men looking at the same coin from different points of view would *prima facie* be said to perceive sensa which are different but which point to the same piece of matter.

Thus we tend *prima facie* to believe in a world which is made up of matter, sensa, and spirit. We have just seen that there is reason to conclude that this *prima facie* appearance is illusory in the case of matter; the question now before us is whether it is also illusory in the case of sensa. The case of spirit will be considered in the next section.

That this *prima facie* appearance is illusory in the case of sensa may readily be shown. If sensa exist, they must have parts within parts to infinity determined on the principle of determining correspondence. But this is impossible, since sensa are not perceived as having any qualities which can give sufficient descriptions in accordance with this principle. Let us note briefly why this is true.

The argument in support of this conclusion is essentially the same as that which led to a similar conclusion in the case of matter. The qualities which the sensa are perceived as having include the qualities that are attributed to matter; and we have already seen that precisely these qualities are not such as to give sufficient descriptions of a series of parts within parts to infinity on the principle of determining correspondence.

It is true that sensa are perceived as having at least two qualities which are not attributed to matter. These are: intensity, as when we perceive a bright light as more intense than a dull light; and extensity, as when we perceive the massiveness of a hot bath. But neither of these will give us a basis for sufficient descriptions of an infinite series of parts within parts. For the difference between the degrees of these qualities is not a third quality of the same sort—the difference between a bright light and a less bright light is not a light of another brightness, nor is the difference between a more and a less extensive pain a pain of another extension. And so it is impossible that a sensum should be divided into parts in respect of either of these qualities.

Sensa therefore lack qualities which can give sufficient descriptions according to the principle of determining correspondence. Consequently we must hold that sensa do not exist as substances. This is, of course, not to deny that they exist in some sense. But in the sense in which they may be said to exist they must have a nature very different from that usually assigned to them; they must have qualities which they are not

perceived as possessing, and which cannot be deduced from any
of the qualities they are perceived as possessing.

(c) *Substance as Spiritual.* In turning to inquire whether
substance can exist as spiritual, we must first undertake to fix
the meaning of spirit. And this may be done, partially at least,
by the following definition: Spirit is the content of any substance
which is a self, a part of a self, a group of selves, or a group
whose members are selves and parts of selves. Any such substance would be called spiritual, though the phrase '*a spirit*'
should be restricted in its application to that spiritual substance
which is a self.

But what are we to understand by a self? Strictly speaking,
the quality of being a self is indefinable; and it is indefinable
because it is ultimate. Nevertheless, this quality is certainly
known. It is that quality which is known to every self-conscious
being since each such being perceives one substance—namely,
himself—as possessing that quality; each self is known to itself
in direct perception. If one doubts whether this statement is
warranted, the following argument may carry conviction. The
proposition, "I am aware of equality," has a meaning, and I
know what the proposition means; therefore I must know each
constituent member of the proposition, and so I must know 'I.'
But whatever is known must be known either by acquaintance
or by description. 'I' cannot be known by description, however,
since either we get no exclusive description or we get two descriptions with no way of knowing that they belong to one
self. Hence it follows that 'I' must be, and is, known by acquaintance, which is equivalent to saying that each must know
the meaning of 'I' and does so by perceiving himself.[34]

[34] The argument is, of course, necessarily much abridged in the summary given here. For the details (and they are necessary if the full force
of the argument is to be felt) the reader should consult Sections 382-393.
The two crucial theses of the argument are: (i) the disjunction with
reference to the two ways of knowing, and (ii) the denial that any self
can be known by description. Of the disjunction McTaggart here offers no
proof, and contents himself with a reference to Russell's article, "Knowledge by Acquaintance and Knowledge by Description." In support of the
second thesis, however, detailed analysis is presented in Sections 383-391
inclusive, in which many points of importance are raised. In Section 392
McTaggart notes the fact that his conclusion stands in opposition to
Bradley's view that whatever is known is *ipso facto* part of the not-self, is,

Thus we may take our provisional definition of spirit as being precise. Spirit is the content of a self or of selves and parts of selves; and the meaning of self, though indefinable, is definite and is directly known by each self-conscious being in his awareness or perception of himself. And we may now proceed to ask whether spirit so defined does exist and, if so, whether there is any reason to suppose that all substance is spirit.

If spirit exists, it must have parts within parts to infinity determined by determining correspondence. Can anything possessing the nature of spirit fulfil this requirement? If not, then we are forced to hold that nothing possessing the nature of spirit can exist. If so, then we are permitted to accept the existence of spirit, since it is clear that *prima facie* spirit claims to exist.

There are three assumptions on the basis of which we can say that spirit may have an infinite series of parts within parts determined by determining correspondence. These assumptions are: (i) that a self can perceive another self, and a part of another self; (ii) that a perception is part of the percipient self; and (iii) that a perception of a part of a whole can be part of a perception of that whole. If these assumptions are granted, the principle of determining correspondence can be established in respect of spiritual substance. Let us suppose a primary whole consisting of two primary parts, B and C, which are selves. The number of primary parts, of course, might be infinite, but the principle would remain the same. Then, by hypothesis, B will perceive himself and C, and will perceive the perceptions which he and C have of themselves and of one another, and the perceptions which they have of these perceptions, and so on to infinity. And B's perceptions of this infinite series of percepta will form an infinite series of perceptions, since he has a separate perception of each perceptum. And since the perceptions of the parts will be parts of the perceptions of the whole, the infinite series will be series of parts within parts. A similar series will occur in C. Thus we shall have a whole of parts within parts to infinity, determined on the principle of determining corre-

in other words, always object and never subject or self. He might also have referred to Kant's famous paralogism on the same topic and to the same effect, but he does not do so.

spondence, since the relation between C and the parts of B or between B and the parts of C is a relation of perception and, on our assumptions, complies with all the conditions with which a relation of determining correspondence must comply.[35] Consequently, if our assumptions are true, we may say spirit exists.

But the three assumptions are true; at least they are not impossible, and we must now see how this is so.

It is sometimes held to be impossible that one self can perceive another self, or a part of another self. But there is no justification for this position. It is true that in present experience no self perceives a state of mind of any other self. I do not perceive any state of mind of any person but myself; I have reason to believe that no person whom I know, either directly or indirectly, has perceived states of mind of any other person than himself; and I have no reason to believe that any person in the universe has done so. But the mere fact that there is no reason to suppose that something does happen is no proof that it could not possibly happen. Therefore it still remains possible that a self might perceive the states of mind of another self, despite the fact that there is no reason to think that in present experience any self actually does so. And this possibility is sufficient for the purposes of the present argument. So we may assume that the question concerning our first assumption is answered affirmatively—a self may perceive another self, or a part of another self.[36]

In addition to introspective evidence, which seems affirmative, but which is by no means conclusive on the point, there are three reasons that would seem to compel the admission that the second of our assumptions is true. (i) The more numerous the perceptions, the 'fuller' the self which has them; and, if this is an appropriate metaphor as it seems to be, it can be so only because

[35] For McTaggart's detailed justification of this statement see Sections 229 and 410.

[36] McTaggart suggests that a possible explanation of the prevailing belief that one self cannot perceive a state of another self is to be found in the failure to note that *having* a state and *perceiving* a state are two quite different things. It is true that not more than one self could have one and the same state; in that event one self would be the state of another self, and this involves a real impossibility. But there is nothing in this to prevent one self's being aware of the awareness of another self.

the perceptions are parts of the self. Again, (ii) B's perception of C makes more direct difference to B than it does to C—the direct difference between B who perceives C and B if he did not perceive C is greater than the difference between C who is perceived by B and C when not perceived by B. In other words, perception makes a greater difference to the percipient than to the perceived; and it is very difficult to understand why this should be, unless perception is a part of the percipient. Finally, (iii) pleasures and pains are parts of the self, and this in itself is sufficient ground for rejecting any argument which assumes that selves cannot have parts. All of these three reasons tend to confirm the theory that perceptions are parts of selves, and there seems to be no valid argument against the theory. We may therefore accept the theory as at least highly probable.

The evidence in support of our third assumption above rests on introspection. It seems clear that, in certain cases at least, we perceive a whole with parts and that the parts are perceived as parts of the whole. For example, I judge that there is at this moment a carpet in this room with a pattern on it, when I have no reason to do so except that, in ordinary language, I see the carpet. In such a case I am perceiving a sensum which is a whole with parts; and my judgment that the carpet is a whole with parts depends on my perception of the whole sensum, and of the parts of the sensum. And it seems clear on introspection that here my perceptions of the parts are parts of my perception of the whole. This becomes specially evident when one considers that, as the details of the pattern of the carpet progressively appear with a gradual increase of light, the change is from a relatively simple perception (the undifferentiated whole carpet) to a relatively complex perception (the carpet as patterned). This is precisely what we should expect to happen if the perceptions of the parts were parts of the perception of the whole. So we may conclude that it is not only possible, but is the empirical fact, that *some* perceptions of parts are parts of perceptions of wholes. And if this is true in some cases, there is no reason why it should not be true in all; therefore, our third assumption is justified.

Thus all three of our assumptions may be accepted as pos-

sible, and even as probable. Consequently we may take the
prima facie existence of spiritual substance as real existence, in
so far as the parts of spiritual substance are perceptions or
groups of perceptions.[37]

Turning, in conclusion, to inquire whether every existent substance must be spiritual, we can see that there is good reason
to hold that such is the case. Of all forms of substance which
have ever appeared to be experienced, only one conforms to the
condition to which every substance as we have seen must conform; and that form is spirit. The other two *prima facie* forms
of substance, matter and sensa, must certainly be said not to
exist as real substances, since they do not fulfil the conditions of
the principle of determining correspondence. Of course, there
does remain the possibility that there is some other form of
substance, which is not spiritual, whose nature is such as to
allow of the determination of its parts within parts to infinity.
But, if there is such substance, there is not the slightest empirical
evidence for it; we cannot even imagine what it could be. Under
these circumstances it would seem that we are logically entitled
to hold that all substance is spiritual—not indeed as a proposition which has been rigorously demonstrated, but as one which
it is reasonable to believe and unreasonable to disbelieve.

With this we are committed to that view of substance which,
according to general usage, may be called by the name of Idealism. Of course, if the name of Idealism is reserved as a name
for a certain sort of epistemological theory, then our view is
not idealistic; since there is in that view no tenet which denies
that a belief is true when, and only when, it corresponds to fact.
The view is rather that of Ontological Idealism, since it holds
that all that exists is spiritual; it is idealistic in the sense in

---

[37] For McTaggart's argument in support of the exclusion of other
prima facie states of selves as real states see Sections 415-425, and Chapters XL, XLI. The argument has been omitted here because it does not
seem indispensable for this summary statement.

A critical comment on the argument of the immediately preceding paragraph above may here be set down. Does the example of the perception
of the carpet prove that the perceptions of the parts are parts of the perception of the whole, or only that the percepta which are parts are perceived as parts of the perceptum which is the whole? There is a difference
of importance here, and clarity as to what is proved is essential.

which the views of Leibniz, Berkeley, and Hegel are idealistic. All that exists is spiritual, the primary parts in the system of determining correspondence are selves, and the secondary parts of all grades are perceptions; selves, therefore, are alone primary parts in the universe, and the universe cannot be a self [38]—such is the view to which our argument has brought us.

APPENDIX

TIME

Like many other idealists, McTaggart holds the thesis that time is unreal and that nothing which exists can really be temporal. The argument which he advances in support of this thesis may be reduced to the following considerations.[39]

As time *prima facie* appears to us, there are two ways of distinguishing positions in time: (i) as present, past, future; and (ii) as earlier, later. For brevity, let us call the first series the A series, and the second the B series. The distinctions of the first series are not permanent, while the distinctions of the second are permanent; an event which is now present, was future, and will be past, while if an event is ever earlier than another it is always earlier. From this fact it might be supposed that the B series is a more important description of time, more essential to its nature, than is the A series. The first question which confronts us, therefore, is whether this is the case or whether it is essential to the nature of time that its events should form an A series as well as a B series.

Is the A series subjective only, while the B series constitutes the real nature of time? On such an hypothesis, change must be possible in the B series taken alone, since by common consent time involves change. But change is impossible in the B series taken alone. An event in the B series (in which the only relations are the permanent ones of earlier and later) always has been an event and always will be one, and cannot begin or cease to be an event. It cannot therefore merge into another event, since at

[38] For the argument on this last point see Section 404. "A whole of which a self is part cannot be a self."

[39] The text of the argument may be found in *The Nature of Existence*, Book V, Chapter XXXIII.

the moment of merging the first event would have ceased to be and another would have begun to be. Consequently, an event in the B series alone cannot change. The only characteristics of an event that can possibly change are its characteristics in respect of the A series; therefore the A series is essential to change and, so, to time; if the B series is to be temporal, it must necessarily involve the A series.

But the A series cannot exist. Past, present, and future are relations—if they are taken as qualities, the argument is not in principle affected—hence they are relative to something else. This something else must be outside of the time-series, since "the relations of the A series are changing relations, and no relations which are exclusively between the members of the time-series can ever change." Consequently, present, past, and future are relations between terms of the A series and an outside entity, X, such that between X and any given term of the A series there is one, and only one, of these relations. To find such an outside entity is not easy, and yet it must be found if the A series is to be called really existent. Furthermore—this is a more positive difficulty—past, present, and future are incompatible determinations, and yet every event in real time must have them all; a past event has been both present and future, a present event has been future and will be past, and a future event will be present and then past. Nor can this contradiction be explained away by saying that one and the same event has these determinations *successively*. In this way the difficulty is not solved, but merely transferred to 'moments'; for what is really said is that an event is present at a moment of present time, past at some moment of future time, and future at some moment of past time. Thus we get the same contradiction, "since the moments at which M has any one of the three determinations of the A series are also moments at which it cannot have that determination." Present, past, and future are as relative with respect to moments as they are with respect to events. The reality of the A series thus leads to inescapable contradiction, and so must be rejected and the reality of time with it. The distinctions of past, present, and future are essential for time; but these distinctions cannot characterize the existent.

CHAPTER IX

VISCOUNT HALDANE (1856-1928)

RICHARD BURDON HALDANE, Viscount of Cloan, was not a philosopher by profession. Throughout his life, however, he was deeply interested in philosophical problems. In his earlier years he had intensive training in philosophical studies under Fraser at Edinburgh and Lotze at Göttingen; in his later years he found time even in the midst of a very busy life as member of Parliament, as Secretary of State for War, and later as Lord Chancellor, to devote himself to systematic philosophical inquiry. The results of his reflections were published in several substantial volumes which place him in the forefront of the representatives of idealistic philosophy in Britain.[1]

In the Preface to his Gifford Lectures he confesses that his chief ground for confidence in the conclusion there defended is "that in substance it has been arrived at long ago. It seems to me," he continues, "that the history of speculative thought, properly read, is no record of discordant hypotheses. It is rather the story of the elaboration of a great conception, in the building up of which, from time to time, construction has been broadened by criticism, and criticism has then been succeeded by more adequate construction. But the main structure of the conception has remained unaltered. Its foundations were laid, more than two thousand years ago, by Aristotle, and these foundations were uncovered, and the structure overhauled, by the great German thinkers who began to interpret Aristotle at the beginning of the last century." He stood by this conviction throughout his life and reaffirms it in the personal statement which he contributed

[1] The most important of his philosophical works are: *The Pathway to Reality* (Gifford Lectures, 1902-1903); *The Reign of Relativity* (1921); and *The Philosophy of Humanism* (1922). An early essay, "The Relation of Philosophy to Science," written in conjunction with his brother, J. S. Haldane, and published in *Essays in Philosophical Criticism* (1883), anticipates the basal theme of his later thought. A popular summary of his mature views is given in the small volume *Human Experience* (1926).

to *Contemporary British Philosophy* shortly before his death: "On the whole, I think that Hegel has come nearer to the ultimately true view than any one since the ancient Greeks."

The influence of Hegel on Haldane was exerted, however, "by his method of approach rather than by his system, or by his detailed theory of the absolute." This method Haldane interpreted to be the disclosure of the character of knowledge by its own self-scrutiny, as exemplified especially in Hegel's *Phenomenology of Mind.* And the outcome of the method he held to be twofold: on the one side, the principle of the foundational character of mind or knowledge, and, on the other side, the corollary doctrine of degrees of reality. A summary statement of each of these will present his own independent formulation of the idealistic argument, which, as we must indicate in conclusion, he thinks is somewhat different in outcome from the formulations of Bradley, Bosanquet, and Pringle-Pattison.

1. Knowledge or Mind as Foundational

The simple statement of this principle is: "There is no world apart from knowledge for which it is there." [2] And the reason for the principle is that a world apart from knowledge or mind is meaningless: "The relation of mind to nature is a foundational one, and it lies in this, that there can be no meaning in any object-world that is not object-world for a knower. If there can be no meaning for the object there can be accordingly no existence for it. For existence involves meaning, and is not a fact unless it is significant." [3] This position seems paradoxical because of a confusion between two meanings of knowledge or mind, and this confusion must first of all be cleared away.

On the one side and most obviously, mind may be identified with an object among other objects, falling together with and conditioned by a physical organism, and possessing knowledge as a sort of instrument which it makes use of in apprehension. As thus taken mind and its knowledge are natural products of the order of events, and are conditioned by environing circum-

[2] *Human Experience*, p. 22.

[3] *The Reign of Relativity*, p. 169. The pagination throughout is that of the first edition of this volume; but the quotations are identical in the third edition.

stances. But this is not all there is to mind and knowledge. For immanent in them, thus taken, and as their implied foundation, there is an ideal system wider in range and quality. In the finite individual neither mind nor knowledge reaches its final or complete expression; on the contrary, each transcends itself in seeking its own fulfilment. Its range appears narrow, not because its nature is narrow, but because of the hindrances due to the organic form in which it finds expression. Its nature is a larger entirety within which it tends to bring itself at every turn.

If mind and knowledge are taken in the narrower sense, they cannot be held to be foundational. To hold that there is no world apart from mind and knowledge in this sense is to assert what clearly is not so and to involve oneself in the paradoxes of mentalism. In the wider sense, however, mind and knowledge are foundational of both apprehension and what is apprehended. Within the larger entirely falls the distinction between subject and object, as well as the whole meaning of reality. And these two points call for separate statement.

Taken *per se*, subject is clearly an abstraction; so is object. This is true because each is only an aspect of a larger whole— the whole of meaning. The 'I' is the center to which all meanings are referred, and the 'not-me' is that which is there *for* me; and the whole meaningful experience is foundational to the distinction between the center and that which is there *for* it. "Except as it is for me the world is incapable of interpretation. Object and subject therefore cannot be looked on as two things existing independently or as separate entities of any kind. They are rather different aspects in an integral process or spiritual activity, a whole within which both fall as aspects." [4] Apart from this whole the distinction between subject and object is entirely meaningless. "In our experience, in its fullest aspect as a form of knowledge, we find that to know means to be neither only subject nor only object, but that these are the moments in a larger entirety, which is the actual fact of knowledge within which they are distinguished." [5]

---

[4] *Ibid.*, p. 166; cf. the entire Chapter VII. Compare Bradley's position on the point.

[5] *Ibid.*, p. 173.

Not only is this larger entirety of mind and knowledge foundational to the distinction between subject and object; it is also foundational to reality itself. The simplest way of approaching the problem of what reality amounts to is to start with experience as real and to watch its implications and changes. Doing this, we find that anything we can call real is so called because of its place in the order of knowledge; its reality, or its lack of it, must be stated in terms of its relation to an ideal knower. "What is obvious is that there is nothing in any particular experience, and equally nothing conceived as lying beyond it, that has a meaning excepting in terms of knowledge. And if existence be only one of these meanings, then to be known in some form is the only way of being real. To be known, I repeat, not as if through a window, by a mind that is *merely* organically conditioned, but as by mind that signifies the system to which the finite intelligence and its object-world alike belong." [6] Reality itself, thus, is an empty abstraction when taken apart from the whole of meaning which is the ideal of finite mind and knowledge.

The general conclusion of this section may be summarily put as follows: "The world that confronts me is actual, and is independent of me, its observer. But that is not the last word about either that world or myself. Both belong to a greater entirety. It is only in so far as they fall within the field of knowledge that they have any meaning or are. The difficulty which realism has had in admitting this has arisen from its assumption that knowledge is the property and instrument of a finite self, the means by which an independent knower lays hold of what is actual apart from himself. But this assumption not only makes the knower different from his knowledge, but implicitly treats the knower as a substance of which knowledge is an activity or property. The knower is thus regarded as finite. In a sense this

---

[6] *The Reign of Relativity*, pp. 137-138; author's italics. This last sentence is quite important for Haldane's thesis: To be real is to be known, but only in the sense of being present to mind as the totality of meanings within which the subject-object distinction falls—as "the self-developing interpretation and expansion of the meanings which are its own creatures, the meanings which make reality what it is, whether for limited purposes we distinguish it as what we call non-mental or not." (*Ibid.*, p. 286; cf. the entire passage.)

is true, as we have already seen, but only when we are concerned with aspects that are far from representing the whole truth. Knowledge cannot really be an instrument wielded *ab extra*, because it is that within which all reality, whatever be its nature, falls. Moreover, knowledge cannot itself be expressed in terms that go beyond itself. It is the foundation of all reality, of the percipient mind, whether nascent or fully developed, as much as of that which is perceived. Because, at the stage at which we exist as individual human beings, it expresses itself in the form of an organism, the conscious self makes itself actual in finite form, the form of the intelligent self with a physical aspect. This fact is its 'That,' from which we start and must start, and our task does not go beyond the explanation of what it signifies. . . . It is by making use of a single kind of conception, and assuming it to be exhaustive, that we come to think of the mind as one thing and its object as another thing, with knowledge as a property by which the first can reach the second. But closer attention shows that mind is much more than an individual thing and, taken apart from the abstract fashion in which we are apt to regard it, is not different in nature from knowledge itself. Our experience is thus potentially and implicitly complete knowledge. It is our human conditions that prevent it from becoming this explicitly. Yet, inasmuch as we are inherently more than we take ourselves to be, no ideal short of perfection in knowledge can ever satisfy us." [7]

2. Degrees of Reality

The foundational character of knowledge, linked with the fact that knowledge discloses itself at a variety of levels, leads to another important doctrine, namely, that of degrees of reality. We are now to inquire how this is so.

That there are levels in knowledge has long been recognized. The fact was early forced on the attention of mankind by the necessity of making use of different types of categories and the problems arising in consequence. The fields of matter, life, mind were long ago distinguished; and it was seen that, *prima facie* at least, each called for a different set of explanatory principles.

[7] *Ibid.*, pp. 211-212.

Categories in explanation of matter would hardly fit organic forms, while organisms exhibiting consciously intelligent behavior seem to demand other explanatory concepts than those applicable to merely living forms. With these different types of categories came the problem of their interrelation, and of the facts they describe.

Formerly it was supposed that the facts might be reduced to matter and energy, and the categories consequently to one type. This was the method of the older materialism. But it now seems hopeless to build up the explanation from below. "Morality cannot be reduced to mathematics, and no more can life be resolved into mechanism, or reason into mere instinct." [8] Nor is the suggestion of the New Realists any more satisfactory. They undertake to put the universals and relations of thought into the nonmental world, which for them confronts the mind as something from which the latter is receptive. But herewith the mind becomes like a substance on which impressions are causally effected from without. Among the causes are the very universals whose significance seems to be possible only as belonging to the nature of mind itself. And there is no justification for this, certainly not in scientific methods of treatment.

On the contrary, the methods of science impel us to a very different view. The principle of relativity in recent physics, for example, involves the view that relativity belongs to the very nature of the object in knowledge. The objects constituting our universe will present appearances which differ in every case according to the situation and kind of motion of the observers with their measuring systems; these appearances are the actual reality.[9] Now the principle of relativity as applied to space- and time-relations holds of other forms of knowledge as well, and it is to be regretted that the title 'theory of relativity' was ever appropriated to the extent it has been for Einstein's doctrine, as if it belonged to that doctrine in a special way. It is characteristic of all forms of knowledge. "The different orders in experience appear to imply, as determining their meanings, conceptions of characters logically diverse, like those of mechanism,

[8] *The Reign of Relativity,* p. 133.
[9] Cf. *Ibid.,* Chapters V and VI.

of life, of instinct, and of conscious intelligence. The principle of relativity applies to all standpoints determined by conceptions appropriate indeed to particular orders of knowledge, but thereby of a limiting character. It seems therefore accurate to regard quantitative relativity as only a special illustration of a wider principle." [10] And applying the principle in this wide sense we are brought to the conclusion that the sundry categories enter into the nature of the objects of knowledge as foundational in their structure; the actual turns out to be profoundly dependent on the character of knowledge itself, in the sense that the object of knowledge is relative to knowledge.

Thus the levels of knowledge are, and must always remain, distinct and irreducible. The categories descriptive of conscious intelligence are *sui generis*, and so are those descriptive of life and matter. Each set of categories is applicable only on its own level, and to employ them uncritically as if they could be indiscriminately applied (as materialism does, for instance, or abstract mentalism or panpsychism) is to fall into the fallacy of the confusion of categories. But the irreducibility of the categories is not to be understood to mean that the different levels are separate entities, cut off from each other by sharp lines of cleavage. This would lead into another fallacy equally serious —the fallacy, namely, of hypostatizing phases of knowledge into isolated and independent entities, as when a living organism comes to be regarded as an entity of a kind different from mechanism, or a mind as an entity or kind of thing different from both. From this error we may be saved by remembering that knowledge is basically a structure which is foundational in the particular knowledge of every individual knower, and that the levels of knowledge are phases or aspects of this more comprehensive and basal entirety.

Linking with what has just been said the consideration, already established, that reality falls within knowledge, we arrive at once at the doctrine of degrees of reality. Levels of knowledge are precisely degrees of reality, since reality is unintelligible apart from its relation to knowledge. The principle of relativity thus applies to reality. "The actual is meaningless except

[10] *Ibid.,* p. 125.

in terms of knowledge, and that knowledge can only describe itself if the full variety of its orders is recognised as essentially implied in it." [11] Thus the actual is a variety of orders recognized as essentially implied in it; the orders of knowledge and the orders of reality are in the end indistinguishable.

What has been said about the levels of knowledge, then, holds in principle of the degrees of reality. These degrees are distinct in the sense that they are irreducible each to the others; the assumption that they are reducible rests on a mere confusion, arising from a failure to recognize that knowledge is foundational and that the principle of relativity consequently applies universally. But, on the other side, these degrees are not to be mistaken for separate and isolated entities. Through our various conceptions we isolate only aspects or phases of reality; we do not through them distinguish independent realities as separately existing. This follows immediately from the consideration that our various conceptual forms of knowledge involve, as basal within their meanings, an entirety of knowledge or an ideal whole of meaning.

The doctrine of degrees here stated is intimately connected with the problem of truth. A brief reference to the application of the doctrine to that problem may serve to clarify the doctrine. The important point is the bearing of the doctrine on the distinction between relative and absolute truth.

According to the doctrine of degrees, there is an important sense in which the truth of an idea belongs exclusively to the order or level to which it directly applies. This is the sense in which all of our special conceptions, as, for example, the conceptions of physics or of biology, are true. Conceptions true in this sense, though indispensable instruments of scientific analysis and progress, are only relatively true; they are true only as applying, each exclusively to its own level of reality. A conception which applies to one level may not at all apply to another level. The conceptions of mechanism, for instance, apply to organisms at one level (as machines) but not to organisms at another level (as consciously selective bodies). But, since the levels of reality are not independent entities, but aspects of a larger entirety, a

[11] *The Reign of Relativity*, p. 235.

given conception is not exhaustive of the nature of its level. It is only by abstraction, by shutting out from attention certain aspects of what we observe, that we can employ these conceptions; and the fact that their truth is relative follows directly from this abstractness. Ideally, a true conception in any absolute sense would have to give expression to the whole of meaning which knowledge implies, and so comprehend the universe. Clearly such an ideal is impossible of attainment by any finite mind, conditioned and confined as it is by senses and brain. Our standard of truth as human beings must fall short of this ideal "and be just a working instrument with the aid of which we seek to travel towards the interpretation that is complete." [12] But it is sheer confusion to suppose that, because our conceptual principles are thus instrumental and relative, they do not in any sense express the nature of reality. After all, the facts to which they apply are real facts; and though the conceptions are inadequate in respect of the full nature of those facts (and this inadequacy must never be forgotten in reading their significance), they are not merely illusory or merely instrumental. [13]

3. FINITE CENTERS AND THE ABSOLUTE

The doctrine of degrees set forth in the preceding section bears directly on the problem of the relation of finite individuals to each other and to the universe. We are now to inquire what solution of the problem the doctrine suggests.

That finite individuals are distinct centers of activity and interest is, of course, a matter of common experience, and any theory which involves the denial of such distinctness is, on that account, unsatisfactory. It is very important to note, however, that each finite individual lies, so to say, at different levels and that its distinctness and uniqueness vary in significance as it is viewed in its different aspects. "The distinction of finite centres from each other possesses one significance when we look to their physical aspects, another significance when we find them as organisms obeying the impulses of the species, and a still

[12] *Ibid.*, p. 140; cf. pp. 10 ff., 138 ff.

[13] Compare Haldane's analytical study of Dewey's view of experience and knowledge in *Experience and Nature* (cf. *Human Experience, passim*).

different meaning when we find them as conscious intelligences co-operating in social wholes."

It is even more important to note what this variation amounts to. Taken in its physical aspect, the distinctness of the individual may be defined largely in terms of mere externality and imperviousness. Taken as an organism, however, the individual loses something of its punctual character and an element of identity with other individuals emerges as basal within its uniqueness. As a conscious intelligence its identity with other individuals becomes the important matter and its externality and imperviousness relatively unimportant. "As we reach the highest regions of mind, in art, in religion, in thought, the distinctness of the finite centres still remains. But it remains for purposes which, at this stage, though real, are subordinate. The transition has been to new conceptions, a change which is more than what can be expressed as one in time. It is a transition within mind to higher standpoints and degrees in reality, in which the higher supersede and yet preserve as logical moments those that they transcend." [14] And, be it remembered, this transition to higher standpoints and degrees in reality is necessitated, not by any merely *a priori* considerations, but by the nature of the finite center itself.

Applying the principle here stated to the problem of the relation between finite individuals (and, indeed, all levels or degrees of reality) and the universe taken as ideal for mind and knowledge, we are in position to see that the answer is not obscure. "An ideal and perfect Universe would be one in which the recognition of all these degrees of reality, these stages in the logic of comprehension, took their places in a mind recognised as completely at one with its object, and containing its world in that completeness as a moment in its own creative activity, a self-creation in which end and means were not finally divorced by the time process." [15] Such a mind might be called the Abso-

[14] The quotations here given are taken from Haldane's contribution to a symposium on the question, "Do Finite Individuals Possess a Substantive or an Adjectival Mode of Being?" (*Proceedings of the Aristotelian Society*, 1918, p. 92.) The entire discussion bears directly on the point at issue.

[15] *Ibid.,* cf. p. 95.

lute. Whether it should be described as 'personal' is an open question, which is partly a matter of terminology. But this at least is clear: In such an Absolute, degrees of reality, the distinctness of finite centers, are not dissolved and negated, but are preserved as logical moments in a higher unity which includes them. To image the details of this unity and this inclusion is, of course, not within the power of finite and limited minds; such minds cannot see God. But there is no region, not even the region of the Absolute, which finite minds cannot survey conceptually. And, if we are careful to avoid the fallacy of the confusion of categories, we may conceptually envisage the Absolute as the unity which expresses itself through the differences of finite centers without 'transmuting' or negating them. Such an ideal unity is, in fact, postulated by the common logic of our daily experience; it is precisely the implication of the foundational character of knowledge.

The position here defended is partially opposed to the views of Bradley, Bosanquet, and Pringle-Pattison. A brief consideration of the opposition and the ground for it may serve to emphasize the basal principle which underlies the issue.

Bradley and Bosanquet tend to minimize the distinctness and uniqueness of finite individuals, and to insist that they are transient aspects of reality which are 'absorbed' and 'transmuted' in the Absolute. This emphasis Pringle-Pattison deprecates and urges in opposition the 'imperviousness' and 'otherness' of finite centers, each of which for him remains to the end "the apex of the principle of individuation by which the world exists." [16] All three thinkers agree, however, that the relation between finite individuals and the Absolute is unintelligible and that the Absolute is impenetrable to thought.

If the doctrine of degrees is to be accepted, the controversy with reference to the 'universality' or the 'uniqueness' of the finite individual falls to the ground. For the finite individual is both at once, nor does his uniqueness and imperviousness stand in conflict with his universality. He is neither to the exclusion of the other, but is both at once and is each equally really. Which he is to be taken as, and with what significance he is to

[16] *The Idea of God,* pp. 389-390, note.

be so taken, depends on the level at which he is to be explained; the whole question is one of degree and aspect. But if taken in one aspect, he is not thereby denied the other; and this principle holds even of his relation to the Absolute.

The reason why Pringle-Pattison holds that the relation between the finite individual and the Absolute is "necessarily incomprehensible save by the Absolute itself" is the assumption that from the finite point of view there is a contradiction between the 'uniqueness' of the finite and the 'universality' which must characterize it as an element in the universe. This assumption falls down, however, if the doctrine of degrees is applied to the problem, as we have just indicated. Contradiction between the two characters arises only when either is taken in abstraction from the principle.

Bradley and Bosanquet insist upon essentially the same position. For them, too, the Absolute is impenetrable to thought and the relation which finite centers bear to it remains unintelligible. They base their position on an analysis of knowledge. Since the form of every judgment is essentially relational, they argue, the subject of judgment always falls beyond the predicate (which is necessarily abstract); however extended, the predicate can never contain the whole nature of the subject. Hence it follows that the Absolute, which is the ultimate subject, always lies beyond the reach of our predicates, and is thus impenetrable to thought. This argument we must, in conclusion, briefly examine.

It is to be emphasized, in the first place, that the position, if left standing, brings us to the precipice of skepticism concerning the Absolute. For it logically prevents our getting even negatively at the character of Absolute experience. "If the only way of thinking be relational, and this way cannot be that of truth, what other path to the Absolute can there be? It is the old difficulty which arises when men begin by criticising the instrument of knowledge, and so discredit it and their own criticism along with it. The outcome is not new knowledge but a scepticism which bids us cease endeavour. Faith in the possibility of knowing even so much about the Absolute as is permitted in Mr. Bradley's *Appearance and Reality* and more recent *Essays on Truth and Reality*, or in Professor Bosanquet's

Gifford Lectures or his well-known Eighth Chapter in the last edition of his *Logic,* such faith becomes difficult when abstract thought has been to so great an extent deposed from being a guide to truth, and possibly from being even aware that it is no guide." [17]

The skepticism inherent in the position extends not only to the Absolute, to *ultimate* reality, but, in the second place, it applies much nearer home, to *proximate* reality as well. For, if in the end reality is to fall beyond our explanatory predicates, there would appear to be no reason to suppose that at any point they are in touch with it; if the relational nature of judgment renders impossible predication about the Absolute, it would seem to render impossible predication about any degree or level of it. "If we are debarred from relying on the predication which is the inseparable form of judgment as it is for us we therefore cannot think in any adequate fashion, and consequently we cannot investigate the nature of the real at all." [18]

If this skepticism is taken seriously, it must further be noted, it renders nugatory two doctrines of which Bradley and Bosanquet make so much—the doctrines of the Absolute and of degrees of reality. For the Absolute becomes a vacuous conception in which, to adapt Hegel's phrase, all cows are black, and which consequently loses any claim to being an explanatory principle. And the doctrine of degrees plainly falls to the ground. If the doctrine is to have any meaning, degrees must be determined within judgment; but if judgment nowhere touches the real, how can what falls within it pass as either real or true? "It is only by the instrumentality of thought itself, as we know and rely on it in daily life, that we can even attempt to realise the principle" of degrees.[19] If thought is out of touch with the real, the principle of degrees is therefore without foundation.

There are two possible ways out of such an impotent skepticism. One is the way of mysticism, from which all the results of thinking are expunged. The other, and more significant way, pointed by Bosanquet and Bradley themselves, is through the

---

[17] *Proceedings of the Aristotelian Society,* 1918, pp. 77-78.
[18] *The Reign of Relativity,* p. 203.
[19] *Ibid.,* p. 205.

doctrine that reality is the subject of every judgment. Remaining consistently with this doctrine one is driven to hold that knowledge is foundational, in the Absolute as well as in its degrees, and that reality, whether ultimate or proximate, is not impenetrable to thought. But the implications of this should be well noted. They are that the principle of relativity obtains throughout the realm of finite knowledge, and that the only intelligible conception of finite centers, as of the Absolute, is that they are organizational and not substantival in nature.

CHAPTER X

JOSIAH ROYCE (1855-1916)

AT St. Louis, Missouri, in the year 1867 there was published the first volume of a historically important philosophical journal under the title, *The Journal of Speculative Philosophy*. Its Editor, William T. Harris, was one of the leading spirits of the newly founded "Kant Club" of that city. As its title indicates, the purpose of this new journal was to serve as the organ of 'speculative philosophy.' As expressed by the editor in his address "To the Reader" prefixed to the first volume of the *Journal*, the service which this philosophy was supposed to render to American thought and culture was threefold: (i) to provide a philosophy of religion suitable to the changing views in the realm of theology; (ii) to develop a social philosophy responsive to the new demands of the national consciousness; and (iii) to give systematic expression to the deeper implications of reflection as evidenced particularly in the growing physical sciences. As the editor conceived, each of these tasks was urgently demanded by the circumstances of the age; and since his views are historically important with reference to the motivation underlying the original advocacy in America of the 'speculative philosophy,' they may appropriately be set down here in more detail.

In the first place, attention is directed to the fact that "immense religious movements" were then going on in both England and America. These are summarily characterized as a "widely active" tendency "to break with the traditional, and to accept only what bears for the soul its own justification," which tendency, it is maintained, "can end only in the demand that Reason shall find and establish a philosophical basis for all those great ideas which are taught as religious dogmas." And to this end, it is asserted, the sort of philosophy which is needed is the sort here called 'speculative.' "The vortex between the traditional faith and the intellectual conviction cannot be closed by renouncing the latter, but only by deepening it to speculative insight."

In the second place, it is noted that the national consciousness, but recently subjected to the vicissitudes of civil war, was rapidly changing. It was turning away from a "brittle individualism in which national unity seemed an external mechanism" towards "the other essential phase" of consciousness in which "each individual recognizes his substantial side to be the State as such" and the freedom of the citizen is seen to consist not "in the mere Arbitrary, but in the realization of the rational conviction which finds expression in established law." And the same need for the same philosophy is felt here also: "that this new phase of national life demands to be digested and comprehended, is a further occasion for the cultivation of the Speculative."

Finally, in the third place, there is envisaged a "scientific revolution, working out especially in the domain of physics," which is regarded as particularly important and which gives evidence that in the sphere of reflection itself the older empirical philosophy is played out and the dawn of a new philosophy is breaking. "The day of simple empiricism is past, and with the doctrine of 'Correlation of forces' there has arisen a stage of reflection that deepens rapidly into the purely speculative." Thus did Harris view the situation in America shortly after the middle of the last century; and the new journal devoted to the interests of speculative philosophy was established to meet it.

But what is to be understood by this speculative philosophy? In the very first article of his journal Harris undertakes to answer this question. Speculative philosophy, he there seems to say, is the essential philosophy of all the greater thinkers from Plato downwards. It is suggested by Plato in his famous "line of knowledge" in the *Republic,* accepted with approval by Aristotle in his *Metaphysics,* and adopted by Spinoza in the "scientia intuitiva" of his *Ethics.* It is also generally exemplified in the arts; the results of the speculative thinkers "furnish us in the form of pure thought what the artist has wrought out in the form of beauty." It is even manifested in religion where "the deepest Speculative truth is allegorically typified in a historical form, so that it acts upon the mind partly through phantasy and partly through the understanding"; and in the mystics we find the "transition of Religion into Speculative Philosophy" actually accomplished.

We are further informed that speculative philosophy reaches its fullest expression in the system of Hegel, who, more than any other thinker, succeeded in giving it systematic formulation; for the soul of this philosophy lies in "the comprehension of the negative," and this is most clearly expounded and illustrated in Hegel's dialectical method. "He, then, who would ascend into the thought of the best thinkers the world has seen, must spare no pains to elevate his thinking to the plane of pure thought. The completest discipline for this may be found in Hegel's *Logic*. Let not one despair, though he seem to be baffled seventy and seven times; his earnest and vigorous assault is repaid by surprisingly increased strength of mental acumen which he will be assured of, if he tries his powers on lower planes after his attack has failed on the highest thought." Thus we are led to understand that the system of Hegel is *par excellence* speculative philosophy. Consequently, in turning the pages of the *Journal*, one is not surprised to discover much space devoted to translations of Hegel's writings and to articles on the exposition of his thought.

It is, of course, true and should not be overlooked that early in the nineteenth century, before the establishment of the *Journal*, post-Kantian German philosophy had already begun to exert some influence upon American thought, which thus early was turning away from the point of view of the Enlightenment and seeking a view more congenial to some of the theological drifts of the time. By the middle of the century, largely through American editions of the works of Coleridge and the translations in F. H. Hedge's *German Prose Writers*, many American thinkers were more or less familiar with certain aspects of German romanticism—especially as represented by Schelling. "The immediate result in New England was to turn the minds of some of the younger Unitarian ministers in Boston from the arid Deism, to which a too slavish adherence to the Lockean tradition had brought the theology of their own church, to the philosophy of immanence which was to form the speculative

basis, so far as it had one, of the Transcendentalist movement." [1]

This movement, of course, for a time gained the ascendancy
in American thought through the Concord School. But it was
soon played out, largely because it failed to meet the changed
situation that arose after the Civil War. To meet this situation,
the speculative philosophy was invoked by Harris and his associates and it speedily gained ground. As is usual with innova-
tions in intellectual concerns, the new philosophy was at first
contemned in academic circles, which professed to hold it suspect
on moral and religious grounds. But it was soon generally accepted, and at length was taught in all the leading schools of
philosophy in the country as the 'orthodox' philosophy. With
the decadence of the Common Sense philosophy of Reid and
Hamilton, introduced by McCosh into Princeton University,
realism was supposed to have died; and pragmatism was as yet
hardly born. So at the turn of the century the position of speculative philosophy was on the whole quite secure. It was shaken
only by occasional domestic quarrels between the personalists
and the absolutists.

Beyond question the outstanding representative of the later
fortunes of the idealistic tradition in America is Josiah Royce,
whose labors during the thirty-four years (1882-1916) of his
connection with the department of philosophy at Harvard University exerted a tremendous influence upon both philosophy and
theology in this country. It is no exaggeration to say that Royce
is the only American representative of the movement who has
succeeded in giving expression to a system at all comparable
with those of Bradley and Bosanquet.

Between the idealism of Royce and that of his British colleagues there are differences of importance, two of which are
on basal issues. Royce is much more openly solicitous concerning
the ultimate integrity of the finite individual than is either
Bradley or Bosanquet. And, again, Royce is, in principle, opposed to the negative view of the ultimate significance of

[1] J. H. Muirhead, "How Hegel Came to America," *Philosophical Review*,
Vol. XXXVII, pp. 226-227. This article should be consulted for details of
the history of the idealistic movement in America.

thought, upheld avowedly by Bradley and somewhat hesitantly by Bosanquet.[2] These divergencies between Royce's idealism and that of the British thinkers are brought to a focus in the conception of the Absolute. Bradley and Bosanquet alike regard the thesis that the Absolute is a Self as self-refuting. For Royce the Absolute is not only a Self, but a Self whose nature is such that within it the integrity of finite selfhood is preserved in a manner which to his two English contemporaries would seem wholly untenable.

Royce is aware of this difference, and indeed emphasizes it. He traces it to the greater emphasis which, as we shall see, he himself places upon the purposive or volitional aspect of experience. He insists that "the Absolute Self, even in order to be a self at all, has to express itself in an endless series of individual acts, so that it is explicitly an Individual Whole of Individual Elements. And this," he further urges, "is the result of considering Individuality, and consequently Being, as above all an expression of Will, and of a Will in which both Thought and Experience reach determinateness of expression."[3] The argument by which this general position is supported we are now to follow.

1. PRELIMINARY OBSERVATIONS

In the Preface to the First Series of his Gifford Lectures, delivered at the University of Aberdeen in 1899 under the title of *The World and the Individual,* Royce makes the following statement with reference to the idealistic argument as he himself conceived it: "The philosophy here set forth is the result of a good many years of reflection. As to the most essential argument regarding the true relations between our finite ideas and the ultimate nature of things, I have never varied, in spirit, from the view maintained in Chapter XI of my first book, *The Re-*

[2] In his earlier statements Bosanquet would appear to be more nearly in agreement with Royce on the point; but in the later stages of his thought he seems at times to swing rather sharply in the direction of Bradley's position. I have elsewhere remarked on this vacillation. (Cf. *Philosophical Review,* Vol. XXXI, p. 498 ff.; and Vol. XXXII, p. 618-619.)

[3] Royce, *The World and the Individual,* Vol. I, 588. Cf. the whole "Supplementary Essay" in this volume; and compare the "Supplementary Essay" in Royce's *The Conception of God.*

ligious Aspect of Philosophy. That chapter was entitled 'The Possibility of Error,' and was intended to show that the very conditions which make finite error possible concerning objective truth, can be consistently expressed only by means of an idealistic theory of the Absolute—a theory whose outlines I there sketched. The argument in question has since been restated, and set into relations with other matters, without fundamental alteration of its character, and in several forms; once in my *Spirit of Modern Philosophy* . . . ; again, in the book called *The Conception of God*, where my own statement of the argument has the further advantages of Professor Howison's kindly exposition and keen criticism; and still again, in the paper called 'The Implications of Self-consciousness,' published in the *Studies of Good and Evil*. In the present lectures this argument assumes a decidedly new form, not because I am in the least disposed to abandon the validity of the former statements, but because, in the present setting, the whole matter appears in new relations to other philosophical problems, and becomes, as I hope, deepened in its significance by these relations."

It may legitimately be debated whether in the several formulations of his argument here indicated Royce never varied in principle. At least, as he himself avows, there is a difference in emphasis between the earlier and the later formulations; and it may be questioned whether this difference in emphasis does not at the same time amount to something very like a difference in principle. In these varying formulations one may readily discern a growing tendency to place the emphasis more upon will and purpose and less upon mere cognition, or, at any rate, a tendency to expand the conception of thought so as to include within it more of the volitional and purposive aspects of experience. One may suspect here a progressive modification of some basal importance in the conception of experience itself which plays such an important rôle in the argument. The very title of the chapter in which, as we are told above, the argument is first formulated, "The Possibility of Error," clearly indicates the purely cognitive emphasis; and the same emphasis is present in the first statement of the argument as presented in *The Conception of God*. But in the "Supplementary Essay," included in that volume as a reformulation of the argument in reply to certain objections raised against the first formulation (especially by Howison), the emphasis shifts so as to lay much more stress upon will and its rôle in experience. The voluntary side of experience here emphasized is even more strongly noted, and made even more basal, in the form which the argument finally takes in *The World and the Individual*.

If we were interested in a separate study of the philosophy of Royce on its own account, the details of this apparent transformation would have to be entered upon and appraised. But for our present purpose little, if anything, would be gained by attempting to trace the fortunes of the argument as it grew in the author's mind. What we are now concerned to note is the place which the Roycean argument occupies in the general history of idealistic philosophy. Since we are assured by the author that the argument is "deepened in its significance" as it appears in the Gifford Lectures, we may take it in the setting there given as the basis for our present summary.[4]

After the date of these lectures, Royce gave another formulation to his idealistic argument in a series of volumes beginning in 1908 with the *Philosophy of Loyalty*. The view advocated under this title gradually assumed a more definite form in the author's mind and found progressive expression in its religious and metaphysical context primarily through the Bross Lectures, delivered in the autumn of 1911 at Lake Forest College under the title of *The Sources of Religious Insight*. It found further expression in the two volumes of lectures on *The Problem of Christianity* delivered in 1912 at the Lowell Institute and in 1913 on the Hibbert Foundation at Manchester College, Oxford. These later volumes, Royce thinks, give expression to "a consistent body of ethical as well as of religious opinion and teaching, verifiable, in its main outlines, in terms of human experience, and capable of furnishing a foundation for a defensible form of metaphysical idealism." But he was also of the con-

[4] *The World and the Individual* (1904): First Series, "The Four Historical Conceptions of Being"; Second Series, "Nature, Man, and the Moral Order." The main body of the argument is contained in the First Series.

viction that this teaching is in "essential harmony with the bases of philosophical idealism set forth in earlier volumes." There is reason to doubt whether in this view the author is strictly correct. It would be interesting to summarize this later formulation in some detail for purposes of comparison with the earlier, if space for the task were available. But it is not, and we shall have to content ourselves with the formulation as presented in the Gifford Lectures, since the author himself unquestionably accepted this as representative of his mature views.[5]

2. A General Formulation

The problem of philosophy is, of course, the problem of the nature of reality or Being, and this problem is, for thought, inescapable. All of us, from moment to moment, have experience. This experience is in part mere brute fact: light and shade, sound and silence, pain and pleasure, grief and joy. It is also, and in addition, idealized experience; besides its mere immediacy, it possesses meaning. These two aspects of experience, however, fact and meaning, are not sharply sundered from each other. Facts are always more than that which is merely immediately given; they are shot through with meaning, at least when we are awake and thoughtful, and they cannot be isolated from ideas. In short, experience is always idealized experience; its immediacy is an abstract aspect of it, set apart by artificial analysis. But the meaning of experience is never fully possessed within experience as it flows by; there is always a beyond, and experience is disquiet and unstable. It is therefore inevitable that experience should drive us to war against the essential narrowness of our conscious field; we live, and must live, looking for the whole of our meaning. But that which would end our disquietude is reality or Being; this alone, if

[5] For the quotations in this paragraph, see the Preface to *The Problem of Christianity*. The general drift of this later formulation may perhaps be gathered from the author's statement of its main thesis: "The universe is a community of interpretation whose life comprises and unifies all the social varieties and all the social communities which, for any reason, we know to be real in the empirical world which our social and our historical sciences study. The history of the universe, the whole order of time, is the history and the order and the expression of this Universal Community." (*Ibid.*, Vol. II, 272-273.)

present, would satisfy the demands of experience. Thus it is that the search for reality is for human beings inescapable.

But the search is at best difficult, and much depends on the way one starts. There are two possible ways which may be followed, and these we may distinguish as the way of the World as Fact and the way of the World as Idea. Following the first way, one is satisfied blindly to accept the mere brute reality of facts as they come. But here one is soon "sunk deep in an ocean of mysteries"; for "this World of Fact daily announces itself to you as a defiant mystery—a mystery such as Job faced, and such as the latest agnostic summary of empirical results, in their bearing upon our largest human interests, or such as even the latest pessimistic novel will no doubt any day present afresh to you, in all the ancient unkindliness that belongs to human fortune." There is here, then, no promise of fruitful issue. So we turn to the way of the World as Idea, which we can at once see is much more promising; for here we are approaching the problem of reality "from the side of the means through which we are supposed to be able to attain reality, that is, from the side of Ideas." The fortunes that shall attend us along this way we are now to discover.

At the very beginning, however, it should be clearly noted that the approach to the problem of reality here adopted resolves that problem into two fundamental questions. These are: What is an idea? and: How can an idea be related to reality? The answers to these questions will be our answer to the problem of reality itself, and therefore for us everything will depend upon what answers we find ourselves in the end compelled to give with reference to these two basal issues. This resolution of the general problem must be borne in mind as we proceed.

Before we enter upon this detailed inquiry, a general survey of the route before us and an indication of the goal towards which it leads may assist us in keeping our bearings. "An idea . . . is first of all to be defined in terms of the internal purpose, or, if you choose, in terms of the Will, that it expresses consciously, if imperfectly, at the instant when it comes to mind. Its external meaning, its externally cognitive function as a knower of outer Reality, is thus . . . to be treated as explicitly secondary to this its internal value, this its character as meaning the conscious fulfilment of an end, the conscious expression of an interest, of a desire, of a volition. To be sure, thus to define . . . is not to separate knowing from willing, but it is rather to lay stress, from the outset, upon the unity of knowledge and will, first in our finite consciousness, and later, as we shall see, in the Absolute. Our present statement of our doctrine is therefore not to be accused, at any point, of neglecting the aspect of value, the teleological, the volitional aspect, which consciousness everywhere possesses.[6] We shall reach indeed in the end the conception of an Absolute Thought, but this conception will be in explicit unity with the conception of an Absolute Purpose. Furthermore . . . we shall find that the defect of our momentary internal purposes, as they come to our passing consciousness, is that they imply an individuality, both in ourselves and in our facts of experience, which do not wholly get presented to ourselves at any instant. Or in other words, we finite beings live in the search for individuality, of life, of will, of experience, in brief, of meaning. The whole meaning, which is the world, the Reality, will prove to be, for this very reason, not a barren Absolute . . . but a whole that is just to the finite aspect of every flying moment, and of every transient or permanent form of finite selfhood,—a whole that is an individual system of rationally linked and determinate, but for that very reason not externally determined, ethically free individuals, who are nevertheless One in God. It is just because all meanings, in the end, will prove to be internal meanings, that this which the internal meaning most loves, namely the presence of concrete fulfilment, of life, of pulsating and originative will, of freedom, and of individuality, will prove, for our view, to be the very essence of the Absolute Meaning of the world." [7]

In this preliminary statement we have Royce's expression of his "central thesis" and his outline of the general argument by

[6] Some of Royce's earlier formulations of the argument had been accused of precisely this neglect. See, for example, the criticisms by Mezes and Howison of the argument in *The Conception of God.* See also Royce's reformulation of the argument in the "Supplementary Essay" of that volume, which is much more nearly in the spirit of the Gifford Lectures.

[7] *The World and the Individual,* Vol. I, 41-42.

which it is supported. It will, of course, be evident to the reader that the argument is, in principle, closely allied to those of Bradley and Bosanquet. There is here the same emphasis upon the *nisus* of experience towards its own completion,[8] and the same insistence that such completion is to be found only in the Absolute. But Royce's view of the nature of the Absolute, and particularly of its relation to finite selves, is conceived in terms much more personal. And his formulation of the argument is his own. In that formulation, it will be observed, the distinction between 'internal' and 'external' meanings is of basal importance. Our first advance along the Roycean way of Ideas, then, must lie in the direction of a clear comprehension of this distinction.

3. Internal and External Meaning

By an *idea*, as here used, we are to understand "any state of consciousness, whether simple or complex, which, when present, is then and there viewed as at least the partial expression or embodiment of a single conscious purpose." This usage is not a mere matter of convenience, nor is it arbitrary. This is precisely what an idea actually is as it appears within experience. For example, a brute noise merely heard, or a color merely seen, is not an idea; it becomes so only when it is the concrete embodiment of a conscious purpose, as would be the case if the noise or the color were of such a nature as to cause you to assume an attitude towards it. A melody when sung or a picture when actively appreciated in its wholeness would be an idea. This definition of an idea must be borne in mind throughout. And it is particularly important to note the emphasis upon the element of purposiveness in the idea. One's ideas of things are never merely images of things, but always involve a consciousness of how one proposes to act towards the things of which one has ideas. Always "an idea appears in consciousness as having the significance of an act of will." It is always the embodiment of a conscious purpose.

---

[8] Compare: "That our consciousness, as it comes, means more than it presents, and somehow implies a *beyond* for which it insistently seeks,— this indeed is a central characteristic of our experience, and one upon which all insight and all philosophy depend." (Royce, *The Conception of God*, p. 148.)

Now this purpose, in so far as it gets embodiment in an idea, constitutes the internal meaning of the idea. Thus every idea, since it is at least a partial embodiment of a purpose, necessarily has an internal meaning. It is that which the idea aims to express and which, when expressed, may be said to be the fulfilment of the idea. A distinction may indeed be drawn between the purpose of an idea and its internal meaning. "The purpose which the idea, when it comes, is to fulfil, may first be viewed apart from the fulfilment. Then it remains, so far, mere purpose. Or it may be viewed as expressed and so far partially accomplished by means of the complex state called the idea, and then it is termed 'the present internal meaning of this state.'" It is clear, however, that the distinction here is merely a distinction between different aspects of the same subject-matter. From one point of view the purpose of the idea is mere purpose, and from another point of view it is the idea's internal meaning. Sharply to separate the two is an abstraction; in the end the purpose is inseparable from the internal meaning.

Besides its internal meaning, every idea also has an external meaning; and this is what is commonly understood by the meaning of an idea. The external meaning of an idea is its reference beyond itself to an object to which it refers, its cognitive relation to outer fact. Thus, the melody which I sing and which internally means the embodiment of my purpose at the instant when I sing it, also and externally means, say, a certain theme which Beethoven composed. Your idea of your friend, which embodies some of the love you have for him, also refers beyond itself to your real friend and in some sense resembles him. The external meaning of an idea, then, is the reference of the idea to objects beyond; for the sake of convenience, let us call it the objective reference of the idea.

At first glance these two meanings of the idea stand sharply opposed to each other, and it seems *prima facie* clear that the validity of an idea is determined exclusively with reference to its external meaning. This *prima facie* view, however, will turn out to be mistaken. In the end there is no opposition between the two meanings, and the validity of an idea is determined primarily with reference to its internal meaning. For, in the end, "the final meaning of every complete idea, when fully developed, must be viewed as wholly internal meaning, and . . . all apparently external meanings become consistent with internal meanings only by virtue of thus coming to be viewed as aspects of the true internal meaning." Historically considered, this is no novel position. It is "essentially the same as the consideration that led Kant to regard the understanding as the creator of the phenomenal nature over which science gradually wins conscious control, and that led Hegel to call the world the embodied Idea." But it is a position which is of basal significance, and which is still far too much neglected. The full implications of it we are now to survey. And, as we enter upon this survey, we must once again remind ourselves that the problem before us is the problem of the relation of the World as Idea to the World as Fact. Following the lead of the internal meanings of our ideas, we shall in the end be brought face to face with the full significance of external meanings—the World as Idea, fully developed, discloses merged within it and expressed through it the World as Fact.

4. FALSE LEADS

In the course of the history of philosophy there have appeared three views of Being which must be considered before we can pass on to the development of the view that follows from the principles above stated. These views are essentially false leads, since none of them offers an adequate definition of reality, and all alike fall before critical analysis. But they are historically important, and there are elements of truth in them, the disclosure of which will carry us well forward in our task.[9]

The first of these conceptions is that of realism, according to which the object is wholly independent of the idea which does, or may, refer to it and controls or determines the worth of the idea; for this view, what we 'merely think' makes 'no difference' to fact. The second conception is that of mysticism, for which reality is absolutely immediate and, when found, altogether ends any effort at ideal definition; this view satisfies

[9] For the details of Royce's discussion of these three views, reference should be made to Lectures II-VI of *The World and the Individual*, Vol. I.

ideas by quenching them. The third conception is that of critical rationalism, which blankly identifies reality with validity. For the first conception, to be is to be independent of all ideas and merely existent whether as known or as unknown or even as unknowable; for the second conception, to be is to be immediately present in pure experience wherein ideas have no place; for the third conception, to be is to be valid or to be in essence the standard for ideas. Each of these views has appeared in various forms throughout the history of philosophy, but these historical forms are of no special concern in the present context. The significance of the claims of the three conceptions as definitions of Being is for us the important matter.

(a) If you suppose the realist to be addressing yourself, what he asserts may be put essentially in the following words: "The world of Fact is independent of your knowledge of that world. This independence, and the very reality itself of the world of Fact, are one. Were all knowledge of facts to cease, the only direct and logically necessary change thereby produced in the real world, would consist in the consequence that the particular real fact known as the existence of knowledge would, by hypothesis, have vanished. The vanishing of our knowledge would make no difference in the being of the independent facts that now we know." The basal element in the realist's conception, thus, is the element of independence; and his view stands or falls with that notion.

By way of criticism of this view, it is clear, in the first place, that the realist can never empirically verify his independent beings. He can only presuppose them. You ask him to show you such an independent being. He points at the table or at the stars. But those, for you and for him alike, are empirical objects, bound up in the context of experience. Nor could any possible enlargement of experience ever show anybody a being wholly independent. There is, then, no empirical proof of the realist's position. But, equally, there is no empirical disproof. Since the realist, in his whole view of the nature of reality, begins by abandoning entirely the realm of experience, there is no empirical criterion that can be applied to his theory. The critic, therefore, has no alternative except to examine the inner consistency or inconsistency of the theory itself.

Such an examination, however, soon discloses the basal error involved in realism. The view is simply and directly self-destructive. For if, as the realist holds, ideas and objects are wholly independent of each other, and independent in such a manner that there is, and can be, no inner link between them, it follows at once that the realist's theory (which itself is, of course, an idea) has no relation to any object, and so no relation to any real world of Fact of the sort that the theory defines. Stated otherwise, realism implies an absolute dualism within the world of real being, since the idea is an existent fact and is as real as the object; and this dualism is so sharp that no tie between the two realms is possible. The disappearance of the object would therefore make no difference to the idea. Consequently there is no logical justification for saying that there is a real object which is independent of the idea. Thus "both the realistic definition, and the totally independent beings, prove to be contradictory"; and so realism as a definition of reality must be abandoned.

But there is some truth in the theory, and this must not be overlooked. It is to be found in the positive implication of the breakdown of the realist's position—the implication, namely, that the object of an idea, whatever it may turn out to be, cannot in the end be totally independent of the thought which defines it. The ultimate dualism of the realistic view is false and must be given up; but this means, positively, that idea and object are inseparably linked. And so much is gain.

(b) In a sense it may be said that mysticism is a view of reality which is the logical opposite to realism. But it is necessary to be clear as to what precisely is here to be understood by *mysticism*. By it is meant, not a vague emotional or religious attitude in which all sorts of superstition and beliefs in special revelations may find accommodation, but rather a definite speculative tendency which from time to time has appeared in the history of philosophy and which emphasizes one basal philosophical thesis. Its thesis is that reality is something which is immediate, in the presence of which all thought and ideas are quenched, all finite strivings set at rest, and from which all otherness has disappeared. One might say that the mystic is a pure empiricist, and indeed the only thoroughgoing empiricist in the history of philosophy. His doctrine of immediacy places him at the opposite pole from the realist, who, as we have seen, insists that the real is always beyond, and beyond in such a manner that there is in it no element of immediacy. The emphasis of the mystic is upon internal meanings alone, while the realist regards only external meanings.

If one who is alive to the contradiction involved in the realistic position were to suppose that a safe refuge is to be found in the opposite extreme of mysticism, one would in this supposition be mistaken. For, in its turn, mysticism is not without its fatal weakness, which lies in its view of immediacy. In his polemic against the independent beings of realism, the mystic goes to the extreme of a type of immediacy in which there is no element of transcendence. Hereupon he finds himself in a position which demands the condemnation of all ideas, and this condemnation he forthwith asserts. He wants internal meanings which are absolute, and, not finding them in finite ideas, he seeks for them elsewhere. What he finds is a sort of Absolute wherein thought and finite ideas wholly vanish; and this he identifies with reality, holding all finite experience to be merely illusory. With this he is caught in a contradiction. For his Absolute has its meaning only in contrast with the finite search through which it was found, with the restless ideas that seek it; and, since these by hypothesis are naught, his Absolute cannot be possessed of content and significance. So we may bring the mystic's case to its close by pointing out that his Absolute "is precisely as much, and in exactly the same sense of the terms a Nothing, as, by his hypothesis, his own consciousness is."

But the emptiness of the mystic's conception of Being must not blind us to the fact that in it he emphasizes certain important philosophical doctrines. Among these should be noted his implicit assumption that the real cannot be wholly independent of knowledge, his recognition that within finite experience meanings are never complete but always point beyond to something in which there is promise of their fulfilment, and his insistence that the essential disquietude of the finite may be set at rest in Being alone. In his adherence to these basal truths the mystic is on the right track. What is lacking is his failure to recognize, and to insist upon, the principle that the goal sought must be precisely a fulfilment, and not a bare negation, of the process through which it is to be attained.

(c) From the preceding survey of realism and mysticism we have learned that reality, the meaning which our finite consciousness seeks, cannot be either a merely independent being or a merely immediate datum. What, then, must it be? To this question there is yet another answer demanding investigation, namely that of critical rationalism.

The conception of critical rationalism, we have seen, would identify reality with validity. Before we proceed to estimate this view, we need to understand more precisely what the view in question is; and to this end a few illustrations may help. In ordinary conversation there are many things that are regarded as real, and yet not real in the sense in which the ordinary realist regards his independent beings. Such, for example, are the prices of commodities, the social status of an individual in the community, economic corporations, international treaties, or the constitution of a commonwealth. Likewise, the moral law and such objects as justice or the good are commonly said to be real, and yet the sort of reality attaching to them is not that of atoms or physical entities. In the field of mathematics we find, once more, examples of the same sort of things—examples which for our present purpose are very important. In pure mathematics the student deals with certain objects (the value of π, the root for any algebraic equation of the nth degree, the limits of convergent infinite series, and the like) which *prima facie* appear to be the product of purely arbitrary definitions. But further inspection shows that such is by no means the case; there is here the possibility of error, and the student is in no way at liberty to proceed in an arbitrary manner. In a sense it may truly be said that the mathematician creates his world; "but once created, this world, in its own eternal and dignified way, is as stubborn as the rebellious spirits that a magician might have called out of the deep." After he has built, the mathematician discovers "that the form of his edifice is somehow eternal, and that there are existences which this form has pre-established, so that he himself looks with wonder to find whether this or that object exists in his new world at all." The world of the mathematician exists, then, but how? Certainly not as a realm of 'pure ideas'; and yet, equally certainly, not as the realm of the realist's independent beings or entities.

With these examples in mind, we can more clearly see the thesis of the critical rationalist. For him what exists or has being stands there as the object of 'possible experience' (to borrow a phrase from Kant, who, by the way, is the spiritual father of this way of thinking). Reality is a realm independent of any private or momentary point of view; the thousandth decimal of π sleeps there, whether actually experienced by any one or not. But for the critical rationalist the independence of reality is not that of the realist; on the contrary, reality as conceived by critical rationalism is simply the permanent possibility of the fulfilment of experience—the object of possible knowledge. "If no body had ever recognized the British Constitution, or the prices, credits, debts, marks, and ranks aforesaid, these objects could not be said to be able to retain any being, although now that they are recognized, such objects appear to have a genuine being, and to be relatively independent of this or that individual judgment." And, while the mathematical objects appear to be different in that they seem to have been valid before any mathematician conceived them, they are nevertheless similarly linked with experience; for they "undertake to be real just as objects of possible thought, as valid truths, and not as independent of all thinking processes, whether actual or possible." Such objects, then, are real, but real only in the sense in which they are valid—namely, as the standard of ideas, objects of possible experience. This thesis, generalized to include all reality and being, is precisely the thesis of critical rationalism: Reality is Validity, the Object of possible experience. What, now, are we to say of this conception of reality?

In the first place, it is to be noted that this conception is an inevitable step in the logically necessary modification of realism. Realism, as we have seen, insists primarily upon the independence of the object; and we have also seen the inescapable contradiction involved in this position. Notwithstanding the breakdown of his theory, however, the realist's notion of the independence of the object, when modified, states an important truth, namely, that the object does transcend the momentary idea which refers to it. And this modification of the realist's position leads at once into that of the critical rationalist. Nor is there any great difficulty involved in seeing how this is so. For when the realist once seriously undertakes to make explicit and articulate what is implied in his doctrine of independence, he is inevitably driven to see that all he can mean by it is that the real is precisely the whole in terms of which the ideas, referring incompletely to that reality, are validated. The whole is just the possible experience of which the present incomplete experience is a fragment and in which, if attained, the present fragmentary experience would secure its validation. "Whatever . . . you may attempt to assert, all that your Realism will ever succeed in articulating, is your belief that experience as a whole, that realm of truth of which you regard your present experience as a case and as a fragment, has a certain valid constitution." Thus, by its own inner dialectic, is realism changed into critical rationalism; and we may therefore say that critical rationalism is a transformed and enlightened realism.

From the preceding survey it is evident that critical rationalism is acceptable as far as it goes. And we may here note the basal truth upon which it lays emphasis. That truth, which the critical rationalist observes from the beginning, is "that an experience of facts which send you beyond themselves, and to further possible experience, for their interpretation, is the only conscious basis for any assertion of a Being that is beyond the flying contents of this very instant." "What is, fulfils the meaning of the empirically present idea that refers to the Being in question, and except as fulfilling such a meaning, Being can neither be conceived, nor asserted, nor verified." In the recognition of this fact lies the strength of critical rationalism and its superiority to realism.

But the question still remains whether critical rationalism

goes far enough, whether the realm of validity which is identified with reality can be left standing as *merely* a realm of validity. And we now turn to a brief consideration of this question. The point at issue is, of course, the notion of validity itself, and we must analyze its foundation.

As applied within our experience, the notion of validity has a very definite meaning. Ideas are valid if they are concretely expressed in experience whenever we choose to test them. In this sense, ideas are valid when they are validated, and validation means being brought into the presence of certain empirical facts—sights, sounds, tangible objects, and the like—to which the ideas refer.[10] It is to be noted, however, and for our present purpose it is very important to note, that validity here also refers to possible experience. The testing of the validity of our ideas, from moment to moment, is at once the proof of the existence of a world of possible experience. "One who observes the nature of a realm of abstractly possible experience, does so by reading off the structure of a presented experience. Necessity comes home to us men through the medium of given fact. This is the general result of modern exact Logic. This is the outcome of the recent study of the bases of mathematical science." And it is also implied in an analysis of the principles of the physical sciences, and even of the assumptions of common sense.

You may say then that the notion of validity applies to the world of possible experience in the sense that such a world is there as a standard for testing empirically the validity of our ideas about it. And in this sense to speak of the valid world of possible experience is to be fairly definite in meaning. But it is obvious, as the critical rationalist himself insists, that the world of possible experience has "far more validity than, in our private capacity, we shall ever test. It is thus with common sense, much as it was with mathematics. The mathematician finds his way in the eternal world by means of experiments upon the transient facts of his inner and ideal experience of this instant's contents. The student of science or the plain man

[10] Compare the pragmatic theory of truth as stated especially by William James in his *Pragmatism* and *The Meaning of Truth*. This theory stops at the point here stated, and does not go beyond as Royce, of course, insists an adequate theory of truth must go.

of everyday life believes himself to be dealing with a realm of validity far transcending his personal experience." And the question is inevitable: What is the meaning of validity as applied to this realm of possible experience which is infinitely more extended than actual human experience; what is a valid truth at the moment when nobody verifies its validity?

To this question the critical rationalist has no definite reply. The only answer he can give identifies validity with some vague character which is merely universal and formal—a mere universal law. Thus he leaves us with two quite distinct views of validity on our hands, namely validity as concrete experience and validity as universal form. And the further question is raised: "Can there be two sorts of Being, both known to us as valid, but the one individual, the other universal, the one empirical, the other merely ideal, the one present, the other barely possible, the one a concrete life, the other a pure form?"

For this question the critical rationalist has no reply at all. He simply rests in the dualism, and seems unconscious that his position involves any difficulty. Henceforward in our survey, therefore, we abandon critical rationalism, which we leave behind as incompetent to answer the question it itself has shown to be inescapable. As we proceed, we can now more clearly see that the problem with which we have to deal is the famous problem of Pontius Pilate: What is Truth?

5. THE WAY OF THE "WORLD AS IDEA"

There are two definitions of truth which are commonly offered in answer to the question now before us. These are: (a) Truth is that about which we judge; and: (b) Truth is the correspondence between our ideas and their objects. Each of these definitions is, in its own way, correct, and the two taken together and adequately understood will bring us to the end of our quest. Such an adequate understanding is indispensable to the attainment of the goal, and this, therefore, is the primary purpose of our further analysis. We shall take the definitions in order, our aim being to see the articulate meaning of each and, in the end, the basal implications concerning the nature of Being of the two taken together. As we enter upon this undertaking, we must remind ourselves of the distinction already drawn between the 'internal' and the 'external' meaning of ideas and their final relation to each other. This, as we proceed, will disclose itself as being of fundamental importance. From the beginning we are forewarned by our study of realism, mysticism, and critical rationalism—all of which, as we have seen, break down, largely because all alike fail to grasp one or another aspect of the complex situation lying back of this distinction.

(a) Beginning with the first definition of truth, we must observe in the first place that there is a certain abstraction involved in treating judgments and ideas as if they were separate. In point of fact, judgments involve ideas, and may indeed be said to be simply combinations of ideas. Therefore, truth as related to judgments is inseparable from truth as related to ideas—truth as that about which we judge is linked with truth as correspondence. But a certain convenience in discussion is to be gained by treating the two separately, since each view has within it an emphasis which calls for distinct statement.

The view that truth is that about which we judge is correct, if properly interpreted. Its correct interpretation, however, rests upon the consideration, already advanced, that the internal and external meanings of ideas are indissolubly linked and that internal meanings in the end control. We are now to see how this is so and what, accepting it, we must conclude concerning the nature of Being.

"Ordinary judgments, all of them . . . make some sort of reference to Reality. Never do you judge at all, unless you suppose yourself to be asserting something about a real world. You can express doubt as to whether a certain ideal object has its place in Reality. You can deny that some class of ideal object is real. You can affirm the Being of this or of that object. But never can you judge without some sort of conscious intention to be in significant relation to the Real. The *what* and the *that* are, indeed, easily distinguished, so long as you take the distinction abstractly enough. But never, when you seriously judge in actual thinking, do you avoid reference *both* to the *what* and to the *that* of the universe." [11] The reference to reality may be very indirect, as in judging about centaurs or fairies; but, however indirect, the reference is always there. "To judge is to judge about the Real."

The characteristic of judgment here emphasized may be stated in other words by saying that to judge is to consider internal meanings with reference to external meanings. For, in our present terminology, the *what* is precisely the internal meaning and the *that* is precisely the external meaning; and judgment, we have said, consists in bringing the *what* into relation to the *that*. Henceforward, then, we shall drop the terms 'that' and 'what,' and speak instead of external and internal meanings. And we shall say that both internal and external meanings are involved in all judgments. But what is their relation? This is our further problem.

(i) In the first place, it is clear that they cannot be sundered from each other, but are inseparably joined. This is evident from the very nature of judgment itself, since both internal and external meanings are involved in judgment and since either is meaningless apart from the other. If one objects that this last statement has not been proved, we may remind him of the preceding discussion of realism, mysticism and critical rationalism, which showed that realism and mysticism alike fail because they undertake to keep internal and external meanings separate, and that the superiority of critical rationalism lies in the recognition that the two cannot be wholly sundered. In addition to this reminder, however, we may propose to such an objector that he undertake an experiment. We may ask him to undertake an analysis of judgment, having first arbitrarily sundered internal and external meanings, and to note the result. What he will discover is that "every attempt to judge, even while it recognizes this sundering as sharpest, is an effort to link afresh what it all the time, also, seems to keep apart." [12] Judgment simply cannot stand such dismemberment and live.

[11] *The World and the Individual*, Vol. I, 272-273. This, of course, is a restatement of the position of both Bradley and Bosanquet; and it is for Royce, as for them, basal.

[12] *Ibid.*, p. 273. Royce undertakes to support this position by an analysis of the several forms of judgment "as they appear in the ordinary text-

(ii) The inseparable union of internal and external meanings is shown by a further consideration. It will be recalled that the chief difficulty confronting the critical rationalist in his final account of validity was his identification of his valid external world with the bare universal or ideal and his consequent exclusion of individuality from that world. Why we held this to be a difficulty in his view, we did not there state except indirectly through the question whether such an abstractly ideal or possible world could be identified with the world of reality, and the implied suggestion that it could not be. But the definite reason for this position is not difficult to discover. There can be no doubt that our whole interest in reality is an interest in individuality. For the Other we seek, through all phases of our experience, is that which, if found, "would determine our ideas to their final truth"; and "only what is finally determinate can, in its turn, determine." The Other which we seek, therefore, must be Individual; that alone will satisfy the demands of our experience. Now, neither our internal meanings nor our external meanings, taken separately, are in the least adequate to embody individuality. "Neither do our internal meanings ever present to us, nor yet do our external experiences ever produce before us, for our inspection, an object whose individuality we ever really know as such." For the individual is unique; *"no other* is like him in the whole realm of Being. It is this *no-Other*-character that persistently baffles both the merely internal meaning, and the merely external experience, so long as they are human and are sundered." [13] Thus we are driven to hold either that the deeper demand of experience is baseless and even meaningless, or that internal and external meanings are not sundered; and the first alternative is without warrant.

(iii) Not only are internal and external meanings inseparably joined, they are also mutually determining; and this, as we shall have occasion later to observe at some length, is an aspect of their relation that is of great significance. Internal meanings are in themselves fragmentary and incomplete; they take the form

---

books of Logic" (categorical, hypothetical, and disjunctive). For the details of the analysis, the reader should consult the text, *ibid.,* p. 273 ff.

[13] *The World and the Individual,* pp. 292, 295.

of asking questions. The answers to the questions thus asked are to be found in external meanings, in 'facts,' in external experience; and herein is the determining function of external meanings. But the 'facts' which give the answer are never barely immediate facts; they are *selected* facts, facts that are relative to the questions asked. Only such facts can give significant answers. "What the bare internal meanings, in their poverty, leave as an open question, the external experience shall decide. If you ask, again, What experience? the answer always is, Not *any* experience that you please, but a sort of experience determined by the question asked, viz., whatever experience is apt to decide, between conflicting ideas, and to determine them to precise meaning." [14] And just here is the determining function of internal meanings. So we may say that internal and external meanings are both at once determining and determined: external meanings must answer the questions which the internal meanings ask, but the questioner in every case selects the experiences that are to be permitted to reply to the questions asked.

(iv) Another point of importance remains to be noted. The internal meanings in the end are in a sense supreme. External experience decides whether our ideas about fact can be confirmed, and, in confirming them, furnishes a positive content which internal meanings never can construct for themselves. But external experience alone can never wholly negate our ideas, since there always remains the possibility that something of their internal meaning may fall elsewhere in reality. It is only when the internal meanings themselves acknowledge defeat, it is only when their surrender is a *self-surrender*, that final victory may fall on the side of external experience. "Our will has its limitless opportunity to 'try again'; and external experience never finally disposes of ideas unless the ideas themselves make, for reasons defensible upon the ground of internal meaning only, their own 'reasonable' surrender." [15] The reason for the supremacy here accorded to internal meanings in the relation they bear to external meanings, as well as the ultimate significance of this

[14] *Ibid.,* p. 286.
[15] *Ibid.,* p. 297.

supremacy, will be made clear by our analysis of the correspondence view of truth.

Before passing on to this analysis, however, we may briefly summarize the main results of our investigation of the other view. There are three such results, which may be taken as the essentials of the view that truth means that about which we judge. As to the nature of truth thus conceived, we have found that truth is determinateness of idea and of experience, as opposed to vague possibilities. To judge is to bring the *what* into relation to the *that* and to give definiteness and precision to each. As to the relation between thought and so-called external experience, we have seen that the two are in inseparable union and that internal meanings occupy a privileged position in the relationship. And, finally, as to the nature of reality, we have found that the real is the individual; individuality is the Other which our experience seeks. Recalling that from the beginning reality and truth are for us synonymous and putting all three of these conclusions into the form of one general statement, we may now say that reality possesses a peculiar sort of determinateness, namely the determinateness of individuality, and is precisely the complete determination of our own internal meaning. This general conclusion will be further supported and clarified by the analysis of 'correspondence,' upon which we now enter.

(b) The view that truth means correspondence between any idea and its object is indeed a very ancient one. But the definition as it stands is not quite satisfactory, and everybody feels that some mystery lies hidden behind it. The difficulty is in the two relations implied by the definition, namely, the relation involved in the assertion that the true idea must correspond with its object; and the relation involved in the implication that the idea has an object. If this difficulty is to be removed, then, two questions must be answered: (i) What is the relation called *correspondence?* and: (ii) What constitutes the relation called *having an object?* And upon these two questions our analysis of the view will turn.

(i) As to the relation of correspondence between an idea and its object, it may be said, negatively, that a true idea, in corresponding to its object, need not in the least be confined to any particular sort or degree of similarity to its object. There may indeed be similarity, and it may be as close or as remote as you please. But similarity is not essential to the relation of correspondence. "A scientific idea about colors need not be itself a color, nor yet an image involving colors . . . a true idea of a dog need not itself bark in order to be true." The relation of correspondence is something quite different from resemblance.

What, then, is it? The only positive answer that can be given to this question must be stated in terms of purpose. Taken by itself, correspondence may be any sort of relation you please; as so taken it may be defined as the possession, on the part of the corresponding objects, of some system of ideally definable characters that is common to both of them and that is such as to meet the purpose for which the particular correspondence is established. But taken as the relation between a true idea and its object which determines the idea as true, it can .be defined only in terms of the internal meaning of the idea. "The idea is true if it possesses the sort of correspondence to its object that the idea itself wants to possess. Unless that kind of identity in inner structure between idea and object can be found which the specific purpose embodied in a given idea demands, the idea is false. On the other hand, if this particular sort of identity is to be found, the idea is just in so far true." Here, once again, the correspondence may be any sort you please—similarity, correlation, symbolic representation, or whatnot. The essential matter is that it be the sort of correspondence, and precisely the sort of correspondence, which the idea itself intends. It is not mere agreement, but intended agreement, that constitutes truth.

Thus there is no purely external criterion of truth. "You cannot merely look from without upon an ideal construction and say whether or no it corresponds to its object. Every finite idea has to be judged by its own specific purpose. Ideas are like tools. They are there for an end. They are true, as the tools are good, precisely by reason of their adjustment to this end." [16] To ask

[16] *The World and the Individual,* pp. 305, 306, 308. Compare the position here stated with the view of the pragmatists.

which of two ideas is the truer is a vain question; it is like asking which of two different tools is the better tool. The question is sensible if the purpose in mind is specific, but not otherwise. There is no one purely abstract test of the truth of ideas, just as there is no one abstract test of the value of all tools. The embodied purpose, the internal meaning, of the instant's idea is a *conditio sine qua non* for its truth; with reference to this alone does the correspondence between the idea and its object have precision and definiteness.

(ii) The internal meaning of the idea, we have seen, is basal to the relation of correspondence. We are now to see that it is also basal to the relation of *having*, when we say that an idea *has* an object. And when we have seen this, we shall be in position to draw our final conclusion concerning the nature of truth and reality.

It has sometimes been supposed in the history of philosophy that the object of any idea is "that which 'arouses, awakens, brings to pass, the idea in question." This view is commonly expressed in some form of the old Aristotelian metaphor of the seal impressing itself upon the wax. According to this view, when we say that an idea has an object we mean that the object is the cause of the idea. This view, however, is for several reasons inadequate as a definition of the relation between an idea and its object. In the first place, there are many temporal objects of which we have ideas, but which are not now present in time, such as objects in the future or objects in the past; and there seems to be no sense in which we could say that such objects are the causes of the ideas we have about them. Is anything in the future, say my own death, or an eclipse due next year, or futurity in general, the cause of my present ideas? And what is the irrevocable past now doing to our ideas that the fact of its irrevocable absence should, as cause, now be viewed as molding our ideas? Furthermore, there are certain non-temporal objects, such for example as those of mathematics, of which we do without doubt have ideas but with reference to which the causal relation would seem to be meaningless. "Does the binomial theorem act as a seal, or any other sort of cause, impressing its image on the wax of a mathematician's mind? Do the proportions of equations do anything to the mathematician when he thinks of them?" And, finally, it must not be forgotten that there are many causes of ideas which, for the ideas, are never objects at all. The physiological processes, for example, which presumably are constituent elements of the causal conditions of any and all of our ideas, are themselves never objects of ideas except under special circumstances; and when they become so, they are abstracted from their causal nexus and considered in quite a different context. Never, it would appear, are they objects for precisely those ideas of which they are causes.

For these reasons, then, we may say that the relation which we express when we say that an idea has its object is not to be identified with the causal relation between the idea and the object. The relation has to do with the truth or falsity of ideas, and is something quite other than a mere *de facto* connection. How, then, is it to be defined?

This definition must be stated, once again, in terms of the internal meaning of the idea. The object of an idea is the object which the idea means; the object which the idea means is the object which it selects; and the object which the idea selects is the object which it determines as its own object, that is, as the object which is to fulfil its internal meaning of embodied purpose. "If I have meant to make an assertion about Cæsar, you must not call me to account because my statement does not correspond, in the intended way, with the object called Napoleon. If I have meant to say that space has three dimensions, you cannot refute me by pointing out that time has only one. And nowhere, without a due examination of the internal meaning of my ideas, can you learn whether it was the object Cæsar or the object Napoleon, whether it was space or time, that I meant." [17] Thus, when we say that an idea has an object, the relation between the two is the predetermination of the object by the internal meaning of the idea; the object "is selected from all other objects, through the sort of attentive interest in just that object which the internal meaning of the idea involves." The idea's object is precisely the object which the idea intends, and not any other.

[17] *The World and the Individual,* p. 318.

(c) Our conclusion thus far is that the internal meaning of the idea predetermines what object it selects as the object it means, and also predetermines what sort of correspondence it intends to have to this object. And with this conclusion we seem to face a fatal difficulty. For we have said, on the one hand, that the object of a specific idea has no essential character which is not predetermined by the internal meaning of the idea, and also, on the other hand, that the correspondence between the idea and its object is precisely that which the internal meaning of the idea demands. And this seems to exclude the possibility of erroneous ideas and to make truth a mere tautology. How are we to meet this difficulty? With the answer to this question we shall have arrived at our goal, namely, the conception of the nature of Reality itself.

As a first step, we must recall two points which were established by our analysis of the definition of truth as that about which we judge. The first of these was the inseparability of internal and external meanings of ideas. Judgment, we there said, cannot stand if the two are separated, and each turns out to be meaningless apart from the other. The second point was concerned with the supremacy of internal meanings in their inseparable union with external meanings. This supremacy we have here once again emphasized, and we have also seen in greater detail the justification for it. External meaning gets its significance and relevancy in the process of thinking through its relation to internal meaning. It now remains for us to point out that, on the other side, internal meanings are to get their completion through the external meanings which they thus predetermine. External meanings also function in a determining capacity, and through them alone internal meanings come to the realization of their own true implications.

Reminding ourselves of these matters, then, we are in position to go forward to the answer of the question before us. The idea seeks its own, the embodiment of its conscious purpose or will in determinate form. But in thus seeking its own it is also, and for that very reason, seeking its Other, its object, its external meaning. Or, we might equally well put the matter the other way round. The idea seeks its Other, its object, its external meaning; but in thus seeking its Other it is also, and for that reason, seeking nothing but the completion of its own internal meaning, its consciously embodied purpose or will. The apparent paradox here involved falls away when one remembers that the internal and the external meaning of an idea are simply inseparable aspects of one and the same state of consciousness, and that the internal meaning, always fragmentary and incomplete, is continuously challenged by the ever-broadening external meaning. It is clearly enough illustrated in all phases of conscious experience—in the ordinary process of "making up our minds," as well as in the more rigorously reflective procedure of those types of experience which give rise to the mathematical and the empirical sciences.[18]

And now we are at last near the homeland. In seeking its object, the idea (any idea whatever) seeks absolutely nothing but its own explicit, and, in the end, complete, determination as this conscious purpose embodied in this one way. The complete content of the idea's own purpose is the Other that it seeks. The finally determinate form of the object of any finite idea, therefore, is the form which that idea itself would assume should it become a completely determinate idea. And, we can now see, this is equivalent to saying that the object of any idea would in the end be an idea or will fulfilled by a wholly adequate empirical content, for which no other content need be substituted or, from the point of view of the satisfied idea, could be substituted. In other words, the final object of any idea would be an individual.

Correspondence with such an object would constitute the idea true, and in this sense we may define truth as correspondence between the idea and its object. But the object must be the complete embodiment of the purpose or will, the internal meaning, which in the idea, as finite, obtains only a partial embodiment. And this object would also be the real object. Thus we may at last say that truth and reality fall together without discrepancy, and that both alike may be defined as "the complete embodiment, in individual form and in final fulfilment, of the internal meaning of finite ideas."

[18] Cf. *The World and the Individual,* Vol. I, pp. 327 ff.

Nor must it be supposed that such a complete embodiment of finite ideas remains a bare possibility. On such a supposition validity would remain for us an incomplete universal conception, and we should be left standing in the position of the critical rationalist—a position which we have already seen to be untenable as a final resting place. We must go beyond this. If validity is to be given its final meaning, there is then an object more than merely valid in terms of which that meaning is to be conceived. "We have now defined what this object is. It is an individual life, present as a whole, *totum simul,* as the scholastics would have said. This life is at once a system of facts, and the fulfilment of whatever purpose any finite idea, in so far as it is true to its own meaning, already fragmentarily embodies. This life is the completed will, as well as the completed experience, corresponding to the will and experience of any one finite idea. In its wholeness the world of Being is the world of individually expressed meanings,—an individual life, consisting of the individual embodiments of the wills represented by all finite ideas. Now *to be,* in the final sense, means to be just such a life, complete, present to experience, and conclusive of the search for perfection which every finite idea in its own measure undertakes whenever it seeks for any object. We may therefore lay aside altogether our *ifs* and *thens,* our *validity* and other such terms, when we speak of this final concept of Being. What is, is for us no longer a mere form, but a Life; and in our world of what was before mere truth the light of individuality and of will have finally begun to shine. The sun of true Being has arisen before our eyes." [19] And hereupon we finally enter the homeland.

Before passing on to consider the more special constitution of the world which our concept of Being involves, we may pause to note that, once you accept this view of Being, you will accomplish the end which the other views of Being (realism, mysticism, and critical rationalism) actually sought. For, with the realist, you will assert that the object is not only other than the finite idea, but is something that is authoritative over against it. However, you will reject the realistic isolation of the idea from the object, and of the object from the idea, as an inadequate state-

[19] *The World and the Individual,* pp. 341-342.

ment of the relation between the two involved in the notion of correspondence. With the mystic, you will say of the object of any of your ideas: *That art thou,* since you have identified Being with the fulfilment of purpose; but you will deny the mystic's purely negative view of Being, and declare that ignorance expresses, not the nature of true Being, but merely the present inadequacy of our passing idea to its own present and conscious purpose—that the eternal light shineth in our every reasonable moment, and lighteth every idea that cometh into the world. And, finally, you will agree with the critical rationalist that Being is that which gives validity to our ideas and, so, may be called 'possible experience'; but you will also observe that, so long as Being is identified with merely possible experience, it fails to define the Being of the object as Other than the very finite idea which is to regard it as Other, and that Being, when adequately defined, must be not merely possible, but actual, experience. It must take an individual form as a unique fulfilment of purpose in a completed life. Thus we may say that our concept of Being is the synthesis of these three views, and that it goes beyond them precisely because it is such a synthesis; it supplies what each demands, but fails to attain.

6. The World and the Individual

Following the way of the World as Idea, we have been brought to the conception of Being which has been defined in the preceding section. It now remains for us, in conclusion, to inquire what this conception of Being implies with reference to (a) the unity of the world, and (b) the status of finite individuality within it.

(a) Our concept of Being involves the conclusion that the world is one, and is present to the insight of a single Self-conscious Knower. And the proof of this conclusion now stands ready to hand.

In the first place, we have already seen that any finite experience is but a fragment of the object that it means; and we have also seen that the object can have no form of Being that is independent of this meaning. Nor can there be said to be any meaning not now wholly fulfilled in present experience, unless that very meaning is present to an insight in which it is included and completed. And from this it necessarily follows that any fact, which is meant by the finite thinker and yet is not at any instant consciously present to him in its fullness, must be present to some other consciousness, and present there as including and completing what the finite thinker at the moment undertakes to know. In other words, "there can exist no fact except as a known fact, as a fact present to some consciousness, namely, precisely to the consciousness that fulfils the whole meaning of whoever asserts that this fact is real."

And herewith we are committed to the conclusion that the real world is a unity completely present to the consciousness of a universal Knower. For there can be no doubt that there are many finite knowers, many knowing processes, and that these are mutually related or not. Then the fact about their relations exists, but exists only as a known fact. There is therefore a consciousness for which the existence and the relations of these various finite knowers is a known fact; and this implies that one final knower knows all knowing processes in one inclusive act. Assume as much variation and multiplicity in the world of fact as you please, the conclusion is the same. Such multiplicity, if a fact, must be known and therefore must be present to a knower as the fulfilment of his own single meaning. Nor can there be, in such a knower, any nature that is to himself unknown; for such a nature would then be absolutely unknown, and therefore not a fact. Thus our conclusion stands: "What is, is present to the insight of a single Self-conscious Knower, whose life includes all that he knows, whose meaning is wholly fulfilled in his facts, and whose self-consciousness is complete . . . to talk of Being is to speak of fact that is either present to a consciousness or else nothing. And from that one aspect of our definition which is involved in the thesis that whatever is, is consciously known, all the foregoing view of the unity of Being inevitably follows." [20]

In this conclusion concerning the unity of Being there are in-

[20] *The World and the Individual*, p. 400. Royce here gives, in the immediately following pages, empirical considerations that seem to him to lie in support of the thesis presented. But these add nothing new in principle to the argument, and so are omitted from the summary. They do add concreteness to the discussion, however, and should be consulted on that account. Cf. especially pp. 402-413.

volved certain characteristics of that unity, two of which are of basal importance and must here be made explicit. The first is personality—the unity is a Self-conscious Knower, and because it is self-conscious it is also a Person. If, then, we wish to speak in theological terms, we may call the unity of Being God and thus identify the result of our idealistic philosophy with the deepest demand of the religious consciousness. But it must not be supposed that God is the temporal result of any process of evolution, and this is the second point which we are to note. God is conscious, not *in* time, but *of* time, of all that infinite time contains. His consciousness is the whole, the totality, within which the temporal process completely falls and is present all at once. To God all is known, and known as completely fulfilled in present experience. For this experience there is no Other, no beyond—this indeed would be only the meaningless void, the absolute Nothing.

(b) It is an accusation frequently advanced that any view of the world as a rational whole, present in its actuality to the unity of a single consciousness, has no room for finite individuality or for freedom. Such an accusation does not hold against the view we have been defending, however, and we must in conclusion see why.

The unity of Being, or God, we have just said, is not in time. His consciousness is eternal, not temporal. There is nothing mysterious about this, and we bear within our own natures the key to the apparent difficulty. For we are possessed of a time-span of consciousness within which a temporal series or sequence of events, such as a melody for instance, is known at once despite the fact that its elements when viewed in their temporal succession are *not* at once. Now this brief span of our consciousness is a perfectly arbitrary limitation of our own special type of consciousness; conceivably, it might be expanded indefinitely. Suppose it expanded until it took in the whole of time, precisely as our own limited span includes a single melody or rhythm; such a consciousness would be an eternal consciousness. Thus in our own conscious experience we have the analogue of an eternal consciousness; there is no deep and dark mystery here. "Listen to any musical phrase or ryhthm, and grasp it as a whole, and you thereupon have present in you the image, so to speak, of the divine knowledge of the temporal order. To view all the course of time just as you then and there view the whole of that sequence,—this is to be possessed of an eternal type of insight." [21]

It is to be carefully noted, further, that our consciousness of a whole phrase is also a consciousness of the succession in which the elements of the phrase come to us. Indeed, the meaning of the phrase is the meaning of the succession; it is grasped only by observing the succession as something that involves earlier and later elements, each of which has its unique place in the temporal series. And this, we must hold, is in principle true of the eternal consciousness. Such a consciousness does not abstract from, nor fail to take account of, temporal succession; on the contrary, it observes the whole of time only by observing what happens in time and precisely as it happens. For the eternal consciousness the whole temporal order is experienced as a whole, just because it is experienced as an order in which each element is unique— each one *after* its predecessor, and *before* its successor.

In the Absolute's experience of time, therefore, there is nothing at all inconsistent with the presence, within the temporal order, of uniqueness and individuality. On the contrary, if there be unique individuals within that order, they must be observed by the Absolute, since by hypothesis their very uniqueness would be an essential element of the order and would, therefore, have to be experienced by the consciousness to which the order as a whole is present.

Now, that there are unique individuals in the temporal order is clear; we ourselves are such. We certainly are in time, and our very nature strives towards uniqueness and individuality. It is more than a half truth that ". . . the Self sins not through self-assertion but through self-abandonment." We have already seen that there is no necessary incompatibility between our concept of an Eternal Consciousness and this temporal uniqueness of our lives; such uniqueness may find its place in the experience of God. We are now to see that it must find its place precisely there.

---

[21] *The World and the Individual,* Vol. II, 145. Compare the view of Green on the notion of eternal consciousness, and note the basal difference between his view and that of Royce.

First, we recall our former conclusion that the fulfilment of its internal meaning which every idea seeks is found ultimately in the complete life wherein are embodied all meanings, both internal and external. To this we must now add the consideration, obvious enough but hitherto not insisted upon, that in this complete life every internal meaning of every idea necessarily preserves its uniqueness. For each internal meaning, each idea viewed as internally significant, is a typical instance of facts, and of precisely those facts of whose unity the world consists. Now if, as we have argued, the whole world is, as a whole, the unique expression of the conscious purpose and thought to which all meanings are completely present, it then follows that every internal meaning, every finite purpose, precisely in so far as it is, is a partial expression of the Eternal Consciousness.

In the next place, we must observe that the finite individual is in principle identical with will and purpose, with internal meaning. This is particularly evident in the case of the human self, which for us is the typical instance of finite individuality.[22] To be sure, the human self has at times been conceived as a self-encased entity, a spiritual substance; and it has been supposed that such a conception of it offers a sufficient description of its uniqueness. This supposition, however, is wholly vain, since the conception is erroneous. And that it is erroneous may be shown by simple empirical considerations of the genesis of the self and not-self—considerations which clearly indicate that the ego is in its origin secondary to social experience.[23] For our present purpose, it is particularly important to note that these

[22] Royce insists that nature must be teleologically defined, and this view of course follows from his insistence that all facts are known facts. "We have no right whatever to speak of really unconscious Nature, but only of uncommunicative Nature, or of Nature whose mental processes go on at such different time-rates from ours that we cannot adjust ourselves to a live appreciation of their inward fluency, although our consciousness does make us aware of their presence." For Royce's development of this view and his differentiation between it and other historical views similar in import, see Lecture V of the Second Series of the Gifford Lectures (*The World and the Individual,* Vol. II, 207 ff.). Compare his discussion of the place of the self in nature as given in Lectures VI and VII of the First Series.

[23] Cf. *The World and the Individual,* Vol. II, 260 ff. and the essay on "The Anomalies of Self-consciousness" in Royce's *Studies of Good and Evil.* Compare the position of Bradley on the point.

considerations disclose the fact that the contrast of self and not-self comes to us as the contrast between the internal and the external meanings of experience. For the self is just the imperfectly expressed purpose of the moment; and the not-self is the Other, the outer world of expressed meaning taken as in contrast with what, just at this instant of our conscious experience, is observed and, relatively speaking, possessed. In the case of the self, the internal meaning assumes the form of something like a life-plan, an ideal, towards the attainment of which the total life of the individual moves. It is by the possession of this ideal that the self is unique—". . . by this, and not by the possession of any Soul-Substance, I am defined and created a Self."

Summing the implications of the facts thus set forth, then, we may readily indicate the status of the finite human individual in the total scheme of things. The relation between the finite self and the Infinite Self is, in principle, the relation between an internal meaning and its fulfilment in its external meaning. The finite self is in the Infinite Self as an element in the total experience of the universe. And here its individuality is not destroyed, but fulfilled; it is in God, but it is not lost in God. On the contrary, it comes to the actualization of itself precisely through its union with the Eternal Consciousness. For every internal meaning is a unique expression of its ultimate completion.

And herein, it must be noted in conclusion, lies the genuine freedom of the finite individual. For to such an individual we may now say: "You are at once an expression of the divine will, and by virtue of that very fact the expression here and now, in your life, of your *own* will, precisely in so far as you find yourself acting with a definite intent, and gaining through your act a definite empirical expression. We do not say, 'Your individuality causes your act.' We do not say, 'Your free will creates your life.' For Being is everywhere deeper than causation. What you are is deeper than your mere power as a physical agent. Nothing whatever besides yourself determines either causally or otherwise just what constitutes your individuality, for you are just this unique and elsewhere unexampled expression of the divine meaning. And here and now your individuality in your act *is* your freedom. This your freedom is your unique possession. Nowhere else in the universe is there what here expresses itself in your conscious being. And this is true of you, not in spite of the unity of the divine consciousness, but just because of the very uniqueness of the whole divine life. For all is divine, all expresses meaning. All meaning is uniquely expressed. Nothing is vainly repeated; you, too, then, as individual are unique. And (here is the central fact) just in so far as you consciously will and choose, you then and there in so far know what this unique meaning of yours is. Therefore are you in action Free and Individual, just because the unity of the divine life, when taken together with the uniqueness of this life, implies in every finite being just such essential originality of meaning as that of which you are conscious. Arise, then, freeman, stand forth in thy world. It is God's world. It is also thine." [24]

[24] *The World and the Individual,* Vol. I, 469-470. In Lectures **IV-VII** of the second volume of this work Royce's treatment of the notion of causation and its application to psychological experience will be found. And in Lecture **IX** he undertakes to bring out the application of his general theory to the problem of evil, with which should be compared his earlier statement as given particularly in the *Studies of Good and Evil.*

CHAPTER XI

JAMES EDWIN CREIGHTON (1861-1924)

FOR more than thirty years, from 1893 to his death in 1924, James Edwin Creighton was a member of the faculty of the Sage School of Philosophy in Cornell University, and during this long period of service in teaching he was actively connected in an editorial capacity with *The Philosophical Review*. In both capacities, as teacher and as editor, Creighton exerted a marked influence on the fortunes of American idealism. His writings are relatively few, consisting for the most part of occasional articles written in defense of idealism. during the strenuous years of its conflict with pragmatism and, later, with realism. In this debate he proved to be a doughty champion of the cause of idealism, and his articles doubtless gained in significance because of the circumstances that called them forth. But they also possessed an intrinsic worth as contributions to idealistic literature, and go far towards the clarification of the main issues raised by historical idealism. The student who wishes to get a concise statement of the basal tenets of the idealists may well go to those articles by Creighton which have to do with the subject.[1]

Early in his philosophical development Creighton accepted in principle the doctrines developed by Bosanquet in his *Logic*, and these became the foundation of Creighton's own efforts at philosophical construction. To them he adds nothing new; his argu-

[1] The most representative of these articles were collected from the journals by H. R. Smart and published the year following Creighton's death under the title, *Studies in Speculative Philosophy*. To the articles the editor has appended a select bibliography.

General accounts of Creighton's life and thought may be found in the following articles: Frank Thilly, "The Philosophy of James Edwin Creighton," *The Philosophical Review*, Vol. XXXIV, 211-229; George H. Sabine, "The Philosophy of James Edwin Creighton," *ibid.*, pp 230-261; William A. Hammond, "James Edwin Creighton," *The Journal oj Philosophy*, Vol. XXII, 253-256; Katherine Gilbert, "James E. Creighton as Writer and Editor," *ibid.*, pp. 256-264.

ment for idealism is therefore quite in the spirit of Bosanquet. He does, however, clarify the argument by making explicit the type of idealism which seems to him defensible on these principles.

He was convinced that there are two quite distinct types of idealism, and that it is essential that they should be clearly differentiated. Even the representatives of idealism, he thought, are not always clear about the distinction; while the critics, especially the more realistic critics, generally assume that there is only one type and direct their attacks against that to the entire exclusion of what, in Creighton's opinion, is the only tenable form. It seemed to him a matter of constructive moment, then, to differentiate the one type from the other and to urge that attention, on the part of proponents and opponents alike, be converged upon the type which is vital.

For the purposes of the present survey, the chief significance of Creighton's contribution to the idealistic argument lies in his differentiation between these two types of idealism, and his advocacy of the one as over against the other.

1. The Two Types of Idealism

Under this title Creighton published in *The Philosophical Review*, 1917, an article in which he undertakes to make the distinction clear.[2] The types to be distinguished and what is to be gained by distinguishing them are indicated in the opening paragraph of that article: "Criticism of idealism from other schools has served to unite under a common flag philosophical thinkers who are by no means at one either in their presuppositions and methods, or in the general character of their results. The grouping of 'mentalists' and panpsychists under a common label with the exponents of speculative idealism, however explicable historically, has led to much confusion and fruitless controversy. Indeed, there is no better illustration at the present day of the hypnotic power of a label than that afforded by the inability of some recent critics of idealism to distinguish in principle between the different forms of doctrine to which this name is applied. It

---

[2] This article is reprinted in *Studies in Speculative Philosophy*, pp. 256-283.

seems to these critics impossible to disturb their fixed systems of classification. Perhaps feeling that an incurable ambiguity attaches to the word 'idealism,' Professor Bosanquet has repudiated that name for himself and seems to suggest that the name should no longer be used to denote the speculative doctrine which derives from the great writers of the past, but that to describe this the term *speculative philosophy* should be employed.[3] This is a proposal that deserves careful consideration. Even if traditional idealism may not be willing to abandon altogether its historical name, it is none the less essential that it should separate itself sharply from what may be called the hybrid forms which claim alliance with it. And this separation should be thoroughgoing and final, not something perfunctory and formal which still makes possible and sanctions mutual borrowings and accommodations. Traditional idealism, if it is to maintain itself as genuinely 'speculative philosophy,' must discard and disclaim the subjective categories assumed by the modern 'way of ideas' which is most frequently connected with the name of Berkeley. Idealists of this school ought not to allow their affections for 'the good Berkeley' to deter them from repudiating all alliance with his philosophical doctrines. Moreover, if this speculative idealism is to be defended and developed, it must rid itself of the ambiguities and restrictions that have resulted from its association with 'mentalism,' and that seem to make it a doctrine remote from the movements of science and the interests of practical life. By thus repudiating the unnatural alliance with the doctrine of 'mental states' speculative idealism will give evidence, not of weakness or vacillation, but of its vitality and steadfastness in maintaining the continuity of its historical position. At the same time it will strengthen its position by removing the chief grounds of misunderstanding and criticism from without." [4]

Mentalism's claim to the title of 'idealism' arises from the fact that it asserts everything to be mental in character—of the content of mind, or of the substance of mind. For it, material ob-

---

[3] For Bosanquet's suggestion, see his article, "Realism and Metaphysics," *The Philosophical Review*, Vol. XXVI, 4-15, especially p. 6.

[4] *Studies in Speculative Philosophy*, pp. 256-258.

jects, at least so far as they can be known in experience, are real only as existent states of consciousness. They are not frankly accepted for what they are, namely, external existents of non-mental character; on the contrary, they are reduced to internal states and are construed as such. The basal contention of this type of idealism is that, if experience is to be made intelligible, objects must be reduced to terms of mind. Mind and material things must be interpreted as literally identical modes of being. Since it is clearly impossible, however, to identify material objects with the states of consciousness of individual minds, this type of idealism posits an Absolute Mind as a vast receptacle, as it were, in which the order of nature and the objects in that order may find a place. This Absolute Mind is conceived of as an existing psychological consciousness, as a series or perhaps as a *totum simul* of states of mind, in reference to which all existents are ideas. Everything that exists is a state of this all-inclusive consciousness.

Of this type of 'idealism' the system of Berkeley is perhaps the clearest example. There can be no doubt that, in the earlier form of his argument at any rate, Berkeley regards experience as a collection of ideas, each of which has a particular mode of existence and is nothing else than that which at the moment it is perceived to be. The outer order of things he carries over into mind—not the individual mind, to be sure, but the mind of God —and it is there supposed to exist as states of consciousness. This, however, makes no difference in principle. Objects and ideas are identified: To be is to be in mind or to be of the substance of mind. Thus the basal thesis of Berkeley's 'idealism' is the basal thesis of all mentalism, namely that *the object must be reduced to terms of mind.*

This thesis takes other forms in other types of mentalism, as in the panpsychist doctrine; but in this form the principle is not changed. Instead of holding, as Berkeley does, that the mind can know only its ideas, panpsychism holds that mind can know only itself, or that the true object of knowledge must in the end be of the substance of mind.[5] In both cases, however, the same thing

[5] Cf. the views of Ward and McTaggart above, and of Howison and Bowne below.

in principle is clearly said: The object of knowledge must be reduced to terms of mind.

Speculative idealism, on the other hand, denies this thesis *in toto*. It takes the standpoint of concrete experience, which is also the standpoint of common sense and science. It begins by viewing mind and the objective system of nature as distinct, and it never dreams of identifying them; they remain distinct to the end. But speculative idealism does not permit their distinction to blind it to the fact that they are complementary; they are for it what they are in concrete experience, namely inseparably related aspects of that conscious life which is experience. It also accepts as complementary, and obviously so, the relation of the individual mind to the minds of other individuals. In other words, it accepts as complementary the social relationship between mind and mind. Thus for speculative idealism there are three moments or coördinates within experience: the self, other selves, and nature. These are accepted as they present themselves within experience, as irreducible and ultimate distinctions. But, while recognizing their difference, speculative idealism also recognizes their complementary nature and relationship. It does not accept them as discrete existences or entities each with its own independent self-enclosed center; holding on to the standpoint of concrete experience, it accepts them as complementary coördinates within experience.

Adopting this starting point, the logical procedure of speculative idealism consists in reading the implications of experience. This is precisely its task, and its main guarantee against error lies in its keeping clearly in view the basal moments of experience. "Experience is at once an explication or revelation of reality, a comprehension of the minds of one's fellows, and a coming to consciousness on the part of mind of the nature of its own intelligence. Philosophy, insisting on seeing things as they really are, must proceed with this system of relationships in view." [6]

Thus the starting point and the aim of speculative idealism are quite radically different from that of mentalism. There is here no question of reducing objects to terms of mind, either in the sense of Berkeleianism or in that of panpsychism. The aim,

[6] *Studies in Speculative Philosophy*, p. 270.

rather, is simply to gain recognition and explicit statement for what is constantly assumed in every-day experience; and this assumption is the point of departure in the undertaking.

2. THE ARGUMENT FOR SPECULATIVE IDEALISM

It is important, in the first place to note that mentalism is in the end untenable and must be set aside. Its basal weakness is that it logically reduces to subjectivism. If objects are to be reduced to 'ideas' of individual minds, then clearly they are as subjective as are individual ideas or states of consciousness. The mentalists recognize this difficulty and seek to escape it by invoking an Absolute Mind in which objects are to exist in the form of trans-human ideas. But this way of escape is logically futile. "On the one hand, things are not rendered a whit more 'ideal' by thinking of them as states of consciousness of an Absolute mind. Moreover, so long as this Absolute mind is conceived after the analogy of an existing psychological consciousness, as a series or even a *totum simul* of states of mind, it has no principle of connection with objective experience. Absolute idealism of this type is just as much subjective as the view which reduces things to states in the consciousness of a finite individual, and is open to all the objections which are brought against the latter theory. To assert that things exist as elements in an Absolute experience is then in itself only an appeal to a mechanical device which explains nothing, and is in addition unmeaning and arbitrary." [7]

Mentalism, thus, is untenable. Speculative idealism, however, is on quite a different footing. It is founded on the logic of experience itself, the critical process which moves within experience and brings into the open the full implication of the reciprocally determining coördinates of self, other selves, and nature. "Its logic and ideal of truth must be that of the concrete universal; so much is determined by the very form of experience. But the nature of intelligence and the nature of the world must be communicated to the mind gradually through the conscious and critical exchange with its social and physical environment.

[7] *Ibid.*, pp. 263-264. Compare the view of Royce.

We have always to look on ahead for the truth about the mind and reality, rather than to assume that these are existing data from which experience sets out . . . the faith of speculative philosophy is that the mind and things are what they show themselves to be *in the whole course of experience.*" [8] Thus speculative philosophy is as stable as is critical experience itself, since in the end the two are one and the same.

Clearly, the logic which Creighton conceives as underlying speculative idealism is identical with the logic of Bosanquet; there is consequently no need to rehearse it here in detail. Creighton does add, however, certain considerations which throw light on some of the important principles of this logic and set them in bolder relief. These we may in conclusion summarily state.

(a) The first of these is the insistence that, for speculative idealism, there is no 'epistemological' problem in the sense in which the realists love to debate it—in the sense, namely, of a problem as to how the mind as such can know reality as such. The very acceptance by speculative idealism of the standpoint of experience renders this problem obsolete. "Without any epistemological grace before meat it falls to work to philosophize, assuming, naïvely, if you please, that the mind by its very nature is already in touch with reality. Instead, that is, of assuming that there is an entity called mind, and another entity having no organic relation to mind called nature, it assumes on the basis of experience that these realities are not sundered and opposed, but are in very being and essence related and complementary. The relation or rather system of relations that constitute the bond between what we call mind and that which is termed nature it takes not as external and accidental, as if each of these could be real outside of this system, but rather as internal, essential and constitutive. We can think of a mind apart from an objective

---

[8] *Studies in Speculative Philosophy,* p. 274. This fundamental thesis the author develops frequently and in various contexts. Besides the discussion from which the above quotation is taken, the reader should consult especially the following articles: "The Standpoint of Experience"; "Experience and Thought," and "The Determination of the Real." All of these articles are included in the *Studies in Speculative Philosophy.*

order only through an abstraction: to be a mind at all it is necessary to be in active commerce with a world which is more than an order of ideas. If it is said that this is mere assumption, and not proof, I reply that this is the universal assumption upon which all experience and all science proceeds. It needs no proof because it is the standpoint of experience itself." [9]

(b) Closely linked with the preceding point is a further one which is foundational to the argument for speculative idealism. And that is that, as mind is in inseparable relation to the external order, the external order is in inseparable relation to mind. The very least that experience can assume and still remain experience is that what we call nature is something which at least is knowable by mind. The only alternative to this is the assumption that nature is a set of things-in-themselves, having only an external relation to mind. But this assumption is untenable, since it throws us back from experience to the effort to show in abstract terms how experience is made; the futility of this has been demonstrated not only by the failure of mentalism, but also by the inadequacy of Kant's phenomenalism and the necessity under which he found himself in the end to hold that nature must consist of objects of possible experience. Knowability then, is a characteristic of things; if it is the nature of the mind to know, it is equally the nature of things to be known. We, therefore, seem entitled to assert that nature is not complete apart from this relation. This is not to be interpreted to mean that natural objects must exist as representations in the mind: such an interpretation is the error of mentalism. It means only that the relation to mind is a constituent moment or characteristic of things, and is not something added on occasion and from the outside.

(c) A further point to be emphasized is that mind is complementary to mind. The process of thinking necessarily involves social relations among a group of individuals. By general assent

---

[9] *Ibid.*, p. 266; cf. pp. 100-101, 104. Compare the view of Pringle-Pattison as summarized above, pp. 157-158 (*The Idea of God,* pp. 111-112, and the entire Lecture VI). Compare also the view of Hegel as developed in the *Phenomenology of Mind* and summarily stated, for example, in Section 10 of the Introduction to the *Smaller Logic* (translation by W. Wallace).

the notion of an isolated individual is inadequate and misleading when employed to explain the moral, political, and religious experience of the individual; the same notion is equally inadequate and misleading when taken as the basis of logic. "Intelligence constantly looks outward, sharing in communistic fashion its own riches with others, and unhesitatingly appropriating the fruits of other men's labors. In other words, intelligence is openness, participation, making possible the mutual sharing and conflict of minds. Intelligence is not a private endowment that the individual possesses, but rather a living principle which possesses him, a universal capacity which expresses through him the nature of a larger whole in which he is a member." [10] This view of mind follows at once from our notion of experience; for, as we have seen, other minds constitute an important moment within experience, and the development of experience must proceed through the mutual interplay of the individual mind with other minds. As nature is essential to the full growth of individual minds, so are the minds of others essential. To be a mind is to be in commerce with nature and with other minds.

(d) It is quite important to note, further, that nature must be left standing in its own right, and must not be reduced to other minds as panpsychism undertakes to reduce it. The obvious reason for this is that such a reduction gives the lie to what appears to be the plain lesson of direct experience. The deeper, and more significant, reason is that such a reduction knocks the support from under rationality itself. It would appear that "an objective order, unmoved by our clamor, indifferent to our moods, with which we can hold commerce only on nature's own terms," is a necessary element in rational experience. Convert such an order into minds, as panpsychism does, and you have removed the only possible basis for rationality. "We could not have a rational experience in a universe consisting solely of a community of freely acting psychic beings. We need also a material system of things, an order to which we have to submit our intelligence and our will, an order that we are unable to bully or cajole,

---

[10] *Studies in Speculative Philosophy*, p. 57. Cf. the entire Chapter III on "The Social Nature of Thinking."

but which we can learn to control only by understanding and obedience." [11]

(e) Finally, if the principle of an Absolute experience is to have any significance for philosophy it must grow out of the critical process of experience and be justified by this. It cannot be accepted at the outset on the authority of merely formal arguments, but it must emerge as the result of thought in the sense in which thought is the critical process of the whole course of experience. "This category of Absolute mind has meaning and content only when it is exhibited as growing out of the reflective process of experience; it is justified only when it is shown to be a necessary standpoint in order to enable reason to overcome actual difficulties that present themselves within human experience itself. Whether such a conception in the end is indispensable as the goal of speculative philosophy is a question which cannot be answered by any *a priori* method. It is only indispensable if it concretely proves itself indispensable in the process of dealing with genuine problems of experience." [12] Furthermore, if the conception is indispensable and if it is to be anything more than a bare abstraction, it must fulfil, not negate, the demands of experience. "It must be capable of justifying and completing while at the same time transforming by illuminating, the standpoint of common sense and of the special sciences." In short, it must be the fulfilment and completion of the deeper demands of experience as the complementary relationship of self, other selves, and nature; it cannot therefore negate any of these coördinate moments of experience.

[11] *Ibid.,* p. 281. Compare the view of Pringle-Pattison: "Absolutely nothing is gained, and much confusion is introduced, by resolving external nature into an aggregate of tiny minds or, still worse, of 'small pieces of mind-stuff.' It is sufficient for the purposes of Idealism that nature as a whole should be recognized as complementary to mind, and possessing therefore no absolute existence of its own apart from its spiritual completion; just as mind in turn would be intellectually and ethically void without a world to furnish it with the materials of knowledge and of duty. Both are necessary elements of a single system." (*The Idea of God,* pp. 188-189; see the entire discussion of panpsychism, pp. 177-189.)

[12] *Studies in Speculative Philosophy,* pp. 268-269. Compare Haldane's views on the point, *supra,* pp. 247 ff.

Chapter XII

GEORGE HOLMES HOWISON (1834-1916)

In America, as in Britain, the development of the idealistic argument speedily led to a personalistic emphasis which stands in rather sharp opposition to absolutism of the type of that advocated by Bradley and Bosanquet. Royce, as we have seen, tends to emphasize the integrity of the finite individual more explicitly than do his absolutistic British colleagues; and despite his adherence to the conception of the Absolute, this emphasis drives him into certain important modifications of the conception. Indeed, in his later writings he leaves off speaking of the Absolute, and speaks rather of "the still invisible, but perfectly real and divine Universal Community" in which conception he finds the essence of Christianity.[1] In the thought of Creighton this tendency receives expression in the thesis that, whatever in the end may be the demands of monism, they at least cannot be permitted to render nugatory the demands of experience which involves the three dynamic coördinates of the self, other selves, and nature—the Absolute must fulfil, and not destroy, the implications of experience. In the 'personalism' or 'personalistic idealism' of George H. Howison and Borden P. Bowne this emphasis becomes the dominant note.

Like Creighton, Howison wrote comparatively little. He was chiefly influential as teacher and lecturer, in which capacity he exerted a marked influence on the cultural development of the Pacific Coast during the years (1884-1909) of his professorship at the University of California. But he did succeed in giving fairly definite formulation to his idealism in the small volume entitled *The Limits of Evolution and Other Essays Illustrating the Metaphysical Theory of Personal Idealism*, published in 1901 (second and revised edition, 1904).

---

[1] See *The Problem of Christianity*. Compare the thesis developed by Royce in *The Philosophy of Loyalty*.

1. CRITICISM OF ABSOLUTISM

The "foundation-theme" of idealism Howison defines as "that explanation of the world which maintains that the only thing absolutely real is mind; that all material and all temporal existences take their being from mind, from consciousness that thinks and experiences; that out of consciousness they all issue, to consciousness are presented, and that presence to consciousness constitutes their entire reality and entire existence." [2] But this foundation-theme may be uttered in various ways, Howison notes; and he insists that the brand of idealistic philosophy advocated by the absolutists gives to it an interpretation which is wholly untenable. To this type of idealism he is militantly opposed.

His basal objection to absolute idealism, or, as he usually prefers to call it, "Idealistic Monism" or "Cosmic Theism," is that, in one reading, it reduces to solipsism, and, in another, it resolves into a pantheism which logically negates the moral nature of finite individuals. "If the Infinite Self *includes* us all, and all our experiences,—sensations and sins, as well as the rest,— in the unity of one life, and includes us and them *directly;* if there is but one and the same final Self for us each and all; then, with a literalness indeed appalling, He is we, and we are He; nay, He is I, and I am He. . . . Now, if we read the conception in the first way, what becomes of our ethical independence?—what, of our *personal* reality, our righteous *i.e.* reasonable responsibility—responsibility to which we *ought* to be held? Is not He the sole *agent?* Are we anything but the steadfast and changeless modes of His eternal thinking and perceiving? Or, if we read the conception in the second way, what becomes of *Him?* Then, surely, He is but another name for *me*. . . ." Nor is there any principle by which one may determine which of the two readings is to be accepted. "My point against Professor Royce's argument, and against the whole post-Kantian method of construing Idealism, summed up by Hegel and supplied by him with organising logic, is this: By the argument

[2] From Howison's comments on Royce's argument in *The Conception of God,* p. 84.

. . . reading off its result as Idealistic Monism (or Cosmic Theism, if that name be preferred) rather than as Solipsism, is left without logical justification. The preference for the more imposing reading, it seems to me, rests on no principle that the argument can furnish, but on an instinctive response to the warnings of moral common-sense."[3] This more imposing reading, however, does not meet the demands of the moral consciousness; seeking to escape the Scylla of solipsism, it falls into the Charybdis of an all-engulfing pantheism. On either reading, therefore, it is untenable.

The more imposing reading of this type of idealism, universally accepted by its proponents, is as fatal to the reality of the finite individual as is the veriest materialism. Under the sheer evolutionary account of man and his place in nature the finite individual is utterly explained away; he is dissipated into blind forces by the analysis to which such an account subjects him. Essentially the same result follows from Cosmic Theism, when once its implications are followed through; for the immanent God of the cosmic theist is just as much the executive cause of the behavior of the finite creature as is the force or energy of the evolutionary naturalist. Both views alike are logically destructive of the human *person* and the moral order which rests upon him, and for essentially the same reason: in the end both negate "that real freedom which is essential to personality and to the pursuit of the genuine moral ideal." How the finite individual is to be logically saved from this negation is the main theme of Howison's argument for what he calls personal idealism.

2. ARGUMENT FOR PERSONAL IDEALISM

In its essentials this argument is a return to that of T. H. Green, with one basal difference. Like Green's argument, that of Howison stresses the *a priori* contribution of consciousness to the intelligibility of experience and also the denial of the Kantian things-in-themselves. The difference between the two arguments lies in the emphasis by Howison on the unique and indispensable importance of finite consciousness as the source and warrant of

[3] *The Conception of God*, pp. 98-99, 105-106. Italics are in the text.

the knowledge of nature. This emphasis is at once the novelty and the crux of Howison's formulation, as will become clear in a somewhat detailed statement of the argument itself.[4]

The logic of natural science is the logic of induction, that is, the logic by which universal laws of nature are discovered. But this logic rests upon the assumption of an all-pervading rationality in things which cannot be justified by an appeal, however general, to merely empirical observation. Whence, then, is its justification derived? The only possible answer is that it is derived from the systematic nature of mind itself, which adds to merely empirically observed facts the element or characteristic of universality and necessary connection. For in the end it is plain that "the ground of every generalisation is *added in* to the facts by the generalising *mind,* on the prompting of a conception organic in it. This organic conception is, that actual connexions between phenomena, supposing them to be exactly ascertained, are not simply actual, but are necessary. The logic of induction thus rests at last on the mind's own declaration that between phenomena there are connexions which are *real,* not merely apparent, not simply phenomenal, but noumenal; that the reality of such connexions lies in their necessity, and that the processes of Nature are accordingly unchangeable. But the implication most significant of all in this tacit logic is the indispensable postulate of the whole process; namely, that this necessity in the connexion of phenomena *issues from the organic action of the mind itself.*"[5]

The general thesis here stated Howison supports in some detail "by analysing the conception of evolution and noting in the result the conditions essential to the conception of it if it is to be taken as a real principle as wide as the universe of possible phenomena." And he takes the conception of evolution in this wide application, because it was so taken by many thinkers of his day who hoped to build a naturalistic philosophy upon it. A brief summary of the steps in this analysis will serve to place before us the main points in his argument.

[4] The summary of the argument here given is drawn from the volume, *Limits of Evolution.* The quotations are from the second edition of this work.

[5] *Ibid.,* p. 35. All the italics are in the original text.

(a) Three elements *prima facie* involved in the conception of evolution are: Time and Space, Change and Progression, and Causation. Evolution refers to the dynamic aspect of phenomena in which the items in the time-series are viewed as undergoing change marked by stages of increasing complexity and diversity, such that the whole is conceived as attaining a greater fullness and richness despite occasional lapses. And among the items there is supposed to be a necessary connection, a rigid nexus linking one stage in the process with another in that relationship which we call cause and effect. This conception of causation is, in fact, the basal element in the broader conception of evolution.

If, now, we suppose that causal connection is only a natural nexus among phenomena, then it cannot mean anything more than "a regular succession of the past—a sequence merely *de facto*." But this mere sequence is by no means all that causal connection means for the evolutionist; in addition, it means a *"necessary and irreversible* succession, a sequence inevitable forever." And the important question which confronts the philosopher is: Whence comes this necessity in the succession of phenomena? It certainly does not arise from the facts with which experimental observations acquaint us, since such observations, however extended, deal only with particular items in the succession, and necessity is no particular item. It is, rather, a generalization and springs only from "the organic action of mind itself"; it is *"added in* to the facts by the generalising mind." The basal element in the conception of evolution, then, is grounded in mind; it issues from mind alone.

Thus there is embedded in the conception of evolution, and intrinsic to it, a factor of "logical unity" which is not, and cannot be, based on any mere *de facto* sequence of phenomena, but is derived from "the organic or *a priori* activity of thought." This is the only sort of unity which is findable in the evolutionary series, and it is the only sort of unity which could possibly characterize the series. It alone could function among the obvious discontinuities of evolutionary phenomena [6] and intro-

[6] Such discontinuities are the apparent 'breaks' or 'jumps' between the inorganic and the organic and between the merely organic and the psy-

duce that element of necessity apart from which evolution could in no intelligible sense be called a universal law. "The bond of kindred uniting all these beings and orders of being, so contrasted and divergent, so incapable of any merely natural or physical generation one from the other, is the inner harmony between the lawful members in a single intelligible Plan, issuing from one and the same intelligent nature. In short, the only *cosmic* genesis, the only genesis that brings forth alike from cosmic vapour to star, from star to planetary system, from mineral to plant, from plant to animal, from the physiological to the psychic, is the genesis that constitutes the life of logic— the genesis of one conception from another conception by virtue of the membership of both in a system of conceptions organised by an all-embracing Idea. This all-determining Idea can be nothing other than the organic form intrinsic in the self-active mind, whose spontaneous life of consciousness creatively utters itself in a whole of conceptions, logically serial, forming a procession through gradations of approach, ever nearer and nearer, to the Idea that begets them each and all. By this it becomes plain that the theme of evolution, if it is to be indeed cosmic and reign in all phenomena, must have all its previous elements— succession, contiguity, causal connexion, generation (mechanical, chemical, physiological, and psychic)—translated upward in this logical genesis." [7]

(b) Hereupon it becomes also plain that evolution, as applicable on the cosmic scale, is essentially a teleological concept. For the analysis already followed shows that the ultimate and only authentic meaning of causality is to be construed in terms of 'final cause'—"the causality that creates and incessantly recreates in the light of its own Idea, and by the attraction of it as an ideal originating in the self-consciousness purely." Causality is precisely the causality of self-consciousness. Apart from self-consciousness there is, strictly speaking, no causality but only transmission. Taken by itself alone and in abstraction from consciousness, nature is "only a passive transmitter." But

chical forms. It is these discontinuities that mark the 'limits' of evolution, which, Howison thinks, remain insurmountable so long as evolution is naturalistically conceived.

[7] *Limits of Evolution*, pp. 37-38.

this is not the nature with which the evolutionist is concerned; the nature of his conception is that which the conception of evolution scientifically describes, and this nature in last analysis has its genesis in intelligence. "Thus Teleology, or the Reign of Final Cause, the reign of ideality, is not only an element in the notion Evolution, but is the very vital cord in the notion."

Our general conclusion may now be gathered together and summarily set down. We have demonstrated "that evolution not only is a fact, and a fact of cosmic extent, but is a necessary law *a priori* over Nature. But we learn at the same time, and upon the same evidence, that it cannot in any wise affect the *a priori* self-consciousness, which is the essential being and true *person* of the mind; much less can it originate this. On the contrary, we have seen it is in this *a priori* consciousness that the law of evolution has its source and its warrant." [8]

(c) Since the conception of evolution is only a striking example of scientific categories in general and of the process of inference by which they are attained, and since its basal element —namely, the conception of causation—is foundational to scientific knowledge, we may generalize the principle disclosed by its analysis. The logic of science itself, we may say, finds "its source and its warrant" in *a priori* self-consciousness. All necessity among phenomena springs from the organic action of mind, is a 'logical unity' which issues only from intelligent nature; and the logic of science is bottomed on this necessity. The world of science, then, we may hold is founded in *a priori* consciousness.

But we may, and must, go farther. Not merely the world of science, as a phenomenal order, is founded in *a priori* consciousness; so also is the world of reality. Either things-as-they-are conform to our *a priori* conceptions, or they must be identified with things-in-themselves, wholly independent of our *a priori* conceptions. In the latter case, however, things-as-they-are remain entirely unintelligible to us, and even the assertion that they exist involves a contradiction. We are therefore driven to accept the first alternative. But, accepting this alternative, we ground things-as-they-are in *a priori* consciousness. The logic of this becomes clear when once the nature of *apriority*, which

[8] *Limits of Evolution*, pp. 39-41.

underlies all generalization, is adequately apprehended. "To say
that a notion is *a priori* is to say that its being a spontaneous
thought of ours exhausts its existence completely; that the entire
being of it is in a native energy of our consciousness, and that
this elemental *discharge* from consciousness is the whole meaning
of the corresponding name. For instance, our pure thoughts corresponding to the words *space, time, cause,* are upon the *a priori*
theory exactly and utterly what Space, Time, and Cause re-
spectively *are.* Anything short of this view would render apriority null. For if there were anything *extra mentem* to which,
even possibly, the *a priori* elements corresponded, we could never
then be certain that they *originated* in our consciousness at all
—we should remain in a quandary as to whether they did or did
not. Yet from our consciousness they *must* originate if they are
to have that absolute universality, and that necessity of application to their objects, with which we incontestably think them.
. . . To make the thing-in-itself a genuine form *a priori* is therefore to *exclude* its existence in any other sense. But this annuls
the desired phenomenalistic conjecture of its *perhaps* absolute
existence; we have committed ourselves irretrievably to the judgment *There are no things-in-themselves.*" We must be serious
with the doctrine of apriority, then, or the generalizations of
science lose their universality and necessity. But, taking the
doctrine seriously, we are compelled to deny the existence of
things-in-themselves; for the doctrine, carried to its completion,
involves the conclusion that "the cognition belonging to each
mind is the *indispensable* condition of the existence of reality." [9]

(d) Another point in the preceding analysis should be carefully noted, and it carries us another step forward in our argument. It is this: The *a priori* consciousness in which the inductive logic of science and reality find their ground is, in the first
instance at least, that of finite beings. There are indeed other
issues involved, and these must be faced below. Meanwhile, we
are to note that the immediate requirements of our analysis
"point us, first and unavoidably, to the intelligence immanent in
the field of evolution, the intelligence of man and his conscious
companions on the great scene of Nature; and, at closest hand

[9] *Ibid.,* pp. 163-164, 170. The italics are in the text.

of all,—first of all,—to the typical intelligence of man simply. The whole question, so far as anything more than conjectural evidence is concerned, is man's question: he is the witness to himself for evolution; in *his* consciousness, directly, and only there, does the demand arise for an explanation of it; in himself he comes upon the nature of mind as directly causal of the form in Nature. . . ." [10]

Herewith we are committed to the important conclusion that the finite individual is indefeasibly real, and not merely a phenomenal appearance of some deeper reality. Since the finite individual is the proximate form of that *a priori* consciousness which is the "source and warrant" of all scientific generalization, the conclusion is inescapable that the reality of the finite individual must first of all be explicitly admitted. The mind of man is not a mere phenomenon, like objects in space and time; it "is transcendentally different from these, and noumenal."

This basal truth is denied alike by evolutionary naturalism and monistic idealism. "In neither view is *a priori* consciousness admitted in the individual person as individual, nor in the human mind at all, as *specifically* human." The former undertakes to explain consciousness as a natural product of the process of evolution; while the latter throws *a priori* consciousness into God or the Absolute, "to be thence gradually imparted to minds as they are slowly created by the process of psychic evolution." [11] But neither view can stand. The naturalistic evolutionist is guilty of the absurdity of trying to explain exclusively in terms of the evolutionary process, as a causal result of it, that which is logically prerequisite not only to its conception but also to its very existence. And the monistic idealist fails to note that "the proper interpretation of *a priori* consciousness, at the juncture where it is established, is at most, and at next hand, as a human, not a divine, original consciousness, and, indeed, as a consciousness interior to the individual mind." [12]

---

[10] *Limits of Evolution*, p. 42.

[11] *Ibid.*, pp. 44-45. Cf. Green's view to the effect that finite consciousness is a 'reproduction' in time of the 'eternal consciousness' in nature.

[12] *Ibid.*, p. 45. The conclusion here stated and the general line of argument leading up to it are well summarized by the author in a later essay

(e) But we must go beyond this. To say that "the cognition belonging to each mind is the indispensable condition of reality" is not equivalent to saying, and must not be interpreted as equivalent to saying, that it is the sole and sufficient condition. In point of fact, it is not so. For, as we may now assure ourselves, the sufficient condition of reality is nothing short of the "consensus of the whole system of minds, including the Supreme Mind, or God." What are the grounds of this assurance?

As a first step in answer to this question we may pause to make explicit a very important implication of the position already reached concerning the noumenal nature of the finite individual—the implication, namely, of immortality and personal freedom. The doctrine of apriority, as we have seen, means that the spontaneous forms of consciousness are foundational to reality. Now what we call the soul is simply "the system of our several elements of consciousness *a priori.*" And hence it directly follows that the soul is foundational to reality, is therefore itself real or, in other words, is immortal. "The objector who would open the eternal permanence of the soul to doubt, then, must assail the proofs of *a priori* knowledge; for so long as these remain free from suspicion, there can be no real question as to what they finally imply. The concomitance of our two streams of experience, the timed stream and the spaced stream, raised from a merely historical into a necessary concomitance by the

on "The Right Relation of Reason to Religion": "Every act of induction, every case of generalisation,—that is to say, of prophetic universalisation from the relatively few single cases that constitute its observed foundation, —is a direct appeal from the limitations of observation to the essential and all-pervading rationality of things. However far the finite *results* of induction may fall short of assuring us of this pervading rationality, the secret of the inductive *method* is our unreserved committal to its reality. But there can be no ground for such a universal rationality in facts themselves, as they are simply and historically presented; our first strict statement about it must be, that it is *a pure addition to the facts, made by the spontaneous instinct of our minds.* . . . The latent logic of the method of induction therefore leads us, first of all and directly, not to the existence of a personal God, nor even to that of the impersonal God, immanent in Nature, to which the evolutional pantheist concludes, but, on the contrary, to a rational *nature* everywhere present and regulative, and only to a person or persons as these are necessarily presupposed in such a nature. Nor does taking the next step of passing to these persons bring us to God, but only, at nearest hand, to men." (*Ibid.,* pp. 274-276. The italics are all in the original text.)

argument that refers it to the active unity of each soul as its ground, becomes the steadfast sign and visible pledge of the imperishable self-resource of the individual spirit." And with this we have also affirmed the freedom of the finite individual. For when we speak of a mind as free, all we can mean is that it is "independently self-active, self-moved from within"; and this is only another way of saying that it is underived, self-subsistent, or eternal. The proof of immortality is also the proof of freedom.[13]

But what are the implications of freedom? Under what conditions is the finite individual genuinely free? The answer lies near, and with it we reach the goal of our quest.

In the first place, freedom implies that the individual is self-defining; its nature is essentially its own, underived *ab extra*. In other words, the free spirit is "intrinsically individual." But, in the second place, the free spirit is also intrinsically universal. Self-definition involves difference; "and difference, again, implies contrast, and so *reference to others*." The free spirit thus is of a dual nature; it is indefeasibly itself, but it is also and necessarily related to other spirits. Precisely because it is itself, it stands in this necessary relation to others. "In this fact we have reached the essential form of every spirit or person—the organic union of the particular with the universal, of its private self-activity in the recognition of itself with its public activity in the recognition of all others. That is, self-consciousness is in the last resort a *conscience*, or the union of each spirit's self-recognition with the recognition of all."[14] The very nature of the self is bound up with the existence of other selves: ". . . the very deepest principle of our conscious lives" is "the consciousness of our relation to other minds."

The view here stated may be oriented historically and also clarified by a brief statement of the basal modification of the Kantian view which it implies. The conclusion at which we have arrived means in principle a denial of Kant's sharp separation between the theoretical and the practical consciousnesses. In opposition to that dualism, the present thesis is that the practical or

---

[13] *Limits of Evolution*, pp. 298, 308, 328, 329.
[14] *Ibid.*, p. 353.

moral consciousness is foundational within the theoretical in the sense that the latter, when sounded by analysis, is seen to rest on the former. The logical roots of every mind's nature are exactly this recognition of itself through its recognition of others, and the recognition of others in this very act of recognizing itself. Hence, the moral life is not only primordial in the nature of mind; but what we call moral consciousness—as if thereby we would divide it permanently from the remainder of consciousness, and count this remainder mere knowledge or mere aesthetic discernment as the case may be—turns out in fact to be the primary logical ground of all other possible consciousness.[15]

Thus the conception of a society of minds is logically involved in the individual mind, is, indeed, foundational within the organic unity of individual mind. Hence it is foundational to the source whence springs, in the first instance, the rationality of things upon which the logic of induction rests. "What we reach, then, as the all but direct implication of induction, is *the reality of a universal rational society.*"[16]

With the recognition of the reality of such a rational society we are brought to a position from which the necessity of admitting the reality of a personal God is readily seen. For such a society is a community of free individuals; and the freedom of each member of the community implies the actualization, in the form of a supremely free Self, of the common nature within which the freedom of each member of the society participates. In other words a nature common to all members of the society is the logical ground of the freedom of each member; and if the freedom of each is real, this common nature is also real. But this common nature must be self-conscious intelligence, the ideal Type to which all finite intelligences approximate and with reference to which all finite intelligences are defined. Thus each member of the society "in the very act of defining his own reality, defines and posits God as real—as the one Unchangeable Ideal

---

[15] Cf. *Ibid.,* pp. 308 ff. Note: "This primal consciousness of our relation to others is the real secret of our belief in noumena, and contains their only true meaning; and it supplies the element which carelessly and wrongly united with Space and Time gives rise to a sensuous misinterpretation of things-in-themselves" (p. 167).

[16] *Ibid.,* p. 276; Howison's italics.

who is the indispensable standard upon which the reality of each is measured. The price at which alone his reality as self-defining can be had is the self-defining reality of God. If he is real, then God is real; if God is not real, then neither can *he* be real." [17]

Thus we have reached our journey's end. We set out to define the nature of the real world within which we find ourselves, and we have arrived at the conception of the "City of God" as the full form of that definition. There are two characteristics of this City which we should note in conclusion. The first characteristic is that it is a City of free citizens, each self-subsistent, though not self-contained, and all in mutually free relationship with the realized common Ideal, a personal God, who also is perfectly free and self-subsistent and exists, not as an all-encompassing and all-devouring Absolute, but only as *primus inter pares*. The second characteristic of the City is that it has foundations which are in no danger of being undermined by the sapping processes of skepticism or agnosticism standing on scientific results; for these foundations rest, not upon the results of science, but upon its very method.

[17] *Limits of Evolution*, p. 355. Howison's italics.

CHAPTER XIII

BORDEN PARKER BOWNE (1847-1910)

LIKE Creighton and Howison, Borden Parker Bowne was very influential as a teacher of philosophy. During the period of his professorship in Boston University, from 1876 until his death, many students who later became teachers of philosophy or allied subjects came under his tutelage and carried away a deep impression of both the man and his vision. And his influence extended far beyond his classroom. His voice was potent in the councils of his own religious communion, and his writings had considerable effect on leaders in other religious creeds. Among technical philosophers other than his own students, however, Bowne's influence has been quite limited; he is seldom quoted or referred to in philosophical debates. One may venture the guess that this neglect is the result of a tacit assumption that Bowne is primarily a theologian and not strictly a philosopher at all— an assumption which finds partial justification at least in Bowne's not infrequent impatience with views opposed to his own and his rather obvious preoccupation with vivid and fixed religious convictions which often seem to color, if not to warp, his consideration of technical philosophical issues. But, whatever the explanation, this neglect is not warranted. Despite his limitations of style and his apparent dogmatism, Bowne dealt with most of the issues with which philosophers are wont to concern themselves; and he offered a definite metaphysical view supported by reasoned considerations which, whatever in the end one may think of them, are at least debatable.

To his particular type of idealism Bowne preferred to apply the label of 'personalism.' His basal view is little different from that of Howison. His argument in support of it is essentially the same, but in a more detailed form and with a difference which in some more or less important respects supplements Howison's formulation and fixes attention specifically upon considerations not specially emphasized by the California philosopher. This difference is sufficiently significant to warrant in the present survey a separate chapter devoted to a summary of Bowne's position.[1]

1. THE METHOD

"The question, What is reality? can only be answered by telling how we must think about reality." This is Bowne's statement of his basal assumption—an assumption which, in his opinion, is sufficiently guaranteed by the consideration that any alternative is intolerable. He does not mean to assert here, however, that there is any sort of 'correspondence' between thought and reality —certainly not "in the sense that we can first know things by themselves, and then form conceptions of the things already known, and finally compare the things and the conceptions in order to note their correspondence." What is intended is, rather, that peculiar relation between thought and things which is disclosed by the validity of our thoughts about things. "The validity is the only correspondence, and this can be determined only by the self-evidence or necessity with which the conception imposes itself on the mind."[2]

The starting point in the process of determining the nature of the real, that is, of discovering how we must think about reality, is, of course, experience. We take the data which experience presents to us, and on the basis of these data we seek to determine what thoughts are necessary; such thoughts, we then say, are valid of things and consequently are revelatory of the nature of reality. There is, in the process, no question of telling how things come to be; the whole process is directed simply towards under-

---

[1] The argument as here summarized is taken from the revised edition of Bowne's *Metaphysics* (1898); first edition (1882). The same argument in a more popular dress is presented in his *Personalism* (1908)—the N. W. Harris Lectures, delivered at Northwestern University in 1907. Bowne's other important philosophical works are: *The Philosophy of Theism* (1887), and *The Theory of Thought and Knowledge* (1897).

For a sympathetic account of Bowne by a former pupil, the reader should consult the article, "Personalism and the Influence of Bowne," by E. S. Brightman, read at a session of the Sixth International Congress of Philosophy, Harvard University, 1926, and published in the *Proceedings* (pp. 161-167) of that society.

[2] *Metaphysics*, p. 3. Cf. *Theory of Thought and Knowledge*, especially Part I, Chapters I-III, and Part II, Chapters I-II.

standing the data experience presents. We take the data as presented, and we introduce into them what modifications are necessary to make our conceptions adequate and harmonious; the
justification of the modifications is within the subject-matter
with which we are dealing. Our method, thus, is critical; it is the
method of critical experience. And it is based on the faith that
what in the end enlightened experience compels us to think about
reality must be accepted as our only answer to the question:
What is reality?

The same view of the method of philosophy may, indeed, be
expressed in terms of the familiar distinction between appearances and reality. These terms are notoriously ambiguous, however; and if this phraseology is to be used, the terms should be
carefully defined. It is at times supposed that appearance is mere
illusion and that reality is an unknowable something that stands
behind this illusory appearance. But this is a gross mistake, and
it should be corrected. The true relation between appearance and
reality is not that of opposition and exclusion, as if what 'appears' could not also be real. Appearance is also in its own way
reality. The difference between the two can only mean that what
we call the real is "the ontological and causal ground of the apparent." So the antithesis is not between the apparent and the
real, as if the apparent were wholly unreal or a mere phantasm.
The antithesis is rather between two sorts of reality—namely,
phenomenal reality and ontological or causal reality. It is quite
important for the further argument that these two senses of the
real be kept distinct, and that both be sharply distinguished
from mere illusion and sheer error.

On the basis of this distinction we may say that the task of
metaphysics is to pass from appearance to reality—that is, it
"may be conceived as an attempt by a study of phenomenal
reality to pass to a consistent and adequate conception of the
causal reality." Phenomenal reality (those elements of experience given in sense-intuition) furnishes the grounds of our inferences; ontological or causal reality (those elements of experience
given in thought) is the outcome of the adequate completion of
these inferences. "When we study the former we find ourselves
unable to rest in it as final; and thus we are compelled to pass

behind the intuitions of sense to the unpicturable constructions of thought." [3]

It must be explicitly borne in mind from the beginning, however, that mere forms of thought have in themselves no guarantee that there is a reality corresponding to them; real thoughts must have a filling from concrete experience. Thoughts "have application only as we find some concrete experience which illustrates them. Otherwise they are abstractions without any real content, or they are formal principles which float in the air until some concrete experience tells us what their actual meaning is." [4] This is a basal principle which is involved in the logic of any sane metaphysics, and must be borne in mind throughout. What is genuinely thinkable must be a "clear notion," and every clear notion must be translatable into terms of concrete experience.

Passing, then, from phenomenal reality to ontological or causal reality, carefully assuring ourselves meanwhile that all our thoughts are genuinely thinkable in terms of concrete experience, we may be assured that we have attained a true insight into the nature of ontological or causal reality. What are the steps in this passage? What is the adequate interpretation of phenomenal reality with which noumenal or causal reality is to be identified? These are the questions before us.

2. Being as Active

Since things exist or have being, the first step in our interpretation of phenomenal reality must be to inquire what, precisely stated, the notion of 'being' is to mean for us. We must ask: What is that mark or characteristic common to all things which exist or have being and absent from non-existent things or things which do not have being?

It may at first sight appear that mere 'given-ness' in phenomenal experience is the essential characteristic of being. But this is clearly untenable, since it involves the conclusion that what is not thus given does not exist, and this conclusion is contrary both to common sense and to reflection. Some things (like pleasures and pains) have being in this sense, but there are other

[3] *Metaphysics*, p. 9.
[4] *Personalism*, pp. 177-178; cf. the whole of Lecture II.

things (like material objects) which exist even when not given in experience. Wherein lies their existence or being?

The only answer to this question seems to be that the being of such things consists in some power of action inherent in them. "Things, when not perceived, are still said to exist, because of the belief that, though not perceived, they are in interaction with one another, mutually determining and determined." [5] Power of action, then, must be taken as the distinctive mark of being. This view alone will save us from becoming followers of Berkeley. The same conclusion is forced upon us by the consideration that the notion of being is precisely the notion which we posit as the explanation of all phenomenal reality, and that the only "clear notion" of being which will perform this logical function is that of an agent which is causal and active. There is no possibility of remaining by the empty notion of pure being; we must pass on to ask concerning the significance of the notion when translated into terms of concrete experience. And hereupon we see quite clearly that "the notion vanishes altogether, unless it take up into itself the thought of definiteness and the thought of causality. Only the definite and only the active can be viewed as ontologically real." [6] Being, therefore, as ontologically real, must be definite and active—that is, must be "a definite causal agent."

Several difficulties seem to lie in the way of accepting this conception of being, and a consideration of these may serve to clarify the ground on which the conception rests. In the end we shall find that all these supposed difficulties result from a failure to distinguish between phenomenal and ontological reality.

The first of these arises from the assumption that there are many objects in experience which are undeniably real and also undeniably inert and active—namely, physical objects. But this assumption is unfounded. The inactivity of such objects is apparent only, as indeed the science of physics itself teaches us; conceptually, everything here stands in the most complex relations of interaction with everything else. Nor is this view contradicted by the law of inertia of matter, which says only that a material element does not have spontaneity with reference to its

[5] *Metaphysics*, p. 16.
[6] *Ibid.*, p. 17.

own space-relations, and not that a material element is ultimately or ontologically static and inert. Wherever one looks in the world of matter, if one looks beyond its phenomenal reality, one finds nothing in conflict with the conception that ontologically material being is active and causal. There is here, then, nothing which contradicts our conception of being.

Another supposed difficulty is at first glance more serious, but little reflection is required to remove it. When we say that all being is active, it may be supposed that we have given no definition of being itself but have only indicated a characteristic which being *per se* must have; and hereupon we are apparently confronted with a distinction between being *per se* and the power or activity which somehow attaches to it. It is indeed true that being *per se* and the power which belongs to it can be detached in abstract thought. But they cannot be detached in reality, nor can a clear notion of their detachment be formed. If one attempts to think their separation concretely, one is at once caught in the clutches of insoluble contradictions. For what is the relation between them, if in fact they are separate?

To this question there is no clear answer. To say that power 'inheres' in being is meaningless. Being *per se* as distinct from power does not account for power, any more than the abstract notion of a triangle accounts for its several sides and angles. The plain truth is that the distinction here is merely a logical one and has no ontological significance. Ontologically considered, being is in activity as the triangle is in its sides and angles.

The same point is clear, if we approach the matter from the side of power alone. Power *per se* is only an abstraction and cannot inhere in anything, just as being *per se* is an abstraction and cannot include anything. The separation between being and power is a logical distinction only, and cannot be accepted as of ontological significance. There is no core of being which has power, for the notion 'core of being' is not a "clear notion." The being of things is in their activity, and not in any 'lump of being' in them.

Such objections as these, then, may be set aside as merely thoughtless assumptions which further thought, based on a clear grasp of the distinction between phenomenal and ontological reality and of their peculiar relation to each other, speedily clears away. "Phenomenal reality is revealed in the contents of sense-intuition; but ontological reality can be grasped only by the unpicturable notions of the understanding. Its nature is a problem for thought, not for sense. We must rise from the world of lumps into a world of energy." [7] And, having so risen, we are face to face with the ontological notion of being.

3. THE NATURE OF A THING

Even so, however, our interpretation of being is by no means complete. Thus far we have determined the nature of things in so far as they can be said to have being or to exist. But we have not distinguished them from one another as individual things. We must now inquire into the essence of things as peculiar and individual.

The conclusion here is indeed not far to seek; it follows directly from that already attained. We have seen that whatever truly exists must be viewed as active, and that activity constitutes the nature of being. Differences among the natures of individual things must, therefore, be defined as differences in the form or kind of activity. "It is in this law that the definiteness of a thing is to be found; and it is under this general form of a law determining the form and sequence of activity that we must think of the nature of the thing." [8]

In opposition to the view here advanced, it has at times been supposed that the nature of things is to be defined in terms of sense-qualities. But this supposition is entirely without foundation and involves us in all sorts of logical difficulties. The notion of a nature applies to all things, but sense-qualities belong only to sense-objects. Furthermore, sense-qualities disclose, not what the sense-objects really are, but only how they affect us. Again, things are always in interaction with one another, and this inter-

---

[7] *Metaphysics*, p. 28. The question may be raised whether the position here stated is quite in harmony with the thesis above defended that thoughts "have application only as we find some concrete experience which illustrates them" (*supra*, p. 318). Bowne vacillates between these two views of thought, and he seems not to be quite clear between them. To what extent the vacillation leads him into inconsistencies is an interesting problem for the student of his system.

[8] *Ibid.*, p. 30.

action is also an expression of their natures; but the interaction itself is neither a sense-quality nor an aggregation of sense-qualities. Finally, the same thing is found to have different sense-qualities which are incommensurable among themselves. If, for instance, one special sense-quality (color, for example) is supposed to define the nature of a thing, then other incommensurable sense-qualities do not, even though they somehow belong to the thing. This we must accept unless we are to fall into the absurdity of holding that a given thing has as many natures as it has sense-qualities and thereby deny the unity of the thing. For these reasons, then, the identification of the nature of a thing with a sense-quality must be given up; in the end, such a view even denies that the thing has a nature.

The impossibility of finding the nature of a thing in its sense-qualities has led to the attempt to find it in some 'essence' behind the qualities. From this attempt two quite different views of the nature of the thing have resulted. One of these is that the essence or nature of the thing is itself without quality of any kind; the other is that it has qualities, but that these are unknown. The first of these views may be set aside at once as worthless, since it identifies the nature of the thing with the notion of being *per se* which we have already been forced to discard. The second view, however, has not as yet been considered in principle and deserves special comment here.

It is clear that there is a peculiar logical difficulty involved in the statement that the nature of a thing is in qualities which are unknown; for the statement seems to assert both that the nature of a thing is known and that it is not known. Even if this logical consideration be left aside and the thesis allowed to stand as not self-contradictory, it may readily be shown to be a thesis in which thought cannot rest. Change is a characteristic of things, but not of qualities; we say that things change their color, for example, but never that one color changes into another. If, then, the nature of a thing is a quality—whether known or unknown makes no difference to the point—the thing could not possibly change; it would remain always simple and unchangeable. Hence the dilemma: Either the nature of a thing is not a quality, or the thing cannot change. But there seems to be no possibility of denying that things actually do change. Consequently, the view that the nature of the thing is a quality, known or unknown, must be denied. If the quality is said to be unknown, the view is not thereby made more tenable but is only complicated by a further difficulty. "On these two accounts, therefore—(1) the unchangeability of qualities, and (2) the necessary changeability of things—we deny that any simple quality or combination of qualities can ever represent the nature of a thing." [9]

So we are apparently justified in reaffirming our original thesis that the nature of a thing is "that law or principle which determines the form and character of its activity." But, lest this thesis itself land us in the difficulties attaching to the notion of being *per se*, it must be guarded against misunderstanding. It does not intend to draw any distinction between the nature of the thing and the law of its activity; on the contrary, it affirms their identity in the thing. "The definite thing is the only reality; and the distinction of thing and law is in our thought. Being without law is nothing; and law without being is also nothing." [10]

Our general conclusion thus far, then, is this: "Being in distinction from non-being finds its mark in causality. Things find the definiteness which they must have in order to exist at all in the law of this causality. Differing things find the ground of their difference in the different laws of the respective causalities. To know this law is to know the thing in itself, or in its inmost essence." [11] From this we may go forward by inquiring into the significance of the fact that the thing appears to be permanent in the midst of change. Can this element of permanence be retained in being; and, if so, how?

4. Permanence as Personal

It is no solution of this problem to hold that the thing itself is changeless, while its qualities change. On the one hand, such a view is logically untenable since the hypothesis of a changeless thing would be useless to meet the situation; even granting

[9] *Metaphysics*, p 38.
[10] *Ibid.*, pp. 41-42.
[11] *Ibid.*, p. 43.

that such a changeless thing exists, it could not be the ground of its changing qualities. In point of fact, on the other hand, this view is not at all different from the view that the nature of things lies in a core of being—a view from which our previous discussion has already driven us. The nature of the thing, we have learned, must lie in its special activity; and this excludes any view which would account for the permanence of the thing by appealing to some static identity which lies back of the thing's changing qualities as their ground.

The true answer to our question is suggested by a consideration of what is involved in our knowledge of change. "The knowledge of change depends on some fixed factor, which, by its permanence, reveals the change as change." Thus, if all things (including the thinking subject) were in mere flux, there could be no knowledge of change; the theory that all things are in flux would itself then be impossible. To make the theory intelligible, we must have at least an abiding and permanent knower. A permanent subject, therefore, is necessary in the knowledge of change; and such a permanent subject we consciously experience in ourselves. And from this we may go on to the conclusion that a permanent subject is necessary to bring the changing qualities of a thing into unity. For a permanent thing is entirely unintelligible unless "its successive phases shall admit of being gathered up into a law-giving expression which shall express for thought the nature of the thing." No mere idea of the thing, however, can serve as such "a law-giving expression"; the idea as such is timeless and has in it no succession, whereas this law-giving expression must include within itself the whole series of the thing's changing states and must bring the members of the series into unity. The idea of the thing must, therefore, be conceived as being realized successively, if it is to be identified with such a law-giving expression. "And to complete the thought, we are thrown back upon the conception of an underlying intelligence which is at once the seat of the idea and the source of the realizing energy." [12].

Thus we are driven to seek for a solution of the problem of

[12] *Metaphysics*, pp. 60, 61, 62.

permanence in change on the personal plane. So long as we remain on the impersonal plane and think of things as mere material elements, the problem is an insoluble puzzle. Here change is mere change without permanence (a Heraclitic flux), and permanence is mere permanence or bare identity without difference (the Eleatic 'being'). If we put the problem on the personal plane, however, it is readily solved; for in self-conscious spirit we find concrete union of change and permanence— permanence through change, and change in permanence. "If, then, the idea of being must include permanence as well as activity, we must say that only the personal truly is. All else is flow and process. . . . As abstract principles, change and identity are in mutual contradiction, and they remain so until they are carried up to the plane of conscious thought, and are interpreted not as abstract conceptions, but as concrete manifestations of the living intelligence which is the source and reconciliation of both." [13]

5. Efficient Causality

The thesis here arrived at receives its final justification in a thoroughgoing analysis of the meaning of causality. The nature of a thing, we have already seen, lies in the law of causality which determines its activity. If, then, we can discover what this law concretely means, we shall thereby attain insight into the nature of the thing and, so, into the nature of being. This analysis, too, will lead us to the thesis that "only the personal truly is"; for in the end volitional causality is the only conception of ontological causality in which we can rest.

As an indispensable preliminary to any serious discussion of the conception of causality, an insidious ambiguity must be cleared away. Causality may have either one of two quite different meanings, and it is essential for clear thinking about the problem that these two meanings be kept distinct. On the one hand, causality may refer to a group of conditions together with an event which arises when the conditions are fulfilled; the total group of conditions is the cause, and the event following upon them is the effect. This sort of causality we may call

[13] *Ibid.*, pp. 65, 67.

"causality in the inductive sense." On the other hand, however, causality may mean productive efficiency or dynamic determination; in this sense of the term, a cause is the determinative ground of events. In this meaning causality may be called metaphysical, as distinguished from the other which is phenomenal.

Causality in the inductive sense is very important practically; indeed, the chief part of practical wisdom lies in knowledge of it. But this type of causality is not here under consideration. Our exclusive interest in this discussion is in metaphysical causality. The question before us is: What is the nature of causality in the sense in which causality is the efficient and determining ground of events?

It is sometimes supposed that such causality may be adequately conceived as a system of independent material things endowed with forces whereby they mutually determine one another through interaction. In this supposition two notions are of basal importance, namely 'system' and 'interaction'; and in examining the claims of the supposition these notions call for analysis.

In order that any system whatever should exist for thought the members of the system must admit of being brought into relations under the various categories of thought and of being united into a logical whole. Furthermore a system which is intelligible must be a system of law, so that definite antecedents will have definite consequents; and this, in turn, demands an exact adjustment of all interacting members to each other. Such are the main characteristics of a conceptual system—a system of thought.

Now it is very important to note that such a system is wholly meaningless, because impossible, apart from a unifying mind. "The mind must comprise the many conceptions in the unity of one consciousness, must distinguish, compare, and relate them, and thus unite them into one systematic whole." [14] For a conceptual system, then, mind is foundational.

Of course, a real causal system, whose nature we are here primarily interested in defining, is not a merely conceptual

14 *Metaphysics*, p. 72.

system; it is a system of things apparently independent of mind. Nevertheless, the immediately preceding remarks are not irrelevant to our inquiry. They direct attention to the supreme condition of the existence of any conceptual system, and raise the very pertinent question as to what, in the real causal system, is to take the place of mind in the conceptual system. If there is to be a causal system, something must there perform the function which mind performs in the conceptual system. Can 'interaction' among the things in the causal system perform this function, as is sometimes supposed? What does the notion of such interaction involve?

In reply to this question several considerations are relevant. In the first place, there is no proper experience of interaction. We do, indeed, at times speak of experiencing interaction between mind and body; but this way of speaking is, in point of fact, a mistake, since what we experience are merely changes (mental or physical) and not any connections between them. Interaction, then, is not a datum of experience, but a problem of thought. In the second place, many traditional notions of interaction among independent beings (such as the transference of a state or condition by one thing to another, or a passing influence from one thing to another, or a play of forces between different things) have been advanced. But none of these notions meet the issue. Analysis discloses that all of them are concerned only with the phenomenal aspects of causality, and are based upon an inductive study of the laws of the reciprocal changes of things; therefore, even if true, they throw no light on the problem we are here concerned with. They refer to inductive causality, and do not at all touch the problem of metaphysical causality. In the third place, and most important of all, the notion of interaction among mutually independent things involves a flat contradiction; for, by definition, the independent must contain within itself the ground of all its determinations, whereas that which is in interaction with other things must have the ground of its determinations partly at least in the other things that go to make up the interacting system. The two conceptions of 'interaction' and 'mutually independent things,' therefore, cannot logically be combined. If things interact, they necessarily constitute a system and are consequently not independent; if they are mutually independent things, they do not constitute a system and therefore cannot possibly interact.

Thus interaction implies unity among the interacting elements. Consequently, the very notion of interaction compels us to forego the attempt to conceive it as "a transitive causality playing between things; it is rather an immanent causality in a fundamental unitary being"—namely, the system within which the interaction falls.[15] But what is this "unitary being"? Can we say of it nothing more concrete than that it is a system?

From what has just been said it is clear that, if there is to be a system, there must be some dynamic bond underlying the members of the system. A system cannot be defined in terms of its several members taken separately; it must be conceived with reference to some sort of basal unity. We have also seen that the unity of any system, in so far as system is an object of thought, lies in mind or intelligence. In the conceptual system unity is furnished by an idea which is ultimately grounded in intelligence. All of this we have seen. We must now see that intelligence must be posited as the ground of any real system.

The reason for this conclusion is that any real system must be thinkable, and the only system which is thinkable, concretely thinkable, is that which is founded in active intelligence. Suppose, for example, that we try to introduce real unity among things by the notion of 'potentiality.' This is to delude ourselves with the supposition that an abstract notion can furnish the ground of an interactive system. All that potentiality means or can mean, when we say that the later members of a series are 'potential' in the earlier, is that the members of the series are somehow connected in a system; it does not in the least tell us *how* they are connected, and to imagine that it does so is to rest satisfied with a purely verbal explanation. What is lacking is the metaphysically essential matter—namely, the ground on the basis of which potentiality is itself concretely thinkable. And this ground we find only in active intelligence.

Thus we conclude that the "unitary being" of an interactive

15 *Metaphysics*, pp. 80-83.

system of real things is active intelligence. "The free and conscious self is the only real unity of which we have any knowledge, and reflection shows that it is the only thing which can be a true unity. All other unities are formal, and have only a mental existence. But formal and real unities alike exist only for and through intelligence."

The system within which causal interaction falls, then, is a system founded on the unity of intelligence which is actual and personal; and so causality, like permanence, finds its final explanation on the personal plane—the plane, that is, of free and self-conscious intelligence. "Living, active intelligence is the condition both of conceptual and of metaphysical unity. Volitional causality, that is, intelligence itself in act, is the only conception of metaphysical causality in which we can rest. Science may study the laws of sequence and reciprocal change under the name of causation, and there is no objection, so long as we understand that this is not causation at all. But when we come to proper efficiency, it is either volitional causality or nothing." [16] The metaphysical categories of causality and unity, the two basal elements of an interactive system, simply contradict themselves until they are realized in active intelligence.

6. The World-Ground

A further point remains to be emphasized. The ground of an interactive system, we have seen, lies in intelligence, which is the condition of such a system. The further point is that this ground must be all-inclusive. In order to function as the ultimate ground of the system, that is, as the principle in terms of which the system finds its final explanation, this intelligence must itself be fundamental and independent; otherwise it itself would call for another principle with reference to which it is to be explained, and this to another, and so on indefinitely. The only way out of this infinite regress is to posit an ultimate ground of unity, a necessary unitary being. Thus, interactive systems imply an ultimate intelligence, "What we call the interaction of the many is possible only through the immanent action of the one fundamental reality. This being, as funda-

16 *Ibid.*, pp. 91, 92.

mental and independent, we call the infinite, the absolute, the world-ground." [17]

In calling it the infinite, the absolute, or the world-ground, however, we do not mean to separate it from the phenomenal order, to deny that it involves relations, or to define it as the stuff or raw material out of which things are made. As infinite, it is the self-sufficient source of the finite; as absolute, it is without relation to an external environment which restricts and determines it; as the world-ground, it is "that basal causality by which the world is produced and maintained." In short, it is the "cause and reason" of everything else; whatever is true or rational or real in the world finds its source and explanation in this ultimate and independent being.

The question which here presses upon us concerning the relation between this infinite world-ground and the finite aspects of the phenomenal order of things and persons may be approached, first, from the standpoint of the finite and, secondly, from the standpoint of the infinite. From the first point of view, the relation may be defined as that of determining causality (for the impersonal finite—the material order) or of creation (for the personal finite—the social order). From the second point of view, the relation may be defined as that of a plan or purpose. These two points may be made clearer by a brief analysis of the facts involved.

As we enter upon this analysis, it is essential that certain conclusions emerging from the preceding discussion be clearly kept in mind. They are: (a) the infinite is not to be thought of as a passive substance, but rather as a unitary and indivisible intelligent agent; and (b) the finite is not to be conceived either as parts of the infinite or as modes of the infinite, as if the infinite were on the one side capable of spatial division or on the other capable of being modified at a point by a finite existent. All such expressions about the infinite involve the confusion that the infinite is some sort of pure substance or core of being.

Purging our minds of this confusion and holding to the notion of the infinite as the intelligent cause of the universe, we can

[17] *Metaphysics*, pp. 92-93.

see that, from the side of the finite, only two views of the relation between the finite and the infinite are possible. We may view the finite "as a form of energising on the part of the infinite, so that it has purely phenomenal existence; or we may view it as a substantial creation by the infinite." The first view holds in fact only of the impersonal finite; this finite exists only as a dependent phenomenon, or as a process of energy not its own. With the personal finite, however, the case is different; its relation to the infinite can be only that of creation. The finite is not made by the infinite out of preëxisting material; it is posited in existence by the infinite. We cannot tell how creation is possible, or what in detail it means; but we can clearly see that, if finite persons are to be free,[18] the relation of creature to creator is the only relation which such persons can sustain to the infinite world-ground.

Of course, this relation implies a dependence of the finite on the infinite. Consequently, we must say that the finite has only a limited and relative existence. But the meaning of this must be clearly grasped or, once again, we may fall into serious error. What is meant is not that the finite is merely an impotent shadow of the infinite Substance, as it is in the system of Spinoza, for example, or in other similar pantheistic systems. What is meant is, rather, that the finite is not self-sufficient and independent in its activity. But this is not to be understood as excluding the possibility that the finite is possessed of a measure of self-direction and self-control—a possibility, indeed, which in ourselves is directly experienced as an actuality. How the dependence and the independence of the finite person are to be reconciled is quite beyond us to fathom. We only know that we cannot interpret his life without admitting both. On the side of the finite we have thinkers and doers, possessed of "an inalienable individuality and personality"; on the side of the infinite we have a thinker and a doer, characterized by ab-

[18] Freedom attaches, not to the will, but to "the knowing and feeling soul; and this soul determines itself not in the dark of ignorance, or in the indifference of emotionless and valueless life, but in the light of knowledge and with experience of life's values." (*Metaphysics,* p. 415.) The important point for the argument is that it is the 'soul,' not merely the 'will,' which is free; and that this freedom is an inalienable, even if ultimately an inexplicable, trait or characteristic of the soul.

soluteness. The former can be said to be related to the latter only as creatures are related to their creator; but this relation must not destroy either their dependence on, or their independence of, their determining source and ground.

Some further light may be thrown on this relationship, if we approach it from the side of the infinite and inquire what, from this point of view, the relation is. So viewed, it is that of plan or purpose within which room is left for the freedom of finite persons. Only in terms of such a plan or purpose is the relation of the infinite to the finite conceivable. The relation of creation from the side of the infinite means, thus, that the finite is posited as an element within a purposeful order, in which every finite thing—freedom apart—is what it is "solely and only because of the requirements of the fundamental plan."

Thus we are brought to a theistic, not a pantheistic, view of the world as the final conclusion of philosophical speculation. And the general line of argument which has brought us to this conclusion may be summarily stated as follows: "That the world-ground must be conceived as free and active intelligence is the result to which thought continually comes, whatever the line of investigation. If we seek a tenable theory of knowledge we find it only as we reach a basal intelligence.[19] If we seek to bind the many together in an all-embracing system, it is possible only in and through intelligence. If we seek for unity in being itself we find it only in intelligence. If we seek for causality and identity in being we find them only in intelligence. If we would give any account of the intelligible order and purpose-like products of the world, again intelligence is the only key. If, finally, we ask for the formal conditions of reality we find them in intelligence. The attempt to define reality itself fails until intelligence is introduced as its constitutive condition. The mind can save its own categories from disappearing, can realize its own aims and tendencies, can truly comprehend or even mean anything, only as it relates everything to free intelligence as the source and administrator of the system." Against this

19 For Bowne's detailed justification of this thesis, the reader should consult his *Theory of Thought and Knowledge.*

theistic view of the world "there is properly no competing view whatever," but only forms of words which, though indeed often "sonorous and swelling," are "without any rational substance." [20]

[20] *Metaphysics*, pp. 111-112.

PART II

CRITICAL

Chapter XIV

ARGUMENTS AND ISSUES

In Part I of this study the aim was to summarize the arguments for idealism advanced by thinkers who are commonly regarded as outstanding representatives of that type of philosophy in recent British and American thought. These summaries were deliberately made as objective as possible, in the hope that each author might be permitted to speak for himself in his own individual manner. In this second part of the study we are to undertake an estimate of these several formulations and to inquire whether, and how far, idealism as thus defended may stand.

The present chapter is concerned with certain preliminary observations which, it is hoped, will serve to clear the ground for the critical task. Standing on the preceding exposition, it will seek first to indicate what general conclusion is common to all of the statements, then to determine the types of argument advanced in support of it, and finally to note some of the more important divergencies among the idealists themselves and to fix the underlying issues. The critical evaluation of these types of argument and issues will be the task of the chapters following.

1. The Main Idealistic Position

The question: What is idealism? has been frequently asked, but a satisfactory answer is not readily to be had. The reason for this should be clear from our preceding survey. Even when taken within the limits in which this survey moves, idealism shows itself to be a very complicated doctrine. To provide a general formula which applies to all of the types there surveyed is not easy, but it is apparently not impossible; and I wish briefly to indicate what such a formula seems to me to be.

It is sometimes said that idealism is that peculiar philosophical doctrine which denies the existence of matter and affirms

the reality only of mind or spirit. Whether such a description
of idealism is to be accepted depends upon what precisely is to
be understood by it. In a certain sense it is correct, but not in
the sense in which it is ordinarily intended.

The assertion that idealism denies the existence of matter does
not apply, in its *prima facie* meaning, to any of the thinkers
whose views we have been studying; they are not idealists in that
sense. One and all insist that matter in some sense is and that
its nature must find satisfactory explanation in any philosophy
which demands serious consideration. If, however, what is meant
is that idealism denies, not the existence of matter, but its
existence out of any implicative relationship to mind or spirit,
then the assertion would apply without exception; in this sense
they are all idealists. Again, it is not true that idealism affirms
the reality only of mind or spirit, if this is taken to be equivalent
to the denial of the existence of matter as distinguished from its
absolute or independent existence. This assertion is true, however, in the sense in which it means that idealism analytically
resolves matter into a system within which mind or spirit is
held to be of basal logical significance. All of the thinkers we
have studied are idealists in this sense.

And hereupon, we may perhaps venture to affirm, is disclosed
the fundamental tenet of idealism—always with reference, of
course, to the limits of the present study. The real nature of
matter, the tenet is, cannot in the end be adequately conceived
without reference to mind or spirit as logically basal within the
conception. In this sense, but in this sense only, may idealism,
as here contemplated be said to deny that matter exists or to
affirm that all is spirit. For only in this sense is the proposition
acceptable without qualification to those representatives of
idealism with whose views we are here exclusively concerned.

It is, of course, true that these representatives differ more or
less widely among themselves both as to the nature of mind and
as to the relationship which in the end is to be admitted between
mind and matter. And these differences, as we shall have ample
occasion to note, enter significantly into the structure of the
several arguments and give rise to divergent types of idealistic
philosophy. Meanwhile, however, there does seem to be agree-

ment on the general doctrine that mind or spirit is foundational for philosophical construction, and this agreement is the point of importance for our immediate purpose.

To the question: What is idealism? our answer, then, would seem to be: Idealism is that philosophical doctrine which undertakes to show that, in order to think matter or the spatio-temporal order of events in its ultimate nature, we are logically compelled to think mind or spirit along with it as in some sense foundational to it. This answer does not mean very much, to be sure, since as soon as we begin to inquire into the proofs advanced we discover important differences on crucial issues. But the answer is at least sufficiently significant to be of service to us when we come to analyze the different arguments.

2. TYPES OF ARGUMENT

The arguments in support of the idealistic position as summarized above fall mainly into three types, which we may here shortly differentiate as a perliminary to our later detailed analysis. They are: the epistemological argument, the argument *a contingentia mundi*, and the ontological argument.

By the epistemological argument—the term is borrowed from Pringle-Pattison—is intended the type of argument which seeks to ground the idealistic position primarily on cognitive experience, by showing that the ultimate implication of the fact of knowledge is a sentient world. It is, in other words, the argument which proceeds through the supposed logical impossibility of the world's existing out of relation to a conceiving mind, or of not being thought; the basal characteristics of the object of knowledge, it urges, hold in principle of the object *per se*.

The argument *a contingentia mundi* is, in Bosanquet's words, "inference from the imperfection of data and premisses." Assuming that what satisfies the intellect is true and real and taking Creighton's phrase the "standpoint of experience" as its point of departure, it proceeds, through the inner diremption of experience, from fragmentariness to ideal completion under the guidance of the principle of non-contradiction or "the spirit of the whole." If one might suggest the phrase, 'to be is to be known,' as the motto of the first type of argument, the motto of this type is 'to be is to be a whole' or 'a world.'

The ontological argument is that of McTaggart, and is by him contrasted with the epistemological—under which heading presumably he would also include the argument *a contingentia mundi*. The epistemological argument starts from true beliefs, and then proceeds to existence. The ontological argument, on the contrary, endeavors "to determine those general character-istics which apply to existence as a whole, or to everything that exists, whether these things are beliefs or not." [1] Starting from indisputable certainty, it goes through supposedly indisputable steps on to the general idealistic conclusion "that nothing exists but spirit." Thus it undertakes to establish idealism by a chain of strictly deductive proof hanging from necessary propositions; and it is either certain throughout, or there is some error in the chain of reasoning.[2] The law of contradiction is the guide here, and the basal assumption is that what involves contradic-tion cannot be real.

Before passing on to a critical consideration of these arguments we must pause to expand the suggestion made above concerning certain differences among the representatives of idealism and to indicate briefly the underlying issues.

3. TYPES OF IDEALISM

These differences concern points of greater or less significance, but two of them are sufficiently important to give rise to rather distinct types of idealism. (a) One classification may be made with reference to differences of view concerning the different levels of the order of nature. In this classification we have spiritualists and dualists. (b) A second important classification is possible on the basis of different views concerning the relation between the whole of things (the universe) and finite human selves. So classified, idealists are either absolutists (monists) or personalists (pluralists).

[1] *The Nature of Existence,* Vol. I, p. 50.

[2] Of course, McTaggart does not claim that he has given a rigid demon-stration that only spirit exists; but he does claim to have rigidly demon-strated that, among the substances known to us, spirit alone can be real. And, clearly, the conclusion, if established at all, is established by strictly *a priori* reasoning—or, at least, what McTaggart calls *a priori* reasoning.

(a) Spiritualists would reduce the entire order of nature to a society of spirits of various kinds and degrees. We are intimately acquainted with ourselves, both as spiritual centers and as beings continuous with levels of nature below and, presumably, above us. On the basis of this principle of continuity we may hold that the levels below us are spiritual centers analogous to ourselves, and what we call the physical or material order is nothing more than the way in which these lower spiritual centers affect our senses. Likewise, on the other side, the same principle may lead us to the conception of spirits above us up to the Spirit of spirits which in some sense is inclusive of all. Thus, in the view of the spiritualists the universe is a veritable "City of God," whose citizens are spirits only.

The dualists, on the other hand, while not denying the ultimacy of universal mind, deny that the levels of nature can be reduced to a society of minds. They hold that such spiritualistic monadism or panpsychism is an entirely erroneous view of nature. And they oppose to it the view of common sense and science that nature can be conceived only as an order of different levels, which, though systematically connected, are in principle irreducible. They insist that we must admit differences where we find them, and that we find a difference between mind and matter which analysis cannot resolve. Like the spiritualist, the dualist accepts the principle of continuity in nature; but he fails to see why this principle contravenes the necessity of the appropriate application of categories. And to reduce all levels of the order of nature to spiritual centers is, he thinks, a misapplication of categories.

(b) The absolutists are agreed among themselves on the main point at issue with the personalists or pluralists, namely that finite human selves (as, indeed, all levels of the order of nature) are 'elements' or 'aspects' of the sentient order of the universe called the Absolute. But they differ among themselves as to what precisely is to be understood by this relationship. In the view of Bradley and Bosanquet, for example, human selves are cursed by the "vice of finiteness" which, they think, can be cured only by 'sublation' in the Absolute. According to this view, finite mind possesses only an adjectival status, and to conceive it adequately we must dissolve its *prima facie* characteristics of exclusiveness and self-centeredness and view it as a 'degree' of the Absolute. In the thought of Pringle-Pattison and Royce, on the other hand, there is no such "vice of finiteness" in human selves to be cured. According to this view, uniqueness is an essential feature of the human mind which must be retained even in the conception of its relation to the Absolute, since to remove this character is to destroy the individual.

If names are wanted to distinguish these two sorts of absolutists, the second might be called 'personalistic absolutists' and the unmodified term 'absolutist' be reserved for the thoroughgoing monists. But the important matter is not that of names, but the essential point of difference between the two views; and that lies in the relative emphasis placed on the uniqueness of finite human selves. On the one side, it is held to be only, so to say, of an 'adjectival' nature, and is related to the Absolute through its character of universality. On the other side, the emphasis is on the 'substantival' nature of the finite individual, and its uniqueness is retained even in its relation to the all-encompassing whole.

For both types of absolutist, however, there is a serious logical difficulty involved in the conception of the relation between the finite self and the Absolute. For the absolutist, simply so called, the difficulty arises from the fact that the finite self falls so far into the Absolute that its fate is unpredictable; for the personalistic absolutist, on the other hand, the difficulty centers about the recalcitrant nature of the finite self in respect of its 'uniqueness,' which to the end apparently remains external. "When the Absolute falls into water, it becomes a fish," is Bosanquet's epigrammatic way of expressing the fact that the Absolute is not far off from the finite. But what happens to the fish, when it falls into the Absolute? This question, the absolutist confesses, cannot in the end be answered. And the personalistic absolutist, on his side, has difficulty in explaining how the Absolute could ever fall into the water so as to become a fish. In short, the finite individual seems, on the principles of the mere absolutist, too much in the Absolute, and, on the principles of the personalistic absolutist, too little in the

Absolute, for the relationship between the two to be readily intelligible.

Precisely these difficulties, which thus divide the absolutists, give rise to pluralistic personalism which hopes to avoid the dilemma by the expedient of resolving the Absolute into a Society of spirits and conceiving finite selves as members of this Society. Thus, it would appear, the finite self may easily be conceived as 'in' the Absolute and yet possessed of all the 'uniqueness' one could possibly desire. Hereupon, however, the personalists tend to develop a family quarrel about this 'Society.' Some insist that it must be conceived as a systematic collection or grouping of spiritual centers, all of which are finite. On this view, in McTaggart's phraseology, the Universe is "a compound substance" whose content is all substances—"a substance of which all other substances are parts." Others urge, however, that to the group of finite centers must be added an Infinite Self who is the logical 'ground' of the Society of selves. On this view, in Howison's phrase, the Universe is a "City of God" with God (the Infinite Self) as *primus inter pares*. In the phrase of Ward, it is a "Realm of Ends" which is a hierarchy of intelligences and—we must believe, though we cannot certainly prove it so—with an Infinite Intelligence at the top. If this view is called theistic personalism, as its advocates urge, then the other should perhaps be called atheistic to emphasize the main difference between the two. But both agree in denying, as against extreme absolutism, that the Universe can be conceived as an all-inclusive Whole, or Absolute, which swallows up and exhaustively 'includes' the finite self.

The theistic personalist is troubled with essentially the same difficulty which confronts the personalistic absolutist—namely, the problem of the relation between his Infinite Individual (which he generally calls God) and the finite selves within the community of spirits. What, precisely interpreted, is intended by the assertion that the Infinite is the 'ground' of the finite? This question the theistic personalist finds difficult to answer. In the end he falls back into the position that nothing more definite can be said in reply than that the Infinite is the 'actualisation' of the freedom of each member of the community

(Howison), or that the relationship is that of 'creator' to 'creature' the further details of which we cannot comprehend (Bowne). And there is general agreement with Ward that, at this point, knowledge fails us and we must here depend on "rational faith."

The atheistic personalist is not forced to this confession, since he declines to proceed into the difficulties which demand it. There is for him no logical difficulty in stating the relation between the Universe and the substances or finite centers which make up its content, for by definition the Universe is precisely that substance the content of which is thus made up. Even so, however, he in his turn is not without his burdens. For one thing, it is not clear that the difficulties can be throttled by an appeal to definition. And, for another, it is doubtful whether the universe so defined is in any significant sense 'systematic.'

4. UNDERLYING ISSUES

We now pass, in conclusion of this preliminary outline, to a brief statement of some of the more important issues which underlie these differences.

One important issue is the significance of the principle of continuity in nature. This issue underlies the controversy between the spiritualist and the dualist. That there is continuity in nature is admitted by all parties in the controversy; it is also agreed that the principle is quite an important one. The divergence arises concerning the manner of reading the principle. The spiritualist reads it backwards, so to say, and proceeds by analogy from higher to lower levels of the order of nature. The dualist questions the justice of this, and insists that the principle is perverted if used to this end.

A second issue, involved in the same controversy, is the problem of the intelligibility of nature. It is brought to the fore by the criticisms which Creighton and Pringle-Pattison alike advance against the spiritualist's results. "We could not have a rational experience," Creighton objects, "in a universe consisting solely of a community of freely acting psychic beings." And essentially the same point is made by Pringle-Pattison in his insistence that panpsychism abolishes the concept of nature in the ordinary sense and, so, removes both the conditions of individuation and the means of communication among individuals.

At the bottom of the controversy between the absolutist and the personalist, as of that between the absolutist and the personalistic absolutist, lies the problem of individuality. All emphasize the basal significance of the individual for philosophical construction and all seek to express the deeper implications of individuality. But the principle of individuality is variously interpreted, with the result that mind is given diverse readings.

Finally, and closely connected with the preceding issue, is the one involved in the controversy concerning the intelligibility of the Absolute. There is no region, not even the region of the Absolute, Haldane insists, which finite minds cannot survey conceptually. The same point is involved in Creighton's contention that the category of the Absolute "is justified only when it is shown to be a necessary standpoint in order to enable reason to overcome actual difficulties that present themselves within human experience itself." This Bradley admits in principle, but he finds himself driven in the end to maintain that the Absolute, though logically a necessary category, is not intelligible in precisely the sense which Haldane and Creighton desire. The theistic personalists, while denying the conception of the Absolute, take a position with reference to the intelligibility of their Infinite Self essentially at one with Bradley's position in respect of the intelligibility of his Absolute.

These four issues, at least, are involved in the differences among the idealists, and they are sufficiently important to call for separate consideration. Before undertaking this task, however, we must turn back to inquire into the validity of the several formulations given to the general types of argument above outlined.

CHAPTER XV

THE EPISTEMOLOGICAL ARGUMENT

THE epistemological argument undertakes to establish idealism mainly on the basis of the nature and implications of purely cognitive experience. It assumes that such experience is ultimate for analysis and is, therefore, the necessary point of departure for philosophical speculation. The business of philosophy, thus, is to read the implications of cognitive experience —the subject-object relationship—which by a supposedly strict logic leads on to the general idealistic conclusion that mind is foundational to existence and reality. This is the main theme of the epistemological argument.

For a critical evaluation of the argument two basal questions are obviously pertinent. Is the underlying assumption valid? If so, does cognitive experience logically imply an idealistic metaphysics? The first of these two questions may be postponed till we take it up in connection with the analyses of Bradley and Bosanquet. The second question is the one before us in this chapter. Beginning with cognitive experience, we are to ask, for what reasons are we driven by it to the idealistic position?

The reasons are given with varying emphases by Ferrier, Green, Ward, Howison, and Bowne, who depend primarily on this type of argument. These varying emphases express different aspects of the argument, and taken together they apparently exhaust its possibilities. Our convenient method of procedure, therefore, is to follow the several formulations seriatim and to conclude with a general summary comment.

1. FERRIER

Some parts of Ferrier's statement have been effectively criticized by both Grote and Pringle-Pattison. These criticisms have already been noted above [1] and need not here be rehearsed,

[1] See, for the summaries, pp. 67-70, 151 above.

though the points stressed are to some extent involved in the comments that are to follow.

As we have already seen, Ferrier's argument focalizes in a trilemma expressed in the proposition: Reality is that which we know, or that of which we are ignorant, or that of which we neither have knowledge nor are ignorant; and there is no other alternative. Despite the ambiguity in the notion of 'ignorance,'[2] the proposition may here be assumed to be formally exhaustive. The force of the argument, then, lies in the resolution of the trilemma, and we are now to see how that resolution fails at crucial points.

In the first place, the reasoning which underlies the denial that reality can be neither an object of knowledge nor an object of ignorance is, it would appear, wholly circular. Briefly put, it is as follows: If reality be neither an object of knowledge nor an object of ignorance, then it must be "the contradictory"; but it cannot be the contradictory, since there is no contradiction in the assertion that X is real; hence it must be either an object of knowledge or an object of ignorance. The circularity of this reasoning is clear when we recall what is to be understood by "the contradictory." It is "either of the factors of cognition taken by itself, or apart from its co-factor"; in other words, it is either subject *per se* or object *per se*.

Keeping this definition in mind, we now ask: Why is it impossible for reality to be the contradictory? And we find the answer to be: Because there is no contradiction involved in the statement that X is real. But the question still remains whether the second meaning of contradiction here is precisely equivalent to the first. If so, then the statement that there is no contradiction involved in 'X is real' is not necessarily true; X might be real and at the same time 'contradictory' *in this sense*. If not, then the fact that 'X is real' is not contradictory does not at all guarantee that it must be either an object of knowledge or an object of ignorance in the sense of the definition of ignorance. But Ferrier assumes that the two notions of contradiction have the same connotation, that the statement 'X is real' involves no contradiction, and is necessarily true. And hereupon he assumes the point to be proved, since the impossibility of reality's being 'the contradictory' in this sense is precisely equivalent to the impossibility of its being neither an object of knowledge nor an object of ignorance.

If you think you can ferret reality out of the hypothetical status indicated by this third alternative by sending in after it the law of contradiction defined beforehand as the law which negates the possibility of reality's being either subject *per se* or object *per se*, then you simply fail to observe the very pertinent fact that you thereby assume in advance that reality is either an object of knowledge or an object of ignorance. Apart from this assumption there is no force in the assertion that 'X is real' cannot involve a contradiction. The question still remains: Why not? Why may not reality, at least some reality, be object *per se*, or even mind *per se?* It might be so, and yet not involve contradiction in the meaning contemplated—not by Ferrier's definition, of course, but by the implication of his second premise.

The point at issue here leads directly into the principle emphasized by Grote in his criticism of Ferrier's sharp distinction between necessary and contingent knowledge. For Ferrier is here assuming that one may state, on the basis of an abstractly 'necessary' proposition, what existential facts can possibly be. And Grote's query whether this is possible and his suggestion that perhaps after all 'necessity' and 'contingency' are not thus to be sharply sundered, direct attention to a principal of basal significance. But this cannot be pursued further here. Suffice it to say that Grote is anticipating an emphasis made by later idealists, like Bradley and Bosanquet, who elaborate in detail the principle he here suggests.

Even if it be granted, however, that Ferrier has convincingly shown that reality is either an object of knowledge or an object of ignorance as defined, the logical necessity of the transition from the object of ignorance to the object of knowledge is apparently not made out except by definition. What force the transition has rests on the proof that the object of ignorance is in its basal characters at one with the object of knowledge.

And this proof, also, seems circular. For ignorance is defined as merely an intellectual deficiency, which is logically remediable; hence, by definition, the object of ignorance potentially is an object of knowledge and this in principle is the point at issue.

Of course, there is an ambiguity here which vitiates the conclusion that the object of ignorance is an object of knowledge (in Ferrier's sense of subject-object), even assuming that the object of ignorance is potentially an object of knowledge. For there is a distinction between an object of potential knowledge (an object taken as knowable) and an object of actual knowledge (an object taken as known). But this ambiguity, which indeed is basal, will concern us below. So far as the step in the argument immediately before us is concerned, it is sufficient to note that it rests on the assumption that ignorance is potential knowledge, which really assumes that every possible object of ignorance must in some sense be an object of knowledge. It further involves a play on the ambiguity in the term 'object of knowledge.'

If it be granted, once more, that the trilemma with which we began has been satisfactorily resolved and reality has been logically driven from the third through the second to the first alternative and has, in consequence, been shown to be an object of knowledge, the idealistic conclusion which Ferrier thinks he has established has not thereby been proved. That conclusion, it is to be recalled, is that reality must be identified with some-subject-plus-some-object, or, simply, subject-object. If it be assumed that reality is an object of knowledge, does it follow from this that reality must be subject-object? Only on the further assumption that an object of knowledge exists, and must exist, exclusively in relation to some subject. But this assumption Ferrier nowhere justifies.

He would be shocked at the accusation that he does not do so, since the denial is equivalent to a rejection of the validity of the argument of the entire first part of the *Institutes*. But the plain truth seems to be that the argument there presented is vitiated by the ambiguity noted above in the term 'object of knowledge'—an ambiguity, it may be said at once, which is the main root of error in his whole argument and which, therefore, must be made plain.[3]

This ambiguity turns around two meanings of knowledge. In one meaning it is equivalent to the experience of being acquainted with, as when I know the color that is before my eyes; in another meaning it is equivalent to information about something which is not thus directly experienced, as when I know the other side of the moon or the rotundity of the earth. In the first meaning, an object of knowledge is that which is directly known or with which the knower is acquainted; in the second meaning, an object of knowledge is indirectly inferred and not an object of direct acquaintance. Now Ferrier asserts as self-evident that in the first meaning the object of knowledge is subject-object; he assumes that the second meaning makes no difference and that here, too, the object of knowledge is subject-object. But it should be clear that the second is not subject-object in quite the same sense in which the first is. The experience of the color is not a subject-object relationship in precisely the sense in which the inference to the other side of the moon or the rotundity of the earth is such a relationship. In the latter case there is a lack of that direct presence to mind which is the chief characteristic of the former. And this is a difference of considerable logical importance. It is sufficiently marked, at least, to raise the question whether all objects of knowledge, if they are to be identified with the subject-object relationship, are precisely the same in this respect.

But this is not the basically important point. That lies in another side of the ambiguity of the phrase 'object of knowledge.' It is, of course, obvious enough that the relationship of subject-object may itself be an object of knowledge; but it is by no means clear that every object of knowledge is such a relationship. And all that is necessary to see this is to observe what, strictly taken, an object of knowledge actually is. It is simply that which is in some sense, through acquaintance or through inference, known. Now the subject-object relationship may be known, presumably directly known, and thus may be an object

[3] Grote's comment on this point also is quite pertinent and should be consulted. See his *Exploratio Philosophica*, Part I, p. 61.

of knowledge; but so may be thousands of other objects—"the choir of heaven and the furniture of the earth." And there is nothing in cognitive experience to support the contention that these, too, are subject-object relationships.[4]

The only reason why Ferrier supposes there is lies in the fact that cognitive experience itself is always and everywhere a subject-object relationship. Wherever there is knowledge there is a knower and a known, and from this he concludes that whatever is known must always be known. In other words, the ubiquity of the subject-object relationship in knowing experience he reads as implying the impossibility of the existence outside of that relationship of what is known only through it. And, clearly, this is a *non-sequitur;* merely because an object cannot be known unless it is an object to some subject is no reason for supposing that it cannot exist apart from *that subject.* And I want to push the significance of the italics here, since the whole point is in them. If some other subject is substituted, then the whole case is given away; for there is not the slightest shred of logic for dragging in more than one subject, as Ferrier himself has urged in his contention that only one subject is necessary "to save the world from contradiction."

It is true, of course, that Ferrier thinks such a subject should be written with an initial capital; but this seems to me merely another inconsistency in his thought. If the fact that when I know the rose it is necessarily related to me is sufficient to prove that the rose cannot exist except as in a subject-object relationship, then I am forever the subject so far as that rose is concerned; there is no need of any other to "save it from contradiction." If, however, there is need to appeal beyond me to save it from contradiction, then forthwith the ground for supposing that the appeal is to another subject is removed; apparently, then, there is something in the rose which lies beyond the subject-

---

[4] The ambiguity discussed in this paragraph renders impossible acceptance of Ferrier's original proposition as 'necessary' in his sense of the term. The proposition, it may be recalled, is: "Along with whatever any intelligence knows, it must, as the ground or condition of its knowledge, have some cognisance of itself." In one meaning of the term 'knowledge' this proposition may be allowed to stand without question, but not in the other. And the meaning in which it is acceptable is not the meaning which Ferrier intends and which is essential for the purposes of his argument.

object relationship, and thus the camel's nose of transcendence is once for all in the tent.

The whole matter may be put very shortly. We start from human cognitive experience. We then note that that experience is always subject-object. We note further that the object of knowledge, that is, the object known, is always related to a subject, and is necessarily so related. We thereupon conclude that the object known must always and necessarily be known. Now I ask, if this be true reasoning, what subject is it to which the object is necessarily related? And the only logically possible answer I can see for the question is that it must be related to the subject whose knowing of it has proved that it must be known.

But this, of course, is solipsism which Ferrier rejects. I must insist, however, that his rejection of it is inconsistent with his basal principles. The reason why he rejects it is plain, and it is the reason why every one else does so—namely, the fact of the transcendence of the object which the next type of argument to be considered builds upon. But this transcendence must be denied, or at least overlooked, if one is to hold in dead earnest that the thesis, 'to be is to be known,' can be logically founded on the cognitive situation.

Ferrier's attempt to escape these consequences by insisting that it is impossible for us to think what it is impossible for us to know accomplishes nothing to the purpose. If 'to think' and 'to know' are synonymous, then the statement is a mere tautology and adds nothing to the points already considered. Presumably, then, 'to think' and 'to know' have different connotations. Consequently, what is thinkable is presumably significantly distinguishable from that which is knowable. Now, unless the knowable means what is also known, I can see no significant distinction between the thinkable and the knowable. So I would agree that what is thinkable is also knowable, but I would at the same time insist that the fact does not change the logic of the situation above analyzed. If, however, the knowable means what is also known or present to mind, then it seems clear to me that what is thinkable need not be knowable. Indeed, the main business of thought, I should say, consists in going beyond what is knowable in this sense.

To the objection that this is a misinterpretation of Ferrier's position on the point and the countersuggestion that what he means is simply that what is thinkable is like what is knowable, merely in the sense that it must be subject-object, I should reply (to the objection) that in the above remarks I have dealt with the argument by which he tries logically to reduce the object of thought to the object of knowledge; and (to the countersuggestion) that the logic here is exactly identical with that above. If that which is thinkable means that which is thought, *caedit questio;* but if it does mean this, a further question at once arises as to whether there are not many things in the world which are not thinkable. If not, can solipsism in the end be escaped?

The significant points in the above comments can perhaps be thrown into relief by the following questions. What are we to understand by an object of knowledge? Is it the subject-object relationship, or is it the object within this relationship? If the latter, is that object nothing more than what it directly appears to be in the relationship? If so, can solipsism in the end be disavowed? Can it be nothing more, and the argument for an all-inclusive subject at the same time be maintained? Is there any difference between the subject-object relationship in which the object is directly apprehended and that in which it is inferred which is significant with reference to the implications of the relationship in respect of the status of the object? Consideration of these questions will go far towards clearing the issues involved in Ferrier's argument. Such consideration will also, I am persuaded, reveal the fact that the main difficulties in the argument turn upon the ambiguity in 'knowledge' and 'object of knowledge,' and that the argument itself is groundless when that ambiguity is cleared away.

2. GREEN

Green's formulation of the epistemological argument may be resolved into the following theses. A spiritual principle (which Green usually calls the principle of 'understanding' or 'consciousness') is basal within human knowledge as the 'source' or 'ground' of all relations. Nature implies an analogous principle, as basal within it; because nature *for us* (our conception of nature) is precisely "an unalterable order of relations" of which this spiritual principle is the ground, and nature *per se* is as it is for us or it is utterly meaningless and empty. Two main questions are raised by this statement. Is consciousness or understanding the source or ground of relations within cognitive experience? Are we compelled to insist that nature *per se* is identical with our conception of nature, in the sense in which our conception of nature is 'grounded' on the principle of the understanding, or else be driven to the conclusion that nature *per se* is entirely without meaning? These two questions we shall consider in order.

That experience in so far as cognitive is also relational may presumably be taken for granted. Clearly, the experience of things and events as unitary and discrete or as standing connected causally or otherwise, with other things and events is through-and-through a relational experience; the 'unity' and 'discreteness' and 'connectedness' are all relational. On this there is here no question. The question concerns the 'ground' of these relations which, it is agreed all around, are basically involved in cognitive experience. Are we forced to say, with Green, that consciousness or understanding is the only source of these relations?

Before passing on to this question, it seems wise to direct attention to the fact that cognitive experience also involves terms which are intimately bound up with relations. This seems wise, not only because it is a fact which is important for the entire discussion, but also and primarily because Green not infrequently tends to overlook it. Of course, he does not deny it; but at crucial steps in his argument his neglect of it makes his transitions appear much smoother and more plausible than would be the case if the existence of terms in experience were explicitly recognized. The importance of the fact that terms and relations are apparently logically correlatives must not be overlooked or minimized.

The view that consciousness or understanding is the 'source' of relations within cognitive experience may have either one of two quite different meanings. It may mean simply that experience of single things or of groupings of single things is essentially relational in its structure and that to the relational aspect of the experience we are to give the name of consciousness or understanding. Or, it may mean that the relations within such experience are 'contributed' *ab extra* to the terms or *relata* by the principle of consciousness or understanding. According to the first view, the 'source' of relations is logically involved in the *relata,* or terms related; according to the second view, the 'source' of relations is external to the *relata* and logically independent of them. In other words, the first view upholds the implicative attachment of form to content within experience, while the second emphasizes their logical distinctness by assuming that form is introduced into the content, as it were from the outside, by an *a priori* principle.

Green does not clearly distinguish these two views, but vacillates between them in the course of his discussion. In this respect he falls into the same inconsistency which characterizes Kant's treatment of the problem—a treatment with which Green is avowedly in close agreement. It is the second view, however, which Green invariably invokes in support of his position and which is, therefore, basal within his argument. Can this view stand?

In the first place, it is open to the objection which Pringle-Pattison advances against it—namely, that it is based upon an antiquated atomistic psychology.[5] It assumes that the primitive content of experience comes unrelated and wholly lacking in organization; and this assumption constitutes the gravamen of the indictment of experience which is to be carried for ultimate settlement to the *a priori* court of consciousness or understanding. But for such an assumption there is no justification to be found within cognitive experience itself. The given terms do not come without order and system, nor is cognitive experience made through imposing upon a chaotic and disordered material organizing relations derived *ab extra.* On the contrary, relations themselves are also in an important sense given along with the terms; they come as involved within the material of experience. Of course, it is true that thought is necessary to discover what these relations are, since they are not given out-of-hand. It is also true that in the process of discovery the selective (and, in this sense,

[5] For Pringle-Pattison's statement see above, pp. 151-152.

the creative) activity of thought is significantly involved. But the same in principle holds of terms also; they, too, are not given out-of-hand but remain to be discovered, and in their discovery intelligence is significantly involved. This consideration raises an important principle which will from time to time come before us as we proceed. For the moment, however, the chief point is the plea of 'not guilty' which cognitive experience itself makes against the indictment; terms come, it claims, not singly but organized, bringing, so to say, their relations with them. That these relations must be discovered by intelligence is nothing against their empirical claim; they are as little 'made' by intelligence as are the terms which they relate and which, themselves, must be likewise discovered.[6]

If the plea of experience against the indictment is to be accepted as justified, then there is no necessity for an appeal to any *a priori* principle. There is, then, no case. If the form comes with the content, if relations come with the *relata*, whence the need of another 'source'? But if the case is pushed and the appeal is made, the court to which the appeal is here directed is, I think, entirely without jurisdiction. Of what avail to the *relata* are relations derived from a source which is wholly external? That Kant wrestles with this difficulty is, of course, well known. But the lesson to be derived from his struggle, one is inclined to suspect, is not as well known as it should be. Particularly, it seems to be entirely overlooked by Green, who professes to follow Kant so closely in the matter. We may, therefore, profitably dwell for a moment on the main point.

Kant's attempt to meet the difficulty is stated in his famous 'deduction' of the categories of the understanding. Leaving the intricacies of his discussion on one side as here irrelevant, we may go at once to his conclusion which is a virtual denial of the possibility of any sharp separation between form and content within cognitive experience. The relational forms or categories,

---

[6] I am assuming here, of course, that there are no mere data, terms barely given without relations or unrelated. To the extent that this assumption is in error, the above comments are without empirical warrant. That the assumption is in any degree erroneous has, I think, never successfully been shown; and the facts *prima facie* lie in support of it. In any event, Green himself, not only does not doubt it, but explicitly defends it.

he shows in effect, are logically presupposed in our entire spatio-temporal experience; without them, he contends, the 'given,' taken either as spatial or as temporal, could not be as it is experienced, and thence he concludes that such relational forms are foundational within the structure of the given as experienced. Kant, indeed, sees nothing in this conclusion which lies against his initial conception of these forms as a priori. Nevertheless, it is in principle a denial that they can be such; for it affirms essentially that the forms are logically involved within the content of experience and are, therefore, not imposed upon it from without.

Kant fails to see this, probably because he is so concerned to show that "the understanding makes nature" that he simply overlooks the converse implication that 'nature' therefore is instrumental in 'making' the understanding. Whatever may be the explanation of his failure to note the full implications of his conclusion, that failure is nothing against the logic of the situation which demands that the conception of the understanding as a purely a priori 'source' of the organizational forms of experience be forthwith surrendered. That logic, in the end, is simple: Either the forms of the understanding are involved in the content as basal, or, as external, they remain impotent in respect of their organizing function. I think it may be said that Kant in his famous 'deduction' in principle shows this.

Whether Kant shows it or not, it remains true. If form and content are sundered, there is no logical bridge between them, and form cannot function significantly as the organizing principle of content. Either they are together from the beginning and are mutually involved, or they always remain apart.[7] In his criticisms of Kant, Green admits this, and indeed he makes much use of the principle; but in the construction of his own argument he seems entirely to overlook it. His own argument is, in fact, built directly upon the denial of the position, and falls if the position stands.

There is another side to the puzzle, however, which is perhaps

[7] C. I. Lewis has recently made an interesting attempt to escape the difficulty while retaining the dualism between the empirical and the a priori. Despite the excellence of his analysis, however, he seems to me to fail. See his Mind and the World-Order, and my review of the book in The International Journal of Ethics, Vol. XL, 550-556.

even more important for Green's argument. This is the side
which lies in the apparent transcendency of that which is given
within experience. Data appear to be more than merely or exclusively empirical and to come from out-of-doors. This is the
character of the given which, for convenience of reference, we
shall hereafter refer to as its trans-empirical character or aspect.
Clearly, it gives rise to a new problem concerning the organization which characterizes cognitive experience. Even granting that
the problem of the relation between the *a priori* form and the
content of experience has been satisfactorily solved, we are still
confronted by the trans-empirical character of the given and the
question of its relation to this *a priori* form. This question is
especially important for Green's argument, since his idealistic
goal cannot be attained so long as this character of the given remains recalcitrant and merely external to the principle of consciousness or understanding.

That it must not be permitted to remain recalcitrant Green is
clearly aware, and his attempt to render it amenable to the principle of understanding constitutes a second crucial step in his
analysis. This step is taken in the resolution of 'nature *per se*'
into 'our concept of nature,' and we are now to inquire whether
this second step is any more successful than the first.

The apparent trans-empirical character of the given seems to
Kant sufficiently stubborn to force a qualification of his famous
statement, "the understanding makes nature," so as explicitly to
exclude the possible assumption that it also "creates" it. This
respect for 'the other side' of empirical objects, impells Kant to
his notion of the thing-in-itself. But he continues to insist that
the forms of the understanding hold only of the hither side; and
he does so, because he can find no ground in his premises for the
view that these forms apply beyond. That Kant falls into logical
difficulties with reference to these two sides of empirical objects
is, of course, true enough; he himself seems to suspect that something is wrong, and he is not always able to remain consistently
by his first position. In the end, so far at least as 'pure' reason
is concerned, he leaves the notion of the thing-in-itself logically
empty and hence theoretically useless.

Green sees clearly enough what Kant's difficulties are, but it is questionable whether he succeeds in pointing a way out. The only way out which he can see is through the denial of the distinction between the two aspects of the empirical object and the application of the forms of the understanding to nature in the entirety of its meaning. In other words, he insists that we must deny any distinction between nature *per se* and our concept of nature, and that we must consequently hold that understanding not only 'makes' nature but 'creates' it as well. However, there seem to be some rather formidable difficulties in this way out.

Green thinks we must deny the distinction because it leaves us with the insoluble puzzle on our hands as to the connection between the empirical and the trans-empirical aspects of the given, and because the so-called trans-empirical aspect, which cannot itself be an object of knowledge, is consequently entirely without meaning. The first of these reasons is developed at length in Green's criticism of Kant's separation between phenomena and noumena, which he undertakes to show is without warrant. The second is developed in his analysis of 'mere sensation' taken apart from the organizing function of the understanding, which he contends is nothing more than a meaningless abstraction. In all of this there is much of great significance, and many of the detailed points on which Green lays stress are in principle sound. But are the conclusions arrived at equally so?

They rest on a common assumption, and they stand or fall with it. The assumption is that understanding is the only source of relations (and, therefore, of meanings), and relations spring from the understanding in a purely *a priori* fashion. On this assumption, whatever in any sense falls beyond the understanding is *ipso facto* both relationless and meaningless. We have already seen reason to doubt the validity of this assumption, and we shall not here repeat what has been said on the point. But two observations on Green's analysis may perhaps serve to clarify some of the important issues involved.

In the first place, Green seems to be entirely in the right with respect to his criticism of the Kantian notion of the thing-in-itself. As Kant conceives it, the thing-in-itself lies beyond experience in such a fashion that it is not in any manner functionally connected with the principles of the understanding. In this conception, it would appear to be strictly meaningless; it nowhere seems to function, and, as defined, it cannot function, in our meaning-situations. But, if the conception as defined must be surrendered, it does not necessarily follow that there is no need of some other conception of similar intent. Whether there is need of such depends upon the demands of experience itself; and it would appear that the trans-empirical character of experience makes such a demand. Indeed, as we have already observed, it is precisely this character which drives Kant to his conception of the thing-in-itself. The trouble with Kant's conception, then, is not that it is not needed, but that, as defined, it will not meet the need which gave it birth. As Green urges, no experience and no interrogation of experience can bring us any nearer to it, and it is, therefore, useless for experience. But the need remains, and the question is: What revision of the notion of the thing-in-itself will satisfactorily meet that need?

Green is right, once more, when he insists on the failure of Kant's attempt to bridge the chasm between things-in-themselves and empirical objects by appealing to the 'matter' of experience as the aspect of phenomena at which the two are causally connected. On Kant's own principles, this involves him in an inconsistency—the inconsistency, namely, of using the causal relation (which, for him, holds only among phenomena) to connect the empirical with that which by definition is non-empirical. To say that the matter of experience is the effect of things-in-themselves is either meaningless or self-contradictory, Green justly urges, if all that can be said about things-in-themselves is that they belong to a world logically disconnected from the world of experience.

However, having surrendered the conception of things-in-themselves, Green thinks that we are committed to a denial of any dualism whatever in cognitive experience. The only difficulty remaining lies in the apparent irreducible minimum in experience itself as manifested in 'pure' sensation. But such an unaccountable minimum, in Green's opinion, is apparent only, not real or ultimate for analysis. Hereupon, he thinks we may conclude, nature *per se* is logically resolved into nature *for us* and the "spiritual principle," which is foundational in cognitive experience, is thereby shown to be foundational also in nature *per se*. The conclusion does not seem to follow, however, and this brings us to the second observation which I wish to make on Green's analysis.

Having shown, as he thinks, that among the objects of possible experience there are no mere sensations independent of thought, Green fails to observe that he is not on that account entitled to say that no object of possible experience can be possessed of a trans-empirical character. It may very well be true that sensation apart from thought is not found, and is not even findable, within experience. But experience may still be characterized by an 'other side' which in some important sense lies beyond thought —in the sense, namely, that it remains for a thought to discover. This possibility Green overlooks because of his assumption that what is 'in' experience must be there *in propria persona*, so to say, and wholly definable with reference to the understanding taken as an *a priori* principle of organization. For this assumption there is no logical justification, unless it can be shown that the alternative is the status of bare externality such as characterizes the thing-in-itself.

The point here under observation is brought constructively to the fore in the argument *a contingentia mundi*, where, as we shall see below, it is basal. Meanwhile it is to be observed that the disjunction, either the meaningless externality of the thing-in-itself or complete inclusion within experience as a structure of the *a priori* principles of understanding, is not exhaustive. It leaves out of account what seems to be a fundamental feature of cognitive experience itself—namely, self-transcendence or, to use Bosanquet's phrase, "the imperfection of data and premisses."

If the disjunction be taken as exhaustive, however, the logical consequences seem plain. Then, reality must either be said to be unknowable, as Kant is generally reputed to maintain, or human understanding is foundational to those meanings and orders of relations with which it is to be identified. Green explicitly rejects the former alternative as in the end untenable, and he must consequently embrace the latter. But if he does so, he will find that his position turns out to be an acceptance in principle of the predicament from which he is trying to escape. His argument, then, implies, not objective idealism as he thinks, but the very subjectivism and phenomenalism which it was originally designed to refute. For, if the data of experience have no trans-empirical character, then our concept of nature and nature *per se* fall together, but with the disconcerting consequences that nature *per se* is utterly phenomenal and reality nothing more than a creature of our own understanding. Thinking to save the universe from the limbo of unintelligibility to which Kant consigns it when he gives it a 'noumenal' status, Green, by this way of argument, secures its intelligibility at the price of reducing it in principle to a wholly 'phenomenal' status. And the price seems prohibitive, or at least what is gained seems worthless. "If this be so," we may say in paraphrase of Green's own strictures on Kant's position, "the conception of a universe is a delusive one. Man weaves a web of his own and calls it a universe; but if the principle of this universe is that of *a priori* consciousness merely, there is indeed a universe, but not of things-in-themselves as in any sense independently existing apart from human consciousness, nor does there seem to be any reason why there should not be any number of such creations."[8]

In summary of the preceding criticism of Green's statement, we may note that the crucial issues turn around the principle of 'understanding' or 'consciousness' and its relation to the 'content' or 'data' within cognitive experience on the one side, and, on the other, to the trans-empirical character of these data. The chief difficulties of his formulation arise, first, out of his insistence that the given is organized *ab extra* by means of relations that spring exclusively from the 'understanding,' and second, out of his virtual denial of any trans-empirical character to the 'matter' of experience. If the "spiritual principle" contributes the character of relational organization to an alien content, how it achieves this remains a mystery. If the given in experience is devoid of any trans-empirical reference, it is equally mysterious how knowledge can refer to anything which can be called nature in the sense of an objective order, independent of human experience. But Green

[8] For the passage here paraphrased, see Green *Prolegomena to Ethics*, section 39.

insists, and it is essential to his argument that he insist, on both of these conditions.

3. Howison

What has been said above in criticism of Green's argument holds in principle for that of Howison also. In Howison's statement we find the same insistence that mind is the 'ground' of the relational organization of cognitive experience. Generalization, whether in common sense or science, does not in any sense depend on facts or the 'matter' of experience; on the contrary, "the ground of every generalisation is *added in* to the facts by the generalising *mind*, on the prompting of a conception organic in it." "The necessity in the connexion of phenomena *issues from* the organic action of the mind itself." Furthermore, there is the same contention that nature *per se* is in the end to be reduced by analysis into our conception of nature, and that mind is consequently foundational in nature *per se*. "The cognition belonging to each mind is the *indispensable* condition of the existence of reality." [9] And in all of this Howison is essentially at one with Green and is open to the same criticism.

There is an explicit emphasis in Howison's statement, however, which directs attention to somewhat new matters, and which, therefore, calls for separate comment. This emphasis lies in his contention that "the proper interpretation of *a priori* consciousness,[10] at the juncture where it is established, is at most, and at next hand, as a human, not a divine, original consciousness, and, indeed, as a consciousness interior to the individual mind."

This is the emphasis upon which Howison builds his 'personalism' as against the claims of "Idealistic Monism" or "Cosmic Theism"; for upon it rests his doctrine of the indefeasible reality and immortality of the finite human individual mind. The emphasis, therefore, is for him quite important. If it is taken seriously, however, it appears to lead straight to solipsism, so

[9] The italics in all of these quotations are Howison's, and they are for him quite important.

[10] Which *a priori* consciousness, the reader must recall and bear in mind, is the "*indispensable* condition," not only of the constructions of common sense and science, but also of reality.

far at least as cognitive experience can serve as a guide. If the individual mind is, "in the first instance and at next hand," responsible for the organizing principles, the *a priori* consciousness, in which the world of science and the real world alike find their "source and warrant," there is apparently no logical warrant for supposing that it may not remain so to the end of the chapter. On this assumption, it would seem, nature is entirely explicable within the four corners of merely individual cognitive experience, and becomes in the very truth my idea. Let us see in more detail how this is so.

Of course, Howison would object to the justice of this as a criticism of his own position, since he explicitly urges that "the necessity in the connexion of phenomena" cannot be accounted for by reference to a given finite *a priori* consciousness and also says that we must even go beyond social consciousness to a divine consciousness in order to find the ultimate ground of this necessity. But his argument here is not very convincing.

In our search for the "sufficient condition" of reality, why must we appeal beyond the individual mind to the "consensus of the whole system of minds, including the Supreme Mind, or God"? The answer which Howison actually gives to this question is both incoherent and circular.

The answer runs to the following effect.[11] The fact that the *a priori* consciousness which is foundational to reality is, in first instance, that of the finite human individual proves that such an individual is eternal; and this means that it is free; and this, again, means that it is self-defining or "intrinsically individual"; but self-definition involves difference, "and difference, again, implies contrast, and so *reference to others.*" Thus "the very deepest principle of our conscious lives" is "the consciousness of our relation to other minds." In the community of such a rational society there is a common nature within which the freedom of each member of the society participates. This common nature must be actualized, since the freedom of each member implies it. That freedom is actual, and it can only be the ideal Type of each and hence a self-conscious Intelligence. Thus each member of the

[11] For a more detailed summary the reader should consult the statement above, pp. 311 ff., and the references there indicated.

society "in the very act of defining his own reality, defines and posits God as real—as the one Unchangeable Ideal who is the indispensable standard upon which the reality of each is measured."

I have said that this answer is incoherent, and I think little consideration on the reader's part is needed to see that the accusation is justified. I shall pause to direct his attention only to three steps in the argument. The first is from the notion of the 'eternity' of the individual to that of his 'freedom' as a sort of self-activity which posits 'others'; there seems to be nothing within the notion of eternity as defined to warrant the transition. The second step is that which transforms the notion of 'others' as thus posited into the notion of 'other selves'; here, once again, the transformation appears to have been accomplished by sleight of hand. The final step is to the Ideal Type as a self-conscious Intelligence; the peculiar power in the word 'actualisation' by which this transition is brought about remains mysterious. But it is beside our present purpose to pursue these incoherencies further.

I have also said that the answer is circular, and this is more to the immediate purpose. Nor is the circularity difficult to discover. We start from the assumption that a priori consciousness is universal, and we end with the conception of a universal a priori consciousness. What has been accomplished in the process, apparently, is nothing more than the privilege of writing the principle with initial capitals.

Does one object to the assertion that the consciousness from which we start is assumed to be already universal? Then two remarks seem pertinent. The first is that this is the only assumption which will give the process even the semblance of being a logical development. The other, and in the present context the more important one, is that apart from this assumption the danger of falling into solipsism has by no means been escaped, but remains still quite imminent. Furthermore, Howison himself gives the whole case away in his insistence that 'intrinsic individuality' is essentially 'intrinsic universality'—only, he mistakenly supposes he has shown this rather than assumed it from the beginning.

With this position I have no quarrel. On the contrary, I should hold that in principle it is the only one defensible. But I should insist that its implications must not be overlooked. And among them certainly this one appears, namely, that the consciousness of the finite individual, however 'a priori' it may be conceived to be, cannot be said to be foundational to the order of nature. It is partial and incomplete, self-confessedly so, from the beginning; and this character is sufficient to negate any supposition that it at least 'adds in' the principles on which alone science and fact are grounded.

I wish to pursue the point further and backward towards our point of departure in this discussion, by raising the question as to where this element of 'universality' in the individual mind ultimately rests. So far as cognitive experience is concerned, it cannot be found in any merely *a priori* principle within mind itself. Universality is not encased within the individual mind as a sort of *a priori* principle from which one may start as from "a clear and distinct idea." On the contrary, it manifests itself there as the fragmentariness and incompleteness of data and premises; and it stands for thought more as a challenge than as a clear-cut principle on which an *a priori* argument may be securely grounded. In short, it is the trans-empirical character of cognitive experience on which we have been insisting above.

And this, in point of fact, seems to be what Howison has in mind. What he is saying is essentially that nature *per se* is such that it cannot be adequately explained in terms of finite *a priori* consciousness, either individual or social. In other words, he is simply recognizing that the objective order of events, with which in some sense we all identify 'real' reality, is not reducible without remainder to any human cognitive experience of that order, but that, on the contrary, within such experience there is always a logical reference to the order beyond. The question which is basal for him, but which he never definitely faces, is whether such a recognition does not in principle undermine the premises on which his argument is founded.

However erroneous and misplaced, Howison's emphasis has at least one advantage. It makes explicit the basal difficulty of the type of argument we are here considering. If we are to take seriously the thesis that "*a priori* consciousness" is the sufficient principle of all cognitive meanings, then we should be frank enough to agree with Howison that, at least in the first instance and "near at hand," such consciousness is that of the finite human thinker; but we should also be sufficiently consistent, as Howison is not, to follow the thesis through to its logical conclusion. And this would appear to be the conclusion that there is no need of any other "*a priori* consciousness" to satisfy the demands of these meanings. For surely it is clear enough, on the one side, that if *a priori* consciousness is the adequate source of these meanings (relational systems), my consciousness alone should suffice; or that, on the other side, if there is need to appeal beyond my consciousness it is because *a priori* consciousness alone is not an adequate source of such meanings.

4. WARD

In his criticism of what he calls Naturalism, Ward raises certain issues of importance concerning the nature and significance of scientific categories and principles of explanation. As the points here involved will be considered in another context, they may for the moment be omitted. We turn at once therefore to Ward's constructive statement, which alone concerns us in the present context.

For his point of departure Ward takes the position which had already been emphasized, particularly by Ferrier—namely, that cognitive experience is essentially dual in nature, a subject-object relationship which is ultimate for analysis. Starting with this unanalyzable duality of experience, he goes on to argue that organization within experience is the product of the 'activity of the subject.' And, finally, on the basis of the further thesis that nature and 'possible experience' must be one and the same or nature is for us meaningless, he concludes that what holds true of 'possible experience' holds true in principle of nature also, and that nature must consequently be interpreted idealistically. In the main, the logic upon which Ward here depends is the same as that which we have hitherto been considering; but the several steps in his statement raise somewhat different issues, and may, therefore, be separately commented on.

In support of his point of departure, Ward undertakes to show why the attempt to pass from the initial duality of subject-object to a dualism of two distinct entities, subject and object, is logically impossible. In the first place, it does violence to the plain empirical fact that cognitive experience is a subject-object relationship. In the second place, if undertaken it shows itself to be entirely illusory.

With reference to the first of these points, presumably its validity must be granted. So long as and wherever actual thinking takes place, there are necessarily a thinker and an object thought, and these are correlatives; remove either, and the thinking-situation is thereby destroyed. So much at least seems clear. But what does this imply with reference to the status of the object? As soon as this question is raised clarity tends inevitably to merge into obscurity. And it does so because of the ambiguity, noted above in connection with Ferrier, of the term 'object of knowledge.' In the sense in which the object of knowledge is identified with the object *as known*, it seems clearly to exist only as related to the knower. But is this the only sense in which the object of knowledge has a meaning? Is there not logical ground for holding that the object of knowledge is independent of the knower? Is the fact that an object, when known, is necessarily involved in a subject-object relationship in itself sufficient to establish the conclusion that the object exists only in that relationship? Indeed, is it sufficient to prove that it can be conceived as existing only in that relationship?

This question has already been answered in the negative, and the reasons for such an answer have been set forth. Ward thinks the negative answer is unwarranted, however, and he essays to show why it is so. His argument presents nothing new in principle, I think, but it does go fairly directly to the heart of the matter and for that reason is valuable. Essentially it runs as follows. In the first place, dualism is absurd; it divides the two aspects of cognitive experience into separate entities, and thereupon finds itself confronted by an utterly silly question, which Ferrier justly enough formulates thus: "What is the nature of the *connexion between one* thing, one thing which no effort of thought can construe as really two?" In the second place, dualism issues from a process of abstraction, arising within the subject-object relationship and going through three steps which can definitely be traced—namely, the notion of the trans-subjective, the hypothesis of introjection, and the reification of abstractions. Taken together, these are entirely illusory.[12] The two parts of this argument must be separately considered.

The first part focuses attention on the ambiguity already noted and discussed. Assuming dualism, are we then to feel as silly as Ferrier's question would make us? I fail to see why we should be so embarrassed. The sting of the question lies in the phrase "one thing which no effort of thought can construe as really two." If this phrase is denied the sting is lost, and I can discover no sound reason why it should not be denied. The assumption which gives it what strength it possesses is that whatever is thought can be 'construed' only as existing within the situation in which it is thought; that an atom, for example, can be construed only as being precisely and exclusively what it is thought to be. And for this assumption I can see no justification whatever, apart from that which rests on a failure to distinguish between the 'object' as the psychological machinery of thinking and the 'object' as that about which one is thinking. The former cannot be 'construed' as out of relation to subject, but surely the latter can—otherwise thought loses its only ground of 'objectivity.'

The whole point rests on the trans-empirical character of the 'object of knowledge,' and there is no need to repeat further what has been said above about it. The object of knowledge is not—at least, not necessarily, though it may be on occasion—the subject-object relationship. It is that within the subject-object relationship to which thought refers; and, so far as I can see, it may be 'construed' either as dependent on the subject or as independent of the subject, according to the demands of its own nature. If the subject furnishes the context within which the 'construction' of the object logically moves, then the object may be said to be dependent on the subject; otherwise, it must be held to be independent.

It may reasonably be suspected that those who hold that the

[12] For the details, see above, pp. 183-185.

subject-object relationship is "one thing" do so because they fail for the moment to view that relationship from within. Standing on the outside, one has reason to say that the subject-object relationship, as itself thus an object of knowledge, is a relationship of correlative terms which cannot be logically sundered. Viewed from the inside, however, its 'unity' presents quite a different aspect. Now, it is the 'duality,' which at other times is specially emphasized by Ward. And the question is raised as to the sense in which, thus viewed, it may be said to be "one thing." Certainly, it seems not to be so in the sense contemplated by Ferrier's hypothetical question, unless 'duality' is to be given some connotation which renders it hardly distinguishable from blank identity of the terms involved in it. Thus, despite the ambiguities, it would seem fairly clear that, when 'dualism,' as a penalty for its unlawful departure from the primitive 'duality' of cognitive experience, is condemned to go about asking silly questions concerning a connection between "one thing" which even thought cannot sunder, the obvious retort is to ask what in the meanwhile has become of this vaunted 'duality.'

The second part of Ward's argument deals with the essential point, but, I think, not satisfactorily. The crucial notion in what he calls the process of abstraction by which dualism is arrived at is the notion of the trans-subjective. This notion, he says, is a natural outcome of intersubjective intercourse; and intersubjective intercourse is a foundational characteristic of experience on any theory this side of solipsism. It is a nice question whether the sequence is here accurately stated, and, indeed, whether there is any sequence at all or only a distinction between two aspects of the total cognitive situation. In any event, it is clear that for Ward the notion of the trans-subjective is a natural one, and is the one out of which dualism grows. But what is the notion of the trans-subjective? It is the notion of *the* sun, for example, as distinguished from the several 'suns' of several observers. Now is *the* sun to be taken independently of the 'suns' of the several observers or of the 'sun' of any observer, as dualism claims? Not at all, we are assured, and so to take it is to mistake an abstraction for a reality. Because *the* sun is independent of any particular subject is no reason for concluding that it is independent of subject. "Such reasoning is about on a par with maintaining that the British House of Commons is an estate of the realm independent of each individual member and that therefore it might be addressed from the throne, for instance, though there were no members."

It is necessary to be careful here, lest we be led astray by a metaphor. The relation between *my* sun and *the* sun in the cognitive situation when I am said to perceive the sun, is hardly analogous to the relation between an individual member and the House of Commons as an estate of the realm. The two relations would be on a logical parity only if it could be assumed that there is, in the individual member, some character of attachment to the House of Commons such that the member 'refers' to the House as what he 'means'—only, in other words, if there were an implicative relationship between the two. And since there is, and can be, no such attachment between the two, the metaphor obviously breaks down.

But it is not useless. We may employ it the other way round, and perhaps to our enlightenment with reference to the point under discussion. If *the* sun is to bear to *my* sun the relation which the House of Commons bears to one of its individual members—and this is the intent of Ward's use of the metaphor—then *the* sun can be nothing more than the systematic whole, which is made up of *my* sun and the suns of other subjects, as the House of Commons is made up of its constituent members. Now in the case of the House of Commons there is the political fiat with reference to which the House is a systematic whole, and on the basis of which its constituent members and their several functions are determined. But where is the foundation of that systematic whole of which the various suns of various subjects are the constituent members? Unless we place it in the heavens, it seems to be wanting; and, so placed, it bears a striking resemblance to *the* sun of the dualist. If we press the metaphor on this side, *the* sun tends to dissolve into an aggregation of subjective suns powerless to be brought into unity; if we hesitate to press it, we are in danger of falling back into that 'dualism' which asks such foolish questions.

Of course, Ward is perfectly right in his contention that merely because something is independent of a particular subject is no sound reason for holding that it is independent of any and every subject. But it must not be overlooked that it may be; whether it is or not remains an open question. In answer to this further question, Ward falls back on the essential duality of subject and object and assumes that this (in one sense, undoubted) fact of cognitive experience is sufficient in itself to render a negative answer. Such an assumption, however, plunges us once more into the ambiguities of the subject-object relationship. We have already exposed these ambiguities sufficiently to indicate that to prove the ubiquity of the subject-object relationship in existence much more evidence is needed than is furnished by the mere fact of its ubiquity in knowledge.

With reference to the second major step in Ward's statement, namely, the thesis that unity and organization within experience are the work of the 'activity' of the subject, it is only necessary to reiterate the main point already developed in the discussion of the statement given to the principle by Green and Howison. If this contention is to be taken seriously, then why should the content or 'matter' of experience submit to such external organization? The question remains unanswered to the end. Even though the content be abstractly taken as entirely empirical, its organization through principles introduced from some a priori region above is unintelligible, and the unintelligibility is only deepened when the (apparently inescapable) trans-subjective aspect is taken into account.

It is true that in speaking of the 'activity' of the subject Ward generally has in mind not merely the cognitive type of experience, but the emotive and volitional as well. But this inclusive use of the notion does not cause any modification of his view concerning its essentially a priori character. The principle remains the same so far as his general statement is concerned.

In his identification of nature and possible experience and his consequent passage to an idealistic interpretation of nature Ward, in the main, is once more following the logic we have already criticized. His exposition of that logic, however, strikes at least one new note which is important. It comes out most clearly in his treatment of causation. Here he insists that we must sharply differentiate between 'efficient' causality and the sort of causality which is merely a correlation of natural events in space and time. To translate the latter into the former, we must read into it the notions of activity and passivity. And we do this by analogical reasoning on the basis of our own psychological experience. Objects conceived as independent of experience might perhaps be conceived as in causal relation in the latter meaning—though in last analysis even so much concession seems hardly logically justifiable, since thus to conceive such objects means to conceive them as standing in certain spatial and temporal relations and both space and time are 'forms' of the activity of the subject. However, they cannot be conceived to be connected in the former meaning (that is, as standing in the relation of 'efficient' causality) unless their independent status is surrendered and they are "assimilated" to human experience "as primitive man does when he personifies sun and moon, winds and stream, fire and pestilence." Furthermore, 'efficient' causality is real causality, is alone the sort of causality which can be predicated of objects as they really are. Thus a real causal order must be idealistically conceived; and since causation is a basal scientific category and is that which science seeks always to discover, science and its method lie in support of an idealistic philosophy.

For the present purpose, the important point is Ward's statement that causation, conceived on the analogy of human volitional experience, must be read into the universe if the universe is adequately to be understood, and the implication of this that philosophical thought, at least, is frankly anthropomorphic. Ward makes much of this principle in the course of the last stage of his argument. But, since the principle receives even greater stress and plays a more important rôle in the statement of Bowne, its critical consideration may best be taken up in that context.

5. BOWNE

"What is reality? can only be answered by telling how we must think about reality." This is the first assumption on which Bowne's formulation of the epistemological argument rests. And the second is that our conceptions "have application only as we find some concrete experience which illustrates them. Otherwise they are abstractions without any real content, or they are formal principles which float in the air until some concrete experience tells us what their actual meaning is." For the rest, his statement is an iteration of the logic with which we are by this time quite familiar, and it is open to the criticism which is already a thrice-told tale. So we shall focus attention upon the two assumptions upon which Bowne builds.

So far as I can see, the first of these must be made by any one who hopes to build his philosophical house on something more secure than a sort of untutored intuition. Nor do I think that any serious philosopher has ever supposed otherwise, except perhaps verbally. That we must hold the real world to be what we are compelled, on the basis of enlightened experience, to think it to be—this, it would seem, is the only alternative in philosophy to an extreme romanticism, for which one world is as good as another and all are as good as nothing.

But the second assumption, which is the important one for the peculiar nuances of Bowne's argument and without which his statement of 'personalism' entirely breaks down, is on quite a different level. Not only is it theoretically without warrant, but it is practically even dangerous. And I wish briefly to draw out these two assertions, though I confess they seem to me obvious.

One theoretical objection to the assumption is that it is simply contrary to what we actually do when we try to think, as is evident in the procedure of thought at its best, namely in science. And in elaboration, I cannot do better than quote the words of Alexander: "One simple consideration is enough to show that we do not merely construe things on the analogy of ourselves. For there must be something in things which makes the analogy valid, or which gives a handle to the alleged imputation," that is, "the imputation by mind of its own characters to external things." "If all we observe in external events is uniform succession, to impute to one of them the power to produce the other is a fiction, the fiction which Hume set himself to discredit. It may be serviceable anthropomorphism, but it is not science nor philosophy. If there is no power traceable in things, then there is none; if the number of things is due to our counting, then there is no number in the things." [13] To all of this there seems to be no reasonable rejoinder. Thought at its best does not 'impute,' it tries to discover.

Of course, Alexander did not have Bowne in mind when he wrote the passages quoted above, but he did have in mind the sort of doctrine which Bowne preaches, and what he says applies with special force to Bowne's peculiar statement. In the light of these passages, that statement resolves itself into something which approaches an absurdity. What is said is that the 'real' meaning of a given notion is derived, not through the process of interpretation in which the notion functions as an explanatory principle, but through the arbitrary process of supplementing the meaning (if there be any) of the notion thus derived by adding to it—for no apparent reason—something drawn from "concrete experience" and supposedly in some vivid fashion "illustrating" it. Apparently, until this supplementing from the riches of "concrete experience" takes place the notion is merely formal and abstract and, in short, woefully empty; it must "float in the air until some concrete experience tells us what its actual meaning is." Causality, for example, is an abstract and suspended notion so long as it tries to fill itself with meaning and give itself a ground only by looking towards the inferential process that gave it birth; but it becomes quite luminous, rich in meaning and amply grounded, as soon as it looks in the direction of "concrete experience," that is, as soon as we arbitrarily translate it into terms of volition. The same, we are asked to believe, holds in principle of all our scientific and philosophical categories, of 'being,' of the 'nature of a thing,' of 'systematic unity,' and of all the rest; categories without exception get for themselves concreteness and meaning only when elevated to the 'personal' plane of "concrete experience." But in the light of Alexander's thesis all of this is the veriest nonsense. And not in the light of that thesis alone, but in the light of any thesis which holds to the facts with equal clarity, must it appear so.

What Bowne is insisting on here is that all thinking must be picture-thinking if it is to avoid being abstract. This, of course, is in direct contradiction of what he urges elsewhere when he

[13] S. Alexander, *Space, Time and Deity,* Vol. I, 188.

says that, if we are ever to attain reality in thought, "we are compelled to pass behind the intuitions of sense to the unpicturable constructions of thought." But, in his enthusiasm for "illustrations" from "concrete experience," he turns his back on the very important principle thus rightly urged and sets his feet in a path from which science has with slow and painful steps at last won its freedom. And precisely in this lies the practical danger of Bowne's emphasis. In principle it makes dominant the logic of anthropomorphism, despite its occasional obeisance to that of science. Against this logic science has struggled from the beginning, and it has at length won in the struggle; its method is the antithesis of this kind of 'thinking.' And unless philosophy is to follow science whole-heartedly in this respect, the question may very well be raised whether it is in any wise superior to the grossest mythology. Certainly it has no reason to vaunt itself because its mythological character is disguised, nor is that character any the less sinister because it does lip-service to the method and results of science. Indeed, the last resort of dogmatism is that sort of thought which, in the name of "concrete experience," presumes to tell ordinary thought precisely what its "actual meaning" is; and dogmatism thus ensconced is not easily dislodged.

Apart from the defects in Bowne's argument which fall under the general principles developed in the preceding criticisms of Green and Howison, the emphasis here under consideration would seem to be the argument's most serious weakness. That Bowne is always and everywhere an exemplar of the dogmatism involved is not charged. But he not infrequently verges upon it, and the only reason he escapes from it (where he does) is that he espouses principles which are at variance with this peculiar doctrine of the 'concreteness' of thought and its creations.

6. SUMMARY

The preceding survey of the several statements of the epistemological argument has presumably shown that, and why, the idealistic position is not by that argument established. In last analysis, the argument reduces to the contention that because mind is foundational within knowledge it is therefore foundational within reality and existence. The weaknesses of the argument arise primarily out of the ambiguities that swarm around the terms 'knowledge' and 'object of knowledge.' The premise which is crucial is the thesis that the object of knowledge is the real object. This is a thesis of many possible meanings, but the one in which it must be taken if it is to serve the purpose for which it is here invoked is that the object of knowledge is exclusively what at the moment it is known to be. If this meaning is to stand, however, then the apparently trans-empirical aspect of the object of knowledge must be denied. But its denial brings disastrous consequences in its train; for precisely on this aspect of the object of knowledge hangs, in the end, the logical possibility of both the development and the corrigibility of knowledge itself and the consequent escape from the four corners of the subject-object relationship taken merely subjectively and *ad hoc*. Thus, in any event, the argument does not prove what its advocates claim. If its chief premise is denied, the argument proves nothing, of course; but if this premise is affirmed and the fallacy of ambiguous terms carefully avoided in the course of the inference, the argument proves at most a type of phenomenalism which can be saved from solipsism only by a desperate appeal to a 'universal' *a priori* consciousness existing *in limbo*.

Not all idealists, however, are willing to dispose of the apparently trans-empirical character of the object of knowledge so cavalierly or to regard it as an obstacle to be overcome. On the contrary, there are those who build the idealistic position directly upon it, and we are now to inquire into the success of their venture.

Chapter XVI

THE ARGUMENT *"A CONTINGENTIA MUNDI"*

With the general conclusion of the preceding chapter Pringle-Pattison, Creighton, and Haldane are apparently in substantial agreement. According to Pringle-Pattison, the epistemological argument is essentially circular; and, even if it were logically valid, it could prove nothing more significant than that the universe must be conceived as merely registered in a mind which, in Balfour's phrase, is "the bare geometrical point through which must pass all the threads which make up the web of nature"— the 'eye,' as it were, which sees all but which cannot in the least function as an explanatory principle of anything it sees and is, therefore, of no philosophical importance. Creighton urges that the argument, if consistent, leads straight to 'mentalism' and 'subjectivism,' since its basal thesis (that the intelligibility of objects demands that they be reduced either to minds or ideas, in other words that they be 'in' mind or of the substance of mind) is precisely the thesis of a subjectivism which cannot be made one whit more 'objective' by the introduction of an 'infinite' or 'absolute' mind. Haldane in principle agrees with both Pringle-Pattison and Creighton, and for essentially the same reasons.

But these critics are also agreed that a refutation of the epistemological argument is not equivalent to a refutation of idealism, for in their opinion a 'sane' idealism depends on another sort of proof. They are agreed, further, as to the general nature of this other line of proof. A brief survey of their several statements may serve to indicate what it is, and so be useful as an introduction to a critical study of the more detailed statements of the argument given by those who have developed it at greater length. In such a preliminary survey historical justice demands that Grote be set in the forefront, since he had already directed attention to the cardinal principle.

1. THE BASAL PRINCIPLE

Grote's thesis is adumbrated in the passage in which he quarrels with the ambiguity which Ferrier leaves in the term 'object': "Mr. Ferrier hardly sufficiently explains whether he means to pass from the notion of ourselves as knowing, or from knowledge being 'knowledge that we know,' which of itself, I think, is not very important, to the notion of ourselves, or part of ourselves, known in the object, which *is* the important one. It is *this* which really leads on, in the chain of thought, to the notion of knowledge being the meeting, through the intervention of phenomenal matter and the conversion of it into intellectual objects, with the thoughts, proceeding in the opposite direction, of mind or a mind like our own, however wider and vaster." The main point here foreshadowed is brought into bolder relief by his insistence, in distinguishing the philosophical from the "phenomenalist" view, that philosophy begins, not with our bodies, but consciousness and that the certainty of consciousness is also certainly dual— consciousness of ourselves is also consciousness of "an universe." Progress in knowledge consists in making ourselves 'at home' in this universe, and this we do by transforming this (at first) "dim universe" into "fullness and particularity."

The chief emphasis of Pringle-Pattison is on what he calls the "moral impossibility" of conceiving the world as a *res completa* without reference to mind, or "devoid of value." The achievements of science, he maintains, establish two correlative propositions: Man is organic to nature, and nature is organic to man. And these two propositions, he further affirms, together imply an idealistic philosophy—that is, a "sane" idealistic philosophy, for which nature is complementary to mind and mind is complementary to nature. Naturalism fails, because it forgets that nature is organic to man; panpsychism or spiritualism fails, because it forgets that man is organic to nature. The two propositions must be read together, if they are to be correctly read; and, thus read, they give rise to "the doctrine of the self-conscious life as organic to the world or of the world as finding completion and expression in that life, so that the universe, as a complete or self-existent fact, is statable only in terms of mind." This is the doctrine of "the higher naturalism" or a "sane idealism."

For Creighton, "speculative idealism," which is to be sharply distinguished from 'mentalism,' is founded on the logic of experience itself. This logic is that of experience working critically within itself, so to say, and disclosing by degrees the full implications of its reciprocally determining coördinates, the self, other selves, and nature. It is the logic of the "concrete universal," which is inherent in the very process of a self-critical experience. For this logic, Creighton insists, the truth about mind and reality is on ahead and is not a datum from which experience or knowledge sets out. "The faith of speculative philosophy is that mind and things are what they show themselves to be *in the whole course of experience.*" And they thus show themselves to be irreducible correlatives; things are left standing in their own right, but with their relation to mind as a constituent moment and not as something merely added on occasion and from the outside.

At first glance, Haldane's statement appears to be a return in principle to the epistemological argument. Knowledge, he asserts, is foundational to reality in the sense that "there is no world apart from knowledge for which it is there"; and this is so, he argues, because "there can be no meaning in any object-world that is not object-world for a knower. If there can be no meaning for the object there can accordingly be no existence for it. For existence involves meaning, and is not a fact unless it is significant." And all of this seems to be a mere repetition of the erroneous argument with which we have dealt in the preceding chapter. Such an interpretation of Haldane's argument, however, is superficial and unwarranted. The knowledge which for him is foundational to reality is not that which belongs to any finite mind and which is used by it as an instrument of analysis. This, indeed, is the view of knowledge underlying the epistemological argument and, as we have seen, is the main source of its weakness. But this is not what Haldane intends by knowledge when he speaks of it as foundational. He intends, rather, the entirety of meaning within which the subject-object relationship of the older argument falls, and which is involved in that relationship as its ground. "What is obvious is that there is nothing in any particular experience, and equally nothing conceived as lying beyond it, that has a meaning excepting in terms of knowledge. And if existence be only one of these meanings, then to be known in some form is the only way of being real. To be known, I repeat, not as if through a window, by a mind that is *merely* organically conditioned, but as by a mind that signifies the system to which finite intelligence and its object-world alike belong."

The logic here contemplated is quite different from that expressed in the epistemological argument. Instead of arguing exclusively from within the subject-object relationship, Haldane would urge that we must argue on the ground of the totality of meaning which lies beyond that relationship and gives it significance; the relationship is not logically primitive, it is logically derivative and has its ground beyond.

It is clear that in these several statements there is a common emphasis, and it is also clear that in this common emphasis lies the chief difference between this way of approach and that of the epistemological argument. This common emphasis is upon the self-transcendence of experience and knowledge. More fully expressed, it is upon the doctrine that experience in all of its forms is in contact with an order which reaches beyond, that this contact is of such a nature as to imply something about both experience itself and the surrounding order, and that a reading of this implicative attachment may give us an answer to the problem of reality. This is the basal principle of the new argument, some of the phases of which we are now to consider. And it is precisely the principle which, if our preceding analysis is correct, constitutes the main stumbling block for the epistemological type of argument.

This new argument, which Bosanquet has called the argument *a contingentia mundi* or the 'nisus' argument, is developed at length by Bradley, Bosanquet, and Royce, in whose formulations it has received its classic statement. In examining its claims, therefore, we must follow the details of their exposition.

Before proceeding to details, however, one general preliminary remark seems called for. It concerns the conception of the Absolute which all three of these thinkers make so much use of; and it is designed to direct attention to the point emphasized, particularly, by Bosanquet in his insistence that the Absolute "is simply the high-water mark of fluctuations in experience, of which in general, we are daily and normally aware"—a point on which there is unanimous agreement among the three. For them the Absolute means merely that which is real, "really real" as Bosanquet says; and it is a fundamental tenet of their common doctrine that the real is always present in appearances. This, of course, is directly involved in their theory of judgment, and it is the chief point of their doctrine of 'degrees of reality.'

There would seem to be no excuse for thus calling attention to it, were it not for the fact that the thoughtless assumption is so commonly abroad that, when they speak of the Absolute, they intend something quite far off from ordinary experience. What they intend by it, on the contrary, is simply "the general view which satisfies the intellect"; with it we are always linked, both by our logical structures and by the ideals "which operate in morality, in social behaviour, or in religion." Bosanquet's bold way of putting it is, "When the Absolute falls into the water, it becomes a fish." And the point must be borne in mind throughout the discussion. But we must turn from such general exhortation (which, from the point of view of the instructed reader, is in fact superfluous) to a consideration of the detailed statements of the argument under survey, and we begin with that of Bradley.

2. BRADLEY

As we have seen, Bradley's statement is founded on the assumption (which "can neither be proved nor questioned") that "the object of metaphysics is to find a general view which will satisfy the intellect" and that "whatever succeeds in doing this is real and true" and "whatever fails is neither." The conclusion supposedly established is that reality must be conceived as "one individual Experience" which "is above all ideality and relations." Or, in greater detail, reality must be conceived as: manifold, not simple, in structure; systematic, in the sense of 'harmonious' with reference to what it contains; systematic, in the further sense of containing all existence or of being all-inclusive; supra-relational; and of the nature of sentience or mind. But the intellect is essentially relational in character, and hereupon we are confronted by a paradox. The "general view which will satisfy the intellect" turns out to be of such a nature (namely, supra-relational) that it is attainable by the intellect only through its own "happy suicide." Born heir apparent to the infinite riches of reality, the intellect discovers in its final disillusionment that it can enjoy them only vicariously. And in this paradox lies the basal difficulty of Bradley's formulation. Our comments on his statement must therefore first converge around it.

It is clear from the beginning that the difficulty arises from the non-relational or supra-relational character of reality. Because thought is essentially relational and because reality must be held to be supra-relational, reality must be said to lie beyond judgment or thought. Such is the contention. Now presumably there can be no doubt that thought is essentially relational: "Thought is relational and discursive, and, if it ceases to be this, it commits suicide." But there may be a doubt whether reality must be held to be supra-relational, particularly in view of the fact that we start from the initial assumption that reality must be that which 'satisfies' the intellect. What, then, is the ground for this contention, and is it solid?

Before passing on to this question, two remarks on the initial assumption seem called for. The first—which might be taken for granted, were it not for the fact that it has been so commonly overlooked by the critics of the Bradleian argument—is that any attack on merely abstract 'intellectualism' is wholly irrelevant to Bradley's position, and must be seen to be so by any one who is not unmindful of the inclusive connotation which he attributes to "the intellect." The second remark concerns the distinction, within the statement of the assumption, between the 'real' and the 'true'—a distinction which underlies the paradox with which we are here dealing, since that paradox arises out of the irreconcilable discrepancy between the two, even though thought's 'satisfaction' is the criterion of both. And what is here to be specially noted is that the assertion to the effect that the assumption "can neither be proved nor questioned" does not hold with equal force for both. So far as the 'true' is concerned, the assumption could hardly be questioned save by the devotees of 'faith' or 'intuition' in some non-intellectual reference; and even they, doubtless, would in the end have to make the assumption to escape the identification of the 'true' with the outcome of some arbitrary will-to-believe. But, in respect to the 'real,' the assumption is on quite a different footing. On this side, it might readily be objected to, even by those who are committed to it on the side of the 'true'; for on this side it involves a further assumption—namely, that reality is always the subject of judgment—which is not necessarily involved on the side of the 'true.'

The main purpose of the second of these two remarks is to emphasize the fact that Bradley's initial assumption, at least in respect to the 'real,' rests directly upon a certain theory of judgment. To say that it cannot be questioned is, therefore, not quite fair, so far at least as this special emphasis is concerned. That what "will satisfy the intellect" is real may, indeed, be said to follow from the view that reality is the subject of every judgment. But the possibility of calling in question that theory of judgment remains open to any one who sees fit to do so—even to those who are committed to the other thesis that what satisfies the intellect is alone to be taken as true.

Whether this theory of judgment must in the end be accepted is, of course, a basal consideration in connection with a critical estimate of the Bradleian argument. Despite its basal character, however, I shall not here pretend to debate the issue. One reason for this is that space is lacking for anything like an adequate analysis. But the more important reason is that such a discussion would not aid directly in carrying forward the chief purpose of my critical remarks, since the theory in question seems to me essentially sound, and I could do little more than elaborate the grounds of my agreement.

The alternative to the theory seems to me to be a distressing dilemma; its denial is to my mind equivalent to a denial of existential reference in the case either of some or of all meanings, and this apparently involves us in a perplexing dichotomy of meanings in the one case or in a rather complete phenomenalism in the other. Hence, a detailed inquiry at my hands would result in a reaffirmation of the theory; consequently, though it would make my account more comprehensive and might serve to bring other issues to the fore, it would hardly serve to attain the main purpose I here have in mind—namely, to develop differences rather than merely to emphasize agreements. So it seems advisable to leave the question on one side. To those who might feel that this procedure *ab initio* eliminates from consideration what is logically fundamental, I can only say that I agree and explicitly recognize the consequent limitation on the logical adequacy of my critical remarks. But I should reiterate my conviction that, so far at least as this underlying assumption is concerned, the argument must be allowed to stand. I should also urge that acceptance of the assumption makes my criticism internal and, on that account, gives additional significance to whatever point it may have.

The assumption avowedly foundational to Bradley's construction will, therefore, be accepted in principle for the following critical analysis, which will move entirely within it. We are to hold, henceforward, that only what satisfies the intellect is to be taken as either true or real. And we are to inquire, first, whether we are committed to the conclusion that the real must be described as supra-relational. It will be noted that the question before us does not concern the true, which for Bradley is always relational; the issue concerns only the nature of reality.

The answer which Bradley gives to this question is, as he himself insists, based on his doctrine of immediate experience. The real, which on our assumption is the subject of every judgment, is given in immediate experience; here is presented the 'that' which judgment ever seeks to qualify ideally. As so presented, the real is non-relational; and we must suppose that it is intrinsically so, since immediate experience itself is directly sensed as non-relational. Judgment, therefore, is seeking to qualify that which is intrinsically non-relational. But this is vain. Since judgment is essentially discursive and relational, it seeks for subject that which as judgment it can never attain. What will 'satisfy' it, therefore, demands of it its own negation and "happy suicide." So runs Bradley's argument in general outline; and its roots clearly lie in immediate experience conceived as non-relational.

Bradley explicitly directs the attention of his critics to this point; and he notes that, within his premises, his vulnerability is in this heel, if anywhere. But he also insists, correctly enough, that he cannot be successfully attacked if his critics content themselves by simply reiterating difficulties from which he himself hopes to escape by means of the very doctrine in question. He thinks what is called for is rather a discussion of premises and ultimate assumptions; and, with a frankness which ought to be more common than it is in philosophical controversy, he unhesitatingly exposes his own. "If what is given is a Many without a One, the One is never attainable. And, if what we had at first were the mere correlation of subject and object, then to rise beyond that would be impossible. From such premises there is in my opinion no road except to total scepticism. This is the ground, inherited of course from others, on which I may say that I have based myself always. If you take experience as above, then all the main conclusions which I advocate are assuredly wrecked. And nothing, I presume, is gained by simply urging against myself and others a result on which we ourselves have consistently stood." "But is it not better, I would ask once more, to begin by a discussion as to what is actually given in experience? Is it not better to recognize that on this point there is no agreement, and little more than a variety of conflicting opinions? The opinion which I myself, with others, have adopted, may of course be erroneous. But obviously I cannot desert it because certain doctrines, on the rejection of which it was long ago based, are assumed to be true." [1]

In the light of the challenge which Bradley here makes, I wish to inquire whether I find myself committed to his doctrine of immediate experience. But the reader must decide for himself how far he can follow, for here we are touching matters on which preferences are fundamental. The main question before us is, as Bradley rightly urges, "What is actually given in experience?" But before passing on to that, I wish to direct the reader's attention to two points emphasized in the first quotation given above. These are the points stated in the first two sentences, and I will take the second first.

[1] Bradley, *Essays on Truth and Reality*, "Supplementary Note to Chapter VI," pp. 199, 201.

"If what we had at first were the mere correlation of subject and object, then to rise beyond that would be impossible." With this thesis I find myself in hearty agreement. I have already dealt with it at some length in the discussions of the preceding chapter on the epistemological argument, and I shall not here repeat what was there said. I shall only add that I know of no more succinct summary of the main objection to the argument based on the supposed ultimacy of the subject-object relationship than that which Bradley here states. And the objection seems to my mind unquestionably sound. If that relationship is what is given us, and that alone, then beyond it we can never logically proceed, and "total scepticism" is inescapable or an appeal to 'faith' inevitable.

"If what is given is a Many without a One, the One is never attainable." Taking this thesis within its own four corners, I see nothing to boggle at unless something sinister be intended by the initial capitals. Presumably, if this were what is given and we could know that such is the case, we should have to accept it; there is no power on our part to create what is given, or to predetermine (save by abstraction, selection, and rearrangement) its nature. But we could not call it real, or, if we should, we could not then stand by the position that only what is to "content the intellect" is to be so called. For I think we must agree with Bradley that there is no understanding where one must take a mere congeries "in a lump"; and such an hypothetical given is apparently such a congeries and can only be so 'understood.' But what cannot be understood, or rather what can be understood only in this esoteric fashion, certainly does not satisfy the demands of intelligence, whatever else may be said about it. To proceed from one such 'one' to another would be out of the question; there is here no principle of implication along which thought may move.

Indeed, I am willing to go all the way with Bradley here, and accept in principle his general rejection of terms without relations and relations apart from terms as being inherently contradictory. To my mind, terms and relations are correlatives and cannot even be conceived apart. Given a term or a relation, and the other is immediately called for; nor can thought be satisfied until what is missing is somehow supplied. Furthermore, just any term or any relation will not do; the relation demanded is that of the term in question, and the term wanted is that which the relation relates. So, to my mind at least, the matter seems to stand. It, therefore, appears to me vain to talk about bare terms or skeletal relations—as though a given term x might be wholly unrelated, or there could be 'on-ness,' for instance, when nothing is on nothing. In all of this I assume I am simply following Bradley's very significant analysis.

Since this analysis has on occasion been dismissed as futile or even silly, the digression may not be amiss if we dwell on it for a moment. As I understand him, Bradley is not here denying that we can distinguish terms and relations, note their different characteristics, classify and talk about them separately. So far as the principles of his analysis carry, he would have no objection to making use of separate symbols to indicate them; and he could, quite consistently, accept the machinery of these symbols and speak of 'transitive' and 'intransitive' and merely 'non-transitive' relations, and of whatever others there may be. What he does deny, however, is that terms and relations, taken existentially and not merely as abstract symbols, can be conceived apart from each other. The attempt to conceive them apart when thus taken, he contends, involves you in obvious contradiction. This is the basal thesis of his analysis, as I read it. And, for my part, I fail to see where he is not on solid ground.

Nevertheless, to return from this digression, I do not subscribe to Bradley's contention that what is given in immediate experience is non-relational. This contention seems to me neither logically nor empirically grounded, and if taken seriously it undermines the structure of relational experience itself. These points, if true, are certainly important for Bradley's argument, and they need to be drawn out further.

Agreeing in the main, I, nevertheless, doubt the assumption which I seem to find underlying Bradley's contention. That assumption is that, if what is given in immediate experience is not a mere congeries of discrete many's, it must then be a non-relational manifold. But I fail to see that the disjunction here is exhaustive of the logical possibilities. Does not the possibility still remain that what is thus given is a whole involving relations?

If such a possibility is to be rejected on purely logical grounds, then it must be shown to be inherently contradictory. I do not see that Bradley has shown this, nor do I think it can be shown. It is true that Bradley has argued at length against the possibility of a mere aggregate of terms without relations, or bare relations without terms. This he has undertaken to show is inherently contradictory, and I agree that he has here succeeded. But I fail to see how this agreement commits me to the denial of the logical possibility of any sort of relational whole. Suppose the relational whole be conceived, not as a mere congeries, but as a system in which terms and relations are mutually involved, am I then to reject it as self-contradictory merely because I have agreed to reject the congeries as such? If I do so, then I certainly follow the lead of a false logic, or at least a logic derived from an assumption which, unless independently justified, begs the point at issue.

Turning to Bradley's empirical considerations, we come to the heart of the matter, and these considerations present two sides. On the one side, they undertake to show that, psychologically, immediate experience is a non-relational type of experience which underlies relational experience. On the other side, they are directed towards the analysis of different levels of relational experience. These two sides call for separate comment, and we take the latter first.

The important question in connection with Bradley's analysis of relational experience which I wish here to raise is: What does that analysis prove? I do not ask whether it is in the main correct, but only whether, assuming it to be correct, it shows that relational experience is inherently contradictory?

What the analysis shows, to deal with its positive outcome, is that any particular type of relational experience is not in itself complete. From spatial and temporal relationships to that of the self, incompleteness and inadequacy are everywhere present; for everywhere the relationship under survey involves the nisus to its own transcendence, that is, implies in its own structure that it is not all. Let this be granted, but also let what is proved be clearly noted. It is, simply, that any type of relational experience is partially abstract and that, when taken as if it were indicative of the absolute, it is mistaken. For it, there is always a 'beyond' or a 'not-yet'; it is never quite all there is.

Bradley assumes, of course, that his analysis proves more. He thinks it shows that the types of relational experience are severally, not only fragmentary and incomplete, but also inherently inconsistent. But the only justification of this position which is offered us, so far as I can see, is the supposition that a relational whole must *ipso facto* be a mere congeries of bare terms and skeletal relations. If it be so, then it will show itself to be fragmentary and incomplete; it does show itself to be fragmentary and incomplete, and therefore it must be inherently contradictory—thus the argument seems to run. But it is clearly a *non sequitur*, unless the original condition can be shown to be the only one upon which the consequence can supervene. And this, I think, Bradley has nowhere shown.

Have I then, Bradley would doubtless ask, overlooked his very important articles on the subject, such as that on "Association and Thought" or that "On Our Knowledge of Immediate Experience," which are designed to show that, and how, non-relational experience psychologically underlies relational experience, the entire subject-object relationship, and through inner diremption grows into it and functions throughout? To such a query my reply would be that I have indeed taken such analyses into account and have, I trust, been duly impressed by their profundity and significance; but I fail to see how they establish the view either that relational experience is inherently contradictory or that what is given is necessarily non-relational in nature. And I wish briefly to justify my failure on both sides.

There is no question, let it be repeated, about the accuracy of Bradley's analyses of immediate experience psychologically considered. Of course important questions remain, as he himself insists; and there will doubtless always be much uncertainty with reference to a region of experience which lies so far in the hinterland. But let it be granted that the main point holds, namely that psychologically there is an immediate experience which is non-relational in nature and which underlies, both genetically and functionally, our entire relational experience. Does it, I inquire, follow from this that what we have in relational experience is inherently contradictory? I fail to see how it follows; there is nothing in the non-relational character of immediate experience which seems to have any implication whatsoever with reference to the structure of relational experience.

Before leaving this side of the matter, I would press the point that if relational experience is inherently contradictory and if thought is essentially and inevitably relational, we are in a rather distressing predicament. How, then, can relational experience be intelligible, or, on the other hand, how can it be self-contradictory? Can intelligence contradict itself, or can it take for significant that which is contradictory? And what, above all, are we to do with the house which science has built? Such questions are not idle ones, if relational structures are seriously to be denominated inherently contradictory, and the difficulties contemplated are not even touched by the doctrine of 'degrees.'

Passing now to the other side, I ask why, if immediate experience is non-relational, we are by that fact bound to the conclusion that what is given in immediate experience is also non-relational. And with this question we are at what may be said to be the crucial point in Bradley's argument.

If it be objected that such a question is unwarranted, since immediate experience by hypothesis involves no object, the obvious reply is to suggest that we be clear as to what it is we are talking about under the heading of 'immediate experience.' Is it mere psychological feeling taken without reference to anything beyond the 'state,' or is it such feeling contemplated as involving a reference to some sort of a situation which is other than the 'state'? If it is the former, then any question about it which assumes (as the one we are asking does assume) that it 'gives' something other than its mere self is unwarranted. If it is the latter about which we are talking, however, the question is not amiss; for, then, an 'object' in some important sense is logically involved, and one may well ask concerning its character. And, of course, it is the latter meaning which alone leaves an attachment between immediate experience and reality, and which Bradley I take it always intends.

Indeed, Bradley himself raises the same question, at least by indirection, and the answer he gives is enlightening. "How, we must ask, in the cases where my immediate experience does serve as a criterion of truth and fact, is it able to perform such an office?" Such a question, clearly, assumes that immediate experience may give "truth and fact," and may itself indicate that it does so. The answer given to the question may, therefore, aid us in our attempt to discover why, accepting its non-relational character, we are committed to the view that what it brings is also non-relational.

Since the answer is so important, it must be quoted at length: "I can feel uneasiness . . . both general and special apart from any object or at least without regard to any object in particular. Again I can have a sense of uneasiness or its opposite in regard to a particular object before me. I do not, so far, make an object of my uneasiness and hold it before me in one with the object; but so far, without actually doing anything of this kind, I feel the jarring or unison specially together and in one with the object. And we have now to ask how this disagreement can become a contradiction before me in the object, so that I am not merely dissatisfied with that but can go on to reject it as unreal.

"What is required is that the object should itself become qualified by the same content which was merely felt within me. *As soon as this qualification has appeared, I have actually before me in the object that which previously was felt within me to be harmonious or to jar in regard to the object.* The feeling (to speak roughly) remains what it was, but it no longer is merely grouped round and centred in the object. The feeling itself is also before me in the object-world, and the object now confronts me as being itself satisfactory or discordant." [2]

I am not now interested to inquire into the efficacy of this statement as an explanation of the way in which immediate experience functions as a criterion of truth and fact where it does so function. That may, once more, be taken for granted. The point of immediate concern lies elsewhere, and it is indicated by the sentence which I have placed in italics. Put in other

[2] *Essays on Truth and Reality,* pp. 179-180. I have italicized the sentence which is specially important for the present purpose.

words, it is that the relations which analysis of the immediate experience discloses were already implicitly there in the immediate experience. At least, this is the meaning as I get it; and it would appear to have an important bearing on the question before us.

But is this the meaning intended? That it is what is said seems plain. The 'object' as presented in immediate experience gives rise to a "sense of uneasiness or its opposite." At any rate, the immediate experience itself is characterized by such a sense "in regard to a particular object before me." Now, in order to fill out this 'sense' I must qualify the object "by the same content which was merely felt within me." Doing this, I have "actually before me in the object that which previously was felt within me to be harmonious or to jar in regard to the object." In the process whereby immediate experience itself functions "as a criterion of truth and fact," I disclose by intellectual analysis what is involved in the "sense of uneasiness or its opposite" which characterizes immediate experience. I then transfer the results of this disclosure to the object which "now confronts me as being itself satisfactory or discordant." Thus, it would appear, the entire relational machinery of the intellect, through which alone immediate experience functions in the realm of truth and fact, is implicit in the 'object' to which immediate experience vaguely refers and round which it is grouped.

If this be true, then I fail to see that we are committed to the view of the non-relational character of what is given in immediate experience. I likewise fail to see why we are not committed to the opposite view. What intellectual analysis discloses about the 'uneasiness' or its opposite of immediate experience is, apparently, the basis for it. What immediate experience demands in demanding the satisfaction of its 'uneasiness' or 'acquiescence in its unison' is that the object be intellectualized, if I may say so, in the corresponding manner and be shown to be discordant—and thus in need of correction—or harmonious—and thus, so far at least, stable.

Nor are we limited to the statement quoted above for evidence of the view here suggested. Evidence for it is to be found throughout Bradley's actual treatment of the 'that' which immediate experience presents as the 'real' subject of judgment. He constantly insists that judgment is a qualification of this 'that.' This emphasis, indeed, is at the very bottom of his doctrine of degrees of reality, and it would seem that it can mean only one of two things: Either the nature of the 'that' is progressively disclosed through judgmental predicates and is therefore relational, or the 'qualification' of reality in judgment is a falsification and the predicates merely 'float.' But the latter alternative is implicitly denied in Bradley's doctrine of 'degrees,' and is explicitly repudiated in his rejection of his earlier doctrine of 'floating ideas.' The first alternative must, therefore, be accepted, unless a third is possible; and I, at least, can see no third.

Such considerations might be drawn out in greater detail, but space is not available and it is perhaps sufficient for the purposes of this survey to outline the main points. Unless I am mistaken in my estimate of them, they serve to cast doubt on Bradley's proof of his thesis that what is given in immediate experience is non-relational. They even suggest that he has, at times, been forced to assume the opposite. That immediate experience itself is non-relational is no proof that what is given in such experience is non-relational, unless immediate experience tells us so as a matter of "truth and fact." But when immediate experience undertakes to speak on matters of truth and fact, it appeals to relational thought for the expression of what it dumbly intends. When relational thought tells immediate experience that its vague 'uneasiness' or 'unison' is directed upon terms and relations, when thought says that its restless uneasiness really portends incompleteness and contradiction, or that its pleasing unison really portends harmony and coherence—to all of this immediate experience adds a hearty Amen! What it meant all the while, but could not know until thought drew out its object, was a relational structure.

These considerations have been based upon the assumption, explicitly accepted throughout, that immediate experience, psychologically considered, is non-relational. I wish now to raise the question whether this assumption can be left standing.

A convenient point of departure may be found in a quotation from Bradley's *Appearance and Reality*. Feeling, "in the sense of the immediate unity of a finite psychical centre," Bradley there says, "means for me, first, the general condition before distinctions and relations have been developed, and where as yet neither any subject nor object exists. And it means, in the second place, anything which is present at any stage of mental life, in so far as that is only present and simply is." [3] I shall converge the discussion upon these two meanings, and we begin with the second.

Taking the second meaning at the level of relational consciousness, where it is most manageable, one must admit that what is here contended for is basically true. Reflective experience does, at least more often than otherwise, move within immediate experience in this sense. But I see no evidence, no convincing evidence, that such experience is non-relational. On the contrary, it would appear to be always relational, so far at least as it is functionally involved in reflection. What is given, as Dewey has insisted, is also 'taken'; and, I would add, as taken it is relational. In other words, what is present and simply is, when oriented towards the reflective process, becomes ladened with meaning derived from previous reflection. The 'that' which is presented must at least be relevant to the problem in hand, and it is not 'present' for reflection unless it is; but relevancy certainly involves relations, and is indeed itself precisely a relation. Thus it would appear that immediate experience, viewed as the significant background of relational experience, is itself relational.

But, one may object, immediate experience in the end comes before reflection, and if we carry analysis far enough backwards we are driven to view it, not as "the immediate unity of a finite psychical centre" functioning in the reflective process, but as such a unity which is perhaps temporally, and certainly logically, prior to the entire reflective process. And with this we are brought back to Bradley's first meaning, and the one which is for him really basal. Consciousness, he insists, is not original. "What comes first in each of us is rather feeling, a state as yet

[3] Second edition, p. 459. The reader will, of course, not fail to note the similarity between the view here stated and that emphasized, on the one side by James in his 'radical empiricism,' and on the other side by Dewey's doctrine of the pre-reflective level of experience in 'having' or 'enjoying.'

without either an object or subject. . . . Feeling is immediate experience without distinction or relation in itself. It is a unity, complex but without relations. And there is here no difference between the state and its content, since, in a word, the experienced and the experience are one. And a distinction between cognition and other aspects of our nature is not yet developed." [4] What, now, are we to say of this view?

It may be said, in the first place, that if the view is taken as here described it presents us with a troublesome question. Why must not immediate experience be taken as ultimate, since, by hypothesis, there is "no difference between the state and its content"? Literally construed, the description here identifies what is experienced with the experience of it; and there consequently appears to be no reason for going beyond the state itself in order to attain what actually is. Of course Bradley insists that we must go beyond it, if we are to attain what actually is. This is what he is constantly urging, and the chief item in his indictment of James's 'radical empiricism' is that it logically leaves us with bare immediacy as both the beginning and the end. But what is the ground for the transcendence of immediate experience in our search for the real?

This ground Bradley finds in the other aspect of immediate experience, namely its complexity. And such an appeal leads us to a second remark. In making this appeal Bradley is virtually affirming that there is a content to the experience upon which the nature of the experience depends, since the complexity of the experience is definable only in terms of its content. He is, therefore denying, in principle, that here "the experienced and the experience are one" in any literal construction of the statement. This he explicitly admits in the context of the quotation from *Appearance* given above. "Feeling has a content," he there affirms, "and this content is not consistent within itself, and such a discrepancy tends to destroy and break up the stage of feeling." Thus the content of immediate experience is the ground for its transcendence, and Bradley emphasizes this fact everywhere where the logical impossibility of remaining fixed in immediate experience is under consideration.

[4] *Essays on Truth and Reality*, p. 194.

I have insisted upon this difficulty in Bradley's statement, not for the purpose of convicting him of a terminological inconsistency of minor significance, but for the purpose of directing attention to what seems to be a basal ambiguity in his whole treatment of the problem of immediate experience itself. When he wishes to emphasize its non-relational character he appeals to the fact that in the experience "there is no difference between the state and its content"; but when the avoidance of the identification of reality with the 'state' and the consequent solipsism is uppermost in his mind, he turns to the 'content' of immediate experience for deliverance. If the first character of immediate experience is granted, then it is surely non-relational; but then the second character can hardly be entertained, and the road away from solipsism is by no means clear. If, on the other hand, appeal is to be made to the 'content,' then solipsism may indeed be escaped; but the non-relational character of immediate experience is thereby in principle surrendered, or at least seriously compromised.

In the light of what has gone before, the ground of this last assertion may be briefly put. Immediate experience has a content, and this content is admitted to be at least distinguishable from the 'state' of immediate experience. Then, presumably, immediate experience must be said in some sense (no matter how) to 'refer' to this content; the content is *its* content. But we have already seen that this content, when defined as immediate experience itself intends it, turns out to be relational in structure; it is as intellectual analysis discloses it to be. If this be accepted, to call immediate experience itself non-relational is without warrant—unless, indeed, the term 'non-relational' be used to characterize those 'states' which vaguely intend, rather than clearly distinguish, relational systems. Terminological questions apart, however, the important point is that immediate experience is such that it intends (in some perhaps dumb but still significant fashion—significant at least when intelligence gets in its work) a 'content' which, when translated into terms and relations, fulfills the 'urge,' of uneasiness or its opposite, characteristic of the immediate experience whose content it is. If this be true, I see nothing but confusion to be gained by denying that the immediate experience itself is in principle relational.

What I am here contending for, then, is not merely a matter of terminology. And to avoid the supposition that such is the case, I wish in concluding this discussion of the topic to direct attention back to the main point. I am willing to admit with Bradley that we finite human beings have a sort of experience in which "there are no distinctions in the proper sense, and yet there is a many felt in one," and that "such a whole admits in itself a conflict and struggle of elements, not of course experienced as struggle but as discomfort, unrest and uneasiness." I recognize both the epistemological and metaphysical importance of this sort of experience. I have no objection whatever to calling it immediate experience, but I fear further to characterize it as non-relational. I fear this, because of the danger involved in respect of the 'content' of the experience. To go from the non-relational character of the experience to the non-relational character of the 'content' of the experience seems natural, and indeed all but inevitable. But the transition would, I am convinced, be a serious blunder in principle. Nowhere, as it seems to me, has Bradley himself shown the necessity of such a transition; on the contrary, what he says about the criterion-value of immediate experience and his entire polemic against mistaking such experience as *merely* immediate seem to me to lie in support of the view that, however 'non-relational' the experience itself may be supposed to be, it in fact 'intends' a content which is intrinsically relational. And this character of the 'content' is the really important point at issue, not what we are to call the experience itself—except, of course, in so far as this is logically bound up with the other issue.

Hitherto we have been considering immediate experience as Bradley conceives it. We have seen reason to doubt that he has proved what is given in immediate experience to be non-relational. Thus we have called in question the corner-stone of his argument in support of the thesis that reality must be supra-relational. For, on one side at least, the argument is to the effect that reality is given us in immediate experience, and since it is there non-relational it presumably is so throughout. But there is another side to his argument which we have not explicitly considered, and I wish now to turn to it. Since the principles involved have been discussed above, only a brief notice seems called for, and I shall go at once to the main issue.

Reality, we have assumed from the beginning, is that which is to "content the intellect." The 'uneasiness' of immediate experience gives the clue as to what this is. On the one hand, it shows that the object actually given fails to satisfy, and we get the idea that it so fails because it is incomplete. On the other hand, it suggests what the complete object must be, namely, a supra-relational whole in which the uneasiness is set at rest. "We attempt to complete our object by relational addition from without and by relational distinction from within. And the result in each case is failure and a sense of defect. We feel that any result gained thus, no matter how all-inclusive so far, would yet be less than what we actually experience. Then we try the idea of a positive non-distinguished non-relational whole, which contains more than the object and in the end contains all that we experience." [5] Such a whole meets our demand, and the intellect is satisfied; it, therefore, is the real in an ultimate sense.

There are many issues raised here, of course, but the one upon which I wish to dwell and which is central may be indicated by the question: Does the intellect really seek for such "a positive non-distinguished non-relational whole"? I fail to see that it does, or that, if attained, such a whole would 'satisfy' it. Bradley insists that it does, because it seeks that which is given in immediate experience; he urges that the 'whole' would satisfy, but only through the intellect's "happy suicide." And these two points may be separately dealt with.

I have no objection to raise against the view that thought seeks that which is given in immediate experience. This view, I take it, is implied in the theory of judgment within which we are here moving. But what is given in immediate experience has not been shown to be such a 'whole,' as I have tried to indicate above. On the contrary, it seems that what immediate experience really intends is a relational whole. If this be so, then

[5] *Essays on Truth and Reality*, p. 188.

to conclude that what thought seeks—namely, that which is given in immediate experience—is forthwith to be identified with a "non-distinguished non-relational whole" is to go beyond the proof. This remains to be established, and the probabilities at least seem to lie against it. But there is no need to repeat this, and I go on to the consideration of thought's "happy suicide" which the attainment of such a 'whole' demands.

That its 'suicide' is demanded by this consummation is clear enough, but that it is a 'happy' one remains in doubt. "Thought is relational and discursive, and, if it ceases to be this, it commits suicide." And, certainly, it would have to cease to be this if it were to contemplate such a non-relational totality as is here in question. But can it in fact contemplate that which demands its removal? I confess that the answer to this seems to my mind obviously negative; only verbally can we be said to think that, which by its very definition, is unthinkable.

Bradley himself faces the point with admirable frankness, as is his wont when confronted by difficulties which his own theory forces on him. But I do not see that his answer to the question I have raised is satisfactory. That he is directing attention to an important difference when he distinguishes between unintelligibility and inexplicability may be granted; and it may be granted, also, that any general view constructed by mortal mind must in the end leave many details unexplained. But the distinction seems hardly to apply in satisfaction of the difficulty about which we are here concerned. For the Absolute, in its non-relational character, seems not only inexplicable, but positively unintelligible. At least, I think it may be said that Bradley has not shown that it is intelligible.

In the first place, it is not derived by intelligence except, first, through the relational expansion of immediate experience and, then, the subsequent contraction of the work of intellect back into immediate experience. Now the relational expansion of immediate experience is intelligible, provided (but only provided, I would add) that what immediate experience 'intends,' its content, is itself basically relational. But the contraction of the work of intelligence, the submergence of the whole realm of 'appearance,' into a non-relational immediacy is, I submit, strictly unintelligible. It is not done in the name of intelligence, and, therefore, cannot be said to 'satisfy' the demands of intelligence. It is done, rather, in the name of a supposed non-relational immediate experience, whose demands are throughout the driving power tending to the Absolute as defined.

This, then, is my first count against the non-relational Absolute: it is derived, not to "content the intellect," but to ease the 'uneasiness' of a supposed—and, in my view, a mistakenly supposed—non-relational immediate experience. The criterion which we assumed at the beginning and agreed to abide by has, thus, been definitely abandoned along the way. Professedly in search of "a general view which will satisfy the intellect," we have in fact been in search of a cosmic non-relational immediate experience which will give easement to a finite and supposedly non-relational immediate experience. The part which intelligence has played in the drama, so far as I can see, is sadly to submit to the destruction of all its results in the name of a merely immediate experience. Howison is right in saying that whether one calls this Absolutism or simply solipsism is largely a matter of taste so far as the logic of the matter is concerned.

But Bradley is in the end forced to admit that such a non-relational whole can hardly serve as a principle of explanation; and it is in this further sense unintelligible. Of course, he insists that it does explain, and that it alone leaves nothing standing outside as a negative instance. But if it explains, it leaves much unexplained on his own showing. I should, on my own behalf, however, push the statement much farther. I should hold that it not only leaves much unexplained and inexplicable, but also leaves the entire relational level of experience utterly unintelligible. For intelligence moves and has its being in the machinery of terms and relations, and it seems quite empty to say that intelligence, or the intelligible, remains when these are removed. The Absolute may be necessary, but it is not so for intelligence; it may be the ultimately real, but if so intelligence and its works are illusory and there is no virtue in them. To call the non-relational Absolute intelligible is vain; all the billows of unintelligibility have gone over it.

If to the preceding criticisms it should be objected that they overlook the fact of continuity between immediate experience and intelligence, then naturally the whole status of the debate would be at once changed. If by immediate experience is to be understood incipient intelligence or intelligence at a low level, this is no more than what I have been contending for. But, then, the non-relational character of immediate experience is explicitly given up and the reality of relations accepted. Then one could say that the Absolute is that which intelligence demands (if it does), but not the Absolute as the non-relational whole we have been contemplating. Then, in short, we should be relieved of the whole burden of non-relational experience, and definitely committed to the identification of reality with what intelligence and its relational machinery is in the end forced to accept.

Then, too, we should have to view another character of the Absolute in a somewhat different light. The character of all-inclusiveness which Bradley attributes to the Absolute arises, like its non-relational character, not out of the demands of intelligence, but out of the uneasiness of immediate experience. For the argument is essentially that, as stated above, any result gained by the intellect in its efforts to 'complete' the object "by relationa addition from without and by relational distinction from within . . . no matter how all-inclusive so far, would yet be less than what we actually experience." In other words, unless the object is all-inclusive it is not such as to satisfy the demands of immediate experience; however far intelligence may carry us by means of its relational machinery, immediate experience cannot rest until the object is stretched to include all that is.

Holding to the view of the non-relational character of immediate experience and its content, Bradley insists that the object thus stretched must in the end fall over into a 'substantial' unity, in other words, must be equated with the "positive non-distinguished non-relational whole" above announced. And so we reach the conclusion that what is to meet the demands of experience must be a non-relational all-inclusive whole.

It is not clear that the character of all-inclusiveness of the Absolute follows, even if it be granted that immediate experience is non-relational and that the Absolute (reality) must satisfy the demands of experience. It may follow; but, if the first premise is to be taken seriously and immediate experience is to be equated with the 'awareness' of some finite center —which, Bradley generally says, is primarily intended,—solipsism seems much nearer than such absolutism and even blocks the way to it. If immediate experience is to be regarded as in principle extensible through relational experience, however, then it seems quite clear that the all-inclusiveness demanded by experience is not necessarily that of Bradley's Absolute as defined. There remain other possibilities which his argument does not contemplate, and the point is sufficiently significant to call for brief expansion and defense.

That, on this view, immediate experience seeks for totality or all-inclusiveness and will not ultimately be at ease till it is found seems in some sense certainly true. But, on this view, it is equally true that the totality thus demanded by immediate experience is that demanded by intelligence also, namely, a relational whole. And the question is in what sense such a whole must be, or may be, said to be all-inclusive. Now, so far at least as I can see, the only answer is that the all-inclusiveness characteristic of such a whole is precisely what it is disclosed to be through the intellectual development of that which is given in immediate experience. It may turn out to be an all-inclusive whole in the sense of a 'substantial' unity; or, on the other side, it may turn out to be full of 'and's.' But which it is cannot, it would appear, be predetermined by any abstractly logical considerations.

Bradley, of course, thinks otherwise, and his attempt to justify his position discloses what to my mind is its basal weakness. "The whole question," he rightly urges, "may, perhaps, be said to turn upon the meaning and value of the word 'and.' Upon the view which I advocate," he continues, "when you say 'R is a, and R is b, and R is c,' the 'and' qualifies a higher reality which includes Ra Rb Rc together with 'and.' It is only within this higher unity that 'and' holds good, and the unity is more than mere 'and.' In other words the Universe is not a mere 'together' or 'and,' nor can 'and' in the end be taken absolutely.

Relatively—that is, for limited purposes—we do and we must use mere 'and' and mere external relations, but these ideas become untenable when you make them absolute. And it would seem useless to reply that the ideas are ultimate. For the ideas, I presume, have a meaning, and the question is as to what becomes of that meaning when you try to make it more than relative, and whether in the end an absolute 'and' is thinkable." [6]

What this argument seems to assume is that 'and' must be a merely external relation and therefore contradictory, or else the universe must be conceived as an all-inclusive substantial whole. In other words, that 'and' must in the end be taken absolutely, or else it must point to an implicative attachment such that it and what it relates so 'qualify' "a higher reality" that they are 'transmuted' into a relationless unity. This may be so, if immediate experience is non-relational; though, as I have already confessed, I do not clearly see why. But on the assumption on which we are now proceeding, the disjunction is by no means exhaustive. At least two other possibilities remain. One is that the all-inclusive whole may be an aggregate of entities related by 'and's' taken, not absolutely, but relatively. And the other is that the all-inclusive whole may be such that the 'and's' are indicative only of what McTaggart has defined as "extrinsic determination." In neither of these is the 'and' a "mere external relation" in the sense in which Bradley has shown (I think, successfully) that such relations are contradictory; nor is the 'all,' in either case, a substantial whole in the sense in which Bradley's "higher reality" is such.

The point of these remarks, it need hardly be added, is not to show that Bradley's conception of an all-inclusive whole, in respect merely of its all-inclusiveness, is necessarily wrong, or that either of the other two conceptions is correct. The point is, rather, to indicate that his conception is not established by his argument, assuming, as he apparently does throughout, the significant extensibility of immediate experience in relational experience. That only the totality of what is can in the end fully satisfy the intellect may, indeed, be granted. But what the structure of this totality is can be revealed only through the

[6] *Essays on Truth and Reality*, p. 230.

progressive satisfaction of the intellect in its function of extending the 'content' of immediate experience.

When we come to the character of sentience which Bradley attributes to his Absolute, we are at what is perhaps the weakest link in his entire argument. To suppose that reality must be sentient experience because any "piece of existence" which we "find" *ipso facto* "consists in sentient experience," and there is no sense in which we "can still continue to speak of it when all perception and feeling have been removed"—this is to put oneself in imminent danger of mistaking circularity for argumentation. That one cannot speak or think of the real unless it is somehow "sentient experience" may, indeed, be taken for obvious, if one is clear as to what it may legitimately mean. That reality is 'meaningless' unless it "consist in sentient experience" does not follow from that tautology; but we are involved at once in troublesome ambiguities with reference to the term 'meaningless,' and it threatens to cheat us in the end with the very empty assertion that the real must be sentient because it could not have any 'meaning' unless it were sentient—an assertion which obviously is of no value for the argument and, as significant for the argument, is circular. But all of this we have seen in some detail in the preceding chapter, since Bradley's analysis here is in principle a restatement of the epistemological argument there considered.

Bradley's restatement does, of course, add an emphasis which is lacking in the statements of the epistemological argument already discussed, and that emphasis is upon immediate experience. "To be real," he urges, "is to be indissolubly one thing with sentience. It is to be something which comes as a feature and aspect within the whole of feeling, something which, except as an integral element of such sentience, has no meaning at all." But I fail to see that this additional emphasis changes the logic of the situation in any important manner.

Bradley himself has contended that, if one assumes the object to be in indissoluble relation to subject as the advocates of the epistemological argument maintain, it does not follow from such an assumption that reality is this object. Likewise, I think one must say, the fact that reality is given in immediate experience does not prove reality to be itself immediate experience. Reality may be 'presented in' such experience, and yet not be that experience; indeed, Bradley is never weary of insisting that reality is something more.

In point of fact, Bradley's appeal here to immediate experience involves precisely the ambiguity between 'immediate experience' and its 'content' with which we have already dealt. Either the 'content' *is* the immediate experience, or it is not. If it is and if reality is given in such experience—if it is, in other words, the 'content' of such experience—then reality itself is immediate experience and is 'sentient.' If the 'content' is not the experience, however, but is something more, then, even though reality is given only in immediate experience, reality may not itself be such an experience or be sentient. Thus it would appear that, if reality is to be called sentient merely because it "comes as a feature and aspect within the whole of feeling," it is thereby in principle identified with "the whole of feeling" within which it thus comes. But this "whole of feeling" is certainly not the Absolute, whatever else it may be. To transform it into the Absolute—which, of course, is the goal of the argument here—one must loose the 'content' from the 'feeling' within which it comes and give it freedom to expand so as to include all there is beyond this momentary 'feeling.' Once this is done, however, the ground has been irrevocably cut from beneath the assertion that the real "is indissolubly one thing with sentience" or that "except as an integral element of such sentience, has no meaning at all."

The ambiguities here involved are basal, and they may readily be localized. They reside in the following terms: *immediate experience, the content of immediate experience, reality as this content,* and *reality as the Absolute.* These ambiguities have been considered above, and there is here neither need nor space to reconsider them. The one further remark which here seems apposite is that, when once these ambiguities are removed and precise meanings attached to the several terms, it will be evident that the argument either identifies the Absolute with the content of immediate experience and the content with the 'state,' or it leaves the sentience of the Absolute an open question. The latter alternative is the outcome, if the meanings attached to the several terms are what, to my mind, are the only ones proper within the context.

The preceding comments, if sound in principle, have an important bearing on the stability of Bradley's idealistic position. In summary, we may venture to indicate what part of it seems to stand, and what is left on one side as at least open to doubt. The following points seem secure: that the subject-object relationship, strictly taken, is not for analysis ultimate, but rests on immediate experience and finds its matrix there; that what alone in the end we can mean by reality is in some sense 'given' in that experience; that, consequently, reality is that which satisfies the demands of that experience as elaborated through relational experience; and that reality is therefore coherent and systematic. The characters of sentience, supra-relational structure, and 'substantial' wholeness are set apart as not proved. With reference to the supra-relational character, the evidence seems against it. It is derived, not to satisfy the intellect, but to satisfy immediate experience interpreted as non-relational. Once granted, the character negates in principle the results of intellectual analysis. Thus, to attain it and to retain it, the fundamental assumption of the argument from the beginning is relinquished. Furthermore, its attainment involves an interpretation of immediate experience which in the end can hardly stand; for it undermines the very theory of judgment in whose behalf it is ostensibly invoked. In short, the criticisms developed in the discussion would apparently leave us in position to retain Bradley's "all-pervasive relativism," which he avows is "the very soul of the Absolute" which he defends,[7] but with the Absolute shorn of its character of immediacy.

3. BOSANQUET

Bosanquet's statement, like that of Bradley, rests on the assumption that judgment or thought is always and everywhere an ideal qualification of reality and that, consequently, what in the end satisfies intelligence may alone be called reality. As

[7] See his "Concluding Remarks" appended to the *Essays on Truth and Reality*.

was true in the preceding discussion of Bradley's statement, the discussion of Bosanquet's which follows aims to move within this assumption and, so, to be internal to the argument evaluated. The discussion is, therefore, not addressed to those who would *ab initio* deny the assumption. But for such the question remains: What is the alternative and whither does it lead?

Bosanquet regards philosophical speculation as merely the conscious attempt on the part of finite mind critically and systematically to read the deeper implications of both itself and its environment. In the end, he thinks, the lesson is that such a mind is guided throughout by the "spirit of the whole" which is implicit in it and its environment alike and which when made explicit is the Absolute wherein mind 'comes to itself.' The philosophical enterprise, thus, is a sort of Pilgrim's Progress of self-critical experience which 'finds' itself through its own transcendence.

Beginning with experiences that may be said to be immediate, we are asked to note, in the first place, that not all are on the same level in respect of their significance for the quest. Some are more 'central' than others, and this character of centrality is measured by the criterion of 'wholeness' or non-contradiction, including values. Gathering the lesson, to be held and applied throughout, that central experiences are to weigh most heavily in our speculations, we pass with our guide to the other stages of the Pilgrim's Progress. We note that nature can be reduced neither to 'states' of mind nor to psychical centers, but is there in its own indefeasible right as common sense and science alike suppose it to be. Everywhere, however—and this is its character which is central for philosophy—it expresses the "spirit of the whole"; for this in principle is what we call natural law. In organic nature, this spirit "comes alive" in individual centers of activity.

Mind, too, is natural, and not some angel or genius from out-of-doors; and in it the spirit of totality receives fuller expression, and ultimately grows conscious and explicit. On one side, mind is linked with nature 'below' it—not, indeed, mechanistically, as is one natural event with another, but teleologically, as an expression (though richer) of the same spirit of totality which is merely implicit in the inorganic and which in mind becomes explicit and conscious. On the other side and 'above' it, mind is linked with its historical and social environment, penetration into which constitutes its genuine freedom and fullest self-expression. This environment, below and above, in which mind is thus "soaked" is, when adequately comprehended, the Absolute, which is not something far off but "is simply the high-water mark of fluctuations in experience, of which in general, we are daily and normally aware." To it we are bound by our logical structures as well as by the ideals "which operate in morality, in social behaviour, or in religion." We are also bound to it existentially, as included within the spatio-temporal order. This order, however, including ourselves and our ideals and logical structures, can be conceived as 'really' real, rather than merely appearance, only when 'negated' in the Absolute—that is, only when 'transmuted' within the perfect whole in such manner that its fragmentariness is filled out and its incoherencies set at rest.

This "cure of finiteness," we can see, is demanded by the finite itself; but it involves a profound modification of the finite the details of which are beyond us, and in this sense the Absolute is impervious to finite thought. Nevertheless, we can discern its main features. It must be an all-comprehensive and harmonious system, whose nature is in the nature of each of its parts. It must also be sentient, though to call it 'personal' is prohibited by the fact that it can have no 'other' and no 'not-yet.' Since it is beyond time, it cannot be called teleological in any temporal sense; but as a "nexus of relations" in which end and means fall together in such manner that neither is merely external to the other and the interconnection between them is so complete that "no part is idle," it may be called teleological in a profounder meaning.

All of this, in respect of both the tenets and the method, is of course directly in the spirit of Bradley's statement, and Bosanquet himself would be the last to claim that he has added anything radically novel. There is the same insistence that 'real' reality must be an all-inclusive, non-temporal, coherent and sentient system; the same doctrine of 'appearances' and 'degrees'; and the same view of the 'sublation' of appearances in the Absolute. The main line of argument, too, is basically the same—the assumption of judgment as the ideal qualification of reality given in immediate experience; and the demand on the part of intelligence (in the inclusive sense) for its own satisfaction through the expansion of experience, 'real' reality being that which in the end satisfies and the principle of non-contradiction and coherence being the criterion throughout.

But Bosanquet's statement explicitly directs attention to certain points not specially emphasized in Bradley's. Among them, the following are the most important: the identification of the principle of individuality with that of coherence or non-contradiction; the inclusive meaning of 'intelligence,' particularly with reference to the doctrine of the centrality of experiences; the teleological character of the Absolute; and the notion of negativity as a character of the Absolute. The first of these points is of direct concern in connection with the issues raised by the differences between the personalists and the absolutists, and its consideration may, therefore, be postponed for the moment. The other three must be considered in the present context, and we shall take them in the order given above.

In a certain sense, of course, no philosopher, indeed no serious thinker, can escape the notion of centrality of experiences, whatever be the terminology used to indicate it. But the notion is vague and may carry different meanings in different contexts. We are here concerned to inquire what meaning it has for Bosanquet, and whether in this meaning it is a workable concept.

The peculiar meaning which Bosanquet attaches to it may be most readily grasped by noting that feeling and conation, as well as mere cognition, are involved in it. That there is an exclusively cognitive meaning of the notion in the commonly accepted sense of 'relevancy' and 'weight' of evidence he, of course, does not deny. But he urges that the principle involved is not limited to cognition, and that we are forced to apply it in the realms of feeling and will when we undertake to be critical here. There is a relevancy of colors, rhythms, and actions, as well as a relevancy of premises and conclusions; and serious thought necessarily makes use of the fact in one realm as in the others. Nor must we fall into the mistake of supposing that in the different realms there are different sorts of relevancy. The principle is everywhere the same; the criterion throughout is the "spirit of the whole"—"bad taste is bad logic, and bad logic is bad taste." Indeed, the chief advantage arising from the term 'centrality' is precisely its emphasis on the universality of the principle: 'relevancy' has been appropriated by mere cognition and is therefore misleading.

The discovery of central experiences, Bosanquet is aware, is a task of no mean proportions. Indeed, he thinks it is one of the most difficult tasks confronting the philosopher and one which, he at times seems to say, demands a special aptitude, "the penetrative imagination—what Wordsworth was unmatched in." But despite the difficulty, he is convinced that they are discoverable and are, in fact, quite certain, though not 'obvious' as the 'simples' of merely "ingenious ratiocination" are said to be. They are, furthermore, at the bottom of all sane speculation. From them our inferences must start, and to them they must in the end return for validation, if they are to have genuine speculative significance.[8]

That Bosanquet makes much of this doctrine of centrality in the course of his argument is, indeed, true. The question before us is whether he makes too much of it, and whether in the end it vitiates his statement.

The crux of the question lies in the comprehensive meaning which he attaches to the notion of centrality. There is, naturally, no question about the principle in so far as logical relevancy alone is concerned. In this sense, all of us necessarily appeal to the principle in our speculative endeavors: not every fact is relevant to every inference, and among those that are relevant some are more 'weighty' than others. All of this may be taken for granted. The question before us is, rather, about the inclusive meaning which Bosanquet insists upon.

The ground upon which Bosanquet here builds is quite plain. It is the thesis that conation, feeling (significant feeling) and

[8] See, for instance, Bosanquet, *The Principle of Individuality and Value*, p. 246, and pp. 269-270.

cognition are all alike aspects of a deeper unity—the unity, namely, of experience which, as critical, may be called intelligence. If the scope of his notion of centrality is to be condemned, this is the thesis at which the attack must be directed. Unless that thesis may stand, then Bosanquet's conception of centrality falls; and, on the other side, if centrality is to be limited to mere logical relevancy, the thesis is in principle denied. Discussion of the issues here involved need not be entered upon; it is sufficient for present purposes to make the ground of the issues clear.

If the inclusive meaning of centrality is accepted, however, interpretation involves evaluation, thinking is linked in principle with 'imagination,' and hereupon we are confronted by an insidious methodological danger. In philosophical speculation, even at its best, anthropomorphism is never far off; and the inclusion of evaluation as integral to the connotation of centrality may readily serve to bring it nearer. In fact, it is the first step on the all-too-easy road which is paved by emotional metaphors, and at the end of which lies a 'reality' that may be of no more significance than an eulogistic predicate— "what we wish existence to be, after we have analysed its defects and decided upon what would remove them." [9] This danger besets idealistic philosophers particularly; and some at least, as I have indicated in the preceding chapter, do not successfully guard against it.

But Bosanquet does not belong to this group. No one has insisted more vigorously than he that our view of reality must spring only from the faithful apprehension and description of an independent order, and has significance only in so far as it is explanatory of that order. Nor has any one more persistently striven to live up to this creed in philosophical construction. Indeed, he has (not without reason) been criticized for going to the extreme of denying ultimate significance, not only to our wishes and emotional aspirations, but also to our very selves——all in behalf of an order in which we are "soaked" and which will not let us alone but "drives us from pillar to

[9] Dewey, *Experience and Nature*, p. 54. The pagination is of the first edition.

post." Certainly, there is in Bosanquet's statement nothing of
the sort of—one is tempted to say, crude—anthropomorphism
which seems to be involved in the statements of Ward and
Bowne, for example.

It is true that this emphasis upon the inclusive meaning of
centrality leads Bosanquet to deny any philosophical value to
the insights of "ingenious ratiocination," and gives rise to a
certain mystical character in his own philosophy. "With the
strongest predilection for rationalistic simplicity, and after the
most resolute efforts to follow out a realistic empiricism," he
confesses, "I have never in the long run found it possible to
construe the world without an element which might be called
mystical." [10] And he was not able to find this possible because
of his view of centrality of experiences. But his actual procedure in working out his construction of the world offers
no warrant for a critic to seize the term 'mystical' as a convenient handle whereby the construction may without further ado
be set aside as a type of mere 'romanticism' which one may
take or leave at pleasure. Nor is the warning amiss that the
point of such criticism is not turned by simply narrowing the
connotation of centrality so as to equate it with 'relevancy.'
For relevancy itself runs to ground in some sort of direct insight,
as is evidenced by the empirical appeal to 'fact' on the one
side or the rationalistic appeal to 'clear and distinct conception'
on the other. And there is 'romanticism' here, too.

If the point of the attack be, however, that Bosanquet's view
of centrality emphasizes the notion of value as important for
philosophical construction and that this is unjustifiable 'romanticism,' then the criticism stands so far as its statement of fact
is concerned. His view of centrality does precisely this. But
whether this is unjustifiable 'romanticism' remains an open
question. The view itself, if I may repeat this, rests upon a
certain interpretation of the 'unity' of experience, with which
it stands or falls. If left standing, then valuation is necessarily
involved in interpretation. But this need not lead to any ob-

---

[10] *The Philosophical Review*, Vol. XXVI, 5. Compare: "Reality, real
reality, is to me what especially fires the heart and the imagination."
(Bosanquet, *Social and International Ideals*, p. 97.)

jectionable sort of 'romanticism,' provided valuation is made to live up to its claim of being subject to the principles of intelligence. And this, I think, Bosanquet succeeds in accomplishing.

He does not succeed in accomplishing this, however, without a certain amount of troublesome vacillation, which at times threatens circularity in reasoning. Frequently he writes as if the Absolute were both the criterion and the implication of value —as if, in other words, one must assume the Absolute in order to determine centrality and must also hit upon centrality in order to envisage the Absolute. And this looks suspiciously like a vicious circle in his reasoning. But I think it is not, as a slight modification of his terminology may show. What he is saying might be translated to read thus: Centrality and value are determined by the criterion of coherence or 'wholeness,' and when determined they will in the end be seen to imply the perfect embodiment of the criterion which functions in their determination—the Absolute. And there is nothing viciously circular in this. The appearance of vicious circularity in the first formulation arises out of the dual meaning of the term 'Absolute,' which as the criterion means the "spirit of the whole" and as the implication means this spirit perfectly embodied. This dual meaning Bosanquet does not always clearly distinguish.

A sort of circularity is not escaped, indeed, even in the reformulation of his position. For it still remains true that the determination of centrality is implicatively involved in the problem for whose solution it is prayed. This difficulty does not arise, however, from the inclusive meaning of the term; it is present also in the notion of merely logical relevancy and 'weight' of evidence. In this sense, apparently, reason itself is circular; and the puzzle to which this circularity gives birth is at least as old as Plato. If it is vicious, then skepticism seems in principle inescapable and there is no remedy. Whether it is vicious is not, fortunately, here in question; the point to be emphasized is simply that it is not peculiar to Bosanquet's doctrine of centrality, but is involved in the very notion of relevancy apart from which reasoning itself is futile.

But one may insist on asking: What is to be said about the ground on which the notion is based? And obviously such a question is fundamental—so fundamental, in fact, that not even a pretense at an answer can here be made, since it would lead far beyond the limits of this survey. But Bosanquet's answer is clear and definite; the ground lies within experience itself, as an honest observation of it will suffice to show. "If we view experience *bona fide*, and follow where its connections lead us, noting the relation of incompleteness to completeness in all the responses of mind, it does not matter from what point we start. It is like going up a hill; you only need to keep ascending, and you must reach the top. You cannot study thought and not be led to will and feeling, nor will and feeling and not be led back to thought." "For the thought which has become expert in this world, such media as sound, colour, form, rhythm, and metre have undoubtedly a logic and a necessity of their own. The universal—the straining towards the whole—is in them all as in all experience; and it is idle to deny their constructive and creative nisus the name of thinking, because it does not operate through what we call *par excellence* logical language and conceptions attached to words. The rhythm that completes a rhythm, the sound that with other sounds satisfies the educated ear, the colour that is demanded by a colour-scheme, are I take it as necessary and as rational as the conclusion of a syllogism." [11] Such is Bosanquet's reply to any objection against the ground on which his inclusive use of 'centrality' is based. For the present discussion, I am willing to accept the reply as in principle sound; clearly, to argue the issues in detail is here impossible.

In the light of the preceding observations, we may summarily say that there appears to be nothing in the use Bosanquet makes of his peculiar conception of centrality which vitiates his argument. It differs from the ordinary notion of relevancy only by the explicit inclusion of values. But the danger, thus introduced, of muddying inference at its source is, at least in principle, avoided precisely by the fact that values are explicitly, and not covertly, introduced and by the insistence upon a common criterion of 'truth' and 'value.' The ground of the more

[11] *The Principle of Individuality and Value*, pp. 39, 62.

inclusive meaning of centrality is in a prior thesis, which turns on quite different considerations.

Before leaving the topic finally, however, it is important to note that the major tenet of this doctrine—namely, variations in significance among direct experiences—has an important bearing on the general problem of 'immediate' experience and stands essentially in opposition to Bradley's view of its non-relational character. For according to Bosanquet's doctrine, not every experience counts, but only those which are specially significant in respect of intellectual constructions, and what these are enlightened experience alone can tell. If there were a non-relational 'immediate' feeling, it could hardly in any sense be 'central'; and an experience which is not central is, for philosophical speculation at any rate, as good as nothing.

But we must now turn to a consideration of the second of Bosanquet's special emphases set out above for discussion, namely his view of 'teleology' as a character of the Absolute.[12]

In his exceedingly stimulating and helpful consideration of current tendencies in philosophy, Bosanquet lays especial emphasis upon the problem of time and its importance for philosophy. He even regards it as a crucial problem.[13] Debate upon it, he thinks, has divided philosophers into two factions, the distinction at stake being "that between time in the Absolute and the Absolute in time."[14] Those who would place the Absolute in time Bosanquet calls 'progressists'; their demand is that there shall be "absolute and ultimate progress in the real." Over against them are arrayed the 'perfectionists'—if I may be permitted so to name them—who would put time in the Absolute; for them the temporal series is only an adumbration, necessary, to be sure, but an adumbration still, of a deeper totality which in its perfection knows no change and upon which there is no 'shadow that is cast by turning.' For the one group the moral point of view is ultimate; for the other, the religious.

---

[12] Most of what follows on the point is abstracted from my article, "Bosanquet on Teleology as a Metaphysical Principle," *The Philosophical Review*, Vol. XXXII, No. 6, pp. 612 ff.

[13] Bosanquet, *The Meeting of Extremes in Contemporary Philosophy*, p. 217.

[14] *Ibid.*, p. 126.

Bosanquet has himself fully and clearly stated the alternatives as they lie in his mind: "That spatio-temporal existence
must be a succession of events *ad infinitum* is common ground.
Now thought furnishes us with an idea of self-realisation, completeness, perfection, and the succession of events *ad infinitum*
is all the actual existence we have hope of possessing in which
this idea of perfection could be realised. . . . There is a view
of life from which the demand and this condition of its fulfilment can be brought together. This is the moral point of view,
which translates perfection into perfectibility. . . . Nothing is
or can be what it ought to be, but it is always going to be what
it ought to be; and this is a demand which can be fulfilled in
a series of facts. And thus, the moral point of view can, it would
appear, be satisfied by a universe whose total reality is ultimately and actually a succession. . . . For us, on the other
hand, there is another possibility. Let the series be the revelation, springing from an infinite and inexhaustible source, a series
infinite because the source is inexhaustible, but finite because
conditioned by finite spirits. Then we can pass from the moral
point of view to the point of view of religion. . . . For us it
[the Absolute] is the living source of the series, a source with
which we can identify ourselves by faith and will, and therefore can unite ourselves with its perfection, although not in
factual existence transcending the temporal series. Then the
world of realities into which we rise by faith and will, and
which we find suggested everywhere in the spatio-temporal region, and are able in a measure to introduce there in so far as
we live for true values—this is not in ultimate reality a universe
of time and change." [15]

I have quoted thus at length Bosanquet's statement of the
alternative views for two reasons. In the first place, it presents
an antagonism which to his mind seemed fundamental in the
discussion of metaphysical problems and which expresses a
basal dichotomy of contemporary metaphysical thought. In the
second place, and primarily for our present purpose, it gives us
a vivid picture of the general background in the light of which
his analysis of the notion of teleology proceeds. For it is his

[15] *Ibid.*, pp. 215-216.

conviction that the progressist's position is nothing more than "an attractive evasion of the fundamental problem," [16] and that the perfectionist alone has steadfastly faced the issue and satisfactorily solved this inescapable paradox of life. And this conviction is, he thinks, sufficiently guaranteed by an analysis of the category that is inextricably involved in the debate as basal to it—the category of teleology.[17] With this in mind we now turn to a consideration of his analysis.

However one may evaluate finally Bosanquet's analysis of the notion of teleology, it seems clear that the attack which he makes against teleology as progress in a mere series of events is wholly successful. A series in which end and means are sundered, as if the end were only a goal to be attained somewhere in the future and the means only vehicles or instruments for its attainment, cannot stand before serious scrutiny. It is, as Bosanquet clearly shows a deeper penetration to disclose, not even an accurate representation of finite experience, to say nothing of its adequacy as an ultimate conception. In its *prima facie* meaning it is entirely an arbitrary notion and cannot be said to have ontological significance. And any philosophy which would take it in this meaning and give it a metaphysical status must in the end admit its bankruptcy. So much Bosanquet has to my mind conclusively shown.

On the other hand, I do not find that his analysis is wholly free from difficulties, and I wish here briefly to suggest what some of the fundamental ones appear to me to be. A convenient point of departure for this undertaking may be found in the fact that the results which we have found emerging from Bosanquet's study are apparently inconsistent, on one side at least, with explicit statements made by him in other places. For at times he speaks as if he were convinced that teleology can in no sense be taken as a metaphysical principle.

In the opening lecture of the *Principle*, for example, he makes the unqualified assertion: "A teleology cannot be ultimate; it can express nothing but a necessity for change founded upon a whole which constitutes the situation to be modified, and, in

[16] *The Meeting of Extremes in Contemporary Philosophy*, p. 217 and elsewhere.
[17] Cf. *ibid.*, pp. 114, 188.

that, the need for modification." [18] And in his later discussion of the problem as we find it presented in the *Meeting of Extremes* he is perhaps even more explicit: "I have dwelt elsewhere on the self-contradictoriness of a finite teleology as a metaphysical conception. I say finite teleology, for a teleology which is not a feature of a finite being is inconceivable." [19] Such statements might be paralleled by others, and they seem to stand in the way of the results above obtained. These results—gained through deeper penetration into the facts—look in the direction of a redefinition of the notion of teleology to make it fit for metaphysical use. If I am not mistaken, there is a point of considerable significance in this apparent inconsistency.

Of course, the obvious and easy way around the difficulty here is to assume that in statements like those quoted in the preceding paragraph Bosanquet is always thinking of teleology as a psychological and ethical concept. Certainly this simple assumption—in no wise a violent one—is sufficient to relieve him of the charge of formal inconsistency. And if the charge were only one of formal inconsistency I should have no interest in mentioning the difficulty. But there seem to be grounds for holding that the difficulty is of deeper root. To my mind at least, the inconsistency arises out of the author's tendency to overlook the dual meaning attaching to the term 'teleology' which he himself has done so much to bring to light. Taking into consideration Bosanquet's whole attitude on the problem and particularly his criticisms of the position that he is concerned to repel, one can with difficulty avoid the feeling that he himself is not always mindful of his own distinction between teleology in its *prima facie* meaning and teleology in the meaning which a deepening analysis attaches to it. In attacking the progressists, for example, he sometimes appears to think it sufficient to point out that a finite teleology applied to the whole is self-contradictory. The assumption, as I understand it, is that teleology in any other sense is inconceivable. Finite teleology predicated of the infinite is *ipso facto* self-contradic-

---

[18] P. 16.
[19] P. 114. The reference here is to the author's discussion in the Appendix to *The Principle of Individuality and Value*.

tory, hence the end of teleology as a metaphysical idea—such at times is the argument as I read it. And, if I follow aright, the argument neglects the possibility that in some sense teleology may attain unto a metaphysical status—a possibility which Bosanquet has taught me to look upon as at least a very probable hypothesis.

A criticism which reaches further into the matter seems to my mind inevitably to emerge from the preceding considerations, and I shall attempt here briefly to set it down. It appears to be only an extension of the preceding point. Facing the two meanings of teleology so convincingly defined by Bosanquet, one must, it would seem, admit that they are distinct and that any intelligent discussion of the problem at issue must keep them separate. But the question still lingers whether they exhaust the possible meanings of the term, whether a third meaning does not necessarily emerge from the facts, and whether, if this third meaning has factual justification, taking it into account does not change the complexion of the debate in some significant manner. Formally, the question is simple. In a complete disjunction the disproof of one side is a virtual proof of the other. If, then, the two meanings of teleology suggested by Bosanquet exhaust the possibilities, proof that one is self-contradictory leaves the other standing in its own right. But if a third meaning can show claims why it should be considered, the argument is not quite so simple. And, to my mind at least, Bosanquet's argument proceeds upon the assumption that it is founded upon a sharp disjunction.

As I view the matter this assumption is not justifiable, and I wish to urge this point. Between the conception of teleology in its *prima facie* meaning and the conception of it with which Bosanquet's analysis ends I seem to discern a third view. The extremes appear to my mind equally unsatisfactory. If even a quasi-serious analysis of a purposive system cannot stop long at the position that end and means are sharply sundered and only externally connected with each other, it seems equally obvious that no analysis of such a system, however penetrating the analysis may be, can satisfactorily describe it as an 'individuality' untouched by maladjustments; to use teleology in this latter sense is really to stretch the meaning of the word beyond recognition and to transform it into what threatens to become a pure abstraction.[20] Between the view of teleology as applicable only to a series in which the 'end' lies yonder in the future like a point or a star or even a 'divine event,' sharply sundered from present actualities, on the one hand, and the view of it as denoting a perfect dead calm of unruffled satisfaction and non-contradiction, on the other, there still seems another possibility. That is the possibility of conceiving it as symbolizing a process in which are progressively realized precisely those ends that bud and grow within and out of present actualities, and which are thus at once means and ends.

This third conception must, of course, fight its way. Such a teleology may be too finite to be predicable of the infinite, too partial to be applied to the whole, too imperfect to envisage perfection. But, if it can be shown to be a deeper interpretation of such teleological systems as we know than are either of the other conceptions, the question still remains as to what that signifies. Does it signify the total bankruptcy of 'teleology,' or does it demand perchance a revision of our view of 'the infinite' and 'perfection'? If the principle upon which Bosanquet lays frequent emphasis be accepted as the guide of our quest, the latter alternative, it would seem, would have to be accepted. For he constantly urges that we must seek the infinite in the depths of the finite, the perfect in the deep-lying leadings of the imperfect.[21]

---

[20] "If pragmatism often seems to involve a subjective, and therefore, premature, teleology, absolute idealism seems to run the risk—at least equally serious—of losing itself in the contemplation of a perfect whole, conceived so indefinitely as to afford no real standard of evaluation. And, moreover, if value is to be estimated in terms of 'nearness to the ultimate whole,' by what means is the degree of such 'nearness' to be determined? 'That the ideal belongs to the future,' in the sense of belonging merely to the future, is the 'great enemy' not only of 'all sane idealism,' but of all clear thinking, where values are concerned; but to conceive the ideal as intelligible apart from the process of temporal development is to conceive it in the abstract, no matter what the disclaimers, and no matter how often the word 'concrete' is appropriated for the sinister view thus developed." (Ernest Albee, in a review of *The Principle of Individuality and Value*, *The Philosophical Review* (1913), Vol. XXII, 312.)

[21] "The absolute or infinite should present itself to us as more of the finite, or the finite at its best, and not as its extinction. More, not in

This third conception of teleology seems to me to destroy the disjunction which Bosanquet finds to be of such fundamental and fateful importance in contemporary tendencies. The dilemma —either "time in the Absolute" or "the Absolute in time"—is destroyed by the introduction of a third possibility, namely, the Absolute *through* time. The old dichotomy between the 'moral' and the 'religious' points of view is broken down. On the basis of this conception, it is no longer necessary to limit the 'moral' point of view exclusively to the temporal series, turning the religious 'faith and will' out into the—I am tempted to say, barren—calm of an eternally fixed, because ineffably perfect, 'nexus of relations.' On the contrary, the two points of view could be, and would have to be, united as different points of approach to the same reality whose nature is such that its very perfection lies precisely and exclusively within its perfectibility. So at least the matter stands in my mind.

If the conciliatory position here suggested is accepted, of course the non-temporal character of the Absolute is forthwith surrendered, and a qualification of its character of all-inclusiveness is called for. If it is to be rejected, however, one would do far better to deny outright any ontological status to the notion of teleology and frankly limit its application to the region where it would seem to have some significance—namely, the order of appearances in time. Then, the term would clearly retain the temporal reference which is essential to it, or which by common consent is always associated with it; and the Absolute, on its side, would be left standing unambiguously for what it is held to be— a non-temporal and complete "nexus of relations" in which the distinction between 'end' and 'means' is meaningless, because

time nor in quantity, but in completeness, in progress along the path of continuity which is indicated by the nature of things." (*Principle*, p. 255.) This thesis is, of course, maintained in varying phraseology by Bosanquet throughout his writings: it is basal in his thought. I do not not press here the question how there could be 'progress' along any 'path' in a timeless whole. I only urge that, if his principle be correct, as I believe it is, and if a deepening penetration of finite experience substantiates the view of teleology above suggested, then it would seem to be logically necessary to make room in the conception of the 'absolute,' or total system, for such teleological endeavor.

within it there is no 'not-yet' and purpose can play no part. So much terminological precision would, at least, be gain.

One obvious advantage to be derived from it is that it directs attention to one of the most persistent difficulties attaching to this notion of the Absolute as a principle of explanation. That difficulty is the logical relation which the Absolute bears to the spatio-temporal order. To this difficulty both Bradley and Bosanquet are keenly alive, and they constantly strive to remove it. In the case of Bradley, it is (apparently hopelessly) complicated by the supra-relational character attributed to the Absolute; and, as we have already seen, he is in the end virtually compelled to admit its unintelligibility. Bosanquet, too, tends in the end to fall back on 'faith and will' as offering a way out. But he makes a valiant effort to render the way thus offered less dark by his doctrine of 'negativity,' to which we now turn.

The concept of negativity is in principle both old and clear. In at least some of its main features, it has been known in philosophy since the days of Plato; it receives special emphasis in the system of Hegel, and other systems more or less directly derived from it. Nor does the notion lack clarity. Even as worked out by Hegel, it is clear enough to any unprejudiced follower of the dialectical movement pictured in the *Phenomenology* or in the *Logic;* and he who fails to apprehend its basal character as depicted in the logical writings of Bradley and Bosanquet has read those writings to little purpose. Furthermore, the genuine significance of the concept in the field of logical inquiry can hardly be denied; we all depend upon it too constantly and too seriously to doubt its value in the resolution of logical difficulties.

Bosanquet has laid a special metaphysical burden on the conception, however, and the question arises whether this burden can be successfully borne by it. The burden is to cure the "vice of finiteness"; and the question is whether the conception is logically competent to effect that cure. Specifically, we are to inquire, in the first place, whether negativity may be held to be a character of the Absolute; and if so, in the second place, whether as such a character it can serve the purpose for which Bosanquet invokes it.

An affirmative answer to the first inquiry seems possible, only provided two conditions are definitely accepted. The first is that the Absolute must, without any reservations, be conceived as a relational whole. The second is that the 'terms' in this relational whole—that is, whatever entities make up the spatio-temporal order—must severally be left standing in their integrity. And I wish briefly to emphasize the necessity of these conditions, and to indicate some of their more important consequences.

Unless the first condition be met, negativity clearly cannot characterize the Absolute. Negativity is as truly a relationship as is contradiction, which it supersedes; therefore, it can characterize nothing but a relationship, as is true of contradiction. To use Bosanquet's own example, "This colour is both beautiful and ugly," is a peculiar sort of relationship which we call contradiction; and contradiction is nothing but this relationship. What happens, now, when it is transformed into negativity? Nothing, except that the contradiction then becomes "frictionless"; it becomes a new sort of relationship, but it remains a relationship still. So developed, it reads: "This colour by daylight is beautiful and by candle-light is ugly." Hereupon, we have a relationship which we call that of negativity; and negativity is nothing but this particular sort of relationship. Now this principle must be retained everywhere; where there is this sort of relationship, there is negativity; and where there is not this sort of relationship, negativity vanishes. If, therefore, negativity is to be attributed to the Absolute, the Absolute must itself be precisely this special sort of relationship. So much seems obvious.

It should be equally obvious that the terms in the relationship of negativity must be left standing, each in its own right. Otherwise, the relationship itself collapses and negativity goes with it —that is, unless one is willing to embrace the monstrosity of a relationship in which there are no terms to be related. If, in the example above, you take away colors and lights and a 'perceiver,' what remains? With the terms gone, nothing remains; the entire situation simply disappears. Nor is it to be supposed that the terms, though left standing, are in some mysterious fashion 'transmuted' when contradiction is translated into negativity; or, if it be so supposed, the verifiable facts must be left out of the reckoning. In the process of translation, to be sure, the terms are modified in some important sense; but the modification is not a mystery, unless the removal of a contradiction in thought be such, and as modified each term still remains and remains its indefeasible self. This principle, also, must be applied throughout: At no point may the terms be voided, however indirectly through the medium of such metaphors as 'transmutation' or 'sublation,' except on penalty of surrendering outright the relationship in question and, thus, the very ground of the possibility of negativity. If, therefore, negativity is to be a character of the Absolute, within that relationship which then is the Absolute the several terms must not be deprived of their logical integrity. This, too, would appear to be obvious.

On the basis of these two conditions, then, negativity may be predicated of the Absolute. Of such an Absolute, two things may with some certainty be said. In the first place, it simply cannot be non-relational—nor 'supra-relational,' if that is equivalent to non-relational—as is Bradley's. In the second place, it cannot be any sort of a whole such that its 'terms' (what, presumably, is commonly meant by its 'appearances') are 'transmuted' or 'sublated' into non-terms. If it be conceived as either of these, then negativity cannot be a character of it, or else the meaning of negativity as such a character must be quite different in principle from that which belongs to it by definition. Colors, standing in the relationship of negativity, are still colors; and they are still related in the peculiar sense of now 'negating' their original contradictory relation; they are integral terms standing in the relation of 'frictionless' contradiction. This, by definition, is negativity. If the Absolute is different in principle from this sort of relationship on either the side of the terms or the side of the relation, then certainly, whatever characters it may have, negativity as defined cannot be among them.

Attributing negativity to the Absolute, then, and using this character as the principle of explanation of the relation between the Absolute and the spatio-temporal order, we are thereby committed to the view that the Absolute is a relational system within which the terms of that order stand fast. It is not clear, however, to what extent Bosanquet accepts this view. That he deems negativity to be a character of the Absolute is indubitable; and that he thinks this character satisfactorily cures the "vice of finiteness" is equally clear. But it is not clear that he subscribes to the consequences above insisted upon, and this hesitancy calls for comment.

Not infrequently, and especially in his later writings, Bosanquet leans rather strongly in the direction of Bradley's view of the Absolute as non-relational. Particularly does he insist upon the impermeability of the Absolute to thought, and on the assumption that this is a necessary consequence of the relational nature of thought. In his reply to the criticisms of his view advanced by Lord Haldane in the famous Symposium of July, 1918,[22] he definitely commits himself to Bradley's position: "As regards the position of thought in such a whole [that is, the Absolute], the question that presses upon my mind is, 'What do you do with the judgment?' Truth and thought, as we commonly speak of them, are one with the judgment; and so far as this discursive thought is concerned, I think Mr. Bradley's analysis is irrefragable, according to which it points to a unity which it cannot realise." And with this, presumably, Bosanquet accepts the Bradleian non-relational Absolute.

On the side of the finite, again, Bosanquet constantly writes as if its 'cure' through negation in the Absolute involves such a radical transformation in the patient that it is hardly recognizable to intelligence after the cure is effected. It suffers a deep sea-change through 'sublation,' and what remains is apparently nothing but an 'aspect' or 'degree' of the Absolute. This holds equally of so-called finite 'things' and finite 'conscious selves.'

In the Symposium above referred to, where the point is specifically to the fore, we find him affirming that there "is no ultimate reason for taking one complex, at least below conscious individuals, as a single thing more than another. They include one another in innumerable subordinations, from the Sahara, for example, or any patch of it, down to any grain of sand in it. A thing, therefore, as an existence, can have no claim to be an ultimate subject." And the same, in principle, holds of finite 'selves.' "While we serve as units, to speak the language of ap-

---

[22] The papers were published in the *Proceedings of the Aristotelian Society*, Vol. XVIII.

pearance, the Absolute lives in us a little, and for a little time; when its life demands our existence no longer, we yet blend with it as the pervading features or characters, which we were needed for a passing moment to emphasise, and in which our reality enriches the universe." Thus, it would appear, that within the Absolute the finite as such is resolved into 'qualities' or 'characters' of a larger whole; what formerly appeared to be 'terms' are such no longer; their 'existence' is no longer demanded. The "language of appearance" is no longer appropriate, and we must, therefore, remain dumb or learn a new language.

That Bradley's argument in support of the non-relational character of the Absolute is 'irrefragable' we have already seen reason to deny; and Bosanquet adds nothing to it. Whether the view of the 'finite,' especially of finite 'selves,' here advocated may stand will concern us below when we come to consider the differences among idealists on the issue of 'individuality.' The matter to be emphasized in the immediate context is that Bosanquet is here caught in an inconsistency. And his only way out, so far at least as I am able to see, is either to renounce the immediacy of the Absolute with its consequent 'sublation' of the finite or frankly to admit that the conception of negativity has no ontological significance.

In Bosanquet's conception of negativity as a character of the Absolute we have, as it seems to me, a principle of profound importance for philosophical construction. For in it lies the ground of explanation of 'appearance' and 'reality,' of the 'actual' and the 'ideal.' If he would only persistently hold to it in its ontological application, his conception of the Absolute, I am persuaded, would mark a decided advance over Bradley's. But, on the other side, he would have to modify that conception. For one thing, he would have to surrender its immediacy and explicitly conceive it as a relational system; and this would involve a change of view in respect of both its 'sentience' and its all-inclusiveness. Nor can I see that such modification would not be much more in harmony with the basal epistemological premises upon which Bradley and Bosanquet alike build. If, however, the ontological application of the notion of negativity is renounced in behalf of the non-relational or supra-relational character of the

Absolute, then Bosanquet's position coincides in principle with
that of Bradley and is open to the same charge of inconsistency.
For, then, the Absolute loses what is chiefly claimed for it,
namely, significance as an explanatory principle. Whatever else
may then be said of it, it can hardly be said to be the "general
view" which "contents the intellect."

4. ROYCE

Royce's point of departure in his statement of the idealistic
argument is the distinction which we all make between 'fact' and
'idea'; and his development of the argument consists in tracing
the fortunes of this distinction when it is submitted to critical
analysis. Such an analysis, he thinks, discloses the "way of
ideas" as the pathway to reality and this way in the end turns
out to be also the "way of fact"; for reality is thus shown to be
the complete embodiment of ideas in an Individual Life for which
ideas and facts fall together. And this is shown through the resolution of 'internal' and 'external' meanings.

"Any state of consciousness, whether simple or complex, which
when present, is then and there viewed as at least the partial
expression or embodiment of a single conscious purpose"—such a
state of consciousness, we recall, is what is to be understood by
an 'idea.' And the "internal meaning" of the idea is this "single
conscious purpose" thus expressed or embodied. The external
meaning of the idea is some object, which is the idea's object and
to which the internal meaning refers. Thus, the melody I sing
internally means my purpose as I sing it; externally it means,
say, Schubert's "Serenade." There is no antagonism between
these two meanings; on the contrary, they are mutually involved
and complementary. Each has a function in intellectual operations, but in the end internal meaning is logically prior and determining. "The final meaning of every complete idea, when fully
developed, must be viewed as wholly internal meaning, and . . .
all apparently external meanings become consistent with internal
meanings only by virtue of thus coming to be viewed as aspects
of the true internal meaning."

This basal truth has been overlooked by certain approaches to
philosophical issues, such as mysticism or realism or critical

rationalism, which in consequence turn out to be false leads. If it is observed, however, we shall discover at the end of our analysis that "the sun of true Being has arisen before our eyes." Internal meaning is then seen to find its own completion in its external meaning. Then, the Other which all along it has intended falls together with it in a complete Life, a single self-conscious Knower whose external meanings are at one with internal meanings. For such a Knower, its Other is its own and consciously recognized as such. Even finite purposes or internal meanings are partial expressions of its complete internal meaning—my ideas are potentially what God's are actually.

In this summary I have consciously tried to direct attention to what seems to me to be foundational in Royce's statement— namely, internal and external meanings and their implicative relationship. Since these bear the weight of the idealistic argument as Royce presents it, our critical comments must center around them. Do they give an adequate basis for the conclusion which Royce rests upon them? To this question we shall henceforward address ourselves. But before passing on, we may profitably dwell for a moment on a few preliminary observations.

Royce's identification of 'internal meaning' with 'purpose' embodied in an idea marks an interesting development in his philosophy. In his earlier formulations of the argument for idealism his emphasis was, almost if not quite exclusively, on the purely cognitive aspects of experience. This is clearly manifest in his first formulation in the famous chapter on "The Possibility of Error" (Chapter XI, *The Religious Aspect of Philosophy*), and also in the formulations given in *The Spirit of Modern Philosophy* and the original essay in *The Conception of God*. Beginning with the "Supplementary Essay" of the last-named volume, however, the emphasis changes to include the emotional and conative aspects of experience as well as the merely cognitive within a common principle. In the Gifford Lectures this emphasis is made central through the explicit identification of 'purpose' and 'internal meaning' and the equally explicit insistence on the logical priority of internal meanings thus conceived.

It has at times been suggested that this development in Royce's views towards a sort of 'voluntarism' must be explained by the historical circumstance that his earlier statements were subjected to vigorous criticism by pragmatists and 'personal' idealists. There is, of course, some truth in the suggestion, but it seems to me important not to overlook the fact that the development is also a natural one in Royce's thought; it is indigenous to his premises. Doubtless, he was compelled to adjust his doctrines to the external attacks of his critics; but the adjustment was to him quite congenial and only brings out more clearly what was already implicit in his principles.

In any event, Royce in this later emphasis is at one with Bradley and Bosanquet, and the agreement can readily be explained by reference to common principles. Nor must the point of agreement be forgotten, if one is rightly to evaluate the groundwork of the 'idealism' which these three thinkers in common defend. To call them 'intellectualists' and to assume that, having so called them, one has thereby convicted them of failure to take account of the value side of experience, is to neglect much of what they have in principle maintained and to overlook their marked divergence from those who appeal to the 'epistemological' type of argument. For all three alike, values are basal within meaning. And the question really is, as we have already seen at some length in our discussion of Bosanquet's view of centrality, not whether they have failed to give value the consideration it deserves, but whether they have in point of fact placed too much emphasis upon it.

Another preliminary remark is more directly relevant to our later considerations. Not infrequently Royce speaks of 'internal meanings' and 'external meanings,' as if they are actually quite distinct and separate. And this fact tends to confuse his reader, since it is in the main quite clear that he does not intend such a sharp separation—he does not intend it, that is, in the earlier stages of his statement. But as the argument proceeds the author himself seems to be confused; for at a crucial step in his argument, where he is insisting upon the, for him basal, notion of the primacy of internal meaning, the separation seems not only to be accepted but also to become quite significant for the argument itself. This inconsistency we shall have occasion to indicate in more detail below.

Meanwhile, however, it is important to note that Royce does not at the beginning intend any such separation between the two 'meanings.' On the contrary, he holds that the distinction between 'internal' and 'external' falls within one whole of meaning, of which each is only a distinguishable aspect. The distinction between them, as if they were two, arises merely from the terminology employed to indicate them.

It is important to insist, further, that this view of the two as merely aspects of one whole of meaning is the only one which in fact can be admitted. And it is so important that the matter needs quite explicit and unambiguous formulation, since, if it is denied, the whole argument is undermined before it gets started. Clearly, internal meaning apart from external, or *vice versa*, is not a meaning in the full sense of the term. And to build an argument on such a separation is to found it upon nothing more substantial than a blank abstraction.

To formulate the point without terminological ambiguity, only a slight modification of Royce's statement is necessary. The 'object of knowledge,' one might say, using this phrase as presumably less ambiguous than the traditional term 'idea,' is of a dual nature. On one side, it is object *for* the knower; and, on the other side, it is object seen in some sense independent of the knower. And its meaning is also dual. It is meaning for the knower, and it is meaning of the object. This manner of statement has at least the advantage of explicitly emphasizing the duality within the unity of meaning and so avoids the disadvantage of verbally suggesting a separation between the two aspects as though they were distinct logical entities. It thus expresses the relationship which, as I understand, Royce intends to affirm between his internal and external meanings, and which must be affirmed if one is to do anything like justice to the complexity of meaning. I wish to stress this last point.

In the first place, it is clear that there are these two sides to the meaning of the object of knowledge. If, to illustrate, I ask what the 'solar system' means, I ask a question which obviously is ambiguous and cannot be answered without further qualification. Whose 'solar system' is wanted—Plato's, Ptolemy's, Newton's, or whose? Or is it *the* solar system which is in question?

The point here is of course obvious and it, equally obviously, exemplifies a universal epistemological fact—namely, the dual reference of the meaning of an object of knowledge.

It is clear, also, that these two aspects of meaning are inseparably joined, and together constitute the full meaning of the object of knowledge. They may, naturally, be arbitrarily sundered and treated in abstraction; but the fact remains that the full significance of the one implies or involves the other. Either Plato's or Ptolemy's or Newton's 'solar system' is implicatively connected with *the* solar system; and what *the* solar system means wholly apart from theirs and everybody's 'solar system' shows itself in the end to be empty. The full meaning of an object of knowledge cannot be stated except in terms of the two aspects taken together; if they are taken separately and without reference to each other, the meaning is thereby truncated. And this, it should be observed, holds true of all objects of knowledge, even including postulated ones, such as those that make up highly abstract systems like mathematics. For these, too, though in a sense arbitrary, mean more than is involved in the merely internal aspect; they are, as postulated, felt to be arbitrary but, when once postulated, they are arbitrary no longer.

With all of this Royce is in essential agreement. But despite that fact, he seems to me in the course of his argument to depart from the principle involved, as I shall indicate below. And I have thought it necessary to draw out the point in this preliminary statement, in order to emphasize what would appear to be the very important principle in Royce's own distinction and thus to lay the foundation for holding that, when he later departs from it, he thereby falls into error.

Emphasis upon the implicative relationship between internal and external meanings, it should be noted further, brings before us once more the apparent circularity already met with in our consideration of Bosanquet's conception of centrality. For what we have just been emphasizing is only another way of insisting that the aspects of meaning are mutually dependent; neither is complete and stable apart from the other. Viewed from this angle, the emphasis seems to be faithful to experience. The purpose embodied in an object of knowledge functions in the determination of 'relevant' facts, and these in turn enter significantly into the determination of the purpose in whose behalf they are selected. And hereupon we are confronted by the old puzzle about knowledge expressed in the famous question: When we learn do we learn that which we know or that which we do not know? And Plato, at least, had some difficulty in finding an answer.

Royce's distinction between internal and external meanings may contain a clue to the answer. If the paradox arises out of the duality of meaning, as it apparently does, then there are three possible ways out. These are: either to deny the duality outright and retain only one aspect as all there is of meaning; or, accepting the duality as inescapable, to make either the external or the internal aspect logically fundamental.

Denial of the duality seems hardly feasible, and must be excluded as a possibility. In the first place, it flies in the face of experience if ideas do actually carry the dual meaning above outlined. But let us assume that this description of experience is in error, and then inquire what follows. Meaning, then, is either merely internal or merely external. If entirely internal, meanings can have no 'objective' significance; if entirely external, they can in no intelligible sense be *ours*. From which it seems to follow, on the one side, that our meanings are merely capricious and, on the other, that they are wholly beyond us. Nor is it plain that we can get around the first difficulty by holding that mind is 'natural,' or around the second by positing mind as a 'relation.' Mind, however 'natural,' can hardly attach meanings to objects, if by hypothesis meanings are not attached to objects. Nor may a meaning be foreshortened or become erroneous simply by entering into a 'relation' of which it is by definition utterly independent. If mind is to attach meanings to objects, it must discover that they are already attached; and if meanings are to be twisted by a relation, they must be embedded in it. In short, to escape from utter subjectivism on the one side and from a self-refuting objectivism on the other, the duality of meaning will have to be admitted on both sides. And this, in my opinion, Royce has conclusively shown in his analyses of mysticism and realism.

But this is not the context in which to enter upon an extended discussion of possible solutions of the paradox of knowledge. What now concerns us is the way out which Royce himself follows. And in turning to this, we take leave of these preliminary remarks.

Royce's way out, as we have already noted, is through the logical priority of internal meanings. And the conclusion with which he emerges, following this way, is the one with which we are familiar: The Other which we seek in knowledge is the complete embodiment of our internal meanings, and such a complete embodiment is a single Individual Life in which internal and external meanings are in thoroughly harmonious accord. But this way out seems to me to be ill-conceived from the beginning, nor does it lead to the conclusion contemplated. The contention that internal meanings are logically fundamental, I should suppose, is unwarranted; and, even if it be granted, it is hardly sufficient to support the conclusion which Royce advocates. These two observations I wish now to develop.

Royce finds support for his advocacy of the logical priority of internal meanings, in the first place, through an analysis of the notion of correspondence which in some sense, we all admit, is involved in the relation between a 'true' idea and its object. His thesis is concisely expressed as follows: "The idea is true if it possesses the sort of correspondence to its object that the idea itself wants to possess. Unless the kind of identity in inner structure between the idea and object can be found which the specific purpose embodied in a given idea demands, the idea is false. On the other hand, if this particular sort of identity is to be found, the idea is just in so far true." As a description of cognitive experience, I think it must be said, this statement is partly correct, but only partly so, and in the main it is unwarranted.

It is correct in so far as it emphasizes the indispensable rôle played by our conceptual systems in the determination of relevancy. Facts, to be relevant, must be relevant to something; and that to which they are relevant is, I take it, necessarily some point of view. In this sense it is presumably unquestionable that internal meanings are logically fundamental in our intellectual operations. Nor can one avoid the feeling that a frank recognition of this might perhaps spare us much fruitless debate about mere 'data' and absolute 'facts.' For, after all, if I may repeat this, as Dewey has very pertinently observed, a datum is also a 'taken'; and 'facts,' science now stands ready to show us, are shot through with intellectual construction.

Our conceptual structures, however, are not intellectual Melchizedeks, and it is not here irrelevant to insist that they are not. They do not come merely *a priori*, but they grow up within an empirical situation with reference to which they function. Furthermore, once they begin to function in experience, they are not in themselves sufficient guides; they are, rather, under the guidance of the situation within which they function and which may demand their modification indefinitely or even their ultimate rejection. That such is the case would seem to be plainly evident from a simple survey of the fortunes of any idea in its actual functioning; it arises as a tentative hypothesis and is subject to constant redefinition, even after it has been established with sufficient surety to attain the status of a 'fact.' And the principle underlying all of this, I should suppose, has been emphasized and made fundamental in the logic advocated particularly by Royce and his colleagues; it is involved in their theory of judgment.

But in the light of such considerations, it would seem to be entirely inadequate to say, as Royce does, that an idea is true "if it possesses the sort of correspondence to its object that the idea itself wants to possess," or that it is false "unless that kind of identity in inner structure between the idea and the object can be found which the specific purpose embodied in a given idea demands." It would be much more nearly in accord with our actual procedure to say that an idea is true if it possesses the sort of correspondence to the object which the object itself 'wants' it to possess, and that otherwise it is false. At any rate, it is a simple fact of all-too-common experience that an idea may possess the sort of correspondence it wants to its object, and yet be false. Indeed, a fairly good case can be empirically made for the contention that such 'correspondence' almost invariably is characteristic of false ideas, as all forms of wish-thinking, for example, bear witness. On the other side, it not infrequently happens that a true idea turns out to have for its object one whose "inner structure" is quite different from what was demanded by the "specific purpose" embodied in the idea when it was first projected for trial—witness, once more, our struggle with our preconceptions.

Of course, if I may repeat this, Royce is directing attention here to an obvious characteristic of human thought. Our minds are never quite "swept and garnished," and the 'idols' are always with us; nor can we have any 'object' at all except from a 'point of view.' But our main business, as *thinkers,* is to avoid falling down and worshiping our 'idols' or setting up our point of view as an ultimate criterion of existence. And Royce's insistence on the logical priority of internal meanings encourages us to do precisely the opposite.

In this insistence, one cannot but feel, Royce is a victim of the ambiguity in his terminology as above noted. If our internal meanings were from the beginning fixed and definite, if, in other words, we could from the beginning clearly see what we really intend, then our internal meanings might serve satisfactorily as guides of our intellectual progress—assuming, apparently without warrant, that we could make any. Royce's terminological distinction between internal and external meanings seems to serve him as a basis for such a supposition. He is apparently led by the verbal distinction to assume that such distinction is also one of fact, that we really have two meanings distinct and separate; and from this the transition to the logical primacy of internal meaning is easy and, perhaps, even inevitable, since the internal meaning alone is *ours* and the external meaning is beyond us until we can bend it somehow back into the internal meaning. But so long as we hold the distinction to be merely verbal and the two so-called meanings to be only aspects of one meaning-situation, as Royce constantly urges we must, emphasis upon the logical priority of internal meaning, as if it alone must be taken as the criterion of 'correspondence' between a true idea and its object, is seen to be unwarranted and based only upon an abstraction. Then, it would clearly appear, the two aspects of the meaning-situation must develop *pari passu* as the situation itself expands; it is the entire situation and not one aspect alone, the relationship and not one term within it to the exclusion of the other, which controls. To put the matter in its full paradoxical character: What determines the correspondence between the true idea and its object is the correspondence itself.

Another consideration, advanced by Royce in support of his contention that internal meanings are prior, centers round the relation between the idea and its object. What is the relation of 'having,' when it is said that the idea 'has' its object? This relation, too, Royce maintains must be defined in terms of the internal meaning of the idea in question. It cannot be described as causal, since it is plain that the object very frequently is not, and cannot possibly be, in any sense the cause of its idea; and it is equally plain that the cause of the idea is, more often than otherwise, not its object. The relation must be defined, rather, by reference to the idea's internal meaning. "If I have meant to make an assertion about Cæsar, you must not hold me to account because my statement does not correspond, in the intended way, with the object called Napoleon. If I have meant to say that space has three dimensions, you cannot refute me by pointing out that time has only one. And nowhere, without a due examination of the internal meaning of my ideas, can you learn whether it was the object Cæsar or the object Napoleon, whether it was space or time, that I meant." The relation of 'having' between the idea and its object, thus, is determinable only by reference to the internal meaning of the idea; its object is the object it intends, and is no other.

The main point is stated in the last sentence of the quotation, and there is more involved than Royce here explicitly admits. The question may always, and frequently must, be raised as to what object is, in a given instance, actually intended; and this question cannot be answered merely by an examination of the internal meaning taken alone. Suppose I assert that Cæsar crossed the Rubicon, is it indubitable that I really intend the object called Cæsar? Can this be determined merely by an examination of my internal meaning? Simply because I utter the word, 'Cæsar,' is no proof that I in fact intended the historical object; I still might intend the historical object called Napoleon. Nor does there seem to be any way to resolve the matter except by bringing in the context of my avowed internal meaning, in other words, except by examining the external meaning. If I, on examination, follow my assertion about Cæsar into its historical context—the march on Rome, the fatal Ides of March, and the main intervening events—then, presumably, my object is the historical Cæsar. If, however, on such examination, I follow up the crossing of the Rubicon with, say, the retreat from Moscow, the battle of Waterloo, and death on the island of St. Helena, the chances are that I do not intend the historical Cæsar at all, despite my explicit declaration that I do, but have meant the historical Napoleon from the beginning. And further doubt as to which object I do really mean—Cæsar or Napoleon—cannot be resolved by any examination of my internal meaning, for that meaning is precisely what is in question.

The point can, I think, be quite summarily put. In every case where the object of an idea is at all in doubt, the final appeal is necessarily to the external aspect of the meaning-situation, and never merely to the internal. And where there is no doubt as to the object intended this is so because the internal aspect (what is asserted to be the object) is taken without proof or is clearly supplemented by examination of the external. Everywhere, confidence is grounded in the external aspect. The relation of 'having,' when it is said that an idea 'has' an object, it would thus appear, is not determinable by examination of the internal meaning alone. The external meaning must also be examined, and in the end it is the final court of appeal; if the internal meaning remains contradictory of the external, it is set aside as illusory. The object which the idea 'has' is the object which is determinable only by reference to the meaning-situation in its wholeness, and not by reference to one aspect of it—certainly not by reference to that aspect which is the internal meaning.

The main drift of the preceding comments may be focalized in this emphasis upon the 'wholeness' of the meaning-situation, and upon the relative priority of the external aspect. As noted in the beginning, in accordance with Royce's own first emphasis, the meaning-situation is one with dual aspects—call them 'internal' and 'external,' 'subjective' and 'objective,' or what you will. The further emphasis—out of harmony with Royce's assertions but, I must insist, alone consonant with his original position—is that this meaning-situation, in what we call the development of knowledge, goes through a process of self-correction in respect of both the idea's object and its 'correspondence' to its object. This process consists in the continuous modification and redefinition of the internal aspect until it arrives at what is commonly designated as a 'factual' status, and even in this status it is not above further modification and redefinition. The external aspect is deeply involved in the process, and its claims are in the end paramount. Internal meaning is always tentative and, if intelligent, seeks its direction in the external. The assertion that "external experience never finally disposes of ideas unless, for reasons defensible upon the ground of internal meaning only, the ideas themselves make their own 'reasonable' surrender" is at best but a partial truth. In the strict sense of 'internal meaning' as defined—namely, as "the specific conscious purpose" which is expressed in the idea "at the instant when it comes to mind"—the assertion is palpably false. The 'surrender' which ideas make, when they are finally disposed of, is not 'reasonable' because of "reasons defensible upon the ground of internal meaning only"; on the contrary, such 'surrender' is made primarily because of reasons defensible only upon the ground of external meaning and, more often than otherwise, the surrender involves the abdication of the internal meaning. The capitulation takes place, when it does, because it is forced by the demands of the external aspect of the meaning-situation, and it is 'reasonable' precisely on account of this compulsion.

To the objection that the preceding criticism overlooks the important distinction between the partial and complete internal meaning of ideas, the reply is twofold. In the first place, it would appear that the internal meaning is by definition always 'complete' and never 'partial'; it is "the specific conscious purpose" of the moment, and one is at a loss to understand how it could ever be otherwise than 'complete.' If, however, this is held to be a mere terminological evasion of the issue, the second point may seem more weighty. Granting the distinction between the stages of the internal meaning, one must surely admit on consideration that it is nothing to the present purpose. Specifically and actually, the 'partial' alone can function in the reasoning process, since it alone is definitely present in consciousness; the 'complete' is always on ahead, and what it is is problematic so far as the immediate intellectual process is concerned. If, then, the internal meaning is to be made logically fundamental in the process, that can only be the internal meaning taken in its partial and 'immediate' aspect. So the objection lacks significance. It assumes a character of internal meaning which by definition is not permissible; and the distinction between the phases of internal meaning, once granted, will not serve the purpose for which it is invoked.

That Royce does appeal to this distinction is, of course, true. He is compelled to appeal to it in order to escape the vicious circle to which his doctrine of the logical primacy of internal meaning threatens to reduce him. But this appeal is a virtual surrender of the doctrine, since it amounts to placing logical priority in external meaning. And this I wish to develop at greater length.

The threatened vicious circle is quite plain. By hypothesis the 'correspondence' between the idea and its object which is to make the idea true (or false) is determinable only by reference to the internal meaning. Also by hypothesis, what object the idea 'has' (an object to which it is to 'correspond' if true, or fail to 'correspond' if false) is determinable only by reference to the same internal meaning. Since this is true it apparently follows that truth is necessarily a character of all ideas which claim to be true and falsity is necessarily a character of all ideas (if there be any such) which do not claim to be true. For every idea which claims to be true "possesses the sort of correspondence to its object that the idea itself wants to possess," and is, therefore, by definition a true idea. And every idea which claims not to be true, or does not claim to be true, is *eo ipso* an idea whose relation to its object is not "that kind of identity in inner structure between the idea and object" which is demanded by "the specific purpose" embodied in the idea "at the instant when it comes to mind." It is, therefore, by definition false. And all of this threatens us with intellectual ruin, since it makes both truth and error quite capricious.

To escape this catastrophe Royce falls back on the distinction between 'present' internal meaning and internal meaning 'in the long run.' And this, for him, is the only way out. But the question is: Where does it lead him?

The distinction, as I have already urged above, seems to me plainly to contravene the definition of the internal meaning. But I do not wish to press this further. The point of importance here is that the distinction is equivalent to a rejection of the primacy of internal meaning and an acceptance of the primacy of external meaning. And I think this can be readily shown.

The distinction means, I take it, that the 'present' internal meaning is to be identified with "the specific conscious purpose" expressed in the idea of the moment—is, in other words, what we have hitherto been assuming was to be understood by 'internal meaning.' And the internal meaning of 'the long run,' or the 'complete' internal meaning, is to be identified with the full expression of what is implicit in the 'present' internal meaning. The 'complete' internal meaning, therefore, remains to be discovered, and the question is how this can actually be done. It cannot be done by an examination of the 'present' internal meaning, since such an examination cannot possibly reveal what is implicit in it. To bring this out the 'present' internal meaning must be submitted to the hazards of trial and error, and subjected to indefinite qualification in the light of the consequences. But is this not equivalent to saying that the 'complete' internal meaning can be revealed only by following the fortunes of the 'present' internal meaning during the course of its expansion through the ramifications of the external meaning? In other words, the 'complete' internal meaning is identical with the 'present' internal meaning as modified to meet the demands of the external meaning. And, if this be so, there is apparently only a verbal distinction between the 'complete' internal meaning and the external meaning; in fact, the two ultimately coincide. To appeal from the 'present' to the 'complete' internal meaning and to place emphasis upon the latter as the criterion, therefore, is equivalent to admitting the logical priority of external meaning. The internal meaning of 'the long run' terminates in the external meaning.

Thus, I think we may fairly say, Royce in the end gives up his doctrine of the primacy of internal meaning. When confronted by the alternatives, either a surrender of the logical priority of internal meaning or an ultimate chasm between 'truth' and 'reality,' he falls back on the 'complete' internal meaning as a way of escape from the subjectivity threatened by emphasis on the 'present' internal meaning. But the 'complete' internal meaning turns out to be derivative, and not prior, in the intellectual process; or, if prior, then it is only verbally distinguishable from the external meaning.

The primary reason why Royce fails to see this, one cannot but suspect, lies in the terminology with which he is working. Having made a terminological distinction between *internal meaning* and *external meaning*, he forgets his original thesis that the distinction is merely a terminological one and proceeds to treat it as if it were a distinction between separate logical entities. On the basis of this assumption, one may note, it would be as reasonable to argue that reality is to be identified with external meaning, as to argue with Royce that it must be identified with internal meaning. But both lines of argument are equally illogical, since they alike violate the original premise —namely, that *internal* and *external* do not indicate distinct types of meaning, but only aspects of one whole of meaning. For the purpose of getting rid of this sinister terminology I suggested in the beginning of this discussion that it would be better to avoid the term *idea* and speak, rather, of the *object of knowledge;* and to translate *internal meaning* and *external meaning* into internal and external 'aspects' of one meaning-situation, with which the 'object of knowledge' is to be identified. Such a terminological modification would at least relieve us of the pressure arising from an unnoted and disclaimed abstraction. It would also help us to place the emphasis where it properly belongs, namely, on the meaning-situation, and rightly to estimate the relative functional significance in concrete thinking of the 'internal' and 'external' aspects. But there is here no space to develop this further.

If this doctrine of the primary of internal meaning is to be surrendered, however, the sole ground on which rests Royce's view of truth as ultimately embodied in an "Eternal Consciousness" is thereby removed. No longer may we say that the 'idea,' in seeking its Other or Object, is seeking nothing but the completion of its own internal meaning, nothing but its own explicit and, in the end, complete determination as this conscious purpose embodied in this one way. We must say, rather, that it 'seeks' the completion of the meaning-situation, through whose expansion as 'this conscious purpose embodied in this one way,' 'it' runs the risk of indefinite modification and, perhaps, ultimate rejection. Nor does the fact that 'it' selects the 'external meaning' and determines its relevancy change the matter; for, once selected and marked as relevant, the 'external meaning' grows quite imperious and brooks no opposition. The object sought, in short, is the fulfilment of the 'object of knowledge'; and there is no basis within the structure of the process of seeking whereby the nature of that which is to fulfil the 'object of knowledge' may be predetermined.

But there is no need to labor this point further, and I will turn to another matter. Suppose the doctrine of the primacy of internal meaning stands. Is Royce's statement solid? Even if the doctrine be allowed, three difficulties of significance seem to remain. And I wish briefly to indicate what they are.

The first concerns the passage to a unique individual form embodying the fulfilment of the internal meaning. In support of the transition Royce here offers two reasons: first, that only such a unique form can be the completion of the internal meaning; and, second, that the only alternative is the abstract 'possible experience' of the critical rationalist. But neither of these reasons is to my mind convincing.

The first point, I think, turns upon a dubious use of the vague term *purpose*. The idea seeks the 'fulfilment' of the 'purpose' embodied in it, so the argument runs, and the final embodiment of this 'purpose' must itself be 'purposive,' or, better, 'purposeful.' And I see nothing here more significant than a verbal twist. It is all-important to be quite clear as to the 'purpose' which is to receive its final embodiment, and to this end we must stick close to experience. Suppose the experience in question is that of my hearing a noise and wondering what

it signifies. What is the 'purpose' embodied in my 'idea' of
the noise? On one side, presumably, it is my attitude towards
the noise, and *prima facie* my attitude of wonderment. But this
is not the 'purpose' embodied in the 'idea' whose 'fulfilment'
the 'idea' seeks. That 'purpose,' surely, is indicated by the question: What does the noise signify? When the question has been
satisfactorily answered, the 'purpose' has received its final embodiment; if I discover that it signifies danger, or fair weather,
or a mechanical defect in my car, my purpose is so far attained.
Of course, hereupon another 'purpose' may arise, if, for instance,
I wonder what to do about it. But this is not the original 'purpose'; it is simply another one, and its 'fulfilment' is attained
in the same way.

Now, in all of this, where is the reason for maintaining that
what finally embodies the 'purpose' must itself be 'purposeful' in
the sense in which my idea is 'purposeful' or embodies purpose? There seems to be none; and if the matter is pushed,
it becomes a little absurd. There seems to be no reason for
holding that the dangerous situation which 'embodies' the 'purpose' of my 'idea' about the noise must itself be an embodiment
of 'purpose'; and to assert that it is so, raises the interesting
question whether it, too, is burdened with curiosity or is an
'idea.'

Sticking hard by experience, then, there is no justification
for the assertion that what finally fulfils the 'purpose' embodied
in a given idea must itself be a unique form which also embodies
'purpose.' The assertion, when taken seriously, lands us in a
position which has the distressing appearance of being an absurdity. So far as the embodied 'purpose' is concerned, its fulfilment may be in anything (from a concrete conscious life to
the most abstruse set of abstract relations) which satisfactorily meets its demands. What this turns out to be depends
upon the meaning-situation within which the 'purpose' functions, or, if one prefers the statement, upon the specific nature
of the 'purpose' itself which varies with the meaning-situation
in which it functions. Nor, if, neglecting such considerations, one
holds the contrary, can the absurdity of attributing consciousness to any and every object which 'fulfils' the purpose of an

idea be escaped. So much seems clear from the actual functioning of ideas within concrete cognitive experience.

Now, I must insist, this principle holds throughout. When
one begins to talk about the 'final' fulfilment of the 'purpose
embodied in finite ideas,' one has not thereby got beyond the
principle. One can argue that such 'fulfilment' must necessarily
be a Life or Consciousness which embodies 'purpose,' only in
forgetfulness of the fact that, when in experience we speak of
the 'purpose' of an 'idea' seeking 'fulfilment,' we are using the
terms in a special sense and are not thinking of 'purpose' in
its psychological reference to will or impulse. Whether such
a Life or Consciousness is alone the ultimate fulfilment of the
purpose embodied in finite ideas cannot be determined on the
basis of the fact that such ideas necessarily express an attitude
of a conscious being. The only 'purpose' of finite ideas relevant
to the question is that which is an aspect of a meaning-situation. Such a Life or Consciousness, then, may be inferred (if it
may be), not because the finite idea embodies 'purpose' in the
sense of being involved within consciousness as its matrix and
therefore necessarily seeking fulfilment of this purpose in a
'purpose' similarly involved in another consciousness, but because
the finite idea embodies 'purpose' in the sense of an implicative
attachment to an objective situation which in its full revelation
discloses itself to be such a Life or Consciousness. In short, the
'purpose' whose embodiment our ideas seek is not the purpose
explicit in us, but the 'purpose' (meaning) implicit in their
objects.

Turning, now, to the other point mentioned above, we must
admit that critical rationalism, as defined by Royce, cannot
stand. To identify Being with mere abstract possibility is to rob
it of any ultimate significance at all; whatever other characters
may belong to it, it must at least have existence and be in some
sense individual. So much, presumably, may be admitted. But
does this admission commit us to the conclusion that Being
must be a complete conscious Life? Only provided this sort of
'concreteness' is the exclusive alternative to the abstract possibility of the critical rationalist. And I see no reason in the
character of internal meaning for the assertion that such is the

case. As we have just seen, internal meaning finds its fulfilment in any implicative relationship which answers its question and supplements, even perchance by way of rejecting, its own partiality. And, so long as such a relationship is not merely fictitious, however abstract and hypothetical otherwise, it would be concrete and individual in the only sense which the fulfilment of the internal meaning demands that it be concrete and individual. What the internal meaning wants is the object which fills it out *in its capacity as meaning;* and this object need not itself be a conscious Life in order to do this—it may be so, but it may be a stick or a nebula or a mathematical equation, depending upon the meaning-situation whose internal aspect is to be filled out.

A second difficulty in Royce's statement concerns his conception of the comprehensiveness of the individual form with which he identifies real Being. If we admit the doctrine of the primacy of internal meaning, does it follow from this that there is ultimately only one all-inclusive meaning-situation? This follows only if it can be shown that the fulfilment of the internal meaning of any given idea implies the fulfilment of the internal meanings of all ideas. This, of course, is not a logical impossibility. But the question now before us is whether it is actual and can be shown to be so by the fact (granted, for the argument) that the fulfilment of the internal meaning of an idea is the concrete embodiment of that internal meaning. There seems absolutely nothing in the premise to warrant the conclusion, and if it is to be shown the proof must rest on other grounds.

In point of fact, the proof which Royce offers does rest on other grounds. The meaning-situation, he virtually says, proceeds through its own indefinite expansion; and since there is no logical stopping point short of the whole of what is, the meaning-situation must be held to be implicitly all-inclusive. This sort of argument is, of course, identical in principle with the arguments of Bradley and Bosanquet in the same context, and it is open to essentially the same criticism. The point of importance here to be noted is that it definitely abandons the doctrine of the primacy of internal meaning. If this form of argument be valid, its validity is based, not on the demand by internal meaning for its own final 'embodiment,' but on the demand by external meaning that the internal meaning be not permitted to find its final 'embodiment' in any stage of the expansion of the meaning-situation short of all-inclusiveness.

On this side of Royce's statement, it should be noted in passing, we meet again the sinister influence of the ambiguity involved in his conception of internal and external meanings and arising, I venture once more to suggest, from his unfortunate terminology. Here the argument seems actually to be this: The 'fulfilment' of one internal meaning involves in principle the 'fulfilment' of every other internal meaning, because in every instance we have the final embodiment of 'internal meaning.' And this sounds very much like a purely verbal argument, with the *prima facie* evidence at least directly against it. If what has been urged above is correct, what is here affirmed can hardly hold except verbally. The 'fulfilment' of the internal meaning of my idea expressed in my act of whistling Schubert's "Serenade," to go back to actual experience, is not *prima facie* connected with the 'fulfilment' of the internal meaning of my idea expressed in this, my effort to apprehend the intricacies of Royce's statement about meaning; taken *prima facie*, the one is not in the slightest degree relevant to the other. Nor can one logically go beyond this *prima facie* distinctness to the conclusion that ultimately they are one in principle, merely by appealing to the fact that each is a 'fulfilment' of an 'internal meaning.' So to argue is, surely, to forget all that has been admitted, and even urged, concerning the logical inseparability of internal and external meanings and to fall a victim to the ambiguity of the terms involved in the premises.

Passing by the terms to the situation beneath, are we not compelled to hold that the mere fact that two meanings are both 'internal' furnishes no logical ground whatever either for denying their *prima facie* distinctness or for affirming that in the end the 'fulfilment' of the one is relevant to, and implied in, the 'fulfilment' of the other? And one cannot but feel that, on this side of his statement, Royce formulates his argument with an eye merely for the common names and not for the diversities of the actual situation denoted by them.

The third, and final, difficulty mentioned above concerns the relational between the all-inclusive Eternal Consciousness and the temporal order, particularly those items in this order called finite minds. This relation Royce undertakes to define in terms of internal meanings; and his contention is that every internal meaning of a finite mind is a unique, though partial, expression of the internal meaning of the Eternal Consciousness. Now there is a basal difficulty here which centers around the 'uniqueness' of the finite internal meanings or purposes. Granting that an Eternal Consciousness exists, as Royce claims, and remembering that *ex hypothesi* its internal meaning is the 'fulfilment' of all finite internal meanings each of which is a 'unique' expression of it in time, we are at once confronted by troublesome questions.

In the first place, what disposition are we to make of mistaken internal meanings, whether as presenting truth-claims or value-claims? It would appear that we are committed to the position that each such mistaken internal meaning is a 'unique,' hence presumably abiding, expression of the internal meaning of the Eternal Consciousness. Hereupon error and evil threaten to engulf us, since finite internal meanings are, perhaps more often than not, mistaken. But, passing this question by, we are met by another even more formidable: What, on our hypothesis, becomes of finite minds within which these finite internal meanings are embedded? This question is, I say, more formidable than that about evil and error, because it strikes at the very roots of the general argument for absolute idealism which we are in this chapter considering—the argument, that is, which seeks to follow the fragmentary character of finite experience out to its ultimate completion. If the situation be as it is here described by Royce, then apparently the argument *a contingentia mundi* is in principle undermined. I wish to draw out the point.

Assuming that each finite internal meaning—"the specific conscious purpose" embodied in the idea "at the instant when it comes to mind"—is a unique expression of the Eternal internal meaning, then apparently any finite mind can in reality be nothing more than the summation of its numerous internal meanings taken *seriatim* in time. Each such internal meaning would seem to be as real as any other, and the entire content of what we call a given finite mind would be only the aggregate of such unique and separate meanings. This, however, at once destroys the 'organic unity' of finite minds, kills the "spirit of totality" within them, and thus removes the logical foundation of the argument from the fragmentariness of finite experiences. On such an atomistic view of finite mind, no finite experience could possibly be fragmentary, it would appear, and there is, therefore, no point at which the "nisus towards the whole" or the drive towards 'fulfilment' could enter. Hereupon we are confronted by the distressing conclusion that if the relation between the Eternal internal meaning and finite internal meanings be as Royce describes it, then the argument which he advances in support of the Eternal Consciousness must be set aside as entirely illusory; the proof of the position is inconsistent with the truth of it.

But, one may well ask, are we not in this criticism forgetting Royce's emphasis on the 'partiality' and 'incompleteness' of finite internal meanings? The answer is: No. We are not forgetting this emphasis, but only trying to follow out the implications of the other emphasis on the 'uniqueness' of each finite internal meaning as an expression of the Eternal internal meaning. The conclusion to which we have apparently been driven is, simply, that the two emphases cannot stand together, and this can equally well be shown by starting from the other emphasis.

Assuming, from this side, that each finite internal meaning is 'partial' only, let us ask about the implications of this assumption. Now, indeed, we have regained the logical ground of the argument *a contingentia mundi* by escaping from the atomistic view of mind in which the other assumption involved us, and restoring within it the "spirit of the whole." But what is the price we have paid? The price, it would appear, of denying in principle the 'uniqueness' not only of all finite internal meanings, but also of all finite minds. No finite internal meaning is, now, a 'unique' expression of the Eternal. It may, indeed, be said to be a 'unique' expression of the internal meaning of finite mind.

But finite mind itself is not 'unique'; it is always the 'partial' embodiment of a more inclusive meaning, and, ultimately, of the internal meaning of the Eternal Consciousness or Mind. No internal meaning, however inclusive, can be absolutely 'unique' or 'really real' save that of Eternal Consciousness. Nor can the doctrine of 'degrees' redeem the situation. What we are after is an internal meaning whose actual embodiment is, as it stands, a unique expression of the Eternal internal meaning; and such an expression is to be found only in that Eternal meaning itself.

The dilemma, thus, seems plain: Either the argument *a contingentia mundi* is without logical foundation, or the ultimate 'uniqueness' of finite internal meanings, and of finite minds also, must be surrendered. The same dilemma may be equally well expressed from the standpoint of the Eternal Consciousness: Either it is a mere aggregate of finite internal meanings, or no finite internal meaning can for it be wholly 'unique.' There is, I think, no difference in principle between these two statements of the dilemma, and both rest on precisely the same considerations.

If the preceding comments on Royce's statement are basically sound, then that statement cannot stand as presented. Its major weakness lies in the emphasis which is placed on the logical priority of internal meaning within the reasoning process. This emphasis, as expressed, seems at times to be developed in forgetfulness of the reiterated insistence on the implicative relationship btween internal and external meanings, and to have for its chief support a terminological distinction. In any event, it does violence to the empirical consideration that internal meaning is only an aspect of a whole of meaning whose development in reflective experience goes through a sort of self-expansion within which the external aspect is generally imperious. Even if the emphasis be granted, however, it fails to establish the conclusion at which Royce is aiming. The passage to the conception of the actual embodiment in individual form of an internal meaning which is inclusive of all finite internal meanings is not justified by the doctrine. If such a conception is assumed, the relation between the Eternal Consciousness, or all-inclusive whole of meaning, and the internal meanings of finite minds presents us with a troublesome dilemma. If the relation is defined as that between a 'partial' and a 'complete' internal meaning, then the uniqueness of finite minds is endangered; if, on the other side, the uniqueness of internal meanings is insisted on, then, not merely the Eternal Consciousness, but finite mind also is threatened with dissolution into atomic elements, and the logical substructure of the entire statement which Royce has given us is rendered quite insecure.

5. A General Difficulty

The preceding sections of this chapter have been concerned primarily with what appear to be the main points of weakness in the statements of the idealistic argument as given by Bradley, Bosanquet, and Royce. Where, we have been asking, have these several statements chiefly failed? In addition to these special difficulties, however, I seem to discover a general one which is common to all of the statements and with which the difficulties above discussed are more or less directly linked. And in the present section I wish to turn to this.

What this more general difficulty is may perhaps best be stated by an analysis of the doctrine of "degrees of reality." This doctrine, as formulated, involves a rather sharp distinction between 'real reality' (the Absolute) and 'degrees' of reality (appearances). By 'real reality' is intended an ontological entity whose detailed characteristics are variously defined and which is not in any sense relative, but is absolute. By 'degrees' of reality, on the other side, are intended 'wholes' which are not absolute, but relative. The contention is that this distinction is a necessary outcome of the premises foundational to the type of argument we are here following. If this contention is run to ground, however, it will be found to resolve itself into the further contention that there are two sorts of the intellect's 'satisfaction,' namely, an absolute satisfaction or satisfaction in general, and a relative satisfaction or satisfaction with reference to a given situation. It is precisely in this further contention that the difficulty of which I am speaking seems to me to lie.

I am not here raising any question concerning the thesis that what satisfies the intellect is alone to be taken as real. On the contrary, this thesis is here, as throughout the preceding discussion, assumed. On the basis of it, the doctrine of 'degrees' of reality seems to stand, since the intellect's satisfaction is, empirically considered, a matter of degrees. My difficulty, therefore, does not concern the doctrine of degrees of truth and reality. It concerns, rather, the conception of 'real reality' as distinct from degrees. And, if I may go at once to the root of the difficulty, it resolves itself into the assumption that intelligence seeks satisfaction in general, or that there is such a thing as an absolute satisfaction of the intellect which the intellect itself strives to attain.

Now I venture to submit that this assumption is not only not warranted by the premises from which it is supposedly derived, but is even contrary to them. And I think the point at issue may be precisely fixed by asking the question: What is the satisfaction which the intellect actually does seek? The answer given to this question by the proponents of the conception here under criticism is that the intellect actually seeks system, that is, a point of view which is both harmonious and comprehensive. To this answer I should raise no objection, provided it be clearly understood, and explicitly granted, that the system, the harmony and comprehensiveness, which the intellect seeks is inseparably linked with a situation which is always specific and not merely general. This proviso seems to me of the first importance and, unless I am mistaken in what seems to me quite clear, it lies against any conception of 'real reality' except as that conception is involved in the doctrine of degrees to such an extent that it could hardly be called absolute in the sense apparently intended.

This proviso is in principle involved in the theory of judgment which lies at the bottom of the argument *a contingentia mundi*, as I understand that theory. According to the theory, as Bradley has very explicitly and judiciously warned us, the real subject of judgment is not the grammatical subject of the verbalization of the judgment, but is reality itself. But what is this 'reality'? Surely it is the total situation within which the ideational process of judging moves; and surely, also, it is always a specific situation. If, then, when seeking its satisfaction judgment is seeking its subject, the satisfaction sought is definable only with reference to a specific situation.

To speak of the intellect's satisfaction as if it were, or may be, quite general, therefore, would appear to contravene the doctrine that such satisfaction is to be found in judgment. Bradley, at least, admits this explicitly in his emphasis on the 'unintelligibility' of the Absolute; and Bosanquet in the end seems to agree in principle. But both thinkers persist in holding also that the conception of the Absolute may in some meaningful sense be said to 'satisfy' the intellect. What I venture to urge is that this position will have to be abandoned, or the theory of judgment with which we started will have to be disavowed. For the position is equivalent to holding that the 'real reality' which ultimately satisfies is not such that it can significantly function as the subject which the judgment seeks in seeking its satisfaction.

Nor am I able, at present at any rate, to see that a way of escape from this difficulty is offered by expanding judgment to the dimensions of 'experience' and then pointing to the fragmentariness of experience. That experience may in principle be thus conceived I am willing to admit, though with some hesitancy arising from the complexities of the issue; and the fragmentariness of experience, in this or any other definition which is empirically warranted, must, I think, be granted. But I fail to see how these admissions lead to the conception of 'real reality' in the sense of the Absolute. For, after all, experience is itself relative, and its 'transcendence' is concretely conceivable only in terms of this relativity. The satisfaction which 'experience' seeks is still *its* satisfaction; and the relativity of this satisfaction is not in principle escaped by the expansion of the core, so to say, in respect of which it is relative. The difficulty is to understand how the Absolute, in its proper character as Absolute, can function as the 'reality' which is the subject of judgment; and this difficulty is apparently wholly independent of the degree of complexity and comprehensiveness of the judgment in question.

There is indeed an insidious danger involved in the notion of 'experience,' and this should be carefully watched. The term itself is generic, but the fact referred to is always specific; and the danger is that the generic character of the term may obscure the specific character of the referent. Thus, it may be supposed that the 'transcendence' of 'experience' is somehow more 'absolute' in its implications than is the 'transcendence' of experiences—such as particular judgments—which are always in some important manner relative. But if one insists on seeing through the terminology and fixing attention on the fact, the relativity of experience itself should not be difficult to discern. Unless this is done, one may readily fall into the error of supposing that, when one speaks of the fragmentariness of experience in general as if it were free of relativity, something besides a merely verbal object is intended.

Thus, to my mind, the notion of 'real reality' as the Absolute cannot be fitted into the compass of the theory of judgment upon which the argument *a contingentia mundi* is founded. If what satisfies the intellect is alone to be called real, then there seems to be no way—other than a mystical one—of escaping the conclusion that reality must always and everywhere possess the status of a 'degree.'

Presumably it is unnecessary to protest that this does not mean, however, that the notion of 'real reality' is theoretically useless. The proponent of the argument we are considering has a perfect right, despite the preceding criticism, to hold to his conception of 'real reality' and his doctrine of degrees. For this criticism has not called in question the ground on which his conception rests—namely, the character of transcendence which belongs to the object in knowledge. The point of the criticism is, rather, that the conception must be modified so as to adapt it to the logical consequences of the relativity of this transcendence.

And, if I understand aright, this is saying no more than what is admitted in principle by the absolutists themselves when they insist, in the language of Bosanquet, that the Absolute ('real reality') is "simply the high-water mark of fluctuations experienced." For this seems to be an admission that the Absolute functions in concrete experience as relevant to its sundry nuances; and this is what I have been urging must be admitted. I have, indeed, urged more. And I have done so, because I am unable to see why this admission does not militate against the other emphasis of the absolutists upon the Absolute's imperviousness to empirical demands. Particularly am I unable to see why in this other emphasis the absolutists are not open to the criticism of forgetting the ground on which alone their conception of the Absolute rests.

6. Concluding Remarks

Throughout this chapter I have proceeded on the assumption that the theory of judgment underlying the argument surveyed is itself not in question. This procedure presumably has the advantage of rendering the criticisms internal to the argument criticized. But it has the disadvantage of limiting the scope of the criticisms. In this concluding section I wish to remedy this deficiency, partly at least, by indicating briefly the main reasons why to my mind the theory cannot in the end be denied.

In the first place, the character of transcendence in the object in knowledge seems to be indispensable to any sound epistemology. And it is so, if I may repeat this, on both empirical and theoretical grounds. It is the matrix of the problematic aspect of cognitive situations, as well as the foundation of the validity and corrigibility of human points of view and interpretations. Apparently no denial of it can escape the charge of being based upon an arbitrary truncation of actual cognitive experience; and apart from it, so far at least as I am able to see, there is no logical way out of the "ego-centric predicament" and its consequent solipsism.[23]

Again, the denial that reality is always the subject in judgment seems to my mind untenable. It amounts to the contention that reality either is never the subject, or is sometimes so and sometimes not so; and in either case difficulties arise. In the first instance, the possibility of any metaphysics, idealistic or

[23] It seems to me that Dewey does scant justice to this character of experience in his recent Howison Lecture on "Thought and Context," with which I am otherwise in essential agreement. What he there says about the fallacy of 'generalisation' is, indeed, quite in the spirit of what I have urged in the preceding section.

other, is in principle negated; and the difficulty is to remain consistently by this position, since such a negation is itself at bottom a sort of metaphysics and thus seems to be self-refuting. Furthermore, there are some judgments whose subjects are the 'given,' and we do on occasion correct erroneous judgments and successfully distinguish between 'illusion' and 'reality.' In the second instance, a sharp division is drawn between types of judgment; and the difficulty here is to justify the distinction. We do, indeed, distinguish between judgments whose subjects are the 'given' and judgments whose subjects are 'postulates'; but it seems very doubtful that this distinction is equivalent to the dichotomy of judgments in question. The 'given' is also in some fairly definite sense 'postulated,' and postulates are also 'given.' There is a necessity implicated in the most arbitrary assumptions—if, that is, they are such that they can function as subjects in judgment—which links such assumptions with a context whose 'reality' is at any rate not a meaningless problem. But the question of the relation between reality and existence remains an open one.

By way of further clarification of the issue here, it should be noted that the view of judgment in question does not involve the denial of the possibility of relational judgments. In the thesis that reality is the subject of every judgment there is no implication that judgments are limited to "the form which ascribes a predicate to a subject," [24] in such a manner that relational judgments are excluded. This might be true if, for example, Bradley's doctrine of 'immediate experience' is left standing. But the integrity of the view of judgment before us is not bound up with the fortunes of that doctrine. It might be set aside, as I have argued above it must be, and the theory of judgment be retained without the slightest inconsistency. The important point to remember in this connection is that, according to the theory, the form of judgment is not that which ascribes a predicate to a subject so much as it is that which ascribes the subject-predicate relationship to a context which is reality. The form is, not 'A is B,' but 'Reality is such that A is B';

[24] The phrase is Russell's. See his *Scientific Method in Philosophy*, p. 45, and note the context.

and this form in itself certainly does not necessarily exclude the possibility that 'Reality is such that A is related to B.'

The inclusive character attributed to 'intelligence' by the theory is a source of danger in philosophical methodology, as I have indicated in the preceding critical remarks on Bosanquet's view of 'centrality' and elsewhere. But, as I have also suggested there, this danger does not seem to my mind insuperable in principle. And I wish here to add that a denial of this inclusive meaning seems to bring formidable difficulties with it. Apparently, it leaves moral and aesthetic experience without a universal criterion of validity, and hence in a state of hopeless relativism. Or if not this, it at least breaks experience in such a fashion that the criterion of values and the criterion of truth are so sharply sundered as to raise pressing problems of their relation—problems which have long been debated in connection with the same dichotomy apparently made by Kant and, in a more uncompromising form perhaps, by the main pre-Kantian tradition in modern philosophy. If one is to reject the theory on this side, one must be cognizant of these consequential difficulties and—what is more important—be prepared to show how in principle they may be satisfactorily resolved. For my part, however, I cannot at present at least clearly see how this may be done.

That the theory of judgment in question here is itself not without difficulties, I am well aware. But to my mind it is essentially sound, and the remarks of this section may serve to indicate the general direction in which analysis of its grounds seems to me to point. It is apart from the main purpose of the present volume to pursue this analysis further, however, and the theory must be left with what support these general observations may furnish.

Chapter XVII

THE ONTOLOGICAL ARGUMENT

In turning to the argument which McTaggart advances in support of what he calls Ontological Idealism—the idealism allied to that of Berkeley and Leibniz and Hegel, not to that of Kant or that of the so-called neo-Hegelian school—we are taking up a very different type of argument from that considered in the preceding chapter. In fact, the two types are in some respects antithetical in their presuppositions. For the one, philosophical speculation is identical with experience which has become self-critical; and in this sense serious philosophical argument must be only empirical. For the other, however, serious philosophical argument eschews empirical considerations as far as possible and aims at being wholly *a priori;* so far as appeal to experience becomes necessary, philosophical argument is to that extent weakened and certainty lapses into mere probability. There, 'satisfactoriness' is basal and is wholly empirical; here, 'consistency' is fundamental and is, or wishes to be, wholly abstract and *a priori.*

Clearly McTaggart's argument departs quite radically from the view of judgment which underlies the arguments of Bradley, Bosanquet and Royce. And, thus, at the very beginning a clear-cut epistemological issue is raised. This is not the occasion, however, to enter upon an extended discussion of the issue, and I shall content myself with two remarks about McTaggart's position.

The first of these is to direct attention to a point which McTaggart himself emphasizes,[1] namely, that on the basis of his view it is theoretically possible to determine the characteristics of existence without raising the question whether anything does actually exist. That this possibility is involved in his view

---

[1] Cf. McTaggart, *The Nature of Existence,* Sections 45, 55. All other foot-notes in this chapter refer to this same volume.

follows from the essentially *a priori* and non-empirical nature of thought, and the further consideration that actual existence can be determined only by an appeal to perception.

My second remark is that, if this be true, as McTaggart admits it is, then there apparently follows the logical impossibility of holding that the characteristics of existence thus determined *a priori* are predicable of actual existence, except through the medium of an unwarranted assumption that thought has an essential empirical reference. For if by hypothesis thought is *a priori* in the sense that it is entirely non-empirical, then the reason why its categories hold true of experience remains utterly mysterious. Nor is the point here based upon a merely verbal foundation. Its genuine significance is attested by the historical fortunes of the distinction in the hands of Kant and his critics. If it be objected that McTaggart's distinction is not that of Kant, I can here only ask where the difference lies, and go on to point to the fact that, whatever McTaggart means by it, he fails to remain consistent with it in the course of his argument. For many of his supposedly *a priori* statements are groundless if the appeal to experience is denied them; and, as we shall observe in the sequel, the crucial step in the argument can be taken only provided the *a priori* nature of thought is abnegated.

Leaving these preliminary remarks and taking the statement of the argument as it stands, we are now to question its stability. But, first, it may be well to remind ourselves of the main theses.

The idealism which he defends, McTaggart tells us, "rests on the assertion that nothing exists but spirit." This assertion, he says, is established, or at least rendered highly probable, by the consideration that, among the supposed substances *prima facie* known to us, spiritual substance alone can escape a fatal contradiction in its nature. The argument in support of this consideration centers round the following theses: Every substance must necessarily have a sufficient description—a description, that is, which is stated in terms of the characteristics (qualities and relations) of the substance, and which applies only to that substance and applies to it in such a manner that the substance is absolutely identified by the description. But every substance has

parts which are substances, and, therefore, every substance is
infinitely divisible. How, then, under this condition, is a sufficient
description of any substance possible? It is possible only on one
condition, namely, that the principle of determining correspondence obtains within substance; in other words, only provided
there is in substance itself the basis for a chain of implications
running downwards from precedent to sequent sets of parts to
infinity. And this must be such that sufficient descriptions of the
precedent sets of parts imply sufficient descriptions of all the
infinite sequent sets of parts. In no other manner can the infinite
series of parts be other than vicious, and a contradiction in the
nature of substance itself be avoided. Therefore, only substance
in which the principle of determining correspondence obtains can
exist. Spiritual substance is the only substance, among those with
which we are *prima facie* acquainted, in which the principle of
determining correspondence holds. Hence substance must be
spiritual, and spirit alone truly exists.

The main theses here are four: every substance must have a
sufficient description; every substance is infinitely divisible into
substances; the principle of determining correspondence must
obtain within substance; and spirit is the only known substance within which the principle of determining correspondence
obtains. We shall determine these in order.

1. SUFFICIENT DESCRIPTION OF SUBSTANCE

The thesis that every substance must necessarily have a
sufficient description is grounded as follows: Every substance
must be dissimilar to all other substances; every substance must,
therefore, have an exclusive description; hence every substance
must have a sufficient description. What, we must inquire, is
to be said of this reasoning?

That every substance must be dissimilar to all other substances may be permitted to stand, since it follows by definition.
Certainly, every substance must have a nature; and, if there
were no differences between the natures of two substances, it is
difficult to see in what respect they could intelligibly be called
two substances. "The substance is made this substance by its
nature, and, if the nature is the same, the substance is the

same." Hence it follows that substances are *eo ipso* diverse and dissimilar, if a plurality of substances is to be admitted.

If substances are diverse and dissimilar, then each substance must have an exclusive description. This position, too, may be allowed to stand. But a consideration in connection with it needs to be emphasized, since it is both crucial for the argument and indicative of a fundamental difficulty. The point here intended to be asserted is, not that no substance without an exclusive description could be *known* to exist as distinguished from other substances, but that "a substance which is not completely similar to any other substance has necessarily an exclusive description." [2] In other words, an exclusive description is implied in the very nature of a substance, whether known, or even knowable, or not.

The crucial character of this point for the argument is disclosed in the step from the necessity of an exclusive description to the necessity of a sufficient description. That step consists in the assertion that, if a substance had no sufficient description, its exclusive description would involve a vicious infinite, and the substance, therefore, would have no exclusive description, that is, would not be dissimilar to all other substances and, so, would not exist. [3]

The argument here is so extraordinarily subtle and complex that one can hardly be certain of having grasped all of the points. But it seems to my mind fairly clear that these, among other things, are asserted: that the possibility and necessity of a sufficient description of substance depends upon the possibility and necessity of an exclusive description of the same substance; that the possibility and necessity of an exclusive description of substance, in its turn, depends upon the dissimilarity of the given substance to all other substances; that the possibility of this, again, depends on the existence of other substances dissimilar to it and to each other; and, finally, that this series of dissimilar

[2] Section 105.
[3] The difference between an exclusive description and a sufficient description, it must be recalled, is that a sufficient description is a special sort of exclusive description—namely, an exclusive description which does not contain undescribed substances, but is entirely in terms of characteristics (that is, qualities and relations).

substances, if infinite in respect of the characteristic of dissimilarity, is a vicious series. Therefore, it is concluded, the series cannot be infinite and substance must have a sufficient description.

The questions of importance in the present context are: What is meant by calling such a series 'vicious'? and: What is the ground for the condemnation implied in the adjective?

A safe point of departure in the search for an answer may be found in McTaggart's own words: "A must be dissimilar to all other substances. The possibility of this depends on the existence of B, and the existence of B depends on its dissimilarity to all other substances. And this depends on the existence of C, and this on its dissimilarity to all other substances, and so on. If this series is infinite, it is vicious. For, starting from the existence of A, each earlier term requires all the later terms, and therefore requires that the series should be completed, which it cannot be. If, therefore, the series is infinite, A cannot be dissimilar to all other substances—cannot, in other words, have an exclusive description—and so cannot exist. Therefore, if A does exist, the series cannot be infinite." [4]

This statement expresses quite clearly why, in its author's opinion, the series cannot be infinite. It cannot be infinite, because it must be completed if a given substance is to be dissimilar to all other substances—as it must be if it exists and if there is a plurality of substances. But why, one is compelled to ask, must the series be *completed?* Unless I am utterly at a loss in my understanding of the matter, the answer involves the author in a position which, on his own showing, is for him intolerable.

The answer itself seems fairly evident, though it is only implicit. The series must be completed, because, unless it is completed at some point, any attempt on our part to understand the dissimilarity of A to all other substances is futile. And I must insist that, if this reference to human knowledge and the attempt to understand is not introduced into the argument, the series on the showing of the argument is nowise 'vicious,' even though infinite. Apart from such reference, the fact that a given sub-

4 Section 105.

stance is dissimilar to an infinite number of other substances involves no difficulty whatsoever. Certainly there is no difficulty in the mere fact—if it be a fact—that any given substance is dissimilar to an infinite series of other substances, and there is no warrant for calling such a series a vicious infinite. It is only when the notion of some sort of knowledge of such dissimilarity, some sort of 'description' of it, is introduced and the effort definitely made to conceive or 'describe' what it could mean, that any difficulties arise in connection with the series, that any demand for its 'completion' appears, or that, if not completed, it may significantly be called 'vicious.'

McTaggart's statement must be amended, then, if its full meaning is to receive formulation. And the purport of the necessary amendment may conveniently be suggested by the following changes (indicated by italics) in the last two sentences: "If, therefore, the series is infinite, A cannot be *known to be* dissimilar to all other substances—cannot, in other words, *be known to* have an exclusive description—and so cannot *be completely known as it* exists. Therefore, if A does exist, *and if the details of its existence are to be adequately understood by minds like ours,* the series cannot be infinite."

It is, of course, true that McTaggart denies that the necessity for a substance to have an exclusive description rests "on the ground that, without an exclusive description, no one could know it as so to distinguish it from other substances. Such an argument," he insists, "would be invalid on three grounds. In the first place, there seems no necessity that every substance should be capable of being known so as to distinguish it from other substances, since they can be different substances without being known to be different. In the second place, an exclusive description may . . . consist of an infinite number of qualities, in which case it could not be known by minds like ours. In the third place, a substance when directly perceived is known as distinguished from other substances without any description of it being required." [5] For these reasons, then, the question whether an exclusive description may by us be known is entirely irrelevant to its necessity.

[5] Section 105.

Granting that this is true of exclusive description, the question whether it holds of a sufficient description still remains. And there is no clear evidence that it does. So far as exclusive description is concerned, the author here frankly admits that "it may consist of an infinite number of qualities" and that, at least by implication, there is no necessity of the 'completion' of the infinite series. Therefore, it would seem, exclusive description does not contemplate a 'vicious' infinite; our knowledge is not involved in its definition. But the case is otherwise with sufficient description; it arises out of the necessity of the 'completion' of the series, and apart from this necessity the notion of sufficient description has no logical ground. Hence it does not follow that knowledge is not foundational within sufficient description, merely because it is not foundational within exclusive description. Everything which McTaggart here urges about exclusive description may be granted, then, without affecting what has been said above about sufficient description.

Nevertheless, the logical relation between the two conceptions is not quite that which McTaggart maintains it is. He insists that the necessity of an exclusive description is the ground of his demonstration that every substance must have a sufficient description. What his demonstration amounts to, however, is simply the contention that there can be no exclusive description unless there is a sufficient description. Unless the series is completed, he says in the quotation above which states the demonstration of the necessity of sufficient description, "A cannot be dissimilar to all other substances—cannot, in other words, have an exclusive description—and so cannot exist." And this, I submit, is equivalent to saying that the logical possibility of a sufficient description is prerequisite to the logical possibility of an exclusive description. The *demonstration* of the necessity of a sufficient description of substance is, on this showing, the basis of the possibility of an exclusive description, and not *vice versa* as is claimed by the author. What is said—if I may repeat this for emphasis —is that there must be a sufficient description if there is to be an exclusive description, and not that there must be an exclusive description if there is to be a sufficient description.

Now, of course, in a certain sense McTaggart's contention that exclusive description is prior to sufficient description holds true —in the sense, namely, in which sufficient description is by definition a special sort of exclusive description. The two stand related somewhat as genus and species, the differentia being that exclusive description may involve undescribed substances whereas sufficient description is an exclusive description put wholly in terms of 'characteristics.' But the important point here before us concerns 'demonstration' of each. And, at least so far as the argument immediately in hand is concerned, the possibility of exclusive description is implied by the possibility of sufficient description, and not the other way around.

Thus it turns out that, despite the author's assurance that the necessity of exclusive description is in no wise connected with the fact of knowledge, since it arises from the nature of substance itself, the 'possibility' of it at least is intimately bound up with the fact of knowledge. For its 'possibility' rests on the 'necessity' of sufficient description, in the sense that a substance cannot have an exclusive description without a sufficient description; and we have seen reason for holding that the fact of knowledge is foundational within the 'necessity' of sufficient description. In short, exclusive description is a 'necessary' feature of substance even though it be such as "could not be known by minds like ours," and yet there can be no exclusive description of substance unless it be featured also by sufficient description, whose 'necessity' arises out of the fact that the infinite series involved in substance cannot be 'vicious,' cannot, that is, be uncompleted. This fact seems to be wholly without foundation unless knowledge "by minds like ours" is introduced into the situation. Exclusive description, therefore, appears to be both founded on the fact of knowledge and also entirely independent of it.

It is curious that McTaggart should have fallen into what has the appearance of being a flat self-contradiction during the course of his discussion of the description of substances. One darkly suspects that the reason lies in the dual consideration that his method requires him to speak of 'substance' as if it were utterly objective and 'ontological' while he, like the rest of us, is of necessity bound to deal with it as a category of the human mind. What he aims to prove, and by his method is obliged to prove, is that exclusive description and sufficient description belong to the existence of substance *per se.* What he actually proves, and in the nature of the case can only prove, is that such 'descriptions' belong to substance in so far as substance is an object of knowledge for human beings—in so far, that is, as it can by us be adequately 'described.' And one is perhaps not far wrong in suggesting that the whole difficulty rests in the ambiguity of the term 'description.'

The reader will, of course, understand that the preceding criticism is not directed against McTaggart's having made knowledge here logically foundational. It is directed, rather, against his having failed explicitly to recognize that he has done so and that in the nature of the case he could not do otherwise. It amounts, in short, to the contention that he is overtly attempting to do what seems to be logically impossible, and what *is* logically impossible if, for example, Royce's doctrine of the relationship between 'internal meanings' and 'external meanings' is in principle sound. The further suggestion is not irrelevant that the lesson of that doctrine is here the basal issue. If the method of metaphysics is 'ontological' in McTaggart's sense of the term, then the meanings with which metaphysics deals and which constitute its exclusive content are 'external' merely; and the question remains whether there are any such meanings.

With reference to the first thesis of McTaggart's statement, then, it may be permitted to stand provided the 'substance' whose sufficient 'description' is in question is explicitly recognized as being identical with an object of knowledge, and is not, even implicitly, supposed to be a 'substance' *per se,* or to have a merely 'external' meaning. This modification of the statement does, indeed, radically affect the underlying assumption that the method it exemplifies is *a priori.* But, when the connotation of the term 'substance' is changed as indicated, I do not see why the thesis that every substance must have a sufficient description is adversely affected by the preceding criticism. In this interpretation, therefore, the first thesis seems to stand. And we now pass to a consideration of the second, namely, that every substance is infinitely divisible into substances.

2. Infinite Divisibility of Substance

The proof of this thesis, like that of the first, passes through three main steps.

That some substances have parts which are substances is proved by the following considerations. Any group—for example, the group of counties of Great Britain—is a collection formed either of substances, or of collections of substances, or of both. A is a group, if it is a collection of B, C, D, etc., where B, C, D, etc., are substances or collections of substances. But any group is itself a substance, since it has qualities and is related but itself is neither a quality nor a relation.[6] Hence it follows at once that at least some substances have parts which are substances. If, for convenience of reference, we call such substances 'compound' substances, we may say, shortly, that some substances are compound.

But are all substances necessarily compound? The answer must be affirmative. If a substance is not compound, then it must be simple. A simple substance, however, cannot have content, since the content of a substance is precisely that plurality which is identical in different sets of parts and no simple substance can have sets of parts.[7] A simple substance, therefore, is a substance without content. But there can be no substance without content. That such is the case is a synthetic proposition, since the conclusion is not implied in the definition. Nevertheless, the proposition is both self-evident and ultimate. "It is self-evident, because it does not need proof; and it is ultimate because it cannot be proved from any proposition more clearly self-evident."[8] So we may take it as certainly established that there can be no simple substance, and that every substance is, therefore, necessarily compound.

[6] The reader will recall that this is the definition of substance. See Section 67, and elsewhere.

[7] "A Set of Parts of any whole is any collection of its parts which together make up the whole, and do not more than make it up, so that the whole would not be made up if any of those parts, or of their parts, should be subtracted. Thus England, Scotland, and Wales are a set of parts of Great Britain. So are all the counties in Great Britain. And so are England, Scotland, and the counties within Wales." (Section 124.)

[8] Section 167. In the Sections immediately following this one, McTaggart presents considerations which tend to clarify and bolster his argument at this point; but he deems positive proof of the point impossible.

That every substance is necessarily infinitely divisible follows immediately from the above conclusion. For if every substance is compound, it necessarily has parts; and, therefore, it has an unending series of sets of parts, since any part in any set will also be a substance which has sets of parts, each of which will have fresh sets of parts *ad infinitum*. Hence, a compound substance is necessarily infinitely divisible.

A critical examination of this argument must be centered upon the two notions of 'parts' and 'content' of substance. Clearly, these are indicative of points which are fundamental for the argument, and they must be examined with some care.

In connection with the notion of 'parts' of substance, one must carefully note, in the first place, that it is derived entirely by definition. Groups have parts, and groups are by definition substances; therefore, so the argument runs, some substances have parts. In the second place, it must be noted that the identification of a part with a substance, so that one may say that the part of a substance is itself a substance, is also arrived at merely by definition. Groups, by definition, have parts which are either substances or collections of substances or both. Summarized, then, the argument in support of 'compound' substances—that is, substances which have substances for their parts—amounts to this: By definition, a group is a substance; by definition, the parts of a group are substances; therefore, some substances are compound, or have parts which are themselves substances.

So far as I can see, there is nothing to be said about this sort of argument, except to indicate clearly its nature and the precise conclusion which 'follows' from it. It is a purely analytical argument in the worst sense of the word: given such and such definitions of a group and of the parts of a group, then a group is a substance which has substances for its parts. Presumably no one can gainsay this, however unconvincing it may be as an argument. But it is important to make explicit what the 'argument' proves. Granting the definitions, it proves precisely this: Any substance has parts which are substances, *in so far as a substance is to be identified with a group*. And the limitation indicated here by italics must be carefully borne in mind.

Thus limited, however, the conclusion is not equivalent to the thesis which is essential for McTaggart's ultimate purpose. The thesis wanted is that all possible substances necessarily have parts which are substances; for on this thesis alone rest the infinite divisibility of substance, the consequent need of the principle of determining correspondence, and the final conclusion that this principle holds only within spiritual substance. McTaggart, of course, sees clearly enough that the preceding analysis of groups and their parts is not sufficient to meet this further requirement, and that something more is demanded. How he supplies the deficiency we must now inquire.

The argument by which he undertakes to establish this further conclusion is, naturally, very ingenious, but in the end it remains to my mind unsatisfactory. The argument proceeds from the (supposedly proved) proposition, 'Some substances—namely, those which are groups—have parts which are substances,' to the desired proposition, 'All substances whatsoever have parts which are substances,' through the medium of the notion of 'content' of substance. In examining the argument, therefore, it is first of all necessary to be clear concerning the meaning of that notion.

"By Content," McTaggart says in his definition, "I mean that plurality which is identical in the different sets of parts of a group. England, Scotland, and Wales are one set of parts of Great Britain, the counties are another, the parishes and extra-parochial places another. . . . And yet we realize that there is a certain identity between them so that in taking the set of counties and the set of parishes we are not taking two realities, but the same reality over again. It is this that I mean by Content." [9] This, presumably, is clear enough, and calls for no comment other than the remark—which, for our later considerations, is quite pertinent—that the notion of 'content' is here defined exclusively with reference to a group.

Now, on the basis of this notion, the following argument is constructed to prove that no substance can be simple. Every substance must have content, since it is self-evident that a substance without content cannot exist; hence there can be no simple substance, and every substance must be compound—that is, every substance must have parts which are substances. But this argu-

[9] Section 125.

ment is not only unconvincing, it is plainly circular. The whole point of the argument is assumed in the very first premise. If every substance must have content and content be as defined, then 'every substance must be a group' is not proved but assumed; it must be a group, that is, compound, by definition. The question is whether it must have content in the sense in which a group has content, and this question is nowhere answered.

So the further thesis needed for McTaggart's later argument is not established. What he has shown here is simply that any substance which has content, in the sense in which that substance which is a group has content, is infinitely divisible; in other words, that any substance which is a group is infinitely divisible. The thesis wanted, however, is that every substance is infinitely divisible; and the proof of this has not been supplied. Granting that every substance must necessarily have content, it still remains to be proved that that content must be expressed in sets of parts *ad infinitum*.

There is another peculiar twist to McTaggart's argument from group to substance. Having made use of the notion of group and its content to establish, as he thinks, the infinite divisibility of substance, he then rejects the identification of group with substance, at least to the extent of denying that every different group is a different substance. And this denial calls for analysis, since it directs attention to another difficulty which concerns the relation between 'content' and 'parts' of substance.

The denial is plainly enough stated. "Every group, then, is a substance, but is every different group a different substance? The group of the counties of Great Britain and the group of the parishes of Great Britain are different groups. But, as we have seen, they have the same content. Shall we say that they are different substances because they are different groups, or the same substance because they have the same content?" To this question he gives the unequivocal answer: "It seems clear to me that we ought to say that they are the same substance. There is only one difference between them—of two sets of parts, which they both have, one set is the set of members of one group, and the other is the set of members of the other group. This difference only applies to their nature as groups, and does not go beyond it; and, while it certainly prevents their being one group, does not affect the question whether they are one substance. On the other hand, the identity of the substance does seem to be bound up with the identity of content." [10]

Now I am frankly at a loss to understand how on any strict interpretation it is logically possible for the two parts of this statement to stand together without contradiction. If every group is a substance and every substance is dissimilar to every other substance, then how two groups may be the same substance is simply beyond my power to conceive. To say that they are the same substance, though different groups, is, so far at least as I am able to see, equivalent in the premises to saying that two substances are at once different and the same. And unless this is a formal contradiction, I am unable to comprehend why it is not one. Of course I can see, if I may make use of the time-honored example, that there is no contradiction between the assertion that every Hottentot is a man and the denial that every clever Hottentot is a clever man; but I must insist that this is due to a subtle shift in the meaning of the term 'man' from the one statement to the other. After all, the clever Hottentot is a clever man, in the sense in which the Hottentot is a man. And there is, obviously I should suppose, a contradiction between the assertion that every Hottentot is a man and the denial that every different Hottentot is a different man—unless, once more, there is some shift in the connotation of the term 'man.'

This homely example may give us a clue to understanding why McTaggart does not see any such contradiction between his two statements as I insist is there. In the first statement, that every group is a substance, he is thinking of substance merely as that which has qualities and is related without itself being either a quality or a relation. However, in the second statement that not every different group is a different substance, he is adding a further qualification to the notion of substance—namely, identity of content. In the first meaning, every group clearly is a substance; in the second meaning, equally clearly, not every different group is a different substance. Thus, if the shift is permitted, formal contradiction between the two statements is avoided.

[10] Section 128.

But hereupon the argument in support of the infinite divisibility of substance is undermined. That argument, it must be recalled, turns primarily on two considerations: that every group is a substance all of whose parts are substances, and that the 'parts' of the group as a substance and the 'contents' of the group as a substance are so linked that 'parts' may be inferred directly from 'content.' Now I submit that the shift in meaning of 'substance' necessary to avoid the charge of formal contradiction between the two parts of the author's statement negates in principle both of these considerations. And I wish briefly to justify this assertion.

The definition of substance in terms of identity of content involves the ultimate denial that any group which can be considered as a 'part' of another group is a substance, and, conversely, it involves the ultimate affirmation that the only group which can be said to be a substance is the group which can in no sense be a 'part' of another group—is, in short, presumably the 'universe.' To take the example from which McTaggart builds his proof that not every different group is a different substance—if the counties of Great Britain and the parishes of Great Britain cannot be different substances because they have the same content, then as parts of Great Britain they are not substances because as parts they have no content at all. Their content is in fact that of Great Britain itself, which alone in this case is the substance. But it, too, forthwith loses its substantiality, since it in turn is a part of a set of parts of the British Empire, and substantiality must of necessity pass on to that. In the end substantiality passes to the 'universe,' which alone has a content of its own in its capacity of a group which is never a part. In this meaning of the term, thus, it would appear that only the universe is a substance, and none of its parts can be.

If, however, we take the other meaning of substance, as that which is neither a quality nor a relation but has qualities and is related, then every group is a substance and every part of a group to infinity is likewise a substance. But, since no two substances can have the same content and remain two, it would apparently follow that no inference can be made from the content of one substance to the content of another. Hence, if those substances which are groups have parts, this is no basis for making any inference whatsoever about substances which are not groups. So it turns out, on this interpretation of substance, that merely because one substance with a content has parts is no ground for holding that any substance with content must have parts. The contents are by hypothesis different, and what is true of one may not be true of another. In short, on this interpretation there is among substances no identity of content at all, and there is consequently no basis of inference from one to the other.

Indeed, I think the point here may be pressed even further. Not only is there no basis of inference from the content of one substance to that of another, but also there is no basis of inference from the content to the parts of one and the same substance. Because the substance A has a content is no ground for arguing that it has parts, since the content belongs to the substance and not to the parts as parts. In other words, a substance may have content without any implication whatsoever that it has parts; if it has parts, they are 'accidents' and not 'essences.' Here, however, we touch upon another side of McTaggart's conception of substance, which will concern us in our study of his principle of determining correspondence; and further consideration of it may be postponed to that context.

Presumably enough has been said to justify serious doubt whether McTaggart has proved the infinite divisibility of substance. His argument proceeds through two meanings of 'substance,' and on neither meaning will it render the necessary conclusion that every substance has parts which are substances. On the first meaning, defined in terms of content, no parts of a substance can possibly be substances, and apparently in the end only one substance is possible. On the second meaning, defined in terms of uniqueness, the fact that one substance has parts which are substances is no guarantee that all have. Furthermore, strictly speaking, no substance can be a part of anything else, and what is a part is not substantial. On the one meaning, substance is not infinitely divisible into substances because everything must be a 'part' of one substance; and, on the other meaning, it is not so, because no substance can be a 'part' of any other substance. On the one side, we can have, at most, an infinite series of 'parts'; and on the other side, a concatenation of infinite substances.

What is called for, clearly, is a consistent usage of terms. If not every different group is a difference substance, then surely no group, save only that which is not a part of any other group, is a substance strictly taken. But if no group which is also a part is strictly a substance, then no proof has been given by the argument that even *some* substances—to say nothing of *all*—have parts which are substances. And if substance is to be identified with identity of content, the question seems inevitable whether the logic of the situation then arising differs from that of the system of Spinoza, and wherein it differs if it does so. But we must leave this phase of the argument and turn to the third thesis, which is the principle of determining correspondence.

3. Determining Correspondence

A preliminary consideration is necessary to pave the way for a critical evaluation of the principle of determining correspondence. And that concerns the very important distinction which McTaggart draws, and makes much use of in his formulation of the principle, between substance and its 'nature.' This is the distinction which I referred to a page or so back, and it seems to me essentially the same as the distinction there noted between the 'content' of substance and its 'parts.'

The nature of a thing is defined as follows: "Since any two or more qualities form a compound quality, all the qualities possessed by any particular thing form a compound quality. And this compound quality may be called the Nature of that thing." [11] The important point to note here, and bear in mind throughout this discussion, is that the 'nature' of a thing is made up of, constituted by, its qualities; all of its qualities form the compound quality which is identical with its nature. We are further informed that "if there was no difference between the nature of two things, they would be exactly similar"; that "the nature of a substance expresses completely what the substance is"; and that "the substance is made this substance by its nature, and, if the

[11] Section 64.

nature is the same, the substance is the same." [12] We are also at
the same time instructed to draw a sharp distinction between
substance and the nature of substance. Qualities, we are told for
example, "are a manifestation of the nature of the substance, and
not of the substance itself." [13] After we have been introduced to
the notion of 'parts' of substance through the discussion of
groups as indicated above, we are cautioned carefully to distinguish "between the manifestation of the whole and the manifestation of the nature of the whole. A is manifested in the
substances which are the parts of A, while the nature of A is
manifested in the qualities of A, which are parts of that nature
. . . it is obvious that the parts of a substance are substances,
while the parts of the nature of a substance are qualities." [14]

Thus, we are asked to accept three propositions. The first is
that substance and its nature are quite distinct; the nature of
substance is the compound quality formed by all of its qualities,
while the substance is—itself. The second proposition is that
the nature of a substance expresses completely and adequately
what the substance itself is, or that the substance is made this
substance by its nature. And the third proposition is that a given
quality is a 'manifestation' [15] of the nature of a substance,
but not of the substance itself; a substance is 'manifested' only
in the substances which are its 'parts.'

This threefold creed is made foundational within the formulation of determining correspondence. Whether it may serve in
this capacity will be discussed below. For the moment, the compossibility of the items of the creed and the implication of it
with reference to the relation between substance and its qualities
alone concern us.

[12] Sections, 93, 94.
[13] Section 114.
[14] Section 144. The point which McTaggart has primarily in mind in this
passage is the determination of the meaning of 'manifestation.' And in his
discussion of the point he takes it for granted that the distinction between
substance and its nature is an obvious and important one. This fact makes
the passage all the more significant for the present purpose.
[15] "By Manifestation I mean nothing more than the relation between a
whole and its parts, when the emphasis is placed on the unity of the whole
rather than the plurality of the parts, so that the parts are regarded as due
to the differentiation of the whole rather than the whole as due to the
union of the parts." (Section 114.)

In the first place, it is to be observed that a difficulty arises from the first two propositions when taken together. If substance and its nature are logically distinct, one is at a loss to understand why this is not contradicted by the assertion that a substance is made what it is by its nature. On the basis of the distinction, it seems clear enough that a given quality is a "manifestation of the nature of substance and not of the substance itself." But how this can be, if the nature of substance makes substance what it is, is by no means clear. For the nature of a substance is, by definition, the totality of its qualities; and if the substance "is made this substance by its nature," how is it logically possible to hold that any given quality, which by hypothesis 'manifests' the nature of substance, does not also 'manifest' substance itself? It would appear impossible to maintain that a quality which manifests a totality of qualities does not also manifest that which is made what it is precisely, and presumably exclusively, by that totality—unless, of course, there is in the term *manifestation* some magic, not evident in its definition, whereby it can successfully bridge a contradiction.

But let us pass this by, and assume that the distinction between substance and its nature stands as defended. How are we thereby benefitted? Apparently, we now have on our hands the old puzzle about substance *per se* and its attribute *per se*. And there seems to be no reason to hold that in this newer form the puzzle is any more soluble than it was in the older. In principle it is the same abstraction which puts all the contents on one side, leaving the other blank; and when thought tries to envisage that emptiness, it is simply balked or stealthily transfers the empty conception to the other side. If substance is different from its nature, then what content can it possibly have? Or, if it has content, then how can it differ from its nature?

Nor can I see that McTaggart escapes the dilemma by the device of asserting that the content of substance is made up of the substances which are its 'parts,' while the nature of substance is made up of qualities. This, he says, is 'obvious.' But that such is the case may certainly be seriously doubted; and, if it be the case, the principle of determining correspondence is wrecked. Elaboration of these two points will serve the double purpose of linking the point here with what has already been said about the 'parts' of substances, and of leading us into the heart of the next stage in the argument.

With reference to the first point, it is sufficient to refer back to what has been developed in the discussion of McTaggart's argument in support of the infinite divisibility of substance. As we have there seen, the conception of substances as 'parts' of substances is derived from an ambiguous relationship between substance and group. The two are identified for the purpose of deriving the proposition that *some* substances have substances for their parts; and the identification is then denied in principle, in order, on the one side, to avoid the embarrassing conclusion that two different substances may have the same content —a conclusion which, of course, undermines the doctrine of the dissimilarity of substances—and, on the other side, to lay the foundation for the desired universal proposition that *all* substances have substances for their parts. All of this we have discussed in some detail, and there is nothing to be gained by repeating the discussion here. It is here important, however, to insist that the instability of the distinction between substance and its nature is essentially that of the distinction between substance and its parts. In both alike the basal issue is the conception of substance itself. Defined as an exclusive 'punctual' center of content, it can neither be a 'part' of another substance or have a substance for its 'part,' nor can it possess a 'nature' by which it "is made" what it is. If, however, it has substances for its parts, its atomic 'uniqueness' is thereby shattered and it threatens forthwith to dissolve into its 'nature.'

But let us leave these difficulties on one side, for the moment, and assume that substance is distinct from its nature in the sense that what 'manifests' its nature does not 'manifest' *it*, and that it is 'manifested' only in its parts which by hypothesis are substances. Such an assumption, I repeat, undermines the principle of determining correspondence. And I wish now to develop this point.

First of all, a word is necessary to remind us what the principle of determining correspondence is. In its detailed statement that principle is indeed quite complicated, as is evident from the summary given in the preceding part of this study. Fortunately, however, the side of the principle which is here in question is relatively simple, and is adequately presented by the author's summary definition of the principle. The definition is as follows: "A relation between a substance C and the part of a substance B is a relation of determining correspondence if a certain sufficient description of C, which includes the fact that it is in that relation to *some* part of B, (1) intrinsically determines a sufficient description of the part of B in question, B!C, and (2) intrinsically determines sufficient description of each member of a set of parts of B!C, and each member of a set of parts of each of such members, and so on to infinity." [16] And to this definition the author adds, in a footnote, this important and quite significant warning: "The determining correspondence, which is a relation between the two substances, is, of course not to be confounded with the relation of intrinsic determination, which is a relation between certain sufficient descriptions of the two substances."

The principle of determining correspondence, then, is a relation between substances, such that a sufficient description of one substance, which includes the fact that it is in that relation to some part of another substance, intrinsically determines a sufficient description both of the part of the other substance in question and of the parts of that part to infinity. Now it is my contention that this principle is insecurely grounded, if the distinction between substance and its 'nature' is as described above —namely, such that qualities "are the manifestations of the nature of substance, and not of the substance itself."

To see the difficulty, one has but to recall two things: First, that the relation of determining correspondence is a relation between substances and not between qualities of substance; second, that 'sufficient description' and 'intrinsic determination' refer exclusively to qualities and relations, and that the latter means nothing but a relation between the qualities X and Y corresponding to the relation of implication between the two propositions of the statement, 'something has the quality X

[16] Section 202.

implies that something has the quality Y.' [17] Recalling these two facts, one cannot but ask: Upon what logical ground can the principle of determining correspondence rest? And, to put it mildly, the answer to such a question is not clear.

The trouble, concisely put, is that the relation of determining correspondence and the relation of intrinsic determination run in parallel lines, between which, so far as the premises go there is no implicative attachment; and, yet, the implicative attachment is essential for the principle. Determining correspondence is a relation among substances, and intrinsic determination is a relation among qualities; but intrinsic determination among qualities, or among sufficient descriptions of qualities, is supposed somehow to guarantee the correspondence among substances, and for this guarantee no authority seems available.

I do not know that the point of the criticism can be made any clearer nor the warrant for it any sounder by laboring the matter. But it is so important that I will venture to dwell on it for a moment longer in the hope that repetition may aid clarity. The hypothesis is that a certain sufficient description of the qualities of a substance will imply other sufficient descriptions of the qualities of other substances to infinity; and the assumption is that this implicative relationship among the sufficient descriptions of qualities carries with it, or somehow involves, a corresponding relationship among the substances of whose qualities this intrinsic determination holds true.

The difficulty is to find within the premises a ground for this assumption, and that difficulty springs from the separation between substance and its nature implied in the distinction between 'parts' and 'qualities' and in the insistence that substance is 'manifested' only in its 'parts' and not at all in its 'qualities.' So long as this distinction remains, the ground for the assumption is lacking, and the principle of determining correspondence is quite insecurely based. Even though a sufficient description of substance C implies a sufficient description of the part of B which is also a part of C and of all subsequent parts of B!C, the mere fact that the one sufficient description implies the others offers no ground whatsoever for inferring

[17] Sections 102, 108.

any relationship between the several substances—not even that any one is a 'part' of any other, except, of course, in the case of C and C!C where the latter is by a definition a part of the former.

If, then, the principle of determining correspondence is to hold, the sharp separation between substance and its nature must be given up and the statement, "the nature of substance completely expresses what the substance is," must be taken at its face value. Hereupon, however, the principle meets a serious obstacle on the other side, and this must now be indicated.

A concise statement of the difficulty may be helpful as preliminary to elaboration of it. If the nature of substance and substance itself are to be identified in the sense demanded by the principle of determining correspondence—that is in the sense in which intrinsic determination among qualities of substances is logically equivalent to a relation of determination among the substances themselves—then the principle of determining correspondence depends upon the possibility of an intrinsic determination among qualities such that a sufficient description of the nature of one substance implies all of its qualities and all of the qualities of all of its parts to infinity. And such a possibility is, on the author's own showing, entirely lacking.

In elaboration of this statement, attention must be fixed upon the two central points: first, intrinsic determination among *all* the qualities of a given substance; and, second, intrinsic determination among *all* the qualities of different substances so far as they are to stand in the relation of determining correspondence. But, before passing to the consideration of these, it may be well to emphasize the logical need of each.

That both sorts of intrinsic determination are needed for the principle of determining correspondence follows at once from the nature of the principle itself. It presupposes that there is a sufficient description of a given substance which intrinsically determines a sufficient description of a given part of that substance and sufficient descriptions of each member of the set of parts of that part and of each member of a set of parts of each of such members to infinity. A 'sufficient description,' it will be remembered, is an exclusive description stated in terms of characteristics of a given substance; it thus applies to only one substance, and it completely identifies it. Therefore, in the first place, the characteristics stated in the sufficient description of the substance must intrinsically determine what that substance is—that is, on the basis of the assumption on which we are here proceeding, must intrinsically determine the nature of the substance or the totality of its qualities; otherwise, the substance would not be exclusively described and the description, therefore, not a sufficient description. In the second place it necessarily follows that the sufficient description of the substance in question must intrinsically determine all of the qualities of all of the substances standing in the relation of determining correspondence to the substance given, since by hypothesis it intrinsically determines all of the sufficient descriptions of all of these sequent substances. Thus, if "the nature of substance completely expresses what the substance is" then the principle of determining correspondence can stand only provided the sufficient description of the substance with which we begin intrinsically determines all of its qualities and all of the qualities of each member of its sets of parts and of each member of the sets of parts of each of such members to infinity. Otherwise, the series of substances is 'vicious,' and it does not constitute a series standing in the relation of determining correspondence.

Turning now to the question whether intrinsic determination obtains among the qualities of the same substance, we note, in the first place, that some qualities of the same substance do stand in this relation to each other. "The occurrence of blueness as a quality of anything intrinsically determines the occurrence of spatiality as a quality of the same thing." And other examples of the same sort might be given, if one is to appeal to experience. But the point may be established *a priori* on the basis of the nature of substance itself. "Every substance, for example, has the quality of having qualities, and the quality of standing in relations. And each of these qualities is intrinsically determined by the other. For everything which has a quality must stand in a relation—its relation to that quality. And everything which stands in a relation must have a quality—the quality of being a term in that relation." Nevertheless, it is also

clear that "every quality of a substance . . . does not intrinsically determine every other." [18] Some qualities are merely "contingent" in respect of other qualities; for example, the occurrence of blueness as a quality of a thing does not intrinsically
determine the occurrence of hardness as a quality of the same
thing, and if hardness in the thing occurs it is contingent in
respect of blueness. Or, to use the author's example, "dissimilarity to B is contingent to substantiality, for B itself is a substance,
while it is not dissimilar to itself."

The same in principle holds of intrinsic determination among
the qualities of different substances. Qualities in one substance
may intrinsically determine qualities in other substances, but
this is by no means true of all qualities. For instance, "If it is
a quality of one person to be a husband, this determines the
occurrence in some one else of the quality of being a wife";
but, clearly, there are many qualities in the one not intrinsically
determined by qualities in the other. Or, again, to return to
'a priori' considerations, the quality of substantiality in one substance S intrinsically determines the quality of dissimilarity to
S in all other substances; but dissimilarity to any other substance by any other, to X by Y, is not intrinsically determined
by the substantiality of S but is contingent thereto.

Now, if all of this is true as seems to be admitted by the
author, then it certainly appears to do violence to the principle of determining correspondence. For, on the supposition
we are here making, there is no intrinsic determination among
all the qualities of one and the same substance as a ground
even for a significant sufficient description of that substance.
The only sufficient description we could offer would be some
such abstract description as "the most powerful of all beings"

[18] Section 108. Of course, McTaggart insists on another sort of determination, which he calls 'extrinsic' determination, and which obtains among
all qualities of a substance. But it is not the sort of determination which is
basal in the principle of determining correspondence, since "there is no
implication in this new sort of determination." Furthermore, strictly speaking, it is impossible on the basis of the assumption upon which our discussion is here proceeding. For extrinsic determination confessedly holds
"not between two qualities as such, but between two qualities in virtue
of the relation in which they stand to substance"; and our present
assumption is that there is no such significant difference between substance and the totality of its qualities, as is here supposed.

which, as the author admits, is largely meaningless and could not be known by us apart from very much other knowledge. Certainly it is not significant enough to serve as the basis of implication concerning other qualities of the substance, for instance, whether it is virtuous or vicious, God or the devil. And any description which gives such meager information about the substance in question could be called 'sufficient' and could be said to identify it 'absolutely' only in some highly esoteric sense. It certainly could not serve as a promising point of departure for fruitful inference.

Again, the chain of implication from the sufficient description of one substance to sufficient descriptions of its parts to infinity appears to be cut asunder at the very first link. For there apparently is no ground for holding that the sufficient description of any substance can intrinsically determine the nature of any other substance. Nor is the situation modified by the introduction of the relation of 'part' between one substance and the other—not modified, that is, if we are to hold steadfast to the view that the nature of the substance makes the substance what it is. For on that view, the relation of part is derivative and not prior. The problem is to define it in terms of the relation of intrinsic determination between the qualities of one substance and those of another substance which, as thus determined, is to be called a 'part' of the first. And the problem seems to be insoluble, since the relation of intrinsic determination fails to hold between the sufficient descriptions of the substances in question.

Thus, from this side also, the principle of determining correspondence seems to be unstable. If substance is made what it is by its nature, that is, by its totality of qualities, where is the basis of the principle of determining correspondence? This is the question we were to answer. And the answer seems to be: There is none. There is no linkage of intrinsic determination among qualities, whether of the same substance or of different substances, such as the principle presupposes. A sufficient description of a substance cannot intrinsically determine the totality of its qualities, or the totality of the qualities of any other substance even though such a substance be one of its 'parts.' Thus, if substance is to be identified with its nature and its nature with the totality of qualities, the principle of determining correspondence seems to break down.

I have purposely framed the preceding criticism of the principle of determining correspondence so as to emphasize what seems to me the basal difficulty in McTaggart's conception of substance—namely, the difficulty of harmonizing the *a priori* and empirical aspects of the conception. On the one side, substance is conceived as itself, and as so conceived it is somehow different from its empirical nature; on the other side, it is conceived as having an empirical nature, and as thus conceived it is denied "an individuality apart and distinct from its nature." [19] Nor, so far as I can follow him at least, does McTaggart succeed in bringing these two sides of the conception into harmony with each other; on the contrary, he seems to shift from one to the other as the exigencies of the argument require. And on neither side may the principle of determining correspondence find a logical basis. Conceived as *a priori*, substance is not touched by the implicative determination among qualities. Conceived as empirical, the implication among qualities is not sufficiently thoroughgoing and comprehensive to form the sort of implicative chain that is necessary. If I am mistaken in all of this, my mistake may at least serve to direct attention to points of fundamental significance in the principle of determining correspondence and thus indirectly aid in the clarification of the principle itself. If I am not mistaken, the principle stands revealed as lacking a logical foundation.

One final comment on the principle is called for in respect of the function which it performs in the argument as a whole. And, despite the fact that this comment is only a repetition of what has already been said above in connection with the conception of 'sufficient description,' it is specially pertinent here and its repetition in this context is not fruitless.

The function of the principle of determining correspondence in McTaggart's argument as a whole is that it alone serves to redeem the infinite divisibility of substance from 'viciousness.' If substance is infinitely divisible and if every substance must

[19] Section 95.

have a sufficient description, then, we are told, the problem
arises concerning the compossibility of these two necessary properties of substance. Can infinitely divisible substance have a
sufficient description? It can have, so the argument runs, only
provided the principle of determining correspondence holds true
within it. If this principle obtains, the infinite series of parts
of substance is not vicious; if it does not obtain, the series is
vicious and the substance cannot exist.

Now, I ask once again, what does 'vicious' here mean, and
what does its use imply with reference to the 'ontological' method
of argument? The answer, it would appear, must be in principle identical with that already given in reply to the similar
question about 'sufficient description.'

That such is the case follows from the simple consideration
that what the principle of determining correspondence in the
end amounts to is a sufficient description of substance such
that the infinite divisibility of substance is amenable to knowledge—that is, is thinkable without contradiction. The infinite
divisibility of substance is vicious, if it involves us in contradiction when we try to think it; in other words, it is vicious
when we make it an object of knowledge. Thus, the principle of
determining correspondence, like that of sufficient description, is
founded on the fact of knowledge. It holds of substance in so
far as substance is made an object of knowledge, and not
otherwise.

It is true that the discussion of the necessity of the principle
of determining correspondence involves issues not involved in
the discussion of the necessity of sufficient description. For here
the problem concerns the relation between a substance and its
'parts,' while there the problem concerned the 'characteristics'
of substance. Despite the fact, therefore, that the point here is
essentially identical with that considered above in our criticism
of the author's demonstration of the necessity of sufficient description, a survey of it in this new context may aid clarity and
strengthen the criticism there suggested. And, once again, we
shall begin with the author's own statement of his thesis.

"Since A has no simple parts, it will have an infinite number
of sets of parts which are sequent to any given set. And, there-

fore, if its nature presupposes sufficient descriptions of the members of any set of its parts, it will have an infinite number of presuppositions.

"The fact that A has an infinite number of presuppositions may not involve any contradiction. But when we consider the nature of these particular presuppositions, we find that a contradiction is involved.

"We have seen that a sufficient description of any substance is given, if sufficient descriptions are given of all the members of any set of its parts. Now, in the first place, if this were the *only* way in which the sufficient description of a substance could be given, there would be a contradiction. The fact that A is a substance presupposes the sufficient descriptions of the members of a set, M, of its parts. And these sufficient descriptions of the members of M could only be given, on our present hypothesis, by giving sufficient descriptions of the members of sets of their parts. These members of the sets of parts of members of M will also form a set of parts of A—the set N. And, in the same way, sufficient descriptions of the members of N could only be given by giving sufficient descriptions of the members of sets of their parts, which members will form another set of parts of A—the set P. And this process will continue to infinity.

"Such an infinite series will be vicious. For the sufficient descriptions of the members of M can only be made sufficient by means of sufficient descriptions of the members of N, and these by means of sufficient descriptions of the members of P, and so on infinitely. Therefore the sufficient descriptions of the members of M can only be made sufficient by means of the last stage of an unending series—that is, they cannot be made sufficient at all. But the existence of A, which presupposes sufficient descriptions of the members of M, implies that there are such sufficient descriptions. And therefore the fact that there can be no such sufficient descriptions implies a contradiction." [20]

I have quoted this statement at length, because it gives the essentials of the author's argument in support of the logical

[20] Sections 188, 189. For the definition of 'presupposition,' see Sections 183-186 and the summary given in the preceding Part of this study (*supra*, pp. 219-220).

necessity of the principle of determining correspondence—which is held to be the only way of escape from the contradiction here demonstrated—and also because it sets forth clearly the assumption on the basis of which the contradiction in the nature of substance rests. This assumption alone concerns us here.

It will be noted, in the first place, that the contradiction does not arise merely from the nature of substance. It does not follow from the definition of substance; nor does it follow from the elaboration of the definition so as to include the infinite divisibility of substance. It does not even follow from the fact that a given substance 'presupposes' sufficient descriptions of the members of its set of parts and the sets of parts of each of these members and of their members to infinity. "The fact that A has an infinite number of presuppositions," we are explicitly informed, "may not involve any contradiction."

Under what conditions, then, does the contradiction arise? It arises only when one demands that the sufficient descriptions to infinity, which are 'required' by a given substance, be "made sufficient." On the basis of this demand, if the sufficient description of a substance merely presupposes sufficient descriptions of its parts to infinity, the infinite divisibility of substance does involve a contradiction. For then the sufficient descriptions of the members of its set of parts "can only be made sufficient by means of the last stage of an unending series—that is, they cannot be made sufficient at all." But the existence of the substance implies that there are such sufficient descriptions, and therefore, "the fact that there can be no such sufficient descriptions implies a contradiction."

But whence comes this demand that the sufficient descriptions 'required' by substance be "made sufficient," and what is to be understood by this? Apparently the demand springs from "minds like ours," and it means simply that substance in the end must be intelligible to us. It is only because we ask that the sufficient descriptions required by the nature of substance be "made sufficient" that substance 'implies' a contradiction so long as it merely 'presupposes' these sufficient descriptions and does not imply them. The contradiction, in short, is founded on the assumption that substance is an object of human knowl-

edge. Taken by itself, substance raises no such demand; in
its mere ontological nature, it is apparently wholly indifferent
to the demand that the sufficient descriptions it requires be
"made sufficient." Only when the demands of human minds, or
"minds like ours," are introduced into the situation as foundational within the structure of substance itself does the
'making' sufficient descriptions 'sufficient' have any significance
at all.

Thus, it would appear, the fact of knowledge is as foundational in the crucial step to the principle of determining correspondence, as it is in that to the conception of 'sufficient description.' And it is foundational in both instances for one and
the same reason—namely, because, in both, 'substance' ceases
to be treated as a mere 'external' meaning and emphasis is
placed on its 'internal' meaning. In both, it is dealt with, not as
it is, in and for itself alone, but as it is for us or for "minds like
ours." And this change in view, I submit, alone gives significance
to the argument in support of the 'necessity' both of sufficient
description and of determining correspondence.

Presumably, I need hardly repeat the warning that the point
of this criticism is not in opposition to McTaggart's having here
made knowledge foundational. But, since it is important, I will
repeat it, and will add that his having done so is merely an
indication of the weakness of his 'ontological' method throughout. For everywhere, where the necessity arises of describing
'contradiction' in terms which are not tautologous as mere matters of definition, the appeal is to 'experience' in the sense in
which experience involves points of view and, broadly, 'internal'
meanings. Then the 'ontological' method is abandoned. I have
singled out for emphasis these two conceptions, *sufficient description* and *determining correspondence*, because of their importance for the argument as a whole and because they seem
fairly clearly to exemplify the abnegation of the method avowed
at the beginning of the argument.

In the light of the preceding considerations, then, it would
seem quite doubtful whether the principle of determining correspondence is certainly established. Its very definition, as a
relation among the 'parts' of substances, involves the question-

able conception of 'parts' as being themselves 'substances.' The chain of implication on which it is built turns out on analysis to offer at best a very insecure foundation because of the ambiguous relationship in which substance and its nature are left standing. But it is now time to pass on to the final thesis of the argument, and I wish in doing so to raise the question whether McTaggart has proved that spirit is a substance within which the principle of determining correspondence may, as a matter of empirical fact, hold true.

Before entering upon a consideration of this question, however, it should be noted that the argument which McTaggart advances against the existence of 'matter' as a substance and of 'sensa' as substances is in principle the same as one side of the argument which we have above advanced against the principle of determining correspondence. For his contention is that 'matter' and 'sensa' are such that no basis can be found in their qualities for sufficient descriptions which are related in accordance with the principle of determining correspondence. And our contention above was to the general effect that no substance, if by substance is to be understood its 'nature' or totality of qualities, can furnish a ground for the principle. Thus it happens that what McTaggart says against 'matter' and 'sensa' furnishes a detailed commentary on, and in support of, the main thesis of our critical remarks on the general principle of determining correspondence.

But we there maintained that no basis for the principle as defined can be found in the qualities of any substance, however conceived, since the principle assumes intrinsic determination among all of the qualities of a given substance and among all of its qualities and all of the qualities of all of its parts to infinity, and such intrinsic determination seems wanting. McTaggart seems to admit this in the cases of 'matter' and 'sensa,' but he denies it in the case of spirit, which, he insists, is a substance within which the principle of determining correspondence may hold in fact. If this be so, then of course it will be necessary to retract our *a priori* denial. We must, therefore, carefully investigate the claims made in behalf of spiritual substance in this respect. And what are these claims?

4. Substance as Spirit

Substance is spiritual, we are asked to agree, if its content is the content of one or more selves; and the quality of being a self is the "simple quality which is known to me because I perceive —in the strict sense of the word—one substance as possessing this quality," namely myself.[21] In spirit thus defined, we are given to understand, the principle of determining correspondence will hold only if the following propositions are true: (1) that a self can perceive another self, and a part of another self; (2) that a perception is part of a percipient self; (3) that a perception of a part of a whole can be part of a perception of that whole. If these propositions are true, the principle of determining correspondence may be established in respect of spiritual substance, and its *prima facie* claim to existence may be allowed. But the three propositions are true, at least they are not impossible, and so spirit may be held to exist. Such, in brief, is McTaggart's position.

Now it is important to observe, in the first place, that the principle of determining correspondence as exemplified in spiritual substance is modified in such a fashion as to make it quite different from the principle which we have been criticizing. Hitherto, we have been assuming that the principle of determining correspondence involves the conception of sufficient description. And we have assumed this on the basis of the author's analysis of that principle, and the explicit definition of it quoted above.[22] Here, however, we are concerned with a principle which not only does not involve sufficient description, but positively excludes it. And this important point needs drawing out in some detail.

"Let us suppose a primary whole," we are now instructed, "all the primary parts of which are selves. And let us suppose that each of these selves has a separate perception, and only one such perception, of each self, and of each part of each self. And let us suppose, as we have just assumed to be possible,

---

[21] Section 382. Perception is defined as "the awareness of substances as distinct from the awareness of characteristics." (Section 44.)

[22] For the author's analysis and definition of the principle referred to, see *op. cit.*, Sections 197-202.

that when any one of these percepta is part of another perceptum, then any perception of the first will be a part of a perception of the second. We shall then have a series of parts within parts to infinity, determined by determining correspondence." [23] This, in brief, is the author's statement of his view of the conditions of determining correspondence within spirit.

Two points with reference to this statement need emphasis. The first is that there is in it no reference to sufficient description nor to intrinsic determination of one sufficient description by another. The second point is that not only is there no reference in the statement to sufficient descriptions, but the statement excludes the possibility of such reference. For we are here asked to deal with a primary whole, all of whose primary parts are selves; and we have been shown at some length in the chapter immediately preceding the one from which this statement is taken that a self cannot be known by description, but can be known only by 'acquaintance,' since for the self there is no exclusive description.[24] There is, therefore, no sufficient description of a self possible. Consequently the principle of determining correspondence among selves, or spiritual substances, such as we are here asked to contemplate, cannot possibly involve sufficient descriptions and intrinsic determination among them.

Hence, even if we grant that the principle as here defined holds among spirits, our previous criticisms of the principle as stated in terms of sufficient descriptions and intrinsic determination among them is not thereby overthrown. For this statement of the principle is quite different from that criticized. It may be noted in passing, however, that this new formulation of the principle is, indirectly at least, in support of the criticism advanced against the other. For it would appear to indicate that, in the author's own view of the matter, the only satisfactory example of the principle can be found in a type of substance whose parts are determined independently of characteristics and their description. And, as we have already noted, he is brought to this by his failure to find an example in either of

[23] Section 408.
[24] For the argument in support of this, see *op. cit.*, Sections 384-391.

the two other *prima facie* substances, namely, matter and sensa, because sufficient descriptions of them on which the principle of determining correspondence may be based are wanting.

Turning, now, to this new formulation of the principle of determining correspondence as exemplified in spirit, we are to inquire into the stability of its foundations. And these foundations are the above-mentioned three propositions which must be true if the principle is to hold of spirit.

The first of these—namely, that a self can perceive another self, and a part of another self—is, in McTaggart's opinion, guaranteed by the consideration that "that which is aware of this awareness" is not an exclusive description of the substance to which it refers. And the proof of this is that there is no reason for holding that it is "intrinsically impossible that a state of a self may be perceived by two or more selves (one of whom may be the self of which it is the state)." "It is true, no doubt, that in present experience I do not perceive the state of mind of any person but myself. And I have good reason to believe that no one of the persons whom I know, or who have recorded their experience in any way which is accessible to me, has perceived the states of mind of any other person than himself. Nor have I any reason to believe that any person in the universe has done so." But all of this is no reason to suppose that it could not happen, and there is no other reason to suppose that it could not happen. Hence, it is possible that a self should perceive another self or the part of another self. And this possibility is sufficient for the argument.

The crux of this argument lies in the assertion that there is no reason for supposing that the proposition in question cannot possibly be true and the implied assumption that the possibility of its being true is a genuine possibility. Each of these points calls for separate comment, and we shall take the second first.

The assumption that the possibility is a real one, rests ultimately on two considerations: that a self empirically perceives itself, and also parts of itself. Granting both of these to be true, how does that affect the possibility that one self may perceive another self or part of another self? Of course, this possibility remains; but it seems to be none the less abstract, because of the admission that a self may perceive itself and parts of itself. In short, the two questions appear to be quite distinct, logically, and the answer of the one to be without any implication with reference to the other. No presumption that I can perceive another self seems to be established by the fact—if it be a fact—that I perceive myself. And, if this be so, there is nothing in experience to make the possibility a genuine one; and it, therefore, remains an abstract possibility only.

But I think we may go further, and urge that we have reason in experience for doubting the possibility. In the first place, the *prima facie* empirical fact is, not that we perceive other selves, but that we perceive characteristics on the basis of which we judge or infer them. In the second place, it seems doubtful whether what I perceive as myself is what, in empirical fact, the self actually is; for what I perceive is at most, as McTaggart admits, the self of the specious present, but either I am not that merely or my self is incapable of any sort of growth, which latter alternative seems to be contrary to experience. In the third place, even granting that I perceive myself as it actually is, there is a relation, namely the relation of 'being' myself, which does not obtain between two separate selves; and there seems to be evidence that the perception of my self is bound up with this relation in such fashion that the perception may be an expression of it and impossible apart from it. In the fourth place, there is a relation between my self and parts of myself, namely, the relation of 'having,' which does not obtain (as McTaggart, once more, admits) between one self and the parts of another self; and there seems to be evidence that the perception by me of a part of my self is bound up with this relation in such a manner that the perception is impossible apart from that relation.

For these four reasons, then, it appears doubtful that it is possible for one self to perceive either another self or a part of another self. And, added to the consideration that the possibility of a self's perception of itself has no implicative significance with reference to the possibility of the perception of one self by another self, they seriously threaten the first of our three assumed propositions.

The second of these propositions—namely, that a perception is part of a percipient self—is, if I am not mistaken, based on a line of proof which proves too much for the author's purpose, if it proves anything at all. And I shall state the point of criticism as briefly as I can, after I have indicated the line of proof.[25]

My perceptions are so related to me that the condition of my self when I have many as contrasted with its condition when I have few "differs in a way which seems to be appropriately expressed by the metaphor of being fuller." Or, expressed otherwise, our cogitations, volitions and emotions, when taken together, in some sense "exhaust the self." Again, B's knowledge of C makes a more direct—not, be it noted, indirect—difference to B than it does to C; the direct difference "between B who knows C, and B if he did not know C, is greater than the direct difference between C which is known by B, and C if it had not been known to B." For these reasons we may hold that perceptions are parts of the percipient self.

Now the point of my criticism is simply this. If such considerations prove that perceptions are 'parts' of the self, they prove equally that other 'cogitations'—such as awareness of characteristics, judgment, assumptions, and imagings—which, *prima facie* at least are not perceptions, and also volitions and emotions are 'parts' of the self in the same sense. But this proves too much for McTaggart's purpose. For, then, the self involves parts which cannot be brought within the principle of determining correspondence, because none of the cogitations nor volitions nor emotions, except perceptions, is capable "of giving us parts of parts to infinity by means of determining correspondence." Therefore, if any or all of these be admitted into the self as distinct parts, spiritual substance in its turn is also threatened with ruin; it thereupon becomes a 'vicious' infinite.

The way out of the difficulty is to reduce them all to perceptions, of course, and this is the way McTaggart takes. But in doing so, he seems to me to fly in the face of experience. He himself admits that there is a *prima facie* difference between

[25] For the details, the reader should consult *op. cit.*, Section 412.

perceptions and all of these other 'states' of experience; and the only reason he gives for denying the *prima facie* distinction, at least the only reason I can find in his discussion for the denial, is that if they are admitted to the status of parts the principle of determining correspondence fails to hold within spirit. But this way of reasoning begs the question, since the point at issue is whether the principle does hold here any more than in the cases of the other supposed substances, 'matter' and 'sensa.'

The important matter, of course, is whether the reduction is empirically permissible. And I fail to see that it is. Surely, if perception means the awareness of a substance or the part of a substance, then awareness of characteristics is at once excluded by definition; it may be a perceptum, that is, an object of perception, in the sense that one who is aware of characteristics may be aware of his awareness, but the awareness of characteristics as such cannot by definition be a perception. And yet, it would appear to be a proved part of the self, if the arguments given in support of perceptions as parts are to be taken as proving that fact. And the same holds in principle of the other cogitations and volitions and emotions. There is no empirical evidence that they can be reduced to perceptions, and, strictly interpreted, 'perception' as defined can refer to nothing which has to do with characteristics; yet, they are involved in the 'fullness' of the self as truly as are perceptions, and they make as great a 'direct difference' to the self.

Thus McTaggart's proof that perceptions are parts of the percipient self proves too much, since it proves that all 'cogitations,' as well as volitions and emotions, are also parts. And this is too much, because, on his own showing, these additional parts render spirit impervious to the principle of determining correspondence. Nor can these other cogitations or volitions or emotions be denied the status of 'parts' in order to obviate this difficulty; for the question is whether the difficulty can be obviated, and it cannot be satisfactorily answered by simply denying the *prima facie* appearances which tend to show that it cannot be—especially when these *prima facie* appearances are substantiated by the very argument which is taken to prove that perceptions have that status. Furthermore, the very definition of perception ("awareness of substances as distinct from the awareness of characteristics") seems to make it impossible to reduce the other cogitations and volitions and emotions to perceptions, as would have to be the case if they are denied the status of parts, since *prima facie* they do occur in spirit and merely to blot them out is arbitrary. And, finally, there is no empirical justification for their reduction to perceptions.

There are two separate theses in the proof which McTaggart offers for the possibility of his third proposition—that a perception of a part of a whole can be part of a perception of that whole. The first of these theses is that we do in fact perceive a whole with parts—for example, a carpet with a pattern on it—and, therefore, perceive a whole sensum and parts of the sensum. The second thesis is that it does sometimes happen —for example, when a gradual increase in light discloses more details in the pattern of the carpet—that the perception of the part is a part of the perception of the whole. From these two considerations the conclusion is reached that it is at least possible for the perceptions of parts to be parts of perceptions of wholes.[26]

McTaggart insists that the first of these two theses would be generally admitted, and presumably in some sense it would be. But, clearly, it proves nothing to the point, unless it can be further shown that the perception of a whole with parts would be impossible if the perception of the part were not a part of the perception of the whole. Against this, McTaggart recognizes, "It may be argued that we might perceive the whole in one perception, that we might perceive each of the parts in other perceptions, and that we might perceive the relation between the things perceived." And he admits that this does sometimes happen. Thus it is not proved that the perception of a whole with parts is impossible unless the perceptions of the parts are parts of the perception of the whole.

But the second thesis remains, and on it McTaggart really bases his case for the possibility of a perception's having perceptions for its parts. Now, of course, introspection is a notoriously flimsy foundation on which to base the justification of

[26] For the details, the reader should see *op. cit.*, Section 413.

any position; but at times it is perhaps the best available, and the present instance seems to be such an occasion. But does introspection in respect of the example offered tend to support McTaggart's thesis? "If we had separate perceptions of the whole and of the parts of the datum perceived in such an experience," he urges, "the change ought to appear as a change to a state with more perceptions, whereas it seems quite clear in my case that it appears as a change from a relatively simple perception to one which is relatively complex." Now, assuming that such an experience as is here described is an example of perception as McTaggart claims it is, I can see no basis in it for the supposition that a perception may be part of a perception. It does show that a perception may grow in complexity, if by that is meant that the characteristics perceived may gradually become more numerous and intricate. But I fail to see that it shows the perception of one part of the perceptum to be a part of the perception of the whole perceptum; the parts appear to me to lie on the side of the characteristics perceived, not on the side of the perception itself. And I should have supposed that, if a perception of a part be in very truth a part of the perception of the whole, "the change ought to appear as a change to a state with more perceptions." However, I am prohibited from making such a supposition by McTaggart's contention that such would necessarily be the nature of the change if the perception of the part is *not* a part of the perception of the whole.

A more important objection is that which raises specifically the question whether such an experience as is here described is an example of perception at all. And this objection is not without foundation, since there is considerable ground for urging that judgment, which the author sharply distinguishes from perception, is intrinsic to the experience. I do not wish here to draw out this objection in detail, but I do wish to emphasize its significance and to call attention to the fact that McTaggart's entire position with reference to substance and its parts rests ultimately upon a negation of the principles which that objection suggests.

Despite these criticisms of McTaggart's 'proof' of the possibility of his third proposition, that possibility, of course, still remains. But if these criticisms are in principle sound, the possibility is merely an abstract one, and its assumption is arbitrary. It may be that a perception of a part can be a part of the perception of the whole; no one can certainly say that such is impossible. But, on the other hand, it may not be so; and there seems nothing in McTaggart's analysis to establish a presumption that it is so.

We have seen reasons to doubt each of the three propositions which McTaggart says we must assume to be true if the principle of determining correspondence is to hold within spiritual substance. It would, therefore, appear to be doubtful whether it has been proved that the principle does there hold. This is the general outcome of our analysis of the considerations which McTaggart advances in support of his 'idealistic' position. But there is another difficulty remaining in his position, and this I wish now briefly to develop.

Waiving the preceding objections to the propositions which the author insists must be true if determining correspondence is to hold within spirit and assuming, not only that they are or may be true, but that the principle of determining correspondence as thus defined may, and presumably does, hold true within spiritual substance, let us go on to inquire concerning the precise meaning of the position thus attained and whether it is free from difficulties.

The position is that the relation of determining correspondence between substance and its parts to infinity is the relation between two perceptions when one is part of the other. In other words, it is the relation between a self and its parts when the self is aware of its parts, and between one self and another self when one is aware of the other and of parts of the other. In short, the relation of determining correspondence is reduced to selves and perceptions as their only parts. And this position seems to me not wholly free from difficulties.

In the first place, the definition of perception must not be forgotten or modified to meet the exigencies of the occasion. If it is not, then the relation of determining correspondence holds only with reference to selves and their awarenesses of themselves and their awarenesses, and of each other and of each other's awarenesses to infinity. Should this seem to be a rather thin series, one must urge that it alone can follow from the premises; selves and their perceptions are all we have to deal with by hypothesis. Their relation is that of part and whole, and selves have only perceptions for their parts and perceptions are only awarenesses either of selves (that is, wholes of awarenesses) or of other perceptions (that is, other awarenesses).

And this thinness of the series is indicative of another difficulty, namely, the apparent failure of the series to provide any basis for inference or implication. Inference and implication hold only among characteristics, or among propositions about characteristics; but characteristics play no part in the series here in question, and cannot logically have any part in it.

Hereupon, if I am not mistaken, we come at the root of the trouble. The relation of determining correspondence, defined in terms of selves and their awarenesses as here conceived, has no significance with reference to characteristics at all. It holds among substances and their parts, but it has nothing whatever to do with the nature of substances. In other words, the determination of the correspondence of parts of substance to infinity involves no reference to description of substances.

If the effort is made to avoid this difficulty by appealing to the doctrine that "the nature of substance completely expresses what the substance is" and concluding, therefore, that there is no justification for any such sharp separation as is here assumed between substances and their parts on the one side and the nature of substance and characteristics on the other, I should most heartily applaud the effort. But I should also be compelled to urge that the doctrine must be borne in mind throughout the argument, and not violated. And I should insist, further, that if this is done the only ground for the thesis that perception alone (in the sense of mere awareness of substance as distinct from awareness of characteristics and from judgments) can be a part of a self is thereby removed. For surely, on the basis of this doctrine, awareness of substance must involve, as an integral element in its logical structure, awareness of characteristics also.

Thus, even if we grant that determining correspondence holds within spirit on the conditions set out above, we have not achieved a result of any great significance so far as an understanding of our actual world is concerned. We have succeeded in removing the 'viciousness' of spiritual substance, but at the expense of reducing it to a thin series of awareness of awarenesses to infinity within which the relation is so 'immediate' that it seems to have no explanatory function at all. The world of characteristics, the realm of description and implication and inference, in short, the actual world of experience, is, on its side, left standing with all of its 'viciousness' uncleansed because untouched by the redeeming principle of determining correspondence.

In view of the claim which McTaggart makes that the results of his ontological argument are certainly established or there is some mistake in the reasoning by which they have been arrived at, I have felt it incumbent on me in the rôle of critic to set forth in detail the weaknesses of that argument as I understand it. And I have tried to do this in the preceding discussion. His general method seems to me impossible of application, even at his own hands. His analyses appear to be carried forward, where they are consistently developed, largely through more or less arbitrary definitions; and the primary reason why these definitions are not wholly arbitrary is that, in violation of his avowed method of procedure, he from time to time (not merely in the two instances which he acknowledges) appeals to empirical considerations as the basis of his formulation of them. His failure to recognize this appeal is responsible for his assumption that the method possesses a character of apriority and 'necessity' which in fact it does not possess. Furthermore, the argument clearly breaks down at crucial points, unless the 'ontological' method is explicitly disavowed. And all along, the argument is beset by troublesome ambiguities, especially in the basal concepts of 'substance' and of the 'nature' of substance and its 'parts.' These arise, one cannot but feel, from the abstractness of the method on the one side and the intractability of experience in respect of its demands on the other.

All of this I have tried to show in considerable detail. If these criticisms have been based on a misapprehension of the author's argument—as they well may be, either in part or even in whole —they may at least serve the fruitful purpose of turning the reader's attention towards one possible misinterpretation which certainly is not entirely arbitrary and which calls for correction. If they are not based on a misapprehension, then the argument involves inconsistencies and fails to accomplish what McTaggart thinks it accomplishes.

Nevertheless, the argument is not without its positive significance. It focusses attention on fundamentals, it clarifies issues, it forces assent or disagreement in such fashion that the ground of either is readily statable, due allowance being made, of course, for the intrinsic difficulty of the subject-matter dealt with. It presents, in short, a statement characterized by that degree of clarity which is all too rare in contemporary philosophical literature. And, despite my conviction that the statement breaks down in the main, indeed primarily because of it, I wish to protest my other conviction that it is unusually significant in its details. I know of no analysis in recent metaphysics which surpasses it in suggestiveness, no one which is more worthy of the reader's serious and protracted study. Whatever view one may in the end entertain of the general results achieved by it, there cannot presumably be two opinions concerning the analytical acumen exemplified in its structure. It is a statement to which one may frequently return, and always with profit for one's own efforts at metaphysical construction.

5. TIME AS UNREAL

WHILE McTaggart's criticism of the reality of time is not foundational in his general argument in support of his identification of substance and spirit, it does have an important bearing on his general position and on absolutism also. So in conclusion I feel under compulsion to indicate some of the difficulties I find in it, even though my observations must be very briefly and tentatively expressed.

One doubtful step in the analysis seems to be involved in the contention that, if the earlier-later series (called the B series) taken apart from the future-present-past series (called

the A series) is supposed to constitute time, change is logically
impossible. The proof of this contention is as follows: "If N is
ever earlier than O and later than M, it will always be, and
has always been, earlier than O and later than M, since the
relations of earlier and later are permanent. N will thus always
be in a B series. And as, by our present hypothesis, a B series
by itself constitutes time, N will always have a position in a
time-series, and always has had one. That is, it always has
been an event, and always will be one, and cannot begin or
cease to be an event." [27] Now I do not doubt that, in such a
series as is here contemplated, the "relations of earlier and later
are permanent"; but I do seriously question whether they are
necessarily so in the interpretation which excludes the logical
possibility of change in a given event. The assumption of the
argument, if I understand it rightly, is that a given event is
punctiform and static—else why the statement, immediately
following the passage above quoted, that when M changes into
N, M ceases to be an event and N begins to be an event? So
far as I can see, the only reason given for this assumption is
that an event must by hypothesis have a 'permanent' position
in the time-series: and this reason seems to me to involve a
troublesome ambiguity.

In the end, so far as I can discover, the difficulty I feel in
connection with this step in McTaggart's argument arises from
what seems to me to be an unjustifiable use of the term 'event.'
What he is virtually saying is that, in the earlier-later series, a
given event must always be that event. To this I should agree,
but I fail to see in this a denial of the possibility of change
in the event. The reason why McTaggart so understands the
matter, it would appear, is that he is assuming that an event
must be static in a static part of time; my difficulty is to see
how the premises involve this conception of an event or a part
of time, rather than the conception of each as dynamic and
enduring.

Thus I am led to doubt whether McTaggart has proved his
first main thesis, namely, that change is logically impossible in
the B series taken apart from the A series. And if he has not
[27] Section 310.

proved this, then his argument falls, since he has not shown that the A series is essential to time.

His second main thesis that the A series is fatal to the reality of time introduces considerations which call for separate comment. The main points here are: (a) that the "A series depends on relations to a term outside the A series," which term can hardly be found; (b) that the supposition of the reality of the A series involves us in contradiction, since on this assumption every event is past, present, and future, whereas it is clear that no event can logically be more than one; and (c) that the attempt to escape this contradiction by saying that a given event is future, present, and past successively leads at once into an infinite regress, since it amounts to saying that as future the event is at a future moment of time, as present it is at a present moment of time, as past it is at a past moment of time. The specification of successive moments of time involves relations to other terms specified as future, present, and past *ad infinitum*. These three points seem to me severally questionable.

(a) Granting that future, present, and past are relations, I am at a loss to understand why either is necessarily a relation to a term outside the A series—to a term, that is, which itself is neither past, nor present, nor future. The assumption that it is so seems to me to rest upon a very abstract view of the relation in question; for it seems to imply that a relation in time at one end, if I may so speak, is not in time at the other. If a given event, E, is temporally related to X and X itself is non-temporal, then the relation in question would certainly appear to be external in the sense in which, as I think Bradley has shown, it involves a contradiction.

The same point may be put the other way around—that which is out of time cannot be temporally related to an event, and no event can in respect of it be either future or past. If X be non-temporal, every event must in respect of it be present —and present in the sense in which there is no future or past distinguishable from it. So far as such a non-temporal X is concerned, the A series has no meaning whatever, except as a succession of events within a static 'now' which can be charac-

terized as neither future nor past. This much at least, it would
appear, the absolutists have rightly stressed.

But, it may be objected, the preceding remarks only emphasize the point of McTaggart's contention. He affirms that
the A series depends on relations to a term outside the A series,
which can hardly be found. What has here been said is that
such a term is inconceivable. And this would appear to be
nothing more than a strengthening of his position, since it
seems to show that the A series depends on a term which not
only cannot be found but cannot even be conceived without
doing violence to the notion of relation. Wherein, then, does
the sting of these remarks lie?

It lies simply in the observation that the assumption of a
non-temporal reality does not help us in the slightest degree
to explain the A series. If the A series does not imply such a
non-temporal reality but rather seems to be entirely unrelated to it, then such a non-temporal reality can apparently,
in no significant fashion, serve as the basis of that illusion
('misperception,' McTaggart calls it) which is the A series. It
is, therefore, quite groundless to say, as McTaggart does elsewhere, that we can infer the existence of such a non-temporal
reality, called the C series, "from the fact that we do misperceive things as in the A and B series." [28] For, even if we
do misperceive things when we perceive them as in the A and B
series, that does not, and cannot, imply the C series; and the
gratuitous assumption of the C series offers no ground of explanation whatever for the fact of our misperception.

(b) That "present, past, and future are incompatible determinations" is in a sense true, but not in the sense that "no
event can be more than one." An event which is past is not, in
the same reference, either present or future. But on the basis
of empirical considerations one may apparently hold without
contradiction that it may be present or future in some other
reference. The death of Queen Anne, to use McTaggart's example, is past in respect of the accession of George V, but
present in respect of the accession of George I, and future in
respect of the Norman Conquest. Empirically considered, then,

[28] Section 526.

this event may be said to be at once past and present and future.

But McTaggart's main point is, of course, that what is empirically true about the event—that is, what is true of it when it is specified in terms of points of view—is not, and cannot be, true of it absolutely. If the A series be taken as real, in other words, he holds it to be contradictory to say that such an event as the death of Queen Anne could be past and present and future. With reference to this position two observations seem pertinent, though each of them is a repetition of what has been said above. The first is that time, if it is to be an object of knowledge, like any other object can be specified only with reference to points of view. And the second is that contradiction is possible only among objects of knowledge; whatever relations may obtain among merely 'ontological' objects, contradiction is not one of them.

Nor does McTaggart's argument proceed on any other principles. Clearly, on his view, the contradiction arising from the incompatibility of present, past, and future rests on a conception of present, past, and future as in some sense absolute—in the sense, namely, that each is itself in such a manner that it cannot possibly be the others also. If this conception be granted, then it certainly follows that a given event must be one and cannot be more than one; but it follows only from that conception. Even granting the conception, however, the supposed contradiction does not arise until another point of view is added; and that is the further conception that real time is such that a given event must be future, present, and past in the same reference. Without this further conception the contradiction in real time does not arise, since the fact of the incompatibility of the several determinations taken alone does not involve any contradiction.

Thus McTaggart's criticism turns on points of view with reference to the determinations of present, past, and future, and also with reference to real time and the significance of these determinations within it. And on this score his criticism stands on no different principles from those underlying any other. All critical remarks about time necessarily proceed from points of

view empirically oriented, and the question about any set of
remarks is whether the points of view underlying it are well
grounded.

So far as McTaggart's remarks are concerned, it seems to me
that the two conceptions underlying them are not well grounded.
To hold that present, past, and future are incompatible in the
sense defined involves acceptance of an abstract view of temporal relations which in the end is untenable. And the conception of present, past, and future as applying to the same event
in the same reference resolves itself finally into the view above
criticized—the view, namely, that these relations necessarily
involve a term outside the A series.

(c) The preceding remarks hold in principle of what is said
about moments of time, and there is no need to repeat them
here. If by moments of time are meant static instants, then it
is clear that an appeal to them as points of reference for the
specification of present, past, and future is futile, since they
themselves need to be specified to infinity. But why conceive
them so? And if they are conceived in connection with events
as aspects or characters of them, why need they be specified
except by reference to other events? What is there in the nature
of time, conceived as real, which compels thought to go beyond
events to moments of time in its effort to specify temporal
relations, or which involves it in contradiction when it specifies
successive moments by reference to events?

An attempt to discuss these questions in detail would, I think,
develop nothing new in principle beyond what has already been
said in this section. But the questions point to the main difficulty in McTaggart's contention about the 'vicious' infinite
regress involved in the specification of the A series. And the
principles above suggested seem to my mind basal in the resolution of the difficulty.

These principles may, perhaps, be reduced to the consideration
that time is a relation and does not differ logically from other
relations. They turn about the question whether time can be
abstracted from events and, if not, whether any thing more than
events is required for the specification of temporal relations.
Unless I am mistaken, McTaggart goes on the assumption that

such an abstraction not only may but must be made; and that assumption seems to me unwarranted. His implied dichotomy between ontological time and time as conceived by the human mind seems to me here, as elsewhere, to involve him in the inconsistent position of trying to determine contradiction wholly independently of any cognitive reference. It seems also to be subject to the same criticisms which have been advanced against his general "ontological" method in the preceding sections of this chapter.

CHAPTER XVIII

UNDERLYING ISSUES

IN the first chapter of this part of our study we noted different types of idealism as represented by the thinkers here under survey, and we also indicated some of the main issues underlying these differences. In the present chapter we are to inquire more in detail concerning these issues. But before passing on to this inquiry, we must pause to emphasize the issue raised by the different types of argument just discussed—an issue which, in last analysis, is fundamental to all the others and which may be said to be the basal issue involved in the historical development of the idealistic argument.

From the preceding analysis, it should be clear that this issue concerns the meaning of the 'object of knowledge.' The argument *a contingentia mundi* is based on the assumption that the object of knowledge is empirical and also characterized by a fragmentariness (which I have ventured to call its transempirical reference). This fragmentariness is indigenous to it and is at once the impulsion and the guide of the intellectual process. This assumption is in principle denied by both of the other types of argument. The epistemological argument does, indeed, accept the empirical status of the object of knowledge; but in the end refuses to admit its trans-empirical reference. And the ontological argument denies both *ab initio*.

The preceding criticisms of the three types of argument have been based on the conviction that the assumption underlying the argument *a contingentia mundi* is sound in principle and that the difficulties encountered by the several types can be traced to their violation of it. The essential subjectivity implicit in the epistemological argument attaches to the denial of the trans-empirical character of the object of knowledge. The emptiness of the ontological argument grows out of its insistence on

508

the non-empirical character of the object of knowledge. The paradoxes of the argument *a contingentia mundi* in its several forms are closely linked with failure to give due consideration to the correlativity of the relationship between the empirical and the trans-empirical aspects of the object of knowledge.

All of this I have argued above, and there is here no need of its repetition. But it is appropriate to insist that the issue is fundamental within these arguments, and that the resolution of the controversy must in the end turn around the conception of the object of knowledge. It is also appropriate to urge that the issue is fundamental in the traditional controversies among idealists and realists, and that a more precise apprehension of it might lend clarity and rid us of at least merely terminological differences. And, as I hope will become clear as we proceed with the analysis, there is reason to suppose that the issue lies close to the heart of those intra-mural divergencies among idealists, which it is the chief purpose of the present chapter to elaborate.

Turning to these, we shall take them in the order in which they were set down in the summary statement given in the introductory chapter of this part of the study.

1. THE PRINCIPLE OF CONTINUITY IN NATURE

The principle of continuity in nature has played an important rôle in philosophical speculation since the time when the concept of evolution achieved the status of a scientific category. Before that time, of course, the principle was by no means unknown and some philosophers, notably Leibniz, made conspicuous use of it. Since the middle of last century the principle has been generally invoked, or at least its claims for serious consideration in philosophical construction have been commonly recognized. The uses to which it has been put have, indeed, been various, and it has often been prayed in behalf of widely divergent conclusions. On occasion, its availability for philosophical purposes has been called in question. But in the main it has entered significantly into the structure of philosophical systems.

The general historical fortunes of the principle are, however, of no concern to us in the present context. Our concern here is, rather, with the principle in respect of the part it plays in the controversy between those idealists who are also panpsychists or 'spiritualists' and those idealists who are their opponents. More specifically, we are concerned with the issue raised by the different uses of the principle at the hands of Ward on the one side and Pringle-Pattison on the other.

The interpretations given to the principle by these two thinkers stand out clearly enough. They are agreed, as against naturalism or materialism, that the principle cannot be invoked for the purpose of reducing the world to forms of mere matter and motion and of expelling spirit from it. "To understand the world as a whole we must take it as a whole"—this, they both urge, is the basic canon of thought and the rock upon which all materialisms ultimately founder. But here their agreement ends. To the question: What does the principle imply for philosophical construction? they offer different answers. The one is that it implies "spiritualistic pluralism"; the other is that it implies a "higher naturalism." And, on the one side, is the assumption that the principle logically involves the interpretation of the lower forms of nature after the analogy of the higher, the inorganic and merely organic after the analogy of the mental or spiritual; while, on the other side, is the assumption that the principle involves nothing of the sort, but only a recognition of the temporal and presumably causal continuity within the emergence of significant differences in the order of nature. Our present purpose is to inquire concerning the grounds of these assumptions.

In support of spiritual pluralism, there seems in truth to be very little that can be said. In the first place, there appears to be no empirical evidence for it; and, in the second place, it is a dangerous interpretation of the principle. Each of these points may be separately emphasized, though I must confess that both to my mind seem obvious.

It is indeed true enough that we all have to begin in our thinking with the only point of departure we have, namely, experience. It is true also that within that experience there are aspects that are relatively 'immediate,' and, more specifically, we must begin with these. But granting the principle of con-

tinuity as in some sense we must, I fail to see any implication
that the lower orders of nature are to be conceived as 'spiritual'
centers. It is doubtful whether we have a more 'direct' acquaintance with ourselves than we do with sticks and stones
and the starry heavens. Even assuming that we do, it is still
more doubtful that sticks and stones and the starry heavens
must be conceived after our likeness. For *ex hypothesi* what we
begin with is experience, and experience involves sticks and
stones and the starry heavens as obviously as it involves
selves. Even assuming that it involves selves in a manner
in which it does not involve these things, we find in that assumption no compulsion to the inference that these things are
somehow selves. I realize, of course, that I am here making use
of terminology that is shot through with vagueness and ambiguities. But I submit that these are indifferent to the point
in question. Whatever meaning you may attach to *self* and to
things—unless, indeed, the point in question is assumed in the
definition of the latter—there is, in the principle of continuity
and the fact that our philosophical construction must begin with
experience, no logical basis to be found for the conclusion that
things are selves, or are analogous to selves.

Furthermore, a serious methodological danger lies in this interpretation of the principle of continuity. For on the basis of
it we are threatened with an *unbridled* anthropomorphism in
philosophy; and the italics here must I think be allowed to
stand. That anthropomorphism threatens us seems plain, and
in fact it is admitted by the proponents of this interpretation
of the principle. They think to minimize the danger, however,
by denying that the anthropomorphism with which we are
threatened is 'crude.' But I fail to see the reason for this.

In the first place, it is not easy to determine degrees of 'crude-
ness' among types of anthropomorphic interpretations. There
seems to be no ready criterion by which we are enabled
to say whether the 'explanation' of the storm-cloud, for example, by attributing to it a sort of personality, as the savage
does, is more or less 'crude' than that by reference to the more
refined 'spiritual centres' vaguely conceived as 'analogous' to our
'selves.' If there is such a criterion, it would seem to suggest

that explanation in terms of full-blown volition and purpose is less 'crude' than explanation in terms of 'spiritual centres' so poorly defined that they tend to become indistinguishable from the mere 'physical events' which by the hypothesis are excluded.

In the second place, any type of 'explanation' which proceeds through an argument by analogy from ourselves to other things is, from the standpoint of scientific inquiry at any rate, necessarily crude throughout. Its procedure is precisely that against which science has struggled from the beginning. Unless philosophy is in this respect to differ radically from science, insistence upon this method of procedure in philosophical speculation is unwarranted. If it is to differ thus, its method is diametrically opposed to that of scientific inquiry and the results achieved by it are everywhere equally 'crude.' For these reasons it would appear that the anthropomorphism with which this interpretation of the principle of continuity threatens us is unbridled. It is wholly without any logical safeguard, and it sets philosophy against science at its very root.

This anthropomorphic interpretation of the principle of continuity therefore, must be given up. There is apparently no ground for it in the principle itself, and it commits us to a method whose demands are hardly sufficiently rigorous to save us from mistaking metaphors for categories of explanation. The case for the other interpretation, however, is quite different. Much can be said in support of it, and in the main it must be allowed to stand.

"Continuity of process and the emergence of real differences" —these, Pringle-Pattison urges, are the "twin aspects of the cosmic history, and it is essential to clear thinking that the one be not allowed to obscure the other." [1] His position seems to be essentially sound on both points. *Prima facie*, at least, the "twin aspects" are plain enough, and presumably there are no differences of opinion about them thus taken. Differences arise when the effort is made to get beneath the *prima facie* view, and it is in connection with this effort that Pringle-Pattison's second point gains special significance. Naturalism and

[1] *The Idea of God*, p. 103.

'spiritualism' agree in denying the 'reality' of the emergent differences, but differ in their reasons for this denial. Naturalism would base its denial on the ground that the emergent differences can be explained in terms of antecedent conditions, while 'spiritualism' would base its denial on the ground that they can be explained in terms of a common character which, though present throughout, comes clearly to view only at the later or 'higher' level. Their common error, from the standpoint of Pringle-Pattison's "higher naturalism," is in their agreement that the 'reality' of the emergent differences must be resolved by this process of 'leveling'—whether 'upwards' or 'downwards' makes no difference in principle. From this standpoint, no leveling of the differences is possible; they stand as they are, real differences that cannot be resolved, however far 'beneath' the *prima facie* view one may penetrate. And I have ventured to affirm that this position is essentially sound.

It is, of course, impossible here to argue the matter in detail. To undertake to do so would involve us in other issues that could be adequately traced only in an extended statement for which space is not here available. It would also be inappropriate in the present context, where we are primarily concerned to fix the immediate issue and note its ramifications. But a word further in this direction seems called for, particularly by way of making explicit some of the difficulties embedded within the position.

If the position is sound, two questions at least must be satisfactorily answered. The first is: By what criterion are 'real' differences to be determined? The second is: What is to be understood by 'emergence,' when it is said that there is "the emergence of real differences"? Both questions present difficulties which are not easily resolved if the position is true.

The difficulty involved in the first question arises from the fact that there are many differences in "cosmic history" which presumably cannot be said to be 'real' differences in the sense contemplated. For example, there is obviously a difference between the two colors, red and green; and it would appear that this difference is not a 'real' one, in the sense intended, since both can be explained in terms of a common principle, namely vibrations of light-waves. Or, is every distinguishable difference a 'real' difference? In that event, the reality of differences would apparently not be inconsistent with the process of 'leveling down,' as it is assumed to be, and the "lower naturalism" would thereby be admitted in principle. Clearly, in any case, some criterion is called for by which 'real' and 'unreal' differences may be differentiated; and, equally clearly, there is a troublesome problem involved in its definition. Unless there is such a criterion, all distinguishable differences are 'real' differences. And if differences which may be reduced to a common principle of explanation are to be denied the status of 'real' differences, what differences are there which may not be so reduced and why?

Assuming 'real' differences and assuming a criterion by which they may be distinguished from other differences that are not real, we are yet confronted by the question as to what is to be understood by 'emergence' when it is held that these real differences come up in the course of cosmic history. That this question is not easily answered is evidenced by the difficulty met by those who have explicitly undertaken to answer it.[2] Nor is the source of the difficulty in answering far to seek. By hypothesis, 'real' differences in the process of events are (presumably) in some sense irreducible; and yet, on the other side, they 'emerge' in the process and (presumably) as 'natural' parts or elements of it. This state of affairs apparently presents us with a dilemma. If they are irreducible they cannot emerge as 'natural' elements in the process; if they do so emerge they cannot be irreducible. I myself do not believe that this dilemma in the end holds; but it is not without foundation in the position we are here considering, and its resolution calls for a careful examination of the notion of 'emergence.'

2. INTELLIGIBILITY IN NATURE

Underlying the two questions here presented in connection with the thesis of the "higher naturalism" is the second of the

---

[2] Compare, for instance, the views of S. Alexander in *Space, Time and Deity,* and of Lloyd Morgan in *Emergent Evolution* and *Life, Mind and Spirit.*

four issues formulated in our introductory outline of the controversy among the types of idealism—the issue, namely, of the intelligibility of nature. For in the end these two questions state, in different ways, the one question as to whether, on this thesis, nature is intelligible. In passing on to this second major issue, therefore, we are really continuing the discussion of the questions raised above with reference to the "higher naturalism." But I wish to break off the discussion at this point, and turn to the general problem of intelligibility for more or less independent consideration. By following this method we shall have an opportunity to bring together into a more constructive statement many stands of the preceding criticisms of the types of argument considered in this survey. In the end we shall inquire concerning the bearing of the thesis meanwhile formulated on the concept of 'emergence' and on the contention by Creighton and Pringle-Pattison that nature, as interpreted by 'spiritualism,' is necessarily unintelligible.

That the problem of intelligibility is among the basal problems of philosophy is a trite statement, and needs here no emphasis. But, despite its basal character, differences of opinion with reference to its proper solution are marked. Two views have run pretty well through the history of philosophy, and these two are clearly exemplified in the types of argument advanced in support of idealism as here under survey. It is, therefore, appropriate that the present discussion of the problem be oriented with reference to these two views. They are, first, the view represented by the advocates of the argument *a contingentia mundi*, and, second, the view represented partly by the exponents of the epistemological argument but exemplified *par excellence* in the ontological argument of McTaggart.

The major difference between these two views may be shortly and fairly adequately expressed by saying that, for the first, the criterion of intelligibility is the order of existence and, for the second, intelligibility is the criterion of that order. The thesis which I wish here briefly to defend is that each of these views is correct in what it explicitly affirms and between them there is no necessary contradiction. Or, put independently, the thesis is that intelligibility is a characteristic of the order of existence, and it is also a characteristic of intelligence itself, but that this is neither a self-contradictory nor a merely circular statement.[8]

The first consideration to be specially noted is that before thinking can take place at all there must be something to be thought about, some object of thought, and this object (ideally, at least) is the controlling factor in the situation. In whatever sense thought may be creative, it certainly cannot be so in the sense that it creates its own object. Its object, even though purely hypothetical, is there as, in some important sense, a datum which is not created but found; and as a datum it exerts a determining influence in the process of thinking, since the 'necessity' of thought has its habitat in it. That thought is acquiescence under compulsion is a thesis in which we are all at the last compelled to acquiesce. To the extent that thought cuts itself free from this complusion, it tends to depart from its own nature and to fall away into mere 'dreaming' and, carried far enough, even into inanity.

The position here stated is, I think, foundational. The direction in which its justification is to be sought, and (in my opinion) found, lies in rigorous analysis of the actual procedure of intelligence itself. Such an analysis would disclose, I take it, that *prima facie* all our judgments are interpretations of more or less independent situations, that the necessity of thought lies in the situation with which it deals, and that apart from the situation *the necessity of thought* is a meaningless, because empty, phrase. Such an analysis would not in the end go beyond these principles. Of course, the controlling situation need not be a 'datum' in the sense in which a perceived situation is such; but however hypothetical, it still has its categorical aspect, however much it may be a matter of postulates and assumptions these have their own implications and they also have a larger context which makes them amenable to critical consideration and evaluation. Logical possibility is grounded in the 'given.' When not thus grounded, possibility is for intelligence fruitless; it is then vain and void, and vain because void. On this point

---

[8] What follows is partly taken from my article on "Emergence and Intelligibility," *International Journal of Ethics*, Vol. XXXIX, No. 2, p. 154 ff.

McTaggart's difficulties, above discussed, are eloquent witnesses; and the failure of his method turns largely on the fact that he overlooks it.[4] And any other method which overlooks it must pay the price of inconsistency, since thought's 'necessity' ultimately resides in its object and not in the act of thinking itself.

And if this be true, then we are committed to the view that 'existence'—interpreted broadly enough to include postulated objects—is the criterion of intelligibility. What is intelligible and what is not cannot be abstractly determined, but must be determined with reference to the relevant situation; in the abstract and without reference to the given situation, no meaning can be attached to intelligibility. What in the face of a situation we are compelled to affirm is that which is intelligible about the situation, and it is intelligible precisely because we are compelled to affirm it. What is intelligible is what has meaning, and it is intelligible precisely in the sense in which it has meaning. What is unintelligible is what has no meaning, and its unintelligibility is precisely identical with its meaningless character. But what has or lacks meaning, and what meaning it has or in what sense it is meaningless, the object alone can tell us. Intelligibility and unintelligibility are of the object's making, not of our own. The proposition that the moon is made of green cheese may be of the highest significance or it may be utterly silly, and which it is remains for the relevant situation to disclose.

But the object of thought itself at times needs correction. It cannot always be accepted at its face value, and its claims not infrequently may not be allowed. Nor do we hesitate to modify or reject it, as the case may be. And on this side, it would appear, intelligence becomes the criterion of existence. For when the object needs correction, the court of appeal is that of intelligence. Whether the object may stand without correction, if its claims are challenged, or whether it must be subjected to a greater or less degree of modification, or whether,

---

[4] Compare Leibniz's difficulties with his "sufficient reason" and the order of contingent things. Note particularly that he is forced in the end to ground his sufficient reason in 'substance' or a 'necessary being' (*Principles of Nature and Grace*, section 8), just as McTaggart is; and in both alike 'sufficient reason' tends to move in a circle.

perchance, it must be rejected entirely—this is for intelligence to determine.

This, too, is a fundamental character of our cognitive experience, as an analysis of the actual procedure of intelligence, once again, will show. The whole history of science lies in support of it. For the road which scientific development has followed is lined with 'objects of knowledge' which have been discarded because they could not stand the examination that intellectual analysis imposed upon them; and many which have survived have done so at the price of undergoing more or less serious modification to meet the demands of intelligence. The same is, of course, true of the history of philosophy itself.

Hereupon we seem to be caught in a vicious circle. Above, we have urged that the object of knowledge is the criterion of its own intelligibility; but here we are saying that intelligence itself is the criterion. Is this a vicious circle? I do not see that it is, and a few preliminary considerations may indicate the ground for this answer.

These can here be stated only in the merest outline, and I shall set them down in the form of three postulates. The first is a repetition of what has already been urged, namely, that thought is always *of* something and this something controls. The second is that this 'something' is always complex, never quite simple, and that it is systematic in the sense that inference may move from term to term within it. The third, which is perhaps a repetition of the second with a different emphasis, is that this situation presents two distinguishable, but inseparable, aspects: on one side it has the character of immediateness, and on the other it calls for mediation and inference. These three postulates might be summarily stated as follows: There is for thought an object which controls, but the object is complex and may be taken either as 'itself' or as the manifestation of a context of which it is an element and to which it is implicatively attached.

Thus, there are two distinguishable meanings of 'intelligibility.' It may mean the character of the object of thought taken in its immediacy; or it may mean the object of thought taken as an element or part of a larger context. In the first meaning,

everything which we ordinarily speak of as a 'fact,' whether 'real' or 'illusory,' is intelligible; it is what it is immediately taken as, and as so taken it is accepted as intelligible. But, as so taken, it may be mis-taken; and therefore its 'intelligibility' in the second meaning is called for, and can be defined only through further intellectual analysis.

Returning to our dilemma with this distinction in mind, we can see that the circle is not a vicious one. When we say that the object determines intelligibility, what we primarily intend is the assertion that we cannot create our ideas out of nothing, but that they must run with 'fact.' When, on the other hand, we say that intelligence is the criterion of intelligibility, what we primarily intend is the assertion that the datum itself, if demanding correction or modification, is relative to the processes of intelligence—that, in other words, 'fact' is itself an intellectual construction. And, when this distinction with its ground is borne in mind, we can see that it is no merely circular statement to say that the object controls intelligence and yet at the same time the correction of the object is the work of intelligence. For the term 'object' is used in different senses in the statement; and the work of intelligence which 'corrects' the object in the first sense is itself under the control of the object in the second sense. Thus it is the object which controls throughout; and it is only because of an oversight concerning the complexity of the object that the supposition arises that the object itself is corrigible by mere intelligence. What is known or thought is, so far, intelligible simply because it is known or thought; it is such that the thought about it is possible. But what is actually thought is not necessarily what, under the circumstances, ought to be thought; it may need correction. This, however, means only that the immediate thought is not necessarily the final thought, and that the first sort of 'intelligibility' calls for further development. And— this is the important point—this further development is under the control of the farther reaches of the 'object of thought.' If immediate intelligibility is unsatisfactory, it is so because the object of thought is not adequately stated or described in terms of it. What it needs is elaboration into a mediated intellig

bility which spells out the character of its remoter context through intellectual analysis and inference moving within it. Thus, 'to be intelligible is to be' and 'to be is to be intelligible' are both in principle true and express basic aspects of the cognitive situation. But they are not simply convertible propositions, since intelligibility is a matter of degrees measured by penetration into a complex situation, and the degree contemplated by one of the propositions is not necessarily identical with the degree contemplated by the other. Only when the degree of intelligibility involved contemplates the total system, which is the 'object of knowledge' in the case, can the two propositions be said logically to fall together.

Summarizing the results of these general remarks, we may say that the categories of thought are primarily descriptive in the sense that what we are to think about objects, if we think truly, remains for the objects themselves to tell us and is not of our own arbitrary and unguided choice or preference. We think as we must, and we must think as the object of thought dictates. This does not mean, however, that, in the case of nature, the insight of the first look is to be taken as nature's final word about herself. It happens, on the contrary, that she apparently invariably has more to say and that such immediate insight demands correction. This 'more' can be had only by means of processes of inference which go beyond the immediately given. Here we may say, if it pleases us, that our categories tend to become explanatory in some more deeply significant manner. But we certainly go astray if we assume that such explanation, in its turn, is wholly independent of the object's leading, as if the immediately intelligible were sheer error and corrigible only by reference to some abstract a priori intelligence. Such explanation is still description, but mediated description, of the object. It is precisely the outcome of thought's penetration into the object's yonder side and the correlative modification of the first appearance of its hither side in the light thus revealed. By its nature thought is descriptive of objects, but it is not content with immediate appearances; by its nature thought is explanatory of objects, but it is not concerned to impose upon them principles of its own creation. Its

aim, ideally, is to speak the message of nature; but it can do so, adequately, only in so far as it penetrates the farther reaches of its immediate object and continuously reinterprets and rectifies the view of the first look.

This view of intelligence and intelligibility is in principle affirmed by the argument *a contingentia mundi;* but in the course of its development at the hands of the absolutists, the fact that the object controls throughout is in the end forgotten and even implicitly denied. On the other side, the control of the object is implicitly rejected from the beginning by the epistemological and ontological arguments; but in the end this rejection is not consistently maintained. And the difficulties involved in the several statements of these arguments may in the main be traced to the sources here indicated, as the criticisms above expressed have presumably shown in some detail.

But our more immediate concern is to inquire into the bearing of the view on the notion of 'emergence' and the insistence that panpsychism or 'spiritualism' is intrinsically unintelligible. And to this inquiry we now turn.

With reference to the intelligibility of the notion of 'emergence,' two remarks may suffice. The first is that it must be determined only in the light of the relevant facts. The questions about the notion raised above must, indeed, receive a satisfactory answer if the notion is to be said to be intelligible; but what the satisfactory answer is remains for the facts in the case to decide. Is 'mind,' for instance, an emergent difference which is 'real'? What is the ground for holding that it is? What precisely is to be understood by the statement that it is? These are questions which, when answered, disclose its 'intelligibility.' And they can be answered only by an analytical study of 'mind' and its context. The second remark, the converse of the first, is that the intelligibility of the notion of 'emergence' cannot be finally determined by means of general *a priori* principles. There is no justification whatever for throwing it into the outer darkness of unintelligibility merely because it does not satisfy the demands of some preconceived conception as to what it must be if it is to be intelligible; the preconceived conception may itself be groundless,

and the only way to check it is to appeal to the object whose
'emergence' is in question.

The same in principle holds of the position of the 'spiritualist.'
Suppose nature to be as he describes it—an order of 'spiritual
centres' characterized by varying degrees of 'spirituality' and interconnected in such fashion that they act together with the degree of uniformity demanded by the so-called laws of nature. Is
such a description intelligible? Is nature thus described rational?
It is, provided the description proffered is an accurate description
—that is, provided the 'spiritual centres,' thus ordered and uniform, are 'explanatory' concepts demanded by a careful analysis
of the factual situations, the objects, for the explanation of which
they are invoked. Granted that they are accurately descriptive
of the deeper aspects of the *prima facie* view of nature, as is
claimed for them, then they are intelligible and rationally necessary in the only sense in which it is logically possible for any
conceptual constructions to be. If they are not so descriptive,
then they are not intelligible and to assume them is arbitrary.

Whether 'emergence' and 'spiritual centres' are to be taken as
intelligible is, of course, a question which is not just here before
us. I am inclined to think that in some sense the first must be;
and I am convinced that the second cannot be, in the sense intended by the panpsychist. But this is irrelevant. Our present
concern is with the general conditions under which they may, or
may not, be so taken. And if the preceding discussion of intelligibility is sound, those conditions are plain. They may be so
taken, if they are concepts which necessarily grow out of the
analysis of the relevant objects considered in their full sweep.
If they do not thus grow out of such analysis, they may not be so
taken. In the first case, they are intelligible because logically
necessary; in the second case, they are unintelligible because
logically arbitrary. And in each case, logical 'necessity' or the
reverse is defined in terms of the complete object, not in terms of
a priori principles abstractly conceived.

And what is here said holds also of the conception of the Absolute, as indeed of all human conceptions which are to have an
application to existence. The intelligibility of the Absolute rests
upon the ability of the concept to describe, and so to explain, the

ultimate reach of experience. This need not be labored, however, since the thesis above developed holds true of all our intellectual constructions, if it holds true at all, and certainly the Absolute is such a construction.

But it does need to be emphasized, since some of the critics of absolutism have at times written as if they supposed the absolutist to assume that his conception of the Absolute were somehow logically privileged and not subject to the ordinary rules of logical procedure. It is clear that the absolutist assumes nothing of the sort, at least it should be clear to any one who has taken the trouble to become acquainted with his argument. He is perfectly willing to subject the conception to the ordinary tests of intelligibility; and, in the main, he is in agreement with the preceding statement of what those tests concretely are. What he contends is that his conception is required by any adequate analysis of experience, and he is willing to have his conception tried by such analysis.

3. THE PROBLEM OF INDIVIDUALITY

The idealistic critics of the absolutist, clearly cognizant of the ground on which he builds, maintain that the Absolute fails precisely because it cannot stand such trial. The absolutist insists that it is a necessary implication of human experience, while his critics hold that it does violence to the most characteristic aspect of that experience, namely, the experiencer himself. Given the Absolute as defined, they urge, the finite experiencer is not merely 'negated,' as Bosanquet says he is, but his very integrity is undermined. So far from implying the Absolute, finite experience cannot, in their opinion, stand in the face of it—the finite subject of experience cannot look upon the Absolute and live. In the end, they conclude, the truth of absolutism is inconsistent with its being known to be true. And, of course, if this criticism is logically justified it is fatal to the conception of the Absolute.

The differences between the absolutist and his personalistic critics turn primarily upon different readings of the nature of the finite individual. Of course, different views about the Absolute are also involved; but these are consequent, not prior. They fol-

low from the different readings of finite individuality, which are
logically fundamental in the controversy. The point of the controversy may, therefore, be sharpened by a concise statement as
to what these readings are.

And they may be put in few words. The personalist, on his
side, is impressed by the uniqueness and existential distinctness
of the finite individual. For him, the individual is a punctual center of reference, and the essence of its individuality lies in its
unity. This unity he looks upon as indefeasible, and for this
reason he deems the Absolute untenable; if it is to be retained,
this unity is logically disrupted and the essential character of the
finite individual thereby destroyed. The absolutist, however, is
not greatly impressed with the uniqueness of the finite individual.
On the contrary, its unity seems to him a matter of degrees. He stresses, rather, the variations within the individual,
and particularly the discrepancy between the actual and the
ideal. The essential character of the individual he finds in its
quality of universality, and the Absolute he regards as merely
the actualization of this; hence he can say that the Absolute "is
simply the high-water mark of fluctuations in experience, of
which in general, we are daily and normally aware." In short:
the personalist finds the principle of individuality in the "indivisible unity" of the finite subject, whereas the absolutist finds it in
the universality embedded in the fluctuations of the subject's
'content.'

But the chief point of difference does not lie precisely here.
It is not quite fair to the personalist to say that he seeks the
principle of individuality in the "indivisible unity" of the subject, unless it is explicitly understood that this unity is not by
him interpreted as excluding reference to content. He, too, emphasizes content as important within individual experience, and
he has no intention of excluding it. What he is chiefly concerned
to insist upon is that the content always has a center of reference, apart from which it is an abstraction; and further that
this center of reference is indispensable to finite experience, in
the sense that if it is removed experience is rendered null. Thus
the main point of his emphasis is that the uniqueness of the
finite individual must remain inviolate throughout, and any the-

ory which violates it—as, he holds, absolutism does—is on that account to be discarded.

The absolutist, on his side, does not deny that there is such a center of reference in finite experience; and he is willing to admit that, so long as finite experience itself is alone in question, the uniqueness of this center is indispensable. He is quite content to agree with the personalist that there could be no finite experience unless there were an experiencer; remove the experiencer, and the experience vanishes. But finite experience itself points to its own transcendence, he would urge; and this is the main point which he wishes to emphasize. The center of the content is not, he insists, a punctual monad, but it is expansive and shot through with change.

We may, therefore, more precisely fix the point at issue in the controversy by saying that what is in question is the indefeasibility of the center of reference which, it is agreed on both sides, is a basal character of finite experience. The one insists that it is indefeasible, and in doing so he has his eye upon its indispensable rôle within experience; the other insists that it is not so, and here the stress is upon the development of experience and the fact that the center itself is not untouched by the process.

Now, presumably there can be no question that the center of finite experience, or what we commonly call the 'self,' is a thing of degrees and variations and is deeply touched by the experiences which time brings. The fact is so obvious that it has become embedded in our common speech, and systematic analysis does but confirm the insight of common sense. We are more ourselves on some occasions than on others, we 'come to' ourselves, 'make up' our minds, learn to see what we really are and want. And the passing of the years leaves little in us that is unchanged. "If by a miracle a man of 60 could have himself, as a boy of 10, introduced to him and open to his insight, is there anything, apart from external history, or bodily marks, by which he could identify him with himself?" And to the answer which Bosanquet assumes must be given to the question we should all doubtless agree in the principle: There is nothing. " 'Twas I, but 'tis not I" is always, and of all of us, profoundly true. The center of experience is no timeless point or static entity.

This emphasis of the absolutist is, then, rightly placed. However in detail the 'self' may be described, whether as essentially spiritual or as exclusively bodily, no doubt can presumably be entertained concerning its dynamic and variant nature. But there is nothing in this to justify the conclusion that the center of experience, the experiencer, is only 'provisional' and must in the end be held to be unreal. Merely because it changes is no reason for supposing that its ultimate significance must be denied, unless, for other reasons, the ultimate significance of change itself is to be denied.

Of course, the absolutist thinks that there are reasons for the general denial, and it is upon this ground that he condemns the changing self to the status of a mere phenomenon. But these reasons seem hardly convincing, and I wish to digress briefly in order to consider them.

The first reason is that given by Bradley, and it runs to the effect that time is essentially relational and therefore inherently contradictory. If we consider time under a spatial form, as a stream of which past and future are parts, we are told, we are at once troubled by the puzzle about terms and relations. " 'Before in relation to after' is the character of time; and here the old difficulties about relation and quality recommence. The relation is not a unity, and yet the terms are nonentities, if left apart." Nor are we any better off if we concentrate attention on time "as it comes," and avoid the figure of the stream. For thus taken, time is now; and the 'now' is not a point, but a process. But "any process admitted destroys the 'now' from within. Before and after are diverse, and their incompatibility compels us to use a relation between them. Then at once the old wearisome game is played again." Thus, however considered, time involves terms seeking relations, and relations seeking terms, equally in vain.

The argument here clearly assumes a distinction between terms and relations, such that they cannot be intelligibly attached to each other. In so far as such an assumption is well-grounded, as I have insisted above in the discussion of Bradley's general theory of relations, relational experience is *ipso facto* unintelligible and self-contradictory. But the important question here before us is whether, in respect of time, the assumption is well-grounded. If it is, its ground must lie in the character of time itself as an experienced fact; and I can see in the character of time nothing to warrant the basal thesis upon which Bradley builds. That thesis, in last analysis, is that the essential character of time, namely 'before in relation to after,' involves two terms ('before' and 'after') which are diverse and call vainly for a relation, and yet without a relation are 'nonentities.'

I have no objection to the statement here given of the essential character of time; time is at least 'before in relation to after.' But I fail to see that Bradley's reason for holding this character to be logically impossible is sound. That 'before' and 'after' are diverse, is true enough presumably. But are they diverse in the sense that "their incompatibility compels us to use a relation between them"? Why may it not be the case that their 'incompatibility' arises simply from the fact that they are different aspects of a relation which holds within a relationship of which events are the terms related? This I should suppose is the more accurate description of the matter; and I should suppose, further, that it removes any compulsion on us to "use a relation between them" in the sense apparently intended by the expression. If the description is to stand, I can attach no meaning to the statement that a temporal situation calls for a relation which it lacks and which must be introduced *ab extra,* or that the relation which it seems to have is not a 'unity' of the terms supposedly related. Nor am I able to see why the description may not stand.

Thus, it would appear, Bradley's criticism of the reality of time, proceeding from its character, is groundless. It rests upon the assumption that time is a relational process in which there are no unifying relations—no relations, in other words, which relate the terms involved—and in the character of time there seems no clear warrant for this assumption. The reverse assumption that the relations do relate, seems here, as elsewhere where experienced relationships are in question, the necessary one; and there is no reason for denying it—unless, indeed, one has already decided on other grounds that reality and time are logically incompatible concepts.

That the absolutist has other grounds for this decision is, of course, well known. And these lie in the nature of the Absolute. The Absolute is, by definition, all there is, hence it cannot change its nature; and, since the Absolute is synonymous with reality, reality must therefore be timeless and nothing temporal can, as such, be real. So runs the other argument against the reality of time and the temporal. Clearly, its validity depends upon the prior question whether the Absolute as here intended has been proved to be identical with reality; and we have seen reason elsewhere for doubting that this has been done. But if it has not, then this argument against the reality of time is not convincing.

There is no need to repeat here the criticisms of the arguments in support of the Absolute which have been advanced above. It is necessary, however, to point out that, from the point of view of intelligent discussion, condemnation of an apparently basal character of the self in behalf of the claims of the Absolute is a very questionable procedure; the nature of the self is nearer at hand than is the nature of the Absolute, and if the two natures conflict it is important to note on which side the presumption lies. So far at least as I am able to see, it would appear to be more in keeping with our common intellectual procedure to shape the nature of the Absolute, as the "general view" which is to satisfy intelligence, to the demands of verifiable aspects of experience, than to bend these so as to fit them into some preconception of that nature; for this is surely derivative from those, so far at least as human knowledge is concerned, and this fact is quite significant in respect of the question whether the nature of the Absolute is to be invoked in denial of what seems to be an indispensable character of finite experience.

Thus, neither the proffered analysis of the empirical character of experience as temporal nor the appeal to the all-inclusiveness of the Absolute seems to support the absolutist's contention that the center of finite experience is in the end unreal. The analysis assumes a general theory of relations which is questionable; and the appeal to the Absolute assumes that the character of the finite center must be trimmed to the nature of the Absolute, and thus begs the point at issue in the controversy. So far as these general considerations go, therefore, the claims of the finite center appear to stand uncompromised by its temporal character.

But change within the center of experience is not the character of it upon which the absolutist actually builds his case against its reality. The fact that it changes is, indeed, in his opinion, indicative of its essentially phenomenal nature. But, when he is confronted with the question as to what specific character of the finite center of experience seems most definitely to establish its unreality, he points, not to its dynamic character, but to the element of self-transcendence which it manifests. It is unreal, he seems primarily to say, because it always points beyond itself for its own fullest expression and deepest achievement.

That experience exhibits such a character must, I think, once more be admitted. Even the most commonplace experience involves a reference beyond, and this reference becomes more marked as experience grows more critical; in what we are pleased to call the more significant forms of experience, as in scientific achievement or genuinely moral endeavor, it is the paramount feature. And, on the other side, any experience which is not characterized by self-transcendence could be only that of a God or that of "a finite clod untroubled by a spark"; it certainly could not be that of a normal human being. All of this, I say, must be admitted. But what does it prove with reference to the question before us?

According to the absolutist, it proves that the self-centeredness of experience is not a basal character, but is one which is being transcended even before our eyes. The fact that experience 'transcends' itself, and by its very nature must do so, is in his view evidence that the reality of experience lies elsewhere than in its own four corners. And this reality, he maintains, is prefigured in that aspect of experience, namely, its universal character, which makes this transcendence necessary and inevitable. The principle of individuality, therefore, he concludes, is in the universality of experience, and not in its 'uniqueness' or 'existential distinctness.'

In all of this, it would appear, there is an element of important truth. But it does not seem to me that the truth involved is that which the absolutist reads out of it. And I wish briefly to develop this point.

I do not myself doubt that normal human experience at least is characterized by 'self-transcendence,' in the sense that it always involves a reference, more or less significant, beyond what is actually experienced at the moment; nor do I doubt that the significance of the reference increases with broadening and deepening experience. I agree, also, that this reference is possible only through the element of universality within experience—is, indeed, precisely what is to be understood by the element of universality, since it is just the thread which links the experiencer with the world about him. And this, I am willing to admit further, is in itself sufficient to show that the essence of individuality is sought in vain, if it be sought in any sort of 'uniqueness' or 'existential distinctness' which is to be defined in terms of mere exclusiveness or punctual self-centeredness—as was done, for example, by the older soul-substance theory. But I fail to see how it proves that the 'uniqueness' of experience, in any sense, is merely 'provisional' and cannot be allowed to remain.

So far from proving this, as it seems to my mind, the character of self-transcendence proves exactly the opposite. As the reference 'beyond' is given free play and allowed to have its way with the individual, does he become any the less a unique individual as result? Not only do I fail to see that such is the case, but I seem to see that the reverse is the accurate account of the matter: 'personality' and 'uniqueness' are thereby intensified. Of course, self-centeredness as identical with narrowness of vision or contractedness of interests is transcended; but self-centeredness in a deeper sense is enhanced. With the broadening of interests and horizons, there is a concomitant enrichment of the center. The growth of experience, it would appear, is just this dual process: On the one side an advance beyond present attainment in outlook and action, and on the other side a deepening of insight and an intensification of purpose. Nor must the significance of the correlative character of these two aspects of the process be overlooked or neglected. They grow together, it would appear, or not at all; and, if this be true, the self-transcendence of experience inevitably implies—is indeed constituted by—the expansion of the content and the enrichment of the center both of which take place *pari passu.*

The absolutist neglects this, or he would hardly suppose that the self-transcendence of experience can be stated solely in terms of its universality and that the 'subject' aspect is of constantly diminishing significance in the process. He neglects it because of his persistent tendency to identify 'experience' exclusively with its content. Fixing attention on the content, on *what* is thought or done, he forgets the thinker or doer, and especially forgets that what one thinks or does creates a different thinker or doer who is the *sine qua non* of the varying content. If this oversight is not made, it seems even plain that the character of self-transcendence, the principle of individuality, cannot be stated in terms of the universal aspect of experience taken alone. It must also include a reference to the deepening, or at least changing, center of experience, which reference is in fact but the reverse side of the aspect of universality. If, however, the oversight is made, then one must pay the penalty which always follows in philosophical speculation when a bare abstraction is taken seriously.[6]

In the light of the preceding consideration, it is presumably needless for me to state that, in my own view, the controversy between personalist and absolutist concerning the principle of individuality must be decided, in part at least, against the absolutist. In so far as the absolutist maintains that finite individuals as centers of experience are 'provisional' only, and must in the end be 'sublated' or 'transmuted' in Reality, I cannot find in empirical observation any ground upon which he may base his claim. And as against this claim it would appear that the personalist's insistence on the indefeasibility of the 'unity' in finite experience is empirically sounder.

There is intended here, however, no blanket endorsement of the personalist's entire position. I seem to find in that position cer-

[6] Compare Pringle-Pattison's criticism of Bosanquet's view about the 'overlapping' of selves, in the Symposium, *Proceedings of the Aristotelian Society*, July, 1918. "A self may be largely identical in content with other selves, and in that sense we may intelligibly talk of 'overlapping,' but to speak as if their common content affected in any way their existential distinctness is to use words to which I can attach no meaning."

tain emphases that tend to neglect the truth in the absolutist's insistence on the universal aspect of experience. These are mainly two, and I wish briefly to state them in concluding this survey of the controversy.

The first of these is the insistence that the freedom of the individual must be conceived as lying in some fiat of the will or mere act of choice. This seems to me to be a mistaken emphasis. I am indeed committed in principle to the position advocated by Pringle-Pattison: "The authorship of our own acts and our responsibility for them—this is the inmost meaning of our freedom and independence, and any theory is self-condemned which can find no room for this elementary certainty." But it seems to me an error of fact to identify freedom with the mere psychological act of willing or choosing. Here, I think, one must agree rather with Bosanquet: "Nothing can come of nothing; and by itself myself, consisting of its acts, is nothing."

The important point to note in connection with freedom is the universal aspect of experience, the participation of the finite individual in the larger meanings which link him with the world of thought and action beyond; in the end, will is free as thought is free. Of course, it is important not to forget that authorship of acts and responsibility for them is an ineradicable feature of finite experience which no theory should eradicate; and the absolutist is prone to forget this when he comes to speak of the Absolute, however much lip-service he may pay it in his descriptive statements. But it is also equally important not to forget that the content of the act is an ineradicable feature of it, apart from which it is largely empty and meaningless; and this the personalist is at times prone to overlook in his zeal for "existential distinctness."

The second emphasis of the personalist which I deprecate, and which is closely linked with the preceding, if, indeed, it is not at one with it, is the emphasis on the 'exclusiveness' of the individual, as if it were possessed of a nuclear character which somehow remains fixed and impervious to change. Such an emphasis seems to me not different essentially from the soul-substance view, and to involve all of the difficulties of the older theory. Nor can I see how it is to stand, if the correlativeness of center and content of experience is not to be denied. If the absolutist errs (as I think he does) in forgetting the fact that content refers always to a center and is an abstraction outside of the reference, the personalist commits essentially the same error in forgetting that the center is always one term in such a reference and is therefore implicatively involved in the universal character of experience. The content apart from the center is abstract. Agreed; but so is the center apart from the content.

It is just here, as I have tried to indicate in the preceding chapter, that McTaggart's view of the self, especially, seems to be weak and indefensible. It is this separation between center and content, if I may repeat the criticism for purposes of illustrating the point now before us, which underlies the main difficulties attaching to his statement of the principle of determining correspondence as holding within spirit. The self, we recall, is conceived as an exclusive center of being, whose parts are perceptions which manifest it but do not manifest its 'nature' or 'characteristics'; neither the self nor any of its parts, apparently, involves an essential relation to content. Thus there is in the self and its parts no character of universality; the essential character is that of merely "existential distinctness." [7] This is the reason why McTaggart is forced to exclude from his statement of the principle of determining correspondence as exemplified in 'spirit' the notion of 'description' which was basal in his general formulation of the principle; 'description' has to do with content, and 'spirit' is something quite different. And this is also the reason why, as applied to 'spirit,' the principle breaks down; there is nothing in spirit as defined on which the principle may stand, since it presupposes implication and implication presupposes universality.

Thus, to return to our main thread, in adjudicating the controversy between the personalist and the absolutist with reference to the principle of individuality, it is not clear that the verdict may be rendered exclusively in favor of either. Both emphasize important aspects of experience, but both also seem to overlook

[7] The phrase is Pringle-Pattison's, but its use here is mine, not his. However, it seems apt as applied to McTaggart's view, though with a shade of meaning which it does not have perhaps for Pringle-Pattison himself.

equally important matters. At least, the absolutist tends to forget that content apart from a center is an abstraction, and the personalist tends (sometimes, at any rate) to minimize the significance of content in respect of the center. The crucial consideration is the relationship between center and content and the functional nature of the relation; the center is what the content makes it, and the content is as it is delimited by the center. The synthesis of what is explicitly affirmed by each is, thus, called for; and such a synthesis can be achieved only by noting the errors involved in the corresponding implicit denials.

4. THE INTELLIGIBILITY OF THE ABSOLUTE

The absolutist, however, ultimately makes his implicit denial, explicit; and in doing so he carries us over into what undoubtedly is, for many of his critics, the weakest point in his system. I refer, of course, to his insistence upon the necessity of the 'sublation' of finite individuals in the Absolute and the consequent 'unintelligibility' of the conception of the Absolute.

Why the absolutist should deem such 'sublation' necessary is not clear. It certainly is not demanded by experience itself, if the immediately preceding remarks about the growing significance of the center of experience in the course of its development are in principle correct. And one not infrequently is compelled to suspect that the 'necessity' lies rather only in the conception of the Absolute. Given the Absolute, the 'sublation' of finite centers follows inevitably—such seems to be the line of reasoning followed by the absolutist when he is emphasizing the merely phenomenal character of the finite individual. But this line of reasoning, obviously, assumes that the conception of the Absolute must, in any event, be allowed to stand; and to this extent it begs the question which the critic of the Absolute is most desirous of debating, namely, whether the conception of the Absolute is to stand.

If it is to stand, then it must serve as a principle of explanation of experience—that is, it must grow out of experience as a necessary implication of it. So much the absolutist himself admits, at least verbally. But his procedure seems to belie his profession; for he is apparently willing to truncate experience in order to fit it into the conception of the Absolute. Herein lies the

basis of justification for the accusation frequently advanced
against him to the effect that he does not, as he professes, derive
the conception of the Absolute from an analysis and interpretation of experience, but, rather, forcibly bends experience at those
points where it does not readily accommodate itself to the nuances of the conception of the Absolute as more or less arbitrarily
defined.

It is to be noted, further, that the 'unintelligibility' of the
Absolute is intimately connected with this procedure. If the Absolute is of such a nature that finite individuals must be 'sublated'
or 'transmuted' in order to become real parts of it, then it is
inevitable that the Absolute be unintelligible. There is nothing in
experience itself which can function as a ground of the meaning
to be attached to such 'sublation' and 'transmutation.' On the
contrary, there is in experience ground for the contention that
such 'sublation' and 'transmutation' cannot have a meaning for
us; for, apparently, by definition they do violence to a fundamental character of experience—namely, the indefeasibility of its
center of reference—apart from which experience itself ceases to
have any intelligible meaning for us.

Nor does Bradley's ingenious explanation suffice to relieve the
difficulty. What he says is, indeed, plain enough and true enough.
On any finite view, we must agree, some aspects of the world
must be left unexplained in detail, and the real question always
is whether what is left unexplained falls outside of our explanatory system as a negative instance. And what he claims for the
Absolute is also plain. The Absolute, he thinks, is not such an
explanatory system, but one which in principle includes every
aspect of experience—its "main features . . . are within our own
experience." But I fail to see that this claim is true. Its logical
justification, as Bradley conceives it, is partly bound up with his
conception of the non-relational character of immediate experience, which we have criticized elsewhere and need not here reconsider. The point I wish now to emphasize is that the conception of
the Absolute does leave outside as a negative instance the aspect
of experience which we have here been surveying; its 'sublation'
of finite experience is presumably one of its "main features," but
this, to my mind, is certainly not "within our own experience."

On the contrary, what is within our experience negates this feature; and if it is insisted upon, the Absolute plainly leaves the growing significance of the center of experience, as exemplified in the development of that experience, on the outside as a negative instance.

The whole matter may perhaps be put briefly. If the Absolute is to grow logically out of what is "within our own experience," then it must be conceived so as to leave room for finite centers of experience standing in their integrity. If it is not so conceived, it is, so far, arbitrarily conceived and must remain for us unintelligible, not alone in the sense that it leaves much unexplained in detail, as any general view must, but in the further and objectionable sense that one (apparently basal) character of experience is left standing outside as a negative instance. On this point, then, the case of the personalist against the absolutist is essentially sound.

But what is the alternative? On the answer to this question, as we indicated in our introductory chapter, the personalists are not agreed, but divide into three groups. One group, the personalistic absolutist, would hold on to the conception of the Absolute, modified so as to admit the reality of finite centers of experience. A second group, the theistic personalists, would substitute for the Absolute the traditional theological term, *God*, conceived as a purposive intelligence and related to finite centers of experience as *primus inter pares*. The third group, represented by only one among the philosophers dealt with in this survey, namely, McTaggart, would hold that only finite centers of experience are real and that the 'Absolute' must be translated into the 'Universe' which is just the totality of such centers bound together by the principle of "extrinsic determination." Each of these positions involves its own special difficulty, and we may bring this chapter to a close by suggesting broadly what these difficulties are.

For the personalistic absolutist, the main difficulty concerns the intelligibility of the Absolute. And in the end he takes a position on the point which is hardly distinguishable from that of the outright absolutist. The Absolute, he insists, must be so conceived as to include finite centers of experience without destroying them; but how this is to be is to us incomprehensible. The Absolute, further, must be conceived as something quite different from a timeless system of abstract truth, since in it there must be some character corresponding to what in ourselves we call conation and fruition of effort, and yet the Absolute itself cannot be in time since time applied to the whole is unintelligible; but how this can be is, once more, beyond us. And in all of this the personalistic absolutist seems to be but repeating what the absolutist has said. Indeed, the difference between them is one of emphasis. Both agree that "when the Absolute falls in the water it becomes a fish"; the absolutist, however, insists that the fish is unintelligible, since in fact it is the Absolute, while the personalistic absolutist insists that the Absolute is unintelligible, since in fact it ought to be the fish. Meanwhile, the bystander darkly suspects that both are guilty of essentially the same error—the error, namely, of mistaking one object of knowledge for another, and of overlooking the essentially dual character of meanings.

The theistic personalist is at least clear that, if the indefeasibility of the finite center of experience is to be maintained, then the Absolute as defined must be unreservedly given up. But his conception of God apparently bears no more intelligible relation to these indefeasible centers. To say that God is the 'actualisation' of the freedom of each such center or that God is the 'creator' and the center the 'creature' is not very enlightening to one who is intent on intellectual analysis. And when it is further insisted that the 'actualisation' is an Unchangeable Ideal, or that the 'creator' is the "cause and reason" of everything else, one wonders how much farther one can be driven before falling into the Absolute, which one had been told was explicitly discarded. The truth seems to be that the theistic personalists are blowing both hot and cold. Discarding the Absolute, they insist on an ultimate 'Person' among many finite ones; and, magnifying this 'Person' so as to make it in very truth 'ultimate,' they in principle embrace the Absolute. The first emphasis gives them the intellectual advantage of retaining the ultimate integrity of finite individuals, while the second emphasis offers them an opportunity emotionally to bask in the effulgence of the absolutist's broader horizon; but how the two emphases are to be reconciled is not clear, and it would appear to the outsider that one or the other must be definitely abandoned.

The atheistic personalist has no difficulties with any Absolute, written with an initial capital; his troubles arise, rather, from absolutes in lower case. He is so concerned to preserve the existential uniqueness of finite centers, so intent upon their 'essences' as self-encased entities, that he is seriously threatened with the loss of their 'natures.' His 'universe,' in consequence, dissolves into an aggregate of such entities bound together by a principle, namely the principle of "extrinsic determination," which is without logical foundation in the aggregate. Since this point is important with reference to the issue immediately before us, as well as with reference to McTaggart's conception of the Universe as a 'compound substance,' it may to advantage be dwelt upon for a moment and without serious digression.

The principle of extrinsic determination, I have said, is without logical foundation; and I wish first briefly to justify this assertion. The principle is that the qualities of a substance are so related to each other, through their relation to the substance, that if one is changed there is no reason to suppose that the others remain. The assumption on which the principle rests is that any change in the 'nature' of a substance changes the substance; and this assumption carries us at once into the question, sufficiently discussed in the preceding chapter, concerning the relation between a substance and its nature. We have already seen reason to doubt whether this relation is consistently conceived by McTaggart, since at important junctures his argument apparently vacillates in respect of it. The essential point to note here, however, is that the principle of extrinsic determination definitely assumes that with any change in the nature of substance there is a change in the substance itself, and that this change in the substance removes the only possible ground upon which one may rest an inference that the other parts of the nature of the substance in question remain.

Now, applying what is here stated to the substance which is the Universe, we seem to be confronted with the alarming conclusion that what hitherto we have been taught to regard as independently existing substances are not such at all, but only dependent parts of one all-comprehensive substance. For the Universe, we are told, is the one compound substance which includes all substances; and, on the basis of the principle before us, we can say that if any part of the Universe were changed the ground for inference concerning the existence of any other substance whatsoever would thereby be removed. Thus it would appear that the substance which is the Universe is so related to all other substances, which it includes as parts, that it is in some important sense the 'ground' of them. And hereupon we are not far from the position of the absolutist.

But, if it be insisted that these other substances, which are included within this all-comprehensive compound substance called the Universe, are still independent substances existing indefeasibly, then there seems to be no logical basis in the aggregate for the principle of extrinsic determination. For, thus conceived, it is by no means clear that particular substances are made what they are by their natures, in so far as those natures are parts of the nature of that substance which is the Universe. Therefore, there is no clear warrant for the assertion that a change in the nature of the Universe would in any way affect them as substances. Thus, so far at least as the Universe is concerned, the principle of extrinsic determination seems to break down—and in last analysis, it should be added, the Universe is not different from any other substance in this regard.

We are, then, apparently compelled to conclude either that those finite centers called substances are *eo ipso* implicatively attached to their several natures, or that they are in some important sense independent of their several natures. If the first alternative is consistently maintained, then each such finite center is essentially universal, as the absolutist claims it is; and the question is whether its nature can stop short of the nature of the Universe, or, if it does so, whether its nature, and therefore, itself, is in fact anything more than a part or aspect of that inclusive whole. If the second alternative is consistently maintained, then the principle of extrinsic determination breaks down for want of a ground on which to stand, and the Universe dissolves before us into an aggregate of substances. The question then arises as to whether the Universe has any nature at all, or, if so, whether it can be anything more than one among other substances with quite independent natures.

So far as McTaggart's position is concerned, it is clear that the difficulty here is only another illustration of the instability, insisted upon in our preceding analyses of 'sufficient description' and 'determining correspondence,' involved in his conception of substance and its nature. But the difficulty is not limited to his peculiar form of statement; it is more than a terminological difficulty. It is embedded in the very structure of any conception which, like his, wishes to hold that finite centers (however described in detail) are essentially self-encased and exclusive monads. Any 'harmony' among them—'pre-established' or otherwise—which is logically efficacious necessarily does violence to their ontological discreteness; if it does not, then it can be nothing more significant than a sort of *deus ex machina*. Such a conception escapes the Absolute, indeed, but only at the price of a host of absolutes which are entirely unmanageable.

5. Summary

In the preceding consideration of the four points at issue among the representatives of idealism, the primary aim has been to clarify them by indicating the difficulties on both sides. A summary statement in conclusion of the chapter may aid in the accomplishment of this aim.

The principle of continuity is, of course, inescapable. But to read it backwards as supporting anthropomorphism in our intellectual constructions is apparently without warrant. If insisted upon, it converts philosophical speculation into a form of 'insight' which apparently lacks a criterion and which, therefore, constantly threatens to get out of hand. On the other side, however, introduction of the notion of 'emergence' burdens us with the dual task of distinguishing between 'real' and 'unreal' emergents and of defending the notion from the charge of being nothing more than an expression either of ignorance or of unfounded prejudice. Nevertheless, intelligibility cannot be defined without reference to the 'object of knowledge'; and an adequate appreciation of the complexity of such an object, particularly of its dual reference within the cognitive situation, would seem to point a way out of the difficulty by directing attention to the apparently correlative relationship between intelligibility and existence. In the end, the intelligibility of 'emergence' is a question of fact; but 'fact' itself is in an important sense an intellectual construction. And the major problem is to define the paradox without falling into an empty circularity of statement.

In the controversy between the absolutist and the personalist, it seems clear that each is emphasizing an important aspect of finite experience and that the resolution of the controversy lies in rightly harmonizing the different emphases. That finite experience is essentially 'content' seems certainly true, as the absolutist insists; but this is only one side of the total fact. It is, equally essentially, a 'unique centre,' as the personalist urges. It is, in short, center-content; and the one aspect must not be abstracted from the other. If, however, the abstraction is made, the dilemma is inescapable: either the identification of the 'essence' of the finite individual with the element of 'universality' and acceptance of its consequent 'sublation' in the Absolute, or emphasis upon its "existential distinctness" as essential and acceptance of its consequent punctual self-sufficiency.

Nor can I see any way out of the dilemma except through a more faithful following of the implications within the situation which experience offers us, namely, the dual center-content situation. And this way out may also perchance throw light on the problem of the intelligibility of the Absolute, which problem is clearly involved in the relationship here in question. But it should be noted that this way out definitely prohibits any compromises made in behalf of the authority of a supposed *a priori* intellect on the one side or, on the other, the demands of supposed 'immediate facts.' For, viewed in its cognitive reference at least, the center-content totality is just the dual meaning-situation with which we are confronted in judgment and from which all of our inferential processes apparently must set out. Any intellectual construction which proceeds in forgetfulness of either side of the situation and the connection of each with the other thereby loses its logical warrant.

Thus it would appear that the four issues in debate are, in the end, one issue. At least there is one issue towards which they all seem to converge when subjected to rigorous analysis. And that is the issue which we have seen to underlie the divergent types of argument—namely, the precise characteristics of the object of knowledge. If the critical comments expressed in this study are essentially sound, then it is no exaggeration to say that it is this issue from which mainly spring all of the others. And if this be so, the crucial question for the idealistic controversy is: What, precisely defined, are the characteristics of the object of knowledge?

CONCLUDING COMMENT

If the preceding account of the idealistic argument in recent British and American philosophy is tolerably accurate, then it may be safely said that the several historical formulations of the argument have brought to a sharp focus a problem of fundamental importance for philosophical construction. Is meaning, as a characteristic of the cognitive situation, wholly immanent in the situation in which it logically functions, or is it also transcendent in respect of that situation? If the latter, to what does it point? Is it transcendent in the further sense that it is utterly independent of the situation? And, in any case, what is the status of the object *per se* and in what sense may it be said to be meaningful? The answers one gives to these questions, it would appear, will go far towards predetermining one's attitude in respect of the problem of metaphysics and the nature of ontological entities; and any solution suggested for the latter problem will assume a certain solution of the former.

So far as the idealistic controversy here surveyed is concerned, if the critical remarks of this study are essentially sound, the presuppositions of the epistemological and ontological types of argument cannot stand; but that underlying the argument *a contingentia mundi* must be accepted in principle. Assuming either of the first two, we find that the argument built upon it proceeds at crucial points only by violating it; if the presupposition in either case is to remain inviolate, steps indispensable for the argument cannot be taken. But, further, neither of these presuppositions can be assumed, since neither adequately articulates the complexities of the cognitive situation. The 'object' is more than it is known as, but this 'more' is apparently inextricably involved in conceptual construction; and each of the presuppositions in question denies in the end one or the other of these characteristics of the 'object.' It is true that the presupposition of the argument *a contingentia mundi* cannot logically support some of the conclusions professedly derived from it by its proponents; nevertheless, the thesis which constitutes this presupposition seems to be demanded and, in its main tenets at least, must be left standing.

If it is to be left standing, however, the consequences to which one is committed by its acceptance must not be overlooked. What some of these are in respect of the several historical formulations of the argument here under scrutiny I have tried to develop in some detail above. But there are others of significance with reference to some of the basal issues at present in debate among the 'schools,' and in conclusion of this study I wish to raise the question whether the following are not among them: (a) that the denial of ontological signification to knowledge ultimately rests on nothing more stable than an arbitrarily truncated conception of the function of ideas in experience, and the appeal to "animal faith" is necessitated only by oversight of the essentially problematic character of the cognitive situation; (b) that to treat the possible or conceivable, tested only by the abstract principle of contradiction, as if it were an ontological entity is to convert metaphysical speculation into a tumble-ground for fancy; (c) that the worship of 'absolutes' should always be enlightened by explicit recognition of their epistemological setting; and (d) that, generally, all our meanings are in the end grounded in existence, or are embedded in systems based merely on postulates. I am convinced that an affirmative answer must be given to this question in all of its details. But the analytical considerations upon which such a conviction depends lie beyond the scope of the present study.

INDEX